Trade,
balance of payments
and growth

Trade, balance of payments and growth

Papers in International Economics in Honor of Charles P. Kindleberger

Edited by

JAGDISH N. BHAGWATI
RONALD W. JONES
ROBERT A. MUNDELL
JAROSLAV VANEK

1971

NORTH-HOLLAND PUBLISHING COMPANY – AMSTERDAM · LONDON
AMERICAN ELSEVIER PUBLISHING CO., INC. – NEW YORK

Library of Congress Catalog Card Number: 71-157041

ISBN North-Holland: 0 7204 3051 8

ISBN American Elsevier: 0444 10094 6

73 graphs, 13 tables

Publishers:
NORTH-HOLLAND PUBLISHING CO., AMSTERDAM
NORTH-HOLLAND PUBLISHING CO. LTD., LONDON

Sole distributors for the U.S.A. and Canada:
AMERICAN ELSEVIER PUBLISHING COMPANY, INC.
52 VANDERBILT AVENUE, NEW YORK, N.Y. 10017

Printed in the Netherlands

PREFACE

If *Festschriften* were to be written for presentation to a scholar on his approaching the end of his creative years, we could not have even contemplated this volume at the present time. But, had we waited, we might have faced the opposite problem of the contributors themselves having passed beyond their productive years.

Charles Kindleberger has the unique distinction of having written imaginatively and with considerable insight and impact in a number of areas of international economic analysis, extending also to issues in economic history and development. He has combined this with a still rarer success in having produced a vast number of pupils who have achieved eminence in the field of international economic analysis.

The essays presented to him, predominantly by his former students at M.I.T. and associates, reflect Charles Kindleberger's wide range of interests. They are intended as an affectionate tribute, not merely to his great accomplishments as a scholar and teacher, but also to the wit and warmth that are among his endearing characteristics and to his deep and humane concern for individual welfare and social progress.

Cambridge, Massachusetts

Jagdish N. Bhagwati
Ronald W. Jones
Robert A. Mundell
Jaroslav Vanek

CONTENTS

LIST OF CONTRIBUTORS

Bela Balassa
Johns Hopkins University and
International Bank for Reconstruction and Development

Pranab K. Bardhan
Indian Statistical Institute

Trent J. Bertrand
Johns Hopkins University

Jagdish N. Bhagwati
Massachusetts Institute of Technology

Richard E. Caves
Harvard University

John S. Chipman
University of Minnesota

Richard N. Cooper
Yale University

W. M. Corden
Nuffield College, Oxford

Carlos F. Diaz-Alejandro
Yale University

Ronald Findlay
Columbia University

Horst Herberg
University of Western Ontario

Stephen H. Hymer
Yale University

Harry G. Johnson
University of Chicago and
London School of Economics and
Political Science

Ronald W. Jones
University of Rochester

Murray C. Kemp
University of California at Berkeley

Peter B. Kenen
Columbia University

Louis Lefeber
Brandeis University

Staffan B. Linder
Stockholm School of Economics

Ronald I. McKinnon
Stanford University

Robert A. Mundell
University of Chicago

V.K. Ramaswami
Late Chief Economic Adviser,
Ministry of Finance
India

Stephen A. Resnick
Yale University

T. N. Srinivasan
Indian Statistical Institute

Paul A. Samuelson
Massachusetts Institute of Technology

Egon Sohmen
Alfred Weber Institut,
University of Heidelberg

Jaroslav Vanek
Cornell University

Henry Y. Wan, Jr.
Cornell University

PART 1

GENERAL EQUILIBRIUM
AND COMPARATIVE ADVANTAGE

CHAPTER 1

A THREE-FACTOR MODEL IN
THEORY, TRADE, AND HISTORY

Ronald W. JONES

1.1. Introduction

One of the fundamental results in the pure theory of international trade is the factor-price equalization theorem. This result has wider applicability than to the area of trade, for fundamentally it is a statement of the relationship between any economy's commodity prices and the returns to its productive factors, whether or not that economy is engaged in trade. It is not surprising that the prices of commodities into which factors enter as productive agents influence the returns earned by those factors in a competitive market. What *is* surprising is that (under appropriate conditions) the quantities of the factors available for employment in the economy — the factor endowments — have no independent role to play in influencing factor prices. This dependence of factor prices *only* upon commodity prices is the essence of the theorem.

Of course even under the stringent assumptions of the two-commodity, two-factor case, it is not really correct to say that factor endowments have no effect on factor prices independently of commodity prices, for factor prices are uniquely determined by commodity prices only for some *range* of the factor endowments. Should the endowment bundle lie outside this range, the economy would be driven to specialize completely in one of the commodities; with fewer commodities being produced than factors employed, the basis for the theorem disappears.

The two-factor, one-commodity case provides the simplest example of general equilibrium in which factor endowments bear directly upon factor returns[1]. To reach a wider variety of possible applications, however, it is

---

[1] The main field in which such a model is used is obviously not that of international trade but of neoclassical growth. In the one sector, growth model changing capital/labor ratios over time affect the real wage and the rate of profit.

3

necessary to introduce more than one commodity. In this paper I analyze a restricted version of the three-factor, two-commodity case. The restriction is that although three factors of production are employed, only *two* enter into the production of any one commodity. This still allows the straitjacket of the factor-price equalization theorem to be removed, while preserving most of the simple methods of analysis characteristic of the two-by-two model. Furthermore, it is precisely this form of the three-by-two model that has served as the basis for two interesting recent contributions to the literature in the fields of economic history [13] and the theory of capital and international trade [7].

The basic structure of this three-by-two model is developed in the next section, using the framework I employed recently in analyzing the two-commodity two-factor model [5]. Following that, in Section 1.3, I discuss the concept of a *factor-price frontier* for this extended model, as a basis for interpreting Peter Temin's remarks concerning American and British technology in the mid-nineteenth century. In Section 1.4 I turn to a question embedded in Peter Kenen's new concept of the role of capital in production and trade, namely, what is the influence of the rate of interest on relative commodity prices (and therefore on the patterns of comparative advantage). Finally, in Section 1.5, I briefly discuss possible extensions of the model.

1.2. Basic Structure of Model

Let X_1 and X_2 denote the two commodities produced. Sector i makes use of a factor specific to that sector V_i and a factor shared with the other sector, the mobile factor, V_N. If a_{ij} represents the quantity of factor i required per unit output of X_j, the basic competitive equilibrium relations can be set out as in eqs. (1.1) to (1.5). These fall into two groups. The first set, eqs. (1.1) to (1.3), states that the endowment of each factor

$$a_{11}X_1 = V_1 , \tag{1.1}$$

$$a_{22}X_2 = V_2 , \tag{1.2}$$

$$a_{N1}X_1 + a_{N2}X_2 = V_N \tag{1.3}$$

is fully employed in one or more productive sectors. The second set, eqs. (1.4) and (1.5), is a statement of the competitive profit relationships. Here R_i is the "rental" return for the use of one unit of factor i, and p_j is the price of commodity j.

$$a_{11}R_1 + a_{N1}R_N = p_1 \,, \tag{1.4}$$

$$a_{22}R_2 + a_{N2}R_N = p_2 \,. \tag{1.5}$$

I assume throughout that both commodities are produced in positive amounts so that costs per unit of output are reflected exactly in market prices.

In the examples I discuss later in the paper the V_i represent physically different factors of production. However, the model is also capable of reinterpretation as a two-factor, two-commodity model where one of the factors is completely immobile occupationally. For example, V_1 and V_2 may represent capital goods installed in each sector and incapable of being transferred. The crucial consideration is not physical identity but economic identity. With immobilities, the returns to factors R_1 and R_2 need not be equalized in the market.

Eqs. (1.1) to (1.5) could be taken to represent *all* the equilibrium relationships for a competitive economy with fixed factor endowments facing fixed commodity prices only if techniques of production are invariant[2]. Otherwise more information is required to determine which set of a_{ij}, out of all the ones available (shown by the unit isoquants), is chosen in the competitive equilibrium. With competition ensuring that unit costs are minimized, each a_{ij} depends upon the ratio of factor prices in industry j, as shown in eq. (1.6):

$$a_{ij} = a_{ij}\left(\frac{R_N}{R_j}\right). \tag{1.6}$$

The basis for the factor-price equalization theorem is to be found in the competitive profit relations. Consider eqs. (1.4) and (1.5). If this were a model for two commodities and two perfectly mobile factors, R_1 and R_2 would be driven to equality. With the a_{ij} depending upon factor prices, two relationships to determine two factor prices are given once commodity prices are known[3]. However, if V_1 and V_2 are different factors, or specific factors, the profit conditions are insufficient to determine factor returns solely from a

---

[2] With fixed coefficients, however, the resource constraints eqs. (1.1) to (1.3) are overdetermined unless inequalities are introduced. I do not pursue this matter as in general I assume sufficient variability in the a_{ij} to allow all resources to be fully absorbed in productive use.

[3] Of course a factor intensity condition is required as well. It is sufficient in the 2×2 model to have factor proportions *different* in the two sectors. The classic source for a discussion of the intensity conditions, and especially for a general treatment of the case of uneven numbers of goods and factors, is the 1953 paper by Samuelson [10].

knowledge of commodity prices. Use must be made also of the full-employment conditions, with the information they contain as to factor endowments.
Solve eqs. (1.1) and (1.2) for each X_j and substitute into eq. (1.3) to obtain
eq. (1.3'):

$$\frac{a_{N1}}{a_{11}} V_1 + \frac{a_{N2}}{a_{22}} V_2 = V_N . \tag{1.3'}$$

Since the a_{ij} depend on factor prices, eqs. (1.4), (1.5) and (1.3') provide a set
of three relationships in the three factor prices and, as parameters, the two
commodity prices and *all* the factor endowments.

The structure of this 3×2 model is best revealed by considering the way
in which the equilibrium is disturbed by arbitrary small changes in commodity
prices and factor endowments. First I shall examine the equations of change
that are derived from eqs. (1.4), (1.5) and (1.3') to focus on the impact of
parametric changes upon the returns to factors of production. Following that
I shall make use of relationships (1.1) and (1.2) to discuss the effect of
changes on the composition of outputs.

The basic equations of change, revealed by differentiating eqs. (1.4), (1.5),
and (1.3'), are given in eqs. (1.7) to (1.9).

$$\theta_{11}\hat{R}_1 + \theta_{N1}\hat{R}_N = \hat{p}_1 , \tag{1.7}$$

$$\theta_{22}\hat{R}_2 + \theta_{N2}\hat{R}_N = \hat{p}_2 , \tag{1.8}$$

$$\lambda_{N1}\sigma_1\hat{R}_1 + \lambda_{N2}\sigma_2\hat{R}_2 - \{\lambda_{N1}\sigma_1 + \lambda_{N2}\sigma_2\}\hat{R}_N$$

$$= \{\hat{V}_N - \lambda_{N1}\hat{V}_1 - \lambda_{N2}\hat{V}_2\} . \tag{1.9}$$

A '^' over a variable denotes the relative change in that variable (e.g., $\hat{R}_1$ is
dR_1/R_1). The θ_{ij} refers to the distributive share of factor i in industry j,
while λ_{Nj} is the fraction of the mobile factor V_N, absorbed by the j-th industry. In deriving eqs. (1.7) to (1.9) use has been made of two simple relationships involving the relative changes in the input-output coefficients $\hat{a}_{ij}$.
Consider the first industry. With a_{i1} chosen so as to minimize unit cost, the
distributive-share weighted average of the changes in the a_{i1} coefficients
$\{\theta_{11}\hat{a}_{11} + \theta_{N1}\hat{a}_{N1}\}$ must be zero[4]. This directly yields, in eq. (1.7), the

---

[4] Geometrically this states that the slope of the isoquant equals the slope of the
factor-cost line. For a more detailed treatment of these relationships, see Jones [5].

statement that the change in the market price of X_1 must be a positively weighted average of (and therefore trapped between) the changes in individual factor prices. In addition, the *definition* of the elasticity of substitution between factors in the first industry, σ_1, relates the change in the a_{N1}/a_{11} ratio to the change in the factor/price ratio. This, and the comparable definition of σ_2, suffice to yield eq. (1.9).

Formal solutions for the effects on factor returns of changes in commodity prices and factor endowments are provided in eqs. (1.10) to (1.12).

$$
\hat{R}_1 = \frac{1}{\Delta}\left\{\left[\lambda_{N1}\frac{\sigma_1}{\theta_{11}} + \frac{1}{\theta_{11}}\lambda_{N2}\frac{\sigma_2}{\theta_{22}}\right]\hat{p}_1 - \frac{\theta_{N1}}{\theta_{11}}\cdot\lambda_{N2}\frac{\sigma_2}{\theta_{22}}\hat{p}_2\right.
$$

$$
\left. + \frac{\theta_{N1}}{\theta_{11}}\left[\hat{V}_N - \lambda_{N1}\hat{V}_1 - \lambda_{N2}\hat{V}_2\right]\right\}, \tag{1.10}
$$

$$
\hat{R}_N = \frac{1}{\Delta}\left\{\lambda_{N1}\frac{\sigma_1}{\theta_{11}}\hat{p}_1 + \lambda_{N2}\frac{\sigma_2}{\theta_{22}}\hat{p}_2 + [\lambda_{N1}\hat{V}_1 + \lambda_{N2}\hat{V}_2 - \hat{V}_N]\right\}, \tag{1.11}
$$

$$
\hat{R}_1 - \hat{R}_2 = \frac{1}{\Delta}\left\{\left[\frac{1}{\theta_{22}}\lambda_{N1}\frac{\sigma_1}{\theta_{11}} + \frac{1}{\theta_{11}}\lambda_{N2}\frac{\sigma_2}{\theta_{22}}\right](\hat{p}_1 - \hat{p}_2)\right.
$$

$$
\left. + \frac{1}{\theta_{11}\theta_{22}}(\theta_{N1} - \theta_{N2})[\hat{V}_N - \lambda_{N1}\hat{V}_1 - \lambda_{N2}\hat{V}_2]\right\} \tag{1.12}
$$

where

$$
\Delta = \lambda_{N1}\frac{\sigma_1}{\theta_{11}} + \lambda_{N2}\frac{\sigma_2}{\theta_{22}}.
$$

The solution for $\hat{R}_2$ is not explicitly shown, as it can be obtained by permuting subscripts in the solution for changes in the other specific factor R_1. Note that the expression σ_i/θ_{ii} occurs frequently. This is the elasticity of the marginal product curve of the mobile factor in industry i[5]. Thus Δ is a weighted average of these elasticities.

With more factors employed than commodities produced, factor endowments exercise an influence over factor returns independent of commodity prices. The relationships are simple. With commodity prices held constant an increase in the endowment of the mobile factor lowers the return to that

[5] For footnote see next page.

mobile factor and raises the return to both specific factors. By contrast, an increased endowment of either specific factor raises the return to the mobile factor and lowers both R_1 and R_2. Changes in endowments always alter the returns to the mobile factor in a direction *opposite* to the returns to *both* specific factors. This is true because with commodity prices constant, any increase in the return to a factor of production must lower the return to the other factor used in that industry. Thus in eqs. (1.7) and (1.8) an increase in R_N with p_i constant must lower both R_1 and R_2. Although R_1 and R_2 move in the same direction as endowments change, eq. (1.12) explicitly shows that R_1 will undergo a greater *relative* change than R_2 if the share of the mobile factor used in the first industry (θ_{N1}) exceeds its share in the second industry (θ_{N2}).

Turn, now, to the influence of commodity price changes on factor prices. Clearly an equiproportionate rise in both commodity prices (a "pure" inflation) changes all factor prices by the same proportionate amount. Of more

[5] Consider the first industry. The marginal physical product of the mobile factor is given by R_N/p_1. This declines as a_{N1}/a_{11}, the ratio of mobile to fixed factor use, rises. The elasticity of the marginal product curve (defined so as to be positive) is $(\hat{a}_{11}-\hat{a}_{N1})/(\hat{R}_N-\hat{p}_1)$. But by eq. (1.7), $(\hat{R}_N-\hat{p}_1)$ equals $\theta_{11}(\hat{R}_N-\hat{R}_1)$. Given the definition of σ_1, the result follows.

With the model characterized by each sector having a specific factor not used by the other sector, it is not surprising that it is the elasticities of the marginal product curves for the mobile factors that assume importance. A simple graphical device (Fig. 1.1) could be employed to derive some of the results in this model. The marginal

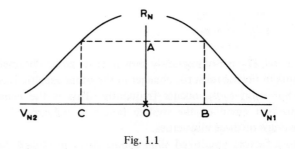

Fig. 1.1

product curves for the mobile factor are put back to back. With given commodity prices and factor endowments the diagram directly gives the solution for $R_N(OA)$ as dependent upon the total quantity of the mobile factor available to the two sectors (*OB* plus *OC* equals V_N). A change in V_i or p_i shifts the appropriate marginal product schedule. An increase in V_N moves both *OB* and *OC* outwards and lowers R_N.

interest is the case in which the system is disturbed by a change in *relative* commodity prices. Suppose the price of commodity 1 rises relatively to that of commodity 2. Then the following relationships hold:

$$\hat{R}_1 > \hat{p}_1 > \hat{R}_N > \hat{p}_2 > \hat{R}_2 \ .$$

The change in each commodity price must be trapped between the changes in the returns to factors used to produce that commodity. Furthermore, the changes in the returns to specific factors are more pronounced than in the return to the mobile factor. Indeed, as the solution in eq. (1.11) shows, $\hat{R}_N$ is a positively weighted average of the changes in each commodity price, a feature of the model that I shall require in Section 1.4.

Factor-price/commodity-price relationships in the standard two-commodity, two-factor model are characterized by what I have called the *magnification effect* [5]. With two mobile factors (and no specific factors), a relative rise in the price of commodity 1 would cause the return to one factor (the factor used more intensively in producing commodity 1) to rise by more (relatively) than either commodity price, and the return to the other factor to rise by less than either commodity price (or perhaps to fall). This is the basis for the Stolper-Samuelson theorem [12], whereby the *real* return to the factor used intensively in a tariff-protected industry is unambiguously raised, regardless of consumption patterns. This magnification effect is preserved in the present model for the specific factors but *not* for the mobile factor. Thus if labor is the single mobile factor, wages calculated in terms of one of the commodities might rise with protection but not in terms of the other commodity.

Note that whereas the fortunes of the specific factors wax or wane together with changes in factor endowments, they move in opposite directions (relative to any other prices) in the face of alterations in relative commodity prices.

Turning to the composition of outputs note from eqs. (1.1) and (1.2) that $\hat{X}_i$ equals $\hat{V}_i - \hat{a}_{ii}$. It would be an easy matter to solve for the change in each output, but consider, instead, the change in the *ratio* of outputs produced. This is given directly by eq. (1.13).

$$\hat{X}_1 - \hat{X}_2 = (\hat{V}_1 - \hat{V}_2) + (\hat{a}_{22} - \hat{a}_{11}) \ . \tag{1.13}$$

If coefficients of production are highly inflexible, output changes are limited to a large extent by changing available quantities of the specific factors. But the intensity with which the specific factors are used depends upon elasticities of substitution and upon changes in all the factor prices, which, by eqs. (1.10) and (1.11), are linked to commodity price and endowment changes. Substitution yields eq. (1.14) for the change in the ratio of outputs produced[6]:

$$(\hat{X}_1 - \hat{X}_2) = (\hat{V}_1 - \hat{V}_2) + \frac{1}{\Delta}\left[\theta_{N1}\frac{\sigma_1}{\theta_{11}} - \theta_{N2}\frac{\sigma_2}{\theta_{22}}\right](\hat{V}_N - \lambda_{N1}\hat{V}_1 - \lambda_{N2}\hat{V}_2)$$

$$+ \frac{\lambda_{N1}\theta_{N2} + \lambda_{N2}\theta_{N1}}{\Delta}\frac{\sigma_1}{\theta_{11}}\frac{\sigma_2}{\theta_{22}}(\hat{p}_1 - \hat{p}_2). \qquad (1.14)$$

For given endowments the coefficient of $(\hat{p}_1 - \hat{p}_2)$ shows the elasticity of substitution along the transformation schedule. Of course this must be positive, and the transformation schedule exhibits the usual bowed-out shape. In the 2 X 2 case (both factors mobile), this result is also obtained *unless* the two industries use factors in the same proportion, in which case the production-possibilities curve is linear. Should this same proviso be applied to the present model? The first question that comes up in this connection is how to compare factor proportions when the two industries each use a factor not employed by the other industry. The answer is found by observing that both industries use the same mobile factor, and the distributive shares of that mobile factor in the two industries can be compared. Consider X_1 to be N-intensive if and only if θ_{N1} exceeds θ_{N2}[7]. As eq. (1.14) shows, even if factor intensities in the two industries are, in this sense, equal, the coefficient of $(\hat{p}_1 - \hat{p}_2)$ still remains finite and, indeed, can be quite small for low values of the elasticities of substitution. When both factors are mobile, the element leading to increasing opportunity costs is the fact that resources initially released by one industry are required in different proportions by the other industry. With some factors specific to an industry, however, expansion of output in that industry must entail adding more of the mobile factor to a fixed quantity of the specific factor (and less of the mobile factor in the other industry), which, by the law of diminishing returns, drives up relative costs in the expanding industry.

---

[6] To solve for $\hat{a}_{ii}$ use two relationships: (1) The θ-weighted average of the changes in input coefficients in the i-th industry is zero, and (2) the definition of σ_i. This yields $\hat{a}_{ii} = -\theta_{Ni}\sigma_i(\hat{R}_i - \hat{R}_N)$.

[7] Thus, referring to eq. (1.12), an increase in the endowment of the mobile factor at constant commodity prices raises, relatively, the return to the specific factor used in the industry making intensive use of the mobile factor. In my treatment of the 2 X 2 case [5], I showed that factor proportions are uniquely related to the size of θ_{ij} compared with θ_{ik} where $k \neq j$.

A question of great interest to trade theory and to the neoclassical theory of growth involves the way in which changes in factor endowments *shift* the transformation curve. The *magnification effect* discussed earlier in connection with price changes is also a feature of the dual relationship between endowment and output changes at constant commodity prices in the traditional 2×2 case[8]. For example, an increase in the endowment of only one productive factor would, at constant prices, raise the output of the commodity using that factor intensively by relatively a greater amount than the factor has increased, and reduce the output of the other commodity. To see how much of this relationship survives in the present 3×2 model, it is necessary to make a distinction between increases in the endowment of the mobile factor V_N and increases in the supply of either specific factor.

Consider the latter effect first. An increase in V_1 would result in greater production of X_1. Unlike the 2×2 case, however, factor prices are adjusting to this change even when commodity prices are being held constant. In particular, the return to the mobile factor rises relative to the return to either specific factor, and this serves to lower the ratio of mobile to specific factor used in the first industry. That is, $\hat{V}_{N1}$, although positive, would be less than $\hat{V}_1$, and therefore $\hat{X}_1$ must fall short of $\hat{V}_1$, thus invalidating this aspect of the magnification effect. However, it is still the case that the output of the other commodity falls, as V_2 is assumed unchanged and some of the mobile factor has been drawn into the expanding industry.

A less extreme change in the composition of outputs results from an increase only in the endowment of the mobile factor (at constant commodity prices). The relative cost of using the mobile factor is cut in both industries, and, since V_1 and V_2 are unchanged, more intensive use of factor N must increase outputs of both X_1 and X_2. As eq. (1.14) shows, this output expansion may not be uniform in the two industries. Two influences operate to alter the relative composition of output: (1) Differences between the two industries in the intensity with which the mobile factor is used. This effect is similar to the *only* explanation for changes in the composition of outputs in the 2×2 case. Other things equal, X_1 expands relatively to X_2 when V_N rises if the distributive share of the mobile factor in the first industry, θ_{N1}, exceeds θ_{N2}. By "other things equal" is meant (2) the elasticities of substitution in the two sectors. Even if factor intensities (as defined in terms of the θ's) are equal as between industries, high values for σ_1 relative to σ_2 allow X_1 to expand relatively to X_2. That is, to preserve the same value for R_N in the

---

[8] This relationship is usually referred to as the Rybczynski theorem. See [9], [4], and [5].

two sectors, most of the increase in N must go into the sector where large increases are required to lower the marginal product of N.

1.3. Factor-Price Frontier

This model can be used to shed light on some queries suggested by Peter Temin's [13] recent discussion of technology in Britain and America in the mid-nineteenth century[9]. The key question I wish to explore is whether one economy can be operating with the same production functions as another and still have higher real wages *and* higher interest rates. An examination of the factor-price frontier for the standard 2 X 2 model suggests a negative answer to this question. But what can be said if technology makes use of three factors of production with the restriction that each sector only uses two factors? This is precisely the model used by Temin; the general properties were discussed in the preceding section. My purpose in this section is to construct factor-price frontiers appropriate to Temin's model.

For this historical interpretation, let labor be the mobile factor, capital be represented by V_1, and land by V_2. Interpret X_1 as the output of manufacturing goods (including machines) and X_2 as the output of the agricultural sector. The special assumptions made are that no land is used in manufacturing activity and no capital is used in agriculture. The interest rate can be associated with the ratio between the returns to capital R_1 and the price of new machines p_1. How the "real wage" is defined makes a considerable difference to the results. To begin with, I make the extreme assumption that only agricultural goods enter into workers' consumption, so that wages R_N need be deflated only by the price of agricultural goods p_2.

A factor-price frontier is a locus of all combinations of factor prices allowed by an economy's given technology[10]. It is not an unambiguous concept. For example, if both factor prices are deflated by the price of the same commodity, the factor-price frontier is dependent only upon the production function for that sector. Thus in eq. (1.7), a relationship between R_1/p_1 and R_N/p_1 is implicitly given — a downward sloping curve whose elasticity is the ratio of distributive shares. If "real" wages were interpreted as R_N deflated

---

[9] I am indebted to Robert Fogel for bringing my attention to this literature. I have had many useful conversations with Fogel and with Stanley Engerman on the material covered in this section. For comments on Temin's article see [2] and [3].

[10] For an early discussion of the concept of a factor-price frontier see Samuelson [11].

by the price of manufactured goods, an economy employing only labor and capital to produce manufactured goods can raise real wages only at a sacrifice of lower rates of interest (rates of profit), regardless of how many factors are used in the rest of the economy. The mid-nineteenth century American economy must have had a superior technology *in manufacturing* if real wages, in this sense of the word, and the rate of interest were higher than in the United Kingdom. This is one extreme, and it is more interesting (and perhaps relevant) to look at the other — letting real wages be defined as R_N/p_2[11].

In a standard 2×2 model with capital and labor mobile, a downward sloping locus relates the wage rate deflated by the price of the consumption good to the rental on capital deflated by the price of the capital good[12]. Each point on the frontier corresponds to a particular commodity price ratio. An increase in the relative price of the labor intensive commodity would raise the real wage and lower the rate of interest. However, such a locus in the 3×2 model of this paper, is *upward sloping*. Suppose the relative price of manufactures rises, and consider the chain of inequalities for commodity and factor prices exhibited in the preceding section. The interest rate has risen ($\hat{R}_1 > \hat{p}_1$) as has the real wage ($\hat{R}_N > \hat{p}_2$). Two countries could have the same technology, but if transport costs or other impediments allowed a higher relative price for manufacturing goods in one of them (say America), both the rate of interest and real wages would have to be higher in that country[13].

But this is not the end of the story, for, unlike the standard 2×2 case, differences in factor endowments exert an independent influence on factor prices. At constant commodity prices, another factor price frontier is traced out if endowments change, and this frontier is negatively sloped. Suppose the supply of one of the specific factors, land, should rise[14]. At constant commodity prices this must raise the real wage and lower the rate of interest — the

[11] To the extent that workers also consumed manufactured goods, the appropriate deflator would be an index of both p_1 and p_2, with weights determined by the share of the two goods in the total budget. The appropriate factor price frontier would lie somewhere between the polar extremes considered in the text.

[12] Although the frontier must be negatively sloped, it *may* be bowed out (concave to the origin). The condition for this to occur is similar to the conditions under which convergence to balanced growth is jeopardized in two-sector growth models, viz. the capital good (manufactures) is capital intensive and elasticities of substitution are "sufficiently" low. For a discussion of this and related matters see the paper by Michael Bruno [1]. In the text, nothing hinges on the concavity of the frontier, only the slope.

[13] Of course *all* factor returns cannot be higher in one country than in another if technologies are identical. In the present example land rents would unambiguously be lower in America.

[14] For footnote, see next page.

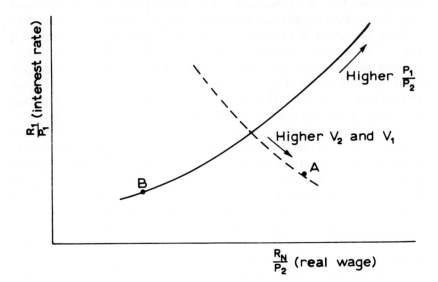

Fig. 1.2. Factor-price frontiers.

returns to mobile and specific factors are affected in opposite directions. In Fig. 1.2 I have shown this second kind of factor price frontier by the down-ward-sloping dotted curve. If the relative price of food was low in America, and if America was land (and capital) abundant (relative to the labor endowment) compared with Britain, both the real wage and rate of interest in America (say at A) could have been higher than in Britain (say at B). These stylized facts are consistent, in this model, with both countries having available the same basic technology.

1.4. Influence of Rate of Interest

In Kenen's treatment of "Nature, Capital, and Trade" [7] the mobile factor is capital. At first glance, Kenen's model seems rather complicated: five different productive activities are considered. However, all this activity can be

[14] From eq. (1.9) it is clear that a more complicated endowment change can just as easily be considered. A pure increase in the endowment of land would have the same kind of impact on factor prices as an increase in the weighted average of land and capital that exceeded any increase in the labor force.

decomposed into three groupings: (1) a standard 2×2 model of the Heckscher-Ohlin variety; (2) a standard two-factor, one-commodity process whereby the capital good is created; and (3) a three-factor, two-commodity model of the type with which this paper is concerned.

Consider, first, the 3×2 section of his model, where he introduces his novel theory of capital. Two factors of production exist in nature, land, and labor (V_1 and V_2). But these factors are inert until and unless they are made productive by an act of investment. In real terms, this can be thought of as, say, the addition of fertilizer to the land or education to the labor. In terms of the abstract model, Kenen posits two production functions ("factor service supply" functions), each of which combines a homogeneous kind of capital (let N equal K) with the specific inert factor (and none of the other factor). In Kenen's treatment, this interaction yields a stream of factor services for a finite number of periods, after which the "improved" factor reverts to its "inert" state unless further investment is undertaken. It is convenient for the present discussion to limit this amount of time (before sudden death depreciation) to one period. Thus at any point of time, the economy has the factor endowment bundle (V_1, V_2, V_K) and has, as outputs, the bundle (X_1, X_2), the quantities of "educated" labor and "fertilized" land[15].

Of course the "output" bundle (X_1, X_2) is really the input bundle for other productive activities. On the one hand, educated labor and improved land are each required to produce both of two commodities (say Y_1 and Y_2) that represent final consumer goods that enter into international trade. Capital is not directly required in these processes, although indirectly it is embodied in X_1 and X_2. On the other hand, the two improved factors are used to produce the capital good.

Kenen is especially concerned with the application of his model to the theory of international trade. Suppose that two countries have identical technologies and engage in free trade in the two goods Y_1 and Y_2. This serves to equalize the returns to the two factors X_1 and X_2 via the usual Heckscher-Ohlin theory. But equal p_1 and p_2 (the returns to the improved factors) do *not* imply the same returns to capital or the inert factors in both countries. As eqs. (1.10) and (1.11) illustrate, differences in factor endowments have an independent bite on R_1, R_2 and R_K. Other things equal, the country with relatively large quantities of capital will have lower

---

[15] Kenen makes stringent assumptions about the form of the factor-service supply function: each is a Cobb-Douglas function ($\sigma_j = 1$) with equal shares of capital ($\theta_{K1} = \theta_{K2}$, a constant). See [7], p. 451, footnote 46 as corrected in the "erratum", p. 658. I am considering the general case.

values for R_K and lower interest rates. The latter follows since the cost of producing the capital good is equated as between countries despite the fact that capital does not enter into trade.

Perhaps the most subtle relationship embedded in Kenen's model connects the rate of interest to the relative price of commodities that enter into trade, and it is this aspect of his model I wish to discuss in this section. To erase the effects of differences in factor endowments per se suppose there exist two countries with identical endowments. Nevertheless, suppose that, before trade, one of the countries has a lower rate of interest than the other. With the opening up of trade, which commodity is exported by the low interest rate country? That is, in Kenen's model, what bias in comparative advantage is imparted by differences in the rate of interest? Equivalently one could reverse the procedure and ask about the effect of a change in the commodity terms of trade upon the rate of interest.

By introducing a make-believe production function, it is possible to get at this relationship and explain the link between relative commodity prices and interest rates using the standard Heckscher-Ohlin factor proportions account of relative prices valid for the 2 × 2 case. The improved factors X_1 and X_2 produce the traded goods Y_1 and Y_2 in a competitive setting. Therefore the relative price of Y_1 and Y_2 is determined in standard fashion by the relative factor price ratio p_1/p_2 or vice versa. It is as if the traded goods were really the improved factors. The hard question concerns the link between the factor price ratio p_1/p_2 and the rate of interest.

The price of the capital good p_K is determined in a competitive model by the cost of production and thus by the technology used and the factor prices p_1 and p_2. Considering small changes, relationship (1.15) connects $\hat{p}_i$ with $\hat{p}_k$, in the same fashion as eqs. (1.7) and (1.8) linked the $\hat{R}_i$ with the $\hat{p}_i$.

$$\theta_{1K}\hat{p}_1 + \theta_{2K}\hat{p}_2 = \hat{p}_K .$$
(1.15)

Now the rate of interest in this kind of model is the ratio of the returns for the use of capital R_K, and the price of the capital good p_K. If there existed a production process whose output was the "services" of capital, and using X_1 and X_2 as inputs, a relationship such as (1.15) for $\hat{R}_K$ could be obtained. Clearly no such physical process exists, but the pricing relationship connecting $\hat{R}_K$ with $\hat{p}_1$ and $\hat{p}_2$ that would be relevant for such a make-believe process *does* exist!

Consider the solution for $\hat{R}_K$ (replace N by K) in eq. (1.11). If endowments are held constant, relationship (1.16) emerges:

$$\theta_{1s}\hat{p}_1 + \theta_{2s}\hat{p}_2 = \hat{R}_K \,,$$ (1.16)

where

$$\theta_{is} \equiv \frac{\lambda_{Ki}\dfrac{\sigma_i}{\theta_{ii}}}{\Delta}$$

and

$$\Delta = \lambda_{N1}\frac{\sigma_1}{\theta_{11}} + \lambda_{N2}\frac{\sigma_2}{\theta_{22}}.$$

The symbols θ_{1s} and θ_{2s} have been used to suggest the distributive shares that would be appropriate in such a make-believe production process. The point is that any increase in the returns to the improved factors filters down and affects, favorably, the return for the service of capital. Of course, by eq. (1.15), such a change would also raise the cost of capital. The change in the interest rate is $(\hat{R}_K - \hat{p}_K)$, and the link between this change and the change in p_1/p_2 (and therefore also the relative prices of the traded commodities) is given simply by comparing θ_{1s} and θ_{1K} (or θ_{1s}/θ_{2s} with θ_{1K}/θ_{2K}). An increase in the rate of interest raises the relative price of the commodity using educated labor relatively intensively (compared with improved land) if and only if educated labor is relatively more important in contributing to the rental on capital goods than it is in contributing to the costs of producing capital goods[16].

---

[16] As remarked in the preceding footnote 15 Kenen considers only the special case in which σ_1 is unity and θ_{K1} equals θ_{K2}. The appropriate comparison in the general case is θ_{1K}/θ_{2K} with θ_{1s}/θ_{2s}. The former exceeds the latter if and only if $p_1 X_{1K}/p_2 X_{2K}$ exceeds K_1/K_2. But if θ_{K1} equals θ_{K2}, K_1/K_2 must equal $p_1 X_1/p_2 X_2$. Therefore in Kenen's case the direction of change in commodity prices given by a change in the interest rate is linked to the comparison between the ratio of the two educated factors in producing $K(X_{1K}/X_{2K})$ and in the economy's endowment bundle (X_1/X_2). As is easily seen, this physical relationship as between factor proportions does not generalize. See Kenen [7], p. 449, and especially eq. (21).

Kenen's special assumptions as to the form of the factor-service supply functions also affect the way in which his transformation curve between X_1 and X_2 (his "gross factor-service frontier", [7], p. 445) shifts with the accumulation of capital. With $\sigma_1 = \sigma_2$ and θ_{K1} equal to θ_{K2} (and therefore θ_{11} also equal to θ_{22}), the coefficient of $\hat{V}_N$ in my eq. (1.14) is zero. An increase in K shifts the $X_1 - X_2$ transformation schedule uniformly outwards from the origin as Kenen demonstrates.

The feature of the 3 × 2 model that permits the financial counterpart of the make-believe production function for the services of capital is clearly (by eq. (1.11)) that the return to capital is derived from the market returns of the improved factors — and that changes in R_K must be a *positively* weighted average of changes in the p_i[17]. It is as if X_1 and X_2 were actually used to produce the services of capital in a competitive market, so that the zero-profit relationship appropriate to such a process would be given by eq. (1.16).

1.5. Possible Extensions of Model

The preceding two sections have served to illustrate two uses that have been made of the model analyzed in Section 1.2. In this concluding section, I suggest briefly how this model might be extended, still falling short of a completely general model in which all three factors can continuously be substituted for each other in producing each of the two commodities.

One suggestion involves allowing all three factors to be used in each industry but a pair of these to be fixed in proportion to each other — always the same pair, but not necessarily in the same proportion as between sectors[18]. Let a_{21} always equal αa_{11} and a_{12} equal βa_{22}. The a_{Ni} can be varied continuously with the bundle of (a_{1i}, a_{2i}). If $\alpha\beta$ is less than unity, the first commodity is distinguished from the second by a more intensive use of factor 1 relative to factor 2 (but not necessarily relative to factor N). The model of Section 1.2 is the special case in which $\alpha = \beta = 0$. Consider the other extreme: If $\alpha\beta = 1$, the model reduces to the familiar two-factor, two-commodity model, where the two factors are N and a particular bundle of factors 1 and 2 (always in the ratio $1/\alpha$ or, equivalently, β). From the production side of the model alone, it is not possible to determine R_1 and R_2 separately, only the return to the composite factor.

For intermediate cases, where $\alpha\beta < 1$, consider the two *different* composite factors: $(a_{11}, \alpha a_{11})$ and $(\beta a_{22}, a_{22})$, with returns R_1^* and R_2^*. In terms of these composite factors the special form of the 3 × 2 model in Section 1.2

---

[17] In either this 3 × 2 model, or in the standard 2 × 2 model, every factor price change is a weighted average of the changes in all commodity prices. However, except for the mobile factor in the 3 × 2 model, one of the weights in each case is *negative* (this is the magnification effect). Therefore such a pricing relationship could not be interpreted as having come from a productive process in which the two commodities are inputs and the service of the particular factor is the output.

[18] I am indebted to Murray Kemp for this suggestion.

is applicable[19]. For example, a change in commodity prices at unchanged endowments has a determinate effect on R_i^* and R_N (as given by a reinterpretation of eqs. (1.10) and (1.11)). These changes in the R_i^*, in turn, determine the changes in the R_i via a set of relationships equivalent to the zero-profit factor-price, commodity price equations of change in the standard 2 × 2 model:

$$\theta'_{11}\hat{R}_1 + \theta'_{21}\hat{R}_2 = \hat{R}_1^* ,$$

$$\theta'_{12}\hat{R}_1 + \theta'_{22}\hat{R}_2 = \hat{R}_2^* ,$$

where

$$\theta'_{ij} \equiv \frac{\theta_{ij}}{\theta_{1j} + \theta_{2j}} .$$

Thus by introducing the notion of composite factors it is possible to decompose a more general 3 × 2 case to the special form of the 3 × 2 model discussed in this paper and the standard 2 × 2 pricing relationships.

An alternative extension focuses on the relationship between V_1 and V_2 instead of introducing all three factors into the production process for any one commodity. Throughout the paper I have assumed that endowments of the specific factors are given as parameters. Suppose, instead, they are outputs of a productive process whereby V_2 can be "converted" into V_1 at increasing opportunity costs. Let the factor endowment ratio V_2/V_1 respond positively to relative returns, R_2/R_1[20]. The basic set of relations (1.7) to (1.9) is altered only in having $\lambda_{N1}\hat{V}_1 + \lambda_{N2}\hat{V}_2$ now depend upon the extent of the change in factor returns R_2/R_1 and the elasticity of substitution σ_V along the transformation locus connecting V_2 and V_1[21].

---

[19] For the concept of elasticity of substitution consider factor N in relation to the composite bundle. For example, define σ_1 as the relative change in (a_{11}/a_{N1}) divided by the relative change in (R_N/R_1^*). Eq. (1.3') changes to

$$\frac{a_{N1}}{a_{11}} \frac{(V_1 - \beta V_2)}{(1-\alpha\beta)} + \frac{a_{N2}}{a_{22}} \frac{(V_2 - \alpha V_1)}{(1-\alpha\beta)} = V_N .$$

R_1^* is merely $R_1 + \alpha R_2$, the cost of the bundle (a_{11}, a_{21}).

[20] In an unpublished manuscript [8], Howard Petith analyzes a two-sector vintage model. Each sector employs a different kind of machine, and these machines, in turn, are jointly produced subject to increasing opportunity costs.

[21] For footnote, see next page.

The model in this paper is the special case $\sigma_V = 0$. As the transformation curve between V_1 and V_2 becomes more elastic, the result of Section 1.2, whereby the change in the return to the mobile factor is trapped between the changes in the commodity prices, is altered to conform more closely with the "magnification" effect of the standard 2×2 model. That is, for sufficiently large σ_V, an increase in the relative price of the N-intensive commodity increases R_N by a proportionately greater amount.

These extensions serve to illustrate how more general cases can be decomposed into the kinds of results familiar from the 2×2 model and the results characteristic of the special form of the 3×2 model examined in this paper.

[21] If R_1/R_2 rises, V_1/V_2 also increases. The sign of $(\lambda_{N1} \hat{V}_1 + \lambda_{N2} \hat{V}_2)$ turns out to depend on a comparison of the distributive shares of the mobile factor V_N in the production of commodities X_1 and X_2. The implication of this is given by eq. (1.12). If the first commodity is N-intensive (in the sense that θ_{N1} exceeds θ_{N2}), compare the impact on the ratio R_1/R_2 of an increase in the endowment of the mobile factor (with constant commodity prices) under the alternative assumptions (1) that V_1 and V_2 remain constant, and (2) that V_1 and V_2 respond to changes in R_1/R_2. In both cases R_1/R_2 rises since X_1 is N-intensive. But in case (2) $\lambda_{N1} \hat{V}_1 + \lambda_{N2} \hat{V}_2$ is positive, thus damping the increase in R_1 and R_2, and in their spread. The possibility of having V_i respond to prices reduces the required extent of the change in prices. For a brief discussion in another context of the importance of terms such as $\lambda_{N1} \hat{V}_1 + \lambda_{N2} \hat{V}_2$ see R.W.Jones [6], p. 330.

References

[1] M.Bruno, "Fundamental Duality Relations in the Pure Theory of Capital and Growth", *Review of Economic Studies*, January 1969.
[2] I.M.Drummond, "Labor Scarcity and the Problem of American Industrial Efficiency in the 1850's: A Comment", *The Journal of Economic History*, September 1967.
[3] R.W.Fogel, "The Specification Problem in Economic History", *The Journal of Economic History*, September 1967.
[4] R.W.Jones, "Duality in International Trade: A Geometrical Note", *Canadian Journal of Economics and Political Science*, August 1965.
[5] R.W.Jones, "The Structure of Simple General Equilibrium Models", *The Journal of Political Economy*, December 1965.
[6] R.W.Jones, "Comments on Technical Progress", *The Philippine Economic Journal*, Second Semester, 1966.
[7] P.B.Kenen, "Nature, Capital, and Trade", *The Journal of Political Economy*, October 1965.
[8] H.Petith, "Substitution in a Vintage Capital Model", Unpublished.

[9] T.M.Rybczynski, "Factor Endowments and Relative Commodity Prices", *Economica*, November 1955.

[10] P.A.Samuelson, "Prices of Factors and Goods in General Equilibrium", *Review of Economic Studies*, XXI, 1953–54.

[11] P.A.Samuelson, "Parable and Realism in Capital Theory: The Surrogate Production Function", *Review of Economic Studies*, XXIX, 1962.

[12] W.F.Stolper and P.A.Samuelson, "Protection and Real Wages", *Review of Economic Studies*, IX, November 1941.

[13] P.Temin, "Labor Scarcity and the Problem of American Industrial Efficiency in the 1850's", *The Journal of Economic History*, September 1966.

CHAPTER 2

FACTOR MARKET DISTORTIONS, THE SHAPE OF THE LOCUS OF COMPETITIVE OUTPUTS, AND THE RELATION BETWEEN PRODUCT PRICES AND EQUILIBRIUM OUTPUTS*

Horst HERBERG and Murray C.KEMP

It is well known that factor market distortions may cause the market-determined locus of competitive outputs to lie inside the technically determined locus of production possibilities[1]. It is also known that, either throughout its length or over a limited range, the locus of competitive outputs may be convex to the origin[2]. Thus if in the standard two-factor, two-product model one factor is paid relatively more in the first industry than in the second the competitive equilibrium might be represented by point P in fig. 2.1.

To those of us brought up on diagrams, fig. 2.1 suggests the possibility that equilibrium outputs may respond perversely to changes in commodity prices, an increase in price being associated with a reduction in output. More specifically, the figure suggests that the price-output relationship will be perverse if and only if the locus of competitive outputs is locally convex to the origin. Our first purpose in writing the present paper is to subject these visual impressions to an algebraic test. It will be shown that the eye is a very unreliable guide; that, in particular, it is possible for the price-output relationship to be normal or conventional even when the locus of competitive outputs is (unconventionally) convex to the origin. For the special case in which production functions are of the constant-elasticity-of-substitution (CES) type, we are able to state conclusions which are more detailed and more precise.

A secondary purpose has been the negative one of correcting what seem

* We acknowledge with gratitude the helpful comments of Ronald W.Jones and Stephen P.Magee.
[1] Hagen [2].
[2] Fishlow and David [1]; Johnson [4].

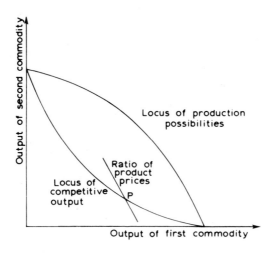

Fig. 2.1

to us to be misunderstandings concerning the shape of the locus of competitive outputs in the face of factor market distortions. This matter is disposed of immediately.

2.1. The Shape of the Locus of Competitive Outputs

General Neo-classical Production Functions
   In a pioneering paper [4], H.G.Johnson reached the following conclusions concerning smooth, strictly quasi-concave, and homogeneous production functions and factor ratios that differ from industry to industry ([4], p. 687n. and p. 689):
   1. If a factor of production receives a relatively higher reward in the industry in which in the absence of factor market distortions it would be applied relatively intensively, then (i) there exists some critical constant degree of distortion such that, if the degree of distortion is less than the critical value, the locus of competitive outputs must lie outside the chord joining its end points; if the degree of distortion is equal to the critical value, the locus of competitive outputs must coincide with the chord joining its end points; and if the degree of distortion is greater than the critical value, the locus of

competitive outputs must lie inside the chord joining its end points. Moreover, (ii) if the degree of distortion exceeds the critical value, the locus must be everywhere convex to the origin.

2. If a factor of production receives a relatively lower reward in the industry in which in the absence of factor market distortions it would be applied relatively intensively, then (i) for each feasible level of output of, say, the first industry there exists some critical degree of distortion such that, at that output, the locus of competitive outputs must lie outside the chord joining its end points, must coincide with the chord, or must lie inside the chord according as, respectively, the actual degree of distortion is less than, equal to, or greater than the critical degree of distortion. Moreover, (ii) the locus must be convex to the origin wherever it lies inside the chord joining its end points.

We hope to show first, by counter example, that Propositions 1 (ii) and 2 (ii) are false and, more broadly, to suggest that the curvature of the locus of competitive outputs at a point cannot be inferred from the relationship of that point to the chord joining the end points of the locus. Later we shall show that Proposition 2 (i) also is wrong.

Throughout the paper it will be assumed (without loss of generality) that in the absence of factor market distortions the first factor would be applied not less intensively in the second industry than in the first. Except where the contrary is indicated, it will be assumed that in the absence of distortions the first factor would be applied more intensively in the second industry than in the first.

Suppose that the first factor receives a relatively higher reward in the second industry. In terms of the box diagram (fig. 2.2) an initial equilibrium is represented by point P on the distorted contract locus, with an isoquant of the first industry tangential of the line X_1X_1, an isoquant of the second industry tangential to the line X_2X_2, and the angle between the two lines determined by the interindustrial difference in the reward of the first factor. (Neither the isoquants nor the contract locus are shown.) That, in spite of the distortion, the second industry uses the first factor relatively intensively is revealed by the slopes of O_1P and O_2P. Now mark off equal distances along O_1P to each side of P, so that $PP_{11} = PP_{12}$, and draw through P_{11} and P_{12} lines which are parallel to X_1X_1 and intersect O_2P in P_{21} and P_{22}, respectively. Evidently $PP_{21} = PP_{22}$. Units of output are chosen so that PP_{11} and PP_{21} correspond to one unit of the first commodity and one unit of the second commodity respectively. Suppose next that below P the isoquant of the first industry curves slowly and therefore hugs the line X_1X_1, and that

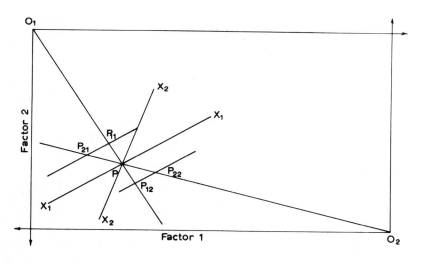

Fig. 2.2

above P the isoquant of the second industry curves sharply and therefore diverges rapidly from the line X_2X_2. Bearing in mind that all of an industry's isoquants are radial blowups one of the other, it then follows that a second point on the distorted contract locus can be found close to P_{21}. Suppose, finally, that above P the isoquant of the first industry curves sharply and therefore diverges rapidly from the line X_1X_1, and that below P the isoquant of the second industry curves slowly and therefore hugs the line X_2X_2. Then a third point on the distorted contract locus can be found very close to P_{12}. Moreover, that isoquant of the second industry which passes through P_{12} will cut O_2P far to the left of P_{22}. Compared to the initial equilibrium, at P, the second equilibrium, near P_{21}, involves an increase in the output of the second industry, and the third equilibrium, near P_{12}, involves a decrease. The increase, however, is greater in magnitude than the decrease. Hence, close to P, the locus of competitive outputs may be convex to the origin; and this is true even though the entire locus must lie above the chord joining its end points.

Suppose again that the first factor receives a relatively higher reward in the second industry but imagine now that the distortion is severe enough to reverse the relative factor intensities of the two industries. Fig. 2.3, which is constructed on the same principles as fig. 2.2, illustrates the possibility. Suppose that above P the isoquant of the first industry curves sharply and that below P the isoquant of the second industry curves sharply. Then one can

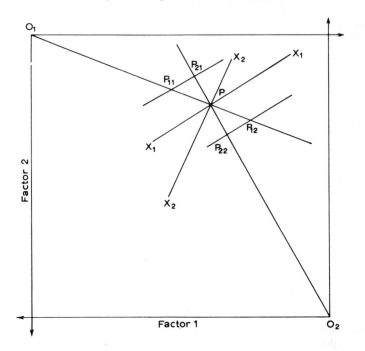

Fig. 2.3

detect the possibility of a second equilibrium involving a unit decrease in the output of the first industry and a less-than-unit increase in the output of the second industry. On the other hand, a unit increase in the output of the first industry necessarily involves a greater-than-unit cut in the output of the second industry. Hence the locus of competitive outputs may have the conventional local curvature; and this is true even though the entire locus must lie below the chord joining its end points, contradicting Johnson's Proposition 1 (ii).

    Imagine, finally, that the first factor receives a relatively higher reward in the first industry, so that the effect of the distortion is to magnify the difference in factor intensities. Fig. 2.4 illustrates the possibility. In this case it is possible to construct examples in which the locus of competitive outputs is locally concave to the origin and examples in which the locus is locally convex to the origin, without regard to the position of the locus in relation to the chord joining its end points. Thus, if the isoquant of the first industry curves sharply below P and the isoquant of the second industry curves sharply above P, then a unit decrease in the output of the first industry may be accom-

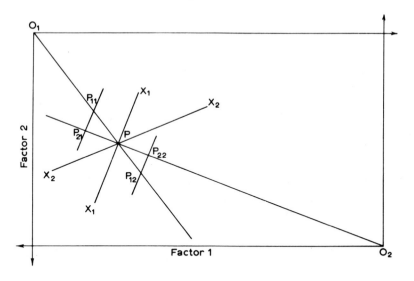

Fig. 2.4

panied by a smaller-than-unit increase in the output of the second industry; and, on the other hand, a unit increase in the output of the first industry must be associated with a greater-than-unit decrease in the output of the second industry. Hence, the locus of competitive outputs may be locally concave to the origin; and this seems to be so whether at the relevant point the locus lies inside or outside the chord joining its end points, contradicting Johnson's Proposition 2 (ii). Alternatively, if the isoquant of the first industry curves slowly above P and the isoquant of the second industry curves sharply below P, then a unit increase in the output of the first industry will be accompanied by approximately a unit decrease in the output of the second industry; and if in addition the isoquant of the first industry curves sharply below P and the isoquant of the second industry curves slowly above P, then a unit decrease in the output of the first industry will be accompanied by a more-than-unit increase in the output of the second industry. Thus the locus of competitive outputs may be locally convex to the origin; and this seems to be so whether at the relevant point the locus lies inside or outside the chord joining its end points.

It seems, therefore, that in no case can the local curvature of the locus of competitive outputs be inferred simply from the position of the relevant point in relation to the chord joining its end points. The curvature of the locus depends partly on the shapes of the two isoproduct curves and hence on the two elasticities of substitution and on their manner of variation along the iso-product curves.

To make further progress, it is necessary to narrow the class of production functions to be studied. Johnson, for example, has studied the class of Cobb-Douglas functions and has shown that, when the first factor is paid relatively more in the industry which in the absence of distortions would use the factor relatively more intensively, the locus of competitive outputs may be locally convex to the origin and, if the locus is locally convex anywhere, it is convex everywhere; and that, when the first factor is paid relatively more in the industry which in the absence of distortions would use the factor relatively less intensively, the locus may change curvature as the production point moves along it. We shall consider the class of CES production functions that contains Cobb-Douglas functions as special cases.

Production Functions with Constant Elasticities of Substitution

We now state a theorem concerning the shape of the locus of competitive outputs when the technology can be summarized by production functions of the CES type with the same positive, finite elasticity of substitution in each industry[3]. First, however, we need some notation and a formal description of the CES production functions.

We begin by writing down the general neoclassical production relationships

$$X_j = F_j(V_{j1}, V_{j2}) \qquad j = 1, 2 \qquad\qquad (2.1)$$

where X_j is the output of the jth industry and V_{ji} is the amount of the ith primary factor of production employed by the jth industry. In view of the homogeneity of F_j, eq. (2.1) can be rewritten as

$$1 = F_j(a_{j1}, a_{j2}) \qquad j = 1, 2 \qquad\qquad (2.2)$$

where a_{ji} is the amount of the ith factor used in producing a unit of the jth commodity. In the special CES case, eq. (2.2) takes the form

$$1 = [(1-\alpha_j)a_{j1}^{-\epsilon} + \alpha_j a_{j2}^{-\epsilon}]^{-1/\epsilon} \qquad \begin{array}{l} \epsilon \neq 0 \\ \infty > \epsilon > -1 \\ 0 < \alpha_j < 1 \end{array} \qquad (2.3a)$$

---

[3] As a by-product we fill a gap in Johnson's treatment of the special Cobb-Douglas case.

or the form

$$\epsilon = 0$$
$$1 = a_{j1}^{1-\alpha_j} a_{j2}^{\alpha_j} \qquad\qquad 0 < \alpha_j < 1 \qquad\qquad (2.3b)$$

where the elasticity of substitution is

$$\sigma = \frac{1}{1 + \epsilon} . \qquad\qquad (2.4)$$

We have assumed that in the absence of factor market distortions the second industry uses the first factor not less intensively than the first industry, so that

$$\alpha_1 \geqslant \alpha_2 . \qquad\qquad (2.5)$$

We have assumed also that the first factor receives a reward which differs from industry to industry. If we denote by μ the ratio of its reward in the second industry to its reward in the first industry, we have

$$\mu > 0, \qquad \mu \gtreqless 1 . \qquad\qquad (2.6)$$

Finally, we introduce the convenient shorthand

$$\beta = \frac{\alpha_1}{1 - \alpha_1} \cdot \frac{1 - \alpha_2}{\alpha_2} \qquad\qquad (2.7)$$

and

$$\gamma = \beta^{\sigma/(\sigma-1)} \qquad\qquad \text{if } \sigma \neq 1 . \qquad\qquad (2.8)$$

Evidently, $\beta \geqslant 1$.

We may now state:

Theorem 1 (CES): I. *Suppose that the two production functions are of the* CES *type, with the same constant, positive and finite elasticity of substitution σ in each industry but with the second industry in the absence of distortions relatively more intensive in its use of the first factor of production ($\alpha_1 > \alpha_2$). Suppose, moreover, that the relative reward of the first factor is higher in the industry in which in the absence of distortions it would be applied relatively intensively (so that $\mu > 1$). Then:*

(a) *If the distortion is insufficiently severe to reverse the relative factor intensities of the two industries ($\mu < \beta$), the locus of competitive outputs is uniformly concave to the origin[4].*

(b) (i) *If the distortion is sufficiently severe to reverse relative factor intensities ($\mu > \beta$) and if the production functions are of the* Cobb-Douglas *type ($\sigma = 1$), the locus of competitive outputs is uniformly convex to the origin[5].*

(b) (ii) *If the distortion is sufficiently severe to reverse relative factor intensities ($\mu > \beta$) and if production functions are not of the* Cobb-Douglas *type, then the locus of competitive outputs is uniformly convex to the origin if*

$$\sigma > 1 \qquad and \qquad \mu < \gamma \tag{2.9}$$

or if

$$\tfrac{1}{2} \leqslant \sigma < 1 \tag{2.10}$$

For $\sigma > 1$ and sufficiently large μ, the locus must be concave to the origin near the axes and convex somewhere else. For $0 < \sigma < \tfrac{1}{2}$ and sufficiently large μ, the locus may be either convex or concave near the axes but must have a convex section somewhere.

II. *Suppose that the two production functions are as specified in I but that the relative reward of the first factor is lower in the industry in which in the absence of factor market distortions it would be applied relatively intensively (so that $\mu < 1$). Then:*

(a) *If the production functions are* Cobb-Douglas, *the locus of competitive outputs may be uniformly convex to the origin, uniformly concave to the origin, or partly concave and partly convex, but it cannot change its curvature more than twice[6]. For sufficiently small distortions (that is, for μ close to unity) the locus is uniformly concave to the origin. For extreme degrees of distortion (that is, for μ close to zero), on the other hand, the locus need not become uniformly convex to the origin. Moreover, if the locus is convex near both of the axes it must be convex everywhere.*

---

[4] This fills the gap in Johnson's treatment referred to in footnote 3.
[5] See Johnson [4], p. 692.
[6] This seems to be a property of Cobb-Douglas loci only.

(b) *If the production functions are not* Cobb-Douglas, *the locus of competitive outputs is uniformly convex to the origin if* $\frac{1}{2} \leqslant \sigma < 1$ *and* $\mu < \gamma$, *and uniformly concave to the origin if* $0 < \sigma \leqslant \frac{1}{2}$ *and* $\mu > \gamma$. *For* $\sigma > 1$ *and* μ *sufficiently small, the locus lies below the chord joining its end points but is concave near the axes and convex somewhere in between. For* $0 < \sigma < \frac{1}{2}$ *and* μ *sufficiently small, the locus may be either concave or convex near each axis but must have at least one convex section. Moreover, near the axis of the first good but not necessarily near the axis of the second good, the locus must lie below the chord joining its end points*[7].

III. *Suppose that the same* CES *production function prevails in each industry (so that* $\alpha_1 = \alpha_2$). *Then for all nontrivial factor market distortions (that is, for all* $\mu \neq 1$), *the locus of competitive outputs is uniformly convex to the origin if* $\frac{1}{2} \leqslant \sigma \leqslant 1$. *Otherwise, the results stated earlier hold with* $\beta = \gamma = 1$[8].

Our proof of Theorem 1 is very long and doubly tedious; but it must be given. It is pleasant to be able to report, however, that readers tempted to jump to Section 2.2 may do so without penalty.

Proof of Theorem 1: The following additional notation will be employed:

V_i The community's endowment of the ith primary factor of production.

σ_j The elasticity of factor substitution in the jth industry.

ρ The ratio of the community's endowment of the first factor to its endowment of the second factor ($\rho \equiv V_1/V_2$).

ρ_j The ratio of the first factor to the second in the jth industry ($\rho_j \equiv V_{j1}/V_{j2}$).

p The relative price of the second commodity in terms of the first.

λ The proportion of the second factor employed by the first industry ($\lambda \equiv V_{12}/V_2$).

We begin by writing four basic relationships on which the rest of the proof rests. From the homogeneity of F_j we have

$$X_j = V_{j2}F_j(\rho_j,1) = V_{j2}f_j(\rho_j) \qquad j = 1, 2 . \qquad (2.11)$$

---

[7] This disproves Johnson's Assertion 2 (i).

[8] In Theorem 2.1 and in later theorems the value $\sigma = 1/2$ appears to be critical; but this is a theoretical artefact. As our later formulae show, what matters is the sum of the two elasticities of substitution minus one. Thus only when the two elasticities are assumed to be equal, as in the present paper, does the value $\sigma = 1/2$ become critical.

In terms of f_j the elasticity of factor substitution may be written

$$\sigma_j \equiv - \frac{f_j'(f_j - \rho_j f_j')}{\rho_j f_j f_j''} \qquad\qquad j = 1, 2\,, \qquad\qquad (2.12)$$

where $f_j' \equiv df_j/d\rho_j$, etc. The marginal conditions of cost minimization are

$$\mu f_1' = p f_2'$$

$$f_1 - \rho_1 f_1' = p(f_2 - \rho_2 f_2')\,. \qquad\qquad (2.13)$$

Finally, the requirement that each factor be fully employed is

$$V_{1i} + V_{2i} = V_i \qquad\qquad i = 1, 2\,. \qquad\qquad (2.14)$$

We seek first an expression for the slope of the locus of competitive outputs. From eqs. (2.11) to (2.14), setting $V_2 = 1$ and recalling that $\rho_1 \neq \rho_2$, we obtain,

$$\lambda \rho_1 + (1-\lambda)\rho_2 = \rho \qquad\qquad (2.15)$$

$$X_1 = \lambda f_1(\rho_1) = \frac{\rho - \rho_2}{\rho_1 - \rho_2} f_1(\rho_1) \qquad\qquad (2.16)$$

$$X_2 = (1-\lambda)f_2(\rho_2) = \frac{\rho_1 - \rho}{\rho_1 - \rho_2} f_2(\rho_2) \qquad\qquad (2.17)$$

$$\frac{d\rho_2}{d\rho_1} = \frac{\sigma_2 \rho_2}{\sigma_1 \rho_1} \qquad\qquad (2.18)$$

$$\frac{dX_1}{d\rho_1} = - \frac{1}{\sigma_1 \rho_1 (\rho_1 - \rho_2)^2} \, [(\rho_1 - \rho)\sigma_2 \rho_2 f_1$$

$$+ (\rho - \rho_2)\sigma_1 \rho_1 (f_1 - \rho_1 f_1' + \rho_2 f_1')] \qquad\qquad (2.19)$$

$$= - \frac{1}{\sigma_1 \rho_1 (\rho_1 - \rho_2)^2} \, [p(\rho - \rho_2)\sigma_1 \rho_1 f_2 + (\rho_1 - \rho)\sigma_2 \rho_2 f_1$$

$$+ (\rho - \rho_2)\sigma_1 \rho_1 \rho_2 f_1'(1 - \mu)] \qquad\qquad (2.20)$$

$$\frac{dX_2}{d\rho_1} = \frac{1}{\sigma_1\rho_1(\rho_1-\rho_2)^2} [(\rho-\rho_2)\sigma_1\rho_1 f_2$$

$$+ (\rho_1-\rho)\sigma_2\rho_2(f_2-\rho_2 f_2'+\rho_1 f_2')] \tag{2.21}$$

$$= \frac{1}{p\sigma_1\rho_1(\rho_1-\rho_2)^2} [p(\rho-\rho_2)\sigma_1\rho_1 f_2 + (\rho_1-\rho)\sigma_2\rho_2 f_1$$

$$- (\rho_1-\rho)\sigma_2\rho_1\rho_2 f_1'(1-\mu)] . \tag{2.22}$$

We observe that, regardless of the value of μ,

$$\text{sign } \frac{dX_1}{d\rho_1} = \text{sign } -\frac{dX_2}{d\rho_1} = \text{sign } (\rho_2-\rho_1) . \tag{2.23}$$

From eqs. (2.20) and (2.22),

$$\frac{dX_1}{dX_2} = -p[1+(1-\mu)\chi] < 0 \tag{2.24}$$

with

$$\chi = \frac{\rho_1\rho_2 f_1' [(\rho_1-\rho)\sigma_2+(\rho-\rho_2)\sigma_1]}{p(\rho-\rho_2)\sigma_1\rho_1 f_2 + (\rho_1-\rho)\sigma_2\rho_2 f_1 - (\rho_1-\rho)\sigma_2\rho_1\rho_2 f_1'(1-\mu)} > 0. \tag{2.25}$$

Finally, if $\rho_1 = \rho_2 = \rho$, it is easy to show that

$$\frac{dX_1}{dX_2} = -\frac{f_1(\rho)}{f_2(\rho)} = -p[1+(1-\mu)\chi^*] = \text{const} < 0 \tag{2.24a}$$

with

$$\chi^* = \frac{\rho f_1'(\rho)}{p f_2(\rho)} > 0. \tag{2.24b}$$

From eqs. (2.24) and (2.25), we see that the sign of d^2X_1/dX_2^2, and therefore the local curvature of the locus of competitive outputs, depends not only on σ_1 and σ_2 but also on their sensitivity to changes in ρ_1 and ρ_2, respectively. Any general, necessary or sufficient, condition for the curvature to be of one kind or the other is bound to be impossibly complicated.

To simplify, we now turn to the special CES case in which $\sigma_1 = \sigma_2 = \sigma$, a positive finite constant. From eq. (2.3),

$$f_j = [\alpha_j + (1-\alpha_j)\rho_j^{-\epsilon}]^{-1/\epsilon} \qquad \begin{matrix} \epsilon \neq 0 \\ \infty > \epsilon > -1 \quad j = 1, 2 \\ 0 < \alpha_j < 1 \end{matrix} \qquad (2.26a)$$

and

$$f_j = \rho_j^{1-\alpha_j} \qquad \begin{matrix} \epsilon = 0 \\ 0 < \alpha_j < 1 \quad j = 1, 2\, . \end{matrix} \qquad (2.26b)$$

From the marginal conditions (2.13),

$$\rho_2 = \eta\rho_1 \qquad (2.27)$$

where

$$\eta \equiv \left(\frac{\beta}{\mu}\right)^{\sigma} \qquad (2.28)$$

and

$$\eta \gtreqless 1 \qquad \text{as} \qquad \mu \lesseqgtr \beta\, . \qquad (2.29)$$

Moreover,

$$\text{sign}\,(\rho_1 - \rho_2) = \text{sign}\,(1 - \eta)\, . \qquad (2.30)$$

From eqs. (2.19) and (2.21), after simplification,

$$\frac{dX_1}{dX_2} = -\frac{\rho(f_1 - \rho_1 f_1') + \rho_1\rho_2 f_1'}{\rho(f_2 - \rho_2 f_2') + \rho_1\rho_2 f_2'} \qquad (2.31)$$

whence

$$\frac{d}{d\rho_1}\,\frac{dX_1}{dX_2} = -\frac{f_1'(f_2 - \rho_2 f_2')B}{\sigma f_1 f_2 [\rho(f_2 - \rho_2 f_2') + \rho_1\rho_2 f_2']^2} \qquad (2.32)$$

where

$$B \equiv 2\rho\rho_2 f_1 f_2 \sigma (1-\mu) + p(\rho-\rho_2)f_2 \left[\rho(f_2-\rho_2 f_2') + \rho_1\rho_2 f_2'\right]$$

$$+ (\rho_1-\rho)\eta f_1 \left[\mu\rho(f_2-\rho_2 f_2') + \rho_1\rho_2 f_2'\right] . \tag{2.33}$$

Now

$$\frac{d^2 X_1}{dX_2^2} = \frac{d}{d\rho_1}\left(\frac{dX_1}{dX_2}\right)\frac{d\rho_1}{dX_2} . \tag{2.34}$$

Hence, if one recalls eqs. (2.23), (2.30), and (2.32),

$$\text{sign}\,\frac{d^2 X_1}{dX_2^2} = \text{sign}\,(\eta-1)B . \tag{2.35}$$

Proposition I(a) follows from eqs. (2.29), (2.33) and (2.35).

We now rewrite B in a form which enables us to attach a sign to it when μ does not lie between 1 and β. From eqs. (2.13) and (2.27),

$$pf_2 = f_1 - (1-\eta\mu)\rho_1 f_1' . \tag{2.36}$$

Hence,

$$B = \rho\rho_2 f_1 f_2 (2\sigma-1)(1-\mu)$$

$$+ (1-\eta\mu)\left[\rho(f_1-\rho_1 f_1') + \rho_1\rho_2 f_1'\right]\left[\rho(f_2-\rho_2 f_2') + \rho_1\rho_2 f_2'\right] . \tag{2.37}$$

Since the square-bracketed terms are positive, the sign of $(1-\eta\mu)$ is of special importance. We note that

$$\text{If } \sigma = 1, \text{ then } 1 - \eta\mu = 1 - \beta < 0 \text{ for all } \mu > 0 ; \tag{2.38a}$$

$$\text{If } \sigma > 1, \text{ then } \gamma > \beta \text{ and } 1 - \eta\mu \gtreqless 0 \text{ as } \mu \gtreqless \gamma ; \tag{2.38b}$$

$$\text{If } \sigma < 1, \text{ then } 0 < \gamma < 1 \text{ and } 1 - \eta\mu \gtreqless 0 \text{ as } \mu \lesseqgtr \gamma . \tag{2.38c}$$

Moreover, γ increases to infinity or falls to zero as μ approaches one from above or below, respectively. From eqs. (2.29), (2.36), (2.37) and (2.38), we infer Propositions I (b) (i), the first sentence of Proposition I (b) (ii), and the first sentence of Proposition II (b).

To squeeze more information from eq. (3.37), it is necessary to consider separately the two cases $\sigma = 1$ and $\sigma \neq 1$. Suppose $\sigma = 1$. Substituting from eq. (2.26b) into (2.37), taking eq. (2.15) into account, and rearranging terms,

$$B = -\frac{\rho_1^2 f_1 f_2}{\mu^2 (1-\alpha_1)(1-\alpha_2)\varphi_2^3}\,(P\lambda^2 + Q\lambda + R) \qquad (2.39)$$

where

$$P = (\alpha_1 - \alpha_2)\alpha_1\alpha_2\psi^2 \qquad (2.40a)$$

$$Q = (\alpha_1 - \alpha_2)(1+\alpha_1+\alpha_2)\varphi_1\psi + (1-\alpha_2)(1+\alpha_1-\alpha_2)\alpha_1\psi^2 \qquad (2.40b)$$

$$R = 2(\alpha_1 - \alpha_2)\varphi_1^2 + (2\alpha_1 - \alpha_2)(1-\alpha_2)\varphi_1\psi \qquad (2.40c)$$

and

$$\varphi_j = \frac{\alpha_j}{(1-\alpha_j)} \qquad\qquad j = 1, 2 \qquad (2.40d)$$

$$\psi = \varphi_2\mu - \varphi_1 \qquad (2.40e)$$

Denote the two roots of B by λ_1 and λ_2. Vieta's rules imply that

(a) $0 < \lambda_1 < \lambda_2 < 1$ if and only if $Q^2 - 4PR > 0$, $Q/P < 0$,

$\qquad (2P+Q)/P > 0$, $R/P > 0$ and $(P+Q+R)/P > 0$; $\qquad (2.41a)$

(b) $0 < \lambda_1 < 1 \leqslant \lambda_2$ if and only if $Q^2 - 4PR > 0$, $R/P > 0$,

$\qquad$ and $(P+Q+R)/P \leqslant 0$; $\qquad (2.41b)$

(c) $\lambda_1 \leqslant 0 < \lambda_2 < 1$ if and only if $Q^2 - 4PR > 0$, $R/P \leqslant 0$,

$\qquad$ and $(P+Q+R)/P > 0$. $\qquad (2.41c)$

In Case (a) the locus of competitive outputs will change its curvature twice, in Cases (b) and (c) only once. In all other possible cases the locus will be either uniformly strictly convex to the origin or uniformly strictly concave. If $\mu > 1$ there are no remaining mysteries; we assume therefore that $\mu < 1$. First, we show that if the locus of competitive outputs is strictly convex to the origin near the axes then it is uniformly strictly convex. Suppose that $d^2 X_1/dX_2^2 \geqslant 0$ for $\lambda = 0$ and $\lambda = 1$ and for some $\mu < 1$. This, together with eqs. (2.35) and (2.39), implies that $R \leqslant 0$ and $P + Q + R \leqslant 0$. Since $P > 0$ and in view of eq. (2.41a) it follows that the inequality $0 < \lambda_1 < \lambda_2 < 1$ cannot hold. Thus Proposition II (a), last sentence, is established. Next we note that, for μ close to one, $P > 0$, $Q < 0$, $R > 0$, $2P + Q < 0$ and $P + Q + R > 0$. On the other hand, for μ positive but close to zero, $P > 0$, $2P + Q > 0$ and $Q^2 - 4PR > 0$; moreover, then

$$Q \lesseqgtr 0 \text{ if } (1-\alpha_1) + (1+\alpha_1)(\alpha_2-\alpha_1) \lesseqgtr 0 \tag{2.42a}$$

$$R \gtreqless 0 \text{ if } 1 + \alpha_2 - 2\alpha_1 \lesseqgtr 0 \tag{2.42b}$$

$$P + Q + R \lesseqgtr 0 \text{ if } 2\alpha_2 - \alpha_1 \lesseqgtr 0 . \tag{2.42c}$$

Thus, for μ positive but close to zero, Q, R, and $P + Q + R$ may be of either sign, depending on the values of α_1 and α_2. For $\mu = 0$, however, $R > 0$ implies $Q < 0$; hence the rest of Proposition II (a) is also established.

Only in the Cobb-Douglas case is B a quadratic function of λ; and only in that case is it true that the locus of competitive outputs is restricted to at most two changes of curvature. When we turn to the case in which $\sigma \neq 1$, we no longer have these convenient properties to draw on and we must be content with conclusions relating to extreme degrees of distortion only. Let us write B explicitly as a function of λ, or $B(\lambda)$. Bearing in mind that $\lambda = 0$, if, and only if, $\rho = \rho_2$ and that $\lambda = 1$ if, and only if, $\rho = \rho_1$, we substitute from eqs. (2.26a), (2.27), and (2.28) into (2.37), to obtain

$$B_0 = \frac{\alpha_2 + (1-\alpha_2)\rho^{-\epsilon}}{\rho^2 f_1(\rho/\eta) f_2(\rho)} B(0) \tag{2.43}$$

and

$$B_1 = \frac{\alpha_1 + (1-\alpha_1)\rho^{-\epsilon}}{\rho^2 \eta f_1(\rho) f_2(\eta\rho)} B(1) , \tag{2.44}$$

where

$$B_0 = (2\sigma-1)(1-\mu)[\alpha_2+(1-\alpha_2)\rho^{-\epsilon}]$$

$$+ (1-\beta^\sigma\mu^{1-\sigma})[\alpha_2+\beta^{-\sigma}\mu^\sigma(1-\alpha_2)\rho^{-\epsilon}]$$

$$= [(2\sigma-1)(1-\alpha_2)\rho^{-\epsilon}+2\sigma\alpha_2] + (1-\alpha_2)\rho^{-\epsilon}\beta^{-\sigma}\mu^\sigma$$

$$- [2\sigma(1-\alpha_2)\rho^{-\epsilon}+(2\sigma-1)\alpha_2]\,\mu - \alpha_2\beta^\sigma\mu^{1-\sigma} \qquad (2.45)$$

and

$$B_1 = (2\sigma-1)(1-\mu)[\alpha_1+(1-\alpha_1)\rho^{-\epsilon}]$$

$$+ (1-\beta^\sigma\mu^{1-\sigma})[\alpha_1\beta^{-\sigma}\mu^\sigma+(1-\alpha_1)\rho^{-\epsilon}]$$

$$= [2\sigma(1-\alpha_1)\rho^{-\epsilon}+(2\sigma-1)\alpha_1] + \alpha_1\beta^{-\sigma}\mu^\sigma$$

$$- [(2\sigma-1)(1-\alpha_1)\rho^{-\epsilon}+2\sigma\alpha_1]\,\mu - (1-\alpha_1)\rho^{-\epsilon}\beta^\sigma\mu^{1-\sigma} \,. \qquad (2.46)$$

Clearly,

$$\text{sign } B_k = \text{sign } B(k) \qquad\qquad k = 0, 1 \,. \qquad (2.47)$$

Suppose now that $\sigma > 1$. Since σ is the highest power of μ in B_0 and B_1, and since $(1-\sigma)$ is the lowest power of μ, eqs. (2.45) and (2.46) imply that

$$B_0 > 0, B_1 > 0 \text{ for sufficiently large } \mu > \beta$$

$$B_0 < 0, B_1 < 0 \text{ for sufficiently small } \mu > 0 \,. \qquad (2.48)$$

From eqs. (2.29), (2.35) and (2.48), d^2X_1/dX_2^2 is negative near both axes if μ is either close to zero or sufficiently large and if σ is greater than one. Under these conditions, therefore, the locus of competitive outputs is strictly concave to the origin near the axes. On the other hand, when $\mu > \beta$ the locus lies below the chord joining its end points. Thus when that condition *also* is satisfied, the locus must be strictly convex to the origin somewhere. The same is true when μ is close to zero for then, as we shall show immediately, the slope of the locus of competitive outputs is numerically less steep than the slope of the chord near the axis of the second good and numerically steeper than the slope of the chord near the other axis. The slope of the chord is

$$S_1 = \frac{-f_1(\rho)}{f_2(\rho)} \tag{2.49}$$

and, from eqs. (2.19) and (2.21), the slope of the locus of competitive outputs is

$$S_2 = -\frac{f_1(\rho) - \rho f_1'(\rho) + \rho \eta f_1'(\rho)}{f_2(\rho\eta)} \qquad \text{when } \lambda = 1 \text{ (i.e., } \rho = \rho_1 \text{)} \tag{2.50a}$$

and

$$S_3 = -\frac{f_1\left(\dfrac{\rho}{\eta}\right)}{f_2(\rho) - \rho f_2'(\rho) + \dfrac{\rho}{\eta} f_2'(\rho)} \qquad \text{when } \lambda = 0 \text{ (i.e., } \rho = \rho_2 \text{)}. \tag{2.50b}$$

For $\sigma > 1$, η tends to infinity, $f_1(\rho/\eta)$ tends to zero, and $f_2(\rho\eta)$ tends to $\alpha_2^{-1/\epsilon}$ as μ approaches zero. Hence, for sufficiently small μ, $|S_3| < |S_1| < |S_2|$, which proves our assertion.

Suppose alternatively that $0 < \sigma < \frac{1}{2}$. The highest and lowest powers of μ in B_0 and B_1 are one and zero, respectively. Without further assumptions about the values of α_1, α_2, ρ, and σ, therefore, the signs of B_0 and B_1 for extreme values of μ cannot be determined. It follows that near the axes the locus of competitive outputs can have every possible curvature. For small μ, moreover, $|S_1| < |S_2|$ but $|S_3| \gtreqless |S_1|$. Even for μ close to zero, therefore, the locus may near the X_2 axis lie above the chord joining its end points. Finally, it seems possible for the locus to be strictly convex to the origin near both axes and concave somewhere in between.

Finally, we note that the case in which $\frac{1}{2} \leq \sigma < 1$ and μ is extreme has already been treated.

That concludes our proof of Propositions I and II. It remains only to consider Proposition III. We now have $\alpha_1 = \alpha_2$ and therefore $\beta = \gamma = 1$. Suppose, first, that $\sigma = 1$. Then, from eqs. (2.29), (2.35) and (2.40),

$$\text{sign } \frac{d^2 X_1}{dX_2^2} = \text{sign}\,(\lambda\mu + 1 - \lambda) \qquad \text{if } \mu \neq 1. \tag{2.51}$$

Thus the locus of competitive outputs is uniformly strictly convex to the origin for all $\mu > 0$, $\mu \neq 1$. Suppose next that $\frac{1}{2} \leq \sigma < 1$. Then, from eqs. (2.29), (2.35), (2.37), and (2.38c),

$$\frac{d^2 X_1}{dX_2^2} > 0 \qquad\qquad \text{if } \mu \neq 1 . \qquad\qquad (2.52)$$

Finally, suppose that $0 < \sigma < \frac{1}{2}$ or $\sigma > 1$. Then, from eqs. (2.45) and (2.46), for extreme values of μ the curvature of the locus of competitive outputs is the same as when $\alpha_1 > \alpha_2$. Thus Proposition III is established.

As a by-product of our proof of Theorem 1 we have the following extremely plausible proposition concerning the relationship between the slope of the locus of competitive outputs and the commodity price ratio[9].

Theorem 2: If dX_1/dX_2 is the slope of the locus of competitive outputs at a point associated with the price ratio p, then

$$\left| \frac{dX_1}{dX_2} \right| \gtreqless p, \text{ as } \mu \lesseqgtr 1 . \qquad\qquad (2.53)$$

Thus if the market of one factor is distorted, the locus will always be intersected by the price line at the equilibrium point.

Proof: The proof is immediate from eqs. (2.24), (2.25), (2.24a) and (2.24b).

2.2. The Relation between Product Prices and Equilibrium Outputs

General Neoclassical Production Functions

We revert for the time being to the more general neoclassical production functions (2.2), and seek a parametric representation of outputs in terms of commodity prices. As a means to that end, we set out equations that give expression to the assumptions of competition, full employment and profit maximization.

The requirement that both factors be fully employed can be expressed as

$$\begin{pmatrix} a_{11} & a_{21} \\ a_{12} & a_{22} \end{pmatrix} \begin{pmatrix} X_1 \\ X_2 \end{pmatrix} = \begin{pmatrix} V_1 \\ V_2 \end{pmatrix} \qquad\qquad (2.54)$$

---

[9] See Hagen [2], p. 508.

Given perfect competition, free entry, and incomplete specialization of production, it follows that in each industry price equals the average cost of production. This equality can be expressed as

$$
\begin{pmatrix} a_{11} & a_{12} \\ \mu a_{21} & a_{22} \end{pmatrix} \begin{pmatrix} w_1 \\ w_2 \end{pmatrix} = \begin{pmatrix} p_1 \\ p_2 \end{pmatrix}
\tag{2.55}
$$

where w_i is the price of the ith factor of production in the first industry, in terms of any *numéraire*, and p_j is the price of the jth product. It remains to give expression to the assumption of profit maximization. Let χ_j be the set $\{(a_{j1}, a_{j2})\}$ each member of which satisfies eq. (2.2):

$$
\chi_j = \{(a_{j1}, a_{j2}) F_j(a_{j1}, a_{j2}) = 1\} .
\tag{2.56}
$$

Then the problem facing the individual firm is that of minimizing its unit costs,

$$
\min_{(a_{11}, a_{12}) \in \chi_1} \quad w_1 a_{11} + w_2 a_{12}
\tag{2.57a}
$$

$$
\min_{(a_{21}, a_{22}) \in \chi_2} \quad \mu w_1 a_{21} + w_2 a_{22} .
\tag{2.57b}
$$

As a necessary condition of cost minimization,

$$
\begin{pmatrix} da_{11} & da_{12} \\ \mu da_{21} & da_{22} \end{pmatrix} \begin{pmatrix} w_1 \\ w_2 \end{pmatrix} = \begin{pmatrix} 0 \\ 0 \end{pmatrix}
\tag{2.58}
$$

where it is understood that the increments da_{ji} are consistent with eq. (2.2).

That completes our specification of the economy. It will prove convenient, however, to place the key equations on a common footing by rewriting eqs. (2.54) and (2.55) in terms of relative changes of the variables. Differentiating eq. (2.54) and rearranging slightly, we obtain

$$
\begin{pmatrix} \lambda_{11} & \lambda_{21} \\ \lambda_{12} & \lambda_{22} \end{pmatrix} \begin{pmatrix} \hat{X}_1 \\ \hat{X}_2 \end{pmatrix} = \begin{pmatrix} \hat{V}_1 \\ \hat{V}_2 \end{pmatrix} - \begin{pmatrix} \lambda_{11}\hat{a}_{11} + \lambda_{21}\hat{a}_{21} \\ \lambda_{12}\hat{a}_{12} + \lambda_{22}\hat{a}_{22} \end{pmatrix}
\tag{2.59}
$$

where $\lambda_{ji} = V_{ji}/V_i$ is the proportion of the community's endowment of the ith factor employed by the jth industry (so that $\lambda_{1i} + \lambda_{2i} = 1$) and where $\hat{X}_1 = dX_1/X_1$, etc. (Notice that λ_{12} is the λ of Section 2.1). In similar fashion, we obtain from eq. (2.55),

$$\begin{pmatrix} \theta_{11} & \theta_{12} \\ \theta_{21} & \theta_{22} \end{pmatrix} \begin{pmatrix} \hat{w}_1 \\ \hat{w}_2 \end{pmatrix} = \begin{pmatrix} \hat{p}_1 \\ \hat{p}_2 \end{pmatrix} - \begin{pmatrix} \theta_{11}\hat{a}_{11} + \theta_{12}\hat{a}_{12} \\ \theta_{21}\hat{a}_{21} + \theta_{22}\hat{a}_{22} \end{pmatrix} \qquad (2.60)$$

where θ_{ji} is the share of the ith factor in the costs of the jth industry (so that $\theta_{j1} + \theta_{j2} = 1$). It is easily verified that

$$\det(\lambda_{ji}) \equiv |\lambda| = \frac{X_1 X_2}{V_1 V_2}(a_{11}a_{22} - a_{12}a_{21}) \qquad (2.61a)$$

and that

$$\det(\theta_{ji}) \equiv |\theta| = \frac{w_1 w_2}{p_1 p_2}(a_{11}a_{22} - \mu a_{12}a_{21}) . \qquad (2.61b)$$

Thus $|\lambda|$ is positive or negative as, in the face of factor market distortions, the production of the first or second commodity is relatively intensive in its use of the first factor of production. On the other hand, $|\theta|$ can be interpreted as a measure of relative factor intensities *in a value sense*. If one puts aside the uninteresting special case in which $\mu = 1$, the determinants $|\lambda|$ and $|\theta|$ may be of opposite sign,

$$|\lambda| \cdot |\theta| \gtreqless 0 \qquad \text{if} \qquad \mu \neq 1 . \qquad (2.62)$$

Our next step is to eliminate the $\hat{a}_{ji}$ from eqs. (2.59) and (2.60) with the aid of eq. (2.58). To convert eq. (2.58) into the required carat form is a trivial matter,

$$\theta_{j1}\hat{a}_{j1} + \theta_{j2}\hat{a}_{j2} = 0 \qquad j = 1, 2 . \qquad (2.63)$$

We next introduce an alternative definition of the elasticity of factor substitution σ_j:

$$\hat{a}_{j1} - \hat{a}_{j2} = -\sigma_j(\hat{w}_1 - \hat{w}_2) \qquad j = 1, 2 . \qquad (2.64)$$

We solve eqs. (2.63) and (2.64) for the a_{ji} and obtain

$$\hat{a}_{11} = -\theta_{12}\sigma_1(\hat{w}_1-\hat{w}_2)$$

$$\hat{a}_{12} = \theta_{11}\sigma_1(\hat{w}_1-\hat{w}_2)$$

$$\hat{a}_{21} = -\theta_{22}\sigma_2(\hat{w}_1-\hat{w}_2)$$

$$\hat{a}_{22} = \theta_{21}\sigma_2(\hat{w}_1-\hat{w}_2)$$

(2.65)

We substitute from eqs. (2.65) into (2.59) and (2.60) and we obtain

$$\begin{vmatrix} \lambda_{11} & \lambda_{21} \\ \lambda_{12} & \lambda_{22} \end{vmatrix} \begin{pmatrix} \hat{X}_1 \\ \hat{X}_2 \end{pmatrix} = \begin{pmatrix} \hat{V}_1 \\ \hat{V}_2 \end{pmatrix} + (\hat{w}_1-\hat{w}_2) \begin{pmatrix} \delta_1 \\ -\delta_2 \end{pmatrix}$$

(2.66)

and

$$\begin{pmatrix} \theta_{11} & \theta_{12} \\ \theta_{21} & \theta_{22} \end{pmatrix} \begin{pmatrix} \hat{w}_1 \\ \hat{w}_2 \end{pmatrix} = \begin{pmatrix} \hat{p}_1 \\ \hat{p}_2 \end{pmatrix}$$

(2.67)

where

$$\delta_1 \equiv \lambda_{11}\theta_{12}\sigma_1 + \lambda_{21}\theta_{22}\sigma_2$$

and

$$\delta_2 \equiv \lambda_{12}\theta_{11}\sigma_1 + \lambda_{22}\theta_{21}\sigma_2 .$$

As our last step, we solve eq. (2.67) for $(\hat{w}_1-\hat{w}_2)$ and substitute in eq. (2.66), then set $\hat{V}_1 = 0 = \hat{V}_2$ and solve for $(\hat{X}_1-\hat{X}_2)$:

$$\hat{X}_1 - \hat{X}_2 = \xi(\hat{p}_1-\hat{p}_2)$$

(2.68)

where

$$\xi = \frac{\delta_1 + \delta_2}{|\lambda| \cdot |\theta|} .$$

(2.69)

It is easily verified that $\delta_1 + \delta_2$ is non-negative. The denominator $|\lambda| \cdot |\theta|$, on the other hand, may be of either sign (see eq. (2.62)). We may be sure therefore that there exist circumstances in which the price-output relationships are perverse; increases in price are associated with decreases in equilibrium output.

The significance of this conclusion would be much enhanced if we could set out, in terms of the basic technical and factor-supply characteristics of the economy, necessary and sufficient conditions for the emergence of each of the two types of price-output relationship, normal and perverse. In particular, it would be of advantage to know whether a normal relationship emerges if, and only if, the locus of competitive outputs is locally concave to the origin and whether a perverse relationship emerges if, and only if, the locus is locally convex. Our attack on these questions has been only partially successful; but some progress has been made.

We begin by noting that in the absence of distortions (i.e., when $\mu = 1$) and provided they do not both vanish the determinants $|\lambda|$ and $|\theta|$ are necessarily of the same sign. Under the same proviso, we may infer from the continuity of the functions $\lambda_{ji}(\mu)$ and $\theta_{ji}(\mu)$ that, for μ sufficiently close to one, the determinants remain of the same sign. For sufficiently small distortions, therefore, the price-output relationships are normal; increases in price are associated with increases in equilibrium output.

With μ unrestricted, however, we are reduced to a dissection of cases.

Case 1a: $|\lambda| < 0$, $\mu > 1$. In this case the first factor is applied relatively intensively in the second industry in spite of the higher reward earned there. Evidently, $|\theta|$ is also negative and therefore $|\lambda| \cdot |\theta|$ must be positive. It follows that the price-output relationships are normal.

Case 1b: $|\lambda| < 0, \mu < 1$. The first factor is used relatively intensively in the second industry but receives there a lower reward. $|\lambda| \cdot |\theta|$ may be of either sign, hence the price-output relationships may be normal as well as perverse, depending on the prevailing circumstances.

Case 2: $|\lambda| > 0$. In this case the first factor is applied relatively intensively in the first industry. From the definitions (2.61a) and (2.61b), it is clear that, for $\mu > 1$ as well as for $\mu < 1$, $|\theta|$ may be negative, $|\lambda| \cdot |\theta|$ negative and the price-output relationships perverse.

We know that in Case 1a the locus of competitive outputs may be locally convex to the origin. Hence, the conjecture that a normal price-output relationship is always associated with local concavity of the locus turns out to be wrong. Nevertheless, as they stand these conclusions are of limited interest. To breathe life into them it is necessary to relate the signs of $|\lambda|$ and $|\theta|$ to the curvature of the locus of competitive outputs. We have not been able to trace this relationship for general homogeneous production functions, but we have been able to do so in the special case in which production functions are of the CES type.

Production Functions with Constant Elasticities of Substitution

Suppose then that production relationships are described by eq. (2.3). In competitive equilibrium, minus the marginal rate of factor substitution must be equal to the ratio of factor rewards:

$$\frac{1-\alpha_1}{\alpha_1}\left(\frac{a_{12}}{a_{11}}\right)^{1/\sigma} = \frac{w_1}{w_2}$$

$$\frac{1-\alpha_2}{\alpha_2}\left(\frac{a_{22}}{a_{21}}\right)^{1/\sigma} = \mu\frac{w_1}{w_2}. \tag{2.70}$$

It follows, taking also eqs. (2.7), (2.28), and (2.61) into account, that

$$a_{12}a_{21} = \left(\frac{\beta}{\mu}\right)^{\sigma} a_{11}a_{22} = \eta a_{11}a_{22} \tag{2.71}$$

$$\text{sign } |\lambda| = \text{sign}(1-\eta) \tag{2.72a}$$

$$\text{sign } |\theta| = \text{sign}(1-\eta\mu). \tag{2.72b}^{[10]}$$

As we already know, and as is also implied by eq. (2.72a),

$$\mu = \beta > 1 \tag{2.73}$$

is the critical degree of distortion beyond which the relative factor intensities of the two industries change.

---

[10] Eqs. (2.35) and (2.37) show that the signs of the determinants $|\lambda|$ and $|\theta|$ are of crucial importance with regard to the local curvature of the locus of competitive outputs. Moreover, comparing these two equations with eqs. (2.68) and (2.69), it is evident that the price-output relationship need not be normal, or respectively perverse, wherever the locus is strictly concave, or respectively strictly convex, to the origin. (Examples will be given later.)

It follows from eqs. (2.38) and (2.72) that $|\lambda| \cdot |\theta|$ is positive if, and only if, (i)$\sigma < 1$ and $\gamma < \mu < \beta$, or (ii)$\sigma > 1$ and either $\mu < \beta$ or $\mu > \gamma$, or (iii)$\sigma = 1$ and $\mu < \beta$. It follows also that $|\lambda| \cdot |\theta|$ is negative if, and only if, (a)$\sigma < 1$ and either $\mu < \gamma$ or $\mu > \beta$, or (b)$\sigma > 1$ and $\beta < \mu < \gamma$, or (c)$\sigma = 1$ and $\mu > \beta$.

It is convenient to examine the Cobb-Douglas and other CES cases separately. Consider first the Cobb-Douglas case ($\sigma = 1$). From eqs. (2.61b), (2.71), and the fact that $\alpha_1 > \alpha_2$, $|\theta|$ is necessarily positive. On the other hand, $|\lambda|$ is positive or negative as μ is less than or greater than β. Thus the price-output relationship is perverse or normal as μ is greater than or less than β, that is, as the distortion is or is not severe enough to reverse the relative factor intensities of the two industries. The interesting case, then, is that in which μ is less than β and sufficiently small to create at least local convexity (to the origin) of the locus of competitive outputs[11]. For in that case the price-output relationship is normal but the locus of competitive outputs per-versely convex to the origin. Thus we have established the following theorem.

Theorem 3 (Cobb-Douglas): If the relative reward of a factor is lower in the industry in which in the absence of factor market distortions it would be applied relatively intensively, then all equilibrium price-output relationships are necessarily normal, an increase in price being associated with an increase in output; and this is so however severe the distortion and whatever the shape of the locus of competitive outputs (it is so, for example, even when the locus is uniformly convex to the origin). If the relative reward of a factor is higher in the industry in which in the absence of factor market distortions it would be applied relatively intensively, then all equilibrium price-output relationships are normal or perverse according as, respectively, the locus of competitive outputs is normally concave to the origin or abnormally con-vex (i.e., as, respectively, the relative factor intensities of the two industries have not been or have been reversed by the distortion).

Let us turn now to the remaining CES cases ($\sigma \neq 1$). From the conclusions summarized two paragraphs earlier, we may infer:

Theorem 4 (CES, $\sigma \neq 1$): The equilibrium price-output relationship is normal when either $\sigma < 1$ and μ lies between γ and β or $\sigma > 1$ and μ lies outside the interval defined by β and γ. If neither condition is satisfied and if μ is different from β and γ the equilibrium price-output relationship is perverse.

---

[11] See Hagen [2], p. 508.

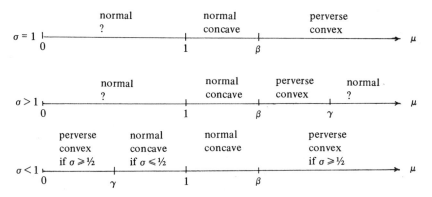

Fig. 2.5. Price-output relationship and shape of the locus of competitive outputs.

Fig. 2.5. provides an illustration. The interesting cases are those in which (i) $\sigma < 1$ and $\mu < \gamma$, so that the price-output relationship is perverse even though no reversal of factor intensities occurs; (ii) $\sigma > 1$ and $\mu > \gamma$, so that the price-output relationship is normal even though the relative factor intensities of the two industries are reversed; (iii) $0 < \sigma < \frac{1}{2}$ and μ extreme, so that the price-output relationship is perverse even though the locus of competitive outputs is locally concave to the origin; and (iv) $\frac{1}{2} \leqslant \sigma < 1$ and $1 < \mu < \beta$, or $\sigma > 1$ and μ extreme, so that the price-output relationship is normal even though the locus of competitive outputs is locally convex. From Cases (iii) and (iv), for example, we learn once again that the conjecture stated on the first page, that perverse price-output relationships are always associated with local convexity of the locus of competitive outputs, and vice versa, is invalid, even when production functions are of the CES type.

We have assumed that only one factor market is distorted. However, this involves no real loss of generality. Thus suppose that distortions are present in both markets, so that

$$\mu_1 f_1' = p f_2'$$

$$\mu_2(f_1 - \rho_1 f_1') = p(f_2 - \rho_2 f_2')$$

where μ_1 and μ_2 are positive, finite constants. Then all of our results carry over, as may be verified by identifying μ, p, p_1, p_2 with $\mu^* = \mu_1/\mu_2$, $p^* = p/\mu_2$, $p_1^* = p_1$, $p_2^* = p_2/\mu_2$, respectively. The reinterpretation of our results is left to the reader.

2.3. Factor Market Distortions and Variable Returns to Scale

Throughout our calculations in Sections 2.1 and 2.2, we have maintained the traditional assumption that returns to scale are constant in both industries. This is not the time to have serious second thoughts about that assumption. Elsewhere, however, we have examined in detail, without the complication of factor market distortions, some of the implications of variable returns to scale [3]. Many of the conclusions of that paper carry over to a context of factor market distortions. In particular this is true of Theorem 2 of [3]. For example, the locus of competitive outputs is convex or concave to the origin in a neighbourhood of zero output for the *j*th industry according as that industry enjoys increasing or decreasing returns to scale, and this is true whatever the degree of factor market distortion and whatever the nature of scale returns in the other industry.

References

[1] A.Fishlow and P.David, "Optimal Resource Allocation in an Imperfect Market Setting", *Journal of Political Economy* LXIX, No. 6 (December 1961) pp. 529-546.
[2] E.E.Hagen, "An Economic Justification of Protectionism", *Quarterly Journal of Economics* LXXII, No. 4 (November 1958) pp. 496-514.
[3] H.Herberg and M.C.Kemp, "Some Implications of Variable Returns to Scale", *The Canadian Journal of Economics* II, No. 3 (August 1969) pp. 403-415.
[4] H.G.Johnson, "Factor Market Distortions and the Shape of the Transformation Curve", *Econometrica* 34, No. 3 (July 1966) pp. 686-698.

CHAPTER 3

TRADE AND FACTOR PRICES IN
A MULTI-COMMODITY WORLD

Jaroslav VANEK and Trent J. BERTRAND [1]

In the present paper we are concerned with situations in which the number of commodities exceeds the number of factors and pursue several objectives. First, we use an approach based on the consideration of a world production possibility surface to, (a) reconsider the question of factor price equalization in the framework of the three-commodity, two-factor model employed in several recent contributions [2]; (b) study the influence of production and demand conditions on the likelihood of factor-price equalization; and (c) extend the analysis from the three to the multi-commodity case (Section 3.2). Second, we explain the need for a substantial amendment of the factor proportions theory of trade for a multi-commodity model and offer a reinterpretation based on previous results obtained by one of the present authors (section 3.3). Finally, a possible explanation for trade in a multi-commodity world is suggested which is especially appealing as a framework for analyzing trade flows between advanced economies (Section 3.4).

3.1. The Production Possibility Surface when Commodities Outnumber Factors

As a preliminary step to our analysis, in this section we investigate the nature of the production possibility surface when commodities outnumber

---

[1] The authors are Professor Kindleberger's students in first and second generation, respectively.

[2] See T.J. Bertrand [1], H.G. Johnson [2], and J.R. Melvin [5]. Earlier papers by Land [3] and Meade [6] also use the two-factor, three-commodity model in discussing factor price equalization.

factors. We can be brief in this presentation because J. Melvin, in a recent contribution, [3] has considered this same question at some length.

We use a three-dimensional diagramatic technique based on the three-commodity (X, Y, and Z) and two-factor (capital K and labor L) case. The production functions for the three commodities are assumed linear homogeneous. Furthermore, it is assumed that these functions fulfill the strong Samuelson no factor intensity reversals assumption; i.e., X, Y, and Z show decreasing capital labor input ratios for any given factor price ratio.

Under these assumptions, a given factor-price ratio will define three rays in the factor space indicating factor input proportions for each commodity. Because of the constant returns to scale assumption, the lengths of each ray measures the output quantity of the respective commodity. In Figure 3.1a, three such rays are plotted in the box diagram defined by factor endowments of a particular country. The ray for the capital intensive product X is drawn from the origin O_1 while that for the labor intensive product Z is drawn from the origin O_2. The intersection of these two rays defines a combination of outputs, $O_1 d$ and $O_2 d$, which is efficient (i.e., the marginal rate of factor substitution is equal in the production of X and Z and factor supplies are fully employed). This combination will therefore contribute a point d to the production possibility curve PP' in the XZ plane of Figure 3.1b. A similar procedure for all feasible factor price ratios will give rise to a series of points forming a contract curve in the box diagram to which will correspond the entire production possibility curve PP' of Figure 3.1b.

With the factor-price ratio used in Figure 3.1a, it is also possible to see the effect of a shift in production from X and Z towards the third good Y with intermediate factor intensity. By sliding the factor input proportions ray for Y along either of the other rays starting from point d, we trace out the reductions in X and Z production required to permit an increased output of Y. For instance, when the Y factor proportions ray takes the position cc', the production of Z and X has fallen by $c'd$ and cd units respectively. Similarly, when the ray takes the position bb', production of X has been reduced to $O_1 b$ and of Z to $O_2 b'$. Finally, when the Y ray takes the position of aa', output of X has fallen to zero; a' will represent a Pareto optimal production combination of Y and Z and will therefore contribute a point a to the production possibility curve $P'P''$ in the ZY plane of Figure 3.1b. The essential aspect of the change in production with fixed factor prices is that

---

[3] J.R. Melvin [5]. As noted by Melvin [5], p. 1249, the nature of the production surface has previously been recognized by P.A. Samuelson [7], Meade [6], and Travis [10].

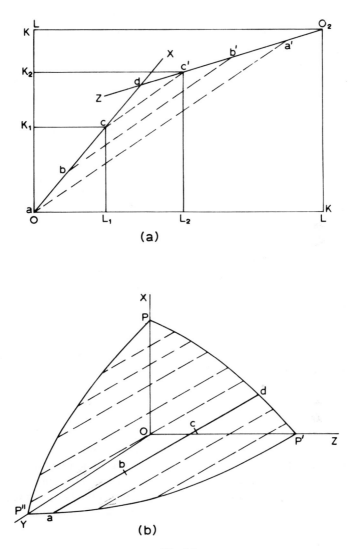

Fig. 3.1

the movement in Figure 3.1b from point *d* to point *a* is linear; that is, if it requires a reduction of 0.5 units of *X* and 1.5 units of *Z* to permit the efficient production of one unit of *Y*, it will require a reduction of 1 unit of *X* and 3 units of *Z* to permit the efficient production of 2 units of *Y*. This is an immediate result of the similarity of triangles traced out by the shifting of the Y factor proportions ray (such as dcc', dbb', and daa'). This process will be repeated for all other factor prices and the three-dimensional production surface of Figure 3.1b will therefore be generated by straight line segments, each corresponding to a different factor-price ratio, running from the XZ plane towards Y. This is so because it will always be possible to reduce output of the X and Z goods in the proportions required to release the factor combination needed for efficient production Y. Here we have dealt with only the three good situations but the extension into the multi-commodity situation is straightforward. Although it cannot be visualized, for instance, with four goods to straight line segments of our Figure 3.1b would become planes in the four-dimensional space.

An interesting result of the nature of this production possibility surface in a world with international differences in production technologies where product prices have no clear relationship to technological conditions in any particular country is that a country will generally — except for sheerest of accidents — produce only as many products as there are factors. This is true because there would be no reason for the price plane to lie along the straight line type production possibility surface derived here. This is not the case if it is assumed, as we do from now on, that production functions are similar for all countries.

3.2. Factor Prices in the Multi-Commodity Model

In this section, we consider the likelihood of factor price equalization when the number of commodities exceeds the number of factors. [4] Under the assumption of identical production functions and no factor intensity reversals, as is well known, [5] factor price equalization requires the potential for efficient production in common of as many commodities as there are factors by the trading countries. "Production in common" means that the marginal rate of factor substitution will be equated between countries; i.e., relative factor prices will be equated. With identical production functions,

---

[4] This question has been the center of considerable debate in the literature. Tinbergen [9] and Land [3] have argued that factor-price equalization would be less likely; Samuelson [7] and Johnson [2] that it would be more likely; Meade [6] that it would be equally likely; and finally Bertrand [1] and Melvin [5] that any conclusion depends on the nature of demand as well as production conditions. In the present paper, we make the minimal assumption on demand that permits conclusions to be derived.

[5] See P.A. Samuelson [7].

absolute factor prices will also be equal. Our approach in this section is therefore to define the areas on the world production surface where this requirement is fulfilled.

In Figure 3.2, a world production surface is constructed from the production blocks of Country I and II. Country I, in the exercise, is assumed to have a higher capital to labor endowment ratio than does Country II. By reversing the axis of the production block of Country I and sliding it along that of Country II so that common marginal rates of transformation, where they exist, slide along each other, the world production surface is traced out by the origin of the production block of Country I. Line segments, such as *ab* and *bc*, it will be noted, are parallel in space because of the common marginal rate of transformation between production of the three goods.

The resulting world production surface consists of four well-defined

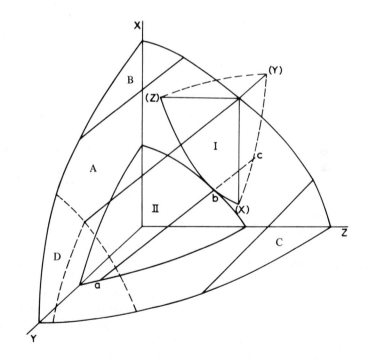

Fig. 3.2

regions: Region A in which both countries produce all three goods: Region B in which Country I produces X and Country II produces X, Y, and Z; Region C in which Country II produces Z and Country I produces X, Y, and Z; and Region D in which Country I produces X and Y and Country II produces Y and Z. As is evident from the method of construction, Regions A, B, and C are ruled surfaces reflecting the nature of the underlying production blocks.

Region A is critical for factor-price equalization. Only in that area is the requirement for factor-price equalization (production in common of as many doos as factors) satisfied. Therefore, factor-price equalization will result only if the world demand point falls within Region A.

While the four regions on the world production surface we have defined exhaust the possible patterns of specialization with the three-commodity, two-factor model, not all four regions need appear on the surface. In Figure 3.3, changes in the world production surface resulting from increasing divergence between the factor endowment ratios of the two countries are demonstrated. In Figure 3.3a, Region A covers all of the world production block which is entirely a ruled surface. This case is only possible when the factor endowment ratios of the two countries are identical. Factor-price equalization will occur regardless of demand conditions. In Figure 3.3b, factor endowment ratios have diverged sufficiently to give rise to a production block similar to that derived in Figure 3.2. Since the reduced A region still includes sections on the $X-Z$, $X-Y$, and $Y-Z$ quadrants, the possibility of factor-price equalization would also exist in any reduced two-commodity, two-factor model. In Figure 3.3c, still greater divergence in factor endowment ratios has reduced the A region to such a degree that in the reduced $X-Y$ or $Y-Z$ model, there would be no possibility of factor-price equalization. However, in the reduced $X-Z$ or three-commodity model the possibility remains. Finally, in Figure 3.3d, the greater divergence in factor endowment ratios has eliminated the critical A region, and there is no possibility of factor-price equalization.

The production conditions and factor endowment ratios underlying the differences between the four examples shown in Figure 3.3 can be studied with the aid of a diagram introduced by H.G. Johnston [2]. In Figure 3.4, the technological relationship between the capital-labor ratios in the three industries is plotted against the ratio between the price of labor w and the price of capital　r. Given a capital-labor endowment ratio, say $(K/L)_{II}$ for country II, the diagram shows that the factor-price ratio could range from $(w/r)_1$ to $(w/r)_2$. Alternatively, given any factor-price ratio, the diagram shows the capital-labor input ratios that would be used in producing the three goods. The correspondence between Figure 3.4 and the world production

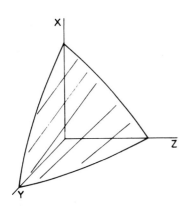
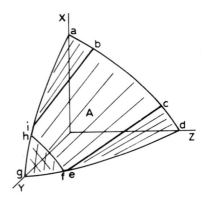
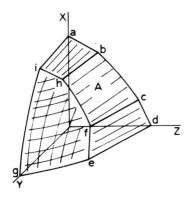
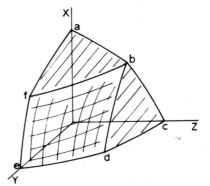

Fig. 3.3

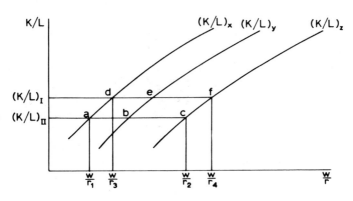

Fig. 3.4

surface can be seen by the relationship between the critical Region A in the latter diagrams and the "overlap" of feasible factor prices defined in Figure 3.4. For instance, if the feasible factor-price ratio range of Country II overlaps with the range $(w/r)^3$ to $(w/r)^4$ defined by the factor endowment ratio $(K/L)_I$ for Country I, the critical Region A will exist on the world production surface. Because there is also an overlap between ab and de and between bc and ef in Figure 3.4, the Region A will include sections on the X-Y and Y-Z quadrants of the world production block; that is, the world production surface will be as shown in Figure 3.3b. The greater the relative overlap in the ranges of possible factor price ratios, the greater is the Region A in relation to the total world production surface.

On the basis of diagrams 3.3 and 3.4 we can define certain factors that tend to increase the likelihood of factor-price equalization. First, and most obvious, the closer factor endowment ratios are in the two countries the more likely is factor-price equalization. Second, the greater the dissimilarity in the production processes the more likely is factor price equalization. By dissimilarity is meant the greater the divergence in factor input ratios at a given factor-price ratio. In Figure 3.4, increasing dissimilarity would correspond to growing distance between the factor input ratio lines for the different goods that would result in increasing overlap of feasible price ranges and a corresponding growth of the critical region A in Figure 3.3. Third, the greater the substitutability in production the more likely is factor-price equalization. This can be seen from Figure 3.4 where greater substitutability is reflected by more positively sloped factor input ratio lines (i.e., a given change in the factor-price ratio will lead to a greater change in factor input proportions) which increases the range of overlap and therefore the critical Region A in Figure 3.3. Fourth, the less extreme are demand conditions the more likely is factor-price equalization. This can be seen from Figure 3.3 where the regions of non-equalization occur when demand is either biased toward Y (leading to the capital abundant country producing X and Y and the labor abundant country producing Y and Z) or biased towards X or Z (leading one country to completely specialize in producing one commodity).

An important question is whether the addition of more commodities increases the probability of factor-price equalization. Reference to our three-good, two-factor model would suggest that factor-price equalization does become more likely, as can be seen with reference to the critical Region A in Figure 3.3. When the third good introduced has an extreme factor intensity, there is a strong expectation that factor-price equalization becomes more likely. For instance, with reference to Figure 3.3c, the probability goes from zero to some positive fraction. When the third good is the intermediate factor intensive commodity Y, comparison of the region A in relation to the total surface with bc in relation to ad in either Figures 3.3b or 3.3c suggests that any increase or decrease in the probability of factor-price equalization is not likely to be too pronounced.

Some approximate arithmetic substance can be given to these expectations in reference to Figure 3.5 where we have linearized the three-commodity, two-factor case similar to that of Figure 3.3b. On the assumption that demand is equally likely to fall anywhere on the production possibility surface, it is easily seen from the relative lengths of the segments that in the two-good case with X and Z the probability of factor-price equalization is 1/2, while with X and Y or with Y and Z, it is 1/4. In the three-good case, this probability is 15/32 or approximately 1/2. In going from the two extreme intensity goods case to the three-good case, there has been no change; but if the original two goods were X and Y or Y and Z, the probability of factor-price equalization doubles. If the selection of the original two goods was at random, the addition of the third good would mean an increase in the probability of factor price equalization from 1/3 (i.e., $1/4 \times 1/3 + 1/4 \times 1/3 + 2/4 \times 1/3$) to 1/2. [6]

It is by no means a simple matter to extend the analysis conducted thus far to a situation involving more than three products. However, the task is not entirely hopeless. Note that already in the case of the two goods — and, of course, two factors of production — the locus of world production points can be approximated by a line. On that line then can be distinguished three segments, the middle one pertaining to solutions with factor price equalization; we recall that that segment can vanish altogether. Such a one-dimensional locus is illustrated in Figure 3.6a.

---

[6] In a recent article in *Economica* [2], H.G. Johnson has argued in terms of the three-commodity, two-factor model that the probability of factor-price equalization is unaffected by the introduction of a commodity with intermediate factor intensity while it is unambiguously increased with the introduction of a commodity with extreme factor intensity. While this conclusion closely parallels our finding here, in our opinion the Johnson argument is incorrect. He treats the probability of factor-price equalization as dependent solely on the overlap of feasible factor prices in trading countries; his conclusion then immediately follows as can be seen with reference to Figure 3.5. However, this treatment ignores the possibility of specialization on two different commodities by the trading countries (i.e., the solutions in the region D of Figure 3.3). Thus, we know that if an intermediate factor intensity commodity with a relatively high demand were introduced, the probability of factor price equalization would likely be decreased whereas the Johnson analysis would show no change in the probability. See T.J. Bertrand [1] for more detailed criticism of the Johnson approach.

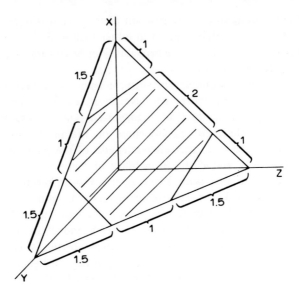

Fig. 3.5

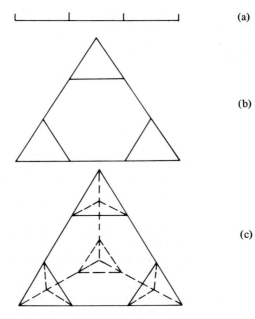

Fig. 3.6

If now we move to three products with two factors, we have the situation just analyzed in this section. The locus of world production points can be approximated by a triangle (suspended by its extremities at the three coordinate axes). The three sides of the triangle, the intercepts with the three coordinate planes, resemble the two-dimensional (two-product) case illustrated in Figure 3.6a; the complete triangle is shown in Figure 3.6b. To get from the totality of possible world production points to those permitting factor-price equalization, we now trunkate the triangle, as indicated in the diagram, by eliminating the areas adjacent to the three axes. We have again postulated that the equalization zone at the intercepts (i.e., along the sides of the triangle) is 1/3 of the total possibility of world production. We know from the analysis of this section that equal zones of equalization at all three sides are impossible, but for the purpose of our exposition we permit ourselves this streamlining because it simplifies the analysis and does not affect significantly its essence. [7] We note that the equalization area now has changed from 1/3 of the total production possibilities for the two-good case, to the hexagon equivalent to 6/9 in the three-good case. Accordingly, with a constant density of probabilities of the world demand points, the probability of factor-price equalization has increased from 1/3 to 2/3.

With four goods and still two factors, we now have four coordinate axes and a four-dimensional space which, of course, we cannot visualize. But since our approximations of the production sets always had one less dimension than the production space, we can still visualize such sets. Assuming again the 1/3 equalization zones at the coordinate-plane intercepts (now six in number) by our averaging, or "streamlining" procedure, we obtain the pattern illustrated in Figure 3.6c. The trunkation at the axis intercepts now is performed by planes, and the (approximate) probability of factor-price equalization now passes from 6/9 for the three-good case, to 23/27 (equals 27/27 minus 4/27), the total production set of 27 equal bodies being reduced by the four adjacent to the axes, as indicated in the diagram. By analogy, and still retaining the 1/3 equalization zone at the coordinate-plane intercepts, we

---

[7] The essence is a convergence towards a higher probability of factor-price equalization. However, the assumption that the average zone of equalization is used for all sides of the world production surface, such as in Figure 3.6b, does give the maximum increase in the probability of factor-price equalization. An indication of the degree of this bias is that when the more realistic zones of 1/2 between X and Z and 1/4 between X and Y and Y and Z (which average to 1/3) are used in the three good case, the probability goes from 1/3 to 1/2 while it is shown that, with the assumption used here, the probability goes from 1/3 to 2/3.

have the approximate probabilities of equalization of 76/81, 237/243, for five, six, etc. products in a two-country and two-factor world.

The results of this extension into the more than three-commodity world should be interpreted as suggestive rather than as rigorously proven or necessary. With different equalization zones at the coordinate-plane intercepts, and nonlinear production sets the precise results will vary from what has just been shown. However, the nature (not magnitude) of the increase in the probability with increasing number of products might be expected to remain the same as that just indicated.

It is also of interest to note some of the properties of the trade solution when the demand and production conditions are such as to lead to factor-price equalization; that is, when world consumption and production falls within the area A of Figure 3.3. Such a case is illustrated for the individual countries in Figure 3.7a and 3.7b. A trading solution in area A of Figure 3.3 means that the price plane defined by common free trade prices will lie along the straight line production possibilities surfaces of the individual countries. There are two important properties of this solution: First, while the requirement for factor-price equalization in the more commodity than factor case is the potential for efficient production of as many commodities as there are factors, with factor-price equalization both countries can efficiently produce all commodities. In Figure 3.7a, Country II has the potential for efficient production of X, Y, and Z along the ray rr as does Country I along the ray $r'r'$. This is not surprising since with the same factor prices and similar technologies, it would be impossible for production costs to diverge between countries. However, the implications are often misunderstood in the literature where an argument for the increased probability of factor-price equalization with more commodities than factors is made on the grounds that the greater the number of commodities the more likely it is to find joint production of at least as many commodities as factors. [8] On a theoretical level, this argument is erroneous and the basis for the increased likelyhood of factor price equalization lies instead on the factors that have been discussed earlier. Either all commodities can be produced in common efficiently (when factor-price equalization occurs) or at most only one commodity could be produced in common by both countries (without factor price equalization).

The second, and closely related, property of the trade solution is the indeterminacy of commodity flows. [9] This is a direct outcome of the ability

---

[8] This argument has been advanced, for instance, by S. Laursen [4].

[9] This indeterminacy of commodity flows has been recognized by Laursen [4], Samuelson [7,8], Travis [10], and Melvin [5].

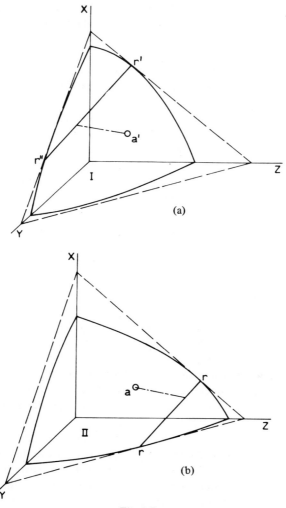

Fig. 3.7

to produce all goods efficiently in both countries when factor prices are equalized. Of course, trade flows will have to balance, but a wide range of production and trade patterns will satisfy this requirement. In Figures 3.7a and 3.7b, let the consumption points of Country II and I be *a* and *a'*. The trade vectors from *a* and *a'* to *rr* and *r'r'*, respectively, must be of equal length and of opposite direction but otherwise are indeterminate. A major implication of this is the inability of the Heckscher-Ohlin factor proportions theory to explain the commodity content of trade, a fact that will be taken up in greater detail in the following section.

3.3. The State of the Factor Proportions Theory and a Suggested Amendment

With factor-price equalization, the commodity structure of international trade is indeterminate; in other words, the factor proportions theory (the principal theory of trade corresponding to the assumptions made) becomes devoid of content in the significant instance of factor-price equalization and more products than factors. A reinterpretation is also required if the number of factors exceeds two since it then becomes impossible to rank commodities by factor intensity.

It is possible to salvage the factor proportions theory in two different — and in the present writers' view — significant respects; this and the remaining section of our article are devoted to the two cases, respectively. Both instances represent realistic generalizations of the factor proportions theory. The first has been developed and proven elsewhere by one of the present authors [11], and thus requires only a brief restatement in the context of the present argument. The second, on the other hand, besides its general quality of a generilization and "saving" of the factor proportions theory also has the particular merit of offering an explanation of the comparative importance of trade among advanced countries that is observable in the real world.

Our first salvaging operation is very simple and proceeds in two distinct stages. First, we must rid ourselves of the indeterminacy. This can be done readily if we conceive of trade as an exchange of productive factor contributions embodied in commodities traded and if only net flows of such contributions across national borders are considered. Note that along the line, plane, or hyperplane ruling the production possibility surface at which the indeterminacy of production occurs, the factor contents of the bill of goods produced by the economy — whether measured in terms of value [10] or in terms of physical inputs — are constant. On the other hand, the specific and unique bill of goods demanded (under the utility maximizing behavior of the consuming public) in the international trade equilibrium also is constant, again whether measured in terms of physical factor contents or factor contents expressed in terms of value. This is obvious because with given and internationally equalized factor prices, to each unit of a specific good

---

[10] Recall also that anywhere along the "ruling" line, factor prices are invariant.

corresponds a unique set of physical and value factor contents. Finally, the difference between the unique and constant factor contents of national consumption and the unique and constant factor contents of national production yields the unique and constant *net* set of factor flows out of (for some factors) and into (for other factors) the economy engaging in international trade in a world of more goods than factors and factor-price equalization. And thus we have disposed of the indeterminacy.

The second step is equally simple: As is well known, the factor proportions theory requires the postulate of identical demand conditions in the trading countries and either unitary income elasticities of all goods or identical incomes for all households. Such assumptions imply that in the international equilibrium two trading partners consume bundles of goods of identical commodity structures. But with factor-price equalization, the factor-content structures (again in value or in physical units) of the consumption bundles must also be the same in the two countries. And obviously, the factor-structure of a "typical" dollar of a country's consumption must be the same as that of world production; this follows from the facts that both trading partners consume the same factor-bundles and that world production equals world consumption. The unique net factor contents of a dollar exported and imported by a country thus are obtained as the difference between the factor contents of a dollar of the (two-country) world output and a dollar of its own national output. This basic finding and the exact analysis leading to it then can be translated into several rigorous theorems, as has been done in [11]. We reproduce here only two of the most general among these:

1. Ranking relative factor endowments of two trading partners (in a two-country world) in the descending order of relative abundance, there will be a breaking point within that ranking between factors on net balance exported and imported.

2. If net factor contents of trade are measured as proportions of national factor endowments (e.g., net factor content equals + 0.1 if national endowment is ten times net factor outflow) then the ranking of relative factor endowments will exactly be reflected by the ranking of net factor flows. [11]

[11] For example, if factor flows measured in this way for Country I in a three-factor model with capital, labor, and natural resources are + 0.3, + 0.1, and − 0.2, then this implies that Country I has the largest capital and smallest natural resource endowment relative to Country II. Similarly, if the ranking of factor endowments is given, the ranking of factor outflows must duplicate it as in our example. Note that a positive sign indicates an outflow and a negative sign an inflow of factor services.

3.4. Some Different Technologies

Our second generalization is more straightforward than the first. We first note that the assumption of identical technologies throughout the world need not be satisfied; indeed, it is most likely that it effectively will not be satisfied. On the other hand, if there are differences in technology, there is no reason to believe that all technologies would be different. More traditional goods can be expected to fulfill the conventional identity postulate, while technologies, actual or potential, of other goods may be different. It is inherent in the nature of the proof of the factor-price equalization theorem that if the number of goods with internationally identical technologies and not subject to specialization is at least as large as that of productive factors, all other assumptions remaining unchanged (including that of no factor reversals), the factor prices again will be equalized internationally, irrespective of the existence of a number of goods with different technologies.

But retaining the (conventional) assumption of constant returns to scale also for the products with different technologies, it immediately follows that with international factor-price equalization there must be complete specialization in all such products. Such a specialization in what we may think of as "new goods" − distinguished from the other goods some or all of which are, so to speak, the "carriers" of factor-price equalization − then can explain a very large volume of trade indeed. It is especially for trade among similar advanced countries where with not too different factor endowments factor-price equalization may well occur, that this explanation of the large volume of trade actually observed is appealing [12]; among other reasons, it disposes of the increasing-returns thesis which, for some widely traded products at least, can hardly be sustained.

The interesting quality of the theory of international trade with some different technologies is that it still falls under our salvaging operation number one. Indeed, even with different technologies, with factor-price equalization the differences in technologies must remain only potential and never can be actual because of the necessity of specialization. Consequently, no single product can be produced by two different techniques or two different factor mixes. But once this is established, the argument of the

---

[12] Note that the welfare benefits from trade based on possibly small differences in technologies may be quite small. The volume of trade should not be used as a proxy for the gains from trade.

preceding section still holds in full as do the theorems there stated and those derived in [11].

It may also be interesting to note that the assumption of no intermediate input-output flows made thus far can also be relaxed without disturbing the amended factor proportions theory of trade of the preceding section. It suffices here to observe that with factor-price equalization — referring here to both primary factors and intermediate goods — factor contents per unit of output must be identical for identical goods throughout the world, and once this is ascertained, the rest of the argument of the preceding section follows.

References

[1] Bertrand, T.J. "Factor Price Equalization when Commodities Outnumber Factors; A Note". *Economica*, February 1969.

[2] Johnson, H.G. "The Possibility of Factor Price Equalization when Commodities Outnumber Factors." *Economica*, N.S. 34 (August 1967) 282–288.

[3] Land, A.H. "Factor Endowments and Factor Prices." *Economica*, N.S. 26 (May 1959) 137–144.

[4] Laursen, S. "Production Functions and the Theory of International Trade." *American Economic Review*, 42 (September 1952) 540–557.

[5] Melvin, J.R. "Production and Trade with. Two Factors and Three Goods." *American Economic Review* 58 (December 1968) 1249–1268.

[6] Meade, J.E. "The Equalization of Factor Prices: The Two Country Two-Factor Three-Product Case." *Metroeconomica*, 2 (December 1950) 129–133.

[7] Samuelson, P.A. "Prices of Factors and Goods in General Equilibrium." *Review of Economic Studies*, 21 No. 1 (1953) 1–20.

[8] Samuelson, P.A. "Summary on Factor-Price Equalization." *International Economic Review*, 8 No. 3 (October 1967) 286–295.

[9] Tinbergen, J. "The Equalization of Factor Prices between Free Trade Areas." *Metroeconomica*, 1 (July 1949) 39–47.

[10] Travis, W.P. *The Theory of Trade and Production*. Cambridge, Mass., Harvard University Press, 1964.

[11] Vanek, J. "The Factor Propertions Theory: The *n*-Factor Case." *Kyklos*, 4 (October 1968).

PART 2

TRADE AND WELFARE

CHAPTER 4

THE GENERALIZED THEORY OF
DISTORTIONS AND WELFARE

Jagdish N. BHAGWATI

The theory of trade and welfare [1] has recently developed independently in seven areas that have apparently little analytical relationship among themselves:

1. The Suboptimality of Laissez-Faire Under Market Imperfections: It has been shown that, when market imperfections exist, laissez-faire (otherwise described as "a policy of unified exchange rates" [5]) will not be the optimal policy. Among the market imperfections for which the suboptimality of laissez-faire has been demonstrated are four key types: (i) factor market imperfection, a wage differential between sectors; [2] (ii) product market imperfection, a production externality; [3] (iii) consumption imperfection, a

---

[1] This paper is the result of thinking and research over a period of many years, originating in my 1958 paper on immiserizing growth [1] and developing considerably since my joint paper with the late V.K. Ramaswami in 1963 [2] on domestic distortions. Since 1965, T.N. Srinivasan and I have collaborated on research in related matters, pertaining to the theory of optimal policy intervention when noneconomic objectives are present [7], a subject pioneered by Max Corden's brilliant work [12]. In many ways, therefore, this paper has grown out of the ferment of ideas in Delhi during 1963–1968, when Srinivasan, Ramaswami, and I happened to work together and independently on the diverse subjects which are brought together in this paper. The work of others, particularly Murray Kemp [23], [24] and Harry Johnson [18], has also contributed to the development of my thinking. The influence of Meade's work must also be acknowledged.

[2] I assume here that the wage differential is "distortionary" and cannot be attributed to legitimate economic grounds, such as disutility in occupations where the higher wage is charged. For a detailed discussion, see Fishlow and David [13] and Bhagwati and Ramaswami [2].

[3] See Kemp [21], Chapter 11, for a fuller discussion of alternative types of production externalities. I have in mind here the case of a "pure" production externality of the Meade variety, as set out in footnote 10 later.

consumption externality; [4] and (iv) trade imperfection, monopoly power in trade. [5]

2. Immiserizing Growth: Examples have been produced where a country, after growth (in factor supplies and/or technological know-how), becomes worse off, phenomena described as *immiserizing growth*. I produced an example of such a phenomenon in 1958 [1] (as also did Harry Johnson independently at the time) where growth led to such a deterioration in the country's terms of trade that the loss from the worsened terms of trade outweighed the primary gain from growth. Subsequently, Johnson [19] produced another example of immiserization, in which the country had no ability to influence her terms of trade but there was a tariff (which is necessarily welfare reducing in view of the assumed absence of monopoly power in trade) in both the pregrowth and the postgrowth situations, and growth impoverished the country in certain cases. I later produced yet other examples of immiserizing growth [6], one in which there was a wage differential in the factor market, and another in which the country had monopoly power in trade (as in my original 1958 example), but the country had an optimum tariff (before growth) which became suboptimal after growth.

3. Ranking of Alternative Policies under Market Imperfections: For the four major imperfections described earlier, the optimal policy intervention has been analyzed by several economists. Hagen [16] has argued that the optimal policy for the case of the wage differential would be a factor tax-cum-subsidy. For the production externality, Bhagwati and Ramaswami [2] have shown that the optimal policy intervention is a production tax-cum-subsidy. For the consumption externality case, it follows from the general arguments in Bhagwati and Ramaswami [2] that a consumption tax-cum-subsidy ought to be used. Finally, for the case of monopoly power in trade, it has been known since the time of Mill and has been demonstrated rigorously by (among others) Graaff [14] and Johnson [17] that a tariff is the optimal policy. Recent work of Bhagwati, Ramaswami, and Srinivasan [8] has then extended the analysis, for each market imperfection, to the ranking of *all* alternative policies: the tariff (trade subsidy) policy, the production tax-cum-subsidy policy, the consumption tax-cum-subsidy policy, and the factor tax-cum-subsidy policy. [6]

---

[4] Instead of a consumption externality, one could assume a situation in which sellers charge a uniform premium on a commodity's import and production price.

[5] The precise sense in which monopoly power in trade represents a market imperfection, in the trade sector, is that foreign prices will not equal the marginal, foreign rate of transformation (as discussed later in the text).

[6] Since the production tax-cum-subsidy policy is equivalent to a tax-cum-subsidy

4. Ranking of Tariffs: Yet another area of research in trade and welfare has raised the question of ranking policies that constitute impediments themselves to the attainment of optimality. Thus, for example, Kemp [22] has analyzed, for a country without monopoly power in trade (and no other imperfections), the question as to whether a higher tariff is worse than a lower tariff. Similarly, Bhagwati and Kemp [10] have analysed the problem for tariffs around the optimal tariff for a country *with* monopoly power in trade.

5. Ranking of Free Trade and Autarky: A number of trade theorists have compared free trade with autarky, when there were market imperfections such as wage differentials (Hagen [16]) and production externality (Haberler [15]), to deduce that free trade was no longer necessarily superior to self-sufficiency. Melvin [26] and Kemp [23] have recently considered the comparison between free trade and autarky when there are commodity taxes.

6. Ranking of Restricted Trade and Autarky: Aside from the case in which trade is tariff restricted (wherein the comparison between restricted trade and autarky becomes the comparison of tariffs discussed in item 4) Bhagwati [4] has considered the ranking of other policies (e.g., production tax-cum-subsidies) that restrict trade and autarky.

7. Noneconomic Objectives and Ranking of Policies: Finally, a number of economists have addressed themselves to the question of optimal policy intervention when the values of different variables are constrained, as noneconomic objectives, so that full optimality is unattainable. Four key types of noneconomic objectives have been analyzed. Corden [12] has shown that a production tax-cum-subsidy is optimal where the constrained variable is production (for reasons such as defense production). Johnson [18] has shown a tariff to be optimal when imports are constrained instead (in the interest of "self-sufficiency"). Bhagwati and Srinivasan [7] have demonstrated that a factor tax-cum-subsidy is optimal when the constrained variable is employment of a factor in an activity (i.e., in the interest of "national character") and a consumption tax-cum-subsidy when the constrained variable is domestic availability of consumption (i.e., to restrict "luxury consumption"). Bhagwati and Srinivasan have also extended the analysis to the ranking of *all* policy instruments for a number of these noneconomic objectives.

This paper is aimed at putting these diverse analyses into a common

given to *all* factors (used in production) of an equivalent and uniform magnitude, the factor tax-cum-subsidy policy referred to in this paper relates to a tax-cum-subsidy policy that applies in a *discriminatory* fashion between or among factors.

analytical framework. This results in the logical unification of a number of interesting and important results, leading in turn to fresh insights while also enabling us to derive remarkable "duality" relationships between the analysis of policy rankings under market imperfections and policy rankings to achieve noneconomic objectives.

4.1. Alternative Types of Distortions

It can be readily shown, in fact, that the diverse results reviewed so far belong to what might aptly be described as the theory of distortions and welfare.

The theory of distortions is built around the central theorem of trade and welfare: that laissez-faire is Pareto optimal for a perfectly competitive system with no monopoly power in trade.[7] Ruling out the phenomenon of diminishing cost of transformation between any pair of commodities (i.e., the concavity of the production possibility set in the familiar, two-commodity system),[8] the Pareto optimality of the laissez-faire policy follows quite simply from the fact that the economic system will operate with technical efficiency (i.e., on the "best" production possibility curve, if we think again of two commodities for simplicity). The economic system will also satisfy further the (first-order) conditions for an economic maximum: DRT = FRT = DRS (where DRT represents the marginal rate of transformation in domestic production, FRT represents marginal foreign rate of transformation, and DRS represents the marginal rate of substitution in consumption).[9]

---

[7] The classic proof of this proposition is in Samuelson [28]. For later treatments, see Samuelson [29], Kemp [22] and Bhagwati [4] and [5].

[8] The phenomenon of diminishing marginal cost of transformation can arise either because of increasing returns [21, Ch. 8] (which is a purely technological phenomenon) or because of factor market imperfection in the shape of a wage differential [2] [13] [20]. The phenomenon has to be ruled out so as to eliminate certain well-known difficulties that it raises (requiring in particular the distinction between global and local maxima [30] and attention to second-order conditions and possibilities of inefficient specialization [27]).

[9] Equalities have been used in stating the first-order conditions, for each pair of commodities, so as to preserve simplicity; they imply, of course, incomplete specialization in production and consumption. Inequalities can be introduced easily, but nothing essential would be gained by way of additional insights. The simplifying assumption of a two-commodity system will also be used through the rest of the paper; this does not critically affect the analysis, although problems associated with devising optimum policy *structures* (e.g., the optimal tariff structure [14] in the case of monopoly power in in trade) are naturally not raised in consequence.

The theory of distortions is then concerned with the following four pathologies which may characterize, singly or in combination, the economic system:

Distortion 1: FRT ≠ DRT = DRS
Distortion 2: DRT ≠ DRS = FRT
Distortion 3: DRS ≠ DRT = FRT
Distortion 4: Nonoperation on the efficient production possibility curve.

"Endogenous" Distortions

These distortions (implying departures from full optimality) may arise when the economy is characterised by *market imperfections* under a policy of laissez-faire. Thus, the presence of national monopoly power in trade will lead to Distortion 1, because foreign prices will not equal FRT. The case of the Meade type of production externality [10] leads to Distortion 2. Distortion 3 will follow when sellers of the importable commodity, for example, charge a uniform premium on imported as well as home-produced supplies. Distortion 4 follows when there is a factor market imperfection resulting from a wage differential, for a factor, between the different activities. [11] In these cases, therefore, the resulting distortions (arising from the market imperfections) are appropriately described as "endogenous" distortions.

"Policy-Imposed" Distortions

On the other hand, the four varieties of distortions listed earlier may be the result of economic policies, as distinct from endogenous phenomena such as market imperfections. Thus, Distortion 1 will arise for a country with no monopoly power in trade if the country has a tariff; it will also arise for a country with monopoly power in trade if the tariff is less or greater than the optimal tariff. Distortion 2 will follow if the government imposes a production tax-cum-subsidy. Distortion 3 will be the consequence similarly of a consumption tax-cum-subsidy policy. Finally, the adoption of a factor

---

[10] This externality can be formally stated as follows [21, p. 128]: For linearly homogeneous production functions $x = x(K_x, L_x)$, $y = y(K_y, L_y, x)$ it can be shown that, with y entrepreneurs not having to pay for their "input" of x, the economy will be characterised by Distortion 2.

[11] A constant wage differential will also lead to Distortion 2; in this instance, we have a case of two distortions occurring at the same time. In fact, the wage differential case leads also to the possibility of a concave production possibility set, as we have already noted; furthermore, as Bhagwati and Srinivasan [11] have shown, the response of production to relative commodity price change also becomes unpredictable, a question, however, of no welfare significance in the context of this paper.

tax-cum-subsidy policy will result in Distortion 4. [12] These are instances therefore of "policy-imposed" distortions.

But as soon as we probe the reasons for the existence of such policy-imposed distortions, two alternative interpretations are possible. Either we can consider these policies as *autonomous* (i.e., a tariff, which leads to Distortion 1, may for example be a historic accident), or we may consider these policies as *instrumental* (a tariff, leading to Distortion 1, may be the policy instrument used in order to reduce imports) – as in the case of the theory of noneconomic objectives when Distortion 1 is created through the deployment of a tariff when the objective is to reduce imports in the interest of "self-sufficiency".

We thus have altogether three sets of "causes" for the four varieties of distortions that can be distinguished: *endogenous*; *autonomous, policy-imposed*; and *instrumental, policy-imposed*. The entire literature that I reviewed earlier can then be given its logical coherence and unity around these alternative classes and causes of distortions.

Before formulating the general theory of distortions and generalizing the theorems discussed in the introduction into other areas, it would be useful to underline the precise manner in which these theorems relate to the different varieties of distortions that we have distinguished so far.

1. The theorems on the suboptimality of different market imperfections clearly relate to the theory of endogenous distortions. Within a static welfare context, they demonstrate that these market imperfections result in the different types of Distortions 1–4, thus resulting in the breakdown of the Pareto optimality of laissez-faire in these cases.

2. The theorems on immiserizing growth, on the other hand, relate to the comparative statics of welfare when distortions are present. The theorems developed in this literature involve cases in which growth takes place under given distortions, either endogenous or policy imposed, and the primary improvement in welfare (which would have accrued if fully optimal policies were followed both before and after growth) is outweighed by the accentuation of the loss from the distortion in the postgrowth situation [6].

Thus, in the original Bhagwati example of immiserizing growth, the assumed free trade and hence failure to impose an optimum tariff (to exploit the monopoly power in trade) in both the pregrowth and the postgrowth situations involves welfare-reducing "distortionary" policies in both situa-

---

[12] A constant rate of factor tax-cum-subsidy will also produce Distortion 2, as in the case of a constant wage differential. However, as we shall see later, a variable factor tax-cum-subsidy policy can be devised which produces *only* Distortion 4.

tions. Immiserization occurs therefore because the gain, which would necessarily accrue from growth if the optimal tariff were imposed in both situations, is smaller than the incremental loss arising from the accentuation (if any) in the postgrowth situation of the welfare loss resulting from the "distortionary" free-trade policy (implying an endogenous Distortion 1 in this instance) in both situations.

Harry Johnson's example of immiserization where the country has no monopoly power in trade but a tariff (which thus constitutes an autonomous policy-imposed Distortion 1) in both the pregrowth and the postgrowth situations, is to be explained in terms of the same logic. In the absence of monopoly power in trade, the tariff is necessarily "distortionary" and, compared with the fully optimal free-trade policy, causes a loss of welfare in each situation. If the growth were to occur with free trade, there would necessarily be an increment in welfare. However, since growth occurs under a tariff, there arises the possibility that the loss from the tariff may be accentuated after growth, and that this incremental loss may outweigh the gain (that would occur under the optimal, free-trade policy), thus resulting in immiserization. Thus, the policy-imposed distortion (i.e., the tariff) generates the possibility of immiserizing growth.

3. The theorems that rank alternative policies under market imperfections are addressed to a different range of questions. They relate to endogenous distortions, of each of the four varieties we have distinguished, and then seek to rank the different, available policy instruments (extending to the full complement: production, consumption, trade, and factor tax-cum-subsidies) in relation to one another and vis-a-vis laissez-faire itself. The problem has been posed in this fashion by Bhagwati, Ramaswami, and Srinivasan [8] in their recent work.

4. The theorems of Kemp [22] and Bhagwati and Kemp [10], which rank tariffs in relation to one another, however, belong to a yet different genre. They relate to policy-imposed distortions, autonomous in the sense defined in this paper, and aim at ranking different levels at which policy may impose the specified distortion (e.g., Distortion 1 in the cases in which tariffs are ranked).

5. The ranking of free trade and autarky under situations involving market imperfections or taxes involves, on the other hand, a comparison of essentially two levels (the zero tariff level and the prohibitive tariff level) at which a policy-imposed distortion (the tariff) is used, in a situation which is itself characterized by another distortion (either endogenous, such as the wage differential in Hagen [16], or policy-imposed, such as a tax on consumption of a commodity).

6. The ranking of a situation with trade restricted by a nontariff policy with a situation of autarky (with therefore an implicit, prohibitive tariff) involves an altogether different type of comparison: of one distortion with another, both autonomous policy-imposed in Bhagwati's analysis [4].

7. The theory of noneconomic objectives [7], on the other hand, relates to the optimal nature of intervention and the ranking of alternative policies, when certain variables are precluded from specified ranges of values in the interest of "noneconomic" objectives. It is therefore, from an analytical point of view, a theory of how optimally (i.e., at minimum cost) to *introduce* distortions in the economic system, when the attainment of the full optimum is precluded by the noneconomic-objective constraints and also of what the relative costs of alternative policies or methods of introducing such distortions, in pursuit of the noneconomic objectives, are. It is thus a theory pertaining to the ranking of instrumental, policy-imposed distortions, with each distortion being defined under a common set of economic and noneconomic constraints.

It is clear, therefore, that these diverse theorems relate to different types of distortions and raise a number of diverse questions relating thereto. But as soon as we grasp this central fact, it is possible to unify and extend the entire body of this literature and thus to develop a general theory of distortions and welfare.

4.2. Distortions and Welfare: General Theory

This generalized theory of distortions and welfare can be developed in terms of seven central propositions.

Proposition 1:
There are four principal types of distortions:
    1. FRT $\neq$ DRT = DRS;
    2. DRT $\neq$ DRS = FRT;
    3. DRS $\neq$ DRT = FRT; and
    4. Nonoperation on the efficient production possibility curve.

These, in turn, can be caused by factors that are:
    1. Endogenous;
    2. Autonomous, policy-imposed; and
    3. Instrumental, policy-imposed.

This proposition is merely a recapitulation of the concepts and analysis developed in the preceding section and requires no further comment. Note merely, by way of reemphasis, that in each of the $(4 \times 3 = 12)$ distortionary situations, the economic system departs from full Pareto optimality.

Proposition 2:

    i. Optimal policy intervention, in the presence of distortions, involves a tax-cum-subsidy policy addressed directly to offsetting the source of the distortions, when the causes are endogenous or autonomous, policy-imposed. Dual to (i) is the theorem that:

    ii. When distortions have to be introduced into the economy, because the values of certain variables (e.g., production or employment of a factor in an activity) have to be constrained, the optimal (or least-cost) method of doing this is to choose that policy intervention that creates the distortion affecting directly the constrained variable.

These two propositions, which constitute a remarkable duality of theorems, extend between themselves to all the classes of Distortions 1 to 4 and their three possible causes, endogenous, autonomous policy-imposed, and instrumental policy-imposed. Furthermore, each proposition is readily derived from the theorems on market imperfections and on noneconomic objectives.

Proposition 2(i) was formulated, in essentially similar form, by Bhagwati and Ramaswami [2] and later by Johnson [18], for the case of endogenous distortions. For Distortion 1, resulting from monopoly power in trade under laissez-faire, it is well known that the optimal policy intervention is a tariff. For Distortion 2, Bhagwati and Ramaswami showed that the optimal policy was a production tax-cum-subsidy. For Distortion 3, correspondingly, the optimal policy is a consumption tax-cum-subsidy. Finally, when a wage differential causes Distortion 4, Hagen [16] showed that the optimal intervention was through a factor tax-cum-subsidy. In each instance, therefore, the policy required is one that directly attacks the source of the distortion.

It follows equally, and trivially, that if these distortions are autonomous policy-imposed, the optimal intervention is to eliminate the policy itself: hence, again the optimal policy intervention is addressed to the source of the distortion itself. Thus, with a suboptimal tariff leading to Distortion 1, the optimal policy is to change the tariff to an optimal level (equal to zero, if there is no monopoly power in trade). Similarly, if a consumption tax-cum-subsidy causes Distortion 3, the optimal policy is to offset it with an equivalent consumption tax-cum-subsidy (which leaves zero net consumption tax-cum-subsidy and thus restores full optimality).

But the extension of these results, via the "dual" Proposition 2(ii), to the class of instrumental, policy-imposed distortions, is far from trivial. And the duality is remarkable. Corden [12] has shown that the optimal policy, if the binding noneconomic constraint relates to production, is a *production* tax-cum-subsidy. Johnson [18] has demonstrated that the optimal policy, if the binding noneconomic constraint relates to import (export) level, is a *tariff or trade subsidy*. Bhagwati and Srinivasan [7] have extended the analysis to show that, if the binding noneconomic constraint relates to the level of employment of a factor of production in a sector, the optimal policy is to use a *factor* tax-cum-subsidy that directly taxes (subsidises) the employment of the factor in the sector where its employment level must be lowered (raised) to the constrained level. [13] They have also demonstrated that the optimal policy for raising (lowering) consumption to a constrained level is a *consumption* tax-cum-subsidy policy.

To put it somewhat differently, a trade-level noneconomic objective is achieved at least cost by introducing a policy-imposed Distortion 1 via a trade tariff or subsidy; a production noneconomic objective by introducing a policy-imposed Distortion 2 via a production tax-cum-subsidy; a consumption noneconomic objective by introducing a policy-imposed Distortion 3 via a consumption tax-cum-subsidy; and a factor-employment (in a sector) non-economic objective by introducing a policy-imposed Distortion 4 via a factor tax-cum-subsidy.

Proposition 3:

i. For each distortion, whether endogenous or autonomous, policy-imposed, in origin, it is possible to analyse the welfare ranking of all alternative policies, from the (first best) optimal to the second best and so on.

ii. a. When distortions have to be introduced into the economy, because the values of certain variables have to be constrained (e.g., production or employment of a factor in an activity), the policy interventions that do this may similarly be welfare ranked. b. The ranking of these policies is further completely symmetrical with that under the "corresponding" class of endogenous or autonomous policy-imposed distortions (e.g., the ranking of policies for production externality, an endogenous Distortion 2, is identical with the ranking of policies when production is constrained as a noneconomic objective).

Since there are four different types of policies (factor, production,

---

[13] Unlike the case of a *constant* wage differential, which also leads to Distortion 2 in addition to Distortion 4, we can devise [7] a variable tax-cum-subsidy that satisfies the constraint on factor employment while creating *only* Distortion 4.

consumption, and trade tax-cum-subsidies), the propositions listed here are aimed at ranking *all* of them for each of the (twelve) varieties of distortions and establishing "duality" relations of the kind we discovered for optimal policies alone in Proposition 2(ii).

Bhagwati, Ramaswami, and Srinivasan [8] have recently analyzed the welfare ranking of all policies for endogenous distortions and establishing the following rankings: [14]

Distortion 1: FRT ≠ DRT = DRS

This is the case of monopoly power in trade. The ranking of policies then is

    i. First best: tariff;

    ii. Second best: either production tax-cum-subsidy or factor tax-cum-subsidy (all policies are superior to laissez-faire but cannot be ranked uniquely vis-à-vis one another). [15]

Distortion 2: DRT ≠ DRS = FRT

This is the case of a pure production externality. The ranking of policies then is

    i. First best: production tax-cum-subsidy;

    ii. Second best: either tariff (trade subsidy) or factor tax-cum-subsidy

---

[14] Their argument is summarised as follows: They use the notation [8] : C_i, X_i denote the consumption and domestic output respectively of commodity i, where $i = 1$, 2. Also, P_c denotes the ratio of the price of the first to that of the second commodity confronting consumers (DRS); P_t denotes DRT = dX_2/dX_1; and P_f denotes the ratio of the world price of the first commodity to that of the second commodity, i.e., the *average* terms of trade. The marginal terms of trade FRT = pf only in the special case in which national monopoly power does not exist.

The welfare function $U(C_1, C_2)$ and the production functions are assumed to be differentiable as required. The U_i denotes the marginal utility of commodity $i (i = 1, 2)$. It is assumed throughout the analysis that under laissez-faire there is nonspecialisation in consumption and production, and that some trade takes place. Then, the following expression, for the change in welfare when there is an infinitesimal movement away from laissez-faire equilibrium, is derived:

$$dU = U_2[dX_1(p_f - p_t) + (X_1 - C_1)dp_f + (p_c - p_f)dC_1$$

If one uses this expression, the different distortions are easily analyzed for alternate policy rankings. Thus, in the case in which DRT ≠ FRT = DRS, which is Distortion 2 in the text just following, the expression reduces to $dU = U_2[dX_1(P_f - P_t)]$ because $P_c = P_f$, $d_{p_f} = 0$ and $p_f \neq p_t$. It follows that either a tariff (trade subsidy) or a factor tax-cum-subsidy that increases (reduces) X_1, if $p_f > p_t$ ($p_f < p_t$), will increase welfare.

[15] For finite tax-cum-subsidies, however, the production tax-cum-subsidy will be superior to the factor tax-cum-subsidy.

(both policies are superior to laissez-faire but cannot be ranked uniquely vis-à-vis each other);

iii. Consumption tax-cum-subsidy will not help. [16]

Distortion 3: DRS $\neq$ DRT = FRT

This is the case in which, for example, the sellers of a commodity charge a uniform premium to buyers over the cost of supplies, whether imported or domestically produced. The ranking of policies then is

    i. First best: consumption tax-cum-subdidy;

    ii. Second best: tariff;

    iii. Production or factor tax-cum-subsidy will not help. [17]

Distortion 4: Nonoperation on the efficient production possibility curve

This is the case in which there is a wage differential, a factor market imperfection. In this case, the ranking of policies is

    i. First best: factor tax-cum-subsidy;

    ii. Second best: production tax-cum-subsidy;

    iii. Third best: tariff (trade subsidy);

    iv. Consumption tax-cum-subsidy will not help. [18]

It is clear that the extension of these rankings to the corresponding cases where the distortions are autonomous policy-imposed (e.g., Distortion 2 resulting from the autonomous levy of a governmental tax, or Distortion 4 resulting from the grant of a governmental subsidy on employment of a factor in one activity) is total and trivial. It is interesting and remarkable, however, that these rankings carry over also to the class of instrumental, policy-imposed distortions.

Thus, for the case of noneconomic objectives, Bhagwati and Srinivasan [7] have provided the basis for analyzing the rankings of different policies, which I now proceed to develop fully:

Trade-level as a Constraint: The ranking of policies in this case is

    i. First best: tariff;

---

[16] This conclusion holds for infinitesimal tax-cum-subsidy. A finite consumption tax-cum-subsidy will actually be worse than laissez-faire in this instance, as it will impose a "consumption loss" on the economy, over and above the loss it is already suffering from the endogenous Distortion 2.

[17] This conclusion again holds only for infinitesimal tax-cum-subsidies on production or factor use. For finite tax-cum-susidies, these policies will necessarily be worse than laissez-faire (unless inferior goods are present).

[18] Again, this conclusion concerning the consumption tax-cum-subsidy must be read in the same sense as in footnote 16.

ii. Second best: either production tax-cum-subsidy or factor tax-cum-subsidy or consumption tax-cum-subsidy (these policies cannot be ranked vis-à-vis one another). [19]

Note the complete symmetry with the rankings under Distortion 1 earlier.

Production level as a Constraint: The ranking of policies in this case is
i. First best: production tax-cum-subsidy;
ii. Second best: either tariff (trade subsidy) or factor tax-cum-subsidy (these policies cannot be ranked vis-à-vis each other);
iii. Consumption tax-cum-subsidy will not help. [20]

Note again the complete symmetry with the rankings under Distortion 2.

Consumption level as a Constraint: The ranking of policies in this case is
i. First best: consumption tax-cum-subsidy;
ii. Second best: tariff;
iii. Production or factor tax-cum-subsidy will not help. [21]

Again, the symmetry with the ranking under Distortion 3 is total.

Factor Employment (in a Sector) as a Constraint: The ranking of policies in this case is
i. First best: factor tax-cum-subsidy;
ii. Second best: production tax-cum-subsidy;
iii. Third best: tariff (trade subsidy);
iv. Consumption tax-cum-subsidy will not help. [22]

In this final case as well, the symmetry with the corresponding Distortion 4 is complete.

Thus, the duality of the policy rankings, for endogenous and autonomous policy-imposed distortions on the one hand and instrumental policy-imposed distortions on the other hand, is altogether complete and remarkable.

Proposition 4:
For each kind of distortion, growth may be immiserizing.
For endogenous and autonomous policy-imposed distortions, belonging to

---

[19] For finite tax-cum-subsidies, however, the factor tax-cum-subsidy policy will be inferior to the production tax-cum-subsidy policy, as Bhagwati and Srinivasan [7] have demonstrated.

[20] This statement must again be read in the same sense as in footnote 16 and footnote 18 earlier.

[21] This statement must be construed in the same sense as in footnote 17.

[22] This statement must be interpreted again in the same sense as in footnotes 16, 18, and 20 earlier.

each of the varieties 1 to 4 that we have distinguished, this proposition has already been demonstrated by Bhagwati [6].

Thus, for example, where Distortion 1 obtains endogenously under laissez-faire because of monopoly power in trade, Bhagwati's 1958 analysis [1] demonstrates the possibility of immiserization. Where Distortions 2 and 4 obtain simultaneously as a result of an endogenous wage differential, the same possibility has again been demonstrated by Bhagwati [6]. Johnson's demonstration [19] of immiserization, when a country has no monopoly power in trade but a tariff, illustrates Proposition 2 for the case of an autonomous policy-imposed Distortion 1.

Note again that the underlying reason for immiserizing growth is that the growth takes place in the presence of a distortion. This distortion produces a loss of welfare from the fully optimal welfare level. Thus, if there is an accentuation in this loss of welfare, when growth has occurred and the distortion has continued, this incremental loss could outweigh the gain that would have accrued if fully optimal policies had been followed in the pregrowth and postgrowth situations [6]. It also follows that such immiserizing growth would be impossible if fully optimal policies were followed in each situation, i.e., if the distortions resulting from the endogenous and policy-imposed causes were offset by optimal policy intervention, as discussed under Proposition 2(i) earlier. [23]

But so far we have discussed only distortions resulting from endogenous and policy-imposed, autonomous factors. However, Proposition 4 applies equally, and can be generalized, to *instrumental* policy-imposed distortions as well.

In complete symmetry with the endogenous and autonomous policy-imposed distortions, the phenomenon of immiserizing growth will be precluded when the constrained variable (e.g., production in the case of a production objective) is attained (in the pregrowth and the postgrowth situations) by optimal policy. On the other hand, immiserization becomes possible as soon as any of the second-best (or third best) policies is adopted to constrain the variable (to a preassigned value in both the pregrowth and postgrowth situations).

This generalization of the theory of immiserizing growth is readily illustrated with reference to production as the constrained variable. Remember that a production tax-cum-subsidy is the optimal policy in this case and a

---

[23] For phenomena of immiserizing growth arising from reasons other than distortions, see Melvin [25] and Bhagwati [9].

tariff a second best policy. Figure 4.1a then illustrates how it is impossible, after growth, to become "worse off" if the production level of a commodity is constrained to the required level by a suitable production tax-cum-subsidy policy. The y production is constrained to level $\bar{y}$; the production possibility curve shifts out from AP to $A'B'$. With a suitable production tax-cum-subsidy used in both the pregrowth and the postgrowth situations, to constrain y production to $\bar{y}$, it is clear that it is impossible to worsen welfare after growth. Figure 4.1b illustrates, however, the possibility of immiserizing growth when the suboptimal tariff policy is followed instead in each case to constrain y output to level $\bar{y}$. Note that this demonstration, where the welfare level reduces after growth to U' from U, does not require the assumption of inferior goods.

Similar illustrations could be provided for the other three cases, where consumption, factor employment in a sector, and trade-level are constrained. In each case, only the pursuit of a suboptimal policy to achieve the specified noneconomic objective could lead to immiserization.

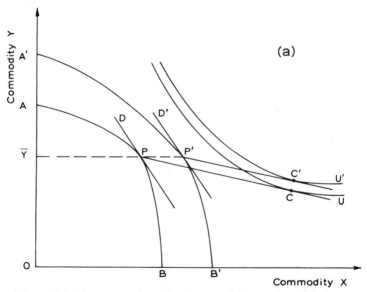

Figure 4.1a. AB is the pregrowth production possibility curve; $A'B'$ the postgrowth production possibility curve. The international price ratio is given at $PC = P'C'$. Production of y is constrained to level $\bar{y}$. A suitable production tax-cum-subsidy takes production, before growth, to P at domestic, producer price ratio DP. After growth, a suitable production tax-cum-subsidy takes producer price ratio to $D'P'$ and production to P'. Welfare level has increased, after growth, to U' ($> U$).

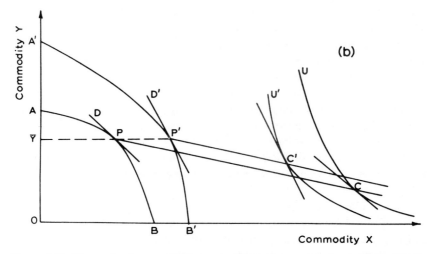

Figure 4.1b. The production possibility curve shifts, after growth, from AB to $A'B'$. In each case, the production of y is constrained to $\bar{y}$ by a tariff. In the pregrowth case, this tariff leads to production at P (with domestic price ratio DP), consumption at C and welfare at U. After growth, production is at P', consumption at C', and welfare has reduced to U' ($< U$), implying immiserizing growth.

Proposition 5:

Reductions in the "degree" of (an only) distortion are successively welfare increasing until the distortion is fully eliminated.

This theorem holds whether we take endogenous or policy-imposed distortions. However, it needs to be qualified, so as to exclude inferior goods for all cases except where a *consumption* tax-cum-subsidy is relevant.

For autonomous, policy-imposed Distortion 1, the Kemp [22] and Bhagwati–Kemp [10] theorems are special cases of Proposition 5: Each further requires the exclusion of inferior goods and attendant multiple equilibria if the possibility of the competitive system "choosing" an inferior-welfare equilibrium under the lower degree of distortion is to be ruled out. [24] In point of fact, identical propositions could be derived for alternative forms of autonomous policy-imposed distortions, factor tax-cum-subsidy, production tax-cum-subsidy, and consumption tax-cum-subsidy. [25]

[24] On this, see Bhagwati [4], Kemp [23], and Bhagwati–Kemp [10].
[25] For the consumption tax-cum-subsidy, the complication arising from inferior goods is not relevant.

Similarly, we can argue that reduction in the degree of each market imperfection will cause a reduction in the degree of its consequent distortion and thus raise welfare. Thus, for example, a reduction in the degree of production externality will reduce the degree of Distortion 2 and increase the level of welfare. [26]

Finally, identical conclusions apply if we reduce the degree of "required" distortion, of the instrumental policy-imposed type, by relaxing the binding constraint on the "noneconomic"-objective variable. Thus, marginally relaxing the constraint on production will suffice to improve welfare. As is clear from Figure 4.2a, the relaxation of the constraint on y production, from $\bar{y}$ to $\bar{y}_n$, will necessarily improve welfare by shifting the "availability line" outwards — if, in each case, the policy. adopted is a production tax-cum-subsidy policy.

If, however, as Figure 4.2b illustrates, a (suboptimal) tariff policy is

[26] Note again the *caveat* regarding inferior goods. This will not apply, however, where the consumption distortion is reduced.

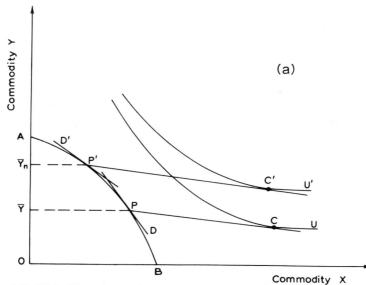

Figure 4.2a. With AB as the production possibility curve, $\bar{y}$ and $\bar{y}_n$ are the successive noneconomic constraints on y production, which are met by use of a suitable production subsidy policy in each case. For $\bar{y}$, production then is at P, consumption at C and welfare level at U. For $\bar{y}_n$, a relaxation in the constraint, production shifts to P' (with producer price ratio at $D'P'$ now), consumption to C', and welfare has increased to U' ($> U$).

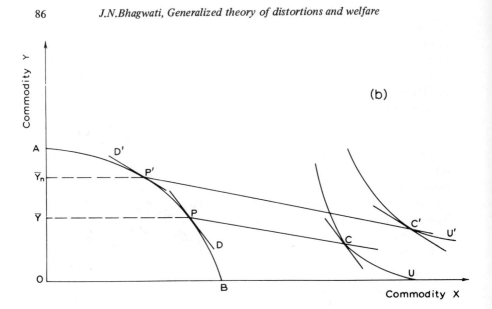

Figure 4.2b. With production of y-commodity constrained successively at $\bar{y}$ and $\bar{y}_n$, a tariff used for that purpose, and production possibility curve AB, the production for $\bar{y}$ constraint is at P, consumption at C and welfare at U. Relaxation in the constraint to $\bar{y}_n$ leads to production at P' and consumption at C' (at price $D'P'$) and welfare increases to U' ($> U$).

followed instead, to constrain y-production to the required level, the result of a relaxation in the constraint is identical; the only qualification is relating to that arising from inferior goods. Further, an identical conclusion holds, as in the case of a production tax-cum-subsidy, for the case of a factor tax-cum-subsidy instead.

Thus, Proposition 5 applies in the case of instrumental policy-imposed distortions, no matter *which* policy is considered (in other words, no matter which distortion is introduced in pursuit of the specific noneconomic objective).

Proposition 6:
   Reductions in the "degree" of a distortion will not necessarily be welfare increasing if there is another distortion in the system.

   This proposition is readily established for endogenous or autonomous policy-imposed distortions.

   Let us first consider a case in which reductions in one distortion *do* lead to improvement in welfare despite the presence of another distortion in the system. Thus, consider the case in which a production externality, an endogenous Distortion 2 where DRT ≠ DRS = FRT, is combined with a consumption tax-cum-subsidy, an autonomous policy-imposed Distortion 3 where DRS ≠ FRT = DRT, but there is no monopoly power in trade. Assume further that the two distortions combine so as to yield altogether the initial situation where DRT ≠ DRS ≠ FRT (so that they are not mutually offsetting as far as one inequality is concerned). In this case, successive reductions in the consumption tax-cum-subsidy will necessarily be welfare increasing, given the production externality; and successive reductions in the production externality will improve welfare (except for the complication introduced by inferior goods). [27]

Next, however, consider the case where there is a production externality (endogenous, DRT ≠ DRS = FRT) combined with a tariff without monopoly power in trade (autonomous policy-imposed FRT ≠ DRS = DRT) and assume that the resulting initial situation is characterized by FRT ≠ DRT ≠ DRS. In this case, successive reductions in the tariff will not necessarily improve welfare steadily, if at all, and the gains may turn into losses. [28] The theorems on the possible inferiority of free trade (i.e., zero tariff) to no trade (i.e., prohibitive tariff) when there is a production externality [15] or a wage differential [2] [16] are only special cases of this general theorem that illustrates Proposition 6.

It is interesting to note further that this theorem can with equal insight be analyzed in terms of Proposition 4 if we recognize that, if optimal policies are followed in *both* the autarkic and the trading "situations", the trade situation must necessarily enable the economy to be "better off" − as is obvious to trade theorists familiar with the Baldwin-envelope technique. If then there is a distortion common to both situations, as with an endogenous wage differential or production externality or with an autonomous policy-imposed production tax-cum-subsidy, the transition to the (free) trading situation may well be immiserizing (i.e., therefore, free trade inferior to autarky) if the loss from this distortion is accentuated and outweighs the primary gain from the shift to (free) trade itself.

---

[27] These conclusions can also be derived by reference to the Bhagwati-Ramaswami-Srinivasan [8] formula, in footnote 14, which reduces for this case to $dU = U_2[dX_1(p_f - p_t) + (p_c - p_f)dC_1]$.

[28] This is seen again by examining the Bhagwati-Ramaswami-Srinivasan formula which reduces, in this instance, to $dU = U_2[dX_1(p_f - p_t) + (p_c - p_f)dC_1]$. It is clear then that a reduction in the tariff, by affecting both X_1 and C_1 may worsen rather than improve welfare; and that the welfare effect of successive tariff changes need not be unidirectional.

Proposition 7:

Distortions cannot be ranked (uniquely) vis-à-vis one another.

This is a readily apparent proposition and applies clearly to all the classes of distortions we have discussed.

Bhagwati's demonstration [4] that Kemp's theorem [22] of the superiority of tariff-restricted trade over no trade will not extend to cases where the trade is restricted instead by policies such as consumption and production tax-cum-subsidies becomes intuitively obvious as soon as it is seen that it falls into the class of theorems belonging to Proposition 7. For, in this instance, two distortions are being compared: (i) a consumption tax-cum-subsidy leading to Distortion 3, DRS $\neq$ DRT = FRT, with a situation of autarky and hence implicit prohibitive tariff, thus involving Distortion 1, FRT $\neq$ DRT = DRS; and (ii) a production tax-cum-subsidy leading to Distortion 2, DRT = DRS = FRT, with autarky involving Distortion 1, FRT $\neq$ DRT = DRS. In principle, of course, the demonstration of impossibility of unique ranking between autarky and restricted trade could be carried equally into the case where trade-restriction occurs via use of a factor tax-cum-subsidy involving Distortion 4 along with 2.

4.3. Concluding Remarks

We have thus succeeded in unifying a considerable body of literature on the welfare economics of trade into a series of major propositions that constitute a generalized theory of distortions and welfare. Aside from the intrinsic elegance of such unification, this has resulted in a number of insights into, and extensions of, the theorems to date in this significant area of economic policy.

References

[1] Bhagwati, J. "Immiserizing Growth: A Geometrical Note." *Review of Economic Studies*, 25 (June 1958).

[2] Bhagwati, J., and Ramaswami, V.K. "Domestic Distortions, Tariffs and the Theory of Optimum Subsidy." *Journal of Political Economy*, 71 (February 1963).

[3] Bhagwati, J. "Non-Economic Objectives and the Efficiency Properties of Trade." *Journal of Political Economy*, 76 (October 1968).

[4] Bhagwati, J. "Gains from Trade Once Again." *Oxford Economic Papers*, 20 (July 1968).

[5] Bhagwati, J. *The Theory and Practice of Commercial Policy*. Frank Graham

Memorial Lecture (1967), Special Papers in International Economics No. 8, Princeton University, 1968.

[6] Bhagwati, J. "Distortions and Immiserizing Growth: A Generalization," *Review of Economic Studies*, 35 (November 1968).

[7] Bhagwati, J. and Srinivasan, T.N. "Optimal Intervention to Achieve Non-Economic Objectives." *Review of Economic Studies,* 36 (January 1969).

[8] Bhagwati, J., Ramaswami, V.K. and Srinivasan, T.N. "Domestic Distortions, Tariffs and the Theory of Optimum Subsidy: Some Further Results." *Journal of Political Economy*, 77 (November/December 1969).

[9] Bhagwati, J., "Optimal Policies and Immiserizing Growth." *American Economic Review*, 59 (December 1969).

[10] Bhagwati, J. and Kemp, M.C. "Ranking of Tariffs under Monopoly Power in Trade." *Quarterly Journal of Economics*, 83 (May 1969).

[11] Bhagwati, J. and Srinivasan, T.N. "The Theory of Wage Differentials: Production Response and Factor Price Equalisation", *Journal of International Economics*, 1 (February 1971).

[12] Corden, W.M. "Tariffs, Subsidies and the Terms of Trade." *Economica*, 24 (August 1957).

[13] Fishlow, A. and David, P. "Optimal Resource Allocation in an Imperfect Market Setting." *Journal of Political Economy*, 69 (December 1961).

[14] Graaff, J. "On Optimum Tariff Structures." *Review of Economic Studies*, 17 (1949–1950).

[15] Haberler, G. "Some Problems in the Pure Theory of International Trade," *Economic Journal,* 30 (June 1950).

[16] Hagen, E. "An Economic Justification of Protectionism," *Quarterly Journal of Economics*, 72 (November 1958).

[17] Johnson, H.G. *International Trade and Economic Growth*, London: George Allen and Unwin Ltd, 1958.

[18] Johnson, H.G. "Optimal Trade Intervention in the Presence of Domestic Distortions." in R.E. Caves, H.G. Johnson and P.B. Kenen (eds.), *Trade, Growth and the Balance of Payments*, Amsterdam: North-Holland Publishing Company, 1965.

[19] Johnson, H.G. "The Possibility of Income Losses from Increased Efficiency or Factor Accumulation in the Presence of Tariffs." *Economic Journal*, 77 (March 1967).

[20] Johnson, H.G. "Factor Market Distortions and the Shape of the Transformation Curve." *Econometrica*, 34 (July 1966).

[21] Kemp, M.C. *The Pure Theory of International Trade*. Englewood Cliffs, N.J.: Prentice-Hall, 1964.

[22] Kemp, M.C. "The Gain from International Trade." *Economic Journal*, 72 (December 1962).

[23] Kemp, M.C. "Some Issues in the Analysis of Trade Gains." *Oxford Economic Papers*, 20 (July 1968).

[24] Kemp, M.C. and Negishi, T. "Domestic Distortions, Tariffs and the Theory of Optimum Subsidy," *Journal of Political Economy*, 77 (November/December 1969).

[25] Melvin, J. "Demand Conditions and Immiserizing Growth." *American Economic Review*, 59 (September 1969).

[26] Melvin, J. "Commodity Taxation as a Determinant of Trade." University of Western Ontario, *mimeographed,* 1968.

[27] Matthews R.C.O. "Reciprocal Demand and Increasing Returns." *Review of Economic Studies,* 17 (1949–1950).

[28] Samuelson, P.A. "The Gains from International Trade." *Canadian Journal of Economics and Political Science*, 5 (May 1939).

[29] Samuelson, P.A. "The Gains from International Trade Once Again." *Economic Journal*, 72 (December 1962).

[30] Tinbergen, J. *International Economic Cooperation*, Amsterdam: North-Holland Publishing Company, 1946.

CHAPTER 5

TRADE AND MINIMUM WAGE RATES

Louis LEFEBER *

5.1. Introduction

Though trade theory is one of the oldest subjects of economic analysis and the effect of free trade on industrialization has been a matter of debate at least since Manoilesco, yet studies of growth and development in the context of the international economy are of comparatively recent vintage. For those that exist, we are indebted to such scholars as Charles Kindleberger, who as students of both trade and development theory have combined the relevant tools of the two disciplines for analyzing the postwar changes in international economic relationships and their implications for growth and development.

Some of these changes reflect altered attitudes toward poverty and economic retardation. Though the distribution of resources continues to be skewed, it is no longer believed that the prevailing extreme inequality among nations and persons is either right or in the long run necessary, and in both industrial and undeveloped economies increasing attention is being given to the question of the international and national redistribution of incomes. At the same time the fact remains that the institutional and organizational means for effecting redistribution are limited and the related problems are only imperfectly understood. In this respect the insights offered by trade theory do not go beyond those obtained from the analysis of purely competitive

* The author is Professor of Economics at Brandeis University and currently Visiting Professor at the Institute of Economic Growth, Delhi. He is indebted to T.N. Srinivasan for substantive comments and very helpful discussions and to the late V.K. Ramaswami for some good talks on this and related topics. He is also grateful to the editors, in particular to Jagdish Bhagwati, for their comments. For the errors the author alone is responsible.

markets. Arguments for free trade as an instrument of international welfare maximization can only be sustained on the dubious assumption that the international distribution of income is optimal. When it comes to trade-induced changes in domestic welfare, trade theory sidesteps the issue when it invokes the well-known compensation principle without considering the actual problem of its implementation. [1]

The problem of compensation or income redistribution is particularly difficult when the institutional means for direct income transfers are not adequate. This is likely to be the case in low income countries if redistribution is to be undertaken in favor of the unemployed or underemployed. Then increasing the demand for labor and the rate of employment at given minimum wage rates may be the only effective policy. This is all the more so since the adverse effects of such a redistribution policy on savings and investment are likely to be less important than in the case of direct income transfers, because the beneficiaries of the redistribution, i.e., those who would otherwise not be gainfully employed, add their own labor to the productive effort.

Nonetheless, such a redistribution policy based on the use of minimum wages is unorthodox and not without its own difficulties. Instead of neutral income transfers the policy makes use of the price mechanism; if carelessly employed it may bring about distortions to resource use, such as excessively high capital intensities in production instead of the desired distribution of income. [2] In fact, minimum wages may themselves be the cause of unemployment and since they can be effective means for redistribution only if a high rate of employment can also be maintained, carefully planned direct or indirect additional controls may also be required to ensure an adequate demand for labor. [3] In particular, if the wage rate considered to be socially optimal is higher than corresponds to labor's marginal productivity in any and

---

[1] For the compensation principle see Samuelson [10].

[2] Wage rigidity or stickiness has been discussed by several trade theorists. For a review and extension of the relevant trade literature see Bhagwati [1]. These contributions are concerned with distortions to the price system and resource allocation in the context of what Bhagwati classifies as the "Traditional Objective Function." Such departures from the traditional as involving utility maximization over time with given minimum wages or the purposeful use of the price system for redistribution and the relationship between employment, consumption, savings and growth have been explored only in the context of a closed economy by int. al. Chakravarty [2], Marglin [8] and [9], Sen [12] and Lefeber [4].

[3] The administration of these too, of course, requires adequate institutions. It would be futile to argue without further reference to legal, administrative, and political

all feasible patterns of full employment resource use, the free market in autarky cannot be expected to employ the entire supply of labor. In other words, a state of underemployment or surplus labor is the outcome. If then those who are left unemployed by the free market are also to benefit from minimum wage income redistribution, the government must intervene to increase the rate of employment.

It is evident that unless additional measures are used to increase the rate of saving, an increase in employment and redistributed consumption can be attained in the autarkic economy only at the cost of a diminished rate of domestic investment. Hence, government intervention to increase employment must reflect a social judgement that it is desirable to sacrifice some future satisfaction for larger current redistributed consumption. It will be seen that the same welfare problem of balancing current and future needs is also present in the open economy. But it is to be expected that the outcome of free trading, though uniquely determined by market forces, cannot be characterized for policy purposes in terms of a unique underemployment equilibrium point, as is the case in autarky. Instead, depending on the terms of trade and relative factor intensities, a range of outcomes is possible with very different implications for welfare.

If it is assumed that all profits are saved and all wages are consumed, free trade can never lead to a lower rate of investment than attainable in autarky.[4] Then at one extreme of the range of feasible outcomes is the possibility that free trade with minimum wages will lead to increased investment *and* to full employment consumption even if in autarky unemployment would prevail. If this is the case, income redistribution is accomplished without sacrifice and with no other government intervention but the

---

structure what the relative difficulties are. However, two points can be made. First, since here the need is for making the use of labor relatively cheaper than the use of capital, in addition to the tax-subsidy policies discussed in this paper, alternative and more or less direct policies to operate through foreign exchange or credit markets can also be devised. (Since these have to be tailored to suit the requirements of particular circumstances, e.g., how to induce an increased demand for labor in family farming, they cannot be taken up here.) Second, even if the organizational difficulties were the same, but if the savings effects of redistribution through employment were more favorable than those of direct income transfers, the use of minimum wages combined with employment creation would still be justified.

[4] The assumption does not necessarily imply that there is no consumption by capitalists but that it would have to be proportional to employment or capital stock so that profits are net of consumption. Of course, if the capital stock is state owned, the problem does not arise at all.

enforcement of the minimum wage legislation. At the other extreme is the possibility that free trade will result in at least as much investment as attainable in autarky, but employment and consumption will be lower than the autarkic rate. If the purpose of minimum wages is to redistribute consumption through employment, free trade in such cases may lead to lower welfare than the free market in autarky. Furthermore, since such an outcome is possible with no increase in domestic investment, compensation would not be feasible either, and only purposeful policies aimed at increasing the demand for labor could improve on the market outcome.

Finally, there is the possibility that investment and consumption will be higher than in autarky but that full employment consumption can not be attained through free trade. In fact, it will be demonstrated that if the wage good is the export good, full employment can never be attained through free trade, no matter how favorable the terms of trade for the export of the consumer good. It follows that manipulation of the terms of trade can have no effect on wage good production and employment beyond that point where the marginal *physical* product of labor in that sector just equals the wage rate. The problem does not arise in the same form with the output of nonwage good sector, i.e., the production and export of investment goods. The reason is that the profit maximizing rate of employment is determined by the equality of the *value* of the marginal product and the money wage rate, magnitudes that do depend on the terms of trade. Hence, given sufficiently favorable terms of trade for the export of investment goods, full employment can be reached through trade even if the export good is relatively less labor intensive than imports.

In contrast to the autarkic free market solution, where unemployment is inevitable and private and social interests can coincide only when society places all the weight on growth and none on current consumption per se, the outcome of free trade may be consistent with more humane concepts of welfare. This is clearly the case when trade leads to full employment at the socially optimal wage rate and, depending on the nature of the welfare function, it may also be the case if full employment is not attained but a higher than the autarkic rate of employment and wage consumption results. But when this is not the case, nondiscriminatory tax and subsidy policies which do not depend on or interfere with the direction of trade flows can be devised for bringing about the social good also in the open economy.

5.2. Autarky When the Supply of Wage Goods Constrains Employment

Assume that in autarky two outputs, consumer goods (C) and investment goods (I) can be produced with two inputs, labor (L) and capital (K) whose quantities are given in the initial period. The production relationships are such as to permit continuous factor substitution, and increasing returns to scale are ruled out. The labor force is growing at a known rate (n) and the capital stock increases according to the rate of investment determined by purely competitive free market forces or government policy. The wage rate (w) is institutionally fixed in terms of the consumer good at some minimum level that in any and all full employment patterns of resource use exceeds the real value of the marginal product of labor in either industry and is sufficiently high to motivate labor to seek employment. [5] Employed workers consume their entire wages and consumption by the owners of capital is included in the form of surplus value. [6] Hence, rents (profits) are net of consumption and are fully reinvested.

In such an economy, the level of employment clearly determines the minimum demand for consumer goods. Conversely, the available supply of C may restrict the rate of employment below full employment, in which case the unemployed must live on public or private support or retire to a subsistence sector outside the monetised economy. If such unemployment cannot be eliminated in the short run (i.e., with given capital stock) [7] by competitive market forces, a state of surplus labor exists. [8] This is necessarily the case if, as assumed in this analysis, in full employment w exceeds the marginal product of labor in the consumer good industry (MPL_C) or if the market value of w (the monetized wage rate) exceeds the value of the marginal product in either industry. Then profit maximizing employers would

---

[5] Note that under these conditions the institutionally fixed wage rate would never be exceeded in the free market; hence, the fixed wage rate is necessarily a minimum wage rate. Accordingly, the two terms can be used interchangeably without any ambiguity. Furthermore, since the wage rate is fixed in terms of the consumer good, it represents also the real wage rate.

[6] Alternatively, capitalists' consumption could be directly proportional to the capital stock. The customary but not necessarily more realistic assumption that consumption is a function of profits would complicate this analysis.

[7] The terms *short run* and *long run* denote states in which the capital stock is fixed at its initial level or growing, respectively.

[8] This definition is consistent with Lewis' concept of infinitely elastic supply of labor [6].

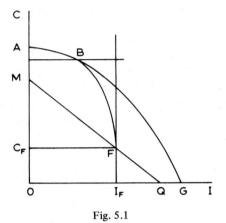

Fig. 5.1

be motivated to restrict employment so as to obtain a marginal product commensurate to w.

The production possibility relationships for such an economy are shown in figure 5.1. [9] The social transformation function (*STF*) represented by the curve *AG* is drawn up on the assumption that there is no wage-consumption constraint on employment, i.e., as if the wage rate were determined in a competitive free labor market instead of institutionally fixed. In this analysis, however, the production possibilities are limited by the given wage rate and the consequent minimum consumption requirements corresponding to any rate of employment. Assuming that the minimum wage-consumption demand in full employment corresponds to *B*, autarkic production cannot take place along the *BG* segment of the *STF* because the feasible levels of consumption do not sustain the fully employed labor force. Nonetheless, autarkic investment can be increased beyond the rate corresponding to *B*. Since on the *STF* the wage rate (the marginal demand for *C* by the last unit of employed labor) by assumption exceeds the MPL_C (which is also the marginal supply of *C* owing to the last unit of labor in the *C* sector), it is possible to liberate inputs from *C* for transfer into *I* by reducing the rate of employment. In fact, in such a situation profit maximizing employers would want to do just that and would continue doing so until employment was reduced to that rate where given the capital stock the marginal productivity of labor is commensurate to

---

[9] The detailed analysis and the derivation of the transformation function and the feasibility function specific to the given wage rate are provided in Lefeber [4]. In addition, the appendix to this paper contains the relevant mathematical framework.

w. Assuming that this is attained at F, the feasibility function corresponding to w (FF_w) consists of the arc ABF.

The segment AB of the STF is feasible since the supply of C exceeds the minimum demand imposed by full employment wage consumption. In other words, consumption does not constrain employment. Along the segment BF, on the other hand, the increase in I at the cost of C correspondingly and increasingly constrains employment below the full employment rate. At F, where the MPL_C equals w, the FF_w comes to its end. There the marginal demand for C is the same as its marginal supply in response to the last unit of labor and nothing could be gained from a further reduction of employment. In fact, it would result in raising the marginal products above the wage rate and given the consumption constraint, both outputs would have to be reduced. In other words, from that point on, the FF_w would have to bend backward. It follows that its slope must be vertical at F. [10]

It is evident that in autarky F represents the only point on the FF_w which is consistent with a profit maximising competitive free market solution; at all other points the wage rate exceeds the marginal product of labor. [11] For this reason and because rents (profits), being net of consumption, are fully reinvested, the free market solution also represents the investment or growth maximizing point on the FF_w.

At F only that much C is produced which is needed exactly to sustain the investment maximizing rate of employment. In other words, at that point consumption is an *intermediate* activity. It follows that only if the social valuation of consumption per se is zero, will the welfare optimal resource use correspond to the free market solution at F where the FF_w (i.e., I as function of C and w) reaches its extreme point and the slope turns vertical. But the fact that at that point the welfare valuation of C qua final good is zero does not imply that its market price (i.e., the price needed to bring forth the last unit of C output) is also zero. Since a positive C output is required to sustain the profit maximizing rate of employment, a nonzero market price for C must also exist.

The autarkic free market price ratio between C and I can be derived in two steps, both relevant to the subsequent trade analysis. The first step consists in

---

[10] See relationship 5.8 of the Appendix. The backward bending segment obtained in response to further reductions in employment is irrelevant to economic decisions and is not shown in the figure.

[11] Throughout this paper the term "free market" is used to denote conditions in which a stable equilibrium can be attained or sustained by decentralised profit maximising decision makers without fiscal intervention.

establishing the conditions of efficient domestic production for any and all feasible output combinations consistent with w but *without* the demand constraints of the analysis. The second step then consists in the identification of the wage-consumption requirements associated with the efficient output combinations so as to divide the C output into its potential final and intermediate uses. It turns out that the final C output (i.e., the surplus over the satisfaction of the wage consumption requirement) as function of I is a transformation function the slope of which is the autarkic free market price ratio between C and I. Given that in this economy there is a final demand only for I and none for C, over and above wage-consumption requirements, the autarkic equilibrium must always be at that point where the C surplus is zero. But when trade is introduced, this will not be the case.

Assume then that w is fixed as before, but that the demand constraints (on C and I) are removed. If constant returns to scale prevail, a straight-line locus of efficient output combinations, such as MQ in figure 5. 1, can be derived by means of an Edgeworth production box whose sides are given by the total amount of capital and labor in the economy. As shown in figure 5.2, for each output there exists an expansion path consistent with least cost hiring when the wage rate is fixed at w. [12] Because of constant returns to scale, these must be straight lines representing constant capital-labor ratios in each activity. [13] The straight-line function MQ is derived by reading off the outputs at those pairs of points on the expansion paths that correspond to any given division of the capital stock between the two sectors. Such a pair of points relating to the output combination at F (which because of free market profit maximization must be on these expansion paths) and the points corresponding to the two vertices of MQ are identified in the Edgeworth box. Since labor is in excess supply at any pair of points on the two expansion paths, MQ must be a straight-line function with slope determined by the ratio of the fixed capital output ratios in the two sectors. Furthermore, because labor is in excess supply also at M and Q, the entire length of the line MQ, as represented in figure 5.1, must lie inside the region defined by the STF. [14]

---

[12] The contract curve from which the STF is derived is indicated by the dotted line in Figure 5.2.

[13] As is well known, given constant returns to scale, the marginal product of a factor is function of factor proportions alone.

[14] Note the analogy to activity analysis. Once the wage rate is fixed, technology is also fixed and capital is the only scarce input. Then the outputs at the two vertices M and Q are fully determined and the line MQ is the linear combination of the outputs at the two vertex points.

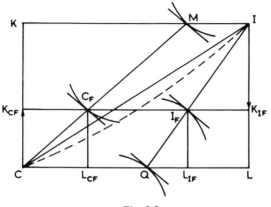

Fig. 5.2

Though the equality of labor's marginal product to w is satisfied every-where along MQ, if the wage consumption constraint is reimposed, it is not a market transformation function between final outputs. To obtain that, the part of C which is needed for wage consumption and therefore represents an input or real cost of production must be subtracted from the output of C. To this end the rate of employment (E) corresponding to any output combination must be ascertained. It is evident that the rate of employment will not, in general, be constant along MQ but that it will be some variable but convex (linear) combination of the employments at M and Q, respectively. Hence wage consumption, i.e., wE as function of I, will also be a convex (linear) combination of the consumption requirements at these two extreme points. Such a wage consumption function is shown by the line $C_M N$ in figure 5.3. [15]

The difference between MQ and $C_M N$ represents the surplus (deficit) of C

---

[15] Figure 5.3 reproduces MQ of Figure5.1. The F, which is uniquely determined free enterprise point, is also marked. Note that $C_M N$ has a negative slope, implying that C is relatively labor intensive as in Figure 5.2. In the converse case the wage consumption function would have to be upward sloping.

The wage consumption function is derived as follows: Assume that if specialization takes place at M, the wE_M is at C_M which is greater than C_F. But because F must also be a linear combination of the wage consumptions at M and Q, the point C_Q (i.e., wE_Q) is determined by the intersection of a straight line through the points C_M and F with a vertical line at Q. The intersection is denoted by N. If C were the relatively less labor intensive output, C_M would be lower than C_F and the wage consumption function would have a positive slope.

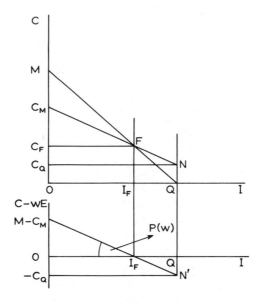

Fig. 5.3

over and above the wage-consumption requirement. This is shown by the straight line function $(M-C_M)N'$ in the lower part of figure 5.3. That portion of this relationship where the surplus is positive (i.e., from $M-C_M$ to I_F) is the transformation function between C for final (nonwage consumption) use and I. [16] But because in autarky there is no demand for final (nonwage) C output, the autarkic solution must always correspond to I_F. Nonetheless, the rate at which final C can be exchanged for I is given by the slope of this transformation function which then represents the autarkic price of I in terms of C. [17] Since this price is function of w, it will be denoted by $P(w)$. [18]

[16] Sukhamoy Chakravarty pointed out to me the analogy to Samuelson's net-net national product concept obtained by deducting the wage bill and other factor payments from the net national product. See Samuelson [11].

[17] Note that the wage rate, the profit rate and the price ratio are constant for any and all output combinations along this transformation function. Thus it also satisfies the conditions underlying Marx's labor theory of value. For an exhaustive analysis of Marxian economics see the forthcoming paper by Sukhamoy Chakravarty entitled "An Essay on the Marxian Theory of Value."

[18] Note that $P(w) \lessgtr OM/OQ$ (i.e., the slope of MQ) as the capital labor ratio in C, i.e., $k_C \lessgtr k_I$ (i.e., the capital labor ratio in I). This directly follows from the fact that if $k_C \lessgtr k_I$, the slope of the wage consumption function C_MN is negative, zero, and positive, respectively.

5.3. Free Trade at Minimum Wages

Assume now that the economy has access to international markets where the demand for, and supply of, both goods are infinitely elastic at given international market prices. Then the demand constraints operating in this economy can be satisfied either from domestic or foreign sources. Entrepreneurs, however, will be interested in trading only if the after trade profits are at least as great as in autarky. Accordingly, if all savings must be invested domestically, trade will be preferred to autarky if the after trade supply of investment goods (domestically produced and/or imported) is greater than the autarkic I output at F. In figure 5.4 a straight line drawn through F perpendicularly to the I axis cuts away that portion of the space where the minimum profit requirement cannot be satisfied. [19] Any outcome to the left of this vertical line is inconsistent with free trade equilibrium because of inadequate profitability, and points on the vertical line itself represent indifference between free trading and autarky. Furthermore, since trade must also satisfy the wage consumption requirement, it follows that for any international terms of trade the profitability of trade must depend on the trade induced changes in labor utilization. In figure 5.4, so as to be consistent

[19] Figure 5.4 reproduces the STF along with the full employment consumption point B, the locus of efficient output combination MQ and the autarkic free market point F. The segment BF of the FF_w is not shown since it represents a constraint only in autarky and not in the open economy. MH and KQ are parallel to each other and their slope corresponds to $P(w)$, i.e., to the slope of the transformation function $(M-C_M)I_F$ shown in Fig. 5.3.

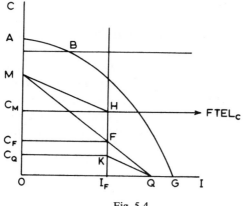

Fig. 5.4

with previous diagrams, it is assumed that C is relatively labor intensive so that specialization in C increases the demand for wage consumption. [20]

Consider now the relationship MQ which represents the entire C output as function of I. If the wage consumption constraint can be satisfied by trading, its entire length represents feasible output combinations. Furthermore, since the free market hiring condition of equating the MPL to w is satisfied everywhere on MQ, no output combination would be produced which is inside the delineated region. But because MQ is linear, if trade develops specialization in one or the other commodity is to be expected. Assuming that specialization takes place at M, the surplus of C over the wage consumption requirement of the employment at M is shown in figure 5.4 by MC_M. In fact the triangle MC_MH exactly corresponds to the feasible region enclosed by the transformation function $(M-C_M)I_F$ of figure 5.3 and the slope of MH is identical to $P(w)$. If MC_MH represents a trade triangle, the surplus MC_M of the C output is exported in exchange for an amount of I which exactly corresponds to I_F; hence, profits from trading are identical to these in autarky. Similarly, KI_FQ represents a trade triangle in response to specialization at Q (i.e., the export of QI_F in exchange for the import of C_Q) which exactly corresponds to region I_FQN' of figure 5.3, so that in this case too the profits are the same as in autarky. From this it follows that if the international terms of trade are identical to the autarkic price ratio, special-ization, and free trade are feasible in either direction but entrepreneurs are indifferent between autarky and trade.

Given that the international terms of trade, $P(I)$ is smaller than $P(w)$, so that specialization in C does take place, the relevant free trade equilibrium locus $(FTEL_C)$ for alternative $P(I)$ can readily be derived. In the absence of any final domestic demand for C over and above the wage consumption require-ment, all equilibria must lie on the horizontal line corresponding to C_M and to the right of H. Accordingly this line to the right of H, as shown in figure 5.4, is the $FTEL_C$.

The more the terms of trade favor the export of C, the further to the right of H the free trade equilibrium will be and the larger profits and domestic investment will be. Nonetheless, entrepreneurs will not have the motivation — in spite of the prevailing excess supply of labor — to increase the output of C above the vertex point at M by hiring more labor. This is the case because the addition of another unit of labor to the rate of employment needed for specialization at M would raise the domestic demand for C by w but —

---

[20] In this there is no loss of generality, for in the opposite case when C is relatively less labor intensive, an exactly analogous argument holds.

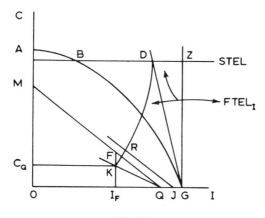

Fig. 5.5

because of diminishing returns to scale in factor substitution — would increase the total output of C only by less than w. Consequently profits in terms of the exportable C surplus and domestic investment would diminish. Thus, *if C is the export good, free trade cannot increase employment above the rate needed to specialize at M, and hence, it cannot lead to full employment.*

The case is different if the terms of trade favor specialization in I. Then if in keeping with the previous discussion I is relatively less labor intensive than C, specialization at Q will require a lower rate of employment and wage consumption than production in autarky. Assume that if specialization takes place at Q the wage consumption requirement is at C_Q as shown in Figure 5.5. [21] If $P(I)$ is equal to $P(w)$, entrepreneurs will be indifferent between autarky or specialization at Q. But because in I production the optimal rate of employment is determined by marginal *value* instead of physical products, it is evident that if $P(I)$ exceeds $P(w)$ entrepreneurs will find it profitable to hire more labor so as to produce more I than corresponds to Q. [22] Accordingly, as successively higher $P(I)$ make for increasing profit-

[21] Figure 5.5 reproduces the relevant elements of the previous Figure 5.4.

[22] That this must be the case can readily be deduced from the condition of profit maximizing employment. If $P(I)$ denotes the terms of trade and F_L stands for the MPL_I, then for a profit maximum $P(I)F_L = w$. Since w is by assumption fixed, a given increase in $P(I)$ warrants just that increase in employment and induced decrease in F_L which keeps the *real* value of the marginal product constant. It is to be noted that in order to attain the full employment point G on the *STF*, the terms of trade must exceed the slope of the *STF* at G. This is true because the wage rate by assumption exceeds the real value of the marginal product in full employment; hence, a suitably larger price ratio

ability, the profit maximizing outputs will be realized by corresponding increases in the rate of employment. The limit is attained at G where unemployment is eliminated so that the entire labor supply is employed in the production of I. Thus, in contrast to the case of C exports where specialization is confined to M, in the case of I exports the profit maximizing output falls within the range QG on the I axis. It follows that given a sufficiently favorable terms of trade larger than $P(w)$, *the export of I in the free market can bring about a higher rate of employment than corresponds to specialization at Q and can, in the limit, result in full employment.*

The free trade equilibrium locus when I is the export good ($FTEL_I$) is shown in Figure 5.5. Specialization at Q takes place when $P(I)$ equals $P(w)$ with trade equilibrium at K where wage consumption is satisfied from imports and investment corresponds to the autarkic rate. Accordingly the $FTEL_I$ begins at K. For successively higher terms of trade the I output exceeds Q. The after trade investment is higher than I_F but because the profit maximizing employment is also higher, so is the after trade supply of C for wage consumption. The trade equilibria for successively higher terms of trade are shown by the arc KD. [23] They are obtained by drawing each successively higher terms of trade line from a correspondingly higher rate of I output on QG until the vertex at G is reached. For example, the terms of trade line JR whose slope corresponds to the slope of MQ will start out from some point to the right of Q — say at J — and will denote a free trade equilibrium to the right of MQ at R which may or may not represent a higher rate of wage consumption than the one at autarky. Full employment trade equilibrium — as argued in footnote 22 — can be attained only at some terms of trade which is higher than the marginal rate of substitution of the STF at G. Such a price line is shown by GD. The after trade availability of C must now correspond to the full employment wage consumption requirement so that the trade equilibrium point D must lie on a horizontal line at the level of B. Even higher price ratios must result in equilibrium points on the same horizontal line to the right of D, the limit being a zero international price for C at Z. Accordingly the $FTEL_I$ consists of the arc KD and the line segment DZ.

---

than corresponds to the marginal rate of transformation is required to compensate for the excess of w over the real value of the marginal product. Note that the real value of the marginal product is evaluated in terms of the price ratio corresponding to the marginal rate of transformation, in this instance at G.

[23] As shown by the arc KD, equal increments in investment are attained at the cost of increasing wage consumption requirements. This is because of diminishing returns to employment combined with a constant amount of capital.

The derivation of the two *FTEL* when *C* is relatively less labor intensive than *I* is exactly analogous to the earlier cases. The conclusion that full employment may be attained through free trade only if *I* is the export good remains unaffected. The only difference is because, as explained in the previous section, $P(w)$ is then greater than the slope of *MQ* and hence the position of the two trade triangles representing indifference between trade and autarky is correspondingly inverted. Specifically, the trade triangle representing specialization at *M* will lie below *MQ* and the one corresponding to *Q* will show a trade equilibrium point outside the region defined by *MQ*.

5.4. Welfare and Trade with Minimum Wages

The welfare implications of free trade with minimum wage rates can be summarized as follows:

1. Free trade ensures at least as much investment as is attainable in autarky.

2. If the wage good is the export good free trade can not lead to full employment, because then specialization is confined to a single point below the *STF* where unemployment is prevalent. If *I* is the export good full employment can be attained through free trade if and only if the terms of trade exceed the *MRT* of the *STF* at its vertex on the *I* axis.

3. It is possible for free trade to result in a lower than the autarkic rate of employment and redistributed consumption. This, in fact, is the necessary outcome if $k_C > k_I$ when *C* is the export good. If $k_C < k_I$ and *I* is the export good, this outcome is also possible but the adverse effect of the lower relative labor intensity in *I* production may be outweighed by an increased demand for labor in response to a sufficiently high terms of trade.

4. If the export good is labor intensive, free trade always results in larger employment and redistributed consumption than obtainable in autarky. [24]

If *w* is the socially optimal wage rate and the welfare goal is to maximize the rate of investment or growth, any and all free trade equilibria — including those that result in a lower than autarkic current redistributed consumption — are welfare optimal. [25] Thus the welfare implications of the free trade

---

[24] When the capital-labor ratio happens to be identical in both sectors, the autarkic price ratio $P(w)$ coincides with the slope of *MQ*. Then wage consumption is the same as at C_F for all output combinations on *MQ*.

[25] With constant returns to scale investment maximization is equivalent to growth maximization, as long as unemployment prevails. Hence if the free trade equilibrium calls for full employment production at *G*, diminishing returns to scale would set in and growth would have to slow down to approach the rate of growth of the labor force.

equilibrium are not essentially different from those of the autarkic free market solution.

If surplus labor prevails, and in the absence of government intervention, the free market solution may also be the fastest route to full employment at some institutionally set minimum wage rate. [26] Such a path may have great appeal in countries where institutional means for income redistribution (i.e., taxation and subsidization) or other welfare remedies which can be applied in the short run do not exist. On the other hand, if the government is able and willing to intervene, it can induce a higher than free market rate of employment and redistributed consumption even in the short run. In autarky this requires a move along the FF_w away from F toward A so that current consumption is increased at the cost of lowering the rate of investment and growth. However, since in autarky F represents the only free market solution, any other output combination requires either centrally controlled resource allocation or decentralized means for inducing a more labor intensive technology than used in the free market. [27]

If the economy is open to international trade and effective government intervention can be obtained, in contrast to autarky where production is confined to the FF_w, the entire STF becomes accessible. In that case, however, even if the intervention is indirect, so that production and trade decisions are made by decentralized, profit maximizing entrepreneurs, trade is no longer free in the sense that the intervention must be specifically designed to ensure that production satisfies the national and international market constraints while, at the same time, it takes place at an appropriate point on the STF. It is, of course, evident that if the STF is nonlinear, full specialization may not be indicated. Instead, depending on the tangency between the STF and the international price line, some of both goods will be produced. The question than is what will determine the direction and size of trade.

Production on the STF implies that the full employment wage consumption requirement must be met. Point B in Figure 5.5 denotes that output combination on the STF where the domestic C output exactly corresponds to this full employment wage demand. If the tangency of the international terms of trade to the STF is to the left of B, a domestic consumer good surplus is indicated and the export of C and the import of I is called for. Thus, the arc

---

[26] See Lefeber and Chakravarty [5].

[27] Decentralized intervention consists in a payroll subsidy financed by profit taxation. For the required size of the tax-subsidy scheme and its relationship to the price structure, see Lefeber [4].

AB represents the *C export range* on the *STF*. If, on the other hand, the tangency is to the right of *B* so that the domestic *C* output is not sufficient to satisfy the wage consumption need, *C* must be imported in exchange for *I*. Accordingly, the arc *BG* represents the *I export range*. It follows that in the absence of any final (nonwage) domestic demand for *C*, all full employment trade equilibrium points must lie at the intersection of the international price line with a horizontal line through and to the right of *B*. Such a line representing the social trade equilibrium locus (*STEL*) is shown in Figure 5.5. Note that if *I* is the export good, the *STEL* is naturally truncated at *Z*, while in the limiting case of full specialization in *C*, given successively lower *P(I)*, there is no limit to the attainable after trade supply of *I*.

The relationship cf the two export ranges to each other, as determined by the position or the height of the *STEL*, is function of the given wage rate. If *w* is raised, the minimum full employment consumption requirement is also raised and the *STEL* shifts upward. The opposite is the case if *w* is lowered. The pattern of trade flows is correspondingly affected. An increase in *w* naturally narrows the *C* export range so that the range of price ratios (terms of trade) which can motivate *C* exports is also narrowed. In other words, a wage increase reduces the *opportunities* for *C* export as well as diminishes the *size* of the exportable surpluses. The *I* export range, on the other hand, increases. If then as a consequence of such change the point of tangency between the price line and the *STF* were to fall into the *I* export range when previously it was in the *C* export range, the economy would have to become an importer instead of exporter of consumer goods.

If trade equilibria on the *STEL* are welfare optimal, the underlying concept of social welfare has something akin to investment maximization as its goal. However, in contrast to the free market, in this case it is pursued subject to a full employment consumption constraint. Viewed in this light the welfare function consists of a fixed coefficient relationship between *C* and *I* arranged not on a ray from the origin (as in linear programming) but along the *STEL* which is function of the socially optimal wage rate. The implication is that the residual output after the satisfaction of the full employment consumption requirement is used entirely for capital formation so that all after trade supplies of *C* and *I* must lie on the *STEL*. It is to be noted that this concept of welfare, with the unique exception of a tangency at *B*, always requires some trade for the attainment of the social optimum. Is also follows that with the exception of those instances where free trade does lead to full employment, the welfare optimal trade equilibrium requires a sacrifice in potential investment for the sake of increased current satisfaction. In other words, for any terms of trade (except those which result in free market specialization at the *I* vertex of the *STF* and hence in free trade equilibria on the *STEL*) the after trade supply of *I* for domestic investment is always larger in the free market than in the social optimum. At the same time all free market equilibria which imply full employment are socially optimal.

Social profit maximization requires the observance of the marginal equivalences as if the wage rate were determined in a competitive free labor market instead of being institutionally fixed. The full employment institutional wage consumption requirement (to be exact, the excess over what the consumption from the competitive market wage would amount to) must then be covered from the national product. Accordingly, government intervention is needed to resolve the problem caused by the excess of the minimum wage over the marginal product of labor. If then intervention is to be based on decentralized means, the government must make the socially optimal resource use the most profitable alternative. As pointed out earlier, this can be achieved by a payroll subsidy in *both* industries which is then financed by a matching profit taxation. The size of the subsidy for each unit of employed labor corresponds to the difference between the wage rate and the real value of the marginal product of labor evaluated in terms of the international price ratio in each sector at the point of tangency. The profit tax needed to cover the cost of the total subsidy exactly corresponds to the excess of what would be the return to capital over and above the value of the after trade supply of domestic investment if wages were determined in purely competitive labor markets. [28] If the appropriate domestic output combination is attained, international trade yields the desired domestic supplies without further need for intervention. It is noteworthy that such an intervention is neutral in the sense that it does not depend on or in any essential sense interfere with the direction of trade flows but depends only on the relationship of the wage rate to the real value of the marginal product in both industries at the welfare point of production.

The above concept of welfare is, however, less than general. It represents a single rigid constraint which forces or brings about a *temporal* correction of the inequity of the current functional distribution of income by means of consumption redistribution to a fully employed labor force. Beyond that it does not provide any scope for balancing the satisfaction of current and future generations. But what if the growth rate in full employment is lower than the rate of growth of the labor force? Or if full employment cannot be attained in the short run because of incipient labor redundancy (implying a linear *STF*), or for any other reasons? An applicable concept of welfare

[28] See Lefeber [4]

would have to permit substitution between current and future consumption or, to suit the framework of this analysis, between current consumption and investment. Then the full employment constraint can be eliminated, but in addition to the wage rate another policy parameter must be introduced. In the most general case this would have to be the social rate of discount but if investment is substituted for the rate of growth of consumption in the welfare function, it would be the desired social average rate of saving.

5.5. Trade and Growth

Whatever welfare function is specified, if redistribution depends on employment at minimum wage rates, the parameters would have to be so selected as to permit a rate of economic growth (or capacity to absorb unemployment) which exceeds the rate of growth of the labor force. For any given wage rate, the maximum rate of growth of the capital stock in autarky or in the open economy corresponds to the ratio of the free market rate of investment to the initial capital stock. If there is initial unemployment, as may well be the case in the free market (and given appropriate assumptions including an absence of technological change), the economy can grow at that rate indefinitely, and if it is growing faster than the potential labor force, at least until full employment is attained. At that point, as is well known, the growth of the economy has to slow down and approach the growth rate of the labor force. Once full employment is attained either in the long run or in the short run (i.e., without capital accumulation) through trade with or without government intervention, a slowdown can be avoided only with the help of a continuous technological change of an appropriate type or by an acceleration of the growth of the labor force itself. It is interesting to note that Charles Kindleberger, in his explanation of the sustained rapid growth in certain European countries after the Second World War, identified migration as one of the basic contributing factors. [29]

If, on the other hand, the rate of growth of the capital stock were less than that of the labor force, the economy would gradually have to approach a state of labor redundancy which could no longer be absorbed through free trade or government intervention. Such a tendency would, of course, be in conflict with any reasonable concept of welfare and would, in the long run, defeat all efforts to redistribute consumption by means of employment. Then the wage rate itself could not be socially optimal and would have to be

[29] See C.P. Kindleberger [3].

correspondingly adjusted downward so as to obtain a suitable increase in the
after trade supply of investible resources.

5.6. Conclusion

In conclusion, the analysis of trade with minimum wages is of more than
academic interest. It is not only because minimum wages are increasingly used
as tools, however insufficiently understood, of income redistribution. More
important is the fact that as a general rule the outcome of free trade with
minimum wage rates will not be socially optimal without additional government intervention. Then, particularly if decentralized policies are to be relied
on to sustain a nonmarket equilibrium, the structure of the different possible
free rate equilibria must be clearly understood. This is the case because such
policies can only be derived from the observed differences between the price
structure associated with the free market and the desired welfare optimal
solution.

Studies in project valuation methods give increasing attention to the use of
international prices for the estimation of domestic social costs and benefits. [30] However, since welfare in the open free market economy is not
necessarily higher than in autarky and the attainment of a welfare optimal
trade equilibrium cannot be taken for granted, international prices can be
guides to social investment decisions only if there is adequate intervention to
ensure welfare optimal resource use in all markets.

Appendix

Assume that I, I_T, C, C_T represent the total domestic supplies and the
traded amounts of C and I and that L_I, L_C, K_I, K_C are the labor and the
capital inputs into the two outputs. The C_T and I_T have opposite signs and
are entered negatively or positively according to the direction of trade flows.
Also, w is the real wage rate fixed in terms of C at a level which exceeds
labor's marginal product in C (f_L) in any and all full employment patterns of
resource use. The total supplies of capital and labor at time t are given by
$K(t)$ and $L(t)$. P_I and P_C are arbitrary weights and $P(I)$ is the fixed
international price of I in terms of C.

Assume constant returns to scale in all activities. The economy is then
described by the following set of relationships:

[30] See, e.g., I.M.D. Little and J.A. Mirrlees [7].

$$U = P_I I + P_C C ,\tag{5.1}$$

$$I = F(K_I, L_I) + I_T ;\tag{5.2}$$

$$C = f(K_C, L_C) + C_T ;\tag{5.3}$$

$$C \geqslant w(L_I + L_C) ;\tag{5.4}$$

$$K_i + K_C = K(t) ;\tag{5.5}$$

$$L_I + L_C \leqslant L(t) ;\tag{5.6}$$

$$C_T - P(I)I_T = 0 .\tag{5.7}$$

In autarky, C_T and L_T are zero and the balance of payments relationship (1.7) vanishes. The *STF* and FF_w of figure 5.1 are derived by maximizing equation 5.1 for alternate values of P_I and P_C, subject to relationships 5.2 to 5.6. However, in the case of the *STF*, it is assumed that $w = 0$, and for the derivation of the FF_w, the w is entered with its given value.

If P_I and P_C are so selected that in the solution 5.4 is binding and relationship 5.6 is nonbinding (i.e., when employment is constrained by the supply of C so that production takes place below the *STF* such as on the arc *BF* in Figure 5.1), the condition of being on the FF_w is given by [31]

$$P_I/P_C = (f_L/F_L)w/(w - f_L) .\tag{5.8}$$

If $P_C = 0$, then the problem reduces to maximizing I subject to relationships 5.2 to 5.6. In that case in order for equation 5.1 to be at its maximum, the inverse of equation 5.8 must vanish. This takes place when $w = f_L$, i.e., when the condition of profit maximizing hiring is fulfilled. It follows that the output combination consistent with the maximum attainable rate of investment (at F in Figure 5.1) corresponds to the profit maximizing free market solution. Then if the Lagrangean multipliers U_I and U_C are interpreted as the market prices of I and C, respectively, the autarkic price ratio $P(w) = U_I/U_C$ is given by

$$P(w) = f_L/F_L = f_K/F_K .\tag{5.9}$$

Since $f_L = w$ at the free market point, all equilibrium output and input variables as well as capital labor ratios (k_I and k_C) are fully determined and

---

[31] Equation 5.8 is obtained by first partially differentiating the Lagrange function $P_I I + P_C C - U_I(I - F) - U_C(C - f) - U_w(wL_I + wL_C - C) - U_K(K_I + K_C - K)$ with respect to the input variables, and then by eliminating the Lagrangean multipliers from the resulting differential relationships. For a more detailed treatment see Lefeber [4].

can be solved for. [32] By adopting the notation $g(k_C)$ for $f(1,k_C)$ and $G(k_I)$ to represent $F(1,k_I)$, the free market equilibrium values of the capital labor ratios which satisfy the minimum wage (denoted by k^*_C and k^*_I) can be solved for by first recognizing that

$$g(k_C) - k_C g'(k_C) = w, \tag{5.10}$$

which determines k^*_C, and that

$$\frac{g(k^*_C) - k^*_C g'(k^*_C)}{g'(k^*_C)} = \frac{G(k_I) - k_I G'(k_I)}{G'(k_I)} \tag{5.11}$$

which then yields the value of k^*_I.

Given that the capital labor ratios are determined by w and in autarky remain invariant whether or not equation 5.4 need be satisfied, the relationships constraining free market choices, e.g. those in Figures 5.2 and 5.3, can be deduced by recognizing the fact that there is a structural analogy between this problem and activity analysis. Accordingly MQ of Figures 5.1 and 5.3, i.e., the locus of efficient output combinations for a given w, is described by the following expression:

$$C = (K/k^*_C)g(k^*_C) - \frac{g(k^*_C)/k^*_C}{G(k^*_I)/k^*_I} I, \tag{5.12}$$

where the constant term represents the C output at the vertex M and the slope corresponds to the ratio of the outputs at the two vertices M and Q.

Since L_C and L_I are C/g and I/G, respectively, wage consumption as function of I (i.e., $C_M N$ in Figure 5.3) is derived from equation 5.12 by means of dividing through by $g(k_C)$, adding L_I on both sides and multiplying by w.
Thus

$$w(L_C + L_I) = wK/k^*_C - \frac{w(k^*_C - k^*_I)}{k^*_C G(k^*_I)} I. \tag{5.13}$$

The slope of this line is negative or positive as k^*_C is greater or smaller than k^*_I.

The market transformation relationship or C surplus as function of I i.e.,

---

[32] For the explicit solution of a system of differential relationships such as 5.1 to 5.6 when $P_C = 0$, see Lefeber and Chakravarty [5].

$(M-C_M)N'$ in Figure 5.3, is obtained by subtracting equation 5.13 from equation 5.12. Denoting the C surplus over wage consumption by C_S, we have

$$C_S = (K/k_C^*)(g-w) - \frac{k_I^*g - w(k_C^* - k_I^*)}{k_C^*G} I.$$ (5.14)

The derivation of equations 5.12, 5.13, and 5.14 is exactly analogous to the argument in the text in which the derivation of these relationships was based on taking convex combinations of values of variables at vertex points. However, if the slope of equation 5.14 is identical to the autarkic price ratio $P(w)$, then according to equation 5.9 it must also be identical to the ratio of the marginal products. To verify this it is sufficient to show that the difference between $P(w)$ and the slope of equation 5.12 correspond s to the slope of equation 5.13. [33]

Denoting the slope of equation 5.12 by $R(w)$, we write

$$P(w) - R(w) = (g'/G') - \frac{g/k_C}{G/k_I}.$$ (5.15)

By factoring out $g'(G/k_I)$ we obtain

$$P(w) - R(w) = \frac{g'}{G/k_I} \left[\frac{G}{G'k_I} - \frac{g}{g'k_C} \right].$$

By substituting equation 6.11 and reordering terms, we get

$$P(w) - R(w) = \frac{k_I g'}{G} \left[\frac{g}{G'} \frac{k_C - k_I}{k_C k_I} - \frac{k_C - k_I}{k_I} \right]$$

Finally, by reordering terms, substituting equation 5.10 and cancelling, it is shown that

$$P(w) - R(w) = \frac{k_I g'(k_C - k_I)}{G k_C k_I g'} \frac{w}{} = \frac{w(k_C - k_I)}{G k_C},$$ (5.16)

which is exactly the slope of equation 5.13. Hence, $P(w)$ is indeed identical to

[33] I am indebted to T.N. Srinivasan for this proof.

the slope of equation 5.14. Furthermore, it follows that $P(w) \gtreqless R(w)$ as $k_C \gtreqless k_I$.

References

[1] Bhagwati, J. "The Theory and Practice of Commercial Policy: Departures from Unified Exchange Rates." *Special Papers in International Economics,* No. 8, Princeton University Press, 1968.

[2] Chakravarty, S. *Capital and Development Planning.* Cambridge, Mass: The M.I.T. Press, 1969.

[3] Kindleberger, C.P. *Europe's Postwar Growth: The Role of Labor Supply.* Cambridge, Mass: Harvard University Press, 1967.

[4] Lefeber, L. "Planning in a Surplus Labor Economy." *American Economic Review,* Vol. LVIII, No. 3, Part 1 (June 1968) 343–373.

[5] Lefeber, L., and Chakravarty, S. "Wages, Employment and Growth." *Kyklos, Vol. XIX, No. 4 (October 1966) 602–619.*

[6] Lewis, W.A. "Development with Unlimited Supplies of Labor." *The Manchester School,* Vol. 22 (May 1954) 139–192.

[7] Little, I.M.D. and Mirrlees, J.A. *Manual of Industrial Project Analysis in Developing Countries, Volume II, Social Cost Benefit Analysis,* Organization for Economic Cooperation and Development, Development Centre, Paris, 1969.

[8] Marglin, S.A. *Industrial Development in the Labor-Surplus Economy: An Essay in the Theory of Optimal Growth,* Preliminary, mimeographed, 1966.

[9] Marglin, S.A. "The Rate of Interest and the Value of Capital with Unlimited Supplies of Labor." Ed. Karl Shell, *Essays on the Theory of Optimal Growth,* 141–164, Cambridge, Mass: 1967. The M.I.T. Press.

[10] Samuelson, P.A. "The Gains from Internation Trade Once Again." *Economic Journal,* Vol. 72 (December 1962) 820–829.

[11] Samuelson, P.A. "A New Theorem on Nonsubstitution." Ed. H. Hegeland, *Money, Growth and Methodology; Essays in Honor of Johan Akerman,* Lund: 1961. Gleerup.

[12] Sen, A.K. *Choice of Techniques.* London: Oxford University Press, 1960.

PART 3

TRADE AND GROWTH

CHAPTER 6

THE EFFECTS OF TRADE ON THE RATE OF GROWTH

W. M. CORDEN

This paper shows how opening-up an economy to trade may affect its rate of growth. * One country's growth in the closed economy is compared with its growth under free trade in an open economy. Given production functions are assumed and the focus is on capital accumulation effects. The paper is an attempt to marry modern trade theory with neoclassical growth theory. If international trade theory is to be a useful aid to thought on practical issues it clearly must include a rigorous theoretical analysis of the effects of trade on growth. This is at least as necessary as the analysis of the effects of growth on trade, on which there is now a valuable body of theory. The growth effects of trade to be discussed here are not necessarily the most important ones in practice but are those that emerge most clearly from a simple neoclassical model. [1] It seems sensible to begin by rigorously exploring this type of model, though further advance on this front will clearly require departures from the neoclassical assumptions. Most of the ingredients will be familiar to students of growth theory, but a novel effect is introduced in Section 6.5 in the form of the "factor-weight" effect. Essentially it is argued that opening-up trade may affect the rate of growth through (1) the "impact" effect (Section 6.2), (2) the effect of the gains from trade raising the rate of capital accumulation, or, in short, the "gains from trade" effect (also Section 6.2),

---

* I am indebted to J.S. Flemming, S. Goldman, I.M.D. Little, R.I. McKinnon, M.D. Steur, and L.R. Webb for valuable comments on an earlier version of this paper, and, I am especially grateful to John Black who has greatly assisted in the development of the argument at every stage and in sorting out numerous difficulties. He has developed the analysis further in [4]. An early version of the paper was presented before the Conference of the Association of University Teachers of Economics at York, England, in March 1968.

[1] See Section 6.9 for references to some other effects.

(3) the "substitution" effect operating through a change in the relative price of investment-goods (Section 6.3), (4) the income distribution effect (Section 6.4), and (5) the "factor-weight" effect (Section 6.5). The effects of the opening-up of trade on the path to the steady state are discussed principally in Sections 6.2 and 6.6. Up to Section 6.6 it is assumed that the country concerned is small, facing given terms of trade; terms of trade effects are considered in Section 6.7. The analysis is extended to tariff changes in Section 6.8. I begin with a brief description of the static characteristics of the model.

6.1. The Static Foundations

The model used in this paper is slightly unusual. The aim is to take into account two separate distinctions between goods, that between consumption goods and investment goods and that between exportables and importables. This problem could be solved by having a simple two-good model where the consumption good is the exportable and the investment good the importable, or vice versa. [2] In such a model, when the price of importables relative to exportables changes the price of investment goods relative to consumption goods changes to the same extent. This would be a special case of the more general model to be used here. The justification for using this model will be given shortly. First let us expound it.

Final usage or "absorption" by the country under consideration consists of two goods, the investment good I, and the consumption good C. The prices of these two goods are P_i and P_c. Real income, output and expenditure, denoted by Y, are always equal, namely to the sum of I and C produced and absorbed. Now I and C are each produced by two inputs, M and X, and each has a constant-returns-to-scale production function with continuous substitution between these inputs. The prices of the two inputs are p_m and p_x. The price ratio p_i/p_c is related to the price ratio p_m/p_x. If I is M intensive relative to C (so that, at a given p_m/p_x, I would employ a higher ratio of M to X than would C) then a rise in p_m/p_x will involve a rise in p_i/p_c; and vice versa if C is the M intensive product. [3] The two inputs, M and X, are in turn produced by

---

[2] As in Oniki and Uzawa [14], Bardhan [2], and Baldwin [1].

[3] The two-good model, where I and C *are* X and M, gives the extreme cases for the relationship between p_m/p_x and p_i/p_c, the two changing then in the same proportion. (The signs of the changes will be the same if I is M intensive and opposite if C is M intensive). When I and C use both X and M, then p_i/p_c will change less than proportionally with p_m/p_x,

two primary factors of production, capital K and labor N. Here also there is in each case (for M and for X) a constant-returns-to-scale production function with continuous substitution between the two primary inputs. It is important to note that the primary factors are inputs only into M and X, and not directly into I and C. The prices of the two factor services are the real wage w and the real rental on capital goods r, and the factor ratio r/w is related to the p_m/p_x ratio in the same way as the p_m/p_x ratio is related to the p_i/p_c ratio. Thus, if M is capital intensive relative to X, a rise in r/w will be associated with a rise in p_m/p_x, and vice versa if M is the labor intensive product. Hence there are three price ratios in the model and two factor-intensity conditions. In a closed economy, we would be able to determine equilibrium prices and outputs if we knew the stocks of N and K, the four production functions and the final demand function. The latter expresses the community's demand for investment goods relative to consumption goods. When the country's propensity to save (i.e., invest) is constant this demand function has the characteristic that the income and price elasticities of demand for I and C are unity. In an open economy, we must specify also which factors and products are traded. We shall assume that only M and X are traded; there are no primary factor movements in or out of the country and all I and C are produced within the country, though from produced factors that may have been imported. Hence for the two traded goods, we also require a foreign offer curve. The elasticity of foreign reciprocal demand is assumed infinite (terms of trade given) up to Section 6.7. Balance of payments equilibrium as well as full employment is also assumed.

In Sections 6.2 and 6.3 it will be assumed that the factor intensities (labor or capital intensities) do not differ between M and X. This has two implications: First, when the economy is opened to trade and the domestic M/X price ratio falls as a result, the primary factor price ratio r/w does not alter. Second, if in the process of growth this primary factor ratio r/w alters, the M/X price ratio need not alter. Geometrically, the M/X transformation curve will be a straight line and even if N and K are growing at different rates the transformation curve will expand in an "unbiased" way, its slope remaining constant. By contrast, in Sections 6.4, 6.5, and 6.6 the M/X factor intensities will be assumed to differ. Hence, when the M/X price ratio alters as a result of opening trade the income distribution will change. Geometrically, the M/X transformation curve will be concave to the origin and (if N and K are growing at different rates) will expand in a "biased" way; if capital is growing faster than labor the bias will be towards the capital-intensive good.

In Sections 6.2, 6.4, 6.5, and 6.6 it will be assumed that the factor intensities (M intensities) do not differ between I and C. Hence opening of trade, or a change in primary factor prices, will not affect the p_i/p_c ratio. By contrast, in Section 6.3 the M intensities of I and C will be allowed to differ, and hence the implications will be explored of the opening of trade altering the p_i/p_c ratio through the alteration in p_m/p_x.

We therefore consider in the following pages three cases: (i) in Section 6.2 there are no factor-intensity differences between M and X nor between I and C: this is the *simplest model*; (ii) in Section 6.3 there are such differences between I and C (but not between M and X); and (iii) in Sections 6.4, 6.5 and 6.6 there are differences between M and X (but not between I and C).

What is the point of our model with its two-tiered production structure? Why not just have a two-good model where one good is the investment good and the importable (or exportable) and the other the consumption good and the exportable (or importable)? This would draw too sharp a distinction between investment and consumption goods as they enter foreign trade; since there would only be two goods, each would have to double duty as an import or export and as investment or consumption good. But the multitude of goods entering foreign trade is largely intermediate inputs entering both consumption and investment without being uniquely associated with either. Hence neither consumption nor investment is likely to consist wholly of importables or exportables. Our model, limited and highly formal as it may seem, is meant to be realistic in this respect. Furthermore, the model makes it possible to analyze the effects of trade on growth in separate elements, one at a time. The opening of trade alters the domestic M/X price ratio. We can allow this to affect the primary factor price ratio while not altering the I/C price ratio, so that we can ignore complications that result from a change in the I/C price ratio. Also, we can allow it to alter the I/C price ratio without affecting the primary factor price ratio, so that other complications can be ignored. We have then a device of great analytical convenience.

6.2. The Simplest Model

We start with a growing, closed economy with two factors of production, labor and capital, and an aggregate constant-returns-to-scale, neoclassical production function that may be thought of as being built up from the constant-returns-to-scale production functions of I, C, M and X.[4] The growth

---

[4] We have thus a "two-level" production function. See Black [3] on the derivation of such "two-level" or derived production functions. Note that there is no index number problem because we are at this stage holding the price ratio between the two final goods, C and I, constant.

rate of labor is given exogenously, there is no technical progress, investment is brought into equality with savings by the rate of interest, and the savings propensity is given and uninfluenced by the level of income per head, income distribution, or the rate of interest. [5] For exposition we shall assume that at a point in time t_0, at which our story begins, the rate of growth of capital is greater than the given rate of growth of labor.

Now in year t_0 the economy is opened up to trade. There are the familiar static gains from trade, so that real income rises. The assumption at this stage that the factor intensities do not differ between M and X means that the country will specialize in X, and that income distribution will not be affected by the change. The assumption that the M intensities do not differ between I and C means that opening-up trade has not altered the relative price of investment goods to consumption goods. The main point to be developed at this stage is that the economy will be able *to absorb* or use more goods and services in real terms, whether consumption or investment goods. The effect will now be the same as if there had been a one-and-for-all technical improvement. The opening of trade has shifted outwards the economy's "absorption-possibility" frontier. [6]

What then is the effect on the rate of growth? We may distinguish two effects, (i) the impact effect, and (ii) the capital accumulation effect. The latter has (a) an immediate implication, and (b) a steady-state implication. All these effects are identical with those that would result from a once-and-for-all technical improvement. If by growth, we mean not growth of output but growth of real income or absorption, then the impact effect is obviously to raise the rate of growth temporarily in year t_0 and to fall back again in the subsequent year. We assume that the economy's adjustment to trade — its reallocation of resources — is completed within the year t_0. This temporary effect will not play any significant part in our analysis. The capital accumulation effect is perhaps not so obvious. A permanent rise in real income or absorption has resulted. With a constant savings propensity, some part of the increase will then be saved and invested. Thus the absolute amount of investment in year t_0 and all subsequent years will rise above what it would have been otherwise. If one starts with a given capital stock at time t_0, a rise in the rate of growth of capital will result. And this will pull up with

[5] Hence we have an elementary form of the neoclassical growth model as described by Meade [12], Solow [17], and Swan [18].

[6] The term "absorption" is used to emphasize that we are concerned not just with consumption possibilities but with possibilities of consuming *or investing*. Alternative terms might be "situation-possibility" frontier or "availability" frontier or envelope.

it the rate of growth of output. If K = capital stock, dK = increase in capital stock, s = savings propensity, Y = real income (absorption), then $dK/K = sY/K$, and the opening-up of trade has raised Y.

This capital accumulation effect of the gains from trade has an implication for the steady state and for the path toward the steady state that will be explained geometrically later. The main point is that in the closed economy, with capital growing faster than labor, and hence output growing more slowly than capital, the capital-output ratio would have been steadily rising, hence, the rate of growth of capital and of output steadily falling. This is an oft-told neoclassical tale: output and capital growth approach the given labor growth rate — that is, there is a tendency towards a steady state. [7] The effect of the opening-up of trade on the movement to a steady state is simple if we assume that the international terms of trade are given to the country and do not change over time. Thus we may suppose that the rest of the world is already in its steady state. The opening-up of trade has displaced K/Y downwards, and so raised dK/K. But, given our simplifying assumptions, there will still be a movement toward a steady state, the growth rate of which will still be determined by the given labor growth rate. While in nonsteady-state situations the opening-up of trade raises the rate of growth for more than just year t_0, it does not alter the steady-state rate of growth.

Figure 6.1 shows rates of growth of real income, capital, and labor on the vertical axis and the output-capital ratio (Y/K) on the horizontal. [8] The horizontal line nn' shows the given labor growth rate. For a given savings propensity, the straight line through the origin Ok shows the rate of growth of capital at various levels of Y/K. The rate of growth of output (real income in the open economy) is given by the line yy'. The constant-returns-to-scale

[7] There is a qualification here, fully expounded by Pitchford [15]. If capital is initially growing faster than labor and the elasticity of substitution is very high, it is possible that in the steady-state capital and output grow at a faster rate than labor. This is the more likely the greater the savings propensity and the smaller the rate of growth of labor. If labor were initially growing faster than capital then, if the elasticity of substitution were very low, the marginal product of labor might fall to zero so that in the steady-state capital and output would grow more slowly than labor. These results are not possible if the elasticity of substitution is unity. Sato [16] has suggested that, in the light of empirical evidence about the values of the relevant parameters, these results are improbable. Even if in the steady-state capital, output and labor would grow at the same rate, it is possible, when the elasticity of substitution is greater than unity, that a rising capital-labor ratio, while leading to a fall in the rate of growth of capital leads, for a time, to a *rise* in the rate of growth of output, though eventually it must fall to the given rate of growth of labor.

[8] The diagram comes from Swan [18].

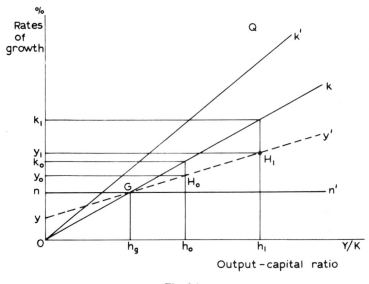

Fig. 6.1

assumption means that when capital and labor are growing at the same rate, output must also grow at that rate, so that all three lines intersect at G. The yy' line would be a straight line as drawn only with a Cobb-Douglas production function (output growth being a weighted average of labor and capital growth, with the weights constant), but this assumption is not essential to our argument. [9]

At time t_0 in the closed economy, Y/K is h_0 and hence the rate of growth of output is y_0. The system would tend towards the steady state at G where Y/K is h_g and the rate of growth is n. The opening-up of trade in time t_0 displaces Y/K to the right, to h_1. Temporarily — just in that year and with a given amount of investment — it raises the rate of growth to some point, such as Q, shown in the diagram vertically above h_1. This is the impact effect, and will henceforth be ignored. We proceed to the capital accumulation effect. The rate of growth of capital will increase from k_0 to k_1 simply because Y/K

[9] Note that if either of the two Pitchford cases applied [15, page 496] the yy' line would not intersect nn' at G but would meet Ok' at a point to the right of G or meet nn' somewhere to the left of G. The point made at the end of footnote 7 means that the curve nn' need not be monotone; even if it intersects nn' at G, it may be positively sloping over a range to the right of G if the elasticity of substitution is greater than unity.

has risen while the savings propensity has remained constant. And this pulls up the rate of growth of output (real income) to y_1. If there were not diminishing returns to capital because capital is growing faster than labor, it would stay at that level (unlike the rise owing to the impact effect which is temporary in its very nature). But in fact, with the capital-labor ratio steadily rising, and hence the output-capital ratio (Y/K) steadily falling, the economy will tend to the steady state at G, moving this time not from H_0 to G, as in the closed economy, but from H_1 to G. In the steady state Y/K will be the same as in the closed economy. [10]

This is a growth-orientated diagram and can be misleading. This type of approach tends to give the impression that only growth rates matter, and especially the growth rates in the steady state. It seems that the gains from trade eventually disappear, and for those who regard "eventually" as more interesting than "now" this could be a short step to saying that (in this type of model) there are no gains from trade. But this would be quite wrong, as becomes clear from Figure 6.2. The vertical axis shows output or real income per head (Y/N), and the horizontal axis, time t. At time t_0, Y/N is j_0. The production function relates Y/K to Y/N, so that j_0 could be derived from h_0 in Figure 6.1 and the production function. In the closed economy Y/N would rise, since, with capital growing faster than labor, output would also be growing faster than labor. It would approach the steady state Y/N, namely j_g, which is uniquely related by the production function to the steady state Y/K, namely, h_g. Thus the closed economy path of Y/N is given in Figure 6.2 by the line $H_0\alpha$.

Now the economy is opened-up in time t_0, thus raising real income or absorption per head to j_i. The vertical distance H_0H_1 represents the static gains from trade, expressed on a per-head basis. It yields the impact effect on the rate of growth. If this gain did not grow with the economy and there were no change in capital accumulation as a result of the opening-up of trade it would simply be carried forward over time, Y/N in every subsequent year being greater than otherwise by the amount H_0H_1. The path of Y/N would then be $H_1\beta$. But in fact it will grow with the economy. In the present model, with the terms of trade given from outside and constant, and no "biases" in the growth pattern because the factor intensities between M and X are

---

[10] While H_1 will in this simple model be on the straight line GH_0 extended, (so that opening up trade does not alter at time t_0 the relative weights attaching to the capital and labor growth rates in determining the rate of growth of output), the economy will not move from H_1 to G along yy', but rather along a curve above yy'. This follows from an argument in Section 6.6, but is a refinement that does not affect the argument so far.

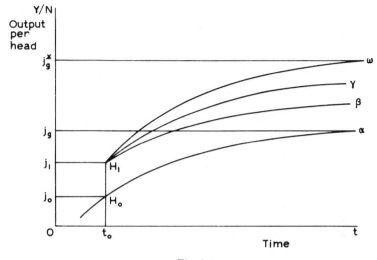

Fig. 6.2

assumed not to differ, the gain from trade will remain a constant proportion of income and so will grow at the same rate as income. In Section 6.6 this question of the growth in the gains from trade will be looked at again for the case where the factor intensities between M and X do differ. The present assumption makes the opening-up of trade the equivalent of a Hicks-neutral technical improvement. It means that in Figure 6.2 the growth path will be given by the curve $H_1\gamma$, which is a constant proportion above $H_0\alpha$.

Finally, we must allow for the effect of the opening-up of trade raising the rate of capital accumulation. This, as we have seen, raises the rate of growth above what it would be otherwise, the excess of the open economy over the closed economy rate of growth declining towards zero as the steady state is approached. Hence Y/N grows faster than indicated by $H_1\gamma$ (which assumed a constant rate of growth, other than in year t_0). The path of Y/N is now given by $H_1\omega$. The steady-state real income per head will now be j_g^*. This should be compared with the steady-state income per head in the closed economy, namely j_g. Both are associated with a Y/K of h_g. But in the open economy it is possible to have a higher income per head for any given Y/K than in the closed economy since the economy has, in fact, become more productive.

The gains from opening-up the economy at any time after t_0 can now be broken down into three elements. [11] The first is the static gain from trade

---

[11] This analysis should help to clarify the discussion of these issues, involving much the same variables, in Linder [11, pp. 60–73].

$H_0 H_1$. The second is the growth of the static gain over time; the gain grows (given our present assumptions) in proportion to closed economy output; its growth is measured by the vertical distance between $H_1 \beta$ and $H_1 \gamma$. The third results from the rise in the rate of growth caused by the increase in capital accumulation and might be described as the "growth gain" from opening-up trade. It is measured by the vertical distance between $H_1 \gamma$ and $H_1 \omega$. The growth gain results when parts of the static gain are invested. It thus represents a particular allocation of the static gain — an allocation which raises real income in the future rather than consumption now — and thus is not additional in a welfare sense. Any trade policy that raises real income creates a static gain and, for any given propensity to save, also raises the rate of growth. Thus the growth effect may reinforce but does not alter policy arguments based on static effects.

The argument developed so far does not depend wholly on the precise assumptions under which it has been developed. Quite generally one can argue as follows: Opening trade or altering trade restrictions may bring about static gains or losses, the subject matter of the static theory of trade and welfare. These depend on factor endowments and intensities, on economies of scale, domestic distortions, the flexibility of factor prices, terms of trade effects, the tariff structure, and so on. The message of our capital accumulation effect is simply that if the marginal propensity to save and invest is positive the growth will rise if the static gains rise and fall if the static gains fall. Further, it is not necessary to assume that the marginal propensity to save is constant or equal to the average propensity. It is necessary only that it is positive. One could make the savings propensity a positive function of real income per head or perhaps dependent on a utility function of some kind. [12] One could construct a realistic model of a closed subsistence economy with zero net savings; when it is opened-up to trade net savings begin for the first time, the gain from trade thus being the initiator of growth.

6.3. The Relative Price of Investment Goods

We now assume that opening the economy to trade alters the price relationship between investment goods and consumption goods. Hence the importable/exportable intensities (the M intensities) must differ as between I

---

[12] See, for example, Baldwin [1], where the propensity to save depends on the marginal productivity of capital and a simple time-preference function. A steady-state tendency still emerges.

and C. Opening-up trade lowers the domestic prices of importables relative to the prices of exportables. If then I is the M intensive good, the price of I relative to the price of C will fall while if C is the M intensive good, the relative price of I will rise.

A constant savings propensity means that the proportion of expenditure on investment is constant. When the relative price of I changes as the result of opening-up trade the ratio of I to C must then change. Thus, if investment goods are M intensive, so that the relative price of I falls, the ratio of I to C must rise. This has effects on capital accumulation. For a given rise in real income at constant prices, the increase in investment will be greater if I is M intensive than if it is X intensive. The argument is illustrated in Figure 6.3. Quantities of I are shown along the vertical axis and of C along the horizontal axis. The "absorption frontier" in the closed economy at time t_0 is KK'; it depends on the stocks of labor and capital, and on the production functions of M, X, I and C. We assume at this stage that the factor intensities (labor or capital intensities) of X and M do not differ so that the absorption frontier is a straight line. The given propensity to save is assumed to be CK'/OK' $(= OB/OK)$ and determines the actual absorption point A, with consumption OC and investment OB. When trade is opened up the absorption frontier expands to EE', its steeper slope reflecting the fall in the relative price of I (with I being M intensive). The new absorption point is A' $(DE'/OE' =$

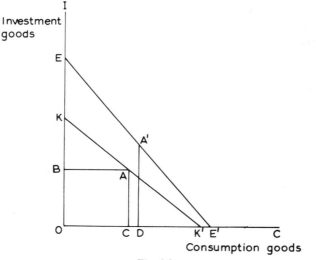

Fig. 6.3

CK'/OK'). The movement from A to A' could be decomposed into an *income* and a *substitution* effect. The first raises absorption of C and I in equal proportion; this is the static gains from trade effect discussed in the previous section. The second switches absorption from consumption to investment in this particular case. The effect is the same as that of a once-and-for-all technical improvement which is *product biased* towards the investment-goods industry. If the relative price of I had risen (if I were X intensive) the "substitution" effect would have led to some fail in investment by comparison with the constant price case.

If the factor intensities (labor or capital-intensities) differed between X and M the transformation curve between them would be concave to the origin rather than a straight line, and the closed economy absorption frontier derived from it in Figure 6.3 would also be concave. But the basic argument would not have changed. There would still be an income and a substitution effect of opening-up trade. Furthermore, this analysis does not really require a constant savings propensity. There is a substitution effect if a fall in the relative price of investment goods causes the ratio of I to C in absorption to rise (or vice versa for a rise in the price ratio); it does not have to rise (or fall) exactly to the extent required to maintain the proportion of expenditure on investment goods constant, because this is the special case where the elasticity of substitution in the static demand or preference function implied in our savings propensity assumption is unity.

It is certainly more plausible to make the weak assumption that there is *some* substitution effect – that is, that a fall in the relative price of I has some effect in raising p_i/p_c (and vice versa) – than to make the strong assumption that the savings propensity is absolutely rigid. Indeed the implausibility of assuming an absolutely constant savings ratio emerges when one asks whether the substitution effect could exactly offset or even more than offset the income effect so that the opening-up of trade leads to no change or even a fall in either consumption or investment. It can be shown that with a constant savings propensity this is indeed possible, and, in certain limiting cases, inevitable. We shall consider this question for the two limiting cases where our model would collapse into a two-good case. The first case is where C uses only X and I only M, so that in fact $C = X$ and $I = M$. Given equal factor intensities between X and M, and so maintaining the straight line case, the points K' *and* E' in Figure 6.3 would coincide. A constant savings propensity would place A' directly above A, so that the opening-up of trade would lead to no immediate change in consumption; all the gains from trade would be invested. The second case is where C uses only M and I only X, so that in fact $C = M$ and $I = X$. In this case the relative price of I would rise and there would be no change in investment, the gains from trade all going into consumption. These are the limiting results which are approached as the difference between the M intensities of I and C increases. But given equal factor intensities between X and M (and hence the straight-line case) it is not possible, with a given savings propensity, for consumption or investment actually to fall.

The possibility that, with a constant savings propensity, the opening-up of trade leads to an absolute fall in consumption or investment arises once we allow the factor intensities between X and M to differ. Again, we consider the limiting cases where the model collapses into a two-good case. In Figure 6.4, M is shown along the vertical axis and X along the horizontal, and the closed economy absorption frontier TT' is concave to the origin. Actual output and absorption in the closed economy are given by the point A, the closed economy price ratio being indicated by the slope of KK'. Closed economy income in terms of X is OK'. If $X = C$ and $M = I$, then the propensity to save is RK'/OK' while if $X = I$ and $M = C$, then it is OR/OK'. If the world price ratio (terms of trade) is given by the slope of EE', the opening-up of trade causes production to shift to P and income in terms of X to fall to OE'. The new absorption point A' must be to the left of A if the proportion of

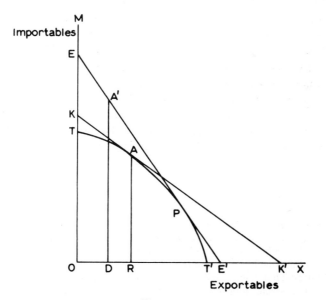

Fig. 6.4

expenditure on the two goods is to stay constant. Thus, if $X = C$ and $M = I$ the propensity to save is now DE'/OE', which must be equal to RK'/OK'. It follows that in this case when $X = C$ consumption must fall absolutely as a result of the opening-up of trade while when $X = I$ investment would fall absolutely. Thus the substitution effect outweights the income effect on that good the price of which has risen relatively. This result is certain in the limiting two-good case. When the difference between the M intensities of I and C is not so extreme the result is still possible, though not certain. The greater this difference in M intensities, the more likely it is. All this depends, it must again be s⸍essed, on the assumption of a rigidly constant savings propensity. But when this assumption leads to such extreme results one must conclude that it is hardly compatible with a plausible intertemporal utility function.

Let us now integrate the substitution effect into our growth model of Section 6.2 and Figure 6.1. The substitution effect means that, in addition to the various effects on the rate of growth discussed in Section 6.2, there are the effects of the change in the relative price of investment goods. If investment goods are M intensive this effect will raise the rate of growth. In Figure 6.1 the Ok line swings then to the left, to Ok', so that for any given Y/K (and with a constant savings propensity) the capital growth rate is higher than before. This higher rate of growth of capital will pull up with it the rate of growth of output. [13] There are thus two capital accumulation effects when trade is opened-up, both raising the rate of growth: first, the capital growth rate rises because Y/K has increased, this being the gains-from-trade effect, and second, the Ok line has swung, this being the substitution effect. The economy again moves towards the steady-state growth rate n. Comparing two cases with the same initial rise in Y/K and Y/N at constant prices, but with relative prices constant in one and the price of investment goods having fallen in the other, the steady state Y/K will be lower, and the steady state Y/N higher, for the latter. The higher steady-state income per head is

---

[13] We now have an index number problem in defining Y, since the relative price of investment goods to consumption goods is no longer constant (as in Section 6.2, earlier). Here Y could be defined as $C + I$ added together at the closed economy prices existing at time t_0, but this would be quite arbitrary. A better approach is to suppose that there is a social utility function with C and I as the arguments, where Y is an indicator of utility. With a constant savings propensity this function would have an elasticity of substitution of unity.

explained by the higher "growth gain" from trade explained in turn by the higher growth up to the steady state. [14]

All these conclusions are reversed when I is X intensive. As we have seen, with a constant savings propensity there is then even the possibility that the substitution effect completely offsets the income effect (if $I = X$ and $C = M$, and if their factor intensities do not differ), or even outweighs it, so that the rate of capital accumulation is actually reduced (if $I = X$ and $C = M$, and the absorption frontier is concave to the origin). [15]

6.4. Income Distribution and the Savings Propensity

Opening-up trade or the imposition of trade restrictions may affect income distribution, and if savings propensities differ between different sectors or factors, they may then affect the overall savings propensity and hence the rate of capital accumulation. This is well-known and was pointed out by Johnson [16] 60 years ago, and is implicit in classical writings and in much modern discussion of trade and growth. We shall now assume (i) that the factor intensities differ between X and M, so that the opening-up of trade shifts income distribution towards the factors intensive in the production of X, (ii) that the M intensities of I and C are identical, so that the relative price of investment goods stays constant, and (iii) that the propensity to save out of profits is greater than that out of wages, each of the sectional propensities being constant; the overall savings propensity is thus a weighted average of the two sectional propensities, the weights depending on the income distribution. If X is capital intensive the overall propensity will rise while if M is capital-intensive it will fall. The rate of capital accumulation will then rise or

[14] Note that when capital is initially growing faster than labor and the elasticity of substitution is very high, the shift in the Ok line, representing a rise in the propensity to save *in real terms,* increases the possibility of the Pitchford case (footnotes 7 and 9); there is thus somewhat more likelihood that the steady state growth rate is above the given labor growth rate.

[15] This is not necessarily an argument for deliberately keeping the economy closed so as to avoid a fall in the growth rate. Incurring this type of static loss in order to raise the rate of capital accumulation is justified only if (a) the socially desired savings propensity is higher than the private one, and (b) first-best policies for raising the savings (i.e., investment) propensity are not feasible. Trade policy affects both the absorption pattern and the production pattern, and the production effect of closing an economy (or restricting trade) would be an unwonted distortion.

[16] An earlier Johnson! See Johnson [8], summarized in Caves [6, Chapter IX], where other discussions of the effects of trade on growth are also reviewed.

fall because of this effect, which has to be added on to the effects already discussed.

The point is quite general and is very relevant in a study of the growth effects of protection. The relevant income distribution effect need not be limited to the distribution between wages and profits as a whole but could concern a shift from one type of profits to another, or perhaps, as between rural rents and urban profits. [17]

The introduction of a differential savings propensity may have various odd results on the path to the steady state. The effects on the closed economy growth path toward (or away from) the steady state will not be pursued here. [18] But consider a rather peculiar result in the open economy, which depends on two special assumptions. First, let us remind ourselves that we are concerned with a small country which faces given terms of trade in the open economy, so that the price ratio between X and M is given from outside. In this type of model, with constant-returns-to-scale production functions and provided there is domestic production of both X and M (nonspecialization), there is (as already pointed out in Section 6.1) a unique relationship between product and factor prices. If the product price ratio is given, the factor-price ratio is then also given. Furthermore, it is well-known from factor-price equalization theory that the *real* values of the factor prices are then also given. It follows that, with the terms of trade p_m/p_c given once trade is opened up, the wage rate w and the rental on capital goods r are given. If the terms of trade do not change while our economy travels towards the steady state — in other words, if the rest of the world is already in *its* steady state — the factor prices must stay constant, at least as long as our country does not specialize.

Now introduce the further assumption that all savings are out of profits. It is a well-known property of growth models that if all savings are out of profits the rate of growth of capital depends solely on the savings propensity

---

[17] Keeping an economy closed or restricting trade may conceivably yield a higher rate of capital accumulation because of this income distribution effect, but it would be a fourth-best policy, even given that the socially optimum savings propensity exceeds the private one. The first-best policy is directly to supplement or subsidize savings or to subsidize the purchase of investment goods, the second-best policy is to redistribute income towards profits directly by subsidizing profits and taxing wages (yielding possibly an undesirable income distribution), the third-best policy is to subsidize directly the capital-intensive industry (shifting income distribution towards profits but creating a production distortion that reduces compensated real income), and fourth-best policy is a tariff on the capital-intensive import (which adds in addition a consumption distortion).

[18] See Hahn and Matthews [7].

out of profits (s_p) and the rental on capital goods r. For if π is absolute profit receipts, then $r = \pi/K$ and $K = I/K = s_p\pi/K = s_p r$. Thus if s_p is constant and r is constant, the rate of capital accumulation k must be constant. We have just seen that in the open economy, if the terms of trade are constant, r must indeed be constant. Hence there is no movement towards a steady state. If capital is initially growing faster than labor, production will become more and more biased towards the capital-intensive good, even though the relative price of this good will not change, until the country becomes specialized in it. From then on the link between product and factor prices will be cut and the movement towards the steady state resumed.

6.5. The Factor-Weight Effect

The next effect to be considered is not on the rate of capital accumulation but on the relative productivity of capital and labor. It arises only if (i) the factor intensities differ between X and M, and (ii) the economy at time t_o is out of its steady state, so that capital and labor are growing at different rates. In addition, we assume, as in the previous section, that I and C do not differ in their M intensities, so that the relative price of investment goods stays unchanged. As in Section 6.2 we have a straightforward aggregate production function. Real income or output Y can be defined in terms of either I or C and depends on inputs of M and X, which in turn depend on inputs of capital and labor and on transformation through trade. If the M, X, and I (and hence C) production functions are constant-returns-to-scale, the aggregate production function which relates output Y to inputs K and N must be also. [19]

Now the point of the *factor-weight effect* is simply that, with a constant-returns-to-scale aggregate production function, the rate of growth of output is a weighted average of the capital and labor growth rates, and the opening-up of trade may change the weights. If y = growth rate of output, n = growth rate of labor, k = growth rate of capital, w = wage rate and r = rental on capital goods, with factor prices equal to values of their marginal products, then in our constant-returns-to-scale model:

$$y = n \left(w \frac{N}{Y} \right) + k \left(r \frac{K}{Y} \right) \tag{6.1}$$

where the expressions in parentheses (the weights) are the factor shares. Now opening-up trade alters Y/N and Y/K in the same proportion. But it may alter

[19] See Black [3] on "two-level" production functions.

the weights by altering the ratio w/r. If X is capital intensive, the opening-up of trade will lead to a shift in output toward the capital-intensive product, substitution of labor for capital in both X and M, and a higher marginal product of capital (and so higher r) and lower marginal product of labor (lower w). If capital is initially growing faster than labor the growth rate then rises. Of course, if M were capital intensive, the growth rate would fall because of this consideration (though on balance it may still increase owing to a rise in the rate of capital accumulation). The main point is that opening the economy to trade alters the relative importance of the two factors of production if X and M have different factor intensities. If it raises the importance of the faster-growing factor, the rate of growth will rise, while if the importance of the faster-growing factor is lowered the growth rate will fall owing to this effect. If there were a single industry in a closed economy, the same effect would result from a *factor-biased*, once-and-for-all technical improvement. In Figure 6.1, when Y/K rises to h_1, the growth rate thus moves to somewhere above or below y_1.

There appears to be no systematic discussion of this effect in the international trade (or the growth) literature. [20] It has been outlined only briefly here and the discussion should be regarded as tentative. [21]

The more general message of the factor-weight effect is that trade or trade restrictions may alter the relative importance of different industries and so indirectly of different factors. If factors are growing at different rates, the overall growth rate may then alter. Since land (natural resources) is usually the slowest growing factor, it follows, for example, that if trade is expanded between a land-scarce country and a land-plentiful one, the rate of growth in the former may well rise and in the latter fall, if other effects are excluded.

But it would be a fallacy to leap to the conclusion that the land-plentiful country should then restrict its trade. Similarly, if capital is growing faster than labor and importables are capital intensive, an economy might indeed grow faster if it were closed than if it were open, but nevertheless it would not gain from staying closed. At every point in time, real income in the closed economy would be below what it would be in the open economy (except in the special case where the closed and open economy price ratios are identical). It could never pay to close an economy or restrict its trade, and

---

[20] The exceptions are Meade [12, Chapter 3], where there is a discussion of the effects of changing factor weights owing to biased technical progress on the rate of growth in the closed economy; and Brown [5, pages 23–34, and pages 57–58], where this is also briefly referred to.

[21] See Black [4] for further development of this subject.

thus to reduce its current income, unless this results in a transfer of real income from present to future, that is, an act of saving and investment. The gain from opening the economy may indeed grow more slowly than closed economy income so that the rate of growth of the two combined — the income of the open economy — would be lower than the rate of growth of closed economy income alone, but this does not alter the fact that at every point in time, other than when closed and open economy price ratios are identical, there is a positive gain from trade. As will emerge more clearly in the next section, the essence of the factor-weight effect is that, with the M/X factor intensities differing, the gain from trade no longer grows in proportion with the economy unless the primary factors of production happen to be growing at the same rate — that is, unless the economy is in a steady state.

6.6. Different Factor Intensities and the Movement Toward the Steady State

In Section 6.2 the movement toward the steady state and the growth in the gains from trade was discussed subject to the assumption that the factor intensities in M and X were the same. In Section 6.5 we have just shown how the rate of growth in year t_0 is affected when the factor intensities in M and X are allowed to differ. Now we shall combine the two analyses and consider the movement from year t_0 toward the steady state and the growth in the gains from trade when the factor intensities between M and X differ. We shall assume away earlier complications by holding the relative price of investment goods constant (the M intensities of I and C are the same) and supposing that the overall savings propensity is not affected by income distribution. We continue to assume that the world terms of trade are given to the country and constant over time, and, as usual, start with capital growing faster than labor.

Now the first point to note is that, both in the closed and the open economy, the system will again move toward the steady state Y/K and rate of growth determined by the given rate of growth of labor. In this model, where there is only one factor that is growing at a given rate, the introduction of the factor weight effect of trade does not affect the steady-state rate of growth. [22] The explanation of the movement toward the steady state is just

---

[22] Black [4] shows that if there is *more than one* "natural" factor — that is, a factor with a given rate of growth — the steady-state growth rate may be affected by opening-up trade. It will be the weighted average of the growth rates of the various "natural" factors; trade may alter the weights. This is an important development of the argument here. It could also be shown that trade may alter the steady-state growth rate if there is technical progress.

as before: the capital accumulation rate declines because the capital-output ratio is rising and keeps on declining until capital is growing at the same rate as labor.

Nevertheless, the factor-weight effect does play a role on the way to the steady state. Consider our Equation 6.1. Once trade is opened up and w and r have attained their new values, they will remain unchanged as long as the country remains unspecialized and the terms of trade are constant. The product price ratio given by the world market will fix the factor prices. But in the movement to the steady state, Y/N rises, and Y/K falls. So the weight attached to k rises while that attached to n falls. Thus, as the overall capital-labor ratio rises the weight attached to capital growth relative to labor growth in determining the output growth rate rises. So, for this reason, the rate of growth will decline more slowly than it would otherwise. [23]

Next consider the changes over time in the gains from trade. In the model of Section 6.2, the static gains from trade grew in the same proportion as the growth of the economy. This depended on the assumption that the factor intensities of M and X were identical. When they are not, then as the capital-labor ratio in the economy rises, the production transformation curve between M and X will acquire an increasing bias towards the capital-intensive good, whichever one it is. With the product price given from outside, this will then lead to an increasing shift in the production pattern towards this good. If M is capital intensive, the output pattern in the open economy will shift increasingly toward M and away from X, growth being thus anti-trade biased. The gain from trade as a proportion of national income will fall, and if biased growth continues, the gain will eventually fall absolutely until imports cease completely and there is no gain from trade at all because there is no trade. Another way of stating this fact is to say that the closed economy price ratio between M and X moves continually closer to the world terms of trade, until the two price ratios are equal, when the gains from trade disappear. But continued growth of capital relative to labor will then turn M into the exportable, so that trade reversal will lead now to the gains from trade

---

[23] Meade [12, Chapter 3] shows that in a closed economy the direction in which the factor weights move in the process of growth depends on whether the elasticity of substitution is greater or less than unity. The open economy case here considered is the equivalent of an elasticity of substitution that is infinite. See also Brown [5]. This discussion relates to the point made in footnote 10. If the factor weights change in the movement toward the steady state, the yy' line will not be a straight line. The argument in the text means geometrically that the open-economy yy' line (not drawn in Figure 6.1) will be concave from below and will generally lie above the closed economy yy' line.

growing more rapidly than the size of the economy. If X were capital intensive — so that the country has even initially a comparative advantage in that product which is intensive in its faster-growing factor — there would right from year t_0 be proportionately growing gains from trade. But this proportionate growth in the gains from trade cannot go on indefinitely. In the movement toward the steady state, the bias in the output expansion will gradually decline and thus modify the growth in the gain. In the steady state itself, there will be no output expansion bias towards X and M, and hence the gains from trade will grow only at the same rate as the economy. Finally, if the factor intensities of M and X were identical there would be no bias in the ouput expansion in the first place, and hence the gains from trade would always grow proportionally with the size of the economy.[24]

6.7. The Case in Which Terms of Trade are Not Constant

The assumption that the world terms of trade are constant will now be removed. The terms of trade may change either as a result of the changing trade offers of the country under consideration, country A, or may change exogenously, that is, the elasticity of the foreign reciprocal demand curve at any point in time may be less than perfectly elastic, or may be infinitely elastic but shifting over time. Of course the terms of trade may change as the combined result of both effects, but this more complex case will not be considered here.[25]

If the foreign reciprocal demand in year t_0 when trade is opened-up is less

---

[24] In Section 6.2 the main analysis assumed a marginal propensity to save equal to the average. But it was pointed out that provided the marginal propensity to save is positive the gain from trade effect will lead to some rise in the rate of capital accumulation. It might be thought that a positive marginal savings propensity, though it has not rested in this paper on an explicit intertemporal utility function, is a sufficiently weak assumption to be reasonable. Yet, taking into account the discussion in the present section, an absolute fall in savings when trade is opened up might be compatible with a plausible intertemporal utility function. All one needs to assume is that the gains from trade are expected to grow over time so that the country is justified in making reduced provisions for what looks like a rosy future, rosier compared to the present than when the economy was closed and expected to stay closed. I owe this point to John Black.

[25] One could analyse this case essentially as an amalgam of the two simpler cases. For complete two-country, two-product, neoclassical growth models in which the terms of trade are endogenous, see Oniki and Uzawa [14], and Bardhan [2], and also Baldwin [1]. None of these compare closed and open economy growth, and in [1] the special assumption is made that investment goods are capital intensive.

than perfectly elastic, a movement from no trade to free trade will involve a static gain as before. While the gain would be greater if the economy had moved not to free trade but to the optimum level of restricted trade, as indicated by optimum tariff theory, nevertheless there must be some gain. [26] So there will be a gains-from-trade effect raising the rate of growth, and substitution, income distribution and factor-weight effects that may go either way. The previous analysis stands completely.

Next assume that country A faces a perfectly elastic foreign reciprocal demand but the terms of trade are exogenously changing over time. To isolate the main effect, assume that the factor intensities of M and X are identical so that we have the simple model of Section 6.2 where, with constant terms of trade, the rise in the growth rate was explained solely by the increase in capital accumulation (apart from the impact effect). But if the terms of trade change, the static gains will grow faster or slower than closed economy output, so that there is an additional (positive or negative) growth effect. An improvement in the terms of trade would shift outwards the absorption-possibility frontier; when the improvement is continuous, we can say that the productivity of transformation through trade is steadily rising. Hence the effect is the same as that of a positive rate of technical progress. The opening-up of trade would then lead to a rise in the growth rate of national income even if there were no increase in the rate of capital accumulation, though (with a positive marginal propensity to save) the rate of capital accumulation will in fact rise over time in relation to its constant terms of trade movement and on balance may no longer decline towards the given labor growth rate.

Now consider the relationship between terms of trade changes and the movement to the steady state. The rest of the world, to be called here country B, may be in or out of its steady state. If it is in its steady state, then its relative prices will be constant. Given the assumption that country A is a very small country that cannot affect prices in country B it follows that country A's terms of trade are then constant. This is the special case considered in earlier sections of this paper. If country A was in its steady state before its economy was opened, it will be jolted out of it by the opening-up of trade and, as has been described earlier, will then begin a movement to a new steady state with a different level of income per head and perhaps output-capital ratio.

If country B is not in its steady state and factor-intensities between its

---

[26] For a formal proof of this see Kemp [9, Chapter 11].

traded products differ, the terms of trade will be changing. And as long as the terms of trade are changing country A cannot, with an open economy, reach its steady state. Momentarily in country A, all factors and outputs may come to grow at the same rate; but if the terms of trade continue changing because country B is not yet in its steady state this cannot last. In other words, in the open economy the small country cannot be in its steady state before the large country is, but the large country does not depend on the small country. If neither country were so small as to be unable to affect the terms of trade, it would be impossible for either country to be in its steady state while the other was not. [27]

6.8. The Effects of Tariffs on the Rate of Growth

An analysis of the effects of opening-up trade on the rate of growth is clearly not of the same practical interest as an analysis of the effects of tariff changes. But the conclusions can readily be adapted to tariff theory. [28] Indeed, this paper was stimulated by an interest in the effects of tariffs and other forms of protection on growth in the belief that it may indirectly shed light on issues of current controversy. It is assumed now that all tariff revenue is automatically redistributed in a nondistorting manner.

First assume that the terms of trade are given. A reduction in tariff barriers has then the same type of effect on the rate of growth as a movement from a closed economy to free trade. It increases the gains from trade and so raises the rate of growth. If I is M intensive, it lowers the relative price of

[27] Mr. Renshaw of Warwick University has pointed out to me the following implication of the factor-weight effect in a two-country world where neither country is small. Suppose that (a) neither country is in its steady state when trade is opened up, (b) capital is growing faster than labor in both, (c) their savings propensities are the same, and (d) there are no factor-reversals. Assume that A has the higher capital-labor ratio, so that (i) A will export the capital intensive and B the labor intensive product, and (ii) A will have the higher income per head. The factor-weight effect will then cause opening-up trade to raise the rate of growth in the richer country A, and to lower it in the poorer country B — though there will also be other effects on the growth rate. But this yields of course no argument from B's point of view for restricting trade to raise its growth rate. It may be more plausible to assume that the richer countries are the land-intensive countries, in which case the factor weight effect will tend to lower growth rates in the richer and raise them in the poorer countries.

[28] No attempt is made here to spell out the effects of a tariff on the path to and the characteristics of the steady state. These can be easily derived by combining the earlier models in the paper with the analysis in this section.

investment goods and so raises the rate of growth further (and lowers the rate of growth if C is M intensive). If X is capital intensive, it shifts income distribution towards profits and so may raise the rate of growth (vice versa if X is labor intensive). Finally, if X is capital intensive and capital is growing faster than labor, then a tariff reduction probably raises the rate of growth by raising the weight of capital in determining output growth (and lowers it if X is labor intensive. [29] All this applies in reverse for an increase in tariffs and is just a revision of our earlier conclusions.

The matter is a little more complicated if the terms of trade are not given, the elasticity of foreign reciprocal demand being less than perfectly elastic. Consider first the gains from trade effect in isolation. There is now an *optimum* tariff at which the gains from trade, defined as including the gains from improved terms of trade, are maximized. Whether a tariff change raises or lowers the gains from trade, and hence the rate of growth, now depends on whether the movement is toward or away from the optimum tariff level. When the tariff is below the optimum an increase raises the rate of growth.

Next consider the substitution, income distribution, and factor-weight effects. These all depend on the direction of the relative price change within the domestic economy brought about by a tariff change. Normally one would expect a tariff reduction to reduce protection of importables, so that, as with the opening-up of trade, it lowers the relative price of M domestically. The substitution, income distribution, and factor-weight effects are then as for the constant terms of trade case, depending on whether I or C is M intensive and X or M is capital intensive. But there is also the paradoxical "Metzler" possibility [30] that a tariff reduction raises the relative price of M domestically, because the effect of a reduced tariff margin over the external (duty-free) price of M has been more than offset by the rise in its external price (the deterioration in the terms of trade). This paradox results when the sum of the foreign elasticity of demand for exports in terms of imports and country A's marginal propensity to import is less than one. In that case, a tariff reduction has substitution, income distribution, and factor-weight effects opposite to those of the constant terms of trade case. The basic analysis required is identical.

---

[29] The word "probably" appears because I have not been able to prove rigorously that the factor-weight effect applies in a simple manner to tariff changes, and there is indeed some doubt whether it does so. This qualification applies to all references to this effect in this section.

[30] Metzler [13].

6.9 **Final Remarks**

One might wonder whether the parts of this paper that have been concerned with the steady state have dealt with anything important. Yet this concern — inherited from the literature of growth theory — can be given a broader interpretation. It may be uninteresting to describe a state which is many years ahead and which may indeed never be reached, since on the way to it parameters are likely to change. But it is of interest to know in which direction growth rates may move and what consequences for real income per head and the growth rate can be expected some years after a particular alteration in trade policy. Focusing on a theoretical ultimate state is thus purely an expositional device. At the same time, a concern *only* with steady states would have obscured significant aspects of the trade and growth process. Notably it would have obscured the factor-weight effect.

The paper has been concerned with only a few effects of trade on growth, and in a highly simplified model. The author does not delude himself that such a model gives a convincing picture of the real world. There are obviously many possible relationships between trade and growth. [31] The relationships that have been discussed here happen to follow naturally from models of trade and of growth that are already familiar. A more complex model might allow the impact effect to be spread over a longer period than just the year when trade is opened up, and more sophisticated assumptions about saving and investment behavior might be introduced; perhaps a plausible inter-temporal utility function might be built explicitly into the model. Economies of scale could be introduced. One could allow the shift either in the production pattern or in the consumption pattern that results from opening up trade to lead to growth-promoting or growth-inhibiting effects through raising or lowering the "learning rate" of the economy. Furthermore, other effects, concerned with technical progress or adaptation, with the inflow of foreign capital in response to trading opportunities, and with the inducement to invest by domestic entrepreneurs, may be at least as important or more important.

One might also have framed the question differently. Instead of asking how opening up trade or a change in trade restrictions affects the rate of growth, one might have assumed an open and possibly unrestricted economy

---

[31] Many of these effects are discussed by Kindleberger [10]. The growth-and-trade theme runs consistently through Charles Kindleberger's writings, especially his historical contributions. The numerous ideas he has thrown out and the interesting relationships he has uncovered offer great scope for incorporation in formal models of trade and growth and for making these more realistic.

to begin with and might have considered how trade and balance of payments effects either fostered or retarded growth. This is the more realistic approach that Kindleberger takes in his discussion of the impact of trade on the rate of growth.[32] He distinguishes between trade as a leading, a balancing, or a lagging sector. The models of export-led growth to which he gives prominence tend to be demand-motored models which assume that increased demand for exports can lead to extra output from existing resources and can induce extra investment; such models can be contrasted with the neoclassical model in the present paper which is essentially supply motored, assuming full employment and full capacity utilization at all times and that investment at any point in time is limited by available savings that do not depend on expected rates of return. Growth in this model is explained by growth in the supply of the factors of production and their productivity, whether internal or through foreign trade. There is clearly scope for the construction of rigorous demand motored models on the lines sketched out by Kindleberger and the authors he cites, and for combining them with supply motored models of the type expounded in this paper.

[32] See [10, Chapter 12].

References

[1] Baldwin, R.E. "The Role of Capital-Goods Trade in the Theory of International Trade". *American Economic Review*, 56 (September 1966) 841–848.

[2] Bardhan, P.K. "Equilibrium Growth in the International Economy". *Quarterly Journal of Economics*, 79 (August 1965) 454–464.

[3] Black, J. "Two-Level Production Functions." *Economica*, 36 (August 1969) 310–313;

[4] Black, J. "Trade and the Long-Run Growth Rate." *Oxford Economic Papers*, 22 (March 1970).

[5] Brown, M. *On the Theory and Measurement of Technological Change.* Cambridge: Cambridge University Press, 1966.

[6] Caves, R.E. *Trade and Economic Structure.* Cambridge: Cambridge University Press, 1960.

[7] Hahn, F.H. and Matthews, R.C.O. "The Theory of Economic Growth: A Survey." *Economic Journal*, 74 (December 1964) 779–902.

[8] Johnson, A.S. "Protection and the Formation of Capital." *Political Science Quart.*, 23 (June 1968) 220–241.

[9] Kemp, M.C. *The Pure Theory of International Trade.* Englewood Cliffs: Prentice-Hall, Inc., 1964.

[10] Kindleberger, C.P. *Foreign Trade and the National Economy.* New Haven: Yale University Press, 1962.

[11] Linder, S.B. *An Essay on Trade and Transformation*, Stockholm: 1961.

[12] Meade, J.E. *A Neo-Classical Theory of Economic Growth.* London: 1962.

[13] Metzler, L.A. "Tariffs, the Terms of Trade and the Distribution of National Income." *Journal of Political Economy* 57 (February 1949) 1–29.

[14] Oniki, H. and Uzawa, H. "Patterns of Trade and Investment in a Dynamic Model of International Trade", *Review of Economic Studies* 32 (January 1965) 15–38.

[15] Pitchford, J.D. "Growth and the Elasticity of Factor Substitution", *Economic Record*, 36 (December 1960) 491–504.

[16] Sato, K. "Growth and the Elasticity of Factor Substitution: A Comment – How Plausible is Imbalanced Growth?", *Economic Record*, (September 1963) 355–361.

[17] Solow, R.M. "A Contribution to the Theory of Economic Growth", *Quarterly Journal of Economics* 39 (February 1963) 355–361.

[18] Swan, T.W. "Economic Growth and Capital Accumulation", *Economic Record*, 32 (November 1956) 334–361.

CHAPTER 7

THE THEORY OF TRADE AND GROWTH: A DIAGRAMMATIC ANALYSIS

Harry G. JOHNSON

The London School of Economics and Political Science and
The University of Chicago

7.1. Introduction

Charles Kindleberger's contributions to the contemporary development of international economics have consisted more in his stimulating and provocative intuitive insights into the problems of international economic policy and his judgment of the practically relevant relationships and facts than in the elaboration of the formal theoretical core of the subject — though others have drawn inspiration for theorizing from his work and his students at M.I.T. have made impressive contributions to the advance of pure international economic theory. International economics specialists, however, must above other economists recognize the principle of comparative advantage. Hence this paper, written in his honor, is concerned with formal theory, specifically some aspects of the theory of international trade and economic growth. Section 7.2 outlines briefly the standard Heckscher-Ohlin model of international trade, in a form which it is hoped is both compact and illuminating. Section 7.3 summarizes the comparative static analysis of the effects of growth on production and trade equilibrium, as developed in the late 1950s by Bhagwati [2], Corden [5], Findlay and Grubert [6], myself [7], and Rybczynski [13]. Section 7.4 applies the analysis to growth models of the standard kind, in which the growth of the labor force is assumed to proceed at an exogenously determined rate, and the growth of the capital stock is made endogenous through the assumption of a fixed savings ratio or savings ratios differing between groups of factor owners. Section 7.5 discusses alternative models of economic growth.

144

7.2. **The Heckscher-Ohlin Model**

The standard Heckscher-Ohlin model assumes, for each country, two factors of production (labor L and capital K), the quantities of which are fixed at any point of time (the endowment or the endowment ratio), which are used to produce two commodities (X and Y) according to constant-returns-to-scale production functions, the commodities being distinguished by the fact that they utilize the factors in different ratios. To avoid complications associated with the possibility of reversal of optimal factor-utilization ratios as the country's factor-endowment ratio changes with growth, it is assumed that X is inherently capital intensive at all possible factor price ratios (the Samuelson strong factor-intensity assumption).

For the construction of a model of the international economy, it is usually assumed that factors and production functions as well as commodities are identical among countries, and the model is simplified by assuming only two countries. These assumptions will be introduced in due course, but for the main purpose of this paper the opening of the domestic economy to international trade can be represented by positing an international price ratio to which the country's economy adjusts. For the analysis of the growth of the domestic economy, this price ratio can either be assumed constant, i.e., unaffected by changes in the country's desire to trade at that price ratio (the small country assumption) or be assumed to vary inversely with the volumes of exports and imports the country supplies and demands at the initial price ratio. Variability of the terms of trade in response to the desired trade volume gives rise, on the one hand, to the possibility of growth entailing a secondary benefit by reducing import demand (export supply) and improving the terms of trade, on the other hand, to the possibility of growth entailing a secondary loss by increasing import demand (export supply) and worsening the terms of trade, and in the extreme, to the possibility of the secondary terms of trade loss outweighing the primary increased-output gain from growth. The conditions necessary to produce this last possibility of "immiserizing growth" [1] have been thoroughly explored and will not be pursued here, the analysis concentrating on the effects of growth on the volume of trade desired at the initial price ratio.

For equilibrium at the fixed world price ratio for commodities, the domestic cost ratio must equal that price ratio; this implies both a unique domestic factor-price ratio and unique factor price ratios in the two industries, which in turn, given the country's endowment ratio, implies a unique allocation of factors to the production of the two commodities. These relations stem from the assumption of constant returns to scale, which makes the factor-utilization ratios depend solely on the factor-price ratio, and, diagrammatically, permits the production functions to be represented by a single isoquant arbitrarily chosen. Fig. 7.1, the familiar Lerner-Pearce diagram, depicts isoquants for X and Y for quantities chosen to exchange one-for-one in the world market. For the domestic cost ratio to be equal to the world price ratio of unity, the economy's factor-price ratio must be the common tangent $M_K M_L$, and the factor utilization ratios must be OR_x and OR_y, respectively. For the economy to be in fact capable of producing some of both goods in equilibrium and in fact have the factor-price ratio $M_K M_L$, the factor-utilization ratios must straddle the economy's overall endowment ratio OR (otherwise the economy would specialize on production of one good and its factor-price ratio would be the tangent to the relevant isoquant at its intersection with OR).

To analyze the allocation of production, it is convenient to choose the isoquants for X and Y as those corresponding to a value of production in each case equal to the country's total national income at world market prices.

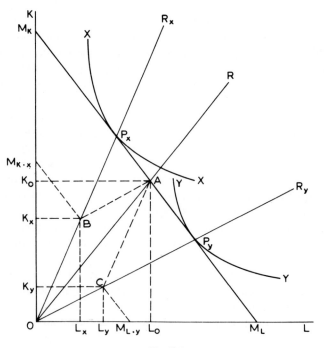

Fig. 7.1

Then point A on OR represents the country's endowment of factors (OK_o of K and OL_o of L), and OM_K and OM_L measure its national income in terms of capital and labor, respectively. The allocation of factors among industries is determined by the requirement that both be fully employed. It can be determined diagrammatically by completing the parallelogram $OBAC$, B giving the factor quantities OK_x and OL_x allocated to X and C the factor quantities OK_y and OL_y allocated to Y. Owing to constant returns to scale, the proportions of X and Y in total national output are represented respectively by the ratios OB/OP_x and OC/OP_y, and the absolute amounts of X and Y produced are proportional to the distances respectively of OB along OR_x and OC along OR_y. For some purposes it is convenient to draw $BM_{K.x}$ and $CM_{L.y}$ parallel to $M_K M_L$ to obtain a representation of the values of the outputs of the two industries in terms of K and L, respectively.

The world price ratio determines the allocation of production between the industries, and the prices of factors both in terms of each other and in terms of the two commodities (since, owing to constant returns to scale, absolute as well as relative marginal products are determined by the factor-utilization ratios). The prices of the factors, the total quantities of the factors, and their allocation among owners, together with the tastes of the factor owners, determine the allocation of the community's total income among expenditures on the two goods; this allocation in conjunction with the production allocation already discussed determines the country's reciprocal demand position in international trade (its net offer of X and demand for Y or vice versa).

The full general equilibrium of the economy could be analyzed on the following lines: (1) Assume for simplicity that the economy is divided into two groups, owners of labor and owners of capital, each group having homogeneous preferences and these preferences differing between groups. (2) Following Laing [9], transform the indifference curves of each group relating to commodities into indifference curves relating to factor combinations, utilizing the relationship between the commodity-price ratio, the factor-price ratios, and the optimal factor-utilization ratios. (3) Insert the two resulting sets of indifference curves into the diagram with origin O. (4) Complete the factor group budget lines $M_{K.x}B$ and $M_{L.y}C$. (5) Find the tangencies of the respective budget lines and preference systems (B' and C', not shown in the diagram). (6) Complete the parallelogram $OB'A'C'$, where A' is a point on $M_K M_L$. The difference AA' would represent the country's reciprocal demand position in terms of factor services demanded and supplied; it could be translated back into commodity demands and supplies by utilizing the factor input coefficients for the two commodities.

This procedure, however, is cumbersome, and the main results to follow do not require a detailed analysis of demand conditions. For simplicity, it will be assumed simply that the country is initially a net exporter of X.

7.3. **The Comparative Statics of Growth**

The apparatus developed in the preceding section can now be applied to the analysis of economic growth. In terms of the model, growth may take two forms, factor accumulation and technical progress. Either factor may increase in quantity, and technical progress may occur in either industry; but all the significant results for one country, on the assumption of fixed terms of trade, can be derived by considering the effects of the accumulation of capital, and of technical progress in the X industry.

The effects of capital accumulation on the economy's production pattern depicted in fig. 7.2 (the isoquants being omitted for simplicity). Capital increase form K_0 to K_0', and the total endowment and its allocation among industries shift from A, B, C, to A',B',C'. Production of Y must fall and that of X increase by more than the total increase in national income $(M_K M_K')$;

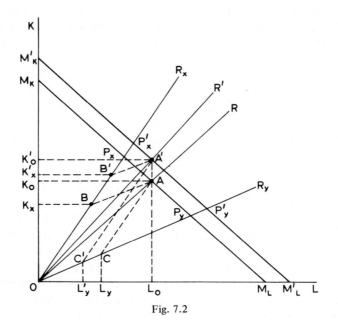

Fig. 7.2

this is most clearly seen from the fact that output of Y is proportional to OC and X to CP_y, and that in the new equilibrium OC' is shorter than OC and $C'P'_y$ longer than CP_y. This is the celebrated Rybczynski theorem:

At constant commodity prices, accumulation of a factor increases the output of the commodity that uses that factor intensively and reduces the output of the other commodity.

On the demand side, the increase in output owing to factor accumulation accrues entirely to the owners of the addition to the stock of the factor, and on the normal assumption of noninferiority of either good in consumption, there will be an increase in demand for both commodities. Thus there must be an increase in the excess of production over domestic demand, or a decrease in the excess of domestic demand over production, for the commodity that uses the augmented factor relatively intensively, the former applying if that commodity is the export good (the case depicted) and the latter if it is the import good. More directly, accumulation of the factor used intensively in production of the export good (capital here) increases the country's supply of exports and demand for imports, and accumulation of the factor used intensively in production of the import good (labor here) decreases the country's supply of exports and demand for imports, at the initial prices. In the former case the country becomes more, and in the latter less, dependent on international trade at the initial world price ratio.

The effects of technical improvement in the X industry on the economy's production pattern are more complex to analyze, for two reasons. First, technical progress changes the relationship between the commodity-price ratio and the factor-price ratio, implying (at constant world prices) a redistribution of income between factor owners. Second, it is necessary to distinguish between capital-saving, neutral, and labor-saving technical progress. Following Hicks (whose definitions are appropriate in this context) technical progress is defined to be capital-saving, neutral, or labor-saving, according as it raises the marginal product of labor proportionately more than, equally with, or less than, the marginal product of capital, and so lowers, leaves unchanged, or raises the ratio of capital to labor that is optimal at a given factor-price ratio.

The effects of neutral technical progress in the X industry are depicted in fig. 7.3, where XX respresents the postprogress location of the original X industry isoquant. To maintain the equality of the cost ratio between the industries with the one-to-one world price ratio, the factor-price ratio must change from the slope of $M_K M_L$ to that of $M'_K M'_L$, the common tangent to the new X and the unchanged Y isoquants. $M'_K M'_L$ represents the original national income at postprogress factor prices, and $M''_K M''_L$ the postprogress

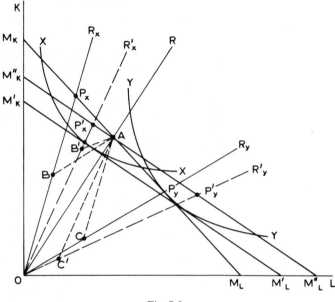

Fig. 7.3

national income. The optimal factor-utilization ratios must change to OR'_x and OR'_y, the capital-labor ratio falling in both industries. Since the capital-labor ratio falls in the Y industry, whose technology is unchanged, the marginal product of labor falls in terms of Y, and since the commodity price ratio is unchanged, the marginal product of labor must have fallen in terms of X as well. In other words, labor loses real income as a result of technical progress in the capital-intensive industry and more than the whole of the benefit of progress accrues to capital.

The factor allocations shift from B,C to B',C' — implying an absolute reduction of production of Y and an increase in the production of X greater than the total increase in national income. This is the analogue for technical progress of the Rybczynski theorem for factor accumulation:

At constant commodity prices, neutral technical progress in an industry increases the output of that industry and reduces the output of the other industry.

But, in contrast to the factor accumulation case, this theorem does not lead unambiguously to the parallel conclusion that neutral technical progress must increase or decrease the economy's dependence on international trade, depending on whether it occurs in the export or the import goods industry.

The reason is the redistribution of income between factors consequent on technical progress: If factor owners have strong marginal preferences for (a relatively high marginal propensity to consume) the commodity that employs their factor intensively, then despite noninferiority the income-redistribution effect may result in demand for the commodity whose production has increased increasing by more than the increase in national income, and possibly by more than the increase in output of that good. The Rybczynski parallel conclusion only holds if this last possibility is excluded by imposing suitable restrictions on factor owner's preferences.

From the analysis of neutral technical progress, it is obvious that the same results follow for the case of capital-saving technical progress in the X industry, which reduces the slope of the optimal factor-utilization ratio with the new technology and the original factor-price ratio to less than that of OR_x, and so accentuates the clockwise rotation of OR'_x. Complexity appears, however, in the case of labor-saving technical progress in the X industry, which rotates the factor utilization ratio with the new technology and the original factor-price ratio counterclockwise and may outweigh the substitution effect of the factor-price ratio change necessary to maintain the original cost ratio so that OR'_x lies counterclockwise in relation to OR_x. In this case, C' must lie right of C, perhaps sufficiently so to represent an increased output of Y, and B' may lie left of B sufficiently to represent a reduced output of X. Hence, even with the restrictions on factor owners' preferences mentioned earlier, no conclusion can be drawn about the effects on export supply and import demand of labor-saving progress in the capital-intensive industry (and similarly of capital-saving progress in the labor-saving industry).

The foregoing analysis of technical progress may be summarized in the proposition that technical progress in an industry must increase the output of that industry and reduce the output of the other, unless progress saves the factor used relatively unintensively in that industry; and that a country's dependence on trade at the initial world commodity-price ratio will increase or decrease according to whether technical progress occurs in its export or import goods industry, unless either progress saves the factor used relatively unintensively in that industry or factor owners have strong marginal preferences for the commodities that use their factors relatively intensively.

While the analysis has thus far rested on the Heckscher-Ohlin assumption of constant returns to scale in production, it can readily be extended to include the effects of factor accumulation in the presence of increasing or decreasing returns to scale, since, on the assumption that they are external to the firm, nonconstant returns to scale can be identified with a technical change in a constant-returns-to-scale production function assumed to apply to individual competitive producers, which technical change is conditional on a change in the industry's total output. For simplicity, the technical change equivalent of nonconstant returns to scale is assumed to be neutral in the Hicks sense.

The effect of an increase in capital in the presence of increasing returns in the X industry is depicted in fig. 7.4, where XX is the national-income equivalent isoquant for the scale of production of X prevailing in the initial equilibrium. It might appear that, given increasing returns in X, this equilibrium must be unstable; but an increase in production of X, which would shift the isoquant left and reduce costs at the initial factor prices, would require a reduction of the capital-labor ratio in both industries and hence a rise in the relative price of capital and cost of X, and this factor-price effect may be assumed to outweigh the scale effect. An increase in the stock of capital must, according to the Rybczynski theorem, lead to an expansion of output of X and contraction of output of Y under constant returns to scale. With increasing returns in X, the X isoquant shifts towards the origin; to maintain the equality of commodity price and cost ratios, the relative price of capital must increase, lowering the capital-labor ratios in both industries and

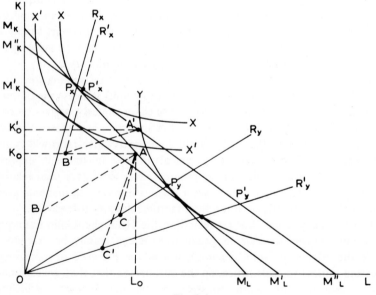

Fig. 7.4

requiring further expansion of X and contraction of Y. Hence in the ultimate equilibrium position (represented by the location of XX at $X'X'$), production of Y must have fallen and of X increased by more than the total increase in national income; and, because the marginal product of labor must have fallen, and that of capital have risen, in both industries, the owners of capital gain more than the whole increase in national income. From this it follows that an increase in the factor used intensively in the export industry, where that industry is subject to increasing returns to scale, must increase the country's demand for imports and supply of exports, except where the redistribution effect outweighs the production effect. It is easily shown that the same conclusion follows if the import goods industry rather than the export industry is subject to economies of scale, and that converse conclusions follow if there is an increase in labor, the factor used intensively in the import goods industry.

Fig. 7.5 depicts the converse case of an increase in the capital endowment

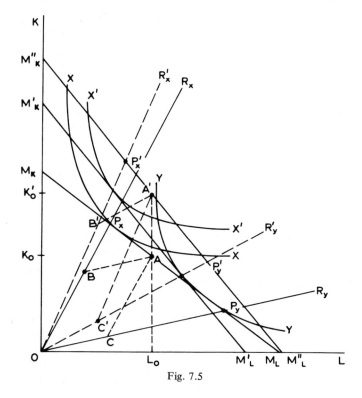

Fig. 7.5

with decreasing returns to scale in the X industry. As the X industry expands to absorb the additional capital, the X isoquant shifts outwards with decreasing returns to scale, and the relative price of labor must rise and of capital fall to maintain equality of the commodity price and cost ratios. In the final equilibrium, production of X must have increased but production of Y may have either increased or decreased (in the diagram C' may fall on a higher or a lower Y isoquant than C), in response to the opposing influences of a higher capital-labor ratio for the economy as a whole, and in the two industries. Also, there will have been some redistribution of income from capital to labor. Hence the effect of capital accumulation on the country's trade dependence is uncertain. The possibility should be noted that, with decreasing returns in the industry intensive in the accumulating factor, national income might actually fall with growth (that is, A' might lie below $M'_K M'_L$ in the diagram). The accumulation of labor rather than capital must (it can easily be shown) reduce the output of X and increase that of Y by more than the total increase in national income, at the same time redistributing income towards capital; ignoring the redistribution effect, the result must be to reduce the economy's dependence on trade. Unlike the case of increasing returns, therefore, when decreasing returns are present in one industry the effects of capital accumulation and labor force growth are asymmetrical: an increase in the factor used intensively in the decreasing returns industry must increase output in that industry but may also increase output in the other industry; an increase in the factor used unintensively in that industry must reduce its output and increase that of the other by more than the whole increase of national income.

7.4. Growth with Endogenous Saving

The analysis of the previous section treated factor accumulation as exogenous. Contemporary growth models treat the accumulation of capital as endogenous, typically by assuming either a given overall savings ratio or given and different savings ratios for the owners of capital and labor; and, to keep the system moving, and specifically to permit it the possibility of a stable long-run equilibrium growth path, it is assumed that the effective labor force grows at an exogenously given exponential rate, either through natural increase or through Harrod-neutral (purely labor-augmenting) technical progress. Interest centers on the questions of convergence on the steady-state growth path from any arbitrary starting point, and of the characteristics of the steady-state growth, including the requirements for maximization of consumption per head on that path (the so-called "golden rule" conditions). These questions become theoretically difficult and exciting only in a model of two or more sectors, differentiated by the production of consumer goods and capital goods. Such models require elaborate mathematics to analyze with full generality (e.g., see [11]); but the important qualitative results can be obtained from conventional trade theory, by making one of the goods in the standard Heckscher-Ohlin model a capital good (for simplicity, one that lasts forever once produced). Further, if one is content to assume convergence on the steady-state growth path and to concern oneself with the characteristics of that path, one can analyze many interesting problems with the traditional geometrical tools.

To begin with the question of convergence on a steady-state growth path, it is obvious from work on the factor-price-equalization theorem that the accumulation of capital relative to labor cannot proceed smoothly if the economy has to pass through a factor-intensity reversal, for (as will be evident from the subsequent analysis) the relative price of one of the commodities will first rise and then fall in this case, and the ratio of the output of that commodity to the other will first fall and then rise, with a constant savings ratio. Hence this possibility is best eliminated by means of the strong factor-intensity assumption. It is also evident that trouble will arise if there are possibilities of multiple equilibrium; hence it is necessary to eliminate the possibility of unstable equilibrium that multiple equilibrium entails. In the standard Heckscher-Ohlin model, the possibility of an unstable closed-economy equilibrium hinges on the income-redistribution effect of an increase in the relative price of a commodity increasing the quantity of it demanded by more than the production and substitution effects reduce excess demand for it, which requires each factor owner to have a marginal preference for the commodity that uses his factor relatively intensively (see [8]). An analogous possibility arises in the two-sector growth model from the assumption that capitalists have a higher marginal (i.e., average) propensity to save than workers. To eliminate this possibility it is therefore necessary to assume *either* that the capital-goods-producing sector is relatively labor intensive, so that a rise in the relative price of capital goods reduces capitalists' income and therefore saving, *or* that the income-redistribution effect is not strong enough to outweigh the increase in production resulting from the price increase. A sufficient condition for the latter is that the elasticity of substitution be unity or greater in both industries. [1]

[1] A simple proof, following Borts [4] is as follows: Define the income of capitalists in terms of capital goods as

Given the exclusion of the possibilities of trouble just discussed, the convergence of the economy on a steady-state growth path follows from the fact that the amount of investment per head required to equip the additions to the effective labor force with the existing capital per head increases proportionately to the existing capital per head, whereas output increases less than proportionately to capital per head, owing to the diminishing marginal productivity of capital. Hence if the overall savings ratio is more than or less than sufficient to maintain capital per head intact, capital per head will rise or fall until savings (the savings ratio times output per head) are just sufficient to maintain capital intact. On the long-run growth path, the savings ratio determines output and consumption per head.

Since a higher ratio of savings raises output per head but reduces the proportion of that output available for consumption, and since output per head does not increase proportionately with increases in the savings ratio and capital per head, there must exist a savings ratio that maximizes consumption per head. This is the problem of the "golden rule" conditions. These conditions can be established by extension of the Heckscher-Ohlin apparatus developed in earlier sections; the following analysis is based on an earlier proof by Laing [10].

Fig. 7.6 is drawn in terms of capital per head of effective labor at a moment of time on the steady-state growth path, the rate of growth of effective labor being n and the production of capital goods per head required to keep capital per head constant over time being nK. For the capital per head OK_0, the production isoquant for capital goods is nK_0, and the economy must allocate to production of it some combination of capital and

$$Y_K = Q_I I + Q_C \frac{1}{p_I} C,$$

where I and C are initial quantities produced of capital goods and consumption goods, p_I is the price of capital goods in terms of consumption goods (initially unity), and Q_I and Q_C are the relative shares of capital in the output of the two goods. Assuming without loss of generality that only capitalists save, their saving ratio being s, and remembering that for small changes $dC \approx -dI$

$$\frac{d(sY_K)}{dI} = s(Q_I - Q_C - Q_C C \frac{dp_I}{dI} + I \frac{dQ_I}{dp_K} \frac{dp_K}{dI} + C \frac{dQ_C}{dp_K} \frac{dp_K}{dI},$$

where p_K is the price of capital services, and dp_K/dI by assumption is positive). For instability the right-hand side must exceed unity; given the fractional nature of Q_I, this is impossible unless at least one of the dQ/dp_K is positive, which required an elasticity of substitution less than unity.

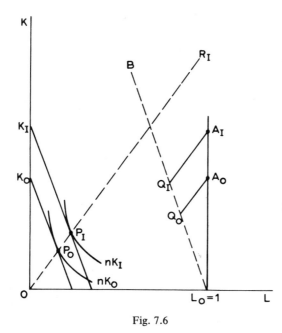

Fig. 7.6

labor falling on that isoquant. Suppose, for a reason to be discussed late, the combination chosen is such as to minimize the value of the services of the existing capital stock in terms of labor; this gives the allocation depicted by P_0 and the factor-utilization ratio shown by OR_I. Draw a line from A_0 (the economy's endowment point) parallel and equal in length to OP_0; this gives point Q_0, representing the resources available for the consumption goods industry. Repeat the process for the larger capital per head OK_1 and investment goods production nK_1, yielding Q_1 as resources available for the consumption goods industry. Then Q_0 and Q_1 must, by similar triangles, lie on a straight line through $L_0 = 1$. This line, L_0B, constitutes the "budget line" of the economy for the production of consumers' goods: it can in effect have more capital for this purpose only by allocating more labor services to the maintenance of capital per head intact. The most efficient way to exchange labor for capital is to maximize the value of labor services in terms of capital services; this accounts for the choice of the factor combination in the investment goods industry that minimized the value of capital in terms of labor. As can readily be seen, the choice of any other factor combination than that represented by OR_I would entail a budget line less steep than L_0B, and so be inefficient. The maximum consumption per head obtainable will be defined by tangency of a consumer goods isoquant with L_0B; for simplicity this may be assumed to occur at Q_1. Wherever it occurs, the tangency implies that the value of consumption goods production is OL_0 in terms of labor, equal to the income of labor, and that the value of investment goods production is equal to the value of capital services. This latter is the "golden rule" condition that total savings should equal the income of capital or that the savings ratio should equal capital's share in total output. Also, dividing the income of capital nK by its quantity yields the alternative condition that the rate of return on capital should equal the rate of growth of the effective labor force.

The convergence of the economy's growth path on a steady-state equilibrium path, and the existence of a maximum-consumption-per-head savings ratio, can be illustrated by an alternative diagrammatic technique, due to the late V.K. Ramaswami (presented sketchily in [12]). Fig. 7.7 is drawn on a per capita basis, and takes as its starting point any arbitrary price ratio between the investment good and the consumption good; for convenience, the price ratio corresponding to long-run equilibrium growth is selected. The right-hand side of the diagram shows the values of outputs per head $M_{I_1}, M_{I_2} ...,$ in terms of investment goods, that the economy could produce with different amounts of capital per head at that price ratio; the 'Rybczynski line" RR is the locus of tangencies of the transformation curves for different amounts of capital with the budget lines $M_{I_1}M_{C_1}, M_{I_2}M_{C_2} ...;$ its

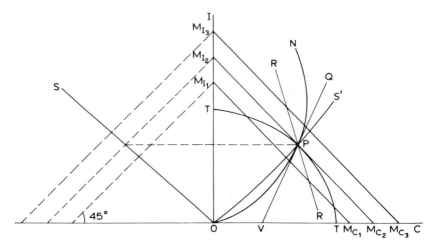

Fig. 7.7

slope with reference to the budget lines embodies the assumption that investment goods are relatively capital intensive. (For points on RR outside this quadrant, the transformation curve has to be conceived of as including negative production of one of the goods). The line VQ is a capital requirements curve; its intersections with the successive budget lines show the production of investment goods required to equip the increment to the effective labor force with the same capital per head as the existing labor force. It cuts the horizontal axis right of the origin because part of existing income is accounted for by labor, whereas increments of income have to be contributed entirely by capital.

Horizontal lines from the intersections of VQ and the budget lines to the relevant transformation curves (not shown on the diagram) trace out the curve ON, which depicts the consumption possibilities per head available to the economy as capital per head varies. It is evident from general geometrical considerations that, as capital per head increases, ON must eventually bend back on itself, indicating a maximum potential consumption per head; this occurs when additional capital per head adds no more to the economy's production potential than is required to meet the associated increment in the capital requirement.

The left-hand side of the diagram represents the savings ratio, in the sense that the intersection of a 45° line from M_K with the savings function OS gives the amount of saving the society will do when it enjoys the income M_I. At any point of time (on any given transformation curve) savings and investment must be equal; hence the production equilibrium of the economy must be such that when output is valued in terms of investment goods at the equilibrium price ratio and multiplied by the savings ratio, the result is equal to the rate of production of investment goods (as illustrated by point P on the transformation curve TT). As the capital stock increases, the production point at the reference commodity price ratio moves northwest along RR whereas the consumption point would move northeast along a vector through O (not shown); to maintain equilibrium the relative price of investment goods must fall and of consumption goods rise, so that income measured in investment goods rises more than proportionately to the increase in capital; hence the fixed saving ratio represented by OS on the left-hand side of the diagram traces out an actual savings curve OS' on the right-hand of the diagram which is concave to the vertical axis. (If investment goods were assumed to be labor intensive, OS' would be concave to the horizontal axis, while the ON curve would have the same shape as in fig. 7.7 — an easier case diagrammatically.)

The intersection of OS' and ON at P determines the characteristics of the long-run equilibrium growth path of the economy in terms of capital, output, and consumption per head. Convergence on this steady-state growth path and the stability of equilibrium are ensured by the fact that up to the intersection, actual investment (saving) exceeds the capital requirement, and vice versa for positions beyond the intersection. (Since the ON curve bends back on itself, this point is perhaps better expressed in terms of consumption falling short of what is consistent with constant capital and output per head to the left of the intersection, and exceeding it to the right of the intersection).

Fig. 7.7, representing the long-run dynamic equilibrium of an economy with a fixed savings ratio and an exogenously given rate of growth of the effective labor force, can be employed to analyze the standard problem of international trade theory in a dynamic context: the opening of the opportunity to trade internationally at a fixed commodity price ratio different from the closed-economy price ratio. There are two possibilities: (i) the fixed international commodity price ratio entails a higher value of consumption goods than the closed-economy price ratio; (ii) the world price ratio entails a higher value of investment goods than the closed-economy price ratio.

The first possibility is illustrated in fig. 7.8, where again investment goods production is assumed to be capital intensive. The availability of a higher price for consumption goods shifts production from P to P' (the capital stock being momentarily held constant) and consumption from P to C' (the increase in income in terms of investment goods increasing saving), the economy becoming an exporter of consumption goods and importer of capital goods. But its saving is now more than sufficient to maintain its capital per head intact, and its capital stock per head starts growing. As it does so, the country's production point will shift to the northwest along the new Rybczynski line $R'R'$. At the new fixed price ratio for investment goods in terms of consumption goods, the country's savings curve will be OS', while its capital requirements curve shifts right to $V'Q'$, reflecting the higher level of consumption the country can attain through trade with any given endowment of capital goods and associated capital requirement. Equilibrium may be reached at the intersection of $V'Q'$ and OS', in which case the economy may still be a net exporter of consumption goods or, as in the case shown, may have been converted from an importer into an exporter of capital goods. Alternatively, complete specialization in the production of capital goods may arrive first, in which case further accumulation of capital will reduce the marginal product of capital in producing capital goods and so further reduce the increment of saving that accompanies an increase in the

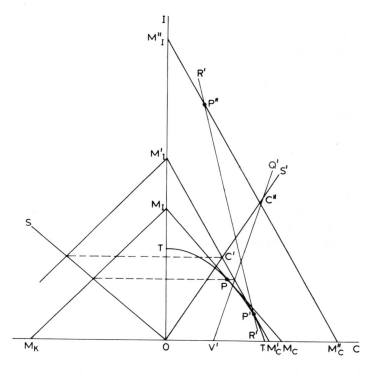

Fig. 7.8

capital stock, equilibrium again being reached when all saving is required to maintain capital per head intact.

If the investment goods industry were labor intensive instead of capital intensive, the accumulation of capital per head consequent on the opening of the opportunity to trade would lead to increasing specialization on the production of consumption goods and import of capital goods. The process might either terminate with the economy incompletely specialized, or result in complete specialization accompanied by a fall in the marginal product of capital in producing consumption goods and hence in its rate of return.

In both cases, the opening of trade leads both to an immediate "static" gain from trade and a longer run gain of consumption per head through the accumulation of further capital.

The second possibility, an increase in the relative price of capital goods, can be analyzed by analogy with fig. 7.8 (which recall assumes capital goods to be capital intensive in production). With a given initial capital stock, the fall in the price of consumption goods and the associated shift to increased production of investment goods lowers income measured in investment goods and reduces saving per head below that necessary to maintain capital per head intact, OS' falling below OP. (The capital requirements line $V'Q'$ again shifts right.) Output per head and consumption per head fall and the economy's production point moves southeast along the Rybczynski line; the final equilibrium may involve imcomplete specialization, with the economy either still exporting capital goods or converted to the export of consumption goods, or complete specialization on the production of consumption goods. If the capital goods industry is labor intensive instead of capital intensive, its output of capital goods must rise as capital decumulates, and it must become relatively more dependent on exports of such goods, in final equilibrium being either incompletely or completely specialized on their production. Whatever the relative factor intensity of capital goods production, the short-run gain in consumption from the opening of the opportunity to trade will be partially, and perhaps more than wholly, offset by a reduction in consumption per head occasioned by capital decumulation.

7.5. Alternative Models of Economic Growth

The argument of the preceding section has assumed, conventionally, that the essence of the growth process can be captured by the assumptions of an exogenously given rate of increase of the effective labor force and a fixed savings ratio (or fixed savings ratios for the two groups of factor owners in the model). Other assumptions are possible. This section briefly explores two alternative models. The first, analyzed elegantly in more detail in a recent paper by Stiglitz [14] retains the assumption of an exogenously determined rate of labor force increase but assumes that saving behavior is governed by time preference, the economy accumulating capital until a minimum rate of interest is attained. The second, which is analogous to a case examined by Bhagwati [3], assumes that the stock of capital is fixed and that labor breeds to the limit of subsistence.

For the time-preference model, it is necessary to assume that investment goods are labor intensive in production; otherwise a random reduction in investment would reduce the rate of interest and so the demand for investment goods rendering the equilibrium of the model unstable. The model is represented in fig. 7.9, where the per capita budget lines M_IM_C have the slope of the commodity price ratio corresponding to the minimum time-preference rate of interest, VQ represents the investment required to keep

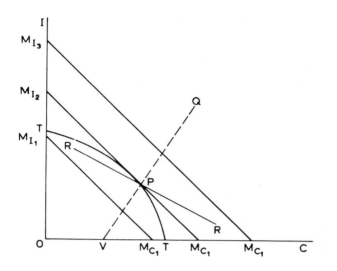

capital per head constant, at the level associated with each budget line it intersects, and RR is the Rybczynski line for the assumed commodity price ratio. On the savings assumptions of the model, RR also depicts the consumption and savings behavior of the community as its income expands; the steady-state equilibrium levels of capital, consumption, and saving (investment) per head are determined by the intersection of the Rybczynski and capital requirements lines at P. (Note that P may involve saving in excess of the "golden rule" requirement.)

The opening of the opportunity to trade at a price ratio different from the closed-economy equilibrium price ratio implies a rate of interest different from the minimum time-preference rate so long as the economy continues to produce both goods. The economy must therefore specialize on the commodity favored by the world price ratio and adjust its capital stock accordingly; further, once specialized, it must adjust the capital-labor ratio in the industry on which it specializes so as to restore the minimum time-preference interest rate.

If the investment-goods industry is favored by the world commodity price ratio, the economy must specialize on that industry. This involves decumulation of the capital stock per head and a consequent reduction of output per head. Since the rate of interest is the marginal product of capital in terms of itself and is determined by the capital-labor ratio in the investment goods industry, restoration of the initial time-preference rate of interest requires utilization of the pretrade capital-labor ratio in that industry, and capital must decumulate until the economy's overall capital-labor is equal to that ratio. In the new equilibrium, the earnings of both capital and labor are the same as before trade in terms of investment goods, but higher in terms of consumption goods. Capital per head and therefore output per head in terms of investment goods are lower than before trade, and consumption per head in terms of investment goods will also be lower than before trade unless the minimum time-preference rate of interest is below the exogenous rate of growth of the labor force (i.e., the economy saves more than the "golden rule" requirement).

If the consumption goods industry is favored by the world commodity price ratio, the economy must specialize on that industry; and this involves accumulation of capital per head for two reasons. The first is that the consumption goods-producing industry is capital intensive relative to the investment goods-producing industry, so that specialization requires capital accumulation. The second is that, at the pretrade capital-labor ratio in the consumption goods industry, the marginal product of capital in terms of consumption goods is unchanged but its value in terms of investment goods is higher; hence the capital-labor ratio in consumption goods must increase to reduce the interest rate (the marginal product of capital in terms of itself) to the long-run equilibrium level. The marginal product of labor must therefore rise in terms of consumption goods, and *a fortiori* in terms of investment goods, while the marginal product and the real income of capital in terms of consumption goods must fall. The increase in capital per head must increase output per head, and will increase consumption per head unless the minimum time-preference rate of interest is below the exogenous rate of growth of the labor force.

The foregoing analysis assumes that the world price ratio is fixed and that the economy must adjust to it (the "small country" assumption). Alternatively, it could be assumed that the country is not negligible in size by comparison with the rest of the world, that the rest of the world is growing at the same exogenously determined rate (this assumption being necessary to permit concentration on the long-run equilibrium growth path) but with a different minimum time-preference rate of interest, and that the world price ratio adjusts to preserve international trade equilibrium. This two-country model permits three possibilities: that the home country specializes and the foreign country does not, the home country adjusting to a world price ratio determined by the foreign rate of time preference — the case already analysed; that the home country remains incompletely specialized, the foreign country specializing and adjusting to its price ratio and interest rate;

and that both countries specialize, the world price ratio lying between the two closed economy price ratios. The range of possibilities can be illustrated by considering the alternative extreme of adjustment by the rest of the world to the home country's time-preference rate and price ratio. In this case, the home country must accumulate or decumulate capital per head depending on whether it initially has a comparative advantage in consumption goods or investment goods — i.e., on whether its rate of time preference is lower or higher than that of the other country. Factor prices will obviously be unchanged in long-run equilibrium, but, if the time-preference rate exceeds the exogenous labor-force growth rate, consumption per head will increase or fall depending on whether the country's time-preference rate is lower than the other country's time-preference rate and capital per head accumulates, or higher and capital per head decumulates; and conversely if the time-prefer-ence rate is below the labor-force growth rate and the country is consequent-ly saving more than the "golden rule" conditions require.

The second model to be analyzed assumes a constant stock of capital and a labor force that breeds to the limit of subsistence, on Malthus-Ricardo lines. (In the Bhagwati analysis [3] on which this model is based, the labor force is instead assumed to be given and the analysis is concerned with the effects of the opening of trade on the amount of unemployment.) Since capital is assumed to be fixed in quantity, the two industries can simply be assumed to produce two commodities, X (capital intensive) and Y (labor intensive), without specification of their nature. It is also necessary to specify the meaning of subsistence; ideally, subsistence should mean a set of equal-utility combinations of X and Y, but for analytical purposes it is simpler to consider subsistence as a fixed marginal product of labor in terms either of X or of Y. This yields four possible analytical cases, corresponding to comparative advantage at the world price ratio in X or in Y, and subsistence fixed in X or in Y.

If the comparative advantage is in X (the capital-intensive industry) and subsistence is also fixed in X, the opening of trade leads to complete specialization in X accompanied by a reduction of the size of the labor force until the labor-capital ratio for the economy is equal to the initial labor-capital ratio in X. Similarly, if the comparative advantage is in Y (the labor-intensive industry) and subsistence is fixed in Y, the country specializes completely on Y, the labor force increasing until the country's overall labor-capital ratio is equal to that initially prevailing in the Y industry. In each case, the purchasing power of wages in terms of the nonsubsistence good increases. If the comparative advantage is in Y, and X is the subsistence good, the country specializes on Y, its labor force increasing until its overall labor-capital ratio is equal to that initially prevailing in the Y industry; but at this labor-capital ratio, while the marginal product of labor in terms of Y is what it was before trade, labor's marginal product in terms of X is higher (because of the lower world cost of X in terms of Y) than in the pretrade situation and the labor force must grow still further to reduce wages to subsistence level. If, on the other hand, the comparative advantage is in X and the subsistence good is Y, the opening of trade brings two conflicting forces to bear on the size of the labor force; specialization on X, the capital-intensive good, at the initial equilibrium labor-capital ratio reduces the overall ratio of labor to capital and hence the labor force, but the increase in the labor-capital ratio in X necessary to reduce the value of the marginal product of labor in X, in terms of Y, to the subsistence level, increases the labor force that can be supported by the given stock of capital. Hence, the labor force may either decrease or increase, depending on whether the lower labor intensity in the X industry as compared with the Y industry dominates the effects of the lower world price of Y, working through the elasticity of substitution of labor for capital in the X industry, or not.

This last model could easily be "dynamized" by introducing a fixed rate of growth of the capital stock, analogous to the exogenously determined growth rate of the labor force employed in previous models. Alternatively, and more elegantly, one of the commodities could be identified as the investment good, and the growth rate of capital assumed to be determined by the rate of interest (the marginal product of capital in terms of investment goods) and the savings ratio of the owners of capital, the other commodity being by definition the subsistence good. The growth rate of the labor force would be determined by the growth rate of capital. The opening of trade, whether the country had a comparative advantage in subsistence goods or in capital goods, would increase the growth rate of capital and therefore of the labor force (after an initial adjustment of labor force to capital stock on the lines outlined earlier) by increasing the rate of interest on the capital stock. In the first case the marginal products of labor and of capital in terms of subsistence goods would remain constant, but the increase in the purchaisng power of consumer goods over investment goods would raise the rate of interest; in the second case the growth of the labor force relative to the capital stock required to reduce the marginal product of labor in terms of investment goods sufficiently to offset the lower relative price of subsistence goods in terms of investment goods would raise the marginal product of capital in terms of investment goods (the rate of interest).

The full details of a model of this kind must be reserved for elaboration in another paper. But such a model has obvious and potentially important implications for the problems of economic development and of the terms of trade between advanced and less developed countries, problems with which Charles Kindleberger has been deeply concerned throughout his professional career.

References

[1] Bhagwati, Jagdish, "Immiserizing Growth: A Geometric Note." *Review of Economic Studies,* Vol. XXV(3), No. 68 (June 1958) pp. 201–205, reprinted as Chapter 13, pp. 325–331 of *Trade, Tariffs and Growth,* op. cit, and as Chapter 18, pp. 300–305 in R.E. Caves and H.G. Johnson (eds), *Readings in International Economics* (Homewood, Ill.: Richard D. Irwin, 1968).

[2] Bhagwati, Jagdish. "International Trade and Economic Expansion." *American Economic Review,* Vol. 48 no. 5 (December 1958), pp. 941–953, reprinted in his *Trade, Tariffs and Growth* (London: Weidenfeld and Nicholson, 1969) Chapter 12, pp. 311–324.

[3] Bhagwati, Jagdish. *The Theory and Practice of Commercial Policy: Departures from Unified Exchange Rates.* (Princeton, N.J.: Princeton University International Finance Section, Special Papers in International Economics No. 8, January 1968).

[4] Borts, G.H. "Professor Meade on Economic Growth." *Economica,* N.S., Vol. 29, no. 113 (February 1962), pp. 72–86.

[5] Corden, W.M. "Economic Expansion and International Trade: A Geometric Approach." *Oxford Economic Papers,* N.S., Vol. 8, no. 2 (June 1956), pp. 223–228.

[6] Findlay, R. and Grubert, H. "Factor Intensities, Technological Progress, and the Terms of Trade." *Oxford Economic Papers,* N.S., Vol. 11, no. 1 (February 1959), pp. 111–121.

[7] Johnson, H.G. "Economic Expansion and International Trade." *Manchester School of Economic and Social Studies.* Vol. 23, no. 2 (May 1955), pp. 95–112, reprinted in *International Trade and Economic Growth* (London: Allen and Unwin, 1958) Chapter 3, pp. 65–93.

[8] Johnson, H.G. "International Trade, Income Distribution and the Offer Curve." *The Manchester School of Economic and Social Studies,* Vol. 27, no. 3 (September 1959), pp. 241–260.

[9] Laing, N.F. "A Diagrammatic Approach to General Equilibrium Analysis." *Review of Economic Studies.* Vol. XXX(1), no. 82 (February 1963), pp. 43–55.

[10] Laing, N.F. "A Geometrical Analysis of Some Theorems on Steady Growth." *Journal of Political Economy,* Vol. 72, no. 4 (October 1964), pp. 476–482.

[11] Oniki, H. and Uzawa, H. "Patterns of Trade and Investment in a Dynamic Model of International Trade." *Review of Economic Studies,* Vol. 32, no. 89 (January 1965), pp. 15–38.

[12] Ramaswami, V.K. "On Two-Sector Neo-Classical Growth." Oxford Economic Papers, Vol. 21, no. 2 (July 1969), pp. 142–160.

[13] Rybczynski, T.M. "Factor Endowment and Relative Commodity Prices." *Economica,* N.S., Vol. XXII, no. 88 (November 1955), pp. 336–341.

[14] Stiglitz, J.E. "Factor Price Equalization in a Dynamic Economy." *Journal of Political Economy,* Vol. 78, No. 6 (November 1970), pp. 456–488.

CHAPTER 8

THE "FOREIGN EXCHANGE GAP" AND GROWTH IN DEVELOPING ECONOMIES

Ronald FINDLAY

The view is now very widely held that the critical bottleneck restricting the rate of growth in the developing countries is the shortage of foreign exchange. The intellectual roots of this concept spread in many directions. The Latin American "structuralist" school has long maintained that the "limited capacity to import" in relation to high and inelastic import requirements has been one of the main factors responsible for the chronic inflation and stagnation in that part of the world. The Indian strategy of development as exemplified in the second Five Year Plan inspired by the theories of Professor P.C. Mahalanobis based on the assumption of a closed economy also encountered the foreign exchange bottleneck as import requirements for new capital goods industries outran the earnings available from stagnant export sectors. Finally there has been the influence of the programming models of Professor Chenery and his various associates that have apparently identified foreign exchange as being the effective binding constraint for many countries.[1] All of these diverse influences have crystal-

* I am grateful to S. Szekeres and R.M. Sundrum for discussions on the subject of this paper and to J. Bhagwati, J. Vanek, and members of seminars at Columbia and M.I.T. for comments on a first draft.

[1] See in particular Chenery, H. and Bruno, M., "Development Alternatives for an Open Economy: the Case of Israel." *Economic Journal*, 1962; and Chenery, H. and Strout, A., "Foreign Assistance and Economic Development," *American Economic Review*, September, 1966. Other contributions to the "gap" theory that might be mentioned are McKinnon, R. "Foreign Exchange Constraints and Efficient Aid Allocation." *Economic Journal*, June, 1964, and Linder, S.B. *Trade and Trade Policy for Economic Development*. J. Bhagwati has drawn my attention to his paper "The Nature of Balance of Payments Difficulties in Developing Countries," in *Measures for Trade Expansion of Developing Countries,* Proceedings of a Japan Economic Research Center Conference), Japan Economic Research Center, October 1966; this paper takes a position similar to the one presented here.

lized in the UNCTAD conferences where the doctrine of the foreign exchange constraint has been developed and institutionalized in the Secretariat, under the leadership of Dr. Prebisch.

While this view has come to be widely held in "development" circles, it appears that there is not much sympathy for it among the majority of professional economists, whose natural reaction on being told that there is a "shortage" of something is to feel that this must be caused by interferences with the free play of the price mechanism, in this case by governments in the market for foreign exchange.

In this paper we shall attempt to examine the foreign exchange constraint doctrine from the standpoint of the pure theory of international trade, hoping to be able to identify precisely the assumptions on which it depends and the manner in which it might restrict the growth rates attainable in developing economies.

8.1

In terms of conventional economic theory, the fundamental constraint on growth is the willingness to save. Given the productivity of capital the greater the willingness of a society to save, that is, to restrain its consumption, the greater will be the growth of its total product. It is, however, asserted that in some cases developing economies may be in a situation where raising the rate of saving will have no effect on the rate of growth which is taken as being determined by the availability of foreign exchange.

The possibility of this can be shown by means of the following simple model. Suppose that a country produces a single commodity that can be used for consumption, investment or export. Imports obtainable at a fixed price in terms of exports are needed only for investment, in fixed proportions with domestic output. Production of domestic output is a function of the stock of capital alone. The working of the model is best explained in Figure 8.1.

The distance OU measures the maximum attainable level of domestic production with the initial capital stock. With a given propensity to consume a distance, OR can be marked off denoting the amount of domestic output consumed. The slope of UV indicates the terms of trade. A family of L-shaped isoquants for investment goods output can be drawn with origin at R, the slope of the line through R indicating the proportions in which domestic and imported inputs are used in investment. The maximum level of investment is measured by RV and domestic output is divided between OR of consumption, RS of investment, and SU of exports which is exchanged for

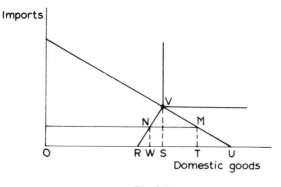

Fig. 8.1

VS of imports. The lower the propensity to consume, the closer will *R* be to the origin and the larger, therefore, will be the level of investment, and, with a given capital-output ratio, the higher the rate of growth.

Suppose, however, that the economy is only able to export *UT* or, alternatively, that *MT* is the maximum level of imports obtainable regardless of the level of exports. In this case the maximum level of investment obtainable is measured by *RN* and *WT* of domestic output will be redundant since only *RW* is required for investment and only *TU* need or can be exported. The "foreign exchange gap" will be measured by the difference between *VS* and *MT*. Under these circumstances reducing the propensity to consume will not raise investment at all but will simply increase the amount of domestic output which is redundant.

The situation can also be represented in terms of a diagram showing the trade off between consumption and investment as in Figure 8.2. The cost of a unit of investment in terms of domestic goods can be obtained by adding the direct input of these goods required per unit of investment to the imported input required, the latter being valued at the fixed terms of trade. If all domestic output is used for consumption, then *OJ* will be the maximum available, and with no constraints on trade, society could transform *OJ* of consumption into a maximum of *OK* investment. Let *HL* and *OL* indicate the levels of consumption and investment that would be chosen in the absence of constraints on trade. If a constraint on trade were to exist such that *OL'* were the maximum feasible level of investment, then reducing consumption below *H'L'* would have no effect on investment and growth since the marginal domestic resources freed would not be transformable into imports which are essential for investment. This is the sense in which it is asserted that the

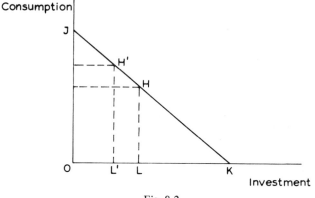

Fig. 8.2

willingness to save and invest on the part of the developing countries is "frustrated" by the foreign exchange constraint.

Several policy implications have been drawn from this analysis. One is the need for export promotion and/or import substitution in the development strategy of the country itself. Another is the need for reduction in the obstacles to trade expansion placed in the way of the developing countries' efforts to penetrate the markets of developed countries. In addition there is the argument that foreign aid will be more productive under these circumstances than in the case where a more conventional shortage of saving is at the basis of the failure for developing countries to grow more rapidly.

This last point can be illustrated in Figure 8.3. With no trade constraint, the maximum level of investment with a given propensity to consume and no foreign aid will be indicated by the point V. If foreign aid of UZ is given, the maximum level of investment will be shifted to V'. Observe that imports do not rise by the full amount of the foreign aid since exports are reduced by SS' in order to release complementary domestic inputs for investment. In the case where the foreign exchange constraint is binding, instead of the saving constraint, there will be redundant domestic output which means that imports for investment purposes can increase by the full amount of the foreign aid. The growth-promoting effect of foreign aid is thus higher in the latter instance. [2] In terms of Figure 8.3 V' will be directly above V and SS' will come out of consumption instead of exports.

[2] This result assumes fixed values of all the relevant parameters. In private correspondence J. Vanek has pointed out that if the marginal propensity to save is

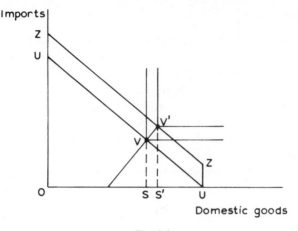

Fig. 8.3

The simple model that we have been discussing appears to elucidate the main propositions of the theory of foreign exchange constraint, stripped of the details of the elaborate programming models in which they are usually embedded. How generally acceptable these conclusions are will naturally depend on how plausible the assumptions are. It is easy to see that the analysis depends critically on the impossibility of substituting domestic for imported inputs into the production of the investment goods sector. While the assumption of rigidly fixed technical coefficients may be valid in each particular line of investment, the overall proportions can be changed by varying the composition of investment so that the model assumes that not only techniques but also demand patterns as well are rigidly determined. The model as presented here assumes that imported goods are not required for consumption purposes, although it would make no difference if there was assumed to be a fixed requirement of imports for consumption as well. In the next section, we shall elaborate the model to include consumption of imported goods, with the proportion of imported and domestic goods consumed depending on relative prices.

greater than the average a process of growth with foreign aid to ease a savings gap will eventually become self-sustaining whereas there is no such automatic mechanism for aid given to ease a foreign exchange gap to become self-liquidating unless specific policies are pursued to that end.

8.2

The extension of the model to handle choice between imported and domestic consumer goods is easily accomplished by an adaptation of the basic diagram of the first section. In Figure 8.4, let OU represent the maximum level of domestic production and the slope of UU', the terms of trade. Given the propensity to save, the line RR' can be determined, indicating the resources available for investment. The point X, where the family of L-shaped isoquants is tangential to RR', determines the imported and domestic inputs into investment as well as serving as the origin for a family of consumption indifference curves. It is convenient, though not strictly necessary for all the results that follow, to assume that these curves are "homothetic." The point V where the indifference curve system is tangential to UU' represents the equilibrium point for the economy as a whole in the absence of any constraints on trade. The higher the propensity to save the higher will be the output of investment goods and the rate of growth.

As before we can imagine that there is a restriction on trade such that $OUYY'$ instead of OUU' becomes the feasible set. The effect of this on growth depends upon whether consumption or investment bears the burden of the reduced opportunities available. In Figure 8.4, it would be possible to maintain the level of investment by switching consumption from V to Y, but since Y could well be below the point on UU' where it is cut by the investment isoquant through X, it is conceivable that there is no reduction in consumption that will allow the desired investment level to be maintained.

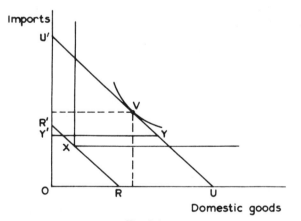

Fig. 8.4

Thus the foreign exchange constraint doctrine would appear to be valid even when there is a choice between imported and domestic consumption.

This conclusion, however, requires further examination. First, we need to be more specific about the constraint on trade. If the limitation is caused by internal factors restricting the supply of exports, the policy implication is obviously that these should be removed. To be relevant the restriction must be one that because of conditions in foreign markets is beyond the control of the domestic authorities. Suppose that world demand is such that the country can export and import at fixed terms up to the point Y but that beyond that point increasing exports results in a constant supply of imports, in other words the demand for exports has unitary elasticity beyond the point Y. The "offer curve" of the rest of the world is, therefore, UYY'.

The equilibrium terms of trade and export-import volumes can be determined by constructing a domestic offer curve to match against the foreign offer curve UYY'. The terms of trade can be varied by rotating UU' on U. Given the propensity to save the resources available for investment at each value of the terms of trade can be obtained by rotating RR' on R, parallel to the rotation of UU' on U. At each value of the terms of trade the tangency of the investment isoquants with RR' will give the imported and domestic inputs required for investment as well as the origin for placing the consumption indifference map to determine the overall pattern of demand for imported and domestic goods by tangency with the parallel UU'. The locus of all these points form the domestic offer curve UVV' in Figure 8.5.

The equilibrium terms of trade will be measured by the slope of UZ where Z is the point of intersection of the domestic and foreign offer curves. The point Z will obviously be inferior to point V, but it should be noted that V is essentially irrelevant to the problem facing the country. It only plays a role if

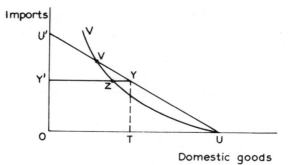

Fig. 8.5

it is assumed that any desired volume of trade can take place at terms equal to the slope of UU', in which case it would represent the equilibrium point. The "foreign exchange gap" analysis starts by calculating foreign exchange required at too favorable terms and thus arrives at a gap by deducting foreign exchange actually available. At the equilibrium terms of trade UZ requirements and availabilities are exactly matched and there is no gap.

As one moves along the domestic offer curve from U to V' the rate of growth will be rising. The fixed propensity to save means that the value of investment in terms of domestic goods is the same all along the offer curve, but since the cost of a unit of investment goods in terms of domestic goods is lower the more favorable the terms of trade the greater will be the increment of capital in real terms and hence the higher the rate of growth as one moves along the domestic offer curve from U to V'. The growth rate of the economy will, therefore, be lower at Z than at V.

The free trade equilibrium point Z, however, is clearly not an optimum point since the point Y which is also on the foreign offer curve would give the same amount of foreign goods for the exchange of less domestic goods. A centrally planned economy, for example, could export UT of domestic goods and import TY of foreign goods. These imports and the remaining OT of domestic goods could then be allocated through the price mechanism, with the relative price of the goods changing until equilibrium is established. The socially desired propensity to save can be introduced by allocating to the investment sector the appropriate fraction of national income evaluated by applying the price ratio at each round of the trial and error process to the combination of OT domestic goods and YT imports.

Alternatively, the state could impose a tariff and redistribute the proceeds in such a way that the domestic offer curve is shrunk in to intersect the foreign offer curve at Y instead of Z. In either case, the slope of the line PP' through Y in Figure 8.6 could represent the equilibrium internal price ratio between the two goods, representing a premium on foreign goods as compared with the external terms of trade represented by the slope of UU'.

The rate of growth of the economy will be higher at Y than at Z. Since the internal relative price of imports is higher at Y than at Z, this statement requires some proof, which is provided in Figure 8.6. The points Z and Y in Figure 8.5 in effect determine two "boxes" of commodity availabilities, which are shown in Figure 8.6. The origin of the consumption indifference map can be placed at the northeast corner of the boxes instead of at the tangency point of the investment isoquants, as in the usual box diagram analysis. Let A be the original equilibrium point inside the box diagram, corresponding to Z. As a result of making the optimal trade restriction

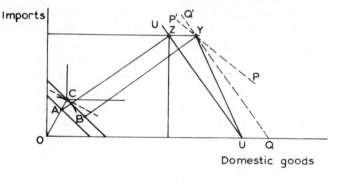

Fig. 8.6

through either state control or tariff policy the point Y becomes attainable, with more domestic goods and the same amount of imports. Suppose that the same internal price ratio were to prevail at Y as at Z, this being indicated by QQ' through Y having the same slope as UU' through Z. With the same propensity to save, C would now represent the equilibrium point for investment goods and B for consumption. Clearly there is an excess demand for imports and excess supply of domestic goods. The relative price of imports has, therefore, to be raised. This will increase national income measured in terms of the domestic good and also raise proportionately the value of investment in terms of domestic goods, since the propensity to save is fixed. The fraction of imports allocated to investment, however, remains the same as at C, since by virtue of the fixed propensity to save, pivoting the relative price line on Y implies pivoting it in parallel fashion on C. In equilibrium the relative price line will have the slope of PP' and the line through C parallel to PP' will be tangential to a consumption indifference curve at C. Investment is, therefore, larger and with the same production of domestic goods the rate of growth corresponding to Y will be higher than that corresponding to Z. Consumers, however, will have less imports at Y than at Z although they will have more domestic goods to compensate for this.

The way Figure 8.6 is drawn assumes that the investment goods sector has a higher ratio of imported to domestic goods at the same price ratio than consumption, but the results will still hold in the opposite case as well.

The analysis so far has assumed a fixed propensity to save. The effect of a change in this propensity on the rate of growth can readily be ascertained for both the free trade and optimal trade cases. The free trade case is analyzed first in Figure 8.7. In this diagram UT and ZT are the volumes of exports and

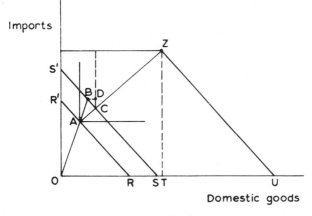

Fig. 8.7

imports respectively and the slope of UZ measures the terms of trade in free trade equilibrium. Here RR' is the line denoting the value of resources devoted to investment corresponding to the original propensity to save. Taking Z as the origin for the consumption indifference map, A is the original equilibrium position where an investment isoquant and a consumption indifference curve are tangential to each other. Suppose now that there is an increase in the propensity to save such that the investment line is shifted from RR' to SS'. The investment equilibrium point shifts to B and the consumption equilibrium point to C resulting in an excess demand for imports of CD and excess supply of domestic goods of BD. The terms of trade will thus move adversely for the country resulting in an exchange of more exports for the same amount of imports. This means that the investment line will swing to the left with the point S remaining fixed which will have the effect of reducing investment below the level attained at B. The question is whether it is possible for this to reverse completely the increase in the propensity to save. The adverse shift in the terms of trade must result in a reduction in consumption demand for imports (since imports are not inferior goods by hypothesis) and so the new equilibrium position must be somewhere on OAB above the point C. But since C is already above A, we see that the terms of trade shift cannot reverse the expansion of investment completely. Thus the greater the propensity to save, the greater the rate of growth. If consumption were more "import intensive" than investment, an increase in the propensity to save will improve the terms of trade and so investment will increase even more in this case.

In the optimal trade situation, the same results will follow except that the availability of each good will be the same before and after the change in the propensity to save, since it is only the internal and not the external price ratio that will be affected by the change in demand.

8.3

In the model of the previous section, we have shown how the equilibrium terms of trade and rate of growth are determined, given the propensity to save. No "foreign exchange gap" appeared since the relative prices of domestic and foreign goods adjust to clear any disequilibrium in the foreign exchange market. This conclusion requires reconciliation with the contention that the nature of the "foreign exchange gap" in developing countries is a situation that no amount of relative price adjustment can alleviate, with the result that the only solution is the provision of the requisite amount of foreign aid. Professor Janoslav Vanek, for example, has recently expressed this point of view. [3]

The difference between our formulation and his is that he takes the rate of growth as given once and for all, so that variation in the relative price of foreign and domestic goods has no effect on the foreign exchange required for investment since fixed proportions of the two types of inputs is of course assumed. With a ceiling imposed on foreign exchange earnings also by hypothesis, we have a situation where both the demand and supply for foreign exchange are perfectly inelastic, with the former exceeding the latter to produce the gap that has to be filled by aid.

It is clear, however, that the postulated conditions cannot hold in any actual market situation. As the terms of trade shift adversely, the real income of the country is reduced, and the maintenance of a fixed investment programme implies that the propensity to save is rising. If the fixed gap theory is interpreted literally, it would imply that the propensity to save can increase to 100 percent and even beyond! What is perfectly correct and reasonable is to point out that if a certain "required" rate of growth is postulated, and the trading conditions facing the country and the propensity to save are also taken as being given, then the required growth rate may not be attainable without foreign assistance. In the absence of such assistance, the growth rate will be reduced to conformity with the other conditions through the

---

[3] Vanek, J. *Estimating Foreign Resource Needs for Economic Development*, (New York: McGraw-Hill Book Co., Inc., 1967), Chapter 6.

adjustment of relative foreign and domestic prices. The price adjustment wipes out the gap through reducing both consumption and investment demand for imports. Thus when critics of the gap theory assert that the so-called gap is only the manifestation of an over-valued currency and when proponents of the theory assert that it is a fundamental "structural" phenomenon, both are in a sense right; while relative price adjustment can close the gap, it cannot do so in a way that leaves the growth rate at the original level.

The question that now arises is whether the postulated growth rate can be attained without foreign aid if there is an increase in the propensity to save, trading opportunities remaining the same. To answer the question let us consider the foreign offer curve UYY' in the diagrams of the previous section. Assume first that imports are required only for investment. With a zero propensity to save, there will of course be no trade and no growth. Increasing the propensity to save will lead to increasing trade volumes and to the rate of growth increasing in the same proportion as the propensity to save since the terms of trade will be constant along the segment UY of the foreign offer curve. Raising the propensity to save beyond the point where the investment isoquant is tangential to UYY' at Y, however, leads to worsening of the terms of trade while leaving the rate of growth, measured in terms of the domestic good, unchanged. The relationship between the saving rate, terms of trade, and the growth rate is depicted in Figure 8.8.

Figure 8.8 shows that OA is the maximum effective propensity to save. Going beyond that leaves the growth rate unchanged and is furthermore "immiserizing" since it reduces consumption as well. If the required growth

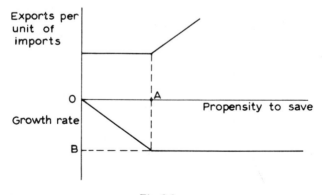

Fig. 8.8

rate is less than *OB* it will be attainable without foreign assistance provided that the propensity to save is sufficiently high. If the propensity to save is not as high as necessary then there is a "saving gap" and the role of foreign assistance in this case is to supplement the inadequate domestic saving. If the desired growth rate is greater than *OB* it is impossible for the country to attain that rate without foreign assistance, whatever the level of its propensity to save. Growth in this case is limited by the "shortage" of foreign exchange in relation to the import requirements of investment.

Suppose now that imports are required for consumption as well. Then the analysis of Section 8.2 for the free trade case indicates that the diagram corresponding to Figure 8.8 will be as shown in Figure 8.9.

The difference from Figure 8.8 is that the growth rate continues to increase as the propensity to save is increased but it cannot go beyond the level *OC* which is the growth rate corresponding to a propensity to save of 100 percent. Thus, unlike the case of Figure 8.8 beyond the level *OA*, increases in the propensity to save are never useless from the point of view of increasing the growth rate, but the marginal effectiveness is nevertheless diminishing. Growth rates higher than *OC* are impossible to attain without foreign assistance. The effect of introducing imports of consumption is thus to extend the growth rates attainable in the absence of foreign assistance from *OB* to *OC*. Of course, in practice, there will be a limit to the extent to

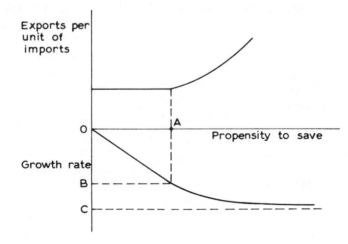

Fig. 8.9

which the propensity to save can be raised so that foreign assistance will be necessary for growth rates lower than OC or even perhaps OB.

It is interesting to note that raising the propensity to save beyond OA in this model makes the country worse off in general, since more exports of domestic goods have to be given for the same volume of total imports but, nevertheless, has a favorable effect on growth through releasing more imports for investment rather than consumption. If there is government intervention to maintain a constant level of exports, the optimal trade case, then the overall availabilities of commodities will remain the same but with an increasing amount of each diverted to investment. The change in relative prices will be purely internal, the external terms of trade being fixed.

Throughout we have been assuming fixed coefficients in investment. Suppose, however, that imported and domestic inputs could be substitued continuously for each other as in a neoclassical production function, but that investment remains more import intensive than consumption. To get even closer to conventional trade theory, let us also assume that the foreign offer curve has the usual convex slope instead of being composed of two linear segments. The analysis of Section 8.2 can be applied readily to this model also and a diagram corresponding to Figures 8.8 and 8.9 obtained. It is obvious that the only difference from Figure 8.9 would be that the linear segments of each curve up to OA would disappear so that we have a smoothly convex curve in each panel of the diagram.

The foreign exchange constraint doctrine has been interpreted here as a ceiling on foreign exchange earnings. It is possible to go further and assert that the foreign offer curve turns downward instead of just flattening out so that more exports result in *less* instead of the same amount of imports. Under these circumstances raising the rate of saving could result in lowering the rate of growth after a point. While foreign demand for exports could well be inelastic for particular countries and commodities, such as coffee from Brazil, it is perhaps rather implausible to expect such a relation to hold for exports as a whole, unless there is some reason for the reduction in consumption to be concentrated heavily on nontradable goods. If such a condition were to hold, however, it then follows that there would again be a limit on the effective rate of saving.

Taking the opposite extreme critics of the gap doctrine frequently point to the experience of Hong Kong, Taiwan, and other countries in attaining very high rates of export growth. Against this view it can be argued that such "export miracles" are possible only for some small countries, so that the doctrine is interpreted to hold for the developing world as a whole and not for every individual country. Such conditions would appear to be likely since labor-intensive manufactures have usually been the goods involved and advanced countries appear to be very sensitive to having their markets penetrated in this sphere. [4]

8.4

The analysis of this paper has attempted to show that the implication derived from the "foreign exchange gap" theory, that increases in the propensity to save may have no effect in raising the rate of growth in less developed countries, is not valid if there are imports for consumption as well as investment. What is true, even under much weaker assumptions about the technology of investment and trading opportunities, is that attempting to raise the rate of growth in a developing country through increasing the propensity to save can run into diminishing returns through worsening terms of trade if investment is more import-intensive than consumption. More saving is never redundant but it can become less and less effective in raising the rate of growth while of course being more and more costly in terms of consumption foregone. If foreign demand for exports is of less than unit elasticity, it is possible for increased saving to reduce the rate of growth.

This formulation of the problem in more familiar terms would appear to be more satisfactory since it can include the usual "gap" model as a special case while retaining the main point of the argument, that limited trading opportunities restrict the growth which less developed countries can attain through their efforts alone.

---

[4] In this connection see the interesting exchange between Myint and Urquidi in *International Economic Relations* edited by P. Samuelson (New York: The MacMillan Co., 1969).

CHAPTER 9

OPTIMUM TRADE AND DEVELOPMENT POLICY IN A DUAL ECONOMY*

Pranab K.BARDHAN

9.1. Trade and the Preobrazhensky Dilemma

The standard aggregative models of development planning for a dual economy incorporate two important institutional assumptions: (a) the industrial sector is more or less under the direct control of the Government, whereas the agricultural sector is largely in the hands of private cultivators and (b) the industrial *real* wage rate is institutionally fixed. These two typical institutional assumptions together with a third institutional presumption — that it is politically difficult to implement any program of substantial *direct* taxation of agriculture in most developing economies — make the problem of ensuring sufficient marketed surplus of food as one of the most important problems of development. For rapid growth of the economy, the planner wants to ensure more production of industrial goods including investment goods, but that involves more industrial employment and transfer of labor from the agricultural sector. Since industrial workers at their low levels of income spend most of their wages on food, thé Government needs more food to feed the growing industrial labor force. Under the institutional assumptions made, the Government is denied both compulsory procurement (such as that in the Soviet Union after agricultural collectivization) and heavy direct taxation of agriculture (such as land taxation in Meiji Japan[1]) as significant ways of tapping the agricultural surplus. Therefore, the only major ways of getting more food are either (a) to exert the Government monopsony power[2]

* I am grateful to Sanjit Bose, Amartya Sen, and T.N.Srinivasan for helpful discussion. Errors are, of course, mine.

[1] For footnote, see next page.

[2] For footnote, see next page.

in buying food by suitably manipulating price policy or (b) to invest more in the production of agricultural inputs that help more food production and therefore sales. The difficulty with (a) is that, if the industrial real wage in terms of food is institutionally given, then higher food prices which might be needed to cajole more sales from farmers will raise the industrial wage bill and thus cut down on the industrial investible surplus and capital accumulation. The difficulty with (b) is that more investment in agricultural inputs will again reduce industrial capital accumulation. The essential trade-offs involved make for an interesting exercise in inter-temporal optimization which has hardly been attempted in the literature[3].

Foreign trade and borrowing enabling imports of food and agricultural inputs are partial ways out of the difficulties mentioned earlier, although more imports mean more diversion of investible resources to the export industries (even assuming that there is no external demand bottleneck limiting export possibilities) and, as for borrowing, much depends on the rate of interest charged and the repayment schedule. Our purpose in this paper is to analyze the problems of optimum development policy in the context of a simple model of such a dual economy open to foreign trade and borrowing.

---

[1] The contribution of land taxes to mobilization of agricultural surplus in Japan after Meiji Restoration has sometimes been overplayed in the literature. Nakamura [13] points out that high rural savings in Meiji Japan were mainly due to the drastic land reforms in early Meiji period which redistributed income from the ruling classes (particularly the *samurai*) of the Tokugawa period to the land-owning classes who had a larger propensity to save, and that direct taxes as proportion of agricultural output were actually much lower in the Meiji period than in the preceding Tokugawa period.

[2] As early as 1926, the Soviet economist Preobrazhenski [15], p. 111, suggested in this context, among other things, the "carrying out on the basis of monopoly a price policy which will be only another form of taxation of private economy".

Preobrazhenski seems to be among the first economists to grapple with the marketed surplus problem and all the dilemmas that arise from rapid industrialization in a partially planned economy where industry is largely state-owned but agriculture is run by private farms: the problems of what he called "primitive socialist accumulation" that were being faced in the Soviet Union of the 1920s. Agricultural collectivization was Stalin's way out of the Preobrazhenski dilemma in the beginning of the 1930s.

[3] Some partial attempts have been made by Findlay [6], Hornby [8], and others. More attention in the literature on dual-economy planning has been concentrated on the intertemporal optimization problem involved in choosing the right techniques of industrial production because of the link between capital intensity of techniques and savings. See Eckstein [5], Sen [17], Marglin [12], and Dixit [3]. The historical-descriptive literature on development of dual economy has also largely ignored the issues raised by the marketed surplus problem. See, for example, Jorgenson [9] and Ranis and Fei [6].

The industrial sector directly controlled by the Government produces two goods, good m — which is either consumable ("textiles") or investible ("machines")[4] — and good n — which is an agricultural input ("fertilizer"). Their production functions are given by

$$F_i = F_i(K_i, L_i), \qquad i = m, n \tag{9.1}$$

where F_i is the output of the ith good, K_i and L_i are the amount of capital and labor employed respectively in producing the ith good. The production functions are assumed to be of constant returns to scale.

The total industrial labor force is given by

$$L = L_m + L_n . \tag{9.2}$$

The industrial wage rate, deflated by the domestic price of food P_f, is an institutionally given constant $\bar{W}$. The total industrial wage bill is therefore given by $P_f \bar{W} L$. Since we are assuming all wages to be consumed,

$$P_f \bar{W} L = P_f C_f + C_m \tag{9.3}$$

where C_f is the amount of food consumed and C_m is the amount of "textiles" consumed by the industrial labor force. Good m is being taken as the numeraire. We shall assume that in the industrial sector the laborers are the only consumers and all remaining industrial surplus is invested.

Total industrial consumption of food is out of supplies from the domestic agricultural sector or imports, so that

$$C_f = S + Z_f \tag{9.4}$$

where S is the surplus of food marketed by the agricultural sector and Z_f is the amount of food imported. It is assumed that all foreign trade (and borrowing) is directly handled by the government and all imported food is distributed only in the industrial sector.

The total amount N of fertilizers used in agricultural production comes either from domestic production of fertilizers in the industrial sector or from imports, so that

---

[4] For simplification we are assuming that "textiles" and "machines" are produced on the same production function.

$$N = F_n + Z_n \tag{9.5}$$

where Z_n is the amount imported of n.

We assume that foreign trade is balanced not instantaneously but over the planning horizon T so that

$$\int_0^T [\bar{P}_f Z_f + \bar{P}_n Z_n + Z_m]\ e^{-rt} dt = 0 \tag{9.6}$$

where $\bar{P}_i$ is the fixed international price of the ith good ($i = f,n$), and Z_m is the amount imported of m (textiles or machines), and r is the given rate of interest at which the country can borrow abroad to cover a current deficit. We are assuming that the country is not a big enough buyer or seller of goods in the world goods market (we shall relax this assumption later) nor a big enough borrower or lender in the world capital market to be able to affect the international prices or the rate of interest.

Vis-a-vis the domestic agricultural sector, the industrial sector faces a marketed-surplus function (offer curve) for food by cultivators, so that

$$S = S(P_f, N) . \tag{9.7}$$

Marketed surplus[5] is directly a function of P_f in the sense that if the Government, the monopsonistic buyer of food, raises its price, more food will be sold by cultivators, i.e.,

$$S_1 = \frac{\partial S}{\partial P_f} > 0 .$$

Marketed surplus also depends on cultivators' use of fertilizers in the sense that new inputs such as chemical fertilizers embody technical progress for traditional agriculture and shift the production functions so that the rise in output brought about by use of fertilizers raises farm sales of food (if farmers' marginal propensity to consume food is less than unity, more output will lead to more sales).

How much fertilizer the farmers would use, of course, depends on the

---

[5] There is a growing volume of literature on estimation of price elasticity of marketed surplus of foodgrains in peasant economies. It is generally agreed that the *long-run* price elasticity of marketed surplus of foodgrains is positive. See Rajkrishna [10], Behrman [2], Bardhan and Bardhan [1].

price of fertilizers they have to pay relative to the price of food at which they can sell their output, i.e., on the ratio P_n/P_f. Thus

$$N = N\left(\frac{P_n}{P_f}\right), \qquad N'\left(\frac{P_n}{P_f}\right) < 0 . \tag{9.8}$$

when the fertilizer-crop price ratio rises, the farmers use less fertilizers. From eq. (9.8), the prices P_f and P_n affect market surplus S of eq. (9.7) in this indirect way as well.

The balance of trade between the industrial and the agricultural sector of the country is given by

$$P_f S = C_m^a + N P_n \tag{9.9}$$

where C_m^a is the amount (and value) of textiles consumed by the agricultural sector. The left-hand side of eq. (9.9) is the value of imports of food by the industrial sector from the agricultural sector, and the right-hand side gives the value of its exports to the agricultural sector. It is to be noted that the Government sells to the agricultural sector both its own output of fertilizers and also all imported fertilizers at price P_n.

As for new investment the choice is to invest in sector m (producing textiles or machines) and/or to invest in sector n (producing fertilizers). But once investment is made and capital is installed in a sector, it is assumed that it cannot be taken out and used in any other sector — the so-called "non-shiftability of capital" assumption. New investment is given by

$$\dot{K} = \dot{K}_m + \dot{K}_n = F_m + Z_m - C_m - C_m^a . \tag{9.10}$$

The extreme right-hand side of eq. (9.10) gives the surplus of investible m available (through domestic production and imports) over consumption of m by both the industrial and the agricultural sectors.

$$\dot{K}_n = \lambda \dot{K} \text{ and } \dot{K}_m = (1-\lambda)\dot{K} \tag{9.11}$$

where λ is the proportion (to be chosen) of new investment devoted to sector n.

It remains to specify the social objective function that the planner is supposed to maximize. We take it as

$$\max \int_0^T U(C_f, C_m) e^{-\rho t} dt + \alpha [K_m(T) + K_n(T)] e^{-\rho T} \tag{9.12}$$

where U is a concave instantaneous utility function, and ρ is a positive and constant rate of time discount, and α is a given constant. (For simplification we are assuming that the planners give equal weight to the terminal capital stocks of the two types.) The immediate objection to such a welfare function is that it ignores the welfare of the agricultural sector, and only consumption in the industrial sector enters as an argument in the utility function. As the experienced reader must have surmised, this is our grudging compromise with analytic tractability in this model of fairly complicated relationships. As a weak excuse, we might point out that in almost all of the dual-economy planning literature cited so far the welfare of the agricultural sector is ignored: for example, it is explicitly ignored in Marglin [12] and Dixit [3] and indirectly ignored by using objectives such as maximizing investment — or maximizing the steady-state rate of growth — as in Hornby [8]. The concentration on the industrial sector is meant mainly to bring out the implications of a policy of rapid industrialization in bold features.

The basic purpose of this paper is not to formulate a national planning model but to formalize the Preobrazhenski problem of optimum "exploitation" of the agricultural sector for the sake of rapid industrialization under some of the institutional constraints mentioned at the beginning of the paper. One may envisage a situation in which the Government, through suitable price policies, tries to squeeze the maximum out of the *kulak*s (who are in many developing countries the major providers of marketed surplus of foodgrains) whereas the non*kulak* subsistence farmers form a self-contained economy that is outside the model[6].

---

[6] Mrinal Datta Choudhuri gave me an ingenious alternative explanation of the model in terms of industrial development of an imperialist economy on the basis of exploiting a colony. The agricultural sector in the paper stands for the colony specializing in primary products. The metropolitan economy produces either good n (which may stand for, say, transportation: think of the British railway investments in colonies in the 19th century) that goes to increase the supply of exports of primary products by the colony, or good m (which is textiles and machines). The model thus analyzes the optimal development policy of an industrializing imperialist economy! It might be interesting to recall that Preobrazhenski talked about "the accumulation in the hands of the State of material means obtained chiefly from sources lying outside the State economic system"; these outside spheres of economy were termed "colonies" and the necessary economic basis of the transition period was, according to him, a relation of "exploitation" between the "metropolis" of State industry and its surrounding colonies, the former drawing in "surplus value" from the latter whereby it expanded the basis of industry, its productivity, and the possibility of living on its own surplus, until finally the petty private economy was crushed out and "engulfed" in the socialist economy. See the discussion by Dobb [4], p. 184, on this point.

9.2. **Optimum investment and trade policy**

Taking all the constraints together, we can now write our Hamiltonian H as given by

$$He^{\rho t} = U(C_f, C_m) - \gamma \left[Z_m + \bar{P}_f Z_f + \bar{P}_n \right.$$

$$\left. \{N\left(\frac{P_n}{P_f}\right) - F_n(K_n, L_n)\} \right] e^{(\rho-r)t} + q\dot{K} \qquad (9.13)$$

where

$$C_f = S\left[P_f, N\left(\frac{P_n}{P_f}\right) \right] + Z_f$$

$$C_m = P_f[\bar{W}L - C_f] , \qquad L = L_m + L_n$$

γ is a constant (as yet) undetermined multiplier

$$\dot{K} = F_m(K_m, L_m) + Z_m + N\left(\frac{P_n}{P_f}\right)P_n - P_f\bar{W}L + P_f Z_f$$

and

$$q = [\lambda q_n + (1-\lambda)q_m]$$

where q_i is the imputed price of investment in industry producing the ith good $(i = m, n)$. The Hamiltonian is to be maximized with respect to the control variables Z_f, Z_m, L_m, L_n, P_f, P_n, and λ. (We shall assume that both food and textiles are consumed and both produced in positive amounts in the industrial sector.) This immediately gives us the following first-order conditions:

$$q - \gamma e^{(\rho-r)t} = 0 \qquad (9.14)$$

$$(U_1 - U_2 P_f) + q(P_f - \bar{P}_f) = 0 \qquad (9.15)$$

where

$$U_1 = \frac{\partial U}{\partial C_f}, \qquad U_2 = \frac{\partial U}{\partial C_m}$$

$$U_2 P_f \bar{W} + q\left[\frac{\partial F_m}{\partial L_m} - P_f \bar{W}\right] = 0 \tag{9.16}$$

$$U_2 P_f \bar{W} + q\left[\bar{P}_n \frac{\partial F_n}{\partial L_n} - P_f \bar{W}\right] = 0 \tag{9.17}$$

$$\frac{\partial S}{\partial P_f}(U_1 - U_2 P_f) + (U_2 - q)\frac{C_m}{P_f} - qS - qN'\left(\frac{P_n}{P_f}\right)\frac{P_n}{P_f^2}(P_n - \bar{P}_n) = 0 \tag{9.18}$$

$$\frac{\partial S_f}{\partial P_n}(U_1 - U_2 P_f) + qN + qN'\left(\frac{P_n}{P_f}\right)\frac{(P_n - \bar{P}_n)}{P_f} = 0 \tag{9.19}$$

$$\lambda \begin{cases} = 1 & \text{if } q_n > q_m \\ \epsilon [0,1] & \text{if } q_n = q_m \\ = 0 & \text{if } q_n < q_m \ . \end{cases} \tag{9.20}$$

The remaining necessary conditions are that $q_i(t)$ are continuous $(i=m,n)$ satisfying

$$\dot{q}_n = \rho q_n - q\bar{P}_n \frac{\partial F_n}{\partial K_n} \tag{9.21}$$

$$\dot{q}_m = \rho q_m - q\frac{\partial F_m}{\partial K_m}. \tag{9.22}$$

The transversality conditions are that $q_m(T) = \alpha = q_m(T)$.

Let us now find out the implications of these optimality conditions.

Take eq. (9.16). With positive marginal utility of consumption of textiles and positive shadow price of new investment q,

$$P_f \bar{W} > \frac{\partial F_m}{\partial L_m}. \tag{9.23}$$

This implies that the industrial wage rate is higher than the (value of) marginal product of labor in industry m. In other words, the optimum technique of production in industry m is more labor intensive under our Ramsey-type social objective function than under the Galenson-Leibenstein [7] type of industrial-surplus-maximizing policy (which equates industrial wage rate with marginal productivity of labor). This confirms the well-known Eckstein-Sen-Marglin result in the literature on choice of techniques. Eq. (9.17) similarly implies that the industrial wage rate is higher than the marginal product of labor in industry n (valued at world price of n).

From eqs. (9.17), (9.18), (9.19),

$$(U_1 - U_2 P_f)\left(\frac{\partial S}{\partial P_f}\frac{P_f}{S} + \frac{\partial S}{\partial P_n}\frac{P_n}{S}\right)S = q\left(C_m^a + \frac{C_m}{P_f\bar{W}}\frac{\partial F_m}{\partial L_m}\right). \tag{9.24}$$

If shadow price of new investment q is positive, the right-hand side of eq. (9.24) is positive.

If one differentiates in eq. (9.7) and uses eq. (9.8),

$$\left(\frac{\partial S}{\partial P_f}\frac{P_f}{S} + \frac{\partial S}{\partial P_n}\frac{P_n}{S}\right) = \frac{S_1 P_f}{S} > 0. \tag{9.25}$$

So if $q > 0$, from eq. (9.24),

$$U_1 - U_2 P_f > 0. \tag{9.26}$$

If one uses eq. (9.26) in eq. (9.15)[7],

$$\bar{P}_f - P_f > 0. \tag{9.27}$$

Eq. (9.27) gives us an interesting result. It means that on the optimum path we should *subsidize* imports of food[8]. The essential reason for this result is as follows: The government as buyer of food has two sources to buy it from, the domestic agricultural sector and the foreign country. With respect to the former the government's purchases affect the price, but this does not occur with respect to the foreign country. It follows from the theory of discriminating monopsony that the buyer tends to have a premium for buying from the more elastic source and in this case this represents the case for subsidizing imports of food from the foreign country[9].

It is more difficult to get an unambiguous result about the optimum trade policy with respect to imports of fertilizers. From eqs. (9.19), (9.24) and (9.25),

---

[7] One may note from the derivation of eq. (9.27), that eq. (9.27) holds even if $q < 0$.
[8] For footnote, see next page.
[9] For footnote, see next page.

$$\text{sign}(\bar{P}_n - P_n)N'\left(\frac{P_n}{P_f}\right)\frac{P_n}{P_f^2} = \text{sign}\left[\frac{NP_n}{C_m^a} \cdot \frac{S_1 P_f}{S} + \frac{\partial S}{\partial P_n}\frac{P_n}{S}\left(1 + \frac{C_m}{C_m^a P_f \bar{W}} \cdot \frac{\partial F_m}{\partial L_m}\right)\right].$$
(9.28)

Let us define $S_1 P_f/S = h_1$, which from eq. (9.7) is the own price elasticity of marketed surplus of food (at a given level of fertilizer use). Let us also define $\partial S/\partial P_n \, P_n/S = -h_2$; from eqs. (9.7) and (9.8), h_2 is the (positively defined) elasticity of marketed surplus of food with respect to changes in fertilizer price. Here h_2 is actually the product of three elasticities, the elasticity of marketed surplus of food with respect to food output (which, with income-elasticity of demand for food less than unity, is larger than one), the elasticity of food crop output with respect to use of fertilizers (which at present low levels of chemical fertilizer use in most countries with traditional agriculture is very high, as indicated by available data[10] of output response to fertilizer trials conducted on farms) and the (positively defined) elasticity of fertilizer

---

[8] The point was first made by Hornby [8], p. 105. But for two reasons his way of deriving this result might mislead a reader about its essential rationale. (1) Hornby derives this result by maximizing the steady-state rate of growth; but it should be clear from our analysis that the result has nothing to do with the steady state or even any kind of dynamic model. It is purely an a-temporal efficiency condition that follows from the theory of discriminating monopsony. (2) Hornby in his model has direct investment by the government in agriculture and he assumes that "the government makes no direct charge for the capital it invests in agriculture". This is not merely an empirically unsatisfactory assumption (it forgets about water rates for irrigation, fertilizer prices, etc., that the government charges in most countries and ignores the interesting problem about deciding their optimum rates); theoretically, it might mislead the reader into thinking that this assumption might be responsible for the case for subsidizing food imports that he derives. This is because, if one assumes that the government charges a positive rate (for simplification, assume that it is constant) for the capital it invests in agriculture with Hornby's eq. (16) in [8], p. 104, modified accordingly, and proceeds with maximization of the steady-state rate of growth; Hornby's result about subsidization of food imports seem to disappear.

[9] What if instead of assuming that the foreign price of food is fixed we take the case where more food imports bid up the foreign price $\bar{P}_f$. In that case eq. (9.15) will be changed to

$$(U_1 - U_2 P_f) + q\left[P_f - \bar{P}_f\left(1 + \frac{d\bar{P}_f}{dZ_f}\frac{Z_f}{\bar{P}_f}\right)\right] = 0 .$$

This means that now we have no unambiguous case for subsidizing food imports: all we can say is that the "optimum tariff" on food imports, even when it is positive, is less than the optimum tariff in the standard literature (which is at a rate equal to the reciprocal of price elasticity of food exports by the foreign country).

[10] For such Indian data, see Panse [14]; for Chinese data see Jung-Chao Liu [11].

use with respect to its price. It seems that in developing economies h_2 is likely to be very high, particularly at low levels of chemical fertilizer use. If h_2 is larger than or equal to h_1,[11] and if $(NP_n/C_m^a) < 1$ (which means, from eq. (9.9), that in the industrial sectors' exports to the agricultural sector sales of consumer goods, textiles, exceed those of agricultural inputs, fertilizers – which is also in general likely to be true), then the right-hand side of eq. (9.28) is negative, so that $\bar{P}_n - P_n > 0$. Under these circumstances the government should also *subsidize* imports of fertilizers. One should keep in mind this holds only under a set of very special assumptions, and in particular these assumptions – such as $h_2 \geqslant h_1$ and $(NP_n/C_m^a) < 1$ – are more likely to be valid at low levels of fertilizer use. As the agrarian economy gets more prosperous (so that h_1 becomes large) and as a substantial quantity of chemical fertilizers gets absorbed in crop production (so that h_2 is not very high and NP_n/C_m^a is larger than before), one can conceivably have a case for taxing imports of fertilizers.

Essentially, the question is whether the Government should subsidize or tax sales of the domestically produced intermediate good (fertilizer) to the agricultural sector. On the one hand, it should tax it (thus improving the industrial sector's terms of trade with the agricultural sector), but on the other, cheaper fertilizer means improved productivity in agriculture (and thus better terms of trade for industry). In the initial stages of development, i.e. at low level of fertilizer use, the latter productivity effect dominates and one gets the case for subsidy. This suggests, as Max Corden pointed out to the author, that the "optimum tariff" in the standard literature may be negative if the country exports a productivity-raising intermediate product that is used in producing exportables in the foreign country.

We have so far tried to find out the implications of our optimality conditions for choice of production techniques and for trade policy. Let us now briefly turn to optimal investment policy in this model.

The first thing to note is that, although we started with smooth neoclassical production functions for the industrial sector, all along the optimum path only one technique (capital-labor ratio) will be used in each industry. Let us explain this.

Since production functions are subject to constant returns to scale in each

---

[11] The value of h_1 is likely to be low in poor agrarian economies, because when the price of food crop P_f goes up, farmers' incomes go up, and even if their income-elasticity of demand for foodgrains is less than unity, it is still quite high (it is about 0.6 in rural India according to National Sample Survey data) and the farmers tend to retain a large proportion of their increased output.

industry, marginal products of each factor is a function only of the capital-labor ratio used in an industry. From eqs. (9.16) and (9.17)

$$\bar{P}_n = \frac{\dfrac{\partial F_m}{\partial L_m}}{\dfrac{\partial F_n}{\partial L_n}}. \tag{9.29}$$

Eq. (9.29) gives K_m/L_m, the capital-labor ratio in industry m, as a unique function of K_n/L_n, the capital-labor ratio in industry n. Now if $q_n = q_m = q$, then eqs. (9.21) and (9.22) give

$$\bar{P}_n = \frac{\dfrac{\partial F_m}{\partial K_m}}{\dfrac{\partial F_n}{\partial K_n}}. \tag{9.30}$$

Eqs. (9.29) and (9.30) imply that K_m/L_m and K_n/L_n are constant, so that on the optimal path only one technique will be used in each industry. If $q = q_m > q_n$, then from (9.14) and (9.22)

$$\frac{\partial F_m}{\partial K_m} = r \tag{9.31}$$

where r is the given rate of interest at which the country can borrow to cover its deficit in balance of trade. From eqs. (9.29) and (9.30), again K_m/L_m and K_n/L_n are fixed. If $q = q_n > q_m$, then from eqs. (9.14) and (9.21),

$$\bar{P}_n \frac{\partial F_n}{\partial K_n} = r. \tag{9.32}$$

Eqs. (9.29) and (9.32) again imply that K_m/L_m and K_n/L_n are fixed.

This result about the constancy of technique in industrial production follows essentially from the constant world relative price of the industrial goods[12] and world rate of interest.

Since they are constant, let us define $\bar{P}_n\, \partial F_n/\partial K_n = a$ and $\partial F_m/\partial K_m = b$.

---

[12] The same result holds even when the world price of n changes with changes in the home country's imports of n, but if the price elasticity of the rest of the world's exports of n is constant.

We shall now see that the optimum investment policy depends on the relative values of a and b. With the help of eq. (9.14) we can now integrate eqs. (9.21) and (9.22) and get

$$q_n(t) = e^{\rho t}\left[q_n(0) - \frac{a\gamma}{r}(1 - e^{-rt})\right] \tag{9.33}$$

$$q_m(t) = e^{\rho t}\left[q_m(0) - \frac{b\gamma}{r}(1 - e^{-rt})\right]. \tag{9.34}$$

From the transversality conditions $q_m(T) = \alpha = q_n(T)$, we can get the values of $q_n(0)$ and $q_m(0)$ and hence eqs. (9.33) and (9.34) may be rewritten as

$$q_n(t) = e^{\rho t}\left[\alpha e^{-\rho T} + \frac{a\gamma}{r}(e^{-rt} - e^{-rT})\right] \tag{9.35}$$

$$q_m(t) = e^{\rho t}\left[\alpha e^{-\rho T} + \frac{b\gamma}{r}(e^{-rt} - e^{-rT})\right]. \tag{9.36}$$

It is immediately obvious from eqs. (9.35) and (9.36) that for any $t < T$,

(i)   If $a > b$, i.e., the constant marginal of product of capital (valued at world prices) is larger for the industry producing fertilizers, then $q_n(t) > q_m(t)$, so that from eq. (9.20), $\lambda = 1$, i.e., all new investment should be devoted to the fertilizer industry;

(ii)   If $a = b$, then $q_n(t) = q_m(t) = q(t)$, so that from eq. (9.20), $1 > \lambda > 0$, i.e., new investment should go to both the industries;

(iii) If $a < b$, $q_n(t) < q_m(t)$, so that $\lambda = 0$, i.e., all new investment should go to the industry producing textiles and machines.

Before concluding, one might extend the model in two ways. First, one may modify the instantaneous utility function in eq. (9.12) by introducing the magnitude of industrial employment L as a separate argument in the utility function so that

$$U = U(C_f, C_m, L), \text{ with } U_3 = \frac{\partial U}{\partial L} > 0. \tag{9.37}$$

Eq. (9.37) implies that in the social objective function a positive weight is attached to the size of the industrial labor force (maybe because of unemployment in the countryside or in nonindustrial service sectors). The reader may check that this will not alter any of the results mentioned in this section; in fact, all of them will be reinforced if we assume $U_3 > 0$.

One might also think of a strong argument for including L as a determinant of S in eq. (9.7). This means that an addition to the industrial labor force by reducing the size of agricultural population may affect the surplus of food marketed. Thus we may have

$$S = S(P_f, N, L). \tag{9.38}$$

It is, however, difficult to be unambiguous about the sign of $S_3 = \partial S/\partial L$. If marginal productivity of labor in the agricultural sector is low then transfer of labor from the agricultural to the industrial sector is likely to raise marketed surplus of food, because with farmers' income elasticity of demand less than unity an increase in their per capita income is likely to raise their sales, so that $S_3 > 0$. But as fertilizers and other new current inputs (like improved seeds) bring technical progress of a kind that is land saving and labor using, it may not be appropriate to assume that labor's marginal productivity in agriculture is or will remain low.

How are our results affected? The results about optimal investment policy are unaltered. If S_3, whether positive or negative, is small in absolute value our results about subsidization of imports of food and fertilizers and about techniques of production being more labor intensive than under a surplus maximization still hold. Our results about subsidization of imports of food will hold even if S_3 has a large negative value.

References

[1] P.K.Bardhan and K.Bardhan, "The Problem of Marketed Surplus of Cereals in India", *Economic and Political Weekly* (Bombay), Vol. 4 (June 28, 1969).

[2] J.R.Behrman, "Price Elasticity of the Marketed Surplus of a Subsistence Crop", *Journal of Farm Economics*, Vol. 48 (November 1966).

[3] A.K.Dixit, "Optimal Development in the Labour-Surplus Economy", *Review of Economic Studies*, Vol. 35 (January 1968).

[4] M.Dobb, *Soviet Economic Development Since 1917*, K.Paul (London: Trench Trubner & Co., Ltd., 1960).

[5] O.Eckstein, "Investment Criteria for Economic Development and the Theory of Intertemporal Welfare Economics", *Quarterly Journal of Economics*, Vol. 71 (February 1957).

[6] R.Findlay, "Capital Theory and Development Planning", *Review of Economic Studies,* Vol. 29 (February 1962).

[7] W.Galenson and H.Leibenstein, "Investment Criteria, Productivity and Economic Development", *Quarterly Journal of Economics*, Vol. 69 (August 1955).

[8] J.N.Hornby, "Investment and Trade Policy in the Dual Economy", *Economic Journal*, Vol. 78 (March 1968).

[9] D.W.Jorgenson, "The Development of a Dual Economy", *Economic Journal*, Vol. 71 (June 1961).

[10] R.Krishna, "A Note on the Elasticity of the Marketable Surplus of a Subsistence Crop", *Indian Journal of Agricultural Economics*, Vol. 17 (July–September 1962).

[11] J.C.Liu, "Fertilizer Application in Communist China", *China Quarterly*, No. 24 (October–December 1965).

[12] S.A.Marglin, "The Rate of Interest and the Value of Capital with Unlimited Supplies of Labour", In: *Essays on the Theory of Optimal Economic Growth*, ed. K.Shell (Cambridge, Mass., M.I.T. Press, 1967).

[13] J.I.Naxamura, *Agricultural Production and the Economic Development of Japan, 1873–1922*, (Princeton, N.J., Princeton University Press, 1966).

[14] V.G.Panse, "Fertilizer Recommendations", Proceedings of the National Seminar on Fertilizers, Fertilizer Association of India, 1965.

[15] E.Preobrazhenski, *The New Economics* (translated by B.Pearce) (New York, Oxford University Press, 1965).

[16] G.Ranis and J.C.H.Fei, "A Theory of Economic Development", *American Economic Review,* Vol. 51 (June 1961).

[17] A.K.Sen, *Choice of Techniques,* (Oxford, Basil Blackwell & Mott, 1960).

PART 4

INTERNATIONAL FACTOR MOVEMENTS

CHAPTER 10

INTERNATIONAL TRADE WITH CAPITAL MOBILITY: A SUBSTITUTION THEOREM

John S.CHIPMAN*

10.1. Introduction

In recent discussions[1] the question has been raised whether and under what conditions it is possible for two countries engaging in trade both to be incompletely specialized, when labor is immobile and capital perfectly mobile between them. This paper is devoted to obtaining conditions for this result, under the traditional assumptions that there are two freely traded commodities as well as two factors of production — one of which (labor) is in fixed supply in each country, and the other (capital) is perfectly mobile between countries and in fixed international supply. Competitive markets and constant returns to scale are assumed. Needless to say, the analysis is equally applicable to a model in which capital is the internationally immobile, and labor the internationally mobile, factor[2].

The main conclusion is that under certain circumstances — to be described presently — in which efficient world production comprises positive outputs of each commodity in both countries, the world production possibility frontier must contain a flat segment corresponding to such output combinations (see fig. 10.1). Thus the international terms of trade will be determinate and unaffected (within specifiable limits) by changes in demand. Within this region, the wage rate in each country and the common rental of capital will be determined independently of demand; adjustment to changes in demand takes place via capital movements between the two countries rather than through

---

* I am much indebted to Ronald Jones for valuable comments.
[1] See Jones [8], and Inada and Kemp [6].
[2] See Mundell [16].

changes in the terms of trade. Since commodity and factor prices are fixed within the region of diversification in production, it follows that firms will choose only one process of production, so there will be effectively "fixed technical coefficients" – hence the term "substitution theorem"[3].

The basic circumstances leading to the above result may be described as follows (see Theorem 2): Consider an equilibrium with positive commodity and factor prices and diversification of production in both countries, and assume that at the equilibrium factor prices, the labor-capital ratios differ as between industries (in each country); then a necessary and sufficient condition that the equilibrium world output point should lie on a flat segment of the world production possibility set is that $\bar{a}_2/\bar{a}_1 \neq \bar{a}_2^*/\bar{a}_1^*$, where $\bar{a}_i$ is the equilibrium labor-output coefficient in the ith industry in the home country, and $\bar{a}_i^*$ the same in the foreign country.

The above condition requires technical coefficients to differ in a certain

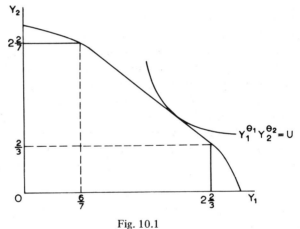

Fig. 10.1

way, namely in terms of their relative labor requirements. In particular, it rules out identical production functions in the two countries combined with absence of factor intensity reversal – the basic assumptions of the factor-price equalization theorem. These assumptions would entail $\bar{a}_2/\bar{a}_1 = \bar{a}_2^*/\bar{a}_1^*$ –

---

[3] See Samuelson [18]. Recently Professor Samuelson has preferred the term "non-substitution theorem" to emphasize the lack of substitution of inputs on the part of firms. On the other hand, the expression "substitution theorem" emphasizes the perfect substitutability in the international production of the two outputs.

a case that may be interpreted as corresponding to the situation in which the flat segment of the production possibility frontier degenerates to a point. In fact, the part of the world production possibility frontier corresponding to diversification may in this case be thought of as composed of a continuum of degenerate flat segments.

The condition $\bar{a}_2/\bar{a}_1 \neq \bar{a}_2^*/\bar{a}_1^*$ will be fulfilled in an equilibrium with diversification if production functions as between the two countries are identical in one industry but not both. In this case, wage rates will be equalized as well as the rental on the internationally mobile capital (Theorem 3); thus, mobility of one factor takes the place of identical production functions in one industry.

Sufficient conditions for the existence of an efficient point with diversification fulfilling the above condition are set forth in Section 10.4 (see Theorem 4). The case of Cobb-Douglas production functions is examined in Section 10.5; the corresponding inequality $\alpha_2/\alpha_1 \neq \alpha_2^*/\alpha_1^*$ in terms of the constant elasticities of outputs with respect to labor inputs turns out, in this case, to be also necessary and sufficient for the existence of a unique positive solution with diversification of production. A numerical example is taken up in Section 10.6. Section 10.7 takes up the question of probabilities, to provide a framework for distinguishing "exceptional" or "coincidental" cases from cases that could be expected to be realized in practice.

10.2. Conditions for Diversification and Nonsubstitution

Let the production functions for commodities 1 and 2 in the home and foreign country be

$$y_i = f_i(l_i, k_i); \qquad y_i^* = f_i^*(l_i^*, k_i^*); \qquad (i=1,2), \qquad (10.1)$$

respectively, where y_i denotes the home output of commodity i, the labor input l_i and the capital input k_i into the home production of commodity i, and starred quantities denote the corresponding entities in the foreign country, following the notation of Kemp [9] and Jones [8]. The f_i and f_i^* are assumed to be concave and positively homogeneous of the first degree; they will further be assumed in this section to be differentiable and strictly quasi-concave, though this requirement is not essential[4].

---

[4] A general treatment would require stating conditions in terms of left and right derivatives, as in Uzawa [22], but this will not be pursued here. A special case of non-differentiability is taken up in the next section.

The factors of production are assumed to be subject to the restrictions

$$l_1 + l_2 \leqslant l \; ; \qquad l_1^* + l_2^* \leqslant l^* \; ; \qquad k_1 + k_2 + k_1^* + k_2^* \leqslant K \; ; \qquad (10.2)$$

where l, l^* are the fixed endowments of labor in the two countries, and K the fixed world supply of capital available to both countries.

Factor-product coefficients will be denoted by

$$a_i = \frac{l_i}{y_i}, \; b_i = \frac{k_i}{y_i} \; ; \qquad a_i^* = \frac{l_i^*}{y_i^*}, \; b_i^* = \frac{k_i^*}{y_i^*} \; ; \qquad (i=1,2) \; , \qquad (10.3)$$

when y_i, $y_i^* > 0$. From the assumed homogeneity,

$$f_i(a_i, b_i) = 1 \; ; \qquad f_i^*(a_i^*, b_i^*) = 1 \; ; \qquad (i=1,2) \; . \qquad (10.4)$$

Let w, r and w^*, r^* denote the wage rate and rental of capital in the respective countries. The minimum unit cost functions are defined, for non-negative w, r and w^*, r^* by

$$g_i(w,r) \quad = \min \{wa_i + rb_i : f_i(a_i, b_i) \geqslant 1\}$$

$$g_i(w^*,r^*) = \min \{w^*a_i^* + r^*b_i^* : f_i^*(a_i^*, b_i^*) \geqslant 1\} \; . \qquad (10.5)$$

These are also homogeneous of degree one and concave (see Shephard [21] and Uzawa [23]). The factor-product ratios entering the minimum unit cost functions (10.5) depend on the factor prices: in case the dependence is unique[5], the functional relationship will be denoted by

$$a_i(w,r), b_i(w,r) \; ; \qquad a_i^*(w^*,r^*), b_i^*(w^*,r^*) \; , \qquad (10.6)$$

where the functions are defined for positive w, r, w^*, r^*.

Let p denote the price of the second commodity relative to the first. As is well known, a point

$$(Y_1, Y_2) = (y_1 + y_1^*, \; y_2 + y_2^*) \qquad (10.7)$$

---

[5] This includes both the case in which the production functions f_i, f_i^* are strictly quasi-concave and the case in which they are of the fixed-coefficient form $f_i(l_i, k_i) = \min(l_i/a_i, \; k_i/b_i)$, etc., provided the functions $a_i(w,r)$, $b_i(w,r)$, etc., are defined for strictly positive w, r.

of efficient world production is one for which there exists a $p > 0$ such that

$$V = Y_1 + pY_2 = y_1 + py_2 + y_1^* + py_2^* \tag{10.8}$$

is a maximum subject to (10.1) and (10.2). An *efficient point with diversification* is defined as a point of efficient world production such that

$$y_i > 0 , y_i^* > 0 \qquad (i=1,2) , \tag{10.9}$$

i.e., each country produces a positive amount of each commodity.

Theorem 1. A necessary and sufficient condition that there be some factor endowments l, l*, K, for which an efficient point with diversification exists, is that the system of equations

$$g_1(w,r) = 1 ; \qquad g_1^*(w^*,r) = 1 ;$$
$$\tag{10.10}$$
$$g_2(w,r) = p ; \qquad g_2^*(w^*,r) = p ;$$

have a solution with $p > 0, w \geqslant 0, w^* \geqslant 0, r \geqslant 0$.

Proof. Form the Langrangean function

$$\varphi(y_1,y_2,y_1^*,y_2^*,l_1,k_1,l_2,k_2,l_1^*,k_1^*,l_2^*,k_2^*)$$

$$= y_1 + py_2 + y_1^* + py_2^* + p_1 [f_1(l_1,k_1)-y_1] + p_2 [f_2(l_2,k_2)-y_2]$$

$$+ p_1^* [f_1^*(l_1^*,k_1^*)-y_1^*] + p_2^* [f_2^*(l_2^*,k_2^*)-y_2^*] + w(l-l_1-l_2)$$

$$+ w^*(l^* -l_1^*-l_2^*) + r(K-k_1-k_2-k_1^*-k_2^*) . \tag{10.11}$$

In accordance with the Kuhn-Tucker theorem [13], in order that (10.8) be maximized subject to (10.1) and (10.2) where $y_i > 0$, $y_i^* > 0$, $l_i \geqslant 0$, $l_i^* \geqslant 0$, $k_i \geqslant 0$, $k_i^* \geqslant 0$, it is necessary and sufficient that there exist $p_i \geqslant 0$, $p_i^* \geqslant 0$ where $i = 1, 2, w \geqslant 0, w^* \geqslant 0, r \geqslant 0$ such that

$$\frac{\partial \varphi}{\partial y_1} = 1 - p_1 = 0 ; \qquad \frac{\partial \varphi}{\partial y_2} = p - p_2 = 0 \tag{10.12y}$$

$$\frac{\partial \varphi}{\partial l_i} = p_i \frac{\partial f_i}{\partial l_i} - w \leqslant 0, \left[p_i \frac{\partial f_i}{\partial l_i} - w \right] l_i = 0 \quad (i=1,2) \qquad (10.12l)$$

$$\frac{\partial \varphi}{\partial k_i} = p_i \frac{\partial f_i}{\partial k_i} - r \leqslant 0, \left[p_i \frac{\partial f_i}{\partial k_i} - r \right] k_i = 0 \quad (i=1,2) \qquad (10.12k)$$

with similar conditions holding in the foreign country, and such that all the multiplier terms in (10.11), following V, vanish.

Conditions (10.12l) and (10.12k) are the necessary and sufficient conditions for minimum cost, and yield the condition that prices equal minimum unit costs, i.e.,

$$wl_i + rk_i = p_i \left[\frac{\partial f_i}{\partial l_i} l_i + \frac{\partial f_i}{\partial k_i} k_i \right] = p_i y_i$$

(summing the equalities in (10.12l) and (10.12k) and using Euler's theorem), hence

$$g_i(w,r) = wa_i + rb_i = p_i .$$

But $p_1 = 1$ and $p_2 = p$ from (10.12y), establishing the first two equations of (10.10); the other two follow similarly.

Q.E.D.

The question of the existence of a solution to the system (10.10) will be taken up in Section 10.4. Suppose, now, that a solution is given. There remains the problem of characterizing the set of combinations (l,l^*,K) of factor endowments that is consistent with this solution; and given any combination (l,l^*,K) in this set, it remains to determine the set of combinations (Y_1,Y_2) of world outputs that correspond to the given solution. The substitution theorem states that if the solution to (10.10) has certain properties to be specified presently, then given any labor endowments l and l^*, there will be a well-defined interval of possible capital endowments K consistent with the solution; and given any K in this interval, there will be a well-defined linear segment of world output combinations (Y_1,Y_2) compatible with the given solution.

From the assumptions of differentiability and strict quasi-concavity of the production functions, it follows (see Shephard [21], p. 11) that the minimum unit cost functions are differentiable for $w > 0$, $r > 0$ and $w^* > 0$, $r^* > 0$, with partial derivatives equal to

$$\frac{\partial g_i(w,r)}{\partial w} = a_i(w,r) \; ; \qquad \frac{\partial g_i^*(w^*,r^*)}{\partial w^*} = a_i^*(w^*,r^*) \; ;$$

$$\frac{\partial g_i(w,r)}{\partial r} = b_i(w,r) \; ; \qquad \frac{\partial g_i^*(w^*,r^*)}{\partial r^*} = b_i^*(w^*,r^*) \; .$$

(10.13)

Let the system (10.10) be written in the form

$$h_1(w,w^*,r,p) = g_1(w,r) \qquad = 1$$

$$h_2(w,w^*,r,p) = g_2(w,r) - p \; = 0$$

$$h_1^*(w,w^*,r,p) = g_1^*(w^*,r) \qquad = 1$$

$$h_2^*(w,w^*,r,p) = g_2^*(w^*,r) - p = 0 \; .$$

(10.14)

The mapping $h = (h_1, h_2, h_1^*, h_2^*)$ is from the nonnegative orthant of the four-dimensional Euclidean space into a subset of the four-dimensional Euclidean space. In view of (10.13), its Jacobian determinant is equal for positive w, w^*, r, p to

$$J(w,w^*,r,p) = \begin{vmatrix} a_1(w,r) & 0 & b_1(w,r) & 0 \\ a_2(w,r) & 0 & b_2(w,r) & -1 \\ 0 & a_1^*(w^*,r) & b_1^*(w^*,r) & 0 \\ 0 & a_2^*(w^*,r) & b_2^*(w^*,r) & -1 \end{vmatrix}$$

$$= a_1^*(w^*,r) \cdot \Delta(w,r) - a_1(w,r) \cdot \Delta^*(w^*,r) \; ,$$

(10.15)

where

$$\Delta(w,r) \quad = \begin{vmatrix} a_1(w,r) & a_2(w,r) \\ b_1(w,r) & b_2(w,r) \end{vmatrix} \; ;$$

$$\Delta^*(w^*,r^*) = \begin{vmatrix} a_1^*(w^*,r^*) & a_2^*(w^*,r^*) \\ b_1^*(w^*,r^*) & b_2^*(w^*,r^*) \end{vmatrix} \; .$$

(10.16)

Suppose (10.14) has a positive solution $\bar{w} > 0, \bar{w}^* > 0, \bar{r} > 0, \bar{p} > 0$; then the cost-minimizing factor-product ratios at these particular factor prices will be denoted

$$\bar{a}_i = a_i(\bar{w}, \bar{r}) ; \qquad \bar{a}_i^* = a_i^*(\bar{w}^*, \bar{r}) ;$$

$$\bar{b}_i = b_i(\bar{w}, \bar{r}) ; \qquad \bar{b}_i^* = b_i^*(\bar{w}^*, \bar{r}) . \qquad (10.17)$$

Similarly, we shall denote

$$\bar{\Delta} = \Delta(\bar{w}, \bar{r}) ; \qquad \bar{\Delta}^* = \Delta^*(\bar{w}^*, \bar{r}) ; \qquad \bar{J} = J(\bar{w}, \bar{w}^*, \bar{r}, \bar{p}) . \qquad (10.18)$$

For these fixed $\bar{a}_i$, $\bar{b}_i$, $\bar{a}_i^*$, $\bar{b}_i^*$, the given solution $\bar{w}$, $\bar{w}^*$, $\bar{r}$, $\bar{p}$ of (10.14) must be a solution of the linear system

$$
\begin{bmatrix}
\bar{a}_1 & 0 & \bar{b}_1 & 0 \\
\bar{a}_2 & 0 & \bar{b}_2 & -1 \\
0 & \bar{a}_1^* & \bar{b}_1^* & 0 \\
0 & \bar{a}_2^* & \bar{b}_2^* & -1
\end{bmatrix}
\begin{bmatrix}
w \\
w^* \\
r \\
p
\end{bmatrix}
=
\begin{bmatrix}
1 \\
0 \\
1 \\
0
\end{bmatrix}. \qquad (10.19)
$$

If $\bar{J} = \bar{a}_1^* \bar{\Delta} - \bar{a}_1 \bar{\Delta}^* \neq 0$, these solution values may be expressed as

$$\bar{w} = \frac{\bar{a}_1^*(\bar{b}_2 - \bar{b}_2^*) - \bar{a}_2^*(\bar{b}_1 - \bar{b}_1^*)}{\bar{a}_1^* \bar{\Delta} - \bar{a}_1 \bar{\Delta}^*} ;$$

$$\bar{w}^* = \frac{\bar{a}_1(\bar{b}_2 - \bar{b}_2^*) - \bar{a}_2(\bar{b}_1 - \bar{b}_1^*)}{\bar{a}_1^* \bar{\Delta} - \bar{a}_1 \bar{\Delta}^*} ;$$

$$\bar{r} = \frac{\bar{a}_1 \bar{a}_2^* - \bar{a}_2 \bar{a}_1^*}{\bar{a}_1^* \bar{\Delta} - \bar{a}_1 \bar{\Delta}^*} ; \qquad (10.20)$$

$$\bar{p} = \frac{\bar{a}_2^* \bar{\Delta} - \bar{a}_2 \bar{\Delta}^*}{\bar{a}_1^* \bar{\Delta} - \bar{a}_1 \bar{\Delta}^*} .$$

The condition $\bar{p} > 0$ then requires that

$$\bar{a}_2^* \bar{\Delta} - \bar{a}_2 \bar{\Delta}^* \neq 0, \text{ and } \text{sign} (\bar{a}_2^* \bar{\Delta} - \bar{a}_2 \bar{\Delta}^*) = \text{sign} (\bar{a}_1^* \bar{\Delta} - \bar{a}_1 \bar{\Delta}^*) . \qquad (10.21)$$

By substitution from (10.20), we find that

$$\bar{a}_1 - \frac{\bar{a}_2}{\bar{p}} = \frac{\bar{\Delta}(\bar{a}_1\bar{a}_2^* - \bar{a}_2\bar{a}_1^*)}{\bar{a}_2^*\bar{\Delta} - \bar{a}_2\bar{\Delta}^*} = \frac{\bar{a}_1\bar{a}_2^* - \bar{a}_2\bar{a}_1^*}{\bar{a}_1^*\bar{\Delta} - \bar{a}_1\bar{\Delta}^*} \cdot \frac{\bar{a}_1^*\bar{\Delta} - \bar{a}_1\bar{\Delta}^*}{\bar{a}_2^*\bar{\Delta} - \bar{a}_2\bar{\Delta}^*} \cdot \bar{\Delta} = \frac{\bar{r}}{\bar{p}}\bar{\Delta} ,$$

and in similar fashion, $\bar{a}_1^* - \bar{a}_2^*/\bar{p} = \bar{\Delta}^*\bar{r}/\bar{p}$; thus, if $\bar{r} > 0$ in (10.20), the determinants $\bar{\Delta} = \Delta(\bar{w},\bar{r})$, $\bar{\Delta}^* = \Delta^*(\bar{w}^*,\bar{r})$ may be expressed as

$$\bar{\Delta} = \frac{\bar{p}}{\bar{r}}\left(\bar{a}_1 - \frac{\bar{a}_2}{\bar{p}}\right) ; \qquad \bar{\Delta}^* = \frac{\bar{p}}{\bar{r}}\left(\bar{a}_1^* - \frac{\bar{a}_2^*}{\bar{p}}\right) , \qquad (10.22)$$

and consequently the Jacobian (10.15) of the transformation (10.14), evaluated at the solution values $\bar{w} > 0$, $\bar{w}^* > 0$, $\bar{r} > 0$, $\bar{p} > 0$, may be expressed as

$$\bar{J} = \frac{\bar{a}_1\bar{a}_2^* - \bar{a}_2\bar{a}_1^*}{\bar{r}} . \qquad (10.23)$$

The property of *absence of factor intensity reversal* is said to hold for the two countries if

$$\Delta(w,r) \neq 0 \text{ for all } w > 0, r > 0 ;$$
$$\Delta^*(w^*,r^*) \neq 0 \text{ for all } w^* > 0, r^* > 0 . \qquad (10.24)$$

This property will not be required in the following theorem; however, it will be necessary to rule out the simultaneous occurrence $\Delta(\bar{w},\bar{r}) = \Delta(\bar{w}^*,\bar{r}) = 0$ at the solution values $\bar{w}$, $\bar{w}^*$, $\bar{r}$. A mild form of (10.24) will be adopted in Section 10.4.

Theorem 2. (Substitution Theorem). Suppose a positive solution $\bar{w} > 0$, $\bar{w}^* > 0$, $\bar{r} > 0$, $\bar{p} > 0$ exists to eqs. (10.10), and that the factor-product ratios (10.17) evaluated at these solution values are such that the determinants (10.22) do not vanish simultaneously, i.e., are such that not both

$$\bar{a}_1 = \frac{\bar{a}_2}{\bar{p}} ; \qquad \bar{a}_1^* = \frac{\bar{a}_2^*}{\bar{p}} \qquad (10.25)$$

hold. Then for any labor endowments l and l^* in the two countries, an efficient point with diversification will exist whenever the world stock of capital lies in the interval

$$\min\left[\frac{\bar{b}_1}{\bar{a}_1},\frac{\bar{b}_2}{\bar{a}_2}\right]l + \min\left[\frac{\bar{b}_1^*}{\bar{a}_1^*},\frac{\bar{b}_2^*}{\bar{a}_2^*}\right]l^* < K < \max\left[\frac{\bar{b}_1}{\bar{a}_1},\frac{\bar{b}_2}{\bar{a}_2}\right]l + \max\left[\frac{\bar{b}_1^*}{\bar{a}_1^*},\frac{\bar{b}_2^*}{\bar{a}_2^*}\right]l^*$$

$$(10.26)$$

Moreover:

(a) *For any K satisfying* (10.26), *if the Jacobian* (10.23) *at the solution values does not vanish, i.e., if*

$$\frac{\bar{a}_2}{\bar{a}_1} \neq \frac{\bar{a}_2^*}{\bar{a}_1^*},$$

$$(10.27)$$

then the world production possibility frontier will contain a nondegenerate flat segment with slope equal to $1/\bar{p}$, of efficient points corresponding to diversification in both countries.

(a-i) *If neither determinant of* (10.22) *vanishes, i.e., if neither equality of* (10.25) *holds, but if* (10.27) *nevertheless holds, then movements along the flat segment correspond to movements of capital between the two countries (see eqs.* (10.33) *later).*

(a-ii) *If one of the determinants of* (10.22) *vanishes, i.e., if one of the equalities of* (10.25) *holds, the world distribution of capital will be fixed and movements along the flat segment will correspond to variations in output in the corresponding country (see eqs.* (10.35) *later).*

(b) *If neither determinant of* (10.22) *vanishes but if the Jacobian* (10.23) *vanishes, i.e., if*

$$\frac{\bar{a}_2}{\bar{a}_1} = \frac{\bar{a}_2^*}{\bar{a}_1^*} \neq \bar{p},$$

$$(10.28)$$

then the flat segment degenerates to a point.

Proof. By Theorem 1, there exist factor endowments l, l^*, K and positive outputs $y_i > 0$, $y_i^* > 0$ $(i=1,2)$ such that (10.7) is an efficient point. Since factor prices are assumed positive, it follows from the Kuhn-Tucker conditions (see the proof of Theorem 1) that factors are fully employed, hence equalities hold in (10.2) and therefore from (10.3) and (10.27) the outputs outputs y_i, y_i^* satisfy

$$\bar{a}_1 y_1 + \bar{a}_2 y_2 = l ; \qquad \bar{a}_1^* y_1^* + \bar{a}_2^* y_2^* = l^* ;$$

$$\bar{b}_1 y_1 + \bar{b}_2 y_2 = k ; \qquad \bar{b}_1^* y_1^* + \bar{b}_2^* y_2^* = k^* ;$$

$$(10.29)$$

where k, k^* denote the amount of capital used in the respective countries, and

$$k + k^* = K .\tag{10.30}$$

Since the y_i, y_i^* are positive, eqs. (10.29) imply

$$\min\left[\frac{\bar{b}_1}{\bar{a}_1},\frac{\bar{b}_2}{\bar{a}_2}\right]\leqslant\frac{k}{l}\leqslant\max\left[\frac{\bar{b}_1}{\bar{a}_1},\frac{\bar{b}_2}{\bar{a}_2}\right];\ \min\left[\frac{\bar{b}_1^*}{\bar{a}_1^*},\frac{\bar{b}_2^*}{\bar{a}_2^*}\right]\leqslant\frac{k^*}{l^*}\leqslant\max\left[\frac{\bar{b}_1^*}{\bar{a}_1^*},\frac{\bar{b}_2^*}{\bar{a}_2^*}\right],\tag{10.31}$$

and since $\bar{\Delta}$ and $\bar{\Delta}^*$ do not vanish simultaneously, strict inequalities must hold in at least one of the pair. Multiplying through by l, l^*, respectively, and adding, we get (10.26).

Now let K satisfy (10.26). Two cases may be considered: (i) the *regular* case, in which both $\bar{\Delta} \neq 0$ and $\bar{\Delta}^* \neq 0$; and (ii) the *singular* case, in which either $\Delta = 0$ or $\Delta^* = 0$, but not both.

(i) If $\bar{\Delta} \neq 0$ and $\bar{\Delta}^* \neq 0$, one may solve both pairs of equations in (10.29) to obtain

$$y_1 = \frac{\bar{b}_2}{\bar{\Delta}}l - \frac{\bar{a}_2}{\bar{\Delta}}k ;\qquad y_1^* = \frac{\bar{b}_2^*}{\bar{\Delta}^*}l^* - \frac{\bar{a}_2^*}{\bar{\Delta}^*}k^* ;$$

$$y_2 = \frac{\bar{a}_1}{\bar{\Delta}}k - \frac{\bar{b}_1}{\bar{\Delta}}l ;\qquad y_2^* = \frac{\bar{a}_1^*}{\bar{\Delta}^*}k^* - \frac{\bar{b}_1^*}{\bar{\Delta}^*}l^* .\tag{10.32}$$

Adding, and making use of eqs. (10.7) and (10.30), we obtain

$$Y_1 = y_1 + y_1^* = \frac{\bar{b}_2}{\bar{\Delta}}l + \frac{\bar{b}_2^*}{\bar{\Delta}^*}l^* - \frac{\bar{a}_2^*}{\bar{\Delta}^*}K - \left[\frac{\bar{a}_2}{\bar{\Delta}} - \frac{\bar{a}_2^*}{\bar{\Delta}^*}\right]k ;$$

$$Y_2 = y_2 + y_2^* = -\frac{\bar{b}_1}{\bar{\Delta}}l - \frac{\bar{b}_1^*}{\bar{\Delta}^*}l^* + \frac{\bar{a}_1^*}{\bar{\Delta}^*}K + \left[\frac{\bar{a}_1}{\bar{\Delta}} - \frac{\bar{a}_1^*}{\bar{\Delta}^*}\right]k .\tag{10.33}$$

If $\bar{J} \neq 0$, the coefficients of k in these two equations are nonzero by (10.21) and their ratio determines the terms of trade $\bar{p}$, given by (10.20), which is the constant rate at which one commodity is transformed into the other as capital moves between the two countries. This establishes part (a-i) of Theorem 2. If $\bar{J} = 0$, the coefficients of k in (10.33) both vanish and Y_1, Y_2 are fixed; thus the flat segment degenerates to a point. This establishes part (b) of the theorem.

The limits between which there is an infinite elasticity of transformation between the world outputs of the two commodities are determined as follows. From (10.31) and the conditions $\Delta \neq 0$, $\Delta^* \neq 0$, we have

$$\min \left[\frac{\bar{b}_1}{\bar{a}_1} , \frac{\bar{b}_2}{\bar{a}_2} \right] l < k < \max \left[\frac{\bar{b}_1}{\bar{a}_1} , \frac{\bar{b}_2}{\bar{a}_2} \right] l ;$$

$$K - \max \left[\frac{\bar{b}_1^*}{\bar{a}_1^*} , \frac{\bar{b}_2^*}{\bar{a}_2^*} \right] l^* < k < K - \min \left[\frac{\bar{b}_1^*}{\bar{a}_1^*} , \frac{\bar{b}_2^*}{\bar{a}_2^*} \right] l^* .$$

Consequently,

$$\max \left\{ \min \left[\frac{\bar{b}_1}{\bar{a}_1} , \frac{\bar{b}_2}{\bar{a}_2} \right] l, K - \max \left[\frac{\bar{b}_1^*}{\bar{a}_1^*} , \frac{\bar{b}_2^*}{\bar{a}_2^*} \right] l^* \right\} < k <$$

$$\min \left\{ \max \left[\frac{\bar{b}_1}{\bar{a}_1} , \frac{\bar{b}_2}{\bar{a}_2} \right] l^*, K - \min \left[\frac{\bar{b}_1^*}{\bar{a}_1^*} , \frac{\bar{b}_2^*}{\bar{a}_2^*} \right] l^* \right\}. \tag{10.34}$$

The two limits of (10.34), when substituted in (10.33), furnish the precise limits between which the marginal rate of transformation between the world outputs of commodities 1 and 2 is constant.

(ii) In the singular case, suppose $\Delta = 0$ for definiteness. Then the left pair of equations of (10.29) have a solution if, and only if, $k/l = \bar{b}_1/\bar{a}_1 = \bar{b}_2/\bar{a}_2$; consequently, the international distribution of capital must be fixed in such a way that $k = \bar{b}_1 l/\bar{a}_1 = \bar{b}_2 l/\bar{a}_2$. This fixes $k^* = K - k$ and the outputs y_1^*, y_2^* in the foreign country, as determined by the pair of equations on the right in (10.32); together with the first equation on the left of (10.29), this yields

$$Y_1 = y_1^* + \frac{1}{\bar{a}_1} l - \frac{\bar{a}_2}{\bar{a}_1} y_2 ;$$

$$\tag{10.35}$$

$$Y_2 = y_2^* + y_2 .$$

The marginal rate of transformation between the two commodities is $\bar{p} = \bar{a}_2/\bar{a}_1$, between the limits $0 \leqslant y_2 \leqslant l/\bar{a}_2$, i.e., for $y_1^* + l/\bar{a}_1 \geqslant Y_1 \geqslant y_1^*$ and $y_2^* \leqslant Y_2 \leqslant y_2^* + l/\bar{a}_2$. A similar analysis holds for the case $\bar{\Delta} \neq 0$ and $\bar{\Delta}^* = 0$, establishing part (a-ii) of the theorem.

In both cases (i) and (ii), we can combine eqs. (10.19) with eqs. (10.29) and (10.30) to obtain

$$Y_1 + \bar{p}Y_2 = (1, \bar{p}, 1, \bar{p}) \begin{bmatrix} y_1 \\ y_2 \\ y_1^* \\ y_2^* \end{bmatrix} = (\bar{w}, \bar{w}^*, \bar{r}) \begin{bmatrix} \bar{a}_1 & \bar{a}_2 & 0 & 0 \\ 0 & 0 & \bar{a}_1^* & \bar{a}_2^* \\ \bar{b}_1 & \bar{b}_2 & \bar{b}_1^* & \bar{b}_2^* \end{bmatrix} \begin{bmatrix} y_1 \\ y_2 \\ y_1^* \\ y_2^* \end{bmatrix}.$$

$$= (\bar{w}, \bar{w}^*, \bar{r}) \begin{bmatrix} l \\ l^* \\ K \end{bmatrix} = \bar{w}l + \bar{w}^*l^* + \bar{r}K .$$

$$(10.36)$$

This states that world expenditure equals world income and is valid for the fixed $\bar{p}$, $\bar{w}$, $\bar{w}^*$, $\bar{r}$ determined by (10.20) as Y_1 and Y_2 vary within the limits described above in cases (i) and (ii). This completes the proof of Theorem 2.

Q.E.D.

Discussion of Theorem 2. At the commodity and factor prices constituting the given solution of eqs. (10.10), the technical coefficients of production are fixed at the values indicated by (10.17). If $\bar{\Delta} = \bar{a}_1\bar{b}_2 - \bar{b}_1\bar{a}_2 = 0$, this implies that the factor proportions are equal in the two industries in equilibrium, hence the isoquants for a dollar's worth of output of the two commodities have a common tangent at the equilibrium wage-rental ratio in the home country. The equivalent condition (10.25) states that the same amount of labor is required to produce a dollar's worth of each commodity. Since the occurrence $\bar{\Delta} = 0$ at equilibrium may be considered entirely coincidental, the hypothesis in Theorem 2 that $\bar{\Delta}$ and $\bar{\Delta}^*$ do not both vanish simply rules out the simultaneous occurrence of these two coincidental events. Case (a-ii) is included in the theorem for logical completeness, but may be regarded as "exceptional" (see Section 10.7); it has been discussed by Samuelson [20], p. 289. In this "singular" case, the world distribution of capital is fixed, and flatness in the world production possibility set results from variation in output in the country in which equilibrium labor-capital ratios coincide in the two industries.

In the "regular" case in which $\bar{\Delta} \neq 0$ and $\bar{\Delta}^* \neq 0$, outputs in the two countries vary in accordance with eqs. (10.32), where the technical coefficients are fixed at the values given by (10.17). These equations imply that, if in either of the countries commodity 1, say, is relatively labor intensive and commodity 2 relatively capital intensive (this will be the case in the home country if $\bar{\Delta} > 0$, and in the foreign country if $\bar{\Delta}^* > 0$), then an increase in the quantity of capital will reduce the country's output of the first commodity, as well as increase the output of the second commodity more than proportionately[6]. This result is known as Rybczynski's theorem (see Rybczynski [17]); however, eqs. (10.32) give much more information than Rybczynski's theorem, namely that the relationship is *linear*[7]. Since this is true in both countries, the relationship between the world outputs Y_1, Y_2 and capital k in the home country is also linear, as shown by eqs. (10.33). In the exceptional case $\bar{J} = 0$, the changes in outputs in one country are exactly balanced by opposite changes in the other country, and world output remains constant as capital moves between them. However, as long as $\bar{J} \neq 0$, outputs change linearly in a nonoffsetting way as capital moves between the two countries[8]. The situation is illustrated in fig. 10.1. In the regular case $\bar{\Delta} \neq 0$, $\bar{\Delta}^* \neq 0$, the condition $\bar{J} \neq 0$ is necessary and sufficient for the existence — for some endowments l, l^*, K — of a nondegenerate flat segment,

---

[6] Divide the left pair of eqs. (10.29) through by l and k respectively; the resulting equations state that the matrix

$$\begin{bmatrix} \bar{a}_1 y_1/l & \bar{a}_2 y_2/l \\ \bar{b}_1 y_1/k & \bar{b}_2 y_2/k \end{bmatrix} = \begin{bmatrix} l^{-1} & 0 \\ 0 & k^{-1} \end{bmatrix} \begin{bmatrix} \bar{a}_1 & \bar{a}_2 \\ \bar{b}_1 & \bar{b}_2 \end{bmatrix} \begin{bmatrix} y_1 & 0 \\ 0 & y_2 \end{bmatrix}$$

is stochastic, i.e., its elements are nonnegative (in fact, positive by assumption) and its row sums are equal to unity. Consequently, its inverse

$$\begin{bmatrix} \dfrac{\bar{a}_1 y_1}{l} & \dfrac{\bar{a}_2 y_2}{l} \\ \dfrac{\bar{b}_1 y_1}{k} & \dfrac{\bar{b}_2 y_2}{k} \end{bmatrix}^{-1} = \begin{bmatrix} \dfrac{1}{y_1} & 0 \\ 0 & \dfrac{1}{y_2} \end{bmatrix} \begin{bmatrix} \dfrac{\bar{b}_2}{\bar{\Delta}} & -\dfrac{\bar{a}_2}{\bar{\Delta}} \\ -\dfrac{\bar{b}_1}{\bar{\Delta}} & \dfrac{\bar{a}_1}{\bar{\Delta}} \end{bmatrix} \begin{bmatrix} l & 0 \\ 0 & k \end{bmatrix} = \begin{bmatrix} \dfrac{l\bar{b}_1}{y_1\bar{\Delta}} & -\dfrac{k\bar{a}_2}{y_1\bar{\Delta}} \\ -\dfrac{l\bar{b}_1}{y_2\bar{\Delta}} & \dfrac{k\bar{a}_1}{y_2\bar{\Delta}} \end{bmatrix}$$

also has row sums equal to unity (see Chipman [3]), that is (in view of (10.32)),

$$\frac{l}{y_1}\frac{\partial y_1}{\partial l} + \frac{k}{y_1}\frac{\partial y_1}{\partial k} = 1 \; ; \qquad \frac{l}{y_2}\frac{\partial y_2}{\partial l} + \frac{k}{y_2}\frac{\partial y_2}{\partial k} = 1 \; .$$

Since one of the terms in each row (depending on the sign of $\bar{\Delta}$) is negative, the other one must be greater than unity. This Leontief property of the above inverse matrix is, in essence, the Rybczynski theorem; compare Jones [7], pp. 560–1 and McKenzie [15], p. 100. As in the case of the Stolper-Samuelson theorem, it does not generalize to more than two factors and products without the addition of further assumptions.

[7] The fact that the Rybczynski loci must be linear does not appear to have been explicitly recognized in the literature; see, for instance, the chart in Samuelson [20], p. 288.

[8] It may appear anomalous that the condition $\bar{J} \neq 0$ always holds when there are Hicks-neutral differences in technology between countries, i.e., $\bar{a}_i^* = \lambda \bar{a}_i$, $\bar{b}_i^* = \lambda \bar{b}_i$, $\lambda \neq 1$; for, from eqs. (10.15) and (10.18), we then have $\bar{J} = \lambda(1-\lambda)a_1\Delta$. This case was brought

as is clear from the discussion following eqs. (10.33); this result is worth recording as a separate

Corollary to Theorem 2. If $\bar{w} > 0$, $\bar{w}^* > 0$, $\bar{r} > 0$, $\bar{p} > 0$ is a solution to eqs. (10.10) such that $\bar{\Delta} \neq 0$ and $\bar{\Delta}^* \neq 0$, and if the world stock of capital satisfies (10.26), then the world production possibility frontier contains a nondegenerate flat segment, with slope equal to $1/p$, if and only if (10.27) holds.

If production functions are identical in the two countries, so are the cost functions, hence any w, r, p that satisfy the cost equations in the home country satisfy those in the foreign country as well. Consequently, eqs. (10.10) have an infinity of solutions with $w = w^*$, and if the absence of factor intensity reversal is assumed (i.e., the inequalities (10.24) , there are no other solutions. This, of course, is simply the factor price equalization theorem (see Samuelson [19]). For each of the solutions of (10.10) with $w = w^*$ the corresponding $J(w,w,r,p)$ must vanish, hence each point on the world production possibility frontier corresponding to diversification in both countries may be regarded as a degenerate flat segment. If reversal of factor intensity can take place, it is quite possible for the world production possibility frontier also to contain a flat segment corresponding to diversification – separated from the factor price equalization region by a zone of specialization – even when production functions are identical in the two countries.

A case of particular interest is that in which $f_i = f_i^*$ for *some i* but not necessarily both. This can occur if, and only if, (see Shephard [21]) $g_i = g_i^*$ for this i; consequently, if (w,r) is a solution of the left pair of equations in (10.10), it must also be a solution of the pair on the right. If the absence of factor intensity reversal is assumed, there can be no other solution. Consequently, we have

Theorem 3. *If eqs.* (10.10) *have a positive solution* $\bar{w} > 0$, $\bar{w}^* > 0$, $\bar{r} > 0$, $\bar{p} > 0$, *and if* $g_i = g_i^*$ *for some i (i.e.,* $f_i = f_i^*$ *for some i), and if conditions*

to my attention by Maria Schmundt. However, it is not compatible with the assumptions of Theorem 2, since it would entail $\bar{r} = 0$ as may be verified from (10.20). This could not be an equilibrium unless marginal productivity of capital became zero for a finite amount of capital and the functions b_i, b_i^* were defined as the minimum capital-output ratios satisfying (10.5). In general, the condition for the flat is given by (10.21) which requires $(\bar{b}_2 - \bar{b}_2^*)/(\bar{b}_1 - \bar{b}_1^*) \neq \bar{a}_2/\bar{a}_1$ in case $\bar{a}_2/\bar{a}_1 = \bar{a}_2^*/\bar{a}_1^*$ – a case which is logically possible but may be considered as being of the same "exceptional" nature as that of (a-ii) in Theorem 2.

(10.24) *hold, then* $\bar{w} = \bar{w}^*$, *i.e., if production functions are identical in one industry and there is no reversal of factor intensity, wage rates as well as rentals are equalized between the two countries.*

10.3. Alternative Formulation in Terms of Activity Analysis

Production conditions, instead of being described in terms of the smooth production functions of (10.1), may be described by the sets of inequalities

$$\sum_{j \in I_1} a_{1j} x_{1j} + \sum_{j \in I_2} a_{2j} x_{2j} \leqslant l \; ; \quad \sum_{j \in I_1^*} a_{1j}^* x_{1j}^* + \sum_{j \in I_2^*} a_{2j}^* x_{2j}^* \leqslant l^* \; ;$$

$$\sum_{j \in I_1} b_{1j} x_{1j} + \sum_{j \in I_2} b_{2j} x_{2j} \leqslant k \; ; \quad \sum_{j \in I_1^*} b_{1j}^* x_{1j}^* + \sum_{j \in I_2^*} b_{2j}^* x_{2j}^* \leqslant k^* \; ;$$

(10.37)

where the I_1, I_2, I_1^*, I_2^* are sets of integers indexing the activities (a_{ij}, b_{ij}), (a_{ij}^*, b_{ij}^*), and where l, l^* are fixed and k, k^* are restricted by

$$k + k^* \leqslant K \tag{10.38}$$

where K is fixed. The variables x_{ij}, x_{ij}^*, k, k^* are assumed to be nonnegative, and the parameters a_{ij}, b_{ij}, a_{ij}^*, b_{ij}^*, l, l^*, K to be strictly positive.

A point of efficient world production is a pair $(Y_1, Y_2) = (y_1 + y_1^*, y_2 + y_2^*)$ where

$$y_i = \sum_{j \in I_i} x_{ij} \; , \qquad y_i^* = \sum_{j \in I_i} x_{ij}^* \; , \tag{10.39}$$

such that

$$V = Y_1 + p Y_2 = y_1 + p y_2 + y_1^* + p y_2^* \tag{10.40}$$

is a maximum subject to (10.37) and (10.38), where $p > 0$. The problem may therefore be formulated as the following linear programming problem (see Dantzig [4]):

$$\sum_{j\in I_1} a_{1j}x_{1j} + \sum_{j\in I_2} a_{2j}x_{2j} \qquad\qquad\qquad \leqslant l$$

$$\sum_{j\in I_1^*} a_{1j}^*x_{1j}^* + \sum_{j\in I_2^*} a_{2j}^*x_{2j}^* \leqslant l^*$$

$$\sum_{j\in I_1} b_{1j}x_{1j} + \sum_{j\in I_2} b_{2j}x_{2j} + \sum_{j\in I_1^*} b_{1j}^*x_{1j}^* + \sum_{j\in I_2^*} b_{2j}^*x_{2j}^* \leqslant K$$

$$\sum_{j\in I_1} x_{1j} + p\sum_{j\in I_2} x_{2j} + \sum_{j\in I_1^*} x_{1j}^* + p\sum_{j\in I_2^*} x_{2j}^* = V = \max, \qquad (10.41)$$

where $x_{ij} \geqslant 0, x_{ij}^* \geqslant 0$.

From the duality theorem of linear programming (see Dantzig and Orden [5]) an equivalent problem is to find a solution $w \geqslant 0, w^* \geqslant 0, r \geqslant 0$ to the linear programming problem

$$wa_{1j} \qquad + rb_{1j} \geqslant 1 \qquad (j\in I_1)$$

$$wa_{2j} \qquad + rb_{2j} \geqslant p \qquad (j\in I_2)$$

$$w^*a_{1j}^* + rb_{1j}^* \geqslant 1 \qquad (j\in I_1^*)$$

$$w^*a_{2j}^* + rb_{2j}^* \geqslant p \qquad (j\in I_2^*)$$

$$wl + w^*l^* + rK = W = \min, \qquad\qquad (10.42)$$

in the sense that a solution to the inequalities of (10.41) exists if, and only if, a solution to the inequalities of (10.42) exists, and moreover, min W = max V.

An efficient point with diversification is given by a solution of (10.41) with $y_1 > 0, y_2 > 0, y_1^* > 0, y_2^* > 0$. However, it is known from linear programming theory (see Dantzig [4]) that if problem (10.41) has a solution, a solution exists with at most three among the variables x_{ij}, x_{ij}^* strictly positive. For diversification, then, there must be an optimal solution with four among $x_{1j}, x_{2j}, x_{1j}^*, x_{2j}^*$ strictly positive (let them be denoted by $x_1 > 0, x_2 > 0, x_1^* > 0, x_2^* > 0$), and such a solution must therefore be *nonunique*. If one denotes the corresponding $a_{1j}, a_{2j}, b_{1j}, b_{2j}$ by $\bar{a}_1, \bar{a}_2, \bar{b}_1, \bar{b}_2$, respectively, an optimal solution of (10.41) is then given by

$$\bar{a}_1 x_1 + \bar{a}_2 x_2 \qquad\qquad\qquad = l$$

$$\bar{a}_1^* x_1^* + \bar{a}_2^* x_2^* = l^*$$

$$\bar{b}_1 x_1 + \bar{b}_2 x_2 + \bar{b}_1^* x_1^* + \bar{b}_2^* x_2^* = K$$

$$x_1 \quad + px_2 \quad + x_1^* \quad + px_2^* \ = V = \max \qquad\qquad (10.43)$$

where $x_1 > 0$, $x_2 > 0$, $x_1^* > 0$, $x_2^* > 0$. From the simplex criterion of linear programming[9], the nonuniqueness entails that all four corresponding inequalities of (10.42) be equalities, i.e.,

$$w\bar{a}_1 \qquad\qquad + r\bar{b}_1 = 1$$

$$w\bar{a}_2 \qquad\qquad + r\bar{b}_2 = p$$

$$w^* \bar{a}_1^* + r\bar{b}_1^* = 1$$

$$w^* \bar{a}_2^* + r\bar{b}_2^* = p$$

$$wl \ + w^* l^* + rK \ = W = \min . \qquad\qquad (10.44)$$

The four equations of (10.44) correspond to those of (10.20), and Theorem 1, therefore, holds in this case as well.

10.4. An Existence Theorem

The results obtained so far are vacuous unless it can be shown that a positive solution to eqs. (10.10) exists. Some precise hypotheses will be formulated in this section, and the existence of a positive solution to eqs. (10.10) under these hypotheses will be proved. The conditions leading to the desired result are, unfortunately, rather complicated to describe, and on the face of it, it is not obvious that they are compatible with the remaining

---

[9] See Dantzig [4] and Dantzig and Orden [5]; for an elementary exposition see Chipman [1]. The conditions (10.44) are also derived in Koopmans [8]; they correspond to the economically obvious requirement that profits (which are required to be nonpositive by the competitive assumption of free entry) be zero on activities actually engaged in.

assumptions that have been made regarding production conditions in the two countries. In order to leave no doubt on this score, the demonstration will be followed in the next section by a discussion of the case of Cobb-Douglas production functions which will be shown, under a certain very simple necessary and sufficient condition, always to allow a positive solution to eqs. (10.10).

The general nature of the problem may first be outlined. The two pairs of equations on the left and right in (10.10) have as their Jacobians the expressions (10.16) (see Samuelson [19], p. 15, Shephard [21], p. 11) and in the two-dimensional case it is known that condition (10.24) is sufficient for the univalence of the respective mappings (10.10). Consequently, we have the inverse functions which may be written (since the price of commodity 1 is held constant at the value 1) as a function of p alone, as

$$w = W(p) ; \qquad w^* = W^*(p) ;$$

$$r = R(p) ; \qquad r = R^*(p) . \tag{10.45}$$

These functions are continuous and differentiable, and their slopes may be expressed as

$$W'(p) = -\frac{b_1 [W(p),R(p)]}{\Delta [W(p),R(p)]} ; \qquad W^{*'}(p) = -\frac{b_1^* [W^*(p),R^*(p)]}{\Delta^* [W^*(p),R^*(p)]} ;$$

$$R'(p) = \frac{a_1 [W(p),R(p)]}{\Delta [W(p),R(p)]} ; \qquad R^{*'}(p) = \frac{a_1^* [W^*(p),R^*(p)]}{\Delta^* [W^*(p),R^*(p)]} . \tag{10.46}$$

The problem is to show that the curves $R(p)$ and $R^*(p)$ have a unique intersection point at values $p > 0$ and $r \geqslant 0$ for which $w \geqslant 0$ and $w^* \geqslant 0$ (see Jones [8], p. 31–33). This is illustrated in fig. 10.2 which is based on a numerical example to be discussed in Section 10.6.

Define

$$\tilde{w}(r,p) = \min \{ w: g_1(w,r) \geqslant 1, g_2(w,r) \geqslant p, w \geqslant 0 \} ;$$

$$\tilde{w}^*(r,p) = \min \{ w^*: g_1^*(w^*,r) \geqslant 1, g_2^*(w^*,r) \geqslant p, w^* \geqslant 0 \} , \tag{10.47}$$

provided the respective sets are nonempty; otherwise define $\tilde{w}(r,p) = \infty$ or $\tilde{w}^*(r,p) = \infty$, respectively. These functions may be given the following interpretation. If the home country faces given world prices 1 and p of the two

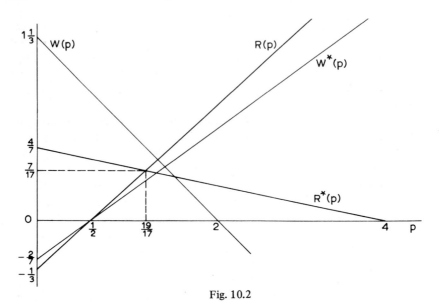

Fig. 10.2

products, and a given rental r on the internationally mobile capital, then competitive equilibrium requires profits to be nonpositive in both industries; if anything is to be produced, however, profits must be zero in at least one industry, and this will occur when $w = \widetilde{w}(r,p)$. Thus $\widetilde{w}(r,p)$ and $\widetilde{w}^*(r,p)$ may be interpreted as the equilibrium wage rates that would be established in the two countries if the prices of the commodities and the rental of capital were given on world markets[10]. Geometrically, $\widetilde{w}(r,p)/r$ is the slope of the tangent (if it exists) to the convex hull of the sets

$$\{(l_1,k_1):f_1(l_1,k_1)\geqslant 1\}, \{(l_2,k_2):f_2(l_2,k_2)\geqslant \frac{1}{p}\}$$

from the point $(0,1/r)$, and the intercept of this tangent on the l-axis is the point $(1/\widetilde{w}(r,p),0)$ (see fig. 10.3). (If no such tangent exists for a given r, $\widetilde{w}(r,p)$ is defined to be zero.)

The following functions will also be defined:

$$\widetilde{g}_i(r,p) = g_i[\widetilde{w}(r,p),r] \; ; \qquad \widetilde{g}_i^*(r,p) = g_i^*[\widetilde{w}^*(r,p), r] \; . \tag{10.48}$$

---

[10] Of course, these could not be full competitive equilibrium wage rates unless r and p were the equilibrium rental and terms of trade, otherwise markets would not be cleared.

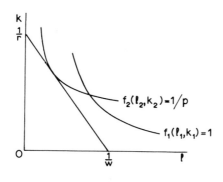

Fig. 10.3

These are the minimum unit costs at terms of trade p and rental r and the wage rates determined by (10.47).

The hypothesis that will now be introduced is modeled after one introduced in a related context by Kuhn [11], [12], pp. 109–110 and modified in Chipman [2], p. 28. In stating the hypothesis it will be tacitly assumed that the two commodities are numbered in such a way that $\Delta(w,r) > 0$, i.e., $b_1(w,r)/a_1(w,r) < b_2(w,r)/a_2(w,r)$, in a certain interval $w_{min} \leqslant w \leqslant w_{max}$, $r_{min} \leqslant r \leqslant r_{max}$. This means that commodity 2 is relatively capital intensive and commodity 1 is relatively labor intensive in the home country, for all w, r in the above intervals. This obviously involves no loss of generality provided $\Delta(w,r)$ is one-signed in the given interval. However, it will be necessary in the following statement to distinguish whether $\Delta^*(w^*,r)$ is positive or negative: if positive, either (a) $a_1/\Delta > a_1^*/\Delta^*$ and the function $R^*(p)$ of (10.45) cuts the function $R(p)$ from above on the left; or (b) $a_1/\Delta < a_1^*/\Delta^*$ and $R^*(p)$ cuts $R(p)$ from below on the left; or (c) $\Delta^* < 0$, hence $a_1/\Delta > a_1^*/\Delta^*$ so $R^*(p)$ cuts $R(p)$ from below on the right. The cases are illustrated in figs. 10.4a, b, and c, respectively, where $R(p)$ is upward sloping and fixed, and where $R^*(p)$ rotates successively in a contraclockwise direction.

Hypothesis 1. There exist two terms of trade $p' < p''$ and six rentals of capital $0 < r_1' < r_2' < r_3'$, $0 < r_1'' < r_2'' < r_3''$ such that the functions $\tilde{w}$, $\tilde{w}^*$ are positive and finite at these values, and such that either
(a) at terms of trade p',

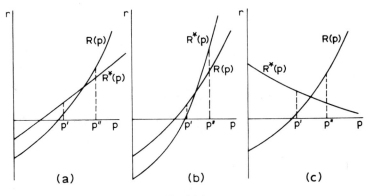

Fig. 10.4

$$\tilde{g}_2(r_1',p')/p' < \tilde{g}_1(r_1',p') ; \qquad \tilde{g}_2^*(r_1',p')/p' < \tilde{g}_1^*(r_1',p') ;$$

$$\tilde{g}_2(r_2',p')/p' > \tilde{g}_1(r_2',p') ; \qquad \tilde{g}_2^*(r_2',p')/p' < \tilde{g}_1^*(r_2',p') ; \qquad (10.49')$$

$$\tilde{g}_2(r_3',p')/p' > \tilde{g}_1(r_3',p') ; \qquad \tilde{g}_2^*(r_3',p')/p' > \tilde{g}_1^*(r_3',p') ;$$

and, at terms of trade p'',

$$\tilde{g}_2(r_1'',p'')/p'' < \tilde{g}_1(r_1'',p'') ; \qquad \tilde{g}_2^*(r_1'',p'')/p'' < \tilde{g}_1^*(r_1'',p'') ;$$

$$\tilde{g}_2(r_2'',p'')/p'' < \tilde{g}_1(r_2'',p'') ; \qquad \tilde{g}_2^*(r_2'',p'')/p'' > \tilde{g}_1^*(r_2'',p'') ; \quad (10.49'')$$

$$\tilde{g}_2(r_3'',p'')/p'' > \tilde{g}_1(r_3'',p'') ; \qquad \tilde{g}_2^*(r_3'',p'')/p'' > \tilde{g}_1^*(r_3'',p'') ;$$

or

(b) the inequalities on the left of (10.49′) and (10.49″) referring to the home country are interchanged with those on the right referring to the foreign country; or

(c) the inequalities on the left of (10.49′) and (10.49″) are retained but those on the right reversed.

Moreover, let r_{min} and r_{max} be the smallest and largest among the above six rentals, and let w_{min} and w_{max} be the smallest and largest values of $\tilde{w}(r,p)$ for $r_{min} \leqslant r \leqslant r_{max}$ and $p' < p < p''$; similarly for w_{min}^* and w_{max}^*. Then

$$\Delta(w,r) \neq 0 \quad \text{and} \quad \Delta^*(w^*,r) \neq 0 \tag{10.50}$$

for all w, w^*, r, on the intervals

$$w_{\min} \leqslant w \leqslant w_{\max} \; ; \quad w^*_{\min} \leqslant w^* \leqslant w^*_{\max} \; ; \quad r_{\min} \leqslant r \leqslant r_{\max} \; . \tag{10.51}$$

In words, the hypothesis may be described as follows: At the lower terms of trade p', there will be a sufficiently small rental r_1' so that both countries will specialize in their capital intensive product (which is commodity 2 in the foreign country in cases (a) and (b) but commodity 1 in case (c)); and a larger rental r_2' so that one of the countries (the home country in cases (a) and (c) and the foreign country in case (b)) will be the first to switch to its labor intensive product; and finally a still larger rental r_3' such that both countries will specialize in their labor intensive product. At the higher terms of trade p'', again there will be a sufficiently small rental r_1'' so that both countries will specialize in their capital intensive product, but now there will be a larger rental r_2'' such that the *other* country — the foreign country in cases (a) and (c) and the home country in case (b) — will be the first to switch to its labor intensive product; finally at rental r_3'' both countries will specialize in their labor intensive product.

Hypothesis 2. For all w, w^*, r on the intervals (10.51),

$$\frac{a_1(w,r)}{\Delta(w,r)} - \frac{a_1^*(w^*,r)}{\Delta^*(w^*,r)} \neq 0 . \tag{10.52}$$

In view of (10.46), this hypothesis ensures that the functions $R(p)$ and $R^*(p)$ have unequal slopes on the interval $p' \leqslant p \leqslant p''$. This is guaranteed automatically in case (c) of Hypothesis 1, corresponding to the case $\Delta(w,r) > 0$ and $\Delta^*(w^*,r) < 0$.

Theorem 4. Under Hypothesis 1, there exists a positive solution $p > 0$, $w > 0$, $w^* > 0$, $r > 0$ to the system of eqs. (10.10). If Hypothesis 2 also holds, this solution is unique in the interval (10.51).

Proof. (Only case (a) of Hypothesis 1 need be taken up; the other two cases may be handled similarly.)

From Hypothesis 1, the functions $\widetilde{w}(r,p')$, $\widetilde{w}^*(r,p')$ are positive and finite on the interval $r_{\min} \leqslant r \leqslant r_{\max}$, and since the sets

$$\{(w,r) \ : \ g_1(w,r) \geqslant 1, \ g_2(w,r) \geqslant p, \ w \geqslant 0, r \geqslant 0\}$$

$$\{(w^*,r) : \ g_1^*(w^*,r) \geqslant 1, \ g_2^*(w^*,r) \geqslant p, \ w^* \geqslant 0, r \geqslant 0\}$$

are closed and convex, the functions $\tilde{w}(r,p')$, $\tilde{w}^*(r,p')$ of (10.47) are convex, hence continuous, functions of r; consequently the functions $\tilde{g}_i(r,p')$, $\tilde{g}_i^*(r,p')$ of (10.48) are continuous functions of r. By conditions (10.49') of Hypothesis 1, it follows[11] that there exist r' and $r^{*'}$ such that

$$r_1' < r' < r_2' \ \text{and} \ \tilde{g}_2(r',p')/p' = \tilde{g}_1(r',p') ;$$

$$r_2' < r^{*'} < r_3' \ \text{and} \ \tilde{g}_2^*(r^{*'},p')/p' = \tilde{g}_1^*(r^{*'},p') . \qquad (10.53')$$

Thus, from (10.53'), (10.47), and (10.48), it follows that $g_2[\tilde{w}(r',p'), r']/p' = g_1[\tilde{w}(r',p'), r'] = 1$ and $g_2^*[\tilde{w}^*(r',p'),r']/p' = g_1^*[\tilde{w}^*(r',p'),p'] = 1$, hence $R(p') = r' < r^{*'} = R^*(p')$ from (10.10) and (10.45). Moreover, $W(p') = \tilde{w}(r',p') > 0$ and $W^*(p') = \tilde{w}^*(r',p') > 0$ by Hypothesis 1.

Likewise, from conditions (10.49'') of Hypothesis 1, there exist r'' and $r^{*''}$ such that

$$r_1'' < r^{*''} < r_2'' \ \text{and} \ \tilde{g}_2^*(r^{*''},p'')/p'' = \tilde{g}_1^*(r^{*''},p'') ;$$

$$r_2'' < r'' < r_3'' \ \text{and} \ \tilde{g}_2(r'',p'')/p'' = \tilde{g}_1(r'',p'') . \qquad (10.53'')$$

Thus, $R^*(p'') = r^{*''} < r'' = R(p'')$, and by Hypothesis 1, $W^*(p'') = \tilde{w}^*(r'',p'') > 0$ and $W(p'') = \tilde{w}(r'',p'') > 0$.

Since the functions $R(p)$ and $R^*(p)$ are continuous (see eqs. (10.10) and the definition (10.45)) and increasing (from (10.46) and recalling that $\Delta(w,r) > 0$ and $\Delta^*(w^*,r) > 0$ in case (a) of Hypothesis 1), there exist $\bar{r} > 0$ and $\bar{p} > 0$ such that $\bar{r} = R(\bar{p}) = R^*(\bar{p})$. This completes the first part of the proof. That uniqueness follows from Hypothesis 2 is obvious.

Q.E.D.

10.5. The Case of Cobb-Douglas Production Functions

Let the production functions be of the Cobb-Douglas form

---

[11] This result follows from Kuhn's theorem [11,12], pp. 109–110 as generalized in Chipman [2], p. 28, for the special two-dimensional case; the proof in this special case is, of course, quite elementary.

$$f_i(l_i,k_i) = \mu_i l_i^{\alpha_i} k_i^{\beta_i} ; \qquad \alpha_i > 0, \beta_i > 0, \alpha_i + \beta_i = 1 \quad (i=1,2) ;$$

$$f_i^*(l_i^*,k_i^*) = \mu_i^* l_i^{*\alpha_i^*} k_i^{*\beta_i^*} ; \qquad \alpha_i^* > 0, \beta_i^* > 0, \alpha_i^* + \beta_i^* = 1 \quad (i=1,2) .$$

$$(10.54)$$

Then it is readily verified that the corresponding minimum unit cost functions are given by

$$g_i(w,r) = v_i w^{\alpha_i} r^{\beta_i} ; \qquad g_i^*(w^*,r^*) = v_i^* w^{*\alpha_i^*} r^{*\beta_i^*} . \qquad (10.55)$$

where

$$v_i = \mu_i^{-1} \alpha_i^{-\alpha_i} \beta_i^{-\beta_i} ; \qquad v_i^* = \mu_i^{*-1} \alpha_i^{*-\alpha_i^*} \beta_i^{*-\beta_i^*} . \qquad (10.56)$$

The eqs. (10.10) therefore become

$$v_1 w^{\alpha_1} r^{\beta_1} = 1 ; \qquad v_1^* w^{*\alpha_1^*} r^{\beta_1^*} = 1 ;$$

$$v_2 w^{\alpha_2} r^{\beta_2} = p ; \qquad v_2^* w^{*\alpha_2^*} r^{\beta_2^*} = p , \qquad (10.57)$$

Define

$$\omega = \log w , \quad \omega^* = \log w^* , \quad \rho = \log r , \quad \pi = \log p \qquad (10.58)$$

and

$$\gamma_i = -\log v_i, \quad \gamma_i^* = -\log v_i^* . \qquad (10.59)$$

Then the system (10.57) can be transformed into the linear system

$$\begin{bmatrix} \alpha_1 & 0 & \beta_1 & 0 \\ \alpha_2 & 0 & \beta_2 & -1 \\ 0 & \alpha_1^* & \beta_1^* & 0 \\ 0 & \alpha_2^* & \beta_2^* & -1 \end{bmatrix} \begin{bmatrix} \omega \\ \omega^* \\ \rho \\ \pi \end{bmatrix} = \begin{bmatrix} \gamma_1 \\ \gamma_2 \\ \gamma_1^* \\ \gamma_2^* \end{bmatrix} . \qquad (10.60)$$

The question of the existence of a unique positive solution $\bar{w} > 0, \bar{w}^* > 0,$ $\bar{r} > 0, \bar{p} > 0$ to (10.57) is then equivalent to the question of the existence of a unique solution to (10.60).

Recalling that $\alpha_i + \beta_i = \alpha_i^* + \beta_i^* = 1$, denote

$$\delta \;=\; \begin{vmatrix} \alpha_1 & \alpha_2 \\ \beta_1 & \beta_2 \end{vmatrix} = \begin{vmatrix} \alpha_1 & \alpha_2 \\ 1 & 1 \end{vmatrix} = \alpha_1 - \alpha_2 \;;$$

$$\delta^* = \begin{vmatrix} \alpha_1^* & \alpha_2^* \\ \beta_1^* & \beta_2^* \end{vmatrix} = \begin{vmatrix} \alpha_1^* & \alpha_2^* \\ 1 & 1 \end{vmatrix} = \alpha_1^* - \alpha_2^* .$$

(10.61)

We verify that

$$\begin{vmatrix} \alpha_1 & 0 & \beta_1 & 0 \\ \alpha_2 & 0 & \beta_2 & -1 \\ 0 & \alpha_1^* & \beta_1^* & 0 \\ 0 & \alpha_2^* & \beta_2^* & -1 \end{vmatrix} = \alpha_1^* \delta - \alpha_1 \delta^* = \alpha_1 \alpha_2^* - \alpha_2 \alpha_1^* ,$$

(10.62)

so that we have the following necessary and sufficient condition for a unique positive solution to (10.57):

$$\frac{\alpha_2}{\alpha_1} \neq \frac{\alpha_2^*}{\alpha_1^*} .$$

(10.63)

We may therefore state:

Theorem 5. Let production functions be of the Cobb-Douglas type (10.54). *Then a necessary and sufficient condition for the existence of a unique positive solution* $\overline{w} > 0$, $\overline{w}^* > 0$, $\overline{r} > 0$, $\overline{p} > 0$ *to the system of eqs.* (10.10) *is that* $\alpha_2/\alpha_1 \neq \alpha_2^*/\alpha_1^*$. *Under these conditions, for all choices l, l* of the labor endowments of the two countries, there exists a world endowment of capital (determined by* (10.26)*) such that the world production possibility set has a flat segment.*

Analysis of the Cobb-Douglas case suggests the use in the general case of the transformation from the logarithms of factor prices to the logarithms of commodity prices. Following Chipman [2], p. 37, [3], define these functions ψ_i, ψ_i^* by

(10.64)

$$\psi_i(\omega,\rho) = \log g_i(e^\omega, e^\rho) \;; \qquad \psi_i^*(\omega^*,\rho^*) = \log g_i^*(e^{\omega^*}, e^{\rho^*}) \qquad (i = 1,2) .$$

Then (10.10) goes over into the system

$$\psi_1(\omega,\rho) = 0 ; \qquad \psi_1^*(\omega^*,\rho) = 0 ; \qquad (10.65)$$

$$\psi_2(\omega,\rho) = \pi ; \qquad \psi_2^*(\omega^*,\rho) = \pi .$$

The question of the existence of a positive solution to (10.10) is equivalent to that of the existence of a solution to (10.65). Making use again of (10.13), we may define the functions

$$\alpha_i(\omega,\rho) = \frac{\partial \psi_1}{\partial \omega} = \frac{wa_i(w,r)}{g_i(w,r)} ; \qquad \alpha_i^*(\omega^*,\rho^*) = \frac{\partial \psi_i^*}{\partial \omega^*} = \frac{w^*a_i^*(w^*,r^*)}{g_i^*(w^*,r^*)} ;$$

$$(10.66)$$

$$\beta_i(\omega,\rho) = \frac{\partial \psi_i}{\partial \rho} = \frac{rb_i(w,r)}{g_i(w,r)} ; \qquad \beta_i^*(\omega^*,\rho^*) = \frac{\partial \psi_i^*}{\partial \rho^*} = \frac{r^*b_i^*(w^*,r^*)}{g_i^*(w^*,r^*)} ;$$

it being understood that w, r, w^*, r^* stand for e^ω, e^ρ, e^{ω^*}, e^{ρ^*} in the above expressions. Here α_i and β_i are the relative outlays on labor and capital in the ith industry in the home country, as functions of the wage rate and rental of capital, and $\alpha_i(\omega,\rho) + \beta_i(\omega,\rho) = 1$ for all ω,ρ; similarly for the foreign country. Define further

$$\delta(\omega,\rho) = \alpha_1(\omega,\rho) - \alpha_2(\omega,\rho) ; \qquad \delta^*(\omega^*,\rho^*) = \alpha_1^*(\omega^*,\rho^*) - \alpha_2^*(\omega^*,\rho^*) .$$

$$(10.67)$$

Analogously to (10.14), the system (10.65) may be rewritten in the form

$$\chi_1(\omega,\omega^*,\rho,\pi) = \psi(\omega,\rho) \qquad = 0$$

$$\chi_2(\omega,\omega^*,\rho,\pi) = \psi(\omega,\rho) \quad - \pi = 0$$

$$(10.68)$$

$$\chi_1^*(\omega,\omega^*,\rho,\pi) = \psi(\omega^*,\rho) \qquad = 0$$

$$\chi_2^*(\omega,\omega^*,\rho,\pi) = \psi(\omega^*,\rho) - \pi = 0$$

where $\chi = (\chi_1,\chi_2,\chi_1^*,\chi_2^*)$ maps the four-dimensional Euclidean space into itself. From (10.66) and (10.67) it follows that the Jacobian determinant of this transformation χ is, as in (10.62),

$$\Theta(\omega,\omega^*,\rho,\pi) = \begin{vmatrix} \alpha_1(\omega,\rho) & 0 & \beta_1(\omega,\rho) & 0 \\ \alpha_2(\omega,\rho) & 0 & \beta_2(\omega,\rho) & -1 \\ 0 & \alpha_1^*(\omega^*,\rho) & \beta_1^*(\omega^*,\rho) & 0 \\ 0 & \alpha_2^*(\omega^*,\rho) & \beta_2^*(\omega^*,\rho) & -1 \end{vmatrix}$$

$$= \alpha_1^*(\omega^*,\rho)\delta(\omega,\rho) - \alpha_1(\omega,\rho)\delta^*(\omega^*,\rho)$$

$$= \alpha_1(\omega,\rho)\alpha_2^*(\omega^*,\rho) - \alpha_2(\omega,\rho)\alpha_1^*(\omega^*,\rho)$$

$$= \frac{ww^*r}{g_2(w^*,r)}\,[a_1^*(w^*,r)\Delta(w,r) - a_1(w,r)\Delta^*(w^*,r)]$$

$$= \frac{ww^*r}{g_2(w^*,r)}\,J(w,w^*,r,p) \tag{10.69}$$

where w, w^*, r, p stand for e^ω, e^{ω^*}, e^ρ, e^π and where the last equality follows from the definition (10.15), and the second-to-last equality makes use of (10.66).

Given a positive solution $\bar{w} > 0$, $\bar{w}^* > 0$, $\bar{r} > 0$, $\bar{p} > 0$ to (10.10), since $g_2(\bar{w}^*,\bar{r}) = p$, it is clear from (10.25) that condition (10.27) of Theorem 2 is equivalent to

$$\frac{\bar{\alpha}_2}{\bar{\alpha}_1} \neq \frac{\bar{\alpha}_2^*}{\bar{\alpha}_1^*} \tag{10.70}$$

where

$$\bar{\alpha}_i = \alpha_i(\bar{\omega},\bar{\rho}) = \alpha_i(\log\bar{w},\log\bar{r})\,; \quad \bar{\alpha}_i^* = \alpha_i^*(\bar{\omega}^*,\bar{\rho}) = \alpha_i^*(\log\bar{w}^*,\log\bar{r})\,. \tag{10.71}$$

Thus, from the Corollary to Theorem 2, if $\bar{\alpha}_1 \neq \bar{\alpha}_2$ and $\bar{\alpha}_1^* \neq \bar{\alpha}_2^*$, then condition (10.70) is necessary and sufficient for the existence — for some stock of capital satisfying (10.26) — of a nondegenerate flat segment.

In the Cobb-Douglas case, α_i and α_i^* are constant functions, and condition (10.70) is also necessary and sufficient for the existence of a unique solution to (10.68). It might be thought that a condition such as $\alpha_2(\omega,\rho)/\alpha_1(\omega,\rho) \neq \alpha_2^*(\omega^*,\rho^*)/\alpha_1^*(\omega^*,\rho^*)$ for all ω, ω^*, ρ, ρ^* might be sufficient for this in general; however, it can readily be shown by counterexamples that this is not the case. Nevertheless, the following proposition can be established:

Theorem 6. Let the functions α_i, α_i^* satisfy

$$0 \ll \alpha_i(\omega,\rho) \ll 1 , \quad 0 \ll \alpha_i^*(\omega^*,\rho^*) \ll 1 \qquad (i=1,2) \tag{10.72}$$

and

$$0 \ll \left| \frac{\alpha_2(\omega,\rho)}{\alpha_1(\omega,\rho)} - \frac{\alpha_2^*(\omega^*,\rho^*)}{\alpha_1^*(\omega^*,\rho^*)} \right| \ll \infty \tag{10.73}$$

uniformly in ω, ρ, ω^*, ρ^*, where $0 \ll x \ll L$ means that $0 < m \leqslant x \leqslant M < L$ for some m, M and all x. Then the system of eqs. (10.65) has a unique solution ω, ω^*, ρ, π.

Proof. Defining $\sigma(\rho)$, $\sigma^*(\rho^*)$ by $\psi_1[\sigma(\rho),\rho] \equiv 0$, $\psi_1^*[\sigma^*(\rho^*),\rho^*] \equiv 0$ and making use of (10.66) and (10.72), we see that the functions σ, σ^* are one-to-one correspondences between the real line and itself. Defining $\tilde{\psi}_2(\rho) = \psi_2[\sigma(\rho),\rho]$ and $\tilde{\psi}_2^*[\rho^*] = \psi_2^*[\sigma^*(\rho^*),\rho^*]$, we see from use of (10.66) and (10.72) that $\tilde{\psi}_2$, $\tilde{\psi}_2^*$ also have this property. From (10.73) we see that $\tilde{\psi}_2 - \tilde{\psi}_2^*$ also has this property, and therefore there exists a unique $\bar{\rho}$ such that $\tilde{\psi}_2(\bar{\rho}) - \tilde{\psi}_2^*(\bar{\rho}) = 0$. Then $\bar{\pi} = \tilde{\psi}_2(\bar{\rho})$, $\bar{\omega} = \sigma(\bar{\rho})$, $\omega^* = \sigma^*(\bar{\rho})$, and the theorem is established.

10.6. A Numerical Example

The following example will illustrate the preceding analysis. It will be constructed by first considering the case of fixed technical coefficients, then finding a full competitive equilibrium that occurs on a flat segment of the world production possibility frontier, and finally by smoothing out the iso-quants in such a way as to leave the competitive equilibrium undisturbed.

Let production functions in the two countries have the fixed-coefficient form

$$f_i(l_i,k_i) = \min\left(\frac{l_i}{\bar{a}_i}, \frac{k_i}{\bar{b}_i} \right); \qquad f_i^*(l_i^*,k_i^*) = \min\left(\frac{l_i^*}{\bar{a}_i^*}, \frac{k_i^*}{\bar{b}_i^*} \right) \qquad (i=1,2) . \tag{10.74}$$

The dual minimum-unit-cost functions then have the linear form

$$g_i(w,r) = w\bar{a}_i + r\bar{b}_i ; \qquad g_i^*(w^*,r^*) = w^*\bar{a}_i^* + r^*\bar{b}_i^* \qquad (i=1,2) . \tag{10.75}$$

Thus eqs. (10.10) are linear; hence as long as

$$\bar{\Delta} = \begin{vmatrix} \bar{a}_1 & \bar{a}_2 \\ \bar{b}_1 & \bar{b}_2 \end{vmatrix} \neq 0, \qquad \bar{\Delta}^* = \begin{vmatrix} \bar{a}_1^* & \bar{a}_2^* \\ \bar{b}_1^* & \bar{b}_2^* \end{vmatrix} \neq 0, \tag{10.76}$$

they may be solved in pairs to obtain the counterpart of eqs. (10.45):

$$w = W(p) \equiv \frac{\bar{b}_2}{\bar{\Delta}} - \frac{\bar{b}_1}{\bar{\Delta}} p \ ; \qquad w^* = W^*(p) \equiv \frac{\bar{b}_2^*}{\bar{\Delta}^*} - \frac{\bar{b}_1^*}{\bar{\Delta}^*} p \ ;$$

$$r = R(p) \equiv \frac{\bar{a}_1}{\bar{\Delta}} p - \frac{\bar{a}_2}{\bar{\Delta}} \ ; \qquad r = R^*(p) \equiv \frac{\bar{a}_1^*}{\bar{\Delta}^*} p - \frac{\bar{a}_2^*}{\bar{\Delta}^*} \ . \tag{10.77}$$

The graphs of these four functions are shown in fig. 10.2 for the case

$$\begin{bmatrix} \bar{a}_1 & \bar{a}_2 \\ \bar{b}_1 & \bar{b}_2 \end{bmatrix} = \begin{bmatrix} 1 & \frac{1}{2} \\ 1 & 2 \end{bmatrix} ; \qquad \begin{bmatrix} \bar{a}_1^* & \bar{a}_2^* \\ \bar{b}_1^* & \bar{b}_2^* \end{bmatrix} = \begin{bmatrix} \frac{1}{2} & 2 \\ 2 & 1 \end{bmatrix} , \tag{10.78}$$

in which $\bar{\Delta}^* = 1\frac{1}{2}$ and $\bar{\Delta}^* = -3\frac{1}{2}$; they are given by

$$w = W(p) = \frac{4}{3} - \frac{2}{3} p \ ; \qquad w^* = W^*(p) = -\frac{2}{7} + \frac{4}{7} p \ ; \tag{10.79}$$

$$r = R(p) = \frac{2}{3} p - \frac{1}{3} \ ; \qquad r = R^*(p) = -\frac{1}{7} p + \frac{4}{7} . \tag{10.79}$$

Solving, we obtain

$$\bar{w} = \frac{10}{17} \ ; \qquad \bar{w}^* = \frac{6}{17} \ ; \qquad \bar{r} = \frac{7}{17} \ ; \qquad \bar{p} = \frac{19}{17} , \tag{10.80}$$

as may also be verified directly from (10.20). If we take, for instance, $p' = \frac{2}{3}$ and $p'' = 1\frac{2}{3}$, it may be verified that case (c) of Hypothesis 1 is satisfied. Condition (10.26) now becomes

$$l + \tfrac{1}{2} l^* < K < 4l + 4l^*$$

and is therefore satisfied by the choice of

$$l = 1 ; \qquad l^* = 1 ; \qquad K = 6 \tag{10.81}$$

(in fact by any K in the interval $1\frac{1}{2} < K < 8$). From (10.34), we obtain $2 < k < 4$ and therefore from (10.33) we find the limits between which the production possibility set is flat (see fig. 10.1):

$$2\tfrac{2}{3} \geqslant Y_1 \geqslant \tfrac{6}{7} ; \qquad \tfrac{2}{3} \leqslant Y_2 \leqslant 2\tfrac{2}{7} . \tag{10.82}$$

To obtain a competitive equilibrium, assume that workers and capitalists in both countries all have identical homogeneous utility functions of the form

$$u = y_1^{\theta_1} y_2^{\theta_2} \quad (\theta_1 > 0, \theta_2 > 0, \ \theta_1 + \theta_2 = 1) . \tag{10.83}$$

Then the competitive equilibrium will necessarily coincide with the point where the aggregate utility function

$$U = Y_1^{\theta_1} Y_2^{\theta_2}$$

reaches a maximum within the world production possibility set. As long as θ_1 lies in the interval

$$0.251 = \frac{6/7}{2\tfrac{2}{3} + \tfrac{2}{3}p} \leqslant \frac{Y_1}{Y_1 + pY_2} = \theta_1 \leqslant \frac{2\tfrac{2}{3}}{2\tfrac{2}{3} + \tfrac{2}{3}p} = 0.782 , \tag{10.84}$$

this maximum will be reached on the flat segment (see again fig. 10.1).

To complete the example, the assumption of fixed technical coefficients will now be removed. Let production functions in both countries have the CES form

$$f_i(l_i, k_i) = \mu_i [\alpha_i l_i^{1-1/\sigma_i} + \beta_i k_i^{1-1/\sigma_i}]^{\sigma_i/(\sigma_i - 1)} \qquad (i = 1, 2)$$
$$f_i^*(l_i^*, k_i^*) = \mu_i^* [\alpha_i^* l_i^{*1-1/\sigma_i^*} + \beta_i^* k_i^{*1-1/\sigma_i^*}]^{\sigma_i^*/(\sigma_i^* - 1)} \qquad (i = 1, 2) \tag{10.85}$$

where

$$\mu_i > 0, \alpha_i > 0, \beta_i > 0, \alpha_i + \beta_i = 1, \sigma_i > 0 ;$$
$$\mu_i^* > 0, \alpha_i^* > 0, \beta_i^* > 0, \alpha_i^* + \beta_i^* = 1, \sigma_i^* > 0 . \tag{10.86}$$

To construct the required example, we need merely set marginal rates of substitution equal to the wage-rental ratios, and solve for β_i, β_i^* to obtain

$$\beta_i = \frac{1}{(1+\kappa_i)}, \qquad \beta_i^* = \frac{1}{(1+\kappa_i^*)} \tag{10.87}$$

where

$$\kappa_i = \left[\frac{\bar{a}_i}{\bar{b}_i}\right]^{1/\sigma_i} \frac{\bar{w}}{\bar{r}}, \qquad \kappa_i^* = \left[\frac{\bar{a}_i^*}{\bar{b}_i^*}\right]^{1/\sigma_i^*} \frac{\bar{w}^*}{\bar{r}}, \tag{10.88}$$

and $\bar{w}$, $\bar{w}^*$, $\bar{r}$ are given the values (10.80). Then the μ_i, μ_i^* are evaluated by setting $f_i(\bar{a}_i,\bar{b}_i) = f_i^*(\bar{a}_i^*,\bar{b}_i^*) = 1$. Choosing, for instance

$$\sigma_1 = 1\tfrac{1}{2}, \quad \sigma_2 = \sigma_1^* = 2, \quad \sigma_2^* \to 1, \tag{10.89}$$

the required production functions (10.85) are

$$f_1(l_1,k_1) = \left(\frac{10}{17}\sqrt[3]{l_1} + \frac{7}{17}\sqrt[3]{k_1}\right)^3 ; \quad f_2(l_2,k_2) = \frac{288}{361}\left[\frac{5}{12}\sqrt{l_2} + \frac{7}{12}\sqrt{k_2}\right]^2 ;$$

$$\tag{10.90}$$

$$f_1^*(l_1^*,k_1^*) = \frac{200}{289}(0.3\sqrt{l_1^*}+0.7\sqrt{k_1^*})^2 ; \quad f_2^*(l_2^*,k_2^*) = 2^{-12/19}l_2^{*\,12/19}k_2^{*\,7/19} .$$

The minimum unit cost functions corresponding to the production functions (10.85) are (see Chipman [2], pp. 59–60])

$$g_i(w,r) \;\; = \mu_i^{-1}(\alpha_i^\sigma w^{1-\sigma}+\beta_i^\sigma r^{1-\sigma})^{1/(1-\sigma)} \qquad (i=1,2)$$

$$\tag{10.91}$$

$$g_i^*(w^*,r) = \mu_i^{*-1}(\alpha_i^{*\sigma^*} w^{*\,1-\sigma^*}+\beta_i^{*\sigma^*} r^{1-\sigma^*})^{1/1-\sigma^*} \qquad (i=1,2) .$$

For the production functions (10.90), we then obtain the corresponding dual cost functions

$$g_1(w,r) = \left[\left(\frac{10}{17}\right)^{3/2} w^{-1/2} + \left(\frac{7}{17}\right)^{3/2} r^{-1/2} \right]^{-2} ;$$

$$g_2(w,r) = \frac{361}{288} \left[\left(\frac{5}{12}\right)^2 w^{-1} + \left(\frac{7}{12}\right)^2 r^{-1} \right]^{-1} ,$$

$$g_1^*(w^*,r) = \frac{289}{200} \left[0.3^2 w^{*-1} + 0.7^2 r^{-1} \right]^{-1} ;$$

(10.92)

$$g_2^*(w^*,r) = 2^{12/19} \left(\frac{12}{19}\right)^{-12/19} \left(\frac{7}{19}\right)^{-7/19} w^{*12/19} r^{7/19} .$$

Substituting (10.80) in (10.92), one verifies that (10.10) holds.

The situation is illustrated in figs. 10.5a and b in terms of the diagrams introduced by Lerner [14]. Suppose $k = 2$; this is shown by the vector $v = (l,k) = (1,2)$ in fig. 10.5 and the vector $v^* = (l^*,k^*) = (1,4)$ in fig. 10.5b. National income is therefore $wl + rk = 24/17$ at home and $w^*l^* + rk^* = 2$ abroad; isoquants are shown in fig. 10.5a corresponding to 24/17 units of commodity a and 24/19 units of commodity 2 (having the same value at price $p = 19/17$), and in fig. 10.5b corresponding to 2 units of commodity 1 and 34/19 units of commodity 2. In the home country the common tangent

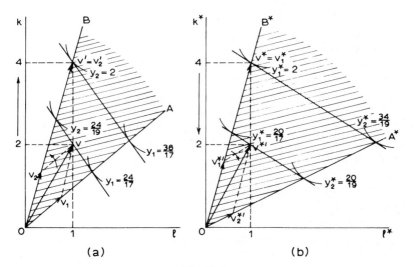

(a)   (b)

Fig. 10.5

to these two isoquants passes through v, and defines the diversification cone AOB, and similarly in the foreign country; at home the factors are allocated in accordance with (10.32) and (10.78), determining the outputs $y_1 = \frac{2}{3}$, $y_2 = \frac{2}{3}$ and hence the vectors $v_1 = (l_1,k_1) = (a_1,b_1)y_1 = (\frac{2}{3},\frac{2}{3})$ and $v_2 = (l_2,k_2)$ $= (a_2,b_2)y_2 = (\frac{1}{3},\frac{4}{3})$ which sum to v, whereas abroad the outputs are (y_1^*,y_2^*) $= (2,0)$ hence the allocation is $v_1^* = (l_1^*,k_1^*) = (a_1^*,b_1^*)y_1^* = (1,4) = v$ and $v_2^* =$ $(l_2^*,k_2^*) = (a_2^*,b_2^*)y_2^* = (0,0)$. Thus the foreign country specializes in commodity 1. When $k = 4$, we have the opposite situation: national income is now $38/17$ and $20/17$ at home and abroad, respectively, the foreign country diversifies and the home country specializes in commodity 2. When $2 < k < 4$, both countries' endowment vectors are inside their respective diversification cones.

10.7. The Question of Probabilities

As is the case with any economic model, and particularly with models of international trade, there are many outcomes that are logically possible but need never be taken account of in practice. These are the "exceptional" outcomes that would occur "by sheer coincidence". While such expressions frequently occur in the literature, they have not been based on any precise or rigorous formulation. An explicit formulation in terms of probabilities is, however, perfectly straightforward and will now be briefly developed.

In accordance with Bayesian ideas, we may consider a well-defined set consisting of 4-tuples of production functions (f_1,f_2,f_1^*,f_2^*) and specify a prior probability distribution over this set. For simplicity and definiteness, I shall consider only the case of Cobb-Douglas production functions; this makes it possible to define the probability distribution over the eight-dimensional space of points $(\mu_1,\alpha_1,\mu_2,\alpha_2,\mu_1^*,\alpha_1^*,\mu_2^*,\alpha_2^*)$ where $\mu_i > 0$, $\mu_i^* > 0$, $0 < \alpha_i < 1$, $0 < \alpha_i^* < 1$, $i = 1,2$. It must be kept in mind that the Cobb-Douglas case has especially favorable properties that are not typical of the general case; however, a general treatment is beyond the scope of this paper, and it will suffice for our purposes to show how an analysis can be carried through in the simplest case.

A prior probability distribution may also be assigned to the set of factor endowments (l,l^*,K), where $l > 0$, $l^* > 0$, and $K > 0$; in particular this will yield a conditional distribution of K given l and l^*. Finally, to obtain utmost simplification on the demand side, we may assume that all individuals in both countries have identical homothetic utility functions; then aggregate demand is independent of the distribution of factors, and we need simply specify a distribution over a class of homothetic utility functions U. Choosing the Cobb-Douglas family as in Section 10.6, this reduces to specifying a probability distribution of the parameter θ_1 over the interval $0 < \theta_1 < 1$. It is natural to assume that the distributions of the production functions, utility functions, and factor endowments are mutually independent.

By Bayes' theorem we have

$$P(H|E) = \frac{P(E|H)}{P(E)} P(H) \qquad \text{if } P(E) > 0, P(H) > 0 ,$$

i.e., the conditional probability of the hypothesis H given the observed event E (the posterior probability of H) is proportional to the product of the likelihood of H, $P(E|H)$, and the prior probability of H, $P(H)$. The object of our analysis is to show that equilibrium on a flat segment of the world production possibility frontier can occur with positive prior probability.

With respect to the distribution of production functions, two extreme assumptions are possible. (1) On the one hand, we can assume that the distribution of production functions is independent as between countries as well as industries; then we can reasonably assume that this distribution is absolutely continuous, and since the set of points in the above eight-dimensional space for which $\alpha_2/\alpha_1 = \alpha_2^*/\alpha_1^*$ has zero Lebesgue measure, condition (10.63) holds with probability 1. Likewise we can conclude that the "singular" case of Theorem 2 has zero probability; therefore from Theorem 5 it follows that a positive solution $\bar{w} > 0$, $\bar{w}^* > 0$, $\bar{r} > 0$, $\bar{p} > 0$ to eqs. (10.10) such that $\bar{\Delta} \neq 0$, $\bar{\Delta}^* \neq 0$, and $a_2/a_1 \neq a_2^*/a_1^*$, will occur with probability 1. (Generally, allowing for production functions other than those of Cobb-Douglas type, one could only say that this probability is positive.) The probability of a flat segment occurring on the world production possibility frontier then reduces to the probability that the inequality (10.26) holds; since $\bar{\Delta} \neq 0$ and $\bar{\Delta}^* \neq 0$ with probability 1, inequality (10.26) defines a nondegenerate interval, so that if the distribution of factor endowments (l, l^*, K) is absolutely continuous, (10.26) must occur with positive probability. Multiplying this by the probability that θ_1 lies in the appropriate interval (computed as in (10.84)), we obtain the probability that equilibrium holds on a flat segment — a positive number. (2) At the other extreme, one might assume that the international diffusion of technical knowledge is so perfect, and that international differences in climate and quality of factors are so negligible, that $\mu_i = \mu_i^*$ and $\alpha_i = \alpha_i^* (i = 1,2)$; then the probability distribution of $(\mu_1, \alpha_1, \mu_2, \alpha_2, \mu_1^*, \alpha_1^*, \mu_2^*, \alpha_2^*)$ is concentrated on a four-dimensional subspace of the eight-dimensional space, and the condition $\alpha_2/\alpha_1 = \alpha_2^*/\alpha_1^*$ holds identically, and a forteriori with probability 1. Then as long as production functions are independently distributed as between industries, there is a zero probability that the world production possibility frontier will have a flat segment. This is the situation that corresponds to the conventional assumptions underlying the factor-price equalization theorem of Lerner [14] and Samuelson [19]. It may be observed that as long as the distribution over the eight-dimensional space of production function parameters is absolutely continuous — which allows the between-country correlation between production function parameters in each industry to be high but less than perfect — there will be a positive probability of equilibrium on a flat segment.

Theorem 3 of Section 10.2 may be approached in the same way. If it is assumed a priori that $\mu_1 = \mu_1^*$ and $\alpha_1 = \alpha_1^*$, then from (10.62) we find that the determinant of the system is $\alpha_1(\alpha_2^* - \alpha_2)$, which vanishes if, and only if, $\alpha_2 = \alpha_2^*$. The set of points $(\mu_1, \alpha_1, \mu_2, \alpha_2, \mu_2^*, \alpha_2^*)$ for which $\alpha_2 = \alpha_2^*$ has Lebesgue measure zero in six-dimensional space, so if the probability distribution over the six-dimensional space is absolutely continuous, condition (10.63) still holds with probability 1. The probability of factor-price equalization will then be equal to the product of the probability that K lies in the interval (10.26) — which is a nonempty interval with probability 1 — and the probability that θ_1 lies in an interval such as (10.84); this probability is a positive number.

References

[1] J.S.Chipman, "Computational Problems in Linear Programming", *Review of Economics and Statistics* 35 (November 1953) 342–349.

[2] J.S.Chipman, "A Survey of the Theory of International Trade: Part 3, The Modern Theory", *Econometrica* 34 (January 1966) 18–76.

[3] J.S.Chipman, "Factor-Price Equalization and the Stolper-Samuelson Theorem", *International Economic Review* 10 (October 1969) 399–406.

[4] G.B.Dantzig, "Maximization of a Linear Function of Variables Subject to Linear Inequalities", in: *Activity Analysis of Production and Allocation* (ed. T.C.Koopmans) (John Wiley & Sons, Inc., New York, 1951) 339–457.

[5] G.B.Dantzig and A.Orden, "A Duality Theorem Based on the Simplex Method", *Symposium on Linear Inequalities and Programming*, Directorate of Management Analysis Service, U.S. Air Force (Washington, D.C., 1952) 51–55.

[6] Ken-ichi Inada and M.C.Kemp, "International Capital Movements and the Theory of Tariffs and Trade: Comment", *Quarterly Journal of Economics* 83 (August 1969) 524–528.

[7] R.W.Jones, "The Structure of Simple General Equilibrium Models", *Journal of Political Economy* 73 (December 1965) 557–572.

[8] R.W.Jones, "International Capital Movements and the Theory of Tariffs and Trade", *Quarterly Journal of Economics* 81 (February 1967) 1–38.

[9] M.C.Kemp, "The Gain from International Trade and Investment: A Neo-Heckscher-Ohlin Approach", *American Economic Review* 56 (September 1966) 788–809.

[10] T.C.Koopmans, "Analysis of Production as an Efficient Combination of Activities", in: *Activity Analysis of Production and Allocation* (ed. T.C.Koopmans) (John Wiley & Sons, Inc., New York, 1951) 33–97.

[11] H.W.Kuhn, "Factor Endowments and Factor Prices: Mathematical Appendix", *Economica*, N.S., 26 (May 1959) 142–144.

[12] H.W.Kuhn, "On Two Theorems in International Trade", *Economia Matematica*, Edizioni Cremonese (Rome, 1967) 105–117.

[13] H.W.Kuhn and A.W.Tucker, "Nonlinear Programming", in: *Proceedings of the Second Berkeley Symposium on Mathematical Statistics and Probability* (University of California Press, Berkeley and Los Angeles, 1951) 481–492.

[14] A.P.Lerner, "Factor Prices and International Trade", *Economica*, N.S., 19 (February 1952) 1–15.

[15] L.W.McKenzie, "International Trade: Mathematical Theory", in: *International Encyclopedia of the Social Sciences* (The Macmillan Company and The Free Press, New York and Glencoe, Ill., 1968) Vol. 8, pp. 96–104.

[16] R.A.Mundell, "International Trade and Factor Mobility", *American Economic Review* 47 (June 1957) 321–335.

[17] T.M.Rybczynski, "Factor Endowment and Relative Commodity Prices", *Economica*, N.S. 22 (November 1955) 336–341.

[18] P.A.Samuelson, "Abstract of a Theorem Concerning Substitutability in Open Leontief Models", in: *Activity Analysis of Production and Allocation* (ed. T.C. Koopmans) (John Wiley & Sons, Inc., New York, 1951) 142–146.

[19] P.A.Samuelson, "Prices of Factors and Goods in General Equilibrium", *Review of Economic Studies* 21 (1953) 1–20.

[20] P.A.Samuelson, "Summary on Factor-Price Equalization", *International Economic Review* 8 (October 1967) 286–295.

[21] R.W.Shephard, *Cost and Production Functions* (Princeton University Press, Princeton, N.J., 1953).

[22] H.Uzawa, "A Note on the Menger-Wieser Theory of Imputation", *Zeitschrift für Nationalökonomie* 18 (Heft 3, 1958) 318–334.

[23] H.Uzawa, "Duality Principles in the Theory of Cost and Production", *International Economic Review* 5 (May 1964) 216–220.

CHAPTER 11

MIGRATION, THE TERMS OF TRADE, AND ECONOMIC WELFARE IN THE SOURCE COUNTRY*

Peter B.KENEN

Those of us whose happier professional duties include the frequent reading of Charles P.Kindleberger's work unite in admiring his intellectual mobility. He has toiled in more fields than many others could cultivate, harvesting rich crops in every one of them. But one constant in a long career is Kindleberger's interest in mobility itself — in the theory and implications of factor movements. His doctoral dissertation dealt with short-term capital[1]. His most recent writings have been concerned with financial integration, direct investment, and other current issues on capital account[2]. Along the way, moreover, he has looked at people, applying the Lewis model to Western Europe's growth and thinking through the implications of emigration from the Mediterranean basin[3].

This brief paper honors him by imitation, the sincerest flattery. It seeks to identify the welfare implications of net emigration, viewed from the standpoint of the source region or country and in the context of the Heckscher-Ohlin model. It proceeds from a single set of assumptions, sufficient to obtain all of its conclusions but has in tow a long mathematical appendix deriving a number of those same conclusions under less restrictive sets of assump-

* I am grateful to Jaroslav Vánek and Ronald Jones for spotting errors in earlier drafts and to several colleagues and students for suggesting improvements and qualifications. Remaining errors and excessive claims to originality are, of course, my own personal achievements.

[1] *International Short-Term Capital Movements* (New York: Columbia University Press, 1937).

[2] *Europe and the Dollar* (Cambridge: The M.I.T. Press, 1966) Chaps. 1, 2, and 5.

[3] *Europe's Postwar Growth: The Role of Labor Supply* (Cambridge: Harvard University Press, 1967) and "Emigration and Economic Growth", Banca Nazionale del Lavoro *Quarterly Review*, No. 74 (September 1965).

tions. In addition to the several standard suppositions of the Heckscher-Ohlin model, listed in due course, it supposes that workers migrate in response to wage differences (or, more precisely, the present value of expected differences), that each migrant takes with him an average-sized family and that no migrant owns any productive property or claims to the income from any such property. These extra suppositions guarantee that migrants gain by moving (if their expectations are fulfilled) and that the welfare gain or loss for persons remaining in the source country depends, in the first instance, on the change in labor's average product (or the present value of future average product). Movements of average-sized families do not change the ratio of labor force to population, so that labor's average product and per capita income, the first approximation to economic welfare, have always to move in the same direction.

11.1. The One-Product Closed Economy

The most common treatment of the problem studied here is a simple aggregate production-function version usually inflicted on unsuspecting students. It derives from the theory of optimum population expounded by Meade[4] and is basic to much recent work on international capital movements, not just migration[5].

Starting with a single product, perfect competition, and constant returns to scale, one commonly invokes the law of variable proportions to ascertain three consequences of net emigration. If the source country is located initially where its marginal product of labor is positive, declining, and smaller than the average product, net emigration has these effects:

1. Total product falls.
2. The marginal product of labor rises and that of capital declines, redistributing income in favor of labor.
3. The average product of labor rises, raising per capita income.

---

[4] James E.Meade, *Trade and Welfare* (London: Oxford University Press, 1955) pp. 84-85. Note, however, the several important qualifications which Meade himself attaches on subsequent pages.

[5] See e.g., G.D.A.MacDougall, "The Benefits and Costs of Private Investment from Abroad: A Theoretical Approach", in: *Readings in International Economics*, eds. R.E. Caves and H.G.Johnson (Homewood, Ill.: Richard D.Irwin, 1968) pp. 172-194.

The second of these three effects does not inhibit definitive inference, because the third effect suggests that, with lump-sum transfers, all remaining residents could be made to gain. If, then, the analysis is sound, public policy should encourage emigration or, at the very least, should not discourage it[6].

But this analysis should not please a sophomore, let alone an author of public policy. Consider a one-product economy with constant returns to scale, described by fig. 11.1[7]. Its initial labor force is OL_0; its capital stock is OK_0; its total output is given by the isoquant P_t; and its wage-rental ratio is given by the slope of P_t at Q_t (by $\tan \beta$). Its national income (in units of capital) is OV_t, of which OK_0 goes to the capitalists and K_0V_t goes to the workers. Now let emigration cut back the labor force to OL_1 and consider the condition of those who stay behind. Prior to emigration, those parties earned OV_0 of income, corresponding to P_0 of output. Emigration, however, reduces available output to P_1, smaller than P_0, reducing, net raising, the welfare of those who stay behind[8]. The conventional analysis falls into error because it compares noncomparable numbers. It compares the average product of the initial labor force (including the emigrants-to-be) with the average product of the final labor force.

Even as amended, however, the model described by fig. 11.1 leaves many questions without answers. One would like to know, for instance, whether the loss of the migrants' tax payments differs from the total cost of the public services that would have been consumed by the migrants and their families. One would also like to know whether the transfer of human capital attending emigration should be treated as a loss to the source country[9]. Most importantly, one would like to know whether this simple analysis can survive

[6] If, of course, the marginal product is declining but equal to average product, there can be no change in the latter or in the welfare of remaining residents. Initial population is, on this view, optimal. If, finally, the marginal product is declining but larger than the average product, emigration will reduce average product and the welfare of remaining residents. Initial population is sub-optimal.

[7] This exposition was suggested by Ronald Jones (who referred me to a similar construction by Harry Johnson). I cannot thank Johnson directly, as his intellectual output far exceeds my bibliographical input.

[8] The new output P_1 will be produced at E, with OL_1 of labor and OK_0 of capital, and there will be a redistribution of income in favor of labor, as the wage-rental ratio at E is larger than $\tan \beta$. This refinement, however, does not undermine the basic analysis or conclusion.

[9] For footnote, see next page.

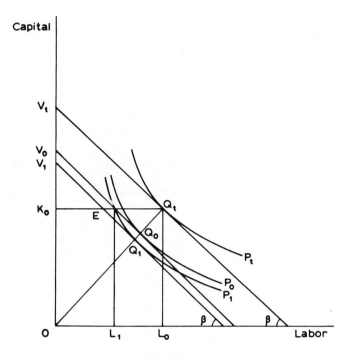

Fig. 11.1.

the introduction of additional commodities and of foreign trade[10]. What follows is an effort to answer this last question (ignoring all the rest).

[9] This is a vexed issue on which much has been written; see, e.g., C.P.Kindleberger, "Emigration and Economic Growth", H.B.Grubel and A.D.Scott, "The International Flow of Human Capital" (*American Economic Review*, Vol. 65 (May 1966) pp. 268-275, and the survey by E.S. Djimopoulos, "Temporary Labor Migration: Effects on the Country of Emigration", International Economics Workshop, Columbia University, 1969 (mimeographed). Clearly, one must avoid double counting. The present value of the human capital embodied in a migrant is part of the present value of his marginal product and has already been subtracted from source-country output. But one has still to ask if some part of that same loss could have been avoided with perfect advance knowledge of the migrant's plans. If employers or government agencies furnish an irretrievable portion of the human capital embodied in a migrant and could have withheld some of that capital for a different use (without impairing the migrant's ability to migrate), one would have to treat that portion of the capital as an *avoidable* loss, if not an additional loss.

[10] MacDougall ("The Benefits and Costs of Private Investment...", pp. 186-188) discusses this issue, but his model does not allow him to study it thoroughly.

11.2. The Two-Product Closed Economy

Consider a single country obeying all the rules of a factor-proportions (Heckscher-Ohlin) model, but, in the first instance, having no foreign trade. It produces two commodities (apples and blankets) under perfect competition and constant returns to scale. It has two factors of production (labor and capital) that are fully employed by its two industries but are used in different proportions by those two industries; let apple production be more capital intensive than blanket production at all sets of factor prices. All persons within the economy have the same tastes, with unitary income elasticities of demand for the two commodities. Each person, moreover, consumes both commodities at all sets of product prices (so that the closed economy must produce both of them)[11].

The relevant circumstances of this economy are described by fig. 11.2. Its initial labor force is B_0L_0; its capital stock is B_0K. The point P_0 lies on the efficiency locus (not drawn here), where the blanket isoquant I_b drawn with reference to B_0, is tangent to the apple isoquant I_a drawn with reference to A_0. The slopes of the two isoquants at P_0 give the initial wage-rental ratio; it is measured by $\tan \beta$. Next, construct A_0G_0 with slope equal to $\tan \beta$. The distance B_0G_0 measures the national income in units of capital, with capital itself earning B_0K and labor earning KG_0. Income per worker is given by B_0G_0/KA_0.

If, now, emigration reduces the labor force to B_0L_1, there will be several major changes in the economy. Note, first, what would happen if there were no change in equilibrium factor and product prices. With constant returns to scale, the new production point P_1 must lie on B_0P_0 and on a line parallel to A_0P_0 drawn from the new factor-box corner A_1; there can be no change in the industries' factor proportions if there is, as yet, no change in factor prices. At P_1, however, blanket output has fallen absolutely [by $(B_0P_0-B_0P_1)/$

---

[11] Note that perfect competition, constant returns to scale, strong factor ordering and incomplete specialization suffice to generate a single-valued functional relationship between marginal products (factor prices) and relative product prices; see, e.g., P.A. Samuelson, *Collected Scientific Papers* (Cambridge: The M.I.T. Press, 1966), Vol. 2, pp. 888-908. This fact is used many times below. The other assumptions concerning demand conditions are used to forecast changes in consumption when we confront income changes and also to construct the representative indifference curve shown in fig. 11.3. If workers and capitalists have the same tastes, with unitary income elasticities, changes in factor prices can have no effect upon the position of a representative (or collective) indifference curve.

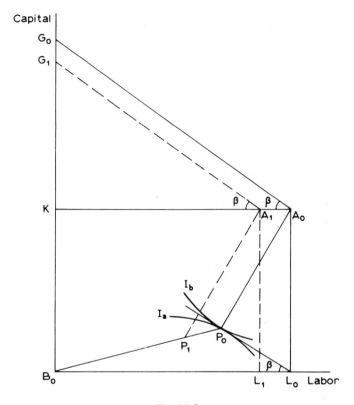

Fig. 11.2.

B_0P_0], while apple output has risen absolutely [by $(A_1P_1 - A_0P_0)/A_0P_0$] [12]. National income has fallen to B_0G_1, but income per worker has risen to B_0G_1/KA_1 [13].

Thus far, it would seem, net emigration benefits the remaining population by raising income per worker. There are, however, two objections to this conclusion. First, it falls into the same trap as the conventional one-product

---

[12] This is a familiar proposition, adapted from T.M.Rybczynski, "Factor Endowment and Relative Commodity Prices", *Readings in International Economics*, pp. 78-89.

[13] In proof, write $B_0G_0/KA_0 = B_0K/KA_0 + \tan\beta$, and $B_0G_1/KA_1 = B_0K/KA_1 + \tan\beta$, so that $B_0G_1/KA_1 - B_0G_0/KA_0 = (B_0K/KA_0)(A_1A_0/KA_1) > 0$.

analysis — comparing noncomparable populations. Second, at unchanged prices, there would be disequilibrium in the product markets.

If, as assumed, emigrants possess no capital, they had no claim to any part of the income B_0K prior to emigration; their total income was G_0G_1, a pro rata share of total labor income. Hence, the constant-price income per worker of a remaining resident was B_0G_1/KA_1 prior to emigration and is not changed by emigration.

If, further, blanket output falls and apple output rises, while the total and average incomes of remaining residents are not changed by emigration, the outflow of workers must generate an excess supply of apples (an excess demand for blankets). Emigration reduces the total demand for both commodities, and there can be no offsetting increase of purchases by those who stay behind. The price of blankets must rise relative to that of apples, and national income must be redistributed in favor of labor (the factor used intensively in the production of blankets). When, finally, this occurs, potential welfare must decline. The gainers (workers) cannot compensate the losers (capitalists).

This last proposition can be proved quite simply. Examine fig. 11.3, the commodity-space counterpart of fig. 11.2. Here, the closed economy's initial transformation curve is $\bar{A}_0E_0\bar{B}_0$, and its initial equilibrium is at E_0 (with product prices given by $\tan\pi$). Its national income is OY_0 measured in apples; it produces and consumes OB_0 of blankets and OA_0 of apples. With net emigration, the transformation curve shrinks and twists becoming $\bar{A}_1E_1\bar{B}_1$. At constant product prices, national income would be OY_1, measured in apples (lower by the Y_0Y_1 generated and received by the now-absent migrants); production would move to OB_1 of blankets and OA_1 of apples; and consumption would move to OB_2 of blankets and OA_2 of apples. There would be B_1B_2 excess demand for blankets and A_1A_2 excess supply of apples. The price of blankets must rise relative to that of apples until the points E_1 and F_1 merge on the new transformation curve. Consider, however, one further property of the income level OY_1. This was the initial income of the nonmigrant workers and capitalists, taken together, so that they were consuming OB_2 of blankets and OA_1 of apples prior to emigration. They were able to attain point F_1 on the "representative" indifference curve U_1. When, then, emigration and the consequent disequilibrium in the product markets drives them to a new consumption point, between F_1 and E_1, it forces them onto a lower indifference curve, reducing the welfare of the remaining population. The higher price of blankets at this new point means, of course, an increase in the wage-rental ratio, so that workers gain and capitalists

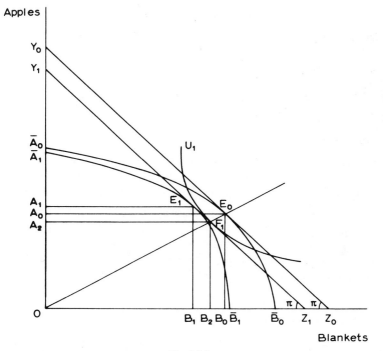

Fig. 11.3.

lose, but the former are unable to compensate the latter by, say, lump-sum transfers; total real income has declined[14].

One can make this last point differently, thereby to stress the vital role of the assumption, soon to be relaxed, that the economy is closed to foreign trade. If the remaining residents of the economy could export A_1A_2 of apples and import B_1B_2 of blankets at relative prices equal to $\tan \pi$, they could produce at E_1 and consume at F_1 (on the indifference curve U_1). Emigration would not alter their welfare. It is the absence of this opportunity that causes the welfare loss[15].

Summarizing for the closed two-product economy, net emigration has these three effects:

[14] See note 11.

[15] Note that immigration has symmetrical effects. Here, the *initial* population enjoys a welfare gain, as immigration generates an excess supply of blankets, reducing their relative price and allowing the initial population to "import" apples from the now larger economy of which they are part. The initial population captures gains from trade.

1. A reduction of total output, measured at constant prices, but no change in the constant-price income per worker of the remaining population.

2. A rise in the price of the labor-intensive product that raises the marginal product of labor and lowers the marginal product of capital, aiding the remaining workers and injuring the capitalists.

3. An overall welfare loss for the remaining population, as the workers cannot compensate the capitalists.

These results affirm the principal conclusions of our amended one-product model. Doing so, incidentally, they contradict the very notion of an optimum population. Whatever the initial population (the capital-labor ratio), emigration will always increase the marginal product of labor but, by the very price effect which guarantees that increase, will always serve to lower overall potential welfare. Workers should oppose public policies restricting emigration (whether or not they plan themselves to emigrate), but the government of a closed economy, concerned about the welfare of all its citizens, should always encourage immigration, not emigration[16].

11.3. The Two-Product Open Economy

We turn now to trading economies and deal, ad seriatum, with three situations: (1) An economy confronting fixed terms of trade (the traditional small-country case). (2) An economy confronting a fixed but imperfectly elastic foreign offer curve. (3) A two-country system in which emigration from the first is immigration to the second, and the global change in the output mix is the chief determinant of the change in welfare.

The first of these three cases is nearly trivial. If product prices are fixed by foreign trade, there can be no price effect, no redistribution of national in-

---

[16] Notice, moreover, that this same argument favors *continuous* immigration..Prior immigrants have only to be viewed as part of the now-initial population, eligible for compensation when further arrivals generate a new excess supply of the labor-intensive commodity and reduce the marginal product of labor. Notice, further, that the argument developed above extends automatically to another set of facts. If the average migrant owns as much capital as the average nonmigrant, leaves its physical embodiment behind, but keeps title to the income, there will still be no change in constant-price income per worker (as the ratio of capital to labor income will not change with net migration), but the price effects described above will still occur (as the ratio of capital goods to labor will still change). These different facts, however, require external commodity trade to effect transfers of property income.

come, and no need for compensation. The excess demand for blankets caused by emigration can be satisfied by larger blanket imports or smaller blanket exports, depending upon the initial trade pattern, and the remaining population is not affected by emigration[17].

The second of these cases is not much more difficult. As before, emigration will generate an excess demand for blankets and excess supply of apples. In this instance, however, prices will change, income will be redistributed in favor of labor, and welfare changes will ensue. If the source country exports blankets (and its remaining residents would also export blankets if prices were unchanged after emigration), the excess demand for blankets as a result of emigration serves to reduce export supply, moving the system along the foreign offer curve and raising the relative price of blankets. This increase in price, however, amounts to an improvement in the terms of trade. Lump-sum transfers, therefore, can increase the welfare of remaining residents[18]. If, contrarily, the source country imports blankets, the excess demand for blankets caused by emigration amounts to an increase in import demand, moving the system along the foreign offer curve in the opposite direction. The resulting increase in the price of blankets amounts to a deterioration in the terms of trade, reducing the welfare of the remaining population[19].

To illustrate these propositions, fig. 11.4a is adapted from fig. 11.2. Here, initial output is at E_0 on the initial transformation curve (not shown) and on the budget line $Z_0 Y_0$, while initial consumption is at F_0, on that same budget line. Export supply is $Q_0 E_0$ of blankets. After emigration, output is at E_1, on the new transformation curve $\bar{A}_1 E_1 \bar{B}_1$, and the budget line $Z_1 Y_1$, while

---

[17] This simplest case could easily be illustrated using fig. 11.3. If, initially, consumption took place at a point on $Y_0 Z_0$ southeast of E_0 (at F_0, not now shown), the economy would be exporting apples in exchange for blankets. Emigration would still shift production to E_1 and consumption to F_1 (but F_1 would lie to the southeast of its present position, on a ray not now shown between the origin, O, and the initial consumption point F_0). There would be a change in the volume of trade, but the remaining residents would stay at their initial consumption point F_1 and on their initial indifference curve, U_1.

Notice, however, that this simplest case begs one important question: What is there to generate the wage differential motivating emigration? We shall not confront this issue until we reach case 3, when it will take on enormous importance. Notice, further, that continuing emigration will eventually terminate blanket production, causing factor-price effects. Commodity prices will still be fixed by trade, but the marginal product of labor will have to rise with any further emigration. This will redistribute income in favor of labor (and may also serve to halt the outflow of labor by closing the initial wage differential).

[18] For footnote, see page 249.

[19] For footnote, see page 249.

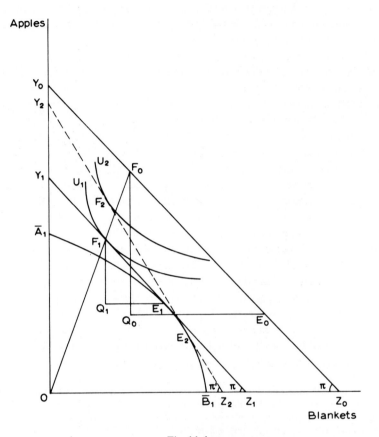

Fig. 11.4a.

consumption is at F_1, at the intersection of $Z_1 Y_1$ and the ray OF_0. Export supply is $Q_1 E_1$ (smaller than $Q_0 E_0$ because F_1 must be southwest of F_0, while E_1 must be northwest of E_0). The budget line $Z_1 Y_1$, however, was that of the remaining population prior to emigration, so that the indifference curve U_1 denotes the initial welfare level of that population. When, then, the reduction of export supply raises the relative price of blankets (from $\tan \pi$ to, say, $\tan \pi'$), the remaining population can achieve the higher welfare level denoted by U_2 [20].

---

[20] For footnote, see next page.

[18] If the remaining residents would import blankets after emigration, emigration could have different welfare implications. An improvement in the terms of trade of the whole economy could be a deterioration in the terms of trade of the remaining population, diminishing its welfare. This possibility is illustrated in the diagram below (a modification of fig. 11.4a in the text). Here, initial exports are $Q_0 E_0$ of blankets, but the

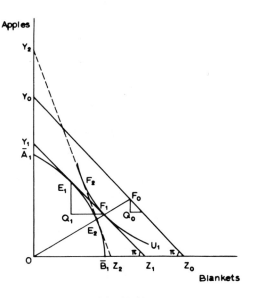

Fig. 11.4b.

constant-price exports of the remaining population would be $Q_1 E_1$ of apples. Emigration will increase the relative price of blankets, as in all other cases studied thus far, but an insufficient increase will leave remaining residents on a representative indifference curve lower than U_1. The new budget line must be steeper than $Z_2 Y_2$ to guarantee an increase in welfare.

[19] Notice the absence of a qualification analogous to that required by the "export" case (and treated in detail in note 18). This is because a country importing blankets prior to emigration has also to do so after emigration. If E_0 were northwest of F_0 in fig. 11.4a, then E_1 would have to be northwest of F_1; E_1 would have to be northwest of E_0 to increase apple output, while F_1 must be on OF_0, southwest of F_0.

[20] The price ratio $\tan \pi'$ will bring equilibrium if one could place the origin of the foreign offer curve at E_2 and have that curve intersect U_2 and $Z_2 Y_2$ at their own intersection, F_2.

To sum up, emigration will increase the economic welfare of the remaining population (by allowing the gainers to compensate the losers) if the source country exports the labor-intensive product (and if the remaining population would do so too in the absence of price changes).

The third case to be considered is the most difficult. Suppose, however, that there is free trade with zero transport costs, so that product prices are the same in both countries under study. Suppose, further, that those countries produce apples and blankets under the same economic conditions, have identical tastes (with unitary income elasticities), but differ in a single, critical way: Let the production functions of one country display a product-neutral, factor-neutral superiority in economic efficiency, thereby to raise its real wage rate and attract the other's labor[21]. This will be the host country; the other will be the source country.

Under these additional assumptions, a migration from source to host country will not affect the incomes of those who remain in the source country, or of the initial host-country residents, until it affects relative prices. It does, however, increase the incomes of the migrants, so that it enlarges total demand for both commodities. This same migration, however, also enlarges constant-price world blanket output and reduces constant-price world apple output, creating an excess supply of blankets and an excess demand for apples, in the world as a whole. It reduces source-country blanket output and enlarges host-country blanket output, but the greater efficiency of the host country makes for a net increase in world blanket output. Similarly, it enlarges source-country apple output and reduces host-country apple output, but the greater efficiency of the host country makes for a net decrease in world apple output. The world price of blankets must decline relative to that of apples, redistributing income in favor of capital within each country[22].

Welfare implications follow directly — and are the opposite of those that were obtained in the closed economy or case (2), earlier. If the source country exports blankets (and its remaining residents would do so too in the ab-

---

[21] If there were no such efficiency difference, the similarity between the two countries would guarantee factor-price equalization under free trade (so long as neither country specialized completely). The introduction of a product-neutral, factor-neutral difference does not prevent the equalization of *relative* factor prices and, therefore, industry factor requirements, but does prevent the equalization of absolute marginal products and, therefore, absolute factor returns. It thereby motivates labor migration (and would cause capital to move along with labor if we were not, arbitrarily, keeping it at home).

[22] Note that this result, if sufficiently extreme, could disappoint the expectations of the migrants themselves and reduce their welfare.

sence of price changes), emigration reduces the welfare of its remaining residents; lump-sum transfers cannot compensate the losers (workers). If, instead, the source country imports blankets, emigration increases the welfare of its remaining residents; lump-sum transfers can be used to compensate the losers.

These results, however, depend uniquely on the choice of reasons for the wage difference needed to explain migration. If efficiency differences had certain biases (product or factor), the argument would change. And if there were no difference of this sort, but a tariff, transport costs, complete specialization, or factor reversals were the cause of higher wages in one country, one might have to use a different approach[23]. There is, in brief, no simple, general method for measuring the consequence of labor migration.

Mathematical Appendix

This appendix furnishes more rigorous proofs of several propositions offered in the text (devoting particular attention to the necessity or sufficiency of the assumptions used in their derivation).

The Basic Model

Consider two commodities ($i = 1,2$) and two countries ($j = 1,2$). Each production function is homogeneous of first degree in labor and capital and is the same in both countries, save for a factor-neutral efficiency term:

$$x_{ij} = a_{ij}[f_i(k_{ij})]\left(\frac{L_{ij}}{L_j}\right), \qquad f_i'(k_{ij}) > 0, f_i''(k_{ij}) < 0 \qquad (11.1)$$

where x_{ij} is ith product output in the jth country (per member of that country's labor force), a_{ij} represents factor-neutral efficiency, k_{ij} is the capital-labor ratio, L_{ij} is labor input, and L_j is the jth country's total labor force. Let $x_{ij} > 0$ at all times.

---

[23] If, for instance, factor reversals were the cause of the wage difference, the welfare changes would be different. Suppose that blankets are labor intensive in the source country and capital intensive in the host country. Migration will reduce blanket output in both countries and will increase apple output, raising the relative price of blankets. This price effect will favor source-country labor and host-country capital, and will increase the welfare of the remaining source-country population if that country (and its remaining population) is the one which exports blankets. In this and other instances, however, migration is apt to be self-limiting; it can, for example, eliminate the factor reversal or complete product specialization that are its initial causes.

With full employment and perfect competition:

$$\sum_i L_{ij} = L_j \tag{11.2}$$

$$\sum_i L_{ij}k_{ij} = L_jk_j \tag{11.3}$$

$$y_{ij}^k = a_{ij}[f_i'(k_{ij})] \tag{11.4}$$

$$y_{ij}^w = a_{ij}[f_i(k_{ij}) - f_i'(k_{ij})k_{ij}] \tag{11.5}$$

where k_j is the jth country's overall capital-labor ratio, while y_{ij}^k and y_{ij}^w are the real wages (incomes) accruing to units of capital and labor, each measured in units of the ith product.

The product-price and factor-price ratios are

$$p_j = \frac{y_{2j}^k}{y_{1j}^k} \tag{11.6}$$

$$v_j = \frac{y_{ij}^w}{y_{ij}^k} \tag{11.7}$$

The demand functions for the first product are

$$c_{1j}^k = g_j^k(y_{1j}^k, p_j) \tag{11.8}$$

$$c_{1j}^w = g_j^w(y_{1j}^w, p_j) \tag{11.9}$$

$$c_{1j} = c_{1j}^w + c_{1j}^k k_j . \tag{11.10}$$

At this juncture, there are 15 endogenous variables for each country (the pairs x_{ij}, k_{ij}, L_{ij}, y_{ij}^k, and y_{ij}^w, plus p_j, v_j, c_{1j}^k, c_{1j}^w, and c_{1j}) and 14 equations (the pairs (11.1), (11.4), (11.5) and (11.7), plus (11.2), (11.3), (11.8), (11.9) and (11.10)). Consider, then three ways to close the system[24].

---

[24] A fourth, closing the economy itself, is to write $x_{1j} = c_{1j}$. This instance, however, is adequately covered in the text and does not, in any case, lend itself to the strategy adopted here.

A. In a single country facing fixed terms of trade

$$p_j = \bar{p} \, . \tag{11.11a}$$

B. In a single country facing a fixed foreign offer curve:

$$(x_{1j} - c_{1j})L_j = s_j(p_j), \qquad (x_{1j} - c_{1j})s_j'(p_j) < 0 \, . \tag{11.11b}$$

C. In a two-country system with no barriers to trade

$$\sum_j (x_{ij} - c_{ij})L_j = 0 \tag{11.11c}$$

$$p_j = p \, . \tag{11.12}$$

In cases (A) and (B), there are 15 equations, equal in number to the endo-genous variables. In case (C), there are 31 equations, equal in number to the 30 national variables plus the additional (common) variable p. In each case, there are four exogenous variables for each country (a_{ij}, k_j, and L_j).

Transformation of the Model
All versions of this model can be written more compactly. Using eqs. (11.1), (11.2) and (11.3),

$$x_{1j} = a_{1j} \, [f_1(k_{1j})] \left[\frac{k_{2j} - k_j}{k_{2j} - k_{1j}} \right] \tag{11.13}$$

where $x_{1j} > 0$ implies $k_{2j} > k_j > k_{1j}$ whenever $k_{2j} > k_{1j}$, as is assumed here-after[25]. Using eqs. (11.1), (11.4) and (11.5), and invoking Euler's theorem:

$$f_i'(k_{ij})(v_j + k_{ij}) = f_i(k_{ij}) \, . \tag{11.14}$$

---

[25] Similarly,

$$x_{2j} = a_{2j}[f_2(k_{2j})] \left[\frac{k_j - k_{1j}}{k_{2j} - k_{1j}} \right] .$$

Or, using eqs. (11.14) and (11.15),

$$x_{2j} = p \left[\left(\frac{v_j + k_{2j}}{v_j + k_{1j}} \right) \left(\frac{k_j - k_{1j}}{k_{2j} - k_j} \right) \right] x_{1j} \, .$$

Then, from eqs. (11.4) through (11.10):

$$p = \left(\frac{a_{2j}}{a_{1j}}\right)\left[\frac{f_2'(k_{2j})}{f_1'(k_{1j})}\right] \tag{11.15}$$

$$c_{1j} = g_j^w(y_{1j}^w, p) + g_j^k(y_{1j}^k, p)k_j \tag{11.16}$$

$$y_{ij}^k = a_{ij}[f_i'(k_{ij})] \tag{11.17}$$

$$y_{ij}^w = y_{ij}^k v_j . \tag{11.18}$$

Now there are nine endogenous variables for each country (the pairs k_{ij}, y_{ij}^k and y_{ij}^w, plus x_{1j} c_{1j} and v_j) and nine equations (the pairs (11.14), (11.17) and (11.18), plus (11.13), (11.15) and (11.16)), plus the common price ratio p and the three versions of (11.11).

Now differentiate eqs. (11.13) through (11.18), using dotted terms to denote percentage rates of change. From eqs. (11.13) and (11.14):

$$\dot{x}_{1j} = \dot{a}_{1j} + Q_j\dot{v}_j - \left(\frac{k_j}{k_{2j}-k_j}\right)\dot{k}_j \tag{11.19}$$

where

$$Q_j = \left(\frac{1}{k_{2j}-k_{1j}}\right)\left[\sigma_{1j}k_{1j}\left(\frac{v_j+k_{2j}}{v_j+k_{1j}}\right) + \sigma_{2j}k_{2j}\left(\frac{k_j-k_{1j}}{k_{2j}-k_j}\right)\right],$$

while

$$\sigma_{ij} = \left(\frac{\delta k_{ij}}{\delta v_j}\right)\left(\frac{v_j}{k_{ij}}\right) > 0 ,$$

so that[26] $Q_j > 0$. From eqs. (11.14) and (11.15):

$$\dot{p} = (\dot{a}_{2j}-\dot{a}_{1j}) + e_j^{pv}\dot{v}_j \tag{11.20}$$

where

$$e_j^{pv} = \frac{v_j(k_{2j}-k_{1j})}{(v_j+k_{1j})(v_j+k_{2j})} > 0 .$$

---

[26] For footnote, see next page.

From eq. (11.16):

$$c_{1j} = E_j^y \dot{a}_{1j} - \left[z_j e_j^{ky} - \left(\frac{k_{1j}}{v_j + k_{1j}} \right) E_j^y \right] \dot{v}_j - E_j^p \dot{p} + z_j \dot{k}_j \qquad (11.21)$$

where $0 < z_j = k_j(c_{1j}^k/c_{1j}) < 1$; where $e_j^{ky} = (\delta c_{1j}^k/\delta y_{1j}^k)(y_{1j}^k/c_{1j}^k) > 0$ and $e_j^{wy} = (\delta c_{1j}^w/\delta y_{1j}^w)(y_{1j}^w/c_{1j}^w) > 0$, so that $E_j^y = [e_j^{wy} + z_j(e_j^{ky} - e_j^{wy})] > 0$; and where $e_j^{kp} = -(\delta c_{1j}^k/\delta p)(p/c_{1j}^k) > 0$ and $e_j^{wp} = -(\delta c_{1j}^w/\delta p)(p/c_{1j}^w) > 0$, so that $E_j^p = [e_j^{wp} + z_j(e_j^{kp} - e_j^{wp})] > 0$. Then, from eqs. (11.17) and (11.18):

$$\dot{y}_{ij}^k = \dot{\alpha}_j^k - \left(\frac{v_j}{v_j + k_{ij}} \right) \left(\frac{1}{e_j^{pv}} \right) \dot{p} \qquad (11.22)$$

$$\dot{y}_{ij}^w = \dot{\alpha}_j^w + \left(\frac{k_{ij}}{v_j + k_{ij}} \right) \left(\frac{1}{e_j^{pv}} \right) \dot{p} \qquad (11.23)$$

where

$$\dot{\alpha}_j^k = \frac{(v_j + k_{2j})\dot{a}_{2j} - (v_j + k_{1j})\dot{a}_{1j}}{(k_{2j} - k_{1j})} ,$$

[26] From note 2, moreover,

$$\dot{x}_{2j} = \dot{a}_{2j} + \left[\left(\frac{v_j + k_{1j}}{v_j + k_{2j}} \right) \left(\frac{k_{2j} - k_j}{k_j - k_{1j}} \right) \right] Q_j \dot{v}_j + \left(\frac{k_j}{k_j - k_{1j}} \right) \dot{k}_j .$$

In consequence,

$$(\dot{x}_{2j} - \dot{x}_{1j}) = (\dot{a}_{2j} - \dot{a}_{1j}) + (T_j k_j) \dot{k}_j - \left[(v_j + k_j) \left(\frac{k_{2j} - k_j}{v_j + k_{2j}} \right) (T_j Q_j) \right] \dot{v}_j$$

where $T_j = (k_{2j} - k_{1j})/[(k_{2j} - k_j)(k_j - k_{1j})] > 0$. Using eq. (11.20), then

$$(\dot{x}_{2j} - \dot{x}_{1j}) = \left[1 + (v_j + k_j) \left(\frac{k_{2j} - k_j}{v_j + k_{2j}} \right) (T_j Q_j) \left(\frac{1}{e_j^{pv}} \right) \right] (\dot{a}_{2j} - \dot{a}_{1j})$$

$$+ (T_j k_j) \dot{k}_j - \left[(v_j + k_j) \left(\frac{k_{2j} - k_j}{v_j + k_{2j}} \right) (T_j Q_j) \left(\frac{1}{e_j^{pv}} \right) \right] \dot{p} .$$

An increase of the capital-labor ratio (or of a_{2j} relative to a_{1j}) will shift the transformation curve, raising x_{2j} relative to x_{1j} at each set of product prices ($\dot{p} = 0$). An increase of p will move an economy along its transformation curve, raising x_{1j} relative to x_{2j}. These familiar results underlie the diagrams used in the text.

while

$$\dot{\alpha}_j^w = \dot{\alpha}_j^k - \left(\frac{\dot{a}_{2j} - \dot{a}_{1j}}{e_j^{pv}}\right).$$

Finally, from eqs. (11.11a) and (11.11b):

$$\dot{p} = 0 \tag{11.24}$$

$$(x_{1j}\dot{x}_{1j} - c_{1j}\dot{c}_{1j}) + (x_{1j} - c_{1j})\dot{L}_j = -e^s(x_{1j} - c_{1j})\dot{p} \tag{11.25}$$

where $e^s = -s_j'(p)[p/(x_{1j} - c_{1j})] > 0$. And from eq. (11.11c):

$$\sum_j [(x_{1j}\dot{x}_{1j} - c_{1j}\dot{c}_{1j}) + (x_{1j} - c_{1j})\dot{L}_j]L_j = 0. \tag{11.26}$$

Factor-Supply Changes and Economic Welfare

Next, postulate a welfare (utility) function for an individual worker or capitalist and the corresponding budget constraint:

$$U_j^t = U_{j.}^t(c_{1j}^t, c_{2j}^t), \qquad t = w, k \tag{11.27}$$

$$(pc_{1j}^t + c_{2j}^t) - y_{2j}^t = 0. \tag{11.28}$$

Maximizing eq. (11.27) subject to (11.28), we have

$$\left(\frac{\delta U_j^t}{\delta c_{1j}^t}\right) = \lambda p \tag{11.29}$$

$$\left(\frac{\delta U_j^t}{\delta c_{2j}^t}\right) = \lambda \tag{11.30}$$

where λ is a Lagrangian multiplier.

Differentiating eqs. (11.27) through (11.30) totally and setting $dU_j^t = 0$, we can solve for the change in y_{2j}^t needed to keep U_j^t constant:

$$\overset{*}{y}_{2j}^t = m_j^t \dot{p} \tag{11.31}$$

where $m_j^t = (c_{1j}^t / y_{1j}^t) \leqslant 1$. Consider, then, two situations:

1. If there are no lump-sum transfers between workers and capitalists, the sign of the realized welfare change is given by:

$$\dot{G}_j^t = \dot{y}_{2j}^t - \overset{*}{\dot{y}}_{2j}^t \ . \tag{11.32}$$

Or, using eqs. (11.22) and (11.23), we have

$$\dot{G}_j^k = \dot{\alpha}_j^k - \left[\left(\frac{v_j + k_{1j}}{k_{2j} - k_{1j}}\right) + m_j^k\right]\dot{p} \tag{11.33}$$

$$\dot{G}_j^w = \dot{\alpha}_j^w + \left[\left(\frac{k_{2j}}{v_j}\right)\left(\frac{v_j + k_{1j}}{k_{2j} - k_{1j}}\right) - m_j^w\right]\dot{p} \ . \tag{11.34}$$

Changes in factor supplies ($\dot{L}_j$ and $\dot{k}_j$) have no welfare impact unless they alter product prices. But when, as their consequence, $\dot{p} > 0$, then $\dot{G}_j^k < 0$ and $\dot{G}_j^w > 0$; this is because

$$\left(\frac{k_{2j}}{v_j}\right)\left(\frac{v_j + k_{1j}}{k_{2j} - k_{1j}}\right) > 1 > m_j^w \ .$$

2. If there are lump-sum transfers, the sign of the realized welfare change is given by:

$$\dot{G}_j = \dot{y}_{2j} - \overset{*}{\dot{y}}_{2j} \tag{11.35}$$

where

$$\overset{*}{\dot{y}}_{2j} = \left(\frac{y_{1j}^w}{y_{1j}}\right)\overset{*}{\dot{y}}_{2j}^w + k_j\left(\frac{y_{1j}^k}{y_{1j}}\right)\overset{*}{\dot{y}}_{2j}^k = \left(\frac{c_{1j}^w + k_j c_{1j}^k}{y_{1j}}\right)\dot{p} = \left(\frac{c_{1j}}{y_{1j}}\right)\dot{p} \tag{11.36}$$

and

$$\dot{y}_{2j} = \left(\frac{y_{1j}^w}{y_{1j}}\right)\dot{y}_{2j}^w + k_j\left(\frac{y_{1j}^k}{y_{1j}}\right)\dot{y}_{2j}^k = \dot{\alpha}_j^k - \left(\frac{y_{1j}^w}{y_{1j}}\right)\left(\frac{\dot{a}_{2j} - \dot{a}_{1j}}{e_j^{pv}}\right)$$

$$+ \left[\frac{v_j(k_{2j} - k_{1j})}{e_j^{pv}(v_j + k_{2j})(v_j + k_j)}\right]\dot{p} \ . \tag{11.37}$$

The last term in eq. (11.37), however, reduces to $(x_{1j}/y_{1j})\dot{p}$, so that eq. (11.35) becomes:

$$\dot{G}_j = \dot{\alpha}_j^k - \left(\frac{y_{1j}^w}{y_{1j}}\right)\left(\frac{\dot{a}_{2j} - \dot{a}_{1j}}{e_j^{pv}}\right) + \left(\frac{x_{1j} - c_{1j}}{y_{1j}}\right)\dot{p} \ . \tag{11.38}$$

Once again, changes in factor supplies leave welfare unaffected unless they alter product prices. Here, however, their price effect is thoroughly familiar: if factor-supply changes improve the terms of trade, they increase welfare; if they worsen the terms of trade, they decrease welfare[27].

We have, therefore, to ascertain the signs of $\dot{p}$ in each version of the model (setting $\dot{a}_{ij} = 0$ to concentrate on changes in factor supplies).

Taking, first, the simplest case, eq. (11.24) now asserts that an economy with fixed terms of trade cannot experience any welfare change consequent upon a change in factor supplies. As $\dot{p} = 0$, by hypothesis, $\dot{G}_j^k = \dot{G}_j^w = \dot{G}_j = 0$.

Taking, next, the other single-country case, we use eqs. (11.19) through (11.21) and (11.25) to write,

$$\dot{p} = \left(\frac{e_j^{pv}}{D_j}\right)\left\{\left[x_{1j}\left(\frac{k_j}{k_{2j}-k_j}\right) + c_{1j}z_j\right]\dot{k}_j - (x_{1j}-c_{1j})\dot{L}_j\right\} \qquad (11.39)$$

where

$$D_j = e_j^{pv}\left[(x_{1j}-c_{1j})e^s + c_{1j}E_j^p\right] + x_{1j}Q_j + c_{1j}\left[z_j e_j^{ky}\left(\frac{k_{1j}}{v_j+k_{1j}}\right)E_j^y\right].$$

The sign of D_j depends entirely on that of its final term (as all other terms are positive). Hereafter, therefore, let all income elasticities be constant, and let workers and capitalists have the same tastes. Under these circumstances, $E_j^y = e_j^{ky}$ and $z_j = k_j/(v_j+k_j)$, the capitalists' share in national income, while the final term of D_j reduces to

$$c_{1j}\left[e_j^{ky}\left(\frac{k_j-k_{1j}}{k_{2j}-k_{1j}}\right)e_j^{pv}\right] > 0.$$

With balanced growth in factor supplies ($\dot{L}_j \neq 0, \dot{k}_j = 0$), the sign of $\dot{p}$ depends entirely upon the trade pattern. If $x_{1j} > c_{1j}$, $\dot{L}_j > 0$ implies $\dot{p} \leq 0$ (giving $\dot{G}_j^k > 0$ and $\dot{G}_j^w < 0$). If $x_{1j} < c_{1j}$, $\dot{L}_j > 0$ implies $\dot{p} > 0$ (giving $\dot{G}_j^k < 0$ and $\dot{G}_j^w > 0$). In either case, of course, $\dot{L}_j > 0$ (overall growth in factor supplies) worsens the terms of trade; $\dot{G}_j < 0$.

With unbalanced growth, the outcome can differ. Consider, in particular, the results of immigration (so that $\dot{k}_j = -\dot{L}_j < 0$). Rewriting eq. (11.39), we have

---

[27] If $x_{1j} > c_{1j}$, then $\dot{p} > 0$ is an improvement in the terms of trade and gives $\dot{G}_j > 0$. If $x_{1j} < c_{1j}$, then $\dot{p} < 0$ is an improvement in the terms of trade and gives $\dot{G}_j > 0$.

$$\dot{p} - \left(\frac{e_j^{pv}}{D_j}\right)\left[x_{1j}\left(\frac{k_{2j}}{k_{2j}-k_j}\right) - c_{1j}(1-z_j)\right]\dot{L}_j$$

$$= -\left(\frac{e_j^{pv}}{D_j}\right)y_{1j}^w\left[\left(\frac{k_{2j}}{k_{2j}-k_{1j}}\right)\left(\frac{v_j+k_{1j}}{v_j}\right) - m_j^k\right]\dot{L}_j . \tag{11.40}$$

As $m_j^k < 1$, this expression takes its sign from $\dot{L}_j$. When, then, $\dot{L}_j > 0, \dot{p} < 0$; $\dot{G}_j^k > 0$, $\dot{G}_j^w < 0$, and the sign of $\dot{G}_j$ depends on the trade pattern. If $x_{1j} > c_{1j}$ initially and (at constant prices) after immigration, $\dot{G}_j < 0$; if, instead, $x_{1j} < c_{1j}$, $\dot{G}_j > 0$.

The two-country situation is more complex; generalized treatment is not too useful. Consider, however, the case of net migration (so that $L_1\dot{L}_1 = -L_2\dot{L}_2$), and use eqs. (11.19) through (11.21) and (11.26) to write

$$\dot{p} = \left(\frac{1}{D}\right)\left\{\left[x_{12}\left(\frac{k_{22}}{k_{22}-k_2}\right) - x_{11}\left(\frac{k_{21}}{k_{21}-k_1}\right)\right]\right.$$

$$\left. - \left[c_{12}\left(\frac{v_2}{v_2+k_2}\right) - c_{11}\left(\frac{v_1}{v_1+k_1}\right)\right]\right\}\dot{L}_1 \tag{11.41}$$

where

$$D = \left[x_{11}\left(\frac{Q_1}{e_1^{pv}}\right) + x_{12}\left(\frac{Q_2}{e_2^{pv}}\right)\left(\frac{L_2}{L_1}\right)\right] + \left[c_{11}e_1^{kp} + c_{12}e_2^{kp}\left(\frac{L_2}{L_1}\right)\right]$$

$$+ \left[c_{11}\left(\frac{k_1-k_{11}}{k_{21}-k_{11}}\right)e_1^{ky} + c_{12}\left(\frac{k_2-k_{12}}{k_{22}-k_{12}}\right)e_2^{ky}\left(\frac{L_2}{L_1}\right)\right]$$

Although $D > 0$, the sign of eq. (11.41) remains in doubt. Additional restrictions are needed. Assume, therefore, that $a_{11} = (1+\gamma)a_{12}$, which assumption (joined to others made earlier) gives $v_j = v_0$, $k_{ij} = k_{i0}$, and $y_{i1}^w = (1+\gamma)v_{i2}^w$, so that $\dot{L}_1$ takes its sign from γ. Further, assume that all tastes are the same and that $e_j^{ky} = 1$. Under this additional assumption,

$$c_{1j} = y_{1j}^k(v_0+k_j)[g(p)] \tag{11.42}$$

where $g(p) = m_j^k = m_j^w \leqslant 1$. Rewriting eq. (11.41), we have

$$\dot{p} = -\left(\frac{1}{D}\right)y_{12}^w\left[\left(\frac{v_0+k_{10}}{v_0}\right)\left(\frac{k_{20}}{k_{20}-k_{10}}\right) - g(p)\right](\gamma\dot{L}_1) . \tag{11.43}$$

As $g(p) < 1$ and $\gamma \dot{L}_1 > 0$, then $\dot{p} < 0$ under all circumstances. Hence, $\dot{G}_j^k > 0$, $\dot{G}_j^w < 0$, and $\dot{G}_1$ takes its sign from the trade pattern. If, at initial prices, $x_{11} > c_{11}$ for the relevant population, $\dot{G}_1 < 0$; if $x_{11} < c_{11}$ for that population, $\dot{G}_1 > 0$.

CHAPTER 12

A SIMULTANEOUS VARIATIONAL MODEL
FOR INTERNATIONAL CAPITAL MOVEMENT*

Henry Y.WAN, Jr.

12.1. Introduction

International capital movement is a time-honored topic in the literature of international economics. Among the recent models, three approaches explicitly take account of the interactions between the lending and borrowing economies. These are represented by: (1) the comparative static analysis of Kemp [1] and Jones [5]; (2) the "golden-rule" model of Negishi [10]; and (3) the "behavioral" growth theory approach represented by Kemp's extension [7] of the Oniki-Uzawa formulation. The first two approaches concentrate upon the consequences of capital movements: the altered capital/labor ratios and the continuous stream of interest payment. The capital movements themselves, e.g., the resource transfers accompanying the making and repayment of a foreign loan, are not considered. The third approach assigns fixed saving ratios to various income shares in the tradition of growth theory. The existence and stability of steady growth paths are the central emphasis of such inquiries, while the direction and magnitude of investment are not studied in much detail.

The present study is of the "rational" growth theory variety. In the tradition of Irving Fisher, and Hicks and Debreu, we postulate that price-taking utility-maximizing individuals ("*kibuzzim*") decide their saving programs

* The genesis of this study dates back to my student days at M.I.T. where inspiration received from Professors C.P.Kindleberger and P.A.Samuelson influenced my research in trade for years to come. Comments by Professor M.C.Kemp and encouragement from Professors J.Stein and G.H.Borts helped the completion of this study. The author is grateful for a research grant received from the Research Committee, University of California, Davis. Mr. Harold Stalford helped to prove part (2) of Proposition 11.

following general equilibrium analysis. Our model is saddled with a battery of simplifying assumptions. Nonetheless, such an undertaking appears to be worthwhile (and thus complementing the received literature) in three aspects:

(a) The comparative evolutions of the international balances for various economies so far defy rigorous theorization. The fascinating yet non-analytic work of Sir G.Crowther in this area has also received little, if any, systematic scrutiny, up to now. We need a dynamic theory providing phase-to-phase descriptions of time paths. This can serve as a measuring rod against the facts of life or the stylized facts of Crowther.

(b) The present theory of general equilibrium emphasizes problems of existence, uniqueness, stability, welfare implications and sensitivity analysis (alias comparative statics or dynamics). In the frameworks of Hicks and Debreu, commodities at different dates are treated as different goods. No information is provided about the time profile of the production and consumption of various commodities, etc., which is implied by any equilibrium. Our model attempts to shed light on the time structures of an equilibrium.

(c) Infinite horizon and a "closed economy" appear to be the twin assumptions à la mode in the optimal growth literature. Since economic agents or planners seldom operate in complete isolation, the simultaneous variational model set up here appears to be the natural extension for optimal growth models. But in making such a transition, the infinite horizon assumption may have to go over board. The non-existence of an equilibrium in some infinite horizon, simultaneous variational models is a by-product of our study which may present certain interesting theoretical implications.

In section 12.2 below we shall consider a finite horizon model. The catenary properties of the equilibrium path when the horizon becomes very long and the consequences of an infinite horizon will be studied in section 12.3. Section 12.4 contains some final remarks. A graphical summary of some time paths of the relevant variables is provided in an Appendix.

12.2. The Finite Horizon Model

Assumptions and Notations

We postulate that each country is made of a large number of entirely identical Sidrauskian families [13]. Rigorous intracountry aggregation becomes possible under constant returns of production. Each of these economic units is a price (interest) taker, facing a system of Walras competition markets, from now to doomsday[1]. Each economic unit maximizes the intertemporal sum of some utility index, the latter being defined over the level of per capita consumption. For all economic units in the world, labor always grows at a certain positive, constant rate. The internationally perfect immobility of labor is matched by the internationally perfect mobility of commodities. Capital good is nondepreciable, perfectly malleable, and directly consumable (e.g., wooden tools can serve as fuel for house heating). Given the time path for the interest rate, this welfare maximization determines a definite optimal consumption path. The interest rate is so determined that the aggregate output for the two economies exactly equals the sum of aggregate consumption and aggregate investment. The initial capital/labor ratios for the two economies may or may not be Pareto optimal. If not, an initial capital transfer is in order under the prodding invisible hand. The terminal capital must be zero: no point to leave consumable resource un-utilized by doomsday. Nor should there be any unsettled foreign borrowing at that ultimate instant; by then un-redeemed claims have no redeeming virtue. These assumptions supply the framework for our model[2].

We shall introduce the following notations:

k_i is the capital/labor ratio for economy i
k_{i0} is the initially endowed ratio for economy i
c_i is the consumption per capita for economy i
v_i is the investment per capita for economy i
f_i is the output per capita for economy i
d_i is the current foreign lending per capita for economy i
u_i is the instantaneous utility indicator for economy i
w_i is the wage rate in economy i
L_{0i} is the initial amount of labor for economy i
θ is the ratio of the population for economy 1 to the total population
n is the population growth rate
r is the interest rate
T is the length of the horizon

[1] I.e., the end of the world.
[2] The underlying mathematical problem is not a standard variational problem. Simultaneous optimizations are carried out vis-à-vis the common equilibrium system of interest rates. The resultant equilibrium is reminiscent of the duopoly model of Roos [11]. It is not a differential game since players in the differential game can select optimal moves with reference only to the present state. In our case, future equilibrium interest rates are needed for deciding current moves.

$i = 1, 2$

u_i and f_i are both supposed to be twice differentiable and concave;
$f_i(0) = 0$, $\infty = f_1'(0) = f_2'(0)$, $0 = f_i'(\infty) = f_2'(\infty)$
$u_i'(0) = \infty$.

Formulation and Equilibrium Conditions

Based upon the previous discussions and the earlier notations, we can develop a formal model in two steps:

1. *The optimization process in each economy.* For economic units in each economy, we have

$$\max \int_0^T u_i[c_i(t)] \, dt \qquad\qquad (12.1)$$

subject to

$$[k_{i0} - k_i(0)] + \int_0^T \{f_i[k_i(t)] - k_i(t) - nk_i(t) - c_i(t)\}$$

$$\exp\left\{- \int_0^t [r(\tau) - n] \, d\tau\right\} dt = 0 \qquad k_i(T) = 0. \qquad (12.2)$$

Expression (12.1) is self-evident, while eq. (12.2) is a "dynamic" budget equation starting that the sum of the initial transfer and the discounted stream of the foreign net investment should be zero over the planning horizon. We note that $(\dot{k}_i + nk_i)$ is the investment per capita, hence $[f_i - (\dot{k}_i + nk_i) - c_i]$ represents the excess of output per capita over expenditure (investment-cum-consumption) per capita. This multiplied by $\exp(nt)$ becomes the foreign investment at t divided by the initial population. The factor $\exp(-_0\!\int^t r \, d\tau)$ is the discounting factor. Combining everything, (12.2) is a dynamic budget equation expressed in "per-initial-capita" terms.

We have not introduced any nonnegative constraints for the following reasons:

(i) $v_i = (\dot{k}_i + nk_i)$ may actually become negative because of our assumption that capital goods are directly consumable. Hence it is possible that consumption exceeds output.

(ii) c_i will always be positive along an optimal path, from our assumption that the marginal utility to consume becomes infinity if consumption becomes zero at any moment. Unless c_i is set to zero throughout the time horizon (obviously a nonoptimal policy), it is impossible to have an optimal c_i path which reaches zero at any one point t_1 and stays at a positive level at another point t_2. Otherwise, making a small "pair-wise" adjustment by decreasing c_i in a small neighborhood around t_2 and increasing c_i in a small neighborhood around t_1, the attainable welfare level will be raised. That is contradictory to the optimality assumption. Hence, $c_i \geq 0$ will be automatically satisfied.

(iii) k_i will always be positive except at the moment T. Suppose this is not true and $k_i(T_1) = 0$ for $T_1 < T$. Since capital is perfectly mobile internationally, capital earns the same rate of returns [see (14)] in both economies. Since by assumption $f_i' = \infty$ if and only if $k_i = 0$ and $i = 1, 2$, the fact that $k_i = 0$ implies $k_j = 0 = k$ $(i \neq j)$ at T. Since $\dot{k} = \theta \dot{k}_1 + (1-\theta)\dot{k}_2 = \theta f_1(0) + (1-\theta)f_2(0) - \theta c_1 - (1-\theta)c_2 - n[\theta(0) + (1-\theta)(0)] = -\theta c_1 - (1-\theta)c_2$, our discussion above ($c_i > 0$ for all t, all i) shows that $\dot{k} < 0$. Hence $k(T_1 + \Delta) < 0$ for some small $\Delta > 0$, which is impossible. Therefore, for any optimal, feasible solution, $k_i = 0$ can only happen at T. But that is already covered by our endpoint condition $k_i(T) = 0$. Hence, $k_i \geq 0$ is again automatically satisfied.

2. *The balance of the aggregate market.* This is represented by two relations:

$$\sum_{i=1}^{2} \left\{ \bar{k}_{i0} - k_i(0) \right\} L_{i0} = 0 \tag{12.3}$$

$$\sum_{i=1}^{2} \{ f_i[k_i(t)] - [\dot{k}_i(t) + nk_i(t)] - c_i(t) \} L_{i0} e^{nt} = 0 \tag{12.4}$$

for all t, where $0 \leq t \leq T$.

Eq. (12.3) states that the initial capital employed, taking the two economies as a whole, must equal to the initial capital endowment. Eq. (12.4) indicates that the foreign borrowing of one economy must be balanced by the foreign lending of the other economy.

Both for mathematical convenience[3] and for subsequent ease in interpretation, we transform eq. (12.2) into its equivalent terms:

---

[3] Eq. (12.2) is an isoperimetric constraint of the Bolza type, not a convenient form for resolution.

$$\bar{k}_{i0} - k_i(0) - d_i(0) = 0 \tag{12.2'}$$

$$\dot{k}_i(t) = v_i(t) - nk_i(t) \qquad\qquad k_i(T) = 0 \tag{12.5}$$

$$\dot{d}_i(t) = \{f_i[k_i(t)] - v_i(t) - c_i(t)\} + [r(t)-n]d_i(t) \quad d_i(T) = 0 . \tag{12.6}$$

Applying the maximum principle, there exist adjoint variables λ_k^i and λ_d^i such that under the optimal control the Hamiltonian

$$H_i = u_i[c_i(t)] + \lambda_k^i(t)[v_i(t)-nk_i(t)] + \lambda_d^i(t)\{f_i[k_i(t)]$$

$$- v_i(t) - c_i(t) + r(t)d_i(t) - nd_i(t)\}$$

is maximized with respect to $c_i(t)$ and $v_i(t)$, implying

$$u_i'[c_i(t)] = \lambda_d^i(t) \tag{12.7}$$

$$\lambda_k^i(t) = \lambda_d^i(t) . \tag{12.8}$$

Moreover, the adjoint variables satisfy the differential equations

$$\dot{\lambda}_k^i(t) = n\lambda_k^i(t) - \lambda_d^i(t)f_1'[k_i(t)] \tag{12.9}$$

$$\dot{\lambda}_d^i(t) = n\lambda_d^i(t) - \lambda_d^i(t)r(t) . \tag{12.10}$$

Furthermore, eq. (12.2') implies a transversality condition[4]:

$$\lambda_k^i(0) = \lambda_d^i(0) \tag{12.11}$$

which can also be deduced from eq. (12.8).

Combining all these conditions, we obtain the twin economic conditions from eqs. (12.8), (12.9) and (12.10),

$$f_1'[k_1(t)] = r(t) = f_2'[k_2(t)] \qquad \text{for all } t \tag{12.12}$$

showing that equal marginal products of capital must rule in a world with perfect capital mobility. From eqs. (12.7) and (12.10),

---

[4] See for instance, p. 162 of Bliss [6] or p. 338 of Hestenes [7].

$$\frac{du'_1[c_1(t)]/dt}{u'_1[c_1(t)]} = -[r(t)-n] = \frac{du'_2[c_2(t)]/dt}{u'_2[c_2(t)]} \qquad (12.13)$$

showing that for both countries, the rate of decrease of the marginal utility indices for all economic units must be equal to the excess of the own rate of interest of capital over the biological interest rate of population growth. Eq. (12.12) is well-known at least since the days of Irving Fisher, and eq. (12.13) is an application of the Koopmans' version of the Keynes-Ramsey saving rule to international economics. The only novelty lies in the implied time profile of international capital movements. To that end, we need further analysis.

The World Economy

At any point of time where the aggregate capital/labor ratio is k, there exists one pair of values (k_1, k_2) such that:

$$\theta k_1 + (1-\theta)k_2 = k \qquad (12.14)$$

$$f'_1(k_1) = f'_2(k_2) \qquad (12.12')$$

which characterizes the efficient allocation of capital. The implied sum $[\theta f_1(k_1)+(1-\theta)f_2(k_2)]$ can be defined as $f = f(k)$, the world maximum output per capita, dependent only upon the value k. The graphical derivation f is rather simple. Plotting θf_1 against θk_1 and $(1-\theta)f_2$ against $(1-\theta)k_2$ and then sliding one graph against the other with the origin of the former moving along the graph of the latter, one can trace out f as depicted in fig. 12.1a. It is easy to show that $f(0) = 0, f' > 0 > f''$.

We now define

$$g(k) = f(k) - nk$$

$$= \dot{k} + \theta c_1 + (1-\theta)c_2 \qquad (12.15)$$

in view of eq. (12.4) and the definitions of θ and k.

Now, from eq. (12.13), we have

$$\dot{c}_i(t) = \left\{ \frac{u'_i[c_i(t)]}{u''_i[c_i(t)]} \right\} \{n - f'[k(t)]\} \qquad i = 1, 2. \qquad (12.16)$$

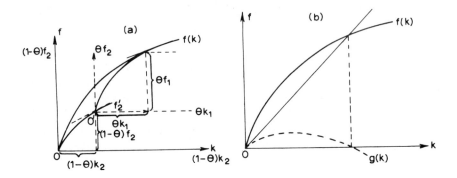

Fig. 12.1.

Given $c_i(0)$, $i = 1$, 2, the simultaneous differential equation system (12.15) and (12.16) is completely determined in its evolutionary path.

For simplicity, we shall assume that u_i exhibits "constant elasticity", i.e., $u_i = c_i^{\alpha_i}$, $1 = 1$, 2. Thus, we have

$$\hat{c}_i(t) = \frac{\hat{u}'_i[c_i(t)]}{(1-\alpha_i)}$$

$$= \frac{(f'-n)}{(1-\alpha_i)} \qquad i = 1, 2 \tag{12.17}$$

where $\hat{x} = d \ln x/dt$ for $x = c_i$ or u'_i.

We shall now examine various special cases of the model.

Differences in the absolute sizes of the economies. Consider two economies which have identical u_i and f_i functions as well as the same initial capital/labor ratio $\bar{k}_{i0}$. Common sense assures us that since all the component economic units ("families") are identical, there will be no lending or borrowing between these two economies despite the disparate sizes of the two countries (i.e., $\theta \neq 1/2$). A rigorous proof can be obtained by noting that in eqs. (12.3) and (12.4), if the terms in the braces { } take the same value, regardless of i, then these brackets must be zero. In other words, neither initial capital transfer, nor subsequent capital movement can ever occur.

Differences in the initial capital/labor ratio endowed. Assuming that $u_1(\cdot) = u_2(\cdot)$ and $f_1(\cdot) = f_2(\cdot)$ but $\bar{k}_{10} \neq \bar{k}_{20}$, we can determine the time paths of consumption and capital per capita as well as the phase-by-phase development of the balance of payments. For definiteness, assume that $\bar{k}_{10} > \bar{k}_{20}$. The results we have are of two kinds:

Result 1. Modes of consumption per capita and capital per capita paths. From eq. (12.17) and the equality between α_1 and α_2, we have

$$c_1(t)/c_1(0) = \exp \int_0^t \frac{(f'-n)d\tau}{(1-\alpha)} = c_2(t)/c_2(0)$$

where α is the common value between α_1 and α_2. We obtain then:

Proposition 1. Under the above assumptions, the consumption per capita of economy 1 is always higher than that of economy 2 by a fixed percentage. The fact $c_1(0) > c_2(0)$ follows later from the lemma for Proposition 5.

Defining $c = \theta c_1 + (1-\theta)c_2$, we have

Corollary: The overall consumption per capita c bears a constant proportion to c_i, for all $t, i = 1, 2$. Also, eqs. (12.15) and (12.17) can be rewritten as

$$\dot{k} = g(k) - c$$

$$\dot{c} = \frac{f'(k)-n}{1-\alpha} \, c \, .$$

Invoking a graphic analysis of Koopmans [9], we have

Proposition 2. The (k,c) path and therefore the (k_i,c_i) path (inasmuch as $k_i = k$ and c_i is proportional to c, $i = 1, 2$) have only three possible modes:
1. First $c(t)$ decreases and then increases; $k(t)$ decreases all the time.
2. The $c(t)$ increases and $k(t)$ decreases all the time.
3. The $c(t)$ increases all the time; $k(t)$ first increases and then decreases.
Mode 1 occurs if and only if $k(0) > k^*$ where $f'(k^*) = n$. Mode 3 occurs if and only if the time horizon is so long that the $c(0)$ chosen is strictly less than $g[k(0)]$.

Result 2. Phase-by-phase analysis of the balance of payments.
Eq. (12.12) leads to

Proposition 3. Under the above assumptions, the initial capital transfer amounts to

$$L_{10}[\bar{k}_{10}-k(0)] = L_{10}(1-\theta)(\bar{k}_{10}-\bar{k}_{20}) \, .$$

The proof follows immediately from the fact that $k_i(t) \equiv k(t)$ for all t and $i = 1, 2$ under the hypothesis of identical production functions.

From Proposition 1 and its corollary, we have

$$c_1(t) > c(t) > c_2(t) \qquad \text{for all } t .$$

From the fact that $f_1(\cdot) = f_2(\cdot) = f(\cdot)$ and $k_1(t) = k_2(t) = k(t)$ for all t, eq. (12.15) leads to

$$f_i(k_i) - v_i(t) = c(t) \qquad \text{for all } t \text{ and } i = 1, 2 .$$

Therefore, we have

Proposition 4. Under the above assumptions, the commodity flow at all points of time, excepting the initial instant, represents a continuous repatriation effort on the part of economy 2. This flow bears a constant proportion to consumption per capita. Here $(f_i - v_i - c_i) = (c - c_i)$ stands for the commodity outflow per capita, which is proportional to c_i following the corollary of Proposition 1.

We now turn to the balance of current account, i.e., the difference between the repatriation flow and the interest flow. The percentage change of the capital account is from eq. (12.6)

$$\hat{d}_i + n = - \frac{c_i(t) - c(t)}{d_i(t)} + f'[k(t)] . \qquad (12.18)$$

Even in the last stage of the three modes in Proposition 2, where $\dot{c}_i > 0 > \dot{k}$, we have no guarantee that $(\hat{d}_i + n)$ will never change sign, will change only once, or will change sign more than once.

However, the analysis of eq. (12.18) yields:

Proposition 5. The $d_i(t)$ can never take opposite signs over the horizon.

This conclusion follows from:

Lemma. $d_i(t)$ and $[c(t) - c_i(t)]$ cannot be both positive. If this condition is violated, then the right-hand side of eq. (12.18) will always be positive and $d_i e^{nt}$ will keep on increasing while $[c(t) - c_i(t)]$ being proportional to $c(t)$

will remain positive. The condition $d_i(T) = 0$ can never be fulfilled in that case.

Summing up, under the above assumptions, we conclude that

1. Economy 2 experiences the status of a "debtor borrower" only in that fleeting initial instant where foreign investment materialized with a quantum jump.

2. It will never develop into a "creditor".

3. It may go through the Crowther stages [3] of the "mature debtor" (i.e., debt increases along with outflows of commodities) and the "debtor repayer" (i.e., debt decreases with outflows of commodities) in that accustomed order, or it may skip the "mature debtor" position altogether or may switch back and forth several times before its terminal entry into the "debtor repayer" status.

As Kindleberger noted (p. 459, 3rd ed.) [11], the item of interest payment makes orderly stage-by-stage progression rather unlikely.

Differences in the production functions. We now assume that $\bar{k}_{10} = \bar{k}_{20}$ and $\alpha_1 = \alpha_2$. However, $f_1(\cdot) \neq f_2(\cdot)$. Obviously, two functions can differ from each other in infinitely many ways. Before going into these matters, we observe that so far as the modes of the (c_i, k_i) paths are concerned, Proposition 1, its corollary, and Proposition 2 hold exactly as before. The association between k and k_i, $i = 1, 2$, needs some analysis in the present context. We note that

$$\dot{k}(t) = \frac{\left(\frac{d}{dt} f'\right)}{f''}$$

$$= \frac{\left(\frac{d}{dt} f_i'\right)}{f_i''} \frac{f_i''}{f''}$$

$$= \dot{k}_i(t) \left(\frac{f_i''}{f''}\right)$$

since $f_i' = f'$ at all times. Now (f_i''/f'') is always positive, being a ratio of negative numbers, k_i is seen to rise and fall with k together, $i = 1, 2$.

The Leontief case. Suppose that

$$f_1(x) = A f_2(x/A) \qquad \text{for all } x \text{ and } A > 1 . \tag{12.19}$$

This corresponds to the Leontief interpretation of the Leontief paradox: the American economy enjoys a technological superiority of the pure "labor-augmenting" type. Analytically, all we need to do is to change the measurement of labor from "natural" to "efficiency" units. Let notations with the tilda sign stand for the same symbols on "efficiency labor" basis, thus:

$$\tilde{k}_1 = \frac{k_1}{A} \qquad \tilde{k}_2 = \frac{k_2}{1} \qquad \tilde{k} = \frac{[\theta A k_1 + (1-\theta)k_2]}{(\theta A + 1 - \theta)}$$

$$\tilde{L}_{10} = A L_{10} \qquad \tilde{L}_{20} = L_{20} \qquad \tilde{k}_{10} = \frac{k_{10}}{A} \qquad \tilde{k}_{20} = k_{20}$$

$$\tilde{f}_1(\tilde{k}_1) = \frac{f_1(\tilde{k}_1)}{A} = f_2(\tilde{k}_1)$$

$$\tilde{v}_1 = \frac{v_1}{A} \qquad \tilde{c}_1 = \frac{c_1}{A} \qquad \tilde{v}_2 = v_2 \qquad \tilde{c}_2 = c_2$$

$$\tilde{\theta} = \frac{\theta A}{(\theta A + 1 - \theta)} .$$

We now have a situation similar to the case of differences in endowed capital/labor ratio. In fact, we observe that

$$\tilde{k}_{10} = \frac{\tilde{k}_{20}}{A} < \tilde{k}_{20} .$$

Therefore, the initial capital movement must be directed into country 1. Moreover, economy 1 will never be a creditor, i.e., $d_1 \leqslant 0$ for all t.
However, we can prove

Proposition 6. Under the above assumptions, $[c_1(t)/c_2(t)] > 1$ for all t.

To prove this result, we first rewrite eq. (12.2) by setting

$$w_i(t) = f[k_i(t)] - k_i(t)f'[k_i(t)] , \qquad i = 1, 2$$

then

$$\bar{k}_{10} + \int_0^T w_i(t) \exp\left\{-\int_0^t [r(\tau)-n]\,d\tau\right\} dt$$

$$+ \int_0^T (\{f_i'[k_i(t)] -n\}k_i(t) - \dot{k}_i(t)) \exp\left\{-\int_0^t [r(\tau)-n]\,d\tau\right\} dt$$

$$- k_i(0) = \int_0^T c_i(t) \exp\left\{-\int_0^t [r(\tau)-n]\,d\tau\right\} dt \ . \qquad (12.2'')$$

Setting $\mu(t) = \exp\left\{-\int_0^t [r(\tau)-n]\,d\tau\right\}$ and using the fact that $f_i'[k_i(t)] = r(t)$ for all t (from eq. (12.12)), we note that $\mu(0) = 1$,

$$- \int_0^T (\dot{\mu}k_i + \dot{k}_i\mu)\,dt = k_i(0) - k_i(T)\mu(T) \ .$$

Eq. (12.2'') therefore becomes

$$\bar{k}_{10} + \int_0^T w_i(t)\mu(t)\,dt - k_i(T)\mu(T) = \int_0^T c_i(t)\mu(t)\,dt \ . \qquad (12.20)$$

From the facts that

$$k_i(T) = 0 \qquad \text{for } i = 1, 2 ,$$

again from eq. (12.17) and the fact that $\alpha_1 = \alpha_2 = \alpha$, say, we have

$$\int_0^T c_i(t)\mu(t)\,dt = c_i(0) \int_0^T [\mu(t)]^{-\alpha/(1-\alpha)}\,dt \ .$$

From eq. (12.20), we finally obtain

$$c_i(0) = \frac{[\bar{k}_{i0} + \int_0^T w_i(t)\mu(t)\,dt]}{\int_0^T [\mu(t)]^{-\alpha/(1-\alpha)}\,dt} \ . \qquad (12.21)$$

Since eq. (12.19) implies $w_1(t) = Aw_2(t)$, we immediately see that $c_1(0) > c_2(0)$ and the proposition is immediate.

The economic content of Proposition 6 is that given equal initial endowments per capita all economic units in an economy enjoying a "Leontief superiority" in production will consume more per capita than those in the other economy by a constant margin at all times.

The "Hicks" difference[5] . This term means

$$f_1(x) = Af_2(x) \qquad \text{for all } x \qquad A > 1 .$$

Suppose f_2 is log linear, then a theorem of Uzawa [14] shows this case reduces to the Leontief difference. However, even when f_i is not log linear, we can still prove:

Proposition 7. Under the above assumptions,

1. There is an initial capital transfer into economy 1.

2. At any point of time, economy 1 enjoys a higher per capita consumption than economy 2.

The verification of 1 is relatively simple. Since $\bar{k}_{10} = \bar{k}_{20} = k(0)$, also $\theta k_1(0) + (1-\theta)k_2(0) = k(0)$, we have

$$\theta[\bar{k}_{10} - k_1(0)] = (1-\theta)[k_2(0) - \bar{k}_{20}] . \tag{12.22}$$

Now after the initial capital transfer, $f_2'[k_2(0)] = f_1'[k_1(0)] = Af_2'[k_1(0)]$. In view of $f_2'' < 0$, $k_2(0) < k_1(0)$, eq. (12.22) indicates that $k_1(0)$ cannot be both greater than or less than $k(0) = \bar{k}_{i0}$ where $i = 1, 2$. Therefore, $k_2(0) < \bar{k}_{i0} < k_1(0)$, as we stated.

Next, to prove 2, we observe for all t that, $f_2'[k_2(t)] = f_1'[k_1(t)] = Af_2'[k_1(t)]$ showing $k_1(t) > k_2(t)$. Therefore,

---

[5] The Leontief difference is akin to the Harrod-neutral technical change. One pertains to cross-country comparison, the other to time series observations. The "Hicks" difference bears a similar relation to the Hicks-neutral technical progress.

$$w_1(t) = f_1[k_1(t)] - k_1(t)f_1'[k_1(t)]$$

$$> f_1[k_2(t)] - k_2(t)f_1'[k_2(t)] \qquad \left(\frac{dw_i}{dk_i} = -k_i f_i'' > 0\right)$$

$$= A\ f_2[k_2(t)] - k_2(t)f_2'[k_2(t)]$$

$$> f_2[k_2(t)] - k_2(t)f_2'[k_2(t)]$$

$$= w_2(t).$$

Since $\bar{k}_{10} = \bar{k}_{20}$, applying eq. (12.21), we have

$$c_1(0) > c_2(0).$$

Hence $c_1(t) > c_2(t)$, for all t.

Differences in Preference functions. We now assume that $f_1(\cdot) = f_2(\cdot)$ and $k_{10} = k_{20}$ but $\alpha_1 > \alpha_2$. Immediately, we have

Proposition 8. Under these assumptions, there is no initial capital movement. This is seen from the fact that

$$r(0) = f'[k(0)]$$

$$= f_i'[\bar{k}_{i0}] \qquad\qquad i = 1, 2.$$

In fact, from $f_1(\cdot) = f_2(\cdot)$, we can deduce that

$$f_i[k_i(t)] - nk_i(t) - \dot{k}_i(t) = g[k(t)] - \dot{k}(t)$$

$$= \theta c_1(t) + (1-\theta)c_2(t) \quad \text{(from eq. (12.15))}$$

$$= c(t),$$

Therefore, the commodity flow between countries can be represented by

$$f_1[k_1(t)] - nk_1(t) - \dot{k}_1(t) - c_1(t) = (1-\theta)[c_2(t) - c_1(t)]$$

$$f_2[k_2(t)] - nk_2(t) - \dot{k}_2(t) - c_2(t) = \theta[c_1(t) - c_2(t)]. \qquad (12.23)$$

In other words, the country which enjoys the higher consumption per capita at any moment must depend upon imported commodities to sustain such a consumption program.

We now use eqs. (12.17), (12.20), and (12.21) to deduce that

$$c_i(t) = \frac{[k(0) + {}_0\!\int^T w(t)\mu(t)dt]\,[\mu(t)]^{-1/(1-\alpha_i)}}{{}_0\!\int^T [\mu(t)]^{-\alpha_i/(1-\alpha_i)}\,dt} \qquad i = 1, 2\,. \qquad (12.24)$$

Assuming that $\mu(t) \leqslant 1$ for all $t \geqslant 0$ and $\mu(t) < 1$ for all $t > 0$, also noting that $\alpha_i/(1-\alpha_i)$ is an increasing function of α_i, we conclude that

$$c_1(0) < c_2(0)$$

$$\hat{c}_1(t) > \hat{c}_2(t) \qquad \text{for } t > 0\,.$$

Moreover, since $\mu(t) > 0$ for all $t \geqslant 0$, the fact that eq. (12.20) implies (because the left-hand side of eq. (12.20) is identical for $i = 1, 2$)

$$\int_0^T [c_1(t) - c_2(t)]\mu(t)dt = 0$$

leads to Proposition 9.

Proposition 9. Supposing $\mu(t) \leqslant 1$ for all $t \geqslant 0$ and $\mu(t) < 1$ for all $t > 0$, then there exists t_0 between 0 and T such that $c_1(t) - c_2(t) \{\gtreqless\} 0$ if and only if $t \{\gtreqless\} t_0$. In other words, the country with a higher "consumption elasticity" of utility will first lend capital to the other country up to a point t_0. It will "live on interest" for a while, enjoying an inward commodity flow without diminishing its foreign investment but finally consumes up its investment as well, just before the doomsday.

Corollary. The $c_1(\cdot)$ and $c_2(\cdot)$ can cross only once. Therefore, the debtor country can never become a creditor. Otherwise, no repayment for the "debtor-turned" creditor is possible.

The construction of a three-dimensional phase diagram according to eqs. (12.15) and (12.16) and the employment of a type of analysis exactly parallel to the two-dimensional diagram of Koopmans establish the following:

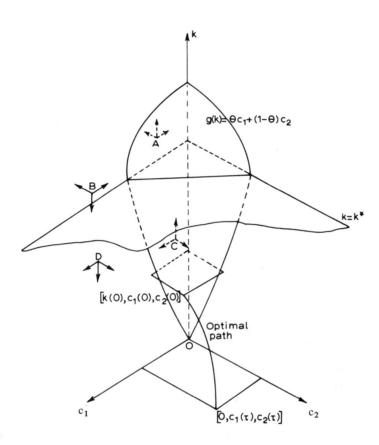

Fig. 12.2.

Proposition 10. If $k(0) < k^*$, then $\mu(0) = 1$ and $\mu(t) < 1$ for all $t > 0$. The phase diagram is shown in fig. 12.2. k^* is such that $g'(k^*) = 0$.

Before we move on to the problem arising from an infinite horizon, we should compare our model with the Kemp 1968 model in one aspect. In the latter model, the saving/income ratio arising out of the profit and wage shares are known constants and the overall saving/income ratio for any country always lies between zero and unity. In our model this is no longer true. During the entire period when (i) the overall capital/labor ratio is both less than k^* and steadily decreasing toward zero while (ii) consumption per capita rises in both countries, the optimal trajectory is inside region D in fig. 12.2. This means the overall saving/income ratio is negative from then on to the end of the world. Since the overall saving/income ratio is the (income) weighted average of the national saving/income ratios, one of these two ratios, at least, must always be negative.

However, the fundamen′al approaches underlying the two models are entirely different. Ours fol′ows the traditional Walras-Hicks-Debreu line with utility maximizing microunits as the basic building blocks. Saving/income ratios at any moment can be derived but are never postulated. Kemp's 1968 model follows the Keynes-Solow-Oniki-Uzawa line, where the micro behavior is assumed to be such as to keep the saving/income ratio (from certain income sources, at least) constant. Reality may lie somewhere in between. But only empirical studies can tell.

12.3. Catenary Properties of the Optimal Path and the Infinite Horizon Model

We shall first study the properties of the optimal path when the time horizon becomes longer and longer. Later in this section, we shall set the horizon to infinity. We shall only consider the case where the two economies differ only in the initial capital endowed per capita. Also the utility function is assumed to be of the constant elasticity type.

Using the phase diagram of Koopmans [8], I have proved elsewhere [15] that as the time horizon lengthens over an increasingly large proportion of the horizon (eventually almost 100% of the time), both the capital/labor ratio and the consumption per capita will approach respectively the limiting values of k^* and $g(k^*)$. This is, of course, the Samuelson-Cass [12], [2] theorem. A graphical sketch is indicated in fig. 12.3.

Consider any rectangle centered at $E = [k^*, g(k^*)]$. Consider also the comparison paths CFD, AE and EB. CFD is tangent to R. AE and EB go to and come from the point E. Suppose the initial capital/labor ratio is $k^1(0) > k^*$ ($k^2(0) < k^*$), also it takes time T_1 along AE to go from $k^1(0)$ to R (along CF to go from $k^2(0)$ to R) and time T_2 along EB to go from R to $k = 0$ (along FD to go from R to $k = 0$). The dotted path is the specific optimal path for given T. When T is large, the dotted path stays for some time inside R. By calculating $\dot{k}$ corresponding to k along the dotted and solid paths, it can be shown that along the dotted path, it takes less than T_1 to enter R and less than T_2 to emerge from R and reach $k = 0$. Hence the sojourn time along the

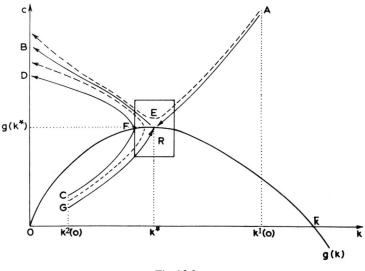

Fig. 12.3.

optimal (dotted) path inside R is at least $(T-T_1-T_2)$. When the horizon T lengthens, obviously the proportion of time in R is:

$$\lim_{T \to \infty} \frac{T - T_1 - T_2}{T} = 1 \, .$$

Since inside R, $|c-g(k^*)| < \frac{1}{2}$ (height of R) and $|k-k^*| < \frac{1}{2}$ (width of R), by choosing smaller and smaller R, one can prove that defining $s = t/T$ (and hence $t = sT$):

$$\lim_{T \to \infty} k(sT) = k^* \qquad\qquad \lim_{T \to \infty} r(sT) = n$$

$$\lim_{T \to \infty} c_i(sT) = \frac{c_i(0)}{c(0)} g(k^*) \qquad\qquad \lim_{T \to \infty} g'[k(sT)] = 0 \, .$$

Here s means the ratio of *time passed* to the *time horizon*.

We can also select R such that $g' < \delta$ and $c > (1-\epsilon)g(k^*)$ inside R. This will be useful for our analysis below.

We now assert that with given $\bar{k}_{10}$ and $\bar{k}_{20}$, hence $d_i(0)$, the longer is the time horizon, the smaller should be the relative international difference of per capita consumption. The proof is as follows:

(1) For $k(0) \geqslant k^*$:

To begin with, let us assume $\bar{k}_{10} > \bar{k}_{20}$ and thus $d_1(0) > 0$. Obviously, $[c_i(t)/c_2(t)]$ is an increasing function of

$$\frac{c_1(0)}{c(0)} - 1 = \frac{1}{\theta + [(1-\theta)/(c_1/c_2)]} \; .$$

Rewriting eq. (12.18), we have

$$d_1(T) = e^{\circ \int^T (g')dt} \; d_1(0) - \int_0^T (c_1 - c) \, e^{-\circ \int^t (g')d\tau} \, dt$$

$$< e^{\circ \int^T (g')dt} \left[d_1(0) - \int_{T_1}^{T-T_2} (c_1 - c) \, e^{-\circ \int^t (g')d\tau} \, dt \right]$$

$$< e^{\circ \int^T (g')dt} \left[d_1(0) - \left\{ \frac{c_1(0)}{c(0)} - 1 \right\} (1-\epsilon)g(k^*) \, e^{-\circ \int^{T_1} (g')d\tau} \right.$$

$$\times \left. \left\{ \frac{1 - e^{-\delta(T-T_1-T_2)}}{\delta} \right\} \right] \tag{12.25}$$

where ϵ and δ can be arbitrarily small positive numbers when a small enough R and a large enough T are selected.

Obviously for any fixed (c_1/c), there exist a large enough T^*, such that whenever $T > T^*$, $d_1(T) < 0$ contradictory to Proposition 5. Hence, when T lengthens, (c_1/c) and hence (c_1/c_2) should be reduced.

(2) For $k(0) < k^*$, a different type of proof is needed:

In this case, Proposition 2 implies that $g' > 0$ for all t. Hence by definition, $\mu(t) = \exp \{ -_0 \int^t g'd\tau \} < 1$. Thus, $[\mu(t)]^{-\alpha/(1-\alpha)} > 1$. But

$$c_1(0) - c(0) = (1-\theta)[c_1(0) - c_2(0)]$$

$$= \frac{(1-\theta)[\bar{k}_{10} - \bar{k}_{20}]}{_0\int^T [\mu(t)]^{-\alpha/(1-\alpha)} \, dt} \qquad \text{(using eq. (12.21) and } w_1 = w_2)$$

$$< \frac{(1-\theta)[\bar{k}_{10} - \bar{k}_{20}]}{T} \; .$$

Hence,

$$\lim_{T \to \infty} [c_1(0) - c(0)] \downarrow 0 .$$

From fig. 12.3, the $c(0)$ is bounded below by the ordinate of the point G located at the intersection of $k = k(0)$ and the GE infinite path. Therefore, again we have

$$\lim_{T \to \infty} \left(\frac{c_1}{c}\right) \downarrow 1 .$$

Incidentally, the above result indicates that for a large enough T, the term $(f_i - v_i - c_i) = (c - c_i)$ will be initially dominated by $f_i'[k_i(0)]\ d_i(0)$. Hence, $d_i e^{nt}$ will increase in the initial period. This corresponds to the Crowther "mature-debtor" category.

Summing up, we have the following results concerning the catenary properties:

Proposition 11. If two economies differ from each other only in initially endowed capital/labor ratios, then when the time horizon is long enough:

1. For a predominantly large portion of the time, the capital/labor ratio, the consumption per capita, and the interest rate will respectively become near to their catenary "limiting" values.

2a. The longer is the horizon, other things remaining equal, the smaller must be the relative difference between the consumption per capita levels for the two economies.

2b. Other things remaining equal, a long enough horizon implies that there is at least an initial period of mature-debtorship for the borrowing economy.

We now turn to the infinite horizon problem, where T is set to infinity in eqs. (12.1) and (12.2)[6]. The condition $k_i(T) = 0$ in (12.5) will be replaced by a natural boundary condition to be determined later. The condition $d_i(T) = 0$ in (12.6) also has to be replaced by something weaker:

$$\lim \inf [d_i(t)\mu(t)] = \underline{D}_i \leqslant 0 \leqslant \bar{D}_i = \lim \sup [d_i(t)\mu(t)] . \qquad (12.26)$$

---

[6] We shall side-step the question of whether we can find convergent objective functionals à la Ramsey-Wieszacker. We are concerned with the *inter alia* consistency between necessary conditions.

The reason of $\underline{D}_i \leqslant 0$ is rather obvious. A claim never realized now nor in the future is as good as no claim. Victims of Schacht's trade policy woke up only too late to this fact. A corollary to this is the fact that if new lendings are always no less than interest receipts, the original claim is never realized. Since $\theta d_1 + (1-\theta)d_2 = 0$, then $\bar{D}_j \geqslant 0$ follows from $D_j \leqslant 0, i \neq j$.

Returning to the limiting values of $k_i = k$ when T is large, we note that any optimal path, if it exists, must exhibit one of the three listed modes (see fig. 3):

1. Reaching $k = 0$ at some finite future date. Now zero capital means zero output, zero rate of accumulation and zero consumption, from this point on until the end of the time horizon. This holds true for both economies. Certainly this is an inferior strategy for both economies. One can simply follow the Ramsey saving rule on an autarkic basis. That will be much better.

2. Approaching the $(\bar{k},0)$ point asymptotically. Again this path is dominated by the autarkic policy of following the Ramsey rule.

3. Approaching $[k^*,g(k^*)]$ asymptotically. We now consider this case in detail:

a. If $d_1(0) > 0$ and $c_1(0) \leqslant c(0)$, obviously $\underline{D}_1 > 0$, thus violating eq. (12.26).

b. If $d_1(0) > 0$, $c_1(0) > c(0)$ then the same argument leading to Proposition 11 implies that there exists T^*, such that $d_1(t)\mu(t) < 0$ for all $t > T^*$. In fact, lim sup $d(t)\mu(t) = -\infty$, thus violating eq. (12.26).

Therefore we have

Proposition 12. For all $k(0)$, there exists no equilibrium for the infinite horizon version of our problem when both economies differ from each other only by the initially endowed levels of capital/labor ratio.

The nonexistence of an equilibrium deserves careful interpretation. It does not imply that autarky is better than developments under any bilaterally arranged international loan. It only states that competitive market forces may fail to guide all parties to a price taker's optimum under a market clearing price system. Using a not quite exact analogy to the theory of games, the competitive equilibrium is like a pure strategy Nash equilibrium. Every player cannot better his lot if every other player plays a given strategy (and hence with the number of players approaching infinity, the price system approaches a constant). The situation where a competitive equilibrium does not exist appears to be similar to the "battle of the sexes" problem. To set (c_1/c_2) to be greater than unity implies a "pay-off vector" beneficial to all economic units in economy 1 but unacceptable to those in economy 2. To set (c_1/c_2) to unity or less than unity implies a "payoff vector" beneficial to all economic units in economy 2 but unacceptable to those in economy 1. However, if one assigns (c_1/c_2) to be some decreasing functions no smaller than unity, then although both economies may fail to reach an optimum position (since Proposition 1 is violated), both economies may be "nearly optimal" in the sense that no feasible path under the given $r(\cdot)$ can provide a level of welfare higher than the assigned path for the respective economies more than an arbitrary small positive number ϵ. This will roughly correspond to the ϵ-optimal equilibrium.

12.4. Final Remarks

The present paper can be generalized in quite a number of directions:
1. The introduction of two or more commodities so that trade can be introduced alongside of investment.
2. The introduction of overlapping generations of individuals whose planning horizon covers only a short timespan.
3. The introduction of an "iterative" variational framework such that one economy consists of price-taking economic units while the other operates under a price-making cartel.

Time and space do not allow us to explore these topics on the present occasion. Suffice it to say, most of these extensions need extensive additional analysis to get economically meaningful results.

On the methodological level, perhaps a much more important modification can be made by introducing interest expectations and explicit mechanisms for adjustments of such expectations. However, the inherent analytical difficulty in this procedure is such that it remains to be seen whether definite conclusions can be obtained along that approach.

Appendix

The purpose of our study is to deduce time paths for certain key variables in an intertemporal equilibrium. We now present a graphical summary of some of these time paths:
I. Two countries differ only in initial endowments.

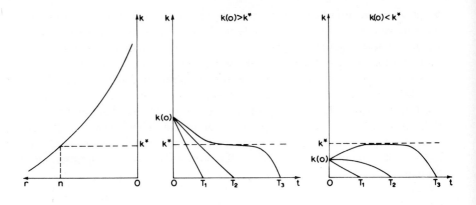

Fig. 12.A1.

(1) Capital/labor ratio — two countries have identical values, all the time (see fig. 12.A1). (T_1, T_2, T_3 stand for three different time horizons, $T_1 < T_2 < T_3$ $k(0)$ is the initial world capital per capita.)

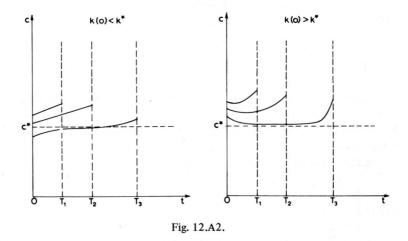

Fig. 12.A2.

(2) Consumption per capita — two countries have levels differing from each other by a constant ratio (see fig. 12.A2).

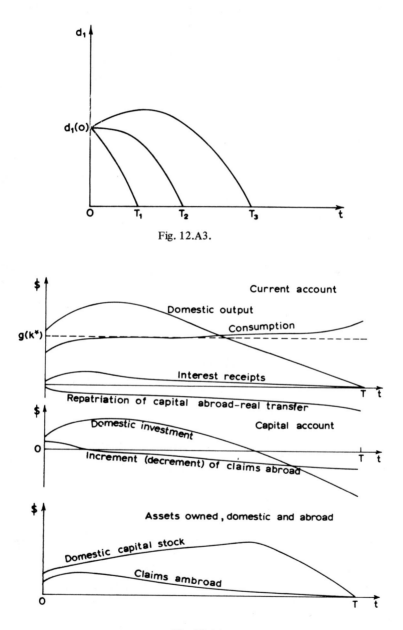

Fig. 12.A3.

Fig. 12.A4.

(3) Claim on foreign country per capita — once a creditor, never a debtor (see fig. 12.A3).

(4) Specimen national accounts for a creditor $[k(0) < k^*]$ per capita basis. (See fig. 12.A4.)

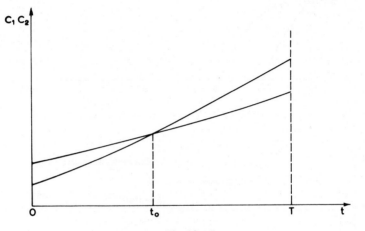

Fig. 12.A5.

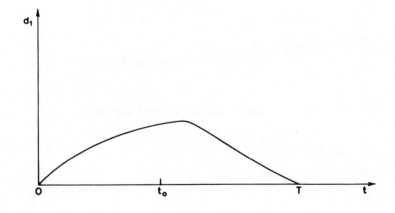

Fig. 12.A6.

II. Two countries differ only in production functions (Leontief case) — similar to the above.

III. Two countries differ only in utility functions (constant elasticity case)

    (1) Consumption per capita (see fig. 12.A5).

    (2) Claim per capita (see fig. 12.A6).

References

[1] G.A.Bliss, *Lectures on the Calculus of Variations* (Chicago, The University of Chicago Press, 1946).

[2] D.Cass, "Optimum Growth in an Aggregative Model of Capital Accumulation", *Review of Economic Studies*, Vol. XXXII (1965).

[3] Sir G.Crowther, *Balances and Imbalances of Payments* (Harvard University Graduate School of Business Administration, Cambridge, Mass., 1957).

[4] M.R.Hestenes, *Calculus of Variations and Optimal Control Theory* (New York: John Wiley & Sons, 1966).

[5] R.Jones, "International Capital Movements and the Theory of Tariff and Trade", *Quarterly Journal of Economics* (Feb. 1967).

[6] M.C.Kemp, "The Gain from International Trade and Investment, A Neo-Heckscher-Ohlin Approach", *American Economic Review*, Vol. LVI (1966) pp. 188-209.

[7] M.C.Kemp, "International Trade and Investment in a Context of Growth", *Economic Record*, Vol. XLIV (1968) pp. 211-223.

[8] T.C.Koopmans, "On the Concept of Optimal Economic Growth", in Salviucci et al., *The Econometric Approach to Development Planning* (Chicago: Rand-McNally & Co., 1966).

[9] C.P.Kindleberger, *International Economics* (Homewood, Ill.: Richard D.Irwin, Inc., 1963) (3rd ed.).

[10] T.Negishi, "Foreign Investment and Long-Run National Advantage", *Economic Record*, Vol. 41 (1965) pp. 628-632.

[11] C.P.Roos, "A Mathematical Theory of Competition", *Journal of Mathematics*, Vol. XLVII (1926) pp. 163-175.

[12] P.A.Samuelson, "A Catenary Turnpike Theorem involving Consumption and the Golden Rule", *American Economic Review*, Vol. LV (1965).

[13] M.Sidrauski, "Rational Choice and Patterns of Growth in a Monetary Economy", *American Economic Review* (May 1967).

[14] H.Uzawa, "Neutral Inventions and the Stability of Growth Equilibrium", *Review of Economic Studies,* Vol. XXVIII (1961).

[15] H.Y.Wan, Jr., *Economic Growth* (Harcourt, Brace & World, Inc., 1971).

PART 5

THEORY OF PROTECTION

CHAPTER 13

TARIFF STRUCTURE AND RESOURCE ALLOCATION IN THE PRESENCE OF FACTOR SUBSTITUTION[1]

V.K.RAMASWAMI and T.N.SRINIVASAN

W.M.Corden [1,2] illuminated understanding of the effects of a tariff when intermediate goods are traded by developing the concept of the effective protective rate. Unlike the nominal protective rate, the effective protective rate takes account of tariffs not only on the final good but also on the imported inputs used in its production. Corden [2, p. 222] defined the concept as follows:

"The effective protective rate is the percentage increase in value added per unit in an economic activity which is made possible by the tariff structure relative to the situation in the absence of tariffs but with the same exchange rate."

He showed, as did H.G.Johnson [4], that if the physical coefficients relating imported intermediate goods and outputs are fixed, a tariff will pull domestic resources toward activities enjoying relatively high effective protective rates.

Given the assumption of nonsubstitutability between imported inputs and domestic factors, one can conceive of the domestic factors as producing a value-added good in each activity, which is combined in fixed proportions with imported inputs in the manufacture of the final good. The relative prices of value-added goods will then depend on the structure of effective protective rates. The effective protective rate for an activity determines the price of its value-added good in precisely the same manner that the nominal tariff rate determines the price of a final good when intermediate goods are not traded. It follows directly from the celebrated Stolper-Samuelson theorem [8] that,

[1] J.Bhagwati, W.M.Corden, H.G.Johnson, J.C.Leith and R.Portes provided useful comments for this chapter.

if there are two activities, the levy of a tariff will pull resources toward the activity enjoying the higher effective protective rate. If there are more than two activities but the number of final goods and the number of domestic factors are equal, and constant returns to scale prevail in each activity, we can conclude that a tariff will pull resources toward the activities enjoying relatively high effective protective rates; for on these assumptions the transformation surface of the value-added goods is concave, and the output mix and resource allocation depend on the effective tariff structure alone. Note that the number of imported inputs used in each activity is of no consequence, given the fixed coefficients assumption.

When substitution between imported inputs and domestic factors is allowed for, alternative definitions of an effective protective rate are possible, depending on the technology used to evaluate it. Corden [3] has provided an ingenious measure of effective protective rates that can predict resource movement, given a special assumption regarding the nature of substitution. Assume that substitution effects are unbiased, in the following sense: When two domestic factors and an imported input are used to make a final good, the quantity of the imported input used per unit of output depends only on the price ratio of the imported input and the final good; and the relative quantities used of the two domestic factors depend only on the ratio of their prices. On these assumptions, we can legitimately conceive of domestic factors as combining to produce value-added goods, which in turn combine with imported inputs to make the final goods. Now define the effective protective rate on an activity as being the proportionate increase in the price of a value-added good resulting from the levy of a tariff. Then we are back in the Stolper-Samuelson world; we can assert that a tariff will pull resources toward activities enjoying relatively high effective protective rates.

Corden has made a valuable analytical contribution in showing that effective protective rate theory is valid on some assumptions, even in the presence of substitution. But there is no reason why substitution should take this particular form. Further, even granted that substitution effects are of this kind, effective protective rates as defined by Corden have no predictive value in practice. The technologies to be utilised in computation cannot be determined unless all production functions are known. We do not in fact know the forms of all production functions for any economy; and, if we did, we need not trouble to compute effective protective rates, for we can instead solve directly for the output mix and resource allocation entailed by a tariff. Corden has no doubt shown that the effective protective rate for an activity on his 1969 definition will lie between the effective protective rates computed on the basis of free trade and posttariff technologies. It is however possible, as Corden himself appreciates, for one activity to have a higher effective protective rate than another activity on the basis of both free trade and posttariff technologies but a lower effective protective rate on the Corden [3] basis. So the Corden [3] measure cannot be applied even if both the free trade and posttariff technologies and prices are known. It is not useful for predicting resource movement when substitution effects are significant, even if these effects are unbiased in Corden's sense.

The Corden definition [3] of an effective protective rate is based on a very special assumption regarding the nature of substitution. Our purpose in this paper is to show by counterexample that, if substitution effects are biased, there cannot exist any definition of an effective protective rate, based on prices of imported inputs and outputs and on technical coefficients alone, that can be used to predict the resource movement resulting from a tariff[2].

We now set out our counterexample. We show that with effective protective rates on any definition whatsoever held constant, a tariff will pull resources and output in one direction on one assumption regarding the overall resource endowment and in the opposite direction on another assumption with regard to the overall resource endowment. We assume that two domestic factors, land and labor, and an imported input, metal, are used in each of the two activities in an economy. Both domestic factors are always fully employed. World prices of metal and of the two outputs are fixed, and are normalized at unity. In each of the two activities, constant returns to scale prevail, and the production function is concave.

---

[2] Corden said in his 1966 paper [2] that effective protective rates measured on the basis of free trade technology would predict resource movement in the presence of substitution. Tan [9] showed, in a brilliant doctoral dissertation submitted to Stanford University, that nothing can be said in general regarding the effects of effective protective rates so defined on resource allocation. He did not however provide a counterexample.

Another possible definition of an effective protective rate is the difference between the ratio of domestic value added in the posttariff and free trade situations on the one hand and unity on the other. Travis [10] and Naya and Anderson [6] have used this definition. We show later that the effective protective rate so defined may not lie between the effective protective rates computed with free trade and posttariff technologies.

We have devised simple counterexamples to both the above measures of effective protective rates. These are not however reproduced, as the counterexample that follows in the above text invalidates any measure whatsoever.

Leith [5, p. 594] provides a valuable analysis of substitution, but concludes that "... the effective protection rate remains the indicator of resource allocation (together with the elasticity of supply of value added) ..." When substitution is biased, the concept of a value-added good which has a supply elasticity is illegitimate.

We write,

1. x_i, y_i for the metal-labor and land-labor ratios in activity i, $i = 1, 2$.
2. L_1 for the amount of labor used in activity 1, the economy's total supply of labor being normalized at unity.
3. y for the total amount of land in the economy.
4. t for the ad valorem rate of subsidy on import of metal. Both outputs are always free of tax or subsidy.
5. f^i for output per unit of labor in activity i, $i = 1, 2$.

The two production functions are

$$f^1 = [0.75+0.25x_1^{-10}]^{-0.01}y_1^{0.9} \tag{13.1}$$

$$f^2 = x_2^{0.20}y_2^{0.65} . \tag{13.2}$$

With these production functions, the equations determining equilibrium input ratios are as follows:

$$0.025[0.75+0.25x_1^{-10}]^{-1.01}x_1^{-11}y_1^{0.9} = 1 - t \tag{13.3}$$

$$0.20x_2^{-0.8}y_2^{0.65} = 1 - t \tag{13.4}$$

$$0.9[0.75+0.25x_1^{-10}]^{-0.01}y_1^{-0.1} = 0.65x_2^{0.20}y_2^{-0.35} \tag{13.5}$$

$$0.075[0.75+0.25x_1^{-10}]^{-1.01}y_1^{0.9} = 0.15x_2^{0.20}y_2^{0.65} . \tag{13.6}$$

Eqs. (13.3) and (13.4) state that the marginal value product of metal in each activity equals its subsidy-inclusive price of $1 - t$. Eq. (13.5) states that the marginal value product of land is the same in each activity. Eq. (13.6) states that the marginal value product of labor is the same in each activity.

Once a subsidy rate t is specified, eqs. (13.3) to (13.6) can be solved to obtain the equilibrium values of x_1, y_1, x_2 and y_2. The factor allocations between activities are then determined from

$$L_1y_1 + (1-L_1)y_2 = y . \tag{13.7}$$

Given y, this equation determines L_1, the amount of labor devoted to activity 1 (the amount of labor devoted to activity 2 will then be $1 - L_1$); and L_1y_1 and $(1-L_1)y_2$ are the amounts of land devoted to activities 1 and 2, respectively.

We specified values 0 and 0.2 for t and 0.10 and 5.00 for y. The solutions[3] for equilibrium factor ratios are listed in table 13.1.

Table 13.1.

Variable	Activity 1		Activity 2	
	$t = 0$	$t = 0.2$	$t = 0$	$t = 0.2$
x	0.6065	0.6301	0.0163	0.0248
y	7.8986	6.4787	0.0753	0.0895

The solutions for factor allocations depend also on the aggregate land availability. These are listed in table 13.2.

Table 13.2.

Total land available	Factor allocation	Activity 1		Activity 2	
		$t = 0$	$t = 0.2$	$t = 0$	$t = 0.2$
0.10	metal	0.001915	0.001035	0.016249	0.024759
5.00	metal	0.381786	0.484271	0.006039	0.005740
0.10	labor	0.003157	0.001643	0.996844	0.998357
	land	0.024938	0.010647	0.075062	0.089353
5.00	labor	0.629491	0.768562	0.370509	0.231438
	land	4.972101	4.979286	0.027899	0.020714

It is obvious from table 13.2 that the imposition of the same subsidy rate of 20% ad valorem on metal shifts *both* labor and land from activity 1 to activity 2 (as compared to the free trade position) when total land available is 0.10 units, while labor and land move in the opposite direction, i.e., from activity 2 to activity 1 (as compared to the free trade position) when total land available is 5.00 units. This conclusively shows that an effective protective rate howsoever defined on the basis of technical coefficients and prices of imported inputs and outputs cannot predict resource movement indepen-

---

[3] We are grateful to Professor K.S.Parikh of the Indian Statistical Institute for solving eqs. (3) to (6) on the IBM-1620 computer of the Indian Planning Commission.

dently of the overall resource endowment, given our assumptions regarding the nature of substitution effects.

Note further that the direction of change of the relative outputs of the two goods resulting from grant of the subsidy will be different, on the alternative assumptions regarding the factor endowment. When the total land supply is 0.10 units, the subsidy not only shifts land and labor to activity 2 but also results in less (more) use of metal in activity 1 (eq. (13.2)). So output of activity 1 declines and that of activity 2 rises. On the other hand, when the total land supply is 5.00 units, the subsidy both moves land and labor from activity 2 to activity 1 and results in less (more) use of metal in activity 2 (eq. (13.1)). Hence in this latter case output of activity 2 declines and that of activity 1 increases[4].

Why is the overall resource endowment of significance? The answer is that when a subsidy is granted the marginal conditions for optimality entail that the land-labor ratios move in *opposite* directions in the two activities. So the allocations of land and labor between the activities consistent with full employment of both factors depend on the resource endowment. Factor

---

[4] We have computed the values of the effective protective rates (EPR) on the basis of free trade (ETEPR) and posttariff (PTEPR) technologies and of a "true" effective protective rate ("true" EPR) defined as the difference between the ratio of domestic value added in the posttariff and free trade situations on the one hand and unity on the other. Let $m_i(t)$ be the equilibrium amount of metal used per unit of output in activity i when the subsidy rate on metal is t. Clearly $t = 0$ represents the free trade situation. The algebraic expressions for the above three measures of EPR (for our model) for activity i can be written with this notation as follows:

$$\text{FTEPR} = \frac{1 - (1-t)m_i(0)}{1 - m_i(0)} - 1$$

$$\text{PTEPR} = \frac{1 - (1-t)m_i(t)}{1 - m_i(t)} - 1$$

$$\text{"True" EPR} = \frac{1 - (1-t)m_i(t)}{1 - m_i(0)} - 1$$

Numerical values for these when t is set at 0.2 are as follows:

Activity	"True" EPR	FTEPR	PTEPR
1	0.0011	0.0275	0.0217
2	0.0000	0.0667	0.0500

It is of interest to note that the "True" EPR for either activity does not lie between FTEPR and PTEPR.

proportions cannot change in opposite directions in the two activities if intermediate goods are not traded and a tariff is levied on a final good; for then the ratios of the marginal physical products of the factors cannot be equal in the two activities in both the free trade and posttariff situations. That is why the Stolper-Samuelson result holds without reference to the factor endowment. But when intermediate goods are traded, domestic factor proportions can change in opposite directions, as in our counterexample. Note that a *reversal* of domestic factor intensities does not take place.

We have shown that when biased substitution takes place effective protective rates on any definition cannot predict resource movement; and that when substitution is unbiased effective protective rates defined so as to indicate resource shifts are either redundant or cannot be computed. But how important is substitution? If it is not, as Corden [3] holds, effective protective rate theory would still be useful. A number of instances come readily to mind in which substitution between domestic factors and intermediate goods would appear to be of significance in the real world. Thus fertilizers are in general a good substitute for land and pesticides are also. The quantities of imported pulp used to make a ton of paper or of imported iron ore used to make a ton of steel will depend in part on the economics of collecting waste paper or scrap for reuse; in poor countries with low wage rates relatively more labor is likely to be applied to such purposes. The output of steel from a blast furnace can be raised by injecting increased quantities of imported petroleum products.

Even when, with any given process, the quantities of imported inputs used per unit of output are invariant with respect to changes in tariff rates, the levy of a tariff can result in a switch of processes that entails substitution. Thus the import of liquid ammonia instead of crude petroleum to make fertilizers may save capital relatively more than labor.

In engineering industries, the various components combined to make a given product may always be the same. But the levy of a tariff may result in some components hitherto domestically produced being imported and in a shift from foreign to domestic sources of supply for other components. This process of substitution may well be biased.

Corden [2] suggested that the annual services of tradable capital goods can be treated in the same way as imported intermediate goods, when it is legitimate to assume a perfectly elastic supply of capital funds on world markets. If then land and labor are domestic primary factors and the annual service of equipment can be treated as an intermediate good, it is clear that there is considerable room for substitution. For example, earth-moving equipment substitutes for labor in construction work. The use of an automatic loom instead of a handloom in the weaving of cloth displaces much labor but virtually no land. The assumption that the supply of capital from abroad is perfectly elastic is however realistic only in exceptional cases; in general, capital must be regarded as a domestic factor of production, inelastic in supply in the short run. Changes in the supply of capital as a result of domestic savings and international capital movements are appropriately taken into account in dynamic analysis.

We must conclude that substitution effects will often be significant and that, therefore, effective protective rates are likely to be a poor guide to the resource movements resulting from the levy of a tariff. This conclusion may appear nihilistic. But in our view, the invalidity of effective protective rate theory is of little practical consequence. The levy of escalated tariffs may or may not pull resources towards the later stages of processing, in either case, rich countries that can raise revenue at less welfare cost in other ways should be advised to abolish all trade barriers. A less developed country may, on the other hand, sometimes be justified in levying trade taxes to collect revenue, particularly when international income transfers are inadequate. But when this is the case, the second-best revenue tariff entailed by the economy's social welfare and production functions must be computed and levied, and the resulting effective protective rates are of no particular significance. Domestic distortions, externalities, and noneconomic objectives are appropriately handled through taxes and subsidies on domestic economic variables[5]. Thus in many situations the optimal policy with regard to foreign trade is non-intervention. When the levy of trade taxes is justified, the optimal tariff must be determined with reference to a specified objective; and the effective protective rates entailed by this tariff are of no relevance.

[5] Ramaswami [7] discusses the optimal policies for handling various distortions, externalities, and noneconomic objectives, and cites earlier papers by J.N.Bhagwati, W.M.Corden, H.G.Johnson, the present authors, and others.

References

[1] W.M.Corden, "The Tariff", *The Economics of Australian Industry*, ed. A.Hunter (Melbourne, Melbourne University Press, 1963) pp. 162–163.
[2] W.M.Corden, "The Structure of a Tariff System and the Effective Protective Rate", *Journal of Political Economy*, LXXIV, No. 3 (June 1966) 221–237.
[3] W.M.Corden, "The Substitution Problem in the Theory of Effective Protection", mimeographed, 1969, a chapter in his book on *The Theory of Protection*, forthcoming.

[4] H.G.Johnson, "The Theory of Tariff Structure with Special Reference to World Trade and Development", *Trade and Development* (Geneva, Institut Universitaire de Hautes Etudes Internationales, 1965) pp. 9–29.

[5] J.C.Leith, "Substitution and Supply Elasticities in Calculating the Effective Protective Rate", *Quarterly Journal of Economics*, Vol. LXXXII, No. 4 (November 1968) 588–601.

[6] S.Naya and J.Anderson, "Substitution and Two Concepts of Effective Rate of Protection", mimeographed, 1968; and *American Economic Review*, in press.

[7] V.K.Ramaswami, "Optimal Policies to Promote Industrialisation in Less Developed Countries", *Essays in Honour of Thomas Balogh*, forthcoming, ed. P.Streeten, mimeographed, 1969.

[8] W.F.Stolper and P.A.Samuelson, "Protection and Real Wages", *Review of Economic Studies*, Vol. IX (November 1941) pp. 58–73. Reprinted in *Readings of the Theory of International Trade* (New York, McGraw Hill Book Co., Inc., Blakiston Division, 1949) pp. 333–357.

[9] A.Tan, "Differential Tariffs, Negative Value-Added and the Theory of Effective Protection", Chapter 3, Ph. D. dissertation (Stanford University, Dept. of Economics, 1968).

[10] W.P.Travis, "The Effective Rate of Protection and the Question of Labor Protection in the United States", *Journal of Political Economy*, Vol. 76, No. 3 (May/June 1968) pp. 443–461.

CHAPTER 14

EFFECTIVE PROTECTION IN DEVELOPING COUNTRIES *

Bela BALASSA

14.1.

Following the introduction of the concept of effective protection in the economic literature, [1] the applicability and usefulness of this concept has come under criticism. Several writers noted, for example, that in the event of substitution among inputs the measurement of effective rates based on the assumption of constant input-output coefficients will be subject to bias. [2] In

* This paper reports on some of the results of the Structure of Protection in Developing Countries project carried out under the auspices of the International Bank for Reconstruction and Development and the Inter-American Development Bank and directed by the present author in his capacity as consultant to the Economics Department of IBRD. The complete results of this inquiry will be published in Bela Balassa and associates, *The Structure of Protection in Developing Countries*, The Johns Hopkins Press, Baltimore, Md., 1971.

The author acknowledges the contributions of the following participants in the research project who undertook the individual country studies: Joel Bergsman and Pedro Malan (Brazil), Gerardo Bueno (Mexico), Teresa Jeanneret (Chile), Stephen Lewis and Stephen Guisinger (Pakistan), and John Power (Malaya, Philippines). The study on Norway was carried out by the author in collaboration with Preben Munthe. Helpful comments were received on an earlier version of the paper from Jagdish Bhagwati and Daniel Schydlowsky.

[1] See H.G. Johnson, "The Theory of Tariff Structure with Special Reference to World Trade and Development," *Trade and Development*, (Geneva: Institut Universitaire des Hautes Etudes Internationales, 1965); B. Balassa, "Tariff Protection in Industrial Countries: An Evaluation", *Journal of Political Economy*, (December 1965), pp. 573–94; W.M. Cordon, "The Structure of a Tariff System and the Effective Protective Rate", *ibid*, (June 1966), pp. 221–237.

[2] See, for example, W.P. Travis, "The Effective Rate of Protection and the Question of Labor Protection in the United States", *Journal of Political Economy*, (May-June 1968), pp. 443–461.

this paper, I wll consider the substitution issue in its relationship to the use of free trade and domestic input-output coefficients in calculating effective rates of protection. Subsequently, empirical results derived by the use of the two sets of coefficients will be presented for the following countries: Brazil, Chile, Mexico, Malaya, Pakistan, Philippines, and Norway. Effective rates estimated at existing exchange rates will be shown first with subsequent adjustments for overvaluation as compared to the free trade situation. Finally, the implications of the findings for efficiency and growth will be noted.

14.2.

It has been suggested that the direction of the bias due to the assumption of constant coefficients in the face of substitution between primary factors taken as a unit and intermediate inputs can be gauged if we consider the measurement of the effective rate of protection — defined as the proportional change in returns to primary factors resulting from protection — as an index number problem.[3] The employment of free trade (presubstitution) input-output coefficients entails an underestimation of the effective rate of protection since we take no account of the gains obtainable through substitution in response to changes in the relative prices of the product and its intermediate inputs. By the same reasoning, the use of postprotection (postsubstitution) coefficients will overestimate the effective rate.[4] Similar considerations apply to substitution among material inputs.[5]

Thus, if we make estimates by using free trade as well as postprotection input-output coefficients, the "true values" of the effective rates can be expected to lie in between the results calculated by the sets of coefficients.

---

[3] This analogy was first pointed out to me in private conversation by Professor Kindleberger.

[4] For proof, see J.C. Leith, "Substitution and Supply Elasticities in Calculating the Effective Protective Rate", *Quarterly Journal of Economics* (November 1968), pp. 588–601.

[5] I am not considering here the possibility that substitution elasticities differed between individual primary factors, on the one hand, and intermediate inputs, on the other, which would make the direction of the bias indeterminate. This possibility, ably discussed in an essay by Ramaswami and Srinivasan in this volume (Chapter 13), undoubtedly has considerable theoretical significance but it is questionable how important it is in practice.

Nor do I consider in this paper the implications for input substitution of changes in factor prices due to protection. On this question, see my "Effective Protection: A Summary Appraisal", prepared for the Conference on Effective Protection, Geneva, December 17–20, 1970.

Defining input-output coefficients under free trade A_{ji} as $a_{ji}P_{jw}/P_{iw}$ and taking the price of the product P_{iw} to be unity, Equation 14.1 is customarily used to estimate the effective rate of protection Z_i from free trade coefficients. [6] In turn, the effective rate of protection is estimated from postpro-

$$Z_i = \frac{W_i - V_i}{V_i} = \frac{[(1+T_i) - \sum_j A_{ji}(1+T_j)]}{1 - \sum_j A_{ji}} = \frac{T_i - \sum_j A_{ji} T_i}{V_i} \quad (14.1)$$

tection coefficients by the use of Equation 14.2 where the values derived from the domestic input-output table are denoted by primed magnitudes and A_{ji}' is defined as $a_{ji}'P_{jd}$.

$$Z_i' = \frac{W_i' - V_i'}{V_i'} = \frac{W_i'}{V_i'} - 1 = \frac{P_{id} - \sum_j A_{ji}'}{\dfrac{P_{id}}{1+T_i} - \sum_j \dfrac{A_{ji}'}{1+T_j}} - 1 \quad (14.2)$$

If material input coefficients are the same under protection as under free trade ($a_{ji}' = a_{ji}$), the primed values of W and V will equal the nonprimed values, and the effective rates of protection derived by the two sets of coefficients will be identical. However, as noted earlier, in the presence of substitution between primary factors, taken as a unit, and intermediate inputs, or among the intermediate inputs themselves, input coefficients will not be the same under free trade as under protection, and the use of the former will understate and that of the latter overstate the true value of the effective rate of protection.

14.3.

These considerations indicate the usefulness of estimating effective rates of protection by the use of both free trade and postprotection input-output coefficients. But, for a particular country, we observe *either* the free trade *or* the postprotection coefficients, depending on the trade policies followed. In the countries considered here, protective measures are applied so that coefficients derived from domestic input-output tables will reflect conditions under protection. In order to make calculations from free trade coefficients, then, one would have to have recourse to "borrowed" coefficients.

[6] The following notation is used: T = the nominal rate of protection, P_w = world market price, P_d = domestic (postprotection) price, V = free trade value added per unit of output, W = value added per unit of output under protection, a_{ji} = the amount of input j used in producing a unit of commodity i.

In "Tariff Protection in Industrial Countries" (see footnote 1), I suggested using for this purpose input-output coefficients derived largely from the input-output tables of Belgium and the Netherlands that have nil or low tariffs and thus approach a free trade situation. [7] The question arises, however, if the same coefficients would apply under free trade conditions to countries with different resource endowments, especially to developing countries.

Such will be the case if (a) production functions are identical among countries or differ only by a multiplicative constant, and (b) there is no substitution between primary factors and intermediate inputs. As regards the first point, the originators of the CES (constant elasticity of substitution) production function have assumed that differences in efficiency are neutral as between countries and have obtained reasonable results under this assumption in a comparison of individual industries in the United States and Japan. [8] United States-Peruvian comparisons tend to support this conclusion. [9] At any rate, there is no definite bias in measurement as a result of differences in production functions.

The direction of the error is uncertain in the presence of substitution between primary factors and intermediate inputs, also. While lower labor costs in developing countries would entail the substitution of labor for intermediate inputs, high capital costs would tend to increase the use of intermediate inputs. At the same time, the magnitude of the error is likely to be small: empirical studies give evidence of little substitutability between primary factors and material inputs [10] and a calculation based on French data showed a substitution elasticity of 0.09 between value added and raw materials. [11] It should be added that substitution among primary factors does not give rise to error since, with the prices of traded goods equalized under free

---

[7] "Tariff Protection," p. 578.

[8] See Kenneth Arrow, H.B. Chenery, B. Minhas, and R.M. Solow, "Capital-Labor Substitution and Economic Efficiency," *Review of Economics and Statistics*, (August 1961), pp. 225–250.

[9] Christopher Clague, "An International Comparison of Industrial Efficiency: Peru and the United States," *Review of Economics and Statistics*, (November 1967), pp. 487–494.

[10] For a survey of the pertinent literature, see H. Theil and C.B. Tilanus, "The Demand for Production Factors and the Price Sensitivity of Input-Output Coefficients," *International Economic Review*, (September 1966), pp. 258–272.

[11] See B. Balassa, S.E. Guisinger, and D.M. Schydlowsky, "The Effective Rate of Protection and the Question of Labor Protection in the United States: A Comment," *Journal of Political Economy*, (July–August 1970), pp. 1150–1162.

trade, value added should be the same irrespective of factor substitution. [12]
Also, with the prices of intermediate inputs being identical everywhere under
free trade, substitution among them cannot take place.

Substitution among intermediate inputs will, however, bias the calculations made for a particular country by the use of free trade and domestic
input-output coefficients in the manner indicated earlier, and thus measurement by the two sets of coefficients serves a useful purpose even if substitution elasticities between primary factors and intermediate inputs were low.
Moreover, such estimates provide an indirect test of the practical importance
of the substitution issue.

14.4.

Available evidence on production functions and on substitution between
primary factors and intermediate inputs thus suggests that the use of "borrowed" free trade coefficients in the place of the country's own free trade
coefficients does not give rise to substantial error, and, whatever the error, it
does not introduce a definite bias in the results. Problems arise, however, in
the practical application of the two sets of coefficients. In this connection,
note should be taken of the sensitivity of the results to errors in observation
and to the weighting procedures applied. I will discuss these problems in the
context of the estimation made for the seven countries under consideration.

Errors may be the result of the incorrect observation of the nominal rates
of protection and the input-output coefficients. The former sources of error
enter irrespective of whether free trade or domestic coefficients are used in
the calculations. By contrast, the latter are of considerably greater importance in regard to the input-output coefficients of developing countries where
data sources are poor than for the free trade coefficients derived from the
input-output tables of developed nations.

Effective rates of protection estimated by the use of domestic coefficients
are especially sensitive to errors of observation since world market value
added is derived as a residual — the difference between the derived world
market value of output and that of intermediate inputs. Errors of observation
may even make the "derived" value added at world market prices negative. [13]

----

[12] It is assumed that value added in nontraded inputs is included with value added in
processing à la Corden. This assumption is also made in all calculations reported in this
paper.

[13] The overestimation of the domestic value of intermediate inputs and the nominal
rate of protection of the product, as well as the underestimation of the domestic value of

It should be emphasized, however, that negative value added at world market prices can also be due to factors other than errors in observation. Possible contributing factors are the purchase of parts and components at prices exceeding the world market price of the assembled product, the use of high-value materials because of import prohibitions, or distortions in relative prices resulting from protection, waste in the production process, and substitution between intermediate inputs and primary factors in response to protection. Moreover, as S.E. Guisinger has shown, negative value added at world market prices may simply reflect the fact that the industry in question could not exist without protection. [14]

The results obtained by the use of free trade coefficients are less sensitive to errors in observation, and such errors cannot give rise to negative value added since value added is not derived as a residual in this case. On the other hand, the use of free trade coefficients does not permit a consideration of wastes of material or the effects of price discrimination on imported inputs.

The comparability of the results also suffers because of differences in product composition and in the weights used in averaging nominal and effective rates of protection. In averaging nominal rates of protection [15] for individual industries, we have used supply weights (domestic production plus imports) in applying domestic coefficients and world trade weights in applying free trade coefficients. The results are thus influenced by the economic structure of the individual countries as compared to the pattern of world trade.

While effective rates of protection have been estimated for individual industries according to the breakdown of the input-output tables, for comparability we have calculated averages for nine industry groups. In the case of

the product and of the nominal rate of protection of intermediate inputs would contribute to such a result.

[14] Stephen E. Guisinger, "Negative Value Added and the Theory of Effective Protection", *Quarterly Journal of Economics*, (August 1969), pp. 415–433.

[15] In the case of the application of quotas or prohibitive tariffs, nominal rates of protection refer to the percentage excess of domestic over world market prices (C.I.F. prices in the case of imports and F.O.B. prices for exports). However, as J.N. Bhagwati has repeatedly shown, quotas are equivalent to tariffs only if we assume universal competitiveness – in foreign supply, in quota holding, and in domestic production (Jagdish Bhagwati, *Trade, Tariffs, and Growth*, Cambridge, Mass: The M.I.T. Press, 1969). Should this not be the case, and should quota allocation be combined with investment licensing, the amount imported will not be the same under the quota as it would be if a tariff equal to the observed price difference were applied (see Bhagwati and Desai, *Planning for Industrialization,* (London: Oxford University Press, 1970, Chap. XVII).

industry data obtained by using domestic coefficients, nominal rates of protection have been averaged by weighting with total supply while effective rates have been weighted by "derived" world market value added. The latter procedure has been used because it alone assures unbiased estimates of effective rates for groups of industries. This is shown in Equation 14.3 where $\overline{Z}$ refers to the average effective protection for the group in question.[16] Finally, world trade weights have been used in averaging effective rates of protection calculated from free trade coefficients.

$$\overline{Z} = \frac{\sum W_i - \sum V_i}{\sum V_i} = \frac{\sum \dfrac{W_i - V_i}{V_i} V_i}{\sum V_i} = \frac{\sum Z_i V_i}{\sum V_i} \tag{14.3}$$

14.5.

The estimates derived by the use of free trade and domestic input-output coefficients for the nine industry groups are shown in Table 14.1 while the industry classification employed is given in the Appendix section. I have further calculated averages of nominal and effective protection for the manufacturing and the primary sectors.

Other things being equal, if substitution effects were important, one would expect the estimates of effective rates of protection calculated by the use of domestic coefficients to be higher than those based on the free trade input-output table because the former would overstate, and the latter understate, the extent of escalation from nominal to effective rates. However, in the majority of industries of the seven countries under study, the use of free trade coefficients gave higher effective rates than did the domestic coefficients. Nor can these results be explained by differences in the industry averages of nominal rates under the two alternatives. While nominal rates for individual industries tend to be higher if weighted by domestic supply rather than by world trade, with the exception of Pakistan and the Philippines the degree of escalation from nominal to effective rates is generally greater if free trade rather than domestic coefficients are used in the calculations.

More generally, we find that the interindustry pattern of effective protection in the individual countries other than Malaya is roughly the same under

[16] I am indebted to Maurice Scott on this point.

Table 14.1

Nominal and effective protection in selected developing countries

		Brazil (1966)		Chile (1961)		Mexico (1960)		Malaya (1965)		Pakistan [e] (1963–64)		Philippines (1965)		Norway (1954)	
		t	z	t	z	t	z	t	z	t	z	t	z	t	z
1. Agriculture, Forestry, and Fishing	D[a]	63	53	42	49	7	3	2	0	7	(−10)	8	0	15	16
	F[b]	50	46	53	58	7	6	17	22	8	−19	31	33	24	34
2. Mining and Energy	D	27	25	8	−2	4	−5	−14	−17	n.a.	n.a.	3	−25	0	0
	F	23	−16	39	72	−1	−13	−2	−8	35	29	11	−9	0	−7
Primary production, Total	D	59	52	28	21	6	1	−2	−6	n.a.	n.a.	7	−1	14	15
	F	38	18	47	64	3	−3	9	8	18	−15	22	14	13	16
3. Processed Food	D	82	87	82	2884	18	6	2	0	133	−307[f]	15	46	11	6
	F	71	92	101	255	13	20	11	7	154	379	38	89	4	0
4. Construction Material	D	79	86	66	64	−4	1	5	−2	54	51	25	50	5	6
	F	67	79	115	154	4	−5	7	9	91	118	42	56	6	8
5. Intermediate Products I	D	92	110	53	70	22	37	−4	−23	44	69	13	16	1	−1
	F	68	115	60	105	14	25	4	9	71	147	18	28	3	3
6. Intermediate Products II	D	c	c	118	159	25	38	9	8	55	188	33	85	7	11
	F	121	187	113	195	33	56	13	25	91	173	34	63	7	14
7. Nondurable Consumer Goods	D	140	173	204	277	25	30	25	64	100	65	22	53	12	16
	F	157	218	188	300	33	45	14	20	112	156	32	46	16	25
8. Consumer Durables	D	108	151	84	101	49	93	1	−2	234	−2100[f]	68	1062	25	38
	F	154	285	95	123	50	85	1	−5	247	510	52	81	27	57
9. Machinery	D	87	100	92	98	29	38	0	−6	86	139	27	103	12	18
	F	80	93	86	97	32	38	5	6	80	110	26	24	12	18
10. Transport Equipment	D	d	d	d	d	26	37	–	–	–	–	29	75	1	−2
	F	26	−26	16	−65	26	30	–	–	–	–	16	−3	1	6
Manufacturing, Total	D	96	113	111	182	24	26	2	−6	85	271	25	61	8	8
	F	86	127	89	158	20	32	8	11	96	188	29	53	6	9

Notes: [a] Estimates based on domestic input-output coefficients.
  [b] Estimates based on free trade input-output coefficients.
  [c] Included with intermediate products I.
  [d] Included with consumer durables.
  [e] In the manufacturing sector, the estimates refer only to producers receiving import privileges.
  [f] Denotes negative value added at world market prices.

Sources: Domestic and free trade input-output tables and information on protective measures. On methods of calculation, see text.

the two alternatives, and differences between the two sets of estimates are apparently owing largely to considerations unrelated to the substitution issue. This can be seen if we examine the results for the seven countries in order of their industrial development and also consider differences in weighting schemes. Using the share of manufacturing output in commodity production as a measure of the degree of industrialization, Norway (60%) occupies first place in the group, followed by Mexico (55%), Brazil and Chile (40–45%) and, at some distance, the Philippines (30%), and Malaya and Pakistan (20%). [17]

In the case of Norway, the results differ little under the two alternatives although effective rates are on the average somewhat higher, and the extent of escalation from nominal to effective rates is slightly greater, if free trade rather than domestic coefficients are used in the calculations. In industries where the effective rates calculated by the use of free trade coefficients are higher than the average, this can be explained by differences in the composition of domestic supply (production and imports) as compared to that of world trade. In the agriculture, forestry and fishing group, the share of forestry and fishing products that receive no protection is much larger domestically than in world trade; in consumer durables, automobiles subject to high tariffs have greater weight in world trade than domestically; and in the transport equipment category, ships with negative effective protection predominate in domestic supply.

Averages of nominal and effective protection for the manufacturing sector are remarkably similar under the two alternatives in Mexico where differences in the rates of protection estimated for individual industries are generally small and fit the pattern observed in Norway. The pattern of escalation from nominal to effective protection is also similar under the two alternatives, the major exception being food processing where the negative effective protection of food exports reduces the industry average calculated from domestic coefficients and results in "reverse escalation".

The use of domestic and free trade coefficients gave by and large similar results in Brazil and Chile, too, although the generally higher nominal protection observed in these countries leads to greater variability in the estimates. As in the case of Norway and Mexico, one also finds that in both countries somewhat higher effective rates of protection and a greater degree of escalation are shown by the use of free trade as compared to domestic coefficients. A major exception is the food processing industry in Chile where, in calcula-

[17] United Nations, *Yearbook of National Accounts Statistics*, except for Brazil where IBRD data were used.

tions made by domestic input-output coefficients, low domestic value added at world market prices has resulted in extremely high effective rates, thus raising the average obtained for the manufacturing sector as a whole. In turn, in primary activities (especially mining), imports under protection raise the estimates obtained by the use of domestic input-output coefficients in Brazil whereas the relative importance of exports has led to the opposite result in Chile.

The preponderance of exports reduces the averages of effective rates of protection derived by the use of domestic coefficients in primary activities in the Philippines, too. At the same time, the high protection of selected durable consumer goods, machinery, and transport equipment raises the averages of effective rates obtained under this alternative while world trade is heavily weighted by durable goods that are not yet produced and receive low or nil protection. In these industries, the low domestic value added in Philippine firms might also have contributed to the observed results. But this is likely to have more to do with the degree of industrial development than with the substitution of intermediate inputs for primary factors.

These differences notwithstanding, the pattern of protection in the Philippines is roughly the same irrespective of whether domestic or free trade coefficients are used in the calculations. Similar conclusions apply to Pakistan. However, in the two countries, averages of effective rates of protection for the manufacturing sector are higher, and the degree of escalation from nominal to effective rates is greater if calculations are made by the use of domestic rather than free trade coefficients.

In the Philippines, the high effective rates of protection of durable goods shown under the first alternative, in Pakistan negative "derived" world market value added leading to effective rates of protection of less than −100% are responsible for these results. [18] While substitution between primary factors and material inputs may occur, the major influences appear to be the high protection of goods entering domestic consumption and the low share of value added in the relatively undeveloped Philippine and Pakistani economies. This conclusion is supported by the observation that the opposite result is shown for intermediate products at lower levels of fabrication and nondurable consumer goods where the industries of the two countries are more fully developed.

[18] While effective rates of protection between nil and −100% indicate discrimination against the industry in question, effective rates between −100 and −∞ result when the "derived world market value" added is negative; i.e., the world market value of intermediate inputs exceeds that of output.

Malaya is an exceptional case inasmuch as the results are affected to a considerable degree by the choice of the input-output coefficients. For several industry groups, including agriculture, forestry and fishing, mining, as well as intermediate products at lower levels of fabrication, the averages of effective protection derived by the use of domestic coefficients are greatly reduced by the large weight of export commodities in total supply. The influence of export commodities is also apparent in averages of effective rates for primary production and for manufacturing; these averages are negative if domestic coefficients are used in the calculations and positive if free trade coefficients are employed. But absolute differences in the sectoral averages are small and the results are characteristic of a country at a low level of development that has not yet embarked on a policy of import-substituting industrialization.

14.6.

Under the assumptions made concerning substitution, comparisons of effective rates calculated at existing exchange rates will provide an indication of the degree of discrimination among domestic activities due to protection. But effective rates will measure the extent of protection of imports, and that of discrimination against exports, under special circumstances only. This would be the case if both the domestic elasticity of supply of exports and the foreign elasticity of demand for exports were infinite so that, in the event protection were eliminated, resources would be reallocated to export industries at constant prices and balance-of-payments equilibrium maintained without a change in the exchange rate. If, however, these assumptions are not fulfilled, the maintenance of balance-of-payments equilibrium would necessitate a devaluation [19] that would in part offset the effects of the elimination of tariffs and other protective measures.

Thus, in the general case, the imposition of protective measures on imports permits balance-of-payments equilibrium to be maintained at a lower exchange rate than under free trade. Correspondingly, effective rates calculated at the existing exchange rate will overstate the extent of protection. In turn, discrimination against export activities is understated because exports are penalized by the low exchange rate associated with protection. Nor will the

---

[19] For a description of the conditions under which the opposite result is obtained, see H.G. Johnson, "A Model of Protection and the Exchange Rate", *Review of Economic Studies*, 2, (1966), pp. 159–167.

absolute magnitudes of effective protection for the individual countries, calculated at the existing exchange rate, be comparable since countries use varying combinations of protective measures and exchange rates.

To measure the extent of protection against imports and that of discrimination against exports while ensuring international comparability, it is necessary therefore to estimate *net* effective protection by adjusting for the overvaluation of the exchange rate as compared to the hypothetical free trade situation. A further adjustment is required if a country was not in balance-of-payments equilibrium at the existing exchange rate in the year for which the calculations have been made.

Logically, the estimation of the difference between the actual and the free trade exchange rate proceeds in two stages. First, one estimates the decrease in exports and the increase in imports that would result from the elimination of protective measures; second, one calculates the extent of the devaluation that would be necessary to remedy the ensuing deficit in the balance of payments. In making calculations, I will assume throughout that the foreign supply elasticity of imports is infinite so that imports are supplied at constant prices. This assumption appears realistic in the case of all the countries under consideration. The other relevant elasticities are to be interpreted as arc elasticities.

Ideally, one should estimate changes in imports as a result of the elimination of protective measures by use of the domestic elasticities of demand and supply, together with data on the share of imports in domestic consumption.[20] This formulation has the advantage that it enables us to utilize information on nominal and effective rates of protection. For the countries under consideration, the necessary information is not available, however, and hence we had to have recourse to the direct method of estimation under which changes in imports (ΔM) are derived on the basis of information on actual imports (M), the elasticity of import demand (η_m), and changes in the prices of imported goods resulting from the elimination of protective measures ($T/1 + T$). The relevant formula is shown by Equation 14.4.

$$\Delta M = \eta_m \frac{T}{1+T} M \qquad (14.4)$$

Changes in exports (ΔX) owing to the elimination of export subsidies (taxes) will depend on the original amount of exports (X), the rate[21] of export

[20] For an application of this method, see my "Tariff Protection in Industrial Countries: An Evaluation."

[21] Here S is positive in the case of subsidies and negative in the case of taxes.

subsidies (S), and the elasticity of supply of foreign exchange (ϵ_f); the latter is, in turn, determined by the elasticities of demand for (η_x) and supply of (ϵ_x) exports. For this purpose we use Equation 14.5:

$$\Delta X = -\frac{\epsilon_x(\eta_x-1)}{\epsilon_x+\eta_x} \frac{S}{1+S} X = -\epsilon_f \frac{S}{1+S} X \tag{14.5}$$

From Equation 14.6 one can estimate the percentage devaluation needed to remedy the deficit that would result from the elimination of protective measures in the case of initial balance-of-payments equilibrium. [22] The formula is composed of the same elements as Equations 14.4 and 14.5 except that the price change caused by the elimination of protective measures is now replaced by that caused by devaluation, with corresponding changes in the signs of the terms representing changes in exports and imports.

$$\Delta X + \Delta M = \left(\frac{R'}{R}-1\right)\left[\frac{\epsilon_x(\eta_x-1)}{\epsilon_x+\eta_x}X - \eta_m M\right] = \left(\frac{R'}{R}-1\right)(\epsilon_f X - \eta_m M) \tag{14.6}$$

In actual estimation, we combine Equations 14.4, 14.5, and 14.6, with account taken of the simultaneity of changes in tariffs, export subsidies, and the exchange rate. The condition for balance-of-payments equilibrium after the elimination of tariffs and subsidies and the compensating devaluation is indicated by Equation 14.7.

$$\epsilon_f\left(\frac{R'}{R(1+S)}-1\right)X - \eta_m\left(\frac{R'}{R(1+T)}-1\right)M = 0 \tag{14.7}$$

In turn from Equation 14.7, the extent of overvaluation can be expressed as compared to the hypothetical free trade situation by the use of Equation 14.8.

$$\frac{R'}{R} = \frac{\epsilon_f X + \eta_m M}{\dfrac{\epsilon_f X}{1+S} + \dfrac{\eta_m M}{1+T}} \tag{14.8}$$

Equation 14.8 is modified in cases when the existing exchange rate does not ensure balance-of-payments equilibrium.

Adjustments for overvaluation as compared to the free trade situation can

[22] Here R refers to the actual exchange rate while R' is the rate that would obtain under free trade.

then be made by utilizing Equation 14.9 which expresses the condition for compensating changes in tariffs, export subsidies (taxes), and exchange rates that would leave domestic prices and the extent of net protection unchanged. [23] Since value added in nontraded inputs is included with value added in processing, this adjustment will not affect the ranking of industries by effective rates.

$$\frac{R'}{R} = \frac{1+T}{1+T'} = \frac{1+S}{1+S'} = \frac{1+Z}{1+Z'} \qquad (14.9)$$

Additional considerations need to be introduced in the case of export industries. It will be recalled that effective rates of protection are estimated under the assumption of constant world market prices, i.e., infinite foreign demand and supply elasticities. To the extent that this assumption is not fulfilled, the degree of discrimination against export industries will be overstated since the lower is the elasticity of foreign demand for a country's exports, the less will the overvaluation of the exchange rate associated with protection reduce the domestic prices of these exports.

Less than infinite elasticities of export demand thus call for an additional adjustment in the estimates of effective protection for export industries. The magnitude of this adjustment will depend on the elasticities of foreign demand and domestic supply of exports. Because of the error possibilities associated with the assumed values of the relevant elasticities for particular products, such adjustments have not been made for individual industries. However, in Table 14.3 later are shown adjusted estimates of nominal and effective protection for primary exports, for the exports of manufactured goods, and for the total exports of the countries in question.

14.7.

We have seen that the estimation of the extent of overvaluation as compared to the free trade situation requires information on the rate of tariffs and other protective measures, the rate of export subsidy, the value of exports and imports, as well as the elasticities of import demand and of export demand and supply. Data on nominal rates of protection are available in the breakdown of the input-output tables, and these have been averaged for total exports and for total imports. In turn, elasticities of demand for the

---

[23] Unprimed magnitudes refer to unadjusted rates of protection and primed magnitudes to adjusted (net) rates.

major export products of the countries in question have been estimated on the basis of information on the elasticity of world demand for the commodity in question and on the share of the country in world exports. For minor exports, assumed values have been used and, in the absence of data for individual industries, we have utilized information available for the country in question and for other countries to derive total import demand and export supply elasticities for each of the countries under study.

The elasticities utilized in the calculations are subject to considerable error. However, a sensitivity analysis of possible values has shown that the range of variation in the extent of overvaluation for realistic assumptions regarding the elasticities is relatively small. I present, therefore, only the results derived on the basis of assumed mean values of the elasticities. The extent of overvaluation estimated on these assumptions is 4% for Malaya and Norway, 9% for Mexico, 15% for the Philippines, 27% for Brazil, 50% for Pakistan, and 68% for Chile.

Adjusting the results of Table 14.1 by the extent of overvaluation, I obtain the estimates of net nominal and effective protection shown in Table 14.2. In the following, I will utilize these estimates to examine (a) the interindustry pattern of protection in the individual countries, (b) the extent of protection of import-competing industries and that of discrimination against export industries, and (c) the extent of discrimination against exports (import substitution) in individual industries.

Apart from Malaya and Norway, there is a strong tendency to discriminate in favor of manufacturing and against primary activities in the countries under study. The existence of such discrimination is already apparent in the observed differences in nominal rates of protection that are substantially higher on manufactured goods than on primary products. Averages of net nominal rates of protection, derived by using domestic input-output coefficients, for primary activities and for manufacturing, respectively, are 25 and 55% in Brazil, −24 and 26% in Chile, −3 and 14% in Mexico, −29 and 23% in Pakistan, and −7 and 9% in the Philippines. [24] Because of escalation in nominal rates of protection, the differences are accentuated in terms of effective rates. Again using domestic coefficients, the results for the two sectors are: Brazil, 20 and 68%; Chile, −28 and 68%; Mexico, −7 and 16%; Pakistan, −40 and 147%; and the Philippines, −14 and 41%.

Discrimination against the mining and energy sector exists also in Malaya and Norway, but in these two countries the system of protection tends to favor agriculture. This result reflects the combined effects of a liberal trade

[24] In the case of Pakistan, the data exclude mining and energy.

Table 14.2

Net nominal and effective protection in selected developing countries

		Brazil (1966)		Chile (1961)		Mexico (1960)		Malaya (1965)		Pakistan[e] (1963–64)		Philippines (1965)		Norway (1954)	
		t	z	t	z	t	z	t	z	t	z	t	z	t	z
1. Agriculture, Forestry, and Fishing	D[a]	29	21	-15	-11	-2	-6	-2	-4	(-29)	(-40)	-6	-13	11	12
	F[b]	18	15	-9	-6	-2	-3	13	17	-28	-46	14	16	19	29
2. Mining and Energy	D	0	-1	-36	-42	-5	-13	-17	-20	n.a.	n.a.	-10	-34	-4	-4
	F	-3	-34	-17	2	-9	-20	-6	-12	-10	-14	-3	-21	-4	-11
Primary Production, Total	D	25	20	-24	-28	-3	-7	-6	-10	n.a.	n.a.	-7	-14	10	11
	F	9	-7	-12	-2	-6	-11	5	4	-21	-43	7	0	9	12
3. Processed Food	D	44	48	8	1676	8	-3	-2	-4	55	-238[f]	0	28	7	2
	F	35	52	20	111	4	10	7	3	69	219	21	65	0	-4
4. Construction Material	D	41	47	-1	-2	-12	-7	1	-6	3	1	9	31	1	2
	F	32	41	28	51	-5	-13	3	5	27	45	26	36	2	4
5. Intermediate Products I	D	52	66	-9	1	12	26	-8	-26	-4	13	-1	1	-3	-5
	F	33	70	-5	22	5	15	0	5	14	65	3	12	-1	-1
6. Intermediate Products II	D	c	c	30	54	15	27	5	4	3	92	16	62	3	7
	F	74	127	27	76	22	43	9	20	27	82	17	42	3	10
7. Nondurable Consumer Goods	D	89	115	81	124	15	19	20	58	33	10	7	34	8	12
	F	103	151	71	138	22	33	10	15	41	71	15	28	12	20
8. Consumer Durables	D	64	98	10	30	37	77	-3	-6	123	-1433[f]	47	915	20	33
	F	100	204	16	33	38	70	-3	-9	131	307	63	58	22	51
9. Machinery	D	48	58	14	18	18	27	-4	-10	24	59	11	77	8	13
	F	42	52	11	17	21	27	1	2	20	40	10	8	8	13
10. Transport Equipment	D	d	d	d	d	16	26	–	–	–	–	13	53	-3	-6
	F	-1	-42	-31	-79	16	19	–	–	–	–	1	-15	-3	2
Manufacturing, Total	D	55	68	26	68	14	16	-2	-10	23	147	9	41	4	4
	F	47	79	13	54	10	21	4	7	31	92	14	34	2	6

Notes: [a] Estimates based on domestic input-output coefficients.
[b] Estimates based on free trade input-output coefficients I.
[c] Included with intermediate products I.
[d] Included with consumer durables.
[e] In the manufacturing sector, the estimates refer only to producers receiving import privileges.
[f] Denotes negative value added at world market prices.

Sources: Table 14.1 and text.

policy for manufactures and the protection of certain segments of agriculture. However, this policy is carried out under different conditions in the two countries, Norway having the most, and Malaya one of the least, industrialized economies in the group.

In Norway's case, trade liberalization in manufactured goods has been considered necessary to remain competitive with other countries at similar or higher levels of development whereas the protection of the agricultural sector has been rationalized on income distributional and on defense grounds. In turn, Malaya began to industrialize through "natural import substitution" and it is not yet clear whether it will follow the example of other developing countries in imposing high barriers on the imports of manufactures. At the same time, Malaya aims at increasing the degree of selfsufficiency in various agricultural commodities through protection.

As noted earlier, the policies followed by Norway and Malaya are in contrast to the system of protection applied in the other countries included in the study which favor manufactured goods over primary products. But one observes considerable differences within the latter group, too. As the figures cited above indicate, the average degree of discrimination in favor of manufactured goods and against primary activities is relatively small in Mexico, it is greater in Brazil and in the Philippines, and it is the most pronounced in Chile and Pakistan.

Further interest attaches to the pattern of protection within the manufacturing sector. If we exclude processed food from our purview and consider machinery as an input, we find the familiar pattern of escalation from inputs to final goods. Rates of effective protection are the lowest on construction materials, followed by intermediate products at lower levels of fabrication, machinery, intermediate products at higher levels of fabrication, and finally consumer goods. Transport equipment is usually in the same group with machinery although the lack of estimates based on domestic coefficients for some countries and differences in the results obtained by the two sets of coefficients for others reduce the reliability of the comparisons.

The observed pattern of protection is largely explained by the structure of nominal rates of protection which rise from lower to higher levels of transformation. Since at the first stage of fabrication raw materials are usually available at world market prices, some escalation in nominal rates is necessary to keep effective rates unchanged from one stage to the next. However, in the countries under consideration with few exceptions nominal rates rise much more than the extent necessary to keep effective rates constant.

Within the consumer goods sector, differences in the effective protection of consumer durables and nondurables seem to depend on the level of industrial development and the size of the domestic market. Consumer durables are protected relatively more heavily in countries at higher levels of industrialization (Norway and Mexico) as the small domestic markets of these two countries provide disadvantages in producing consumer durables where economies of scale are of importance. By contrast, average levels of protection of consumer durables are relatively low in Chile, Malaya, and the Philippines that have not yet embarked on the domestic production of several of these commodities.

Pakistan presents a special case inasmuch as it exports some nondurable consumer goods under a subsidy scheme while domestic production for the small home market requires the high protection of consumer durables. Finally, levels of protection of the two types of consumer goods are about the same in Brazil that aims at selfsufficiency in both of them.

The protection of processed foods in the countries in question does not fit any definite pattern. In Pakistan, the high protection of sugar has raised the average for this industry to a considerable extent; in Chile the desire for selfsufficiency has had a similar effect. In the Philippines, the results depend on the choice of the input coefficients while elsewhere comparative advantage in food products (Brazil, Mexico, and Malaya) or the desire to keep food costs low (Norway) explains the relatively low levels of protection of these commodities.

14.8.

To indicate the extent of net protection of import substitutes and that of discrimination against exports, Table 14.3 provides a summary of estimates for export, import-competing, and non-import-competing industries derived by the use of domestic input-output coefficients. Industries that sell more than 10% of their output have been considered export industries, import-competing industries have been defined as those where imports provide more than 10% of domestic supply while industries with lower import and export shares have been classified as "non-import-competing".

These distinctions could not be made for Brazil and Pakistan. In the former case, the input-output table does not provide sufficient detail to separate exports from the other categories. In the latter, the same commodities often have protected domestic markets and receive export subsidies, so that there is no clear distinction between import substitutes and exports. Nevertheless, on the basis of the data of Table 14.2, some general conclusions can be made for these countries, too.

Table 14.3

Net nominal and effective protection on export, import-competing, and non-import-competing industries

	Chile		Mexico		Malaya		Philippines		Norway	
	Nominal protection	Effective protection	Nominal protection	Effective protection	Nominal protection	Effective protection	Nominal protection	Effective protection	Nominal protection	Effective protection
Export Industries										
Primary	−32	−36	−5	−7	−11	−11	−19	−32	−4	−8
Manufacturing	−	−	6	12	−7	−19	−2	9	−3	−6
Total	−32	−36	−3	−5	−10	−12	−14	−28	−3	−7
Import-Competing Industries										
Primary	−15	−11	−	−	5	1	−2	−2	13	15
Manufacturing	9	14	20	39	2	7	14	39	6	9
Total	1	0	20	39	3	3	7	8	8	12
Non-Import-Competing Industries										
Primary	−22	−23	−1	−7	3	0	3	1	−	−
Manufacturing	39	153	10	5	−3	17	13	86	−	−
Total	38	124	6	−1	3	0	7	9	−	−
All Non-Export Industries										
Primary	−15	−12	−1	−7	4	0	1	0	13	15
Manufacturing	26	68	15	16	2	7	14	57	6	9
Total	17	30	11	6	3	1	7	9	8	12

Note: Export industries comprise industries where more than 10% of production is exported; import-competing industries include industries where imports provide more than 10% of domestic supply; and non-import-competing industries are those where international trade does not exceed 10% in either direction.

Source: See table 14.1.

There are no industries in Norway that could not be classified either as import-competing or as export industries. Also, there are few industries that would come into the nonimport-competing category in Malaya and in such instances there is usually natural protection. In the other five countries, however, a substantial segment of industries are considered "non-import-competing". The industries in question are either on the borderline between import substitution and exports [25] or have prohibitive tariffs. Some of the primary activities, such as forestry and fishing, are borderline cases and usually have negative net effective rates of protection. In turn, the intermediate goods and consumer goods industries included in the non-import-competing category often supply domestic needs behind prohibitive tariff walls. In these industries, domestic competition has generally reduced the domestic price below the sum of the world market price and the tariff but calculations based on price comparisons still show substantial effective protection in Chile and the Philippine although not in Mexico.

With the exception of Norway where agriculture is protected, the net effective rate of protection is usually negative on primary activities classified as import-competing. This conclusion is of especial interest, because in most cases rates of effective protection calculation at existing exchange rates were positive and only adjustment for overvaluation has revealed that the structure of protection indirectly subsidizes imports and thus penalizes the domestic production of primary goods.

Within the manufacturing sector, the net effective protection of import-competing industries is 39% in the Philippines and Mexico, 14% in Chile, 9% in Norway, and 7% in Malaya. The high figure for Mexico is rather surprising; it is largely the result of the high protection of a few intermediate goods and consumer durables (paper and paper products, iron and steel, and motor vehicles) that are produced domestically and are also imported. Mexico suffers in this comparison, because it permits imports in some industries where other countries have achieved selfsufficiency behind high tariff walls. At the same time, the average rate of net effective protection of non-import-competing industries is only 5% in Mexico as against 153% in Chile and 86% in the Philippines. [26]

Since the relative shares of import-competing and non-import-competing industries in the manufacturing sector vary from country to country, special

[25] The problem is here partly that one finds different results depending on whether domestic prices are compared to foreign prices calculated on a C.I.F. or F.O.B. basis. We have used the former alternative in this study.

[26] The 17% effective protection shown in Malaya is greatly affected by the high protection of a single industry, joineries.

interest attaches to results derived by combining the two. One then finds that average net effective protection in these nonexport industries is 68% in Chile, 57% in the Philippines, 16% in Mexico, 9% in Norway, and 7% in Malaya. Brazil belongs in the first-mentioned group as it does not export manufactured goods and the average net protection of its manufacturing sector is 68%. Finally, net rates of effective protection of manufactured goods including exports average 147% in Pakistan.

14.9.

Export taxes, tariffs on inputs used in export industries, and overvaluation of the exchange rate as compared to the free trade situation all contribute to discrimination against exports. Such discrimination, expressed by negative net effective protection, means that the industries in question have to operate with lower value added than they would under free trade. This is because tariffs on inputs increase the cost of production while export taxes reduce the price received in foreign currency and overvaluation lowers the domestic currency equivalent of foreign exchange receipts.

Malaya and the Philippines levy taxes on most primary and manufactured exports; Pakistan and, to a lesser extent, Mexico tax primary exports and subsidize the exports of manufactured goods; apart from taxes on Brazilian coffee exports, there are, however, no export taxes or subsidies in Brazil and none at all in Chile and Norway. Tariffs on inputs increase discrimination against exports to some extent in all countries but especially in the Philippines. Finally, the extent of discrimination against exports due to overvaluation as compared to the free trade situation is measured by the rate of overvaluation itself.

As a result of these influences, there is considerable discrimination against export industries in Chile, Brazil, and the Philippines but much less so in Malaya, Norway, and Mexico. [27] Pakistan provides a special case in as much as it strongly discriminates against primary export industries but tends to favor export industries in the manufacturing sector.

Apart from discrimination against export industries, the system of protection also involves a bias against exporting and in favor of sales in domestic markets in the industries classified as import-competing or non-import-competing. The extent of this bias can be measured by calculating the

[27] The 9% effective rate of protection for Mexico's manufacturing export industries is an average of net discrimination against export products and net protection of import substitutes included in these industries.

percentage excess of domestic value added in import substitution over that obtainable in exporting.

Among the countries in question, Pakistan does not have a bias against exporting in industries receiving special privileges under the Export Bonus scheme. In view of the relatively low levels of protection, this bias is small in Norway, Malaya, and in Mexico also. By contrast, in Brazilian, Chilean, and the Philippine industries there is a considerable bias against exporting. There are even cases where protection raises the cost of inputs to such an extent that exporting at world market prices would require negative value added domestically. [28]

14.10.

One may conclude that, with the exception of Malaya, the interindustry pattern of effective protection in the individual countries is little affected by the choice of the input-output coefficients, and we do not observe the systematic differences in the estimates that would prevail if input substitution were of importance. Differences in the results obtained under the two alternatives are largely explained by considerations unrelated to the substitution issue, such as the level of industrial development and the weighting schemes employed.

Despite differences in the stage of industrial development and the level of protection, we find considerable similarities in the structure of protection of the seven countries under study. The results exhibit the familiar pattern of escalation, with effective rates being generally the lowest on primary commodities, followed by intermediate products at lower levels of fabrication, machinery, intermediate products at higher levels of fabrication, and consumer goods. There is no discrimination against agriculture in Norway and Malaya, however, while the degree of protection of food processing varies among the countries.

Again with the exception of Norway and Malaya, one observes high protection in import-competing industries and a considerable degree of discrimination against export activities. These results have entailed inefficient resource allocation in the countries in question. But, as I have elsewhere argued, [29] the adverse effects of protection on the growth of productivity are likely to be much more important. This conclusion follows since the small

[28] The relevant estimates are shown in the country chapters of *The Structure of Protection in Developing Countries*.

[29] "Growth Strategies in Semi-Industrial Countries," *Quarterly Journal of Economics*, (February 1970).

protected markets limit the possibilities of applying modern, large-scale production methods and, in the absence of effective competition, there are few incentives for technological improvements. Under such circumstances, it is not surprising that industries where the process of import substitution has been completed continue to require high levels of protection.

Continuing protection has also led to a decline in the rate of economic growth in countries such as Brazil and Chile after the process of import substitution had been completed in industries where this is relatively simple. At the same time, in several of the countries under study, the growth rate itself is overstated as the production of the more rapidly growing manufacturing sector is valued at higher than free trade prices. [30]

It would appear, then, that the adoption of a more rational policy of protection would permit an acceleration of economic growth in countries with high levels of protection. This would include reducing the interindustry differences in effective protection, decreasing the extent of import protection, and giving more equal treatment to exports and import substitution in particular industries. A detailed discussion of desirable policy changes, however, falls outside the scope of this paper. [31]

[30] The adjusted growth rates, with the unadjusted figures in parenthesis, for the 1950–65 period are: Brazil, 5.5 (5.6)%; Chile, 3.6 (3.6)%; Mexico, 5.9 (6.0)%; Malaya, 5.1 (5.1)%; Pakistan, 3.0 (3.6)%; Philippines, 4.8 (5.1)%, and Norway, 4.6 (4.5)%. The two figures are identical in Chile where manufacturing grew at a rate not exceeding the average and in Malaya where levels of protection are low (in the latter case, data refer to the 1955–1965 period). Finally, in Norway, the opposite result is obtained because of the low growth rate exhibited by the highly protected agricultural sector. An explanation of these figures as well as a detailed evaluation of the results reported in this paper are given in *The Structure of Protection in Developing Countries,* Chapter 5.

[31] On guidelines for a policy of protection, see *The Structure of Protection in Developing Countries*, Chapter 5.

Appendix

Table 14.4
Composition of industry groups

1. Agriculture, Forestry, and Fishing:	01 Agriculture and forestry, 02 fishing
2. Mining and Energy:	0.3 Solid fuels, 04 gas, 05 iron ore mining, 06 nonferrous metal ores, 07 petroleum and natural gas, 09 other minerals
3. Processed Food:	10 Meat products, 11 other prepared food products, 12 sugar, 13 confectionary, 14 dairy products, 15 cereal products, 16 other food products, 18 oils and fats
4. Construction Material:	08 Basic construction materials, 45 non-metallic mineral products
5. Intermediate Products I :	21 Thread and yarn, 28 lumber, 31 woodpulp, 35 leather, 39 synthetic materials, 40 other chemical materials, 44 petroleum products, 46 glass and glass products, 48 pig iron and ferro-manganese, 49 steel ingots, 54 nonferrous metals
6. Intermediate Products II:	22 Textile fabrics, 29 wood products and furniture, 32 paper and paper products, 37 rubber products, 38 plastic goods, 41 chemical products, 50 rolled steel products, 51 other steel products, 55 metal castings, 56 metal manufactures
7. Nondurable Consumer Goods:	23 Hosiery, 24 clothing, 25 other textile articles, 26 shoes, 33 printing and publishing, 36 leather goods except shoes, 66 precision instruments, 67 toys, sport goods, jewelry
8. Consumer Durables:	62 Automobiles, 64 bicycles and motorcycles
9. Machinery:	57 Agricultural machinery, 58 nonelectrical machinery, 59 electrical machinery
10. Transport Equipment:	60 Shipbuilding, 61 railroad vehicles, 65 airplanes

Notes: Numbers refer to the classification scheme used by the European Common Market.

Sources: Office Statistique des Communautés Européennes, *Tableaux "Entrées-Sorties" pour les pays de la Communauté Européenne Economique,* October 1964.

PART 6

THE TRANSFER PROBLEM

CHAPTER 15

ON THE TRAIL OF CONVENTIONAL BELIEFS
ABOUT THE TRANSFER PROBLEM

Paul A.SAMUELSON*

15.1. Introduction

When Germany was made to pay war reparations at Versailles, economists fell into dispute on the question of whether a unilateral transfer will, aside from the primary burden of the payment itself, also cause a secondary burden as a result of a presumed induced deterioration of the terms of trade of the paying country. In this famous transfer problem debate, Keynes, Pigou, Taussig, Robertson, and many others upheld this orthodox view of presumed secondary deterioration. Ohlin, pointing out that income effects had been neglected, asserted that no such clear-cut presumption was possible; and Viner demonstrated that the classical writers were by no means unanimous in holding to the orthodox position[1]

Analytically, the discussion remained confused, because models involving effective demand and financial considerations were rarely carefully separated from those involving pure barter. (In connection with barter models, even the

* Grateful acknowledgment is made to the National Science Foundation for research support and to Karen H.Johnson for assistance in the preparation of this paper.

[1] See for example the debate and rejoinders of J.M.Keynes and B.Ohlin, *Economic Journal*, Vol. XXXIX (1929) pp. 1-7, 172-182, 400-408. The principal article of each man is reproduced in H.S.Ellis and L.A.Metzler, eds. for the American Economic Association, *Readings in the Theory of International Trade* (Philadelphia: Blakiston Company, 1950) pp. 161-178. For a broad review see J.Viner, *Studies in the Theory of International Trade* (New York: Harper & Brothers, 1937) pp. 326-360. In the Taussig festschrift, "Note on the Pure Theory of Capital Transfer", Chapter 8, in: *Explorations in Economics, Notes and Essays Contributed in Honor of F.W.Taussig* (New York: McGraw-Hill Book Co. Inc., 1937) pp. 84-91. W.W.Leontief provided an alleged possible example in which the secondary burden was on the receiver, and so strongly as to make the payer better off in consequence of its paying a transfer.

great Marshall erred by shifting the paying country's offer curve while leaving that of the receiving country intact.) Empirically, the situation also remained confused, because it was not even clear whether Germany's reparations equalled the unilateral investments made to her from abroad.

Not until the 1930s did Pigou[2] clarify the barter aspects by appeal to an exact Jevons model of exchange. This enabled one to see how much the orthodox result depended upon particular assumptions made about transport costs and impediments in international trade. In two rather exhaustive articles[3], I concluded that, in the absence of transport costs or impediments, the orthodox presumption lacked basis (thus, in a sense, awarding the palm to Ohlin as against the pre-*General Theory* Keynes). With transport costs and tariff impediments, the outcome was shown to be very complex indeed, because once we isolated the crucial income-propensities upon which the result depended, clear-cut presumptions became difficult.

There the matter stood until recently Professor Ronald Jones[4] provided a beautifully simple argument that demonstrates an anti-orthodox (and, hence, partially anti-Ohlin) presumption even in the purest model involving zero transport costs and tariffs. Jones shows that random differences in tastes, which are independent of random differences in comparative advantage, result in countries' tending to import goods that are peculiarly taste-appreciated by them. (If I am a drunkard and you are a fop, I am more likely to export cloth and import rye than vice versa.) In consequence of Jones's hypothesis, my test criteria deduce that the receiving country is likely to have a *deterioration* of its terms of trade, giving to the paying country a secondary blessing rather than the secondary burden of the orthodox school or the zero burden of the Ohlin school.

[2] A.C.Pigou, "The Effects of Reparations on the Ratio of International Exchange", *Economic Journal*, Vol. XLII (1932) pp. 532-542. This is summarized in A.C.Pigou, *A Study in Public Finance*, 3rd ed. (London: Macmillan & Co. Ltd., 1947), Chapter XIX.

[3] P.A.Samuelson, "The Transfer Problem and Transport Costs: The Terms of Trade When Impediments are Absent", *Economic Journal*, Vol. LXII (June 1952) pp. 278-304, and P.A.Samuelson, "The Transfer Problem and Transport Costs, II: Analysis of Effects of Trade Impediments", *Economic Journal*, Vol. LXIV (June 1954) pp. 264-289. Both articles are reproduced in *The Collected Scientific Papers of Paul A.Samuelson*, Joseph E.Stiglitz, ed. (Cambridge, Massachusetts: The M.I.T. Press, 1966) pp. 985-1037. In abridged form these are reproduced in R.E.Caves and H.G.Johnson, eds. for American Economic Association, *Readings in International Economics* (Homewood, Ill.: Richard D.Irwin, Inc., 1968) pp. 115-147.

[4] R.Jones, "The Transfer Problem Reconsidered", *Economica*, Vol. XXXVII (1970) p. 178 ff.

I applaud the Jones result. Yet, even though I know better, I often find myself falling into the orthodox presumption. Why is this? Is it forgetfulness? Is it stupidity? Or is it perhaps that I, along with Keynes and Taussig, have implicitly in mind a tempting model in which the orthodox result is legitimately implied? The present paper explores the affirmative answer to the last question and hopes to throw light on the reasons that earlier writers fell into the orthodox view.

15.2. Partial Equilibrium Models

Implicitly, economists tend to use partial equilibrium models and to combine financial analysis with real. Less systematically, they tend to use simple Ricardian constant costs. Put all this together and you will not be surprised at the orthodox thesis. Moreover, by some sophisticated specifications, these top-of-the-mind notions can be made part of an *exact* general equilibrium model that combines Marshall, Ricardo, and, for that matter, Hume. However, I confine myself here to the transfer problem, leaving for publication elsewhere[5] the rigorous general equilibrium model.

Begin with fig. 15.1 which provides an interesting variant on the familiar back-to-back diagrams of Cournot, Barone, Bickerdike, Joan Robinson, Haberler and many others[6]. In fig. 15.1a one has the usual supply and demand curves for wheat in America expressed in dollars. In fig. 15.1c one has similar curves for wheat but expressed for England in terms of the pound. In fig. 15.1b the foreign exchange rate R, giving the dollar costs of £1 (e.g., $3/£1) is denoted by the slope of the OR ray. (The exchange rate giving the pound cost of $1, $r = 1/R$, is denoted by the slope of the ray referred to the vertical axis, thus preserving symmetry between countries.)

At each exchange rate R, there is determined an equilibrium dollar wheat price P_1, also a pound wheat price p_1, and, finally, the physical (algebraic) export of wheat from America to England. We can write the algebraic export functions as the difference between supply and demand in the respective countries, namely, $E_1(P_1) = S_1(P_1) - D_1(P_1)$ and $e_1(p_1) = s_1(p_1) - d_1(p_1)$ with E_1' and e_1' posited to be positive as a condition of stability. (This says the supply schedule, if negative, must be more vertical than the demand curve, in the usual Walrasian manner.)

[5] P.A.Samuelson, "An Exact Hume-Ricardo-Marshall Model of International Trade", *Jour. Int. Econ.*, Vol. I (February, 1971) pp. 1-18.

[6] For footnote, see page 331.

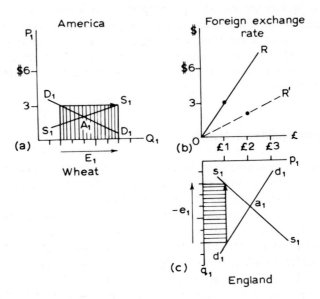

Fig. 15.1. The OR ray in (b) translates each dollar P into its equivalent pound p. Wheat market equilibrium occurs where America's export arrow is just matched by England's import arrow. If wheat were the only good, America at OR would enjoy an export surplus measured in dollars by the rectangle in (a) or in pounds by the rectangle in (c). For one-good balance of payments equilibrium, OR would have to depreciate to OR' so that both rectangles vanish. Any such clockwise move of the ray increases America's exports algebraically and reduces England's algebraic exports. Lowering R lowers all £p's and raises all $\$P$'s. Thus, in a one-good case, an indemnity from America to England moves OR' counterclockwise to OR and induces a necessary depreciation of the payer's currency.

Competitive arbitrage requires that prices in two markets be equal when expressed in common currency units. Hence,

$$P_1 = Rp_1 . \tag{15.1}$$

Finally, equilibrium is determined by the equality of export of wheat from one country with import of wheat in the other; namely, by solving

$$-e_1(p_1) = E_1(RP_1) \tag{15.2}$$

in order to get p_1 as a declining function of R. I.e., appreciating the pound will lower the price of wheat in London. By symmetry, depreciating the dollar relative to the pound (i.e., raising R) will tend to raise the dollar price of

---

[6] As applied to single commodities in international trade, the familiar back-to-back diagram or its equivalent goes back to A.A.Cournot, *Mathematical Principles of the Theory of Wealth* (1938) tr. by Nathaniel T.Bacon (New York: The Macmillan Co., 1927) Chapter X; J.Viner, *Studies in the Theory of International Trade*, pp. 589-591 gives references to Cunyngham (1904), Barone (1908), Pigou (1904) and H.Schultz (1935); also see C.F.Bickerdike, *Economic Journal* XVII (1907) p. 98 for simple Cournot-like formulas; for a nongraphic literary exposition see F.W.Taussig, *Some Aspects of the Tariff Question* (Cambridge, Mass.: Harvard University Press, 1915 and 1931) Chapter I; see also G.Haberler, *The Theory of International Trade* (London: William Hodge & Co., Ltd., 1936) Chapter 15, pp. 227-236, and also the reference there to R.Schuller (1905). Or see P.A.Samuelson, *Economics*, 8th ed. (New York: McGraw-Hill Book Company, Inc., 1970) Chapter 34, pp. 651-653, whose fig. 34-2 has identical functions to those of fig. 15.1 here. The 1967, 1964, and 1958 editions also contain similar diagrams in Part Five.

The Cournot problem has been generalized to any number of commodities and given a solution by S.Enke in "Equilibrium Among Spatially Separated Markets: Solution by Electric Analogue", *Econometrica*, Vol. XIX (January 1951) pp. 40-47; see also P.A. Samuelson, "Spatial Price Equilibrium and Linear Programming", *American Economic Review*, Vol. XLII, No. 3 (June 1952) pp. 283-303, and P.A.Samuelson, "International Price Equilibrium: A Prologue to the Theory of Speculation", *Weltwirtschaftliches Archiv*, Band 79, Weft 2 (Hamburg: Hoffmann & Campe Verlag, December 1957) pp. 181-219; both these articles are reproduced in *The Collected Scientific Papers of P.A. Samuelson*, op. cit., Vol. II, pp. 925-984. Karl Fox and also G.C.Judge and T.Takayama have generalized the problem to multiple commodities.

As applied to exchange rate equilibrium, the earliest exact reference seems to be C.F.Bickerdike, "The Instability of Foreign Exchange", *Economic Journal*, Vol. XXX (1920) pp. 118-122 (which in a sense predates Pigou's 1932 rigor); J.Robinson, *Essays in the Theory of Employment* (London and New York: The Macmillan Co., 1937) pp. 183-228 further advances the subject. For graphical formulation and advance see G. Haberler, "The Market for Foreign Exchange and the Stability of the Balance of Payments: A Theoretical Analysis", *Kyklos*, Vol. III (1949) pp. 193-218 which is reproduced in *International Finance, Selected Readings*, R.N.Cooper, ed. (Harmondsworth, England: Peguin Books Ltd., 1969) pp. 107-134; also G.Haberler, "Currency Depreciation and the Terms of Trade", in: *Wirtschaftliche Entwicklung und soziale Ordnung*, Ernst Lagler and Johannes Messner, eds. (Vienna: Verlag Herold, 1952) pp. 149-158. In the modern literature innumerable writers have worked out elasticity expressions for so-called Marshall-Lerner stability conditions based upon such models. Similar matters are ingeniously formulated in John Burr Williams, *International Trade Under Flexible Exchange Rates* (Amsterdam: North-Holland Publishing Co., 1954). See also T.O. Yntema, *A Mathematical Reformulation of the General Theory of International Trade* (Chicago, Ill.: The University of Chicago Press, 1932), a beautiful work that has never been appreciated at its true worth.

wheat, making the American dollar P_1 an increasing function of the foreign exchange rate.

Fig. 15.1 shows all this. As the pound depreciates, *OR* pivots clockwise. As it does so, American wheat exports decline. When the exchange ray shifts to *OR'* in fig. 15.1b, all trade ceases.

Now suppose that wheat were the only good. Balance-of-payments equilibrium requires an equivalence of aggregate value of exports to aggregate value of imports. If wheat is the only good, this can be realized only when R depreciates to the *OR'* level of zero wheat export. This equilibrium R^* is given by the solution of

$$E_i(RP_i) = -e_i(p_i) \qquad\qquad i = 1 \qquad\qquad\qquad (15.3)$$

$$\sum_{i=1}^{1} p_i e_i(p_i) = p_1 e_1(p_1) = 0 \, .$$

We thus have, in addition to the balance-of-payments equation, an export equation for every good, namely in our case of the single good wheat, eq. (15.2). Hence, we always do have $n + 1$ equations to determine the np's and the equilibrium R^*. From p, we get P by eq. (15.1).

15.3. Exchange Depreciation For The Paying Country

What is the moral? What implication is there for the transfer problem? Suppose America is now to make a unilateral payment to England. How will the previous one-good autarky equilibrium at *OR'* be disturbed? Obviously, *OR'* must pivot upward (counterclockwise) toward *OR*. For such a depreciation of the dollar is the only way[7] that an American trade surplus can be generated.

Thus, the Keynes intuition that the *paying country's exchange rate depreciates* is vindicated in this primitive model. But this tells us nothing about any secondary movement induced in the terms of trade. Indeed, with wheat the only good, there is no price ratio P_1/P_2 for America to compute as a measure of the (so-called *Taussigian net*) terms of trade.

---

[7] The usual perverse violation of Marshall-Lerner stability conditions is *not* possible at a one-good autarky point.

15.4. Constancy of Some Marginal Utility

Before introducing a second good, we must notice that when America produces more wheat than she consumes, this must be financed. Since there is no investment or disinvestment in our model, how can the value of net national product fall short of the value of net national income received from wheat production? Evidently this value of the export surplus is financed by American government taxation of earned income to pay for the reparations. (In England, the reverse problem is easily resolved. English product consumed exceeds income earned domestically by the amount of government subsidy. But how does the English government finance this subsidy? From its "reparation" receipts.)

The reparation is, in effect, paid in wheat. One might even have the American tax and the English subsidy paid in terms of wheat. Everything would then seem to be in terms of wheat, the only good named. If wheat were truly the only economic good, what is the meaning of supply and demand curves? What is the American dollar supply and demand for P_1 in terms of?. What is English pound supply and demand for p_1 in terms of?. On reflection, we realize that "money" must in a rigorous model be a Marshallian euphemism for some domestic good or a host of such goods and factors.

Let us postulate that wheat is producible in each country by labor applied to fixed wheat land. The law of diminishing returns shows up as the rising supply functions. More precisely, suppose we use labor hours as our *numeraire*, so that wage rates, W in America and w in England, are each set equal to unity. Then our functions $S_1(\cdot), D_1(\cdot), E_1(\cdot)$, are really functions of P_1/W. Likewise, we write $s_1(p_1/w), d_1(p_1/w), e_1(p_1/w)$.

But there is still a snag. When governments tax us or subsidize us, particularly if these fiscal variables were payable in wheat rather than in wage units of income, that tax or subsidy can usually be expected to distort and alter the Marshallian demand functions. How does a conscientious Marshallian get rid of this distortion and complication? He can do so if he stipulates that labor has strictly constant marginal disutility (or that leisure, regarded as "money", has strictly constant marginal utility). In this singular model, all consumer-surplus and producer-surplus concepts are valid. And, what is important to an Ohlin skeptic, *all* income effects are exhausted on labor (or leisure), which unlike wheat and other traded goods, are purely domestic goods.

One last caveat if my Marshallian model is to be rigorous: as one moves up the supply curve, the absolute level of rent rises. Property's relative share is given by the ratio of two areas: the producer-surplus "triangle" between the supply curve and the rectangle formed by each supply point all divided by the

rectangle's whole area. However, we need not worry if landlords have different wheat-leisure preferences than workers or worry about intraclass taste
differences. Provided everybody values leisure at constant marginal utility
and is not satiated with it, each person's independent demands for wheat, or
cloth, or steel will be simply added to form nonshifting aggregate demand
functions $D_i(P_i/W)$ and $d_i(p_i/w)$. In order that the supply functions for the
different goods be independent, I postulate the Ricardo-Viner case where
labor is the only transferable input between industries, all wheatlands and
woollands being specialized to single industries and earning simple Ricardian
residual rents. This can justify the independence and invariance of the
$S_i(P_i/W)$ and $s_i(p_i/w)$ functions.

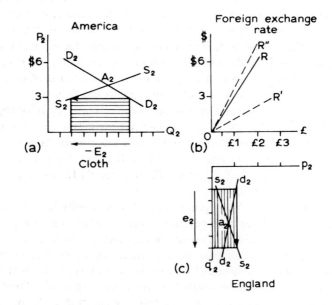

Fig. 15.2. At each exchange rate, cloth equilibrium is found where arrows match as in
fig. 15.1. To find two-good balance of payments equilibrium, pivot ray until in either
country export rectangle(s) cancel out import rectangle(s), as at *OR*. If now America
pays transfer to England, *OR* must shift up to *OR''* and currency of the payer depreciates. Because of Robinson curiosum, such a rise in *R* could perversely improve payer's
terms of trade $P_1/P_2 = p_1/p_2$; but in Ricardian case where *SS* curves are horizontal and
exchange market stable, payer's terms of trade *must* depreciate.

15.5. Many Goods

Now in fig. 15.2 a second good along with wheat is added, say wool or cloth. Now at an exchange rate such as OR, each country has an export advantage in one of the goods, America in wheat and England in cloth. Before reparations the common OR ray in figs. 15.1b and 15.2b provides equilibrium R^* because the export and import rectangles in each country cancel out to zero or balance-of-payments equilibrium.

If we try a higher R, England runs a deficit. If we try a lower R, the dollar (and r) appreciates, and America runs a trade deficit.. The R^* equilibrium is unique and stable[8].

Mathematically, our equilibrium is defined by

$$E_i(RP_i) + e_i(p_i) = 0 \qquad\qquad i = 1, 2, ..., n \qquad\qquad (15.4)$$

defining

$$p_i = p_i[R] \qquad\qquad p_i' < 0$$

$$P_i = P_i[R] \qquad\qquad P_i' > 0$$

and

$$b[R] = \sum_1^n p_i e_i(p_i) = \sum_1^n p_i e_i(p_i[R]) = \sum_1^n p_i e_i[R] = 0, \qquad (15.5)$$

where $e_i'[R] < 0$.

All the ink spilled over so-called Marshall-Lerner stability (for which see Haberler's 1949 *Kyklos* citation of works of Hirschman, A.C.Brown, L.A. Metzler, and others beyond those I had already cited) conditions merely produces breakdowns of the terms involved in $b'[R]$. It suffices to note that $b' < 0$ is not inevitable even though probable in many specifications.

Now return to the transfer problem. If America now pays an indemnity

---

[8] It is well known that great inelasticity of the functions could negate the Marshall-Lerner conditions for such stability. Provided the curves have the usual shapes, there will exist at least one finite equilibrium R^* at which trade balances. Our drawing satisfies stability conditions. And generally the Ricardo constant-cost case, which we shall discuss later, makes for high elasticity and a tendency toward stability.

to England, how must the two-good OR ray of equilibrium rotate to produce an American export surplus? Clearly the dollar must depreciate and OR must move counterclockwise (as to OR'' in fig. 15.2), thereby increasing our wheat export and diminishing our cloth imports. In symbols, if America pays Europe a unilateral transfer of £t, we replace eq. (15.5)'s balance-of-payment condition by $-t$ rather than zero on the right-hand side, namely,

$$b[R] = -t \qquad (15.6)$$

and, provided $b' < 0$, the stable case, we confirm for any number of goods the earlier theorem, namely

Theorem: The exchange rate of the paying country is depreciated by a unilateral transfer.

15.6. Deteriorating Gross-Barter Terms of Trade

Because currency depreciation increases *every* physical export algebraically (i.e., cuts down on any physical import), the paying country is "hurt" by the transfer. This shows that, regardless of what happens secondarily to the (Taussigian net) terms of trade, the 1935 Leontief phenomenon — of an alleged possibility that a transfer can have secondary effects so much opposed to the primary burden as to lead to a utility gain to the payer — definitely cannot happen in our model.

For a two-good model Taussig's "gross barter terms of trade", the ratio of the paying country's physical imports to its physical exports, $e_2[R]/-e_1[R]$ in the wheat-cloth case, must definitely deteriorate. This is because the numerator declines with R and the denominator grows with R. Of course there is nothing very surprising about this result, since one does expect there to be a primary burden.

When we face more than one export and more than one import, and when goods can pass from one category into the other, an index number problem arises for any definition of the terms of trade, gross or net. Our two-good result concerning the deterioration of gross-barter terms of trade can, however, be generalized as follows.

In view of the fact that *every* algebraic export from England is reduced by the transfer receipt, if we can divide the n goods into m American imports $e_i[R]$ and $n-m$ American exports $-e_j[R]$, then for any *fixed* positive weights $(k_1, k_2, ..., k_m, k_{m+1}, ..., k_n)$, the following definition of the gross-barter terms of trade, $\Sigma_1^m k_i e_i [R] / \Sigma_{m+1}^n (-k_j e_j [R])$, will definitely fall, just as in the case of the two-goods example.

15.7. Likely, But Not Inevitable, Secondary Burden

To explain impressionistic views of the past, we have come far enough. In the present partial-equilibrium model (which elsewhere I call the B-R-H model because Bickerdike, Joan Robinson, and Haberler have perhaps written most about it), the transfer *does depreciate* the currency of the paying country[9]. And for the majority of economists, a deterioration of the exchange rate is practically identified with a deterioration of the terms of trade. Indeed some economists even go so far in their thinking as to believe that it is the lowering of the terms of trade that brings about the correction in the trade balance incident to a currency depreciation. This too-facile identification of the terms of trade with the foreign exchange rate has many roots. For one thing, as already mentioned, there is the common confusing together of barter and financial models. Thus an expression such as the Marshall-Lerner elasticity criterion for stability is used interchangeably for (1) a barter model like that involved in Marshall's 1879 *Pure Theory of Foreign and Domestic Commerce* or the Appendix to his 1923 *Money, Credit and Commerce* where reciprocal offer curves cross and (2) a money model such as the B-R-H one now under discussion. (Of course, this model is itself not really a financial model but is also a special kind of barter model, as my version of it makes clear for perhaps the first time.) In the typical two-good barter model of J.S.Mill, Marshall (1879), Edgeworth, and others, stability is restored only by changes in the price ratio of the traded goods or the (net) terms of trade. But such reasoning is not really valid for the model here under discussion.

[9] This result does *not* have to be qualified even for an unstable equilibrium as I shall demonstrate in fig. 15.3. If fixed parities are imposed by the gold standard, the Hume mechanism accomplishes the equivalent result by ultimately lowering the W in the P_i/W expressions and raising the w in the p_i/w expressions so that w/W appreciates by *exactly* the same percentage as does the exchange rate R in my exposition. Part of Keynes's skepticism concerning the feasibility of transfer had nought to do with the change in the terms of trade as much as with his skepticism concerning the ease with which the conventional gold standard mechanism made adjustments under a regime of fixed parities. Perhaps he would have been less skeptical if he had been contemplating a regime of floating exchange rates. In the companion paper already referred to, I prove the illogic of those who oppose floating exchange rates on the grounds of elasticity-pessimism demonstrating that if the econometric conclusions of these critics is correct, then the fixed-parity equilibrium under the Hume mechanism is *also* unstable!

For many years after 1920 when Bickerdike first published such a model, economists took it for granted that exchange depreciation causes a nation's export prices to fall relative to its import prices. Even in the gold-standard case, equilibrium is loosely said to be restored as prices of the deficit country fall relative to prices of the surplus country. (In the referred to companion paper to this one, I analyze the flaw involved in such wording.) Actually, however, as we have seen, and as our diagrams will confirm, when R rises in virtue of depreciation of the dollar, prices of both export *and* import goods fall in dollar terms; and prices of both British imports *and* exports rise in pound terms. Therefore, it is gratuitous to jump to the conclusion that the prices of exports of the depreciating country drop relative to those of its imports.

Yet it was not until the late 1930s that Joan Robinson[10] pointed this out in the literature — much to the surprise of specialists in international trade theory. When they first became aware of the Robinson curiosum, they thought that perhaps her effect was brought about only in cases where the equilibrium was unstable by virtue of reversal of the Marshall-Lerner stability criterion. But it was easy to provide examples of perfectly stable equilibria where the terms of trade actually turned in favor of the depreciating country, and yet depreciation did restore the disturbed equilibrium.

We can state then that it is quite possible for the secondary effects of the transfer payment to go either way: the net terms of trade of the paying country could improve or they could deteriorate as a result of the transfer.

To see this, consider a two-good case of say wheat and cloth. It is easy to construct along Robinson lines an example of a stable system and in which P_1/P_2 *rises* as a result of the transfer rather than falls as the orthodox view would hold. Where economists went wrong in denying this possibility was in comparing prices *across* countries — comparing a P with a p, as for example P_1 with p_1. It is true that the price of cloth has risen in dollars and fallen in pounds. But, since such a ratio is nothing but the exchange rate in a free market, what else could it do when R changes? Such a ratio has nothing to do with a properly computed measure of the terms of trade, which should involve a comparison of export prices with import prices in the same market, whether it be the dollar or pound market. Thus, whatever P_1/P_2 does, so must p_1/p_2 do, since they are the same thing. (I.e., cancelling out R from numerator and denominator of the former will give you the latter, no matter what is the new exchange rate R.) When index numbers of prices become involved, and also certain impediments and costs of trade, one can become

---

[10] J.Robinson, *Essays in the Theory of Employment*, pp. 218-221, particularly p. 219, *n.* 1.

confused on these fundamentals. Such confusions are common in connection with historic discussions of purchasing-power parity, as I have discussed elsewhere[11]; and I fear that sometimes Keynes added to the confusion on this matter.

Although the Robinson curiosum shows that no unambiguous answer is possible concerning the secondary burden of a transfer, economists have tended to think that this phenomenon is abnormal in the sense of being unusual. Because we are discussing what is after all a rather idealized model, I am not sure that sense can be made of a statement that one result is "empirically more realistic" than another. But in any case, economists have often supplied conditions that they hoped were sufficient to rule out the Robinson curiosum. Broadly speaking, they sought such conditions in extreme elasticity of postulated supply. In my present concern to try to explain why older economists fell naturally into the orthodox view, I shall now present a rather extreme case of elastic supply — namely, the classical model of Ricardian constant costs. For, within that model, we shall see that the Marshallian partial-equilibrium approach does lead to deterioration of the terms of trade along the lines of the orthodox presumption.

15.8. Combining Marshallian Curves and Ricardian Comparative Advantage

Because my companion paper elaborates upon the present subject and because my 1962 paper, just cited, presented a complete account of the production side of the many-good Ricardian model, I shall be brief here and omit diagrams.

Now labor is assumed to be the only factor, A_1, A_2, A_3, ... units of American labor being required to produce a unit of goods 1, 2, 3, ... To produce a unit of those same goods in England requires a_1, a_2, a_3, ... units of English labor. Recall that W is the dollar wage rate for American labor and that w is the pound wage rate for English labor. In good classical fashion, we rule out migration between countries. As before, the exchange rate giving the cost of one pound in terms of dollars is R, with $r = 1/R$ being the number of pounds per dollar.

How is supply affected in figs. 15.1 and 15.2? Supply is affected by having the supply curves all become horizontal, in consequence of the Ricardian

---

[11] P.A.Samuelson, "Theoretical Notes on Trade Problems", *Review of Economics and Statistics*, Vol. XLVI, No. 2 (May 1964) pp. 145-154, reproduced in *The Collected Scientific Papers of Paul A.Samuelson*, Vol. II, pp. 821-830.

assumption of constant costs. For example, with labor the only factor and lands ignorable, diminishing returns has no scope. Elsewhere I spell out the minor variations needed in the B-R-H model when it is made Ricardian. (This involves merely introducing some inequalities into eqs. (15.4) earlier.) However, we can dispense with that examination here, because on reflection we notice that the way relative prices change is *completely predictable* from the movement of the exchange rate alone.

For it is an easy theorem in the constant-cost case that depreciating the dollar must reduce all prices of the goods America exports in comparison with those she imports; and it will leave intact the price ratios of all goods that a country continues to produce.

Where are these price ratios to be measured? In England or in America? It does not matter; in a perfect market, the price ratios in one country are identical with those in another, regardless of the production origin of the goods in question.

Specifically, for any two goods that America continues to produce, the price ratio is given by A_i/A_j. For any two goods that England continues to produce, the price ratio anywhere in the world is given by a_i/a_j. The only interesting case then is the comparison, in any one place, of the price ratio of an American export to a European export as R rises. Let us consider the net terms of trade as England sees them between cloth and wheat as measured by p_2/p_1 or P_2/P_1. Using the latter dollar version, one calculates it as the European labor cost of cloth a_2 translated from pounds into dollars by the exchange rate R, all divided by American labor cost (in dollars) of wheat. Hence, so long as each country's cost for its indicated export is the lowest cost anywhere in the world, the expression for England's terms of trade becomes

$$P_2/P_1 = a_2wR/A_1W .$$

This is seen to be linear in the exchange rate and hence grows whenever R grows (up to the point where England is priced out of the market and America's A_2/A_1 takes over or down to the point where America is priced out of the market and a_2/a_1 prevails). Of course a change in the exchange rate might be offset by a wage rise in the depreciating country and a wage fall in the appreciating country. But the real transfer will not be possible unless the wR/W factor in the above expression does in fact rise and that is all we need for the argument. Incidentally, as remarked before in a footnote, although my discussion is couched primarily in terms of flexible exchange rates, it applies fully to the gold standard case of fixed parities: in that case, R stays constant, but, as a result of specie flows or managed money, the called-for percentage changes all take place in the wage ratio w/W.

Let us take stock to see what the Ricardian case has added to the intuitive expectations of literary economists concerning the transfer problem. What constant cost has done is to rule out the Robinson curiosum.

Now any exchange depreciation induced by a unilateral payment must (save in the limiting and frequent case, beloved by Frank Graham, of "limbo" where one country is both producing and importing a good in proportions determined by reciprocal demand and where secondary burdens are nil) create a secondary burden on the paying country in the form of a deterioration of its export prices relative to its import prices. Q.E.D.

My task is completed. I have shown that any economist who reasoned in the back of his mind in terms of simplified partial-equilibrium industries, foreign exchange equilibrium, and comparative cost, could be forgiven from falling into the orthodox presumption in connection with the transfer problem. For that presumption is a valid theorem in terms of the B-R-H model, or at least in my B-R-H-S version of it.

15.9. Comparative-Static Stability in the Large

He who reads and runs can now run. But there are a couple of loose threads that I would like to tie up. First, as mentioned before, there is the possibility of a locally unstable equilibrium. (I must stress that the Ricardian horizontal supply does not, for all its infinite elasticity, rule that out — even if it perhaps makes instability less likely and does negate the Robinson curiosum.) As far as both dynamics and comparative statics are both concerned, such local instability does not — repeat, *not* — change the conclusion that a transfer will end up deteriorating the exchange rate of the payer. This strong conclusion, which might be dignified as being an extension of the "correspondence principle"[12], seems to have been overlooked and misunderstood in the literature. Second, there remains the minor problem of relating this defense of the orthodox position to my earlier 1952 and 1954 exhaustive examination and near rejection of that position.

Fig. 15.3 illustrates a case of multiple equilibrium. Between the two stable equilibria A and C, there is the unstable equilibrium B. Now along comes an indemnity of t paid to Britain (say, in pounds). This shifts my plot of $-b[R]$ to the right. Or what is the same thing, find the new equilibrium in fig. 15.3

[12] For footnote, see next page.

by looking for the intersection of the curve, not as before with the vertical axis, but with the vertical line t distance to the left of the axis. And again one has three equilibria, stable a and c and unstable b.

This accords with the usual discussions. Writers say, "See how the stable A has shifted upward, to a, as the receiving country's currency appreciates. And see how the stable C shifts upward to c. All this is as one should expect: according to the simplest correspondence principle, when an equilibrium is dynamically stable, its comparative statics behaves normally. But see how the unstable B shifts *perversely* to b. This too is in accordance with the correspondence principle that relates perverse dynamics to perverse comparative statics. Now we have room for paradox: if the world begins at the unstable B, America could better her terms of trade by forcing a reparation payment on England!"

Some of this argument is correct. But some is simply wrong. It is true that

---

[12] For the heuristic "correspondence principle", see P.A.Samuelson, *Foundations of Economic Analysis* (Cambridge, Mass.: Harvard University Press, 1947, and in paperback, Atheneum Publishers, New York, N.Y., 1965). Chapters IX, X and Appendixes A, B. As applied to a linear system or to the linear approximation near equilibrium of a nonlinear system — say to $\Delta y_i = A[y_i] + [b_i]$, or to $d/dt[y_i] = A[y_i'] + [b_i]$ — its comparative statics will depend on the nonsingularity of its Jacobian matrix A, while its dynamic properties will depend on the latent roots of A defined by $\det[A-(1+x)I] = 0$, or by $\det[A-xI] = 0$. When a root x_1 becomes or passes through zero, the qualitative dynamic behavior reverses (as from stability to instability) and so too will the comparative static behavior (as from normality to perverseness). As an example, when $k = 1 + x$ in the multiplier expression $1 + k + k^2 + \ldots$ passes through unity and above, dynamic instability occurs; at the same point, the comparative static multiplier expression, $1/(1-k)$ perversely turns negative. But, as will be argued in connection with fig. 15.3 below, $1/(1-k)$ is not really a true comparative static observed phenomenon.

Since 1947, a number of economists have questioned the generality and unambiguity of the correspondence principle; let me make some disclaimers here. When x_1 is complex rather than real and has its real part change sign as x_1 passes through a pure imaginary number or has $|1+x|$ pass through unity, the argument needs modification because only the dynamic behavior is reversed. Furthermore, the heuristic principle works best when A is a definite matrix as in connection with an extremum problem; for then real roots are assured, and not only do we have knowledge about A but also about its principal minors. Similarly if A is a Leontief-Metzler-Frobenius matrix, in which all off-diagonal elements are of one sign and A possesses diagonal dominance, then similar sweeping conclusions are possible about principal minors and the reality of the relevant root; and indeed, as I pointed out in the 1960 Frisch *Festschrift*, my version of the LeChatelier principle holds for such structures. See P.A.Samuelson, "An Extension of the LeChatelier Principle", *Econometrica* 28 (1960) 368-379 (reproduced, with the first paragraph misprint "inelastic" corrected to read "elastic", in: *Collected Scientific Papers I*, pp. 626-637).

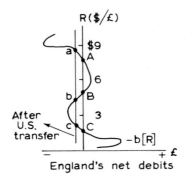

Fig. 15.3. Here is a typical case where elasticity-pessimism does create unstable equilibrium *B* between stable equilibria *A* and *C*. Payment of transfer by America to England
of *t* pounds is like shift of vertical axis leftward by amount *t*. New intersections give
effect of transfer on exchange rate (and in constant cost case, equivalent deterioration of
terms of trade). That stable equilibria shift upward to *a* and *c* is obvious. But conclusion
that unstable *B* shifts to new unstable *b*, thereby perversely improving terms of trade of
payer is quite false. In the short run, transfer produces positive excess demand at *B*; with
such excess demand *R* is dynamically bid up; final equilibrium ends up at *c*. Thus, both
comparatively statically as well as dynamically, payment depresses currency of paper
– even though the unstable branch has opposite slope. The correspondence principal in
the large is thus established for this one-dimensional case.

a system that starts at either stable equilibrium will move upward to the
indicated new equilibrium – with all the effects indicated in the present
paper. But it is simply not true that starting the system at the unstable *B*
equilibrium, and then disturbing it by a payment to England, will cause *R* to
fall – either in the end or at any time during the transitional process.

Let us see what must actually happen. The instant the payment begins
England runs a surplus in the foreign exchange markets (i.e., in the first
instant we move due west of *B*). In the second instant, this bids up the price
of the pound *R*. (This is in accord with the dynamic adjustment equation
that says that dR/d(time) has the algebraic sign of "excess demand" for
pounds.) So in the transition *R rises* just as in the stable cases. In those
stable cases, however, the transition ends when *R* has risen into the new,
nearby, stable equilibrium. What happens in this unstable case? There is no
new, nearby, stable equilibrium, so the transition process just goes on and on.
The *R* continues to rise. Continues to rise forever? No, it cannot rise above
the highest stable equilibrium *c*. And so it rises until that equilibrium is
reached. In short, one always has a comparative-static rise in *R* with or with-

out instability! So one can say that "in the large", as contrasted to local un-stable and irrelevant branches of the $b[R] + t = 0$ relation, the final observed dR/d(transfer) movements have the same positive sign as in the stable case. No matter how many stable and unstable equilibria, *every* initial equilibrium is displaced into a higher stable equilibrium. Q.E.D.

How this sweeping correspondence result must be modified when the prob-lem is more than two dimensional must remain an open question. However, our result does have some policy implications: if momentarily trapped in an unstable equilibrium, and it becomes a nice question as to how *that* could have come about, a country can benefit by using its monopoly power and restricting goods in international trade so as to force the world into a stable equilibrium more agreeable to the country in question. But it cannot do so by throwing its bread on the waters in the form of gifts and transfers. (Also one shudders at the prospect of two von Neumann countries jockeying for position between stable equilibria more agreeable to one than to the other – an indeterminate problem in bilateral monopoly.)

Fig. 15.3 brings out another facet of the policy problem. From Versailles on, Keynes warned that Germany might not have the capacity to pay the imposed reparations. (Some have dismissed this as Francophobia; and in the Weimar republic, Schumpeter made himself rather unpopular by saying that of course Germany *could* pay the reparations if she set her will to it.) Whether Keynes was right in his impressionistic econometrics back in 1919, fig. 15.3 shows that if the vertical line is moved too far westward, there might be *no* possible equilibrium. Making Germany pay so large an indemnity would result merely in an endless depreciation of the mark and galloping inflation inside the country. (Whether the 1920-1923 German hyperinflation had much to do with reparations is not at all clear.)

Finally, there remains the task of reconciling the present strong affirmation of the orthodox position with the earlier skepticism concerning it.

15.10. Reconciliation with 1952-1954 Results

Of my two cited *Economic Journal* articles on the transfer problem, it was the first 1952 one that largely assumed no transport costs and no domestic goods. And it was that article which (the new Jones result aside) demonstrated that Ohlin agnosticism was warranted in criticism of the orthodox presump-tion of a secondary burden, the terms-of-trade charges were shown to depend upon *relative income propensities* for the two goods in the two countries; and with transport costs ignorable and demand not at all localized, the principle of insufficient reason suggested that *any* result was equally likely. How does the present model fit in?

Both wheat and cloth are certainly freely transportable. However, leisure in America and leisure in England are not internationally transferable items. They are domestic goods par excellence, with so to speak infinite transport costs as the result of the usual Ricardian assumptions that factors are immobile in international trade. Recall that leisure and labor are different names, or different aspects, of the same thing. Therefore at first blush, one is inclined to say that the present paper takes one out of the agnosticism of my first paper and into the morass of my second 1954 paper, with its many possible patterns of transport costs[13]. But that would seem too sweeping a conclusion. What use would my first 1952 model be if the existence of any immobile factors were considered to render it inapplicable? It, after all, did allow explicitly for transformation trade-offs between the two goods, with labor and land thus being understood to be in the background; and nothing could be less mobile than land. Therefore, it cannot be the mere presence of localized labor that frees the present inquiry from the conclusions of my first paper.

At a slightly deeper level, it might be argued that "leisure" never entered into my 1952 paper at all. Labor did, but the supply of labor as with the supply of every factor was implicitly taken there as fixed. There was no need, explicitly or implicitly, to consider leisure. In other words, it is the *variability* of the supply of labor or of some domestic good that seems to be involved here. This suggests that the present model falls into the category of what was described on p. 302 of the 1952 article (p. 1099 of my *Collected Scientific Papers*, Vol. II) as follows:

"...To my knowledge the only logically air-tight successful defense of the orthodox view is that given by Viner [*Studies*, p. 348-349], in which he explicitly introduces into the problem transport costs great enough to make international trade prohibitive for some 'domestic commodities'. Naturally a high percentage of our income is spent on such commodities."

Hence it does become likely that my test criterion involving income propensities on food and cloth of payer and receiver, suitably generalized for induced production effects, will indicate the orthodox presumption. As is said in a footnote on the next page of the 1952 article: "Viner's successful vindication of the orthodox presumption was possible because of his (quite realistic) introduction of an element of asymmetry into the problem: his

---

[13] See P.A.Samuelson, *Economic Journal*, 1954, op. cit. The only definite conclusion reached there was that the orthodox presumption had much to be said for it; but where the impediment involved real, exhaustive cost, Ohlin agnosticism seemed justified.

domestic good is made (infinitely) substitutable for the region's export good production and not at all substitutable for the import good production."

Simple mathematical analysis can show that the Ricardian case analyzed here is indeed of this general class involving asymmetric relations between a country's exports and its domestic goods or factors in variable supply.

To show this I shall make use of an Edgeworthian device pioneered by James Meade, the trade-indifference contours. (In the cited Caves-Johnson American Economic Association's reproduction of my 1952-1954 article, I added a 1966 postscript suggesting that my case of variable production could be reduced to "box-diagram" format by the use of the now-familiar Meade device. But for the present purpose, I have to go beyond the usual form of the Meade device and optimize also with respect to labor supply in the background. For example, for prescribed levels of $-E_1$ and $-E_2$, I maximize America's utility from wheat consumed, cloth consumed, and leisure enjoyed, subject of course to the Ricardian labor-cost contraints. This gives me in the end "contours of trade indifference". Fig. 15.4 illustrates these for America and Europe. The European contours are shown as broken lines and are to read from right to left and upside down in the usual box-diagram fashion.

Actually, and this will come as no surprise to students of Kuhn-Tucker nonlinear programming or of Edgeworthian trade theory, these contours will now be parallel straight lines in a large part of the field (i.e., where a country is producing something of both goods), with slope equal to A_2/A_1 or a_2/a_1 as the case may be. Beyond the boundaries of this field, the differences in comparative cost will introduce discernible asymmetries in fig. 15.4's income propensities or Engel's curves. Thus, suppose we begin at a prereparation point where each country is specializing on the good in which it has a comparative advantage. Also, let us evaluate the crucial income propensities there, to see if we do find that they differ in a systematic fashion predictable from comparative-cost theory alone. The answer is, yes. An international income change (because of reparation or anything else) alters the amount exchanged of a country's *export* good alone. In that case, transferring abstract purchasing power from America to England will cause the price of England's export good, cloth, to be bid up (by her) and will cause the price of America's export good, wheat, to be bid down (by the drop in America's income). Thus the orthodox presumption is indeed triumphantly established. Q.E.D.[14]

---

[14] Of course the present theorem is a restatement, from a different point of view, namely the 1952-1954 viewpoint, of what has already been established in this paper.

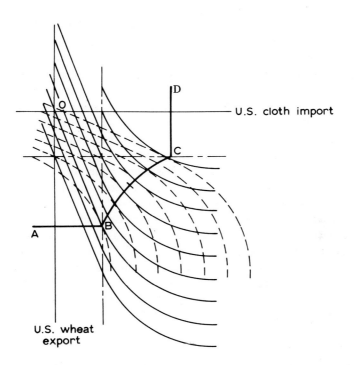

Fig. 15.4. Reading upward and in the usual left-to-right fashion, one sees the American trade-indifference contours. Reading upside down and from right-to-left, one sees the English trade-indifference contours. Directly below the origin, both sets of contours are straightlines determined by comparative cost ratios. In case where America exports wheat and imports cloth, transfer moves equilibrium on the contract curve *CB* toward *B*, necessarily depreciating wheat/cloth price ratio.

A last word. One of the triumphs of the 1952 paper was the demonstration that, for stable systems, no matter what the complexity of conditions in the background, the simple food-cloth income propensities were determinative. What then do *they* tell us about the present case? Because of the assumption that leisure-labor has constant marginal utility, all consumption-income effects for cloth and wheat are zero in both countries. As a result, my 1952 criterion becomes 0/0, an indeterminate number that tells us nothing but which is consistent with orthodox deterioration proved by other methods.

Mathematically, I shall reduce the behavior equations of the problem to the solution of a certain maximum problem for each country. We have seen that the independent demand curves of the different citizens can be horizontally added to get the market demand curves. These individual demand curves are, by virtue of our assumption of constant marginal utility of leisure-labor, identical to marginal utilities for each citizen. When summed horizontally, these marginal utilities provide an aggregate marginal utility function in the sense of being the derivative of its own integral. The integral[15] for each good can be written as the concave function $U_i(Q_i)$ and $u_i(q_i)$, which serve as the Gossen-like utilities for America and England, respectively. Lest anyone raise an eyebrow that I work with a collective concept such as total utility of a country, let me hasten to point out that this is completely rigorous because of my assumption that each person has labor-leisure of constant marginal utility. So long as workers never run out of leisure and provided that they have run into work, all is completely rigorous.

I shall leave to the reader the parallel case of England and shall concentrate on America. Our programming problem is to find the quantities that America is to produce of wheat and cloth, Y_1 and Y_2, so as to maximize national utility. If one selects utility units in such a way that one unit of labor corresponds to one util, and if one eliminates labor by substituting the production-possibility frontier of Ricardo, $L = A_1 Y_1 + A_2 Y_2$, the simple Kuhn-Tucker concave-programming problem results:

---

[15] Except for the algebraic sign of the import variable, these are what I introduced as "social-payoff" functions in the cited articles on spatial and intertemporal price equilibrium: P.A.Samuelson, *American Economic Review*, 1952, op. cit., pp. 283-303 and *Weltwirtschaftliches Arkiv*, 1957, op. cit., pp. 181-219. It may be asked, how are collective indifference curves possible in view of my earlier proof that they exist only when the indifference curves are homothetic and identical between citizens? The present case does not quite fall into that category. But, as has been discussed elsewhere, there is a wider class in which collective indifference contours hold within a range, namely the Gorman-Theil case where all Engel's curves are straight lines with slopes (at each price ratio) common to all the citizens. Now actually the only lines that can stay straight lines through the nonnegative orthant are lines through the origin – my homothetic case. In the present example, where the Engel's curves are lines parallel to the leisure axis, when the individual stops buying leisure, because he cannot afford any, or when he buys 24 hours of leisure because it does not pay him to work at all, we lose the simplifications that constancy of marginal utility does for us in providing solid underpinning for partial equilibrium. So, as in all Gorman-Theil deviations from my narrower conditions, the collective indifference curves will break down as a concept in the large. (Actually, for indemnity large enough, some Englishmen will quit working and some American will find himself working every possible hour. And then partial equilibrium cannot be used.) However, for the purpose of the present exercise, within a range of indemnities, the trick does work even though it cannot work unconditionally.

$$\max_{Y_i} U_1(Y_1 - E_1) + U_2(Y_2) - A_1 Y_1 - A_2 Y_2 = U^*(-E_1, -E_2) \quad Y_i \geqslant 0$$

where the levels of goods imported or exchanged $-E_i$ are taken as given.

The well-known necessary and sufficient conditions for an optimal solution are given by

$$U_i'(Y_i - E_i) - A_i \leqslant 0 ,$$

with the inequality holding only when $Y_i = 0$. This gives us as many conditions as there are goods. After we have substituted these optimal decisions into the maximand, we get the desired U^* function that provides our generalized-Meade, trade-indifference contours. The slopes of these U^* contours are given by the ratios of the partial derivatives of the U function. It is now evident that these slopes are the constant A_2/A_1 where both goods are being produced. Where America is producing wheat alone, our interesting case, the slope is given by $U_2'(-E_2)/A_1$ and the contour is strongly convex. The convex field joins up with the parallel-straightline field at a critical value of $-E_2^*$, and hence the boundary is the vertical line through the point market B in fig. 15.4. To the right of that vertical boundary, the Engel's curves are also vertical lines for America.

By similar mathematical reasoning, the reader will establish that Europe's critical boundary, at which her production of wheat ceases, is the horizontal line through the point C; and her Engel's curves in the interesting region below that boundary all have Engel's curves that are horizontal. And so, utilizing the income propensities of my 1952 paper, we have the asymmetry needed to justify the orthodox position. Q.E.D.

Any reader who wishes to skip this mathematical argument is invited to compare the "contract locus" *ABCD* of fig. 15.4 with the *CC* contract locus of figs. 1 and 2 of my 1952 paper. The techniques developed there, when applied to fig. 15.4 will indeed vindicate the orthodox Keynes-Taussig presumption.

As my colleague Professor Bhagwati has suggested to me after reading a first draft of the present paper, there is an easy heuristic way to understand why the present model results in the orthodox deterioration of the payer's terms of trade: First, assume all prices unchanged. Since income effects go entirely on to the domestic good leisure, there is no change in the amounts consumed of wheat and cloth in either country. So far, then, no presumed change in terms of trade. But recall that the payers are all forced to work more and thereby to produce more of something: under complete specialization, that something can be only the exportable good of the paying country. Similarly, the receivers all work less and produce less of their exportable good. With consumptions otherwise unchanged, an increase in America's wheat production and a decrease in England's cloth production can only result in a deterioration of the terms of trade between wheat and cloth if markets are to be cleared. Q.E.D. I may add: the moral is that, when productions are variable, the criteria of my earlier papers based on consumption propensities, $\partial C_i/\partial I$, have to be modified by income-induced production and cross-effects.

15.11. Conclusion

We have come a long way. The orthodox way of thinking has been in a sense traced down to its possible intuitive origins. But this has been done in a rigorous way only in the context of a very strong model in which the conditions for partial-equilibrium analysis are rigidly met.

I hold no brief for orthodoxy. Actually my own vested interests have been on the other side. But rereading my 1952-54 papers in the light of the present analysis convinces me that these papers underestimate the strength of the orthodox presumption. This is because these papers concentrated on the criterion of income-induced changes in the consumptions of the traded goods. An exception was noted in the Viner airtight successful defence of the orthodox view (1952, p.302 and 1954, p.289) but this was illegitimately treated as an esoteric case. So let me redress the balance here.

In all trade models there are "domestic (i.e., non-traded) factor inputs" in the background and their supplies may well be variable, being subject to income propensities triggered off by transfers. And in most realistic models there do exist transport impediments which create a regime of purely-domestic commodities in each country. These too are subject to income propensities. Finally, although an increased consumption of a domestic or a reduced supply of an input triggered by receipt of a transfer could squeeze the production of *any* good traded internationally, there is perhaps a definite presumption that the competitive squeezing of supply will be greatest for the good which the receiving country is actually exporting — because in some sense it is for that country "relatively important"; and for the paying country, where resources are released by the reparation, the prime effects would seem to be on increasing the supply of the international goods which the payer exports. If this is so, the orthodox or anti-Ohlin presumption is upheld.

Note that no reliance is made here on constancy of marginal utilities or of costs or on the independence assumptions typical of partial equilibrium. The Bhagwati argument paraphrased in the last section could be applied to the general case of a concave production possibility frontier involving two or more traded goods, one or more domestic good in each country, and one or more labor or other input that has normal income effects. I should warn though that the orthodox presumption is not, so to speak, ironclad. This for the reason that we cannot always presume that an indirect income effect impinges relatively most on the good a country exports[16]. A beautiful counterexample is provided by a case involving classical factor-price-equalization. Let every person in both countries have identical tastes for wheat, cloth, and a domestic good bricks at every income level. (I.e., tastes are homothetic and income elasticities unitary.) Land and labor totals are frozen. Production functions are identical geographically. America, being land rich, exports wheat; England exports cloth. Specialization though is incomplete, all goods being produced in positive amounts in both countries. Obviously, the conditions for the factor-price equalization theorem are realized both before and after transfer.

Now America pays a transfer to England. What is the effect on the terms-of-trade of wheat and cloth? Surprisingly, we can assert that all price ratios will remain unchanged, in accordance with Ohlin's anti-orthodox view. To prove this realize that the world is, before and after the transfer, on its pro-duction-possibility frontier producing unchanged totals of the three goods. Totals are preserved because the income effects are so nicely balanced. Given three goods and two factors, there is an indeterminacy of where the total of bricks is to be produced geographically. Without disturbing the equilibrium goods-factor price ratios, if localized demand decrees that more of bricks is to be produced after the transfer in the receiving country and less in the paying country, that can take place. Hence, the only effect of the transfer is to cause the paying country to produce and consume less of its domestic good, and hence produce more of the traded goods; but with its consumption of those goods down, it is now financing the transfer by exporting more than before; in the receiving country, opposite effects take place. But note that this all meshes at unchanged price ratios. Q.E.D.

[16] In my 1954 paper, p.289, this point was already made in answer to a query from Professor Haberler.

PART 7

THE BALANCE OF PAYMENTS

CHAPTER 16

DEVALUATION AND AGGREGATE DEMAND IN AID-RECEIVING COUNTRIES *

Richard N. COOPER

Theoretical discussions of the balance of payments have typically been framed in terms of equilibrium analysis, considering either a movement from one comparative static equilibrium position to another or the dynamic stability of the foreign exchange market about its equilibrium position. Such analysis has generated important propositions; but it misses the central point that balance-of-payments problems as actually encountered usually require an inspection of the consequences of moving from a position of *dis*equilibrium to one of equilibrium. Disequilibrium analysis may provide different conclusions, leading to different policy implications, from the more conventional equilibrium analysis.

For example, it is generally regarded as a truism that currency devaluation is inflationary, except under those circumstances when a devaluation would perversely worsen a country's balance on goods and services. The reasoning underlying this proposition is simple and straightforward: A successful devaluation will increase export receipts and/or divert import demand to domestic substitutes, on both counts adding to the total monetary demand in the economy if monetary policy is suitably permissive; but increases in aggregate demand, reinforced by multiplier effects, will tend to worsen the trade balance. It follows that conscious policies of demand deflation must be undertaken if the beneficial effects of devaluation are not to be partially or even wholly eroded through devaluation-induced increases in total demand.

This paper challenges the theoretical proposition that successful devalua-

* I am grateful to Jagdish Bhagwati, Robert Mundell, and Jaroslav Vanek for comments on an earlier version of this paper, but they are of course absolved of any blame for the final product.

tion is always [1] inflationary and sets out conditions under which the opposite will be true. It attempts to illustrate the influence that an initial position of disequilibrium may exert on the final outcome.

To set the scene more precisely, consider a small country beset by balance-of-payments difficulties. It is a normal importer of capital, fixed in terms of foreign currency, under a foreign assistance program. "Small" here means small enough that the country cannot influence the prices of its imports, and it can neglect secondary repercussions on the rest of the world, but not necessarily so small that it is a price taker in the markets for its principal exports. Assume also that the country's government covers any budget deficit (or discharges a surplus) by borrowing from (or repaying) the central bank, because private capital markets are undeveloped. These assumptions approximate the conditions in many less developed countries in today's world. [2]

The balance-of-payments difficulties may take two different forms: (1) an overall balance-of-payments deficit, involving loss of foreign exchange reserves, the domestic monetary effects of which are automatically neutralized through offsetting domestic credit creation, e.g., through an exchange stabilization account; (2) an overall balance in external payments, maintained by a system of controls over imports. The first situation can obviously last only so long as gold or foreign exchange reserves are available, while the second is subject to erosion through time as the controls are increasingly circumvented. The country is assumed to devalue its currency by enough in the first situation to eliminate the overall deficit or in the second situation to eliminate the controls instituted to suppress the payments deficit.

One can then put the following question: If the economic authorities wish to maintain total demand for domestic output in the country, should their macro-economic policies accompanying devaluation be deflationary or expansionary? As noted earlier, the conventional answer is that they must deflate domestic demand enough to permit an improvement in the trade balance. I will show that under some circumstances the devaluation behaves much like the imposition of an excise tax and offsetting *expansionary* policies are required to maintain aggregate demand.

---

[1] Changes in the distribution of income arising from devaluation, and the effects of these distributional changes on savings and imports, including the possibility of deflation, have been recognized. See Diaz [7].

[2] See C.P. Kindleberger [16].

16.1. The Currency of Measurement

Perhaps the clearest way to demonstrate the possibility that successful devaluation (i.e., one that improves the balance on goods and services [3]) may be deflationary is to contrast the trade position measured in terms of foreign currency with the position measured in domestic currency. A devaluing country is typically interested in improving the current account of its balance of payments in terms of *foreign* currency. Foreign exchange is the scarce resource, of which supplies to the country are inadequate. But the impact of a devaluation on the country's total demand must be measured in terms of *domestic* currency; that is the medium in which domestic income arises and expenditures are made. In equilibrium analysis, this distinction between foreign and domestic currencies is of no consequence. A trade account balanced in one currency will be balanced in the other; a deficit eliminated in foreign currency will also be eliminated in domestic currency. When the relationship between currencies changes, however, the distinction between currencies may be of considerable importance where the initial position is one of imbalance, because the trade position may improve in foreign currency and simultaneously deteriorate in terms of domestic currency. This outcome is possible in many less developed countries, which are capital-importing countries with rather low elasticities of demand for imports.

The possibility of deflationary devaluation can be seen most simply by considering the relationship $B = rD$, where $B = X - M$ is the trade balance measured in terms of foreign currency, r is the foreign-currency price of a unit of domestic currency, and D is the trade balance measured in terms of domestic currency. A devaluation by $\Delta r < 0$ will change the balance measured in either currency, leading to the relationship:

$$\Delta B = (r + \Delta r)\Delta D + D\Delta r = r(1+k)\Delta D + kB, \qquad (16.1)$$

where Δ indicates a change in the variable it precedes and $k = \Delta r/r$, the proportionate devaluation. It is clear from Equation 16.1 that even when ΔB is positive, implying an improvement in the foreign balance, ΔD may be negative, implying a reduction in total demand for domestic output in the devaluing country. This outcome is possible if imports exceed exports ($B < 0$) both before and after devaluation, a condition usually met in devaluing less developed countries. Most analysis of devaluation has neglected this possibility because it assumes that the devaluation is small and trade is initially '

---

[3] Trade balance for short.

balanced ($B = D = 0$). [4] In this case, the change in the balance must have the same sign no matter what the currency of measurement.

But with a trade deficit, the two balances may move in opposite directions, because the relationship between the currencies has changed. The magnitude, measured in domestic currency, of a given deficit in foreign currency will *rise* as a result of devaluation, before any allowance is made for economic adjustments in response to the devaluation. [5]

16.2. Expenditure Effects

To see now what the initial impact of devaluation on domestic income (and output) may be, consider the accounting relationship

$$Y = E + D$$

where Y is domestic output and E is total domestic expenditure. Domestic output will fall if $\Delta E + \Delta D$ is negative. It was argued above that ΔD might well be negative even when the balance improves in terms of foreign currency. But what about the impact of devaluation on domestic expenditure, holding output-constant (i.e., before allowing for income-induced changes in expenditure)?

There are five reasons why a devaluation might affect domestic expenditure directly, leaving aside indirect effects arising from devaluation-induced changes in monetary conditions, on which more will be said later.

First, devaluation may lower real income associated with a given level of output by worsening the terms of trade, and under some circumstances this decline in real income may induce an upward shift in the money level of expenditures by causing a disproportionate reduction in savings. [6]

[4] See the classic analysis by Joan Robinson [18]. Also Alexander [1], Fleming [9], Laursen and Metzler [17], and Tsiang [20]. An exception is Hirschmann [13], who early pointed out the possibility that a change in the balance measured in domestic currency might have the opposite sign from the change in the balance measured in foreign currency, and therefore that successful devaluation might be deflationary *both* in the devaluing country and in the rest of the world. Haberler [11], Harberger [12], and Bernstein [2] also state clearly that the two balances may move in opposite directions, but they carry the analysis no further. Day [6] is concerned with the size of the devaluation required to *eliminate* an initial trade imbalance, and of course a deficit eliminated in one currency will also be eliminated in the other.

[5] This can be seen by rewriting Equation 16.1 as: $\Delta B - kB = r(1+k)\Delta D$. The balance in domestic currency will worsen by a multiple of B even when $\Delta B = 0$.

[6] This is known as the Laursen-Metzler effect. See [17]. There is some question

Second, a devaluation will generally redistribute income as compared with the predevaluation period, toward those factors of production engaged in the export and import-competing industries, away from those engaged in purely domestic industries (and, when devaluation replaces import controls, from the recipients of import licenses). Income redistribution will raise the level of expenditures associated with a constant output if the beneficiaries of the redistribution have a higher propensity to spend than do the losers and lower it if the reverse is true. These distributional effects have on occasion played an important role in the postdevaluation period. According to Diaz, the redistribution from workers to landowners resulting from devaluation of the Argentine peso in late 1958 caused the sharp recession in the following year; a similar development apparently occurred in Finland after the devaluation of 1957. [7] Under different circumstances, of course, the redistributional effects might induce a spending boom.

Third, devaluation may change consumer or investor expectations in a way that alters expenditure. If devaluation is widely anticipated, expenditures on both nontraded and (especially) traded goods may be higher than normal; after devaluation, in contrast, expenditures may be lower than normal during the period in which excessive inventories are being worked off. Expectational effects will not of course last indefinitely, but their impact may be present for a year or more.

Fourth, foreign investors may find the devaluing country a more attractive place to invest, e.g., because exports from it are more competitive in world markets after devaluation or because controls on imports and remittances have been relaxed or removed as a result of devaluation, and they may therefore increase their local currency expenditures in the country. Such an increase in local expenditures by foreign investors may result in either larger or smaller foreign exchange receipts for the country (since each dollar now commands more local currency than it did before devaluation), and the devaluation-induced change in these foreign exchange receipts must be allowed for in reckoning the impact of devaluation on the country's

whether the Laursen-Metzler effect exists at all, since it ignores the influence of a rise in import prices on real balances and hence on saving. See Kemp [15, pp. 277–280], who argues that devaluation-induced changes in the terms of trade will not increase expenditure out of a given money income. In any case, the Laursen-Metzler effect is weakened by an initial excess of imports over exports, and as Jones [14, p. 80] has pointed out, an initial trade deficit may even *reverse* the expected impact of changes in terms of trade on the trade balance, reinforcing rather than weakening the effects of devaluation.

[7] See Diaz [7] and [8] and Gerakis [10].

payments position. As we will see later, if all capital inflows represent private investment in the country, a successfull devaluation is bound to be expansionary, except for the kinds of expenditure effect considered immediately above.

In the long run, private foreign investment increases the total output that can be produced by (and the income that accrues to) a fixed supply of domestic factors of production, thereby breaking the fixed link between factor inputs and total output that has been implicit above.

A fifth possible impact of devaluation on expenditure also arises from increasing the output that can be produced from a fixed amount of factor inputs. [8] When devaluation is substituted for controls on trade and other transactions, real output may increase because resources may be used more efficiently. [9] Real income will rise as a result, but domestic expenditure will presumably rise by less than total output and unless foreign demand increases by the full difference excess supply, hence deflationary pressures, will emerge. This resource allocation effect, when present, will generally have a much longer time dimension than the expectational or even the redistributional effects.

To return to the question of deflationary devaluation, the first (Laursen-Metzler) of these expenditure effects, if it exists, will weaken the tendency toward deflation. The redistributional effect could be either deflationary or inflationary. The expectational effect will generally strengthen the tendency to deflation following devaluation, and so, when it exists, will the Sohmen real income effect. Increased foreign investment, on the other hand, will always weaken it. Hereafter, all of these expenditure effects will be neglected, although we will return to the question of foreign investment later.

Finally, changes in monetary conditions may also affect domestic expenditure. This too will be taken up later.

16.3. Price Elasticities and Devaluation

Whether devaluation is actually deflationary also depends on the responsiveness of the trade balance to changes in relative prices. The more responsive trade is to changes in the exchange rate, the less likely devaluation is to be deflationary. But it will be shown later that devaluation can be

---

[8] Thus our assumption of "constant total output" here becomes "constant domestic inputs," e.g., full employment of domestic resources.

[9] This possibility has been emphasized by Sohmen [19].

deflationary even when the conventional test for successful devaluation, the Marshall-Lerner condition, is met, i.e., even when the sum of the country's price elasticity of demand for imports and the world's price elasticity of demand for the country's exports exceeds unity.

The formal relationships between devaluation, price elasticities, and the change (in either currency) in the balance of goods and services are shown in the appendix to this chapter. These relationships assume that domestic output (income) is unchanged. They are therefore partial relationships, indicating the impetus from devaluation that is transmitted to domestic output and income, not the final impact after induced changes in income and expenditure have taken place. [10] For a small country (implying an infinitely elastic supply of imports) and for a devaluation that is negligibly small, devaluation will have *no* effect on the trade balance measured in foreign currency ($\Delta B = 0$), and before allowing for induced income effects, if

$$\epsilon_m = \frac{X}{M} \left[\frac{\eta_x(1-\epsilon_x)}{\eta_x + \epsilon_x} \right] \tag{16.2}$$

Here ϵ_x is the foreign price elasticity of demand for the country's exports, η_x is the country's price elasticity of supply for exports, and ϵ_m is the country's price elasticity of demand for imports, all defined to be nonnegative. X/M is the ratio of exports of goods and services to imports of goods and services before the devaluation; this ratio is of course insensitive to the currency of measurement.

An analogous condition must be met if devaluation is to have no effect on the balance measured in domestic currency ($\Delta D = 0$):

$$\epsilon_m = 1 - \frac{X}{M} \left[\frac{\epsilon_x(1+\eta_x)}{\eta_x + \epsilon_x} \right] \tag{16.3}$$

Thus, for given values of the other parameters, the requirement of no change in the foreign currency balance imposes one value on ϵ_m, while the requirement of no change in the domestic currency balance imposes another.

In geometrical terms, Equations 16.2 and 16.3 form two boundaries defining three regions in demand elasticity space, one in which the balance deteriorates in terms of both currencies (the conventional case of "perverse"

---

[10] They also assume that the prices of exported goods do not influence the demand for imports and vice versa, i.e., that the cross elasticities between exports and imports are zero. For less developed countries heavily reliant on the export of primary products this assumption is reasonable, especially in the short run.

elasticities), one in which the balance improves in terms of both currencies, and one in which the balance improves in terms of one currency but deteriorates in terms of the other. These boundaries are plotted in Figure 16.1, treating η_x and X/M as parameters.

It can be seen from Figure 16.1 that there may be a substantial range of values for the two demand elasticities for which a successful devaluation ($\Delta B > 0$) may nonetheless be deflationary ($\Delta D < 0$). This outcome cannot occur if $\epsilon_m > 1$, but it can occur for values of ϵ_x greater than unity.

The curvature of the two boundaries is determined by the supply elasticity for exports η_x and is the same for given values of $\epsilon_x < 1$. If η_x is infinitely large, as would be the case when there is unemployment and underutilized capacity in the export industries, then the boundaries become straight lines and the terminal point of the upper boundary ($\Delta D = 0$) on the ϵ_x axis is M/X. If trade is initially balanced ($X/M=1$) then Equations 16.2 and 16.3 are identical, the two boundaries coincide, and the demand-elasticity field is divided into only two regions, one indicating deterioration in the balance and the other indicating improvement. If, in this case, costs are constant ($\eta_x = \infty$), the boundaries coincide in the conventional Marshall-Lerner condition for no change in the balance, $\epsilon_x + \epsilon_m = 1$, shown as a dashed line in Figure 16.1. It can be seen that there may be a substantial subregion, to the right of the dashed line, in which the Marshall-Lerner condition is met and devaluation is nonetheless deflationary.

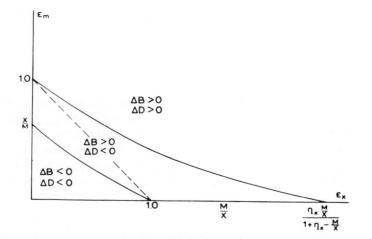

Fig. 16.1

Smaller supply elasticities result in greater curvature of both boundaries toward the origin, and in the limiting case of $\eta_x = 0$ result in the two regions shown in Figure 16.2. [11] In this case devaluation will always improve the foreign balance (provided $\epsilon_m > 0$), in our setting, but it will also always be deflationary if ϵ_m is smaller than $1-(X/M)$, regardless of the value of ϵ_x.

As is well-known, the elasticity formulas used here are normally inappropriate when total supply is less than perfectly elastic and monetary conditions are permissive, for switches in expenditure from imports to domestic goods will raise domestic prices and factor costs, thus weakening or even nullifying the relative price effects of devaluation. However, our focus here is on cases where devaluation is *de*flationary. Domestic spending is switched from domestic products to imports, not the other way around. This possibility does not salvage the formulas as general statements of changes in comparative static equilibrium positions, for the full impact of induced income and monetary changes are not taken into account, but it does show that induced domestic income and price changes may reinforce rather than weaken the relative price effects of devaluation. If the monetary authorities are attempting to maintain balance in the domestic economy before and after devaluation, they may have to take expansionary measures rather than contractionary ones.

---

[11] Here η_x refers to the elasticity of supply of exports, not of the economy as a whole. Short-run export supply could be inelastic even in the presence of unutilized resources if certain resources specific to the export industry (e.g., trees bearing export products) were fully utilized and if local consumption of export products were negligible.

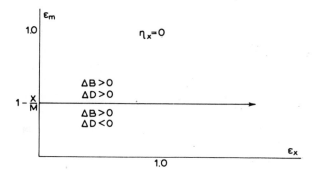

Fig. 16.2

Some comment is in order on the nature of the elasticity of demand for imports ϵ_m. Where imports are unencumbered by controls, this is a conventional price elasticity, indicating the reduction in demand for imports following a rise in their local currency prices, with money incomes unchanged. Where imports are subject to quotas or other controls, however, the "elasticity" here is to be interpreted as the actual change in imports following devaluation, before allowing for changes in money income, but after allowing for removal of controls maintained to suppress the payments deficit. In these circumstances the volume of imports may actually increase, depending on the extent of devaluation required to restore equilibrium without the controls and the degree of competition prevailing within the import sector. In any case, this "quasi-elasticity" may be expected to be small.

Moreover, the time dimension is also important. Price responsiveness, both of supply and of demand, is likely to be higher after economic units have had time to adjust to the new situation. The supply of exports may be quite inelastic in the short run but will become more responsive with the passage of time. If the elasticity of demand for imports is also low, devaluation by a country in deficit may be expected to be deflationary in the short run, as indicated in Figure 16.2. More local purchasing power will be drained away in the purchase of (net) imports. With the passage of time, spending will switch to local products. The boundaries of the middle zone will shift northeastward as supply responds increasingly to the new opportunities. As this occurs, the values for ϵ_m consistent with deflation also increase. The values of ϵ_x consistent with deflation decline but may remain quite high (compare Figure 16.1 with Figure 16.2).

16.4. Discrete Devaluations

The foregoing analysis has assumed that the devaluation is sufficiently small that its magnitude can be neglected in the analysis. Yet in the "adjustable peg" regime of fixed exchange rates prevailing under the rules of the International Monetary Fund, this assumption possibly introduces important error, since devaluations are usually nonnegligible in amount, typically ranging from 10 to 50%. In fact, however, allowance for discrete devaluation does not require substantial modification of the above results except for very large devaluations.

The analogues to Equations 16.2 and 16.3 become quite complex when the effects of a discrete devaluation are taken into account; and of course the results depend on the size of the devaluation itself. The analysis can be simplified by considering only the two extreme conditions on export supply, $\eta_x = \infty$ and $\eta_x = 0$. The geometrical results are shown in Figures 16.3 and 16.4 respectively. They depict k and ϵ_m along the axes, with ϵ_x and X/M treated as parameters. As before, two boundaries, defined by $\Delta B = 0$ and $\Delta D = 0$, divide the field into regions. The rightmost points of the boundaries in Figure 16.3 terminate on the boundary lines of Figure 16.1 (Figure 16.3 has been drawn for $\epsilon_x = 0.5$), where the magnitude of the devaluation is negligibly small. The three parameters ϵ_x, ϵ_m, and k define a three-dimensional space which can be imagined by putting the k axis perpendicular to the page (the $\epsilon_x - \epsilon_m$ plane) in Figure 16.1. Figure 16.3 represents one cross section of that space.

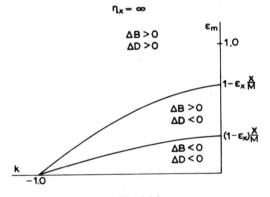

Fig. 16.3

It can be seen in Figure 16.3 that the region of deflationary devaluation narrows as the magnitude of the devaluation increases, but it remains substantial except for very large devaluations. For values of $\epsilon_x < 0.5$, however, the middle region first *increases* its vertical dimension as the devaluation gets larger, then subsequently decreases. [12] Thus in this case a discrete devalua-

[12] To show this, we can set Equations 16.A3 and 16.A4 in the Appendix equal to zero, calculate the slope $(\partial \epsilon_m / \partial k)$ of the two schedules shown in Figure 16.3, and evaluate them at $k = 0$.

(from 16.A3) $\left(\dfrac{\partial \epsilon_m}{\partial k} \right)_3 = \dfrac{X}{M}(1 - \epsilon_x) \left[1 - \dfrac{X}{M}(1 - \epsilon_x) \right]$ at $k = 0$.

(from 16.A4) $\left(\dfrac{\partial \epsilon_m}{\partial k} \right)_4 = \dfrac{X}{M} \epsilon_x \left[1 - \dfrac{X}{M} \epsilon_x \right]$ at $k = 0$.

It can be seen that for $\epsilon_x = 0.5$ these two expressions are equal. For $\epsilon_x < 0.5$, $(\partial \epsilon_m / \partial k)_3 > (\partial \epsilon_m / \partial k)_4$, implying that the region bounded by the two schedules first increases in the ϵ_m dimension as $-k$ becomes larger.

tion runs a somewhat larger chance of being deflationary than is evident from
Figure 16.1.

Figure 16.4 shows the opposite extreme case where exports are completely
inelastic in supply, adding a third dimension k to Figure 16.2. Here the region
of deflationary devaluation is obviously insensitive to the elasticity of
demand for exports, since supply cannot respond. As already noted, in this
case devaluation will always improve the balance measured in foreign
currency.

Figure 16.3 shows that a sufficiently large devaluation will always improve
the trade balance (within the framework of this static analysis), regardless of
the size of the demand elasticities (so long as $\epsilon_m > 0$). Thus the "stability
conditions" so frequently discussed in the literature on exchange rates are not

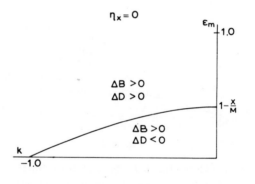

Fig. 16.4

applicable to discrete changes in exchange rates; certain effects that grow
with the magnitude of the devaluation and eventually assure improvement in
the balance are normally neglected. In particular, for a given (discrete)
devaluation, the percentage decline in export prices (leading to loss of foreign
earnings if $\epsilon_x < 1$) will be smaller than the percentage increase in domestic
prices of imported goods (leading to a fall in demand for imports), and this
discrepancy will grow with the size of the devaluation. This effect pointing
toward improvement is reinforced if $X < M$, since the decline in export
earnings applies to a smaller base than the decline in import volume. [13]

---

[13] See the Appendix. The elasticities used here are arc elasticities, and they therefore

16.5. Deflation Reinforces Devaluation

One general conclusion to be drawn from this discussion is that devaluation-induced changes in aggregate demand, far from undoing the effects of devaluation on the trade balance, actually in certain cases can be expected to *reinforce* the effects of devaluation on the balance. It is generally assumed that the price effects of devaluation will be weakened or even eliminated if aggregate money demand is permitted to rise in response to the devaluation.[14] But if devaluation worsens the balance in terms of domestic currency, expenditure on domestic output (hence domestic income) will be depressed and that will contribute toward a further improvement in the balance. In the "Keynesian" case of infinitely elastic supply for both imports and exports, where no government action is taken to compensate for the changes in income but monetary action is taken to hold interest rates constant, the ultimate effect of devaluation on the trade balance (ΔB^*) will be

$$\Delta B^* = \Delta B - (r + \Delta r)\frac{m}{s+m}\,\Delta D = \frac{s}{s+m}\,[\Delta B + k\,\frac{m}{s}\,B] \qquad (16.4)$$

where m is the marginal propensity to import out of additional income, s is the marginal propensity not to spend out of additional income, and foreign repercussions are ignored. Clearly if $\Delta D < 0$, the "final" improvement in the balance will exceed the "initial" improvement. This contrasts with the more usual formulation under these assumptions, $\Delta B^* = [s/(s+m)]\Delta B$, where the final improvement (after allowing for income effects) is clearly less than the initial improvement, and possibly substantially less. This conventional expression is in error even when devaluation is expansionary, since as we have seen ΔD cannot be equated with ΔB except when trade is initially in balance.

This analysis implies that devaluation, even successful devaluation, may generate unemployment and underutilization of capacity and hence without corrective policy may lead to a waste of resources. Under these circumstances, the economic authorities may rightly choose to *expand* total domestic expenditure, contrary to the advice usually given, and they can do so without weakening the "initial" effects of devaluation on the balance (ΔB). However, since for moderate devaluations the devaluation-induced deflation will always be less than the initial imbalance measured in domestic currency, the

take on values appropriate to the devaluation in question. They need not be the same as the elasticities evaluated for small changes in relative prices around the pre-devaluation exchange rate. Obviously, however, if the magnitude of the arc elasticity of demand for imports *declines* sufficiently rapidly as the devaluation is increased, even large devaluations may not improve the trade balance.

[14] See Alexander [1], Black [4] and Tsiang [20].

Table 16.1

Devaluation-Induced Change in Demand as a Percentage of the Initial Level of Imports[a]

Initial trade ratio (X/M)	Proportionate devaluation $(-k)$				
	0.1	0.2	0.3	0.4	0.5
0.9	−0.3	+0.1	1.6	5.0	11.7
0.8	−0.9	−1.1	−0.5	1.7	6.7
0.7	−1.4	−2.4	−2.6	−1.7	1.7
0.6	−2.0	−3.6	−4.8	−4.0	−3.3
0.5	−2.5	−4.9	−6.9	−8.4	−8.3

[a] On the assumption $\eta_x = \infty$, $\epsilon_m = \epsilon_x = 0.5$.
Source: Computed from Equation 16.A4.

permissible expansion is limited. [15] Table 16.1 gives some illustrative values of the impact of devaluation on aggregate demand, relative to the initial level of imports.

These results are perhaps paradoxical. They can be seen from another angle, however, which shows how the devaluation itself generates deflationary pressures that may require conscious expansionary monetary or fiscal actions to offset them. It was assumed that the net capital inflow is fixed in terms of foreign currency and that the proceeds accrue to the government, such as would occur under many foreign assistance programs. Devaluation will raise the local currency proceeds from this capital inflow as well as that from the sale of reserves, and these proceeds will accrue either to the government or to the central bank. Unless the government increases its local expenditures commensurately, the effect will be very much like the imposition of excise taxes on imported goods, an act of contractionary fiscal policy. Given institutional arrangements in most less developed countries, in particular the arrangement whereby government banking is done at the central bank, the contractionary fiscal policy will also be accompanied by contractionary monetary policy.

To be sure, some of these contractionary effects will be offset by the stimulus to exports and rising incomes in the export sector. But if the foreign

[15] This follows directly from Equation 16.1: for successful devaluation ($\Delta B > 0$) of less than 50%, $\Delta D < D$ in absolute magnitudes. This may not be negligible, however. For a country where imports amount to 20% of GNP and exports are only 60% as high as imports, the deflationary impact of a barely successful 50% devaluation would be nearly 8% of GNP.

elasticity of demand for exports is sufficiently low, and if imports exceed exports by a sufficient margin, the contractionary effects exerted on the import side will dominate the expansionary effects on the export side.

The argument that devaluation will not work when an economy is operating at full capacity without additional, complementary monetary and fiscal contraction is inapplicable in this case, for under these circumstances devaluation has, as it were, its own "built-in" contractionary monetary and fiscal measures. [16]

Nothing has been said so far about changes in domestic investment resulting from devaluation-induced changes in domestic monetary conditions. If before devaluation the impact of reserve losses on the domestic money supply was exactly offset by domestic credit creation, and if all capital inflow accrues to the government, then a devaluation that restores payments balance will result in a steady change in the domestic credit base in the amount by which the trade deficit has changed, measured in domestic currency. [17] To the extent that the money supply was rising before devaluation, a deflationary devaluation will automatically dampen, and possibly reverse, the increase. In any case, under the postulated circumstances, a devaluation that reduces the level of spending on domestic output will also reduce the money supply, compared to what it would otherwise be. Because the impact on the money supply is a continuing one, contraction of domestic credit will ultimately reinforce the deflationary expenditure effects by damping down domestic investment.

[16] Tsiang [20], in particular, has argued on the basis of equilibrium analysis that with a "Keynesian" neutral monetary policy — under which the monetary authorities act so as to hold interest rates unchanged — devaluation will not improve the trade balance under conditions of full employment. On the basis of the disequilibrium analysis developed here, in contrast, devaluation will improve the trade balance because the devaluation itself induces the release of more than enough capacity to permit a reduction of the import surplus in real terms.

[17] Let H represent central bank purchases or sales of domestic assets (e.g., loans to the government) per period, and K represent (constant) capital inflow measured in foreign currency. Then the money supply will be unchanging before devaluation if $H = -(1/r)(B + K)$. For a devaluation that restores payments balance, $\Delta B = -(B + K)$, and the per period increase in government receipts from the capital inflow is

$$ -\frac{kK}{r(1+k)} = \frac{1}{r}\Delta B - \Delta D . $$

Thus the increase in government receipts exceeds the government borrowing before devaluation, $(1/r)\,\Delta B$, by $-\Delta D$. Maintaining a constant nominal money supply will therefore require a per period *increase* in government spending or in credit to the private sector by this amount if $\Delta D < 0$. The real money supply will of course fall because of the rise in import prices.

The devaluation will, of course, increase the profitability of investment in the export and import-competing sectors, and to the extent that the resulting incentive to invest is neither blunted by tighter monetary conditions nor offset by reduced investment in the nontrade sector (where profitability has fallen), the initial deflationary impact of the devaluation will be mitigated or even reversed.

Finally, the role of foreign investment inflows must be considered. Two alternative assumptions come to mind: (1) Net capital inflow is fixed in foreign currency but the domestic currency proceeds accrue to private investors rather than to the government, and (2) Net capital inflow is fixed in terms of domestic currency, as might be the case for certain forms of private investment. In the first case, devaluation will lead to larger domestic currency proceeds accruing to the foreign investor, and to the extent that he spends these proceeds domestically (or someone else borrows them for domestic expenditure), this will impart an expansionary force that must be added to the impact of the (domestic currency) change in the trade balance. In the second case, elimination of the payments deficit will require an improvement in the trade balance (in foreign currency) large enough to offset the devaluation-induced decline in capital inflow as well as the initial payments deficit. In either case, and for combinations of them, a devaluation that eliminates the deficit will be expansionary by the amount of the initial payments deficit, measured in domestic currency. [18] If devaluation induces an *in*flow of private foreign capital (because profits in the export industries are higher, etc.), then the improvement in the trade balance required to eliminate the payments deficit is correspondingly reduced, but the foreign investment will provide an expansionary impetus to the economy.

Thus the possibility of deflationary devaluation arises solely (apart from redistributional and other expenditure effects discussed earlier) from the presence of capital inflow accruing to the government, which in turn is assumed not to respond fully and at once to increased "revenues" by increasing its domestic expenditures. This set of circumstances is far more common today than it was in the past, perhaps explaining the earlier neglect of the possibility of deflationary devaluation.

----

[18] Consider the case where initially $B + K < 0$ and capital inflow K is fixed in terms of domestic currency. Then devaluation will result in a proportionate decline in the foreign-currency value of capital inflows, and elimination of the payments deficit will require a correspondingly larger improvement in the trade balance: $\Delta(B + K) = -(B + K)$. Then $\Delta(B + K) = r(1 + k)\Delta D + k(B + K)$, so $\Delta D = -(1/r)(B + K)$, which is positive.

An analogous analysis may be applied when the capital inflow is fixed in terms of foreign currency but the domestic currency proceeds are automatically spent.

16.6. Actual Values of the Parameters

Real world relevance is given to the foregoing analysis because many countries do in fact have substantial and continuing deficits in their trade in goods and services. In 1967 no fewer than 28 countries, listed in Table 16.2, had a ratio of exports to imports of goods and services less than 0.8. Most of these countries were recipients of substantial amounts of foreign assistance. These ratios suggest that the middle region of Figure 16.1 (which is drawn for $X/M = 0.6$) could in fact be an important one.

Data on demand and supply elasticities are much more difficult to obtain. As noted earlier, however, both the elasticity of supply of exports and the elasticity of demand for imports are likely to be small in the period immediately following a devaluation, although they may be expected to increase with time. Second, import demand elasticities in many less developed countries are held down both by the composition of those countries' imports (oriented heavily to raw materials, capital goods, and in some cases food-stuffs) and by import policies that do not permit changes in relative prices to express themselves fully in changing the demand for imports. If imports are already rationed through quotas or exchange licensing, raising the domestic currency price of foreign exchange needed to import may well have little or

Table 16.2
Ratio of Exports to Imports (Goods and Services), 1967

Mali [a]	0.36	Dominican Republic	0.72
Lesotho [b]	0.48	Nicaragua	0.72
Pakistan	0.49	Paraguay	0.72
Dahomey	0.54	Indonesia	0.73
Jordan	0.57	Sierra Leone	0.74
India	0.60	United Arab Republic	0.74
South Korea	0.60	Nigeria	0.74
Somalia	0.62	Costa Rica	0.75
South Vietnam	0.62	Peru	0.76
Tunisia	0.63	Spain	0.77
Malawi	0.66	Guatemala	0.77
Israel	0.68	Mexico	0.77
Greece	0.68	Iceland	0.77
Haiti	0.70	Togo	0.79

[a] 1967/1968
[b] 1966/1967

Source: International Monetary Fund, *Balance of Payments Yearbook*, Volume 20, 1963 −1967.

Table 16.3
Examples of Deflationary Devaluation

Country	Year of devaluation	Change in balance on goods and services in year following devaluation		Column (2) as a percentage of GNP in the year of devaluation
		(in millions of U.S. dollars)	(in millions of local currency)	
		(1)	(2)	(3)
Colombia	1962	30	−1340	4.0
Iceland	1960	2	− 190	2.3
India	1966	202 [a]	−2102 [a]	0.9
Israel	1962	11 [a]	− 460 [a]	6.9
Korea	1961	64	−4300	1.5
Korea	1964	112	− 300	0.1

[a] Two years following devaluation.

Source: *International Financial Statistics.*

no effect on the quantity imported, yet it will reduce purchasing power in the hands of the public. Moreover, if devaluation is accompanied by some relaxation of quantitative restrictions on imports, as it frequently is, the value of imports in *foreign* currency might actually increase. Geometrically, the predevaluation ratio X/M can be regarded as having been lowered, and the middle region of Figure 16.1 is thereby increased in size. Devaluation under these circumstances is even more likely to be deflationary.

Table 16.3 lists several currency devaluations, drawn from the early 1960s, in which the trade balance in fact improved in terms of foreign currency but deteriorated in terms of domestic currency, therefore exerting some deflationary impact on the domestic economy. These figures obviously record influences other than the devaluation alone, but the movement of the trade positions in opposite directions according to the currency of measurement reflects the impact of devaluation on the initial trade deficit when the demand for imports is inelastic. In Israel and India the trade position in foreign currency actually worsened in the year immediately following devaluation, owing in part to import liberalization in each case, but improved sharply in the second year following devaluation though not by enough to reduce the trade deficit in domestic currency as compared with the year preceding devaluation. As already noted, it takes some time, certainly more than a year, for a devaluation to take full effect. [19]

[19] For a summary of the experience following 24 devaluations in capital-importing countries, see Cooper [5].

16.7. Summary

In a range of circumstances common to many less developed countries, successful devaluation will be deflationary rather than inflationary, as is usually supposed. Devaluation will of course increase the domestic prices of imports and import-competing goods; it is precisely this price increase that is deflationary, since higher money payments for imports withdraw purchasing power and thereby reduce expenditures on domestic goods. The outcome is very much analogous to that created by an increase in excise taxes, which raises prices but also reduces excess demand for domestic output. This phenomenon, which might be called the "excise tax effect" of devaluation, may go part way toward explaining the business slumps that have frequently occurred following devaluation by less developed countries. [20]

When these circumstances are met, further deflation through monetary and fiscal policies, usually said to be necessary to make devaluation work, may be both unnecessary and inappropriate. Indeed, there may even be occasions on which *expansionary* policies might accompany devaluation, in order to avoid unnecessary waste of resources, although generally such expansion need not be very large. If deflation is desired on domestic grounds, on the other hand, devaluation may contribute toward that end, and the resulting deflation will reinforce the price-switching effects of devaluation on the trade balance.

Apart from the limitations that have already been mentioned, this analysis makes no allowance for wage-price spiraling following the devaluation-induced rise in domestic prices of foreign trade goods. Cost inflation induced by the devaluation may seriously threaten the success of a devaluation and will always test the nerves of the monetary and fiscal authorities.

Appendix

For a change in exchange rate Δr, holding money incomes and interest rates constant, the balance on goods and services measured in foreign currency B may be expected to change by

---

[20] The underlying analysis is in principle symmetrical, so a foreign aid donor country, with $X/M > 1$ due to outflows of capital, may find that a devaluation will worsen its trade balance in foreign currency but improve it in domestic currency, thus imparting an expansionary impetus to the economy that unless checked will reinforce the initial deterioration in the balance. A necessary (but not sufficient) condition for this unfortunate confluence is $\epsilon_x < 1$.

$$\Delta B = kM \left\{ \frac{X}{M} \frac{\eta_x(1-\epsilon_x)}{\eta_x + \epsilon_x} - \frac{\epsilon_m(1+\eta_m)}{\eta_m + \epsilon_m} \right\} \tag{16.A1}$$

The balance measured in *domestic* currency D will change by

$$\Delta D = kM_d \left\{ -\frac{X}{M} \frac{\epsilon_x(1+\eta_x)}{\epsilon_x + \eta_x} + \frac{\eta_m(1-\epsilon_m)}{\eta_m + \epsilon_m} \right\} \tag{16.A2}$$

where ϵ_m = price elasticity of demand for imports, ϵ_x = price elasticity of foreign demand for the country's exports, η_m = price elasticity of foreign supply of imports, η_x = price elasticity of supply of exports, X = initial level of exports of goods and services, M = initial level of imports of goods and services (subscript d indicates measurement in domestic currency), and $k = \Delta r/r$ = the proportionate change in exchange rate.

Setting Equation 16.A1 and 16.A2 equal to zero, taking limits for $\eta_m = \infty$, and rearranging terms, leads to Equations 16.2 and 16.3 in the text.

Expression 16.A2 was first derived by Joan Robinson [18] although the underlying analysis goes back to Bickerdike [3]. The derivation of both expressions can be found in Alexander [1]. Both of these authors, however, derived the above expressions by neglecting certain interaction terms, a procedure that is justifiable only if k is negligibly small and if interest in the analysis is focussed on stability in the exchange market.

For discrete devaluations of nonnegligible amount, the interaction terms cannot be safely neglected. Unfortunately, including them explicitly involves complex expressions in fractional orders of k and the elasticities. Some idea of the influence of these terms can be gained, however, by considering the two analytically simple cases $\eta_x = \infty$ and $\eta_x = 0$, both for $\eta_m = \infty$, as before, For these cases (shown as Figures 16.3 and 16.4) we have

for $\eta_m = \eta_x = \infty$:

$$\Delta B = kM \left[\frac{X}{M}(1-\epsilon_x) - \frac{\epsilon_m}{1+k(1-\epsilon_m)} \right] \tag{16.A3}$$

$$\Delta D = kM_d \left[-\frac{X}{M} \left(\frac{\epsilon_x}{1+k} \right) + \frac{1-\epsilon_m}{1+k(1-\epsilon_m)} \right] \tag{16.A4}$$

and for $\eta_m = \infty; \eta_x = 0$:

$$\Delta B = kM \left[\frac{-\epsilon_m}{1+k(1-\epsilon_m)} \right] \tag{16.A5}$$

$$\Delta D = kM_d \left[-\frac{X}{M} \frac{1}{1+k} + \frac{1-\epsilon_m}{1+k(1-\epsilon_m)} \right] \tag{16.A6}$$

The elasticities in Equations 16.A3 to 16.A6 are arc elasticities and may therefore vary with the size of the devaluation. They have been somewhat arbitrarily defined here so as to have the desirable property that $\epsilon_x = 1$ will leave total foreign exchange receipts from exports unchanged and $\epsilon_m = 1$ will leave total domestic currency payments for imports unchanged; thus,

$$\epsilon_x = -\frac{\Delta Q}{Q} \left(\frac{q+\Delta q}{\Delta q} \right) \quad \text{and} \quad \epsilon_m = -\left(\frac{\Delta Q'}{Q'+\Delta Q'} \right) \frac{q'}{\Delta q'}$$

where Q is the quantity of exports and q its price in foreign currency, and Q' is the quantity of imports and q' its price in domestic currency. These definitions differ slightly from those normally used for arc elasticities, but the major conclusions from the analysis are not sensitive to this alteration.

Equations 16.A3 and 16.A5 indicate why *some* level of devaluation will succeed in reducing a trade deficit, regardless of the values of the demand elasticities. As long as there is some price sensitivity to the demand for imports ($\epsilon_m > 0$), a sufficiently large devaluation will lead to a fall in import volume that more then compensates for the loss of export receipts, since export receipts will decline at most by $kX(1-\epsilon_x)$ and import volume (= payments, since foreign prices are assumed constant) will fall by $kM[\epsilon_m/(1+k(1-\epsilon_m))]$. For $k<0$, $-k$ (the proportionate fall in export prices) $< -k/(1+k)$ (the proportionate rise in import prices); therefore for k sufficiently close to -1 the reduction in imports will outweigh any reduction in exports.

The elasticity expressions give only the initial impetus to the trade balance, before allowance for induced changes in income and expenditure. A more complete analysis, for the limiting case in which prices of all domestic output (including exports) are unchanged, would start from the identity: $Y = E + D$, whence

$$\Delta Y = \frac{\partial E}{\partial r} \Delta r + \frac{\partial E}{\partial Y} \Delta Y + \frac{\partial D}{\partial r} \Delta r + \frac{\partial D}{\partial Y} \Delta Y \tag{16.A7}$$

or

$$\Delta Y = \frac{\Delta r}{s+m} \left[\frac{\partial E}{\partial r} + \frac{\partial D}{\partial r} \right] \tag{16.A8}$$

where E is aggregate domestic expenditure, $s = 1 - (\partial E/\partial Y)$, and m is the marginal propensity to import ($= -\partial D/\partial Y$). For a discrete devaluation $(\partial D/\partial r)\Delta r$ is given by Equation 16.A4. If in addition $(\partial E/\partial r) = 0$, the total change in the trade balance (in foreign currency) is given by Equation 16.4 in the text. This formulation assumes that credit conditions are maintained so as to avoid shifting the expenditure function.

References

[1] Alexander, Sidney S. "Effects of a Devaluation: A Simplified Synthesis of Elasticities and Absorption Aproaches." *American Economic Review* XLIX (March 1959) pp. 22–42.

[2] Bernstein, E.M. "Strategic Factors in Balance of Payments Adjustment." IMF *Staff Papers*, V (August 1956) pp. 151–169.

[3] Bickerdike, C.F. "The Instability of Foreign Exchange." *Economic Journal* XXX (March 1920) pp. 118–122.

[4] Black, J. "A Savings and Investment Approach to Devaluation." *Economic Journal*, LXIX (June 1959) pp. 267–274.

[5] Cooper, R.N. "An Assessment of Currency Devaluation in Developing Countries." Chapter 13 in Gustav Ranis (ed.), *Government and Economic Development*, New Haven: Yale University Press, 1971.

[6] Day, Alan. "Devaluation and the Balance of Payments." *Economica*, XVII (November 1950) pp. 431–437.

[7] Diaz-Alejandro, Carlos F. "A Note on the Impact of Devaluation and the Redistributive Effect." *Journal of Political Economy*, LXXI (December 1963) pp. 577–580.

[8] Diaz-Alejandro, Carlos F. *Exchange Rate Devaluation in a Semi-Industrialized Country*. Cambridge: The M.I.T. Press, 1965.

[9] Fleming, J. Marcus. "Exchange Depreciation, Financial Policy, and the Domestic Price Level." IMF *Staff Papers*, VI (April 1958) pp. 289–322.

[10] Gerakis, Andreas S. "Recession in the Initial Phase of a Stabilization Program: The Experience of Finland." IMF *Staff Papers*, XI (November 1964) pp. 434–445.

[11] Haberler, Gottfried. "The Market for Foreign Exchange and the Stability of the Balance of Payments." *Kyklos* (1949) pp. 193–218.

[12] Harberger, Arnold C. "Currency Depreciation, Income, and the Balance of Trade." *Journal of Political Economy* LVIII (February 1950) pp. 47–60.

[13] Hirschmann, Albert O. "Devaluation and the Trade Balance: A Note." *Review of Economics and Statistics* XXXI (February 1949) pp. 50–53.

[14] Jones, Ronald E. "Depreciation and the Dampening Effect of Income Changes." *Review of Economics and Statistics*, XLII (February 1960) pp. 74–80.

[15] Kemp, Murray C. *The Pure Theory of International Trade*. Englewood Cliffs, N.J.: Prentice-Hall Inc., 1964.

[16] Kindleberger, C.P., "Liberal Policies vs. Controls in the Foreign Trade of Developing Countries." in J.D. Theberge (ed.), *Economics of Trade and Development*, New York: John Wiley & Sons, 1968.

[17] Laursen, S. and Metzler, L.A. "Flexible Exchange Rates and the Theory of Employment." *Review of Economics and Statistics*, XXXII (November 1950) pp. 281–299.

[18] Robinson, Joan. "The Foreign Exchanges," Chapter 4 in *Readings in the Theory of International Trade*, New York: McGraw-Hill Book Co. Inc., Blakiston Division, 1949.

[19] Sohmen, Egon. "The Effect of Devaluation on the Price Level," *Quarterly Journal of Economics* LXXII (May 1958) pp. 273–283.

[20] Tsiang, S.C., "The Role of Money in Trade-Balance Stability: Synthesis of the Elasticity and Absorption Approaches." *American Economic Review*, LI (December 1961) pp. 912–936.

CHAPTER 17

THE INTERNATIONAL DISTRIBUTION OF MONEY IN A GROWING WORLD ECONOMY

Robert A. MUNDELL

The purpose of this article is to analyze the conditions of world monetary equilibrium in a comprehensive bi-country framework that links inflation, interest rates, money stocks, rates of credit expansion, and the balance of payments in a growing world.

17.1. The Conditions of Monetary Equilibrium

The model we shall introduce for this purpose [1] requires balance in two markets: a market for claims (against money) and a market for capital against money. It assumes that in making the choice between holding money, claims and capital the typical investor balances expected yields on each asset, where expectations are based on an extrapolation of current rates of change. Thus, if prices of commodities are rising at the rate π, it is assumed that they will go on rising at that rate; and similarly for changes in the prices of claims. This assumption, which would be fully justified only in consideration of an economy in growth-inflation equilibrium, enables us to isolate some important comparative dynamic properties of an international economic system, and to develop a convenient representation of it in graphical form.

The line ii in Figure 17.1 refers to the money-claims market in which the nominal interest rate is taken to be a declining function of real money balances, plotted on the abscissa. At low interest rates the community is willing to hold the outstanding stock of securities only if the quantity of real

---

[1] This article will appear in my forthcoming book *Monetary Theory: Inflation, Interest and Growth in the World Economy* (Pacific Palisades, Calif.: Goodyear Publishing Co.).

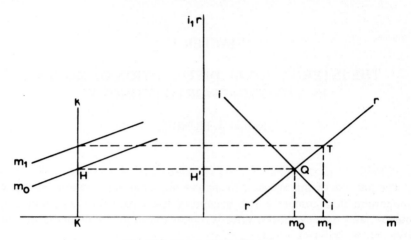

Fig. 17.1. The static equilibrium.

money balances is high. When the rate of interest rises people shift out of money into claims, raising the price level and lowering the real value of money balances. We shall write this function as

$$i = i(m) \qquad\qquad (17.1)$$

where $m = M/P$, the real value of money holdings, and i is the rate of interest paid on claims.

The rr schedule plots the relation between the real rate of interest and the stock of real money balances at which the money-capital market is an equilibrium. It can be derived by making use of the extension of the diagram in the left-hand quadrant. The abscissa in this quadrant measures the quantity of capital, and the schedule KK indicates the stock of capital, a magnitude which is marching to the left over time under conditions of growth but which at any instant can be regarded as given. The line m_0 identifies the schedule of the marginal product of capital corresponding to the quantity of real money balances m_0. This intersects the capital stock schedule KK at the point H and establishes the real rate of interest corresponding to the level of real money balances m_0. Thus Q is one point on the rr schedule.

Consider now an increase in the quantity of real money balances to, say, m_1. This raises the marginal product of capital and shifts the H line upwards, establishing a new point of equilibrium on the rr line at the point T. In a similar way all the points on rr can be established, and it is readily seen that this schedule must have a positive slope. I shall write this function in the form

$$r = r(m) \qquad\qquad (17.2)$$

where r is the real rate of interest.

The equilibrium interest rate and level of real balances is determined, in the absence of growth of capital or money, by the intersection of the two schedules, that is, at the point Q. The equilibrium condition is that $i = r$, so that

$$i\left(\frac{M}{P}\right) = r\left(\frac{M}{P}\right) \qquad\qquad (17.3)$$

determines the equilibrium level of real money balances m_0. At levels of real money balances lower than m_0 the marginal product of real capital is lower than the marginal product of money, and asset holders would shift out of commodities into money lowering the price level and raising the quantity of real money balances. To put the question differently, raising the rate of interest above r_0 would create an excess supply of money and capital and an excess demand for securities, inducing a fall in the rate of interest and a return to the equilibrium at Q. Thus Q is an equilibrium that is stable.

Now consider the effects of taking growth explicitly into account (Figure 17.2). Growth induces an increased desire for liquidity (hoarding) and thus an increase in spending less than the increase in real output. If we define the rate of growth in the demand for real money balances as proportion of the capital stock, we can subtract it from the rr line to get $\lambda\lambda$. For simplicity of exposition, we shall also identify this schedule with the rate of growth of

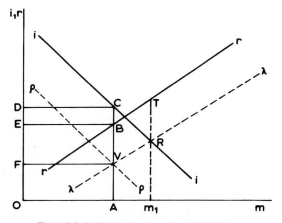

Fig. 17.2. Inflationary growth equilibrium.

output, an identification which is probably a valid approximation for certain types of output increases but is precise only under specific assumptions about the income elasticity of demand for real money balances. [2]

When the economy is growing but the stock of money is constant, the equilibrium will be at R. The price level will be falling at a rate equal to the rate of growth, and the real rate of interest will be higher than the nominal rate of interest by the deflation rate RT. The condition of equilibrium is that

$$i\left(\frac{M}{P}\right) - r\left(\frac{M}{P}\right) = \pi = -\lambda \, ,$$

where π is the rate of inflation and λ is the given rate of growth. Holders of money and claims to nominal income streams will experience capital gains at a rate equal to the rate of deflation.

Now consider the effects of a positive rate of monetary expansion. This can be represented on the diagram by drawing a line $\rho\rho$ beneath ii such that the vertical distance between the two schedules represents the rate of monetary expansion. The equilibrium will then be determined at the point where $\rho\rho$ and $\lambda\lambda$ intersect. Thus, for the schedule drawn in the diagram, a new equilibrium is reached at V. The equilibrium is characterized by the following phenomena:

$$r = OE = \text{the real interest rate;}$$
$$i = OD = \text{the money interest rate;}$$
$$\rho = FD = \text{the rate of monetary expansion;}$$
$$\lambda = FE = \text{the rate of growth;}$$
$$\pi = BC = \text{the rate of inflation.}$$

The equilibrium conditions are as follows:

$$i\left(\frac{M}{P}\right) - r\left(\frac{M}{P}\right) = \pi \, ,$$

[2] Real money balances are a component of wealth and thus affect saving and the rate of interest [see my "Inflation and Real Interest," *Journal of Political Economy* 71 (June 1963) 280–83] while the rate of growth of output itself will be affected by the productivity of capital; on the basis of these considerations the hoarding could be made endogenous to the system. My concern in this article, however, is with the international aspects of a long term model, and it seemed appropriate to avoid overburdening the exposition with details by treating growth exogenously. A more complete analysis is contained in my book on monetary theory (Pacific Palisades, Calif.: Goodyear 1971 V. Chapter 8). The present analysis should be interpreted as tracing out the implications of particular growth rates rather than explaining their determinants.

$\rho = \pi + \lambda$,

$\lambda = \lambda_0$,

$\rho = \rho_0$.

The comparative "statics" of the system are thus established. An increase in the rate of monetary expansion lowers the real interest rate, raises the money interest rate and lowers the level of real money balances. This is readily seen by differentiating the above system and noting that $(\partial i / \partial (M/P) < 0$ and $\partial r / \partial (M/P) > 0$.

17.2. Monetary Interaction Between Economies

Let us now consider the situation that arises when it becomes necessary or useful to divide the world economy into two or more distinct parts. Assume that the two parts use the same money and freely trade in goods but do not lend to one another. What monetary relationships would we expect to emerge? Let us assume first that the money supply in the world as a whole is fixed.

The first relationship is that money will move from slow-growing to fast-growing regions. *The inhabitants of the fast-growing country will keep expenditure below output to generate a balance of payments surplus in order to finance money accumulation.* This will exert deflationary pressure on the world as a whole. The effect, therefore, will be capital gains to the nongrowing region as the real value of their cash balances appreciates permitting them to export over time a fraction of their money stock to the other region. Equilibrium will be achieved when the world price level is declining at the rate sufficient to satisfy the desired increase in the real money stock in the growing country. The growing country finances its accumulations of new real money balances from two sources: (a) imports of money from the other region and (b) rising real value of hoards. The growing region's balance of trade surplus represents a transfer of resources to the nongrowing part analogous to the seigniorage gain when one country alone is the issuer of money.

The equilibrium is represented in Figure 17.3. Let us denote the two countries by A and B, the latter being the growing region. Equilibrium in the absence of growth would be established by the intersection of the rr and ii schedules in the two countries. Growth in B now involves a reduction in expenditure and releasing of goods for export (or reduction of imports) to

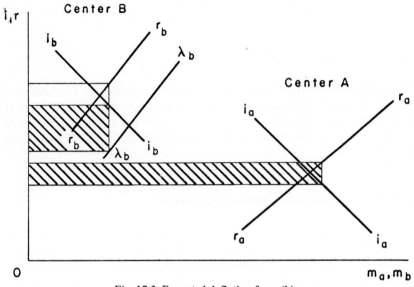

Fig. 17.3. Exported deflation from (b).

finance money accumulation. Deflationary pressure in B then results in a flow of goods to A in return for more imports of money, while the loss of money from A and the hoarding of money in B combine to produce deflationary pressure in the world as a whole. The conditions of equilibrium require that deflation in both countries go on at the same rate because of the connected markets, means that the difference between real and nominal interest rates must be the same in both countries. A second condition is that the desired increase in real money balances in the growing country B be equal to the actual increase generated by the sum of the capital gains on their existing stock of real money balances and B's balance of trade surplus. The latter must be equal to the trade deficit of country A, which in turn has to equal the increase in the real value of existing money balances in A. Taken together these conditions imply that

$$\frac{\lambda_b + \pi}{\pi} = -\frac{m_a}{m_b}$$

where the subscripts identify the countries. This means that the rate of world deflation due to growth in country B is

$$\pi = -\lambda_b \frac{m_b}{m_a + m_b}$$

that is, the rate of growth in B weighted by the size of B in relation to the world as a whole, the weights being the stocks of money. This result can easily be derived from the diagram since it implies that the two hatched areas are equal; they represent the real value of B's trade surplus and A's trade deficit.

It is a short step to take into account growth in country A. Growth in A creates more deflation in the world as a whole and diminishes A's deficit and B's surplus. When A and B grow at the same rate the deficit becomes zero, the appetite for real money balances in both countries being satisfied by the deflation in the world as a whole. This is readily seen from the generalization of the above formula:

$$\pi = -\frac{\lambda_a m_a + \lambda_b m_b}{m_a + m_b}.$$

17.3. Monetary Expansion in One Country

Let us now elaborate the model by allowing for monetary expansion. If, in Figure 17.3, country B had the right to issue money the authorities could create it by purchasing domestic assets and fully satisfy the hoarding demand occasioned by growth and eliminate the balance of payments surplus. Insofar as the balance of payments surplus may be regarded as a tax, the monetary independence implied by the right to issue money would enable the residents of B to avoid paying the tax.

It will be somewhat more instructive, however, if we first analyze the equilibrium that results when country A has the sole right to issue money. Consider in Figure 17.4 a given rate of money expansion in A equal to the vertical distance between $\rho_a \rho_a$ and $i_a i_a$. If A were isolated this would result in inflation in A equal to the rate of monetary expansion and a transfer of resources from A residents to the government of A. But when country B is taken into account the rate of inflation in A is mitigated. *The tax that A's government levied upon its citizens by the issuing of money will be paid partly by B.*

The exact position of equilibrium will again depend on the relative sizes of the two countries. The conditions of equilibrium require that the rates of inflation in the two countries must be the same and that A's deficit equals B's surplus. Thus the two hatched areas must be equal and

$$\rho m_a = \pi(m_a + m_b)$$

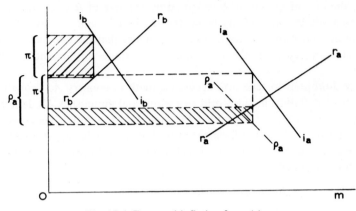

Fig. 17.4. Exported inflation from (a).

or

$$\frac{\pi}{\rho} = \frac{m_a}{m_a + m_b}.$$

This ratio measures the percentage of the tax that is borne by the residents of A, whereas

$$m_b \pi = m_a (\rho_a - \pi)$$

measures the trade surplus of B and the trade deficit of A—the seigniorage tax accruing to A because of its right to issue "world" money.

Let us now analyze the more complete system that emerges when A is issuing money and both countries are growing. How will the new money be distributed between the two countries and what balance of payments configuration will result?

The answers are provided in Figure 17.5. It will be convenient to identify five types of seigniorage arising from the monetary expansion in A. The total seigniorage is $\rho_a m_a$, which represents the purchasing power obtained by A's government when it issues money at the rate ρ_a expressed as a fraction of money held in A. Internal seigniorage is the tax on A's residents and, external seigniorage is the tax on B's residents.

I. The πm_a = internal inflation seigniorage. This is due to the need of residents in A to rebuild cash balance eroded by price inflation.

II. The $\lambda_a m_a$ = internal growth seigniorage. This is due to the need of residents in A to add to real cash balances because of growth. External

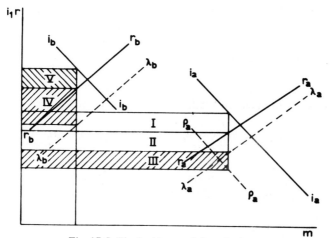

Fig. 17.5. The incidence of the seigniorage.

seigniorage is the tax on B's residents, and is equal to A's balance of payments deficit.

III. Here $(\rho_a - \pi - \lambda_a)m_a$ = external seigniorage. This can be interpreted as the flow excess supply of money in A, her balance of payments "deficit."

IV. The $\lambda_b m_b$ = external growth seigniorage. This arises from the desire of residents in B to acquire money to finance growth.

V. Here πm_b = external inflation seigniorage. This represents the real value of the desired increment in nominal money balances required to compensate for the capital losses suffered on existing balances.

Clearly, when A's ex ante deficit is equal to B's ex ante surplus

$$III = IV + V$$

and the system is in "equilibrium".

It will be convenient to have a symbolic characterization of some of these results. First, from the fact that total seigniorage

$$\rho_a m_a = I + II + III$$

we have

$$\rho_a m_a = \pi m_a + \lambda_a m_a + (\pi + \lambda_b) m_b$$

so

$$\frac{m_a}{m_b} = \frac{\pi + \lambda_b}{\rho_a - \pi - \lambda_a}.$$

Now B's "desired surplus" is

$$(\pi + \lambda_b)m_b$$

and A's "desired deficit" is

$$(\rho_a - \pi - \lambda_a)m_a$$

so that, when the two are in equilibrium the rate of inflation is

$$\pi = \frac{(\rho_a - \lambda_a)m_a - \lambda_b m_b}{m_a + m_b} = \frac{(\rho_a - \lambda_a)(m_a/m_b) - \lambda_b}{(m_a/m_b) + 1} = \frac{(\rho - \lambda_a)\sigma - \lambda_b}{\sigma + 1}$$

where σ is the ratio of money held in A to money held in B. The noninflationary rate of monetary expansion in A is thus

$$\rho = \frac{\lambda_b}{\sigma} + \lambda_a$$

Thus when $\lambda_b = 0$, A's money supply must grow at a rate equal to the rate of growth of her economy if price stability is to be preserved. Other results of this kind are readily obtained from the formula.

17.4. "Defensive" Monetary Expansion in B

The monopolized right to issue money grants to A the possibility not only the right of determining the rate of expansion of the means of exchange and therefore, indirectly, the rate of change in the world price level; and also the means of taxing real resources from the rest of the world in addition to her own citizens. We shall refer to this right as the *issue privilege*. To offset it or to ameliorate its more outrageous effects, country B will create her own currency and confine her losses to the foreign exchange component of the banking assets which are the counterpart of the monetary liabilities. What effect will this have on the equilibrium?

It should be apparent, that, for any given rate of monetary expansion in A, an increase in the rate of *credit* expansion in B is inflationary for the world as a whole. When there is an ex ante deficit in A, the monetary authorities in B accumulate reserves. To resist undesired reserves, they extend domestic credit and, in a sense, engage in competition for seigniorage that would otherwise accrue to A. The result is that the world price level as a whole rises at a more rapid rate than would otherwise occur. Suppose that, from a position of initial equilibrium, growth in B accelerates. This would ordinarily result in a surplus in B as residents hoard, and the result would be a deflation (or a slower rate of inflation) in the world as a whole as the ex ante surplus bids money away from A. But the demand-induced surplus in B can be prevented if B's authorities extend credit assuming that B's money is convertible into A's money and is therefore a perfect substitute for it for internal transactions and provide residents in B with the money they want through domestic banking operations. This prevents deflation or accelerates inflation for if the government in B had not expanded, residents in B would have had to finance growth by sucking money away from the rest of the world.

We might also consider the effects of a credit expansion in B without any initiating increase in hoarding. The effect is to create an excess supply of money and an ex ante deficit in B so that its central bank will lose reserves. Unless the extension of credit in B is large most of its effect will be taken up by a loss of reserves. But if B has initially very large reserves and can therefore afford a large extension of credit, the effects on the world money supply may be substantial and there would result a significant effect on the world price level. For a given rate of monetary expansion in A, the potential increase in the world price level that could be induced by credit expansion in B depends on the ratio of the stock of reserves in B as a proportion of the world money supply. As this fraction increases the power of B to raise world prices is increased.

These results are useful first approximations but they are not exact. To formulate more exact propositions it will be useful, first to present the effects of credit expansion in B diagrammatically, and then to develop the analysis in symbolic terms. It will simplify the diagrammatic exposition somewhat without loss of essential generality if we start off (Figure 17.6) with a situation in which the rate of credit expansion in B is zero and where the rate of monetary expansion in A is such as to ensure price stability in the world at large. A's rate of monetary expansion is AC which exceeds A's rate of growth BC by enough (AB) to finance B's rate of growth DE without any changes in the price level.

Now suppose that from this position, where B is running a surplus to accumulate desired real balances, the central bank in B expands credit by the full amount of the surplus, i.e., at the rate ED. If A now reduced her rate of monetary expansion to BC, then A's deficit and B's surplus would be corrected. But suppose instead that A maintains her rate of monetary expansion at the rate AC. Then the deficit in A is "unwanted" in B and there is an excess supply of money equal to the area $FGDE = ABHJ$, and a corresponding excess demand for goods. The price level must therefore rise to absorb the excess money.

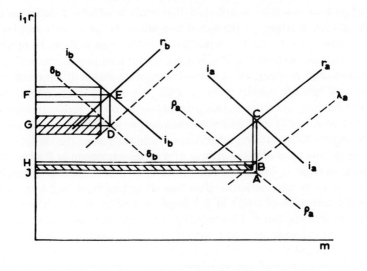

Fig. 17.6. Defensive measures in B.

Where will the new equilibrium be? The answer is found by establishing that level of real balances in A at which the following two conditions are met. First, the excess of the money over the real rate of interest in A must equal the excess in B. Second, the excess of A's rate of monetary expansion over the sum of her rate of growth and the rate of inflation multiplied by her stock of real money balances (A's ex ante deficit) must equal the excess of the sum of the inflation rate and B's growth rate over B's rate of credit expansion multiplied by the stock of real balances in B (B's ex ante surplus). The second condition means that the two hatched areas are equal.

We see, therefore, that B's attempt to eliminate her surplus is not wholly successful. The rate of credit creation DE causes inflation which increases the demand for additional money to compensate for the depreciation on existing balances.

To formulate the results exactly let us write the equilibrium conditions:

$$i_a(m_a) - r_a(m_a) = \pi = i_b(m_b) - r_b(m_b)$$
$$m_a(\rho_a - \lambda_a - \pi) = B = (\pi + \lambda_b - \delta_b)m_b$$

where B is the balance of payments deficit in A (surplus in B) and δ_b is the rate of credit expansion in B. [3] Now it is possible to see that when, initially, $\delta_b = 0$ and $\pi = 0$ the balance of payments deficit of A is

$$(\rho_a - \lambda_a)m_a = B = \lambda_b m_b \ .$$

When B now expands credit at the rate determined by the rate of growth of output, A's deficit becomes

$$(\rho_a - \lambda_a - \pi)m_a = B = (\pi)m_b$$

which is still positive if B's credit expansion results in inflation, as indeed it must since it reduces the excess flow demand for money in A. To correct her surplus by her own action alone B must expand credit at the rate

$$\delta_b = \lambda_b + \pi \ .$$

Now

$$\pi = (\rho_a - \lambda_a)\frac{m_a}{m_a + m_b} + (\delta_b - \lambda_b)\frac{m_b}{m_a + m_b}$$

[3] Differentiation of these equations with respect to δ_b yields

$$\frac{dm_a}{d\delta_b} = m_b \frac{(i'_b - r'_b)}{\Delta} < 0$$

$$\frac{dm_b}{d\delta_b} = m_b \frac{(i'_a - r'_a)}{\Delta} < 0$$

$$\frac{d\pi}{d\delta_b} = \frac{(i'_a - r'_a)(i'_b - r'_b)}{\Delta} > 0$$

$$\frac{dB}{d\delta_b} = \frac{m_b(\rho_a - \lambda_a - \pi) - m_a(i'_a - r'_a)}{\Delta}(i'_b - r'_b)$$

where

$$\Delta = \begin{vmatrix} i'_a - r'_a & r'_b - i'_b & 0 \\ \rho_a - \lambda_a - \pi & \delta_b - \pi - \lambda_b & -m_a - m_b \\ 0 & i'_b - r'_b & -1 \end{vmatrix} ;$$

the inequalities are based on the assumption that $\Delta > 0$.

or simply,

$$\pi = \rho_a - \lambda_a .$$

Thus,

$$\delta_b = \lambda_b + \rho_a - \lambda_a .$$

Country B's expansion rate must exceed her growth rate by the excess of A's rate of monetary expansion over A's growth rate. This is because the inflation itself induced by B's credit expansion increases the hoarding demand for money.

17.5. Conclusion

This article has presented an image of the world payments situation different from that found in the literature and currently used to interpret balance of payments statistics. For a given rate of credit creation in each of the countries the balance of payments is determined by the rates of growth of transactions and output.

In the real world, of course, rates of credit expansion are policy variables and will in most cases be positive functions of domestic growth rates. Domestic growth creates in the first instance a desire for increasing money which reduces expenditure below income, puts pressures on the credit markets, and generates a balance of payments surplus. The additional money will be automatically created as the central bank intervenes in the exchange market to prevent currency appreciation, thus creating domestic money at the same time that it adds to its holdings of foreign exchange reserves. To prevent unnecessary accumulations of reserves the central bank will purchase domestic assets (e.g., government bonds) and satisfy, by internal monetization, the growth induced increases in desired cash. Different central banks of course will pursue different policies; some, for example, will try to maintain the same ratio of foreign reserves to central bank liabilities; others may vary the reserve ratio to keep domestic reserves a given fraction of imports. But in each case the autonomous variable in monetary policy is the rate of internal credit creation (the purchase of domestic assets), while the passive element is the rate of reserve increase. The public determines the quantity of money it wants to hold and the rate at which it is to be increased, while the central bank determines that part of it which will be backed by foreign reserves.

When we take into account interactions with the rest of the world, these propositions need to be adjusted. At the microeconomic level credit expansion has no effect on the money supply. But in the world as a whole a dollar's worth of money created anywhere in the system adds exactly that much money to the money supply of the system as a whole. At the microeconomic level, the national communities determine the quantity of money they want. But at the macroeconomic level the nominal quantity of money is determined by the collective policies of the various central banks, while the world community as a whole determines its real value. If the collective money supply of the world economy is greater than the quantity desired, the world price level will rise until its real value has been adjusted to the level the community wants to hold.

This is not to say, of course, that the policies of various countries are symmetrical with respect to one another. Positions of dominance and subordination arise with respect to the different currencies. In the present configuration of the world economy the other nations keep their currencies convertible into the dollar, not the other way around. The U.S. monetary authorities are not constrained to govern their monetary policy by other than domestic considerations since the only way the foreign central banks can avoid accumulating dollar holdings is by inflating themselves. The struggle on the part of the dominant country to acquire external inflation seigniorage at the expense of foreign countries, and the resistance to paying the imposed tax on dollar balances can readily lead to a situation of competitive inflation.

CHAPTER 18

CURRENCY AREAS AND MONETARY SYSTEMS

Egon SOHMEN

In everyday speech, a common currency area would be a geographical region in all of whose parts a single monetary unit of account is used as a general means of payment. In a well-known paper, Robert Mundell has defined a common currency area as "a domain within which exchange rates are fixed." [1] Although Mundell is careful enough not to say so explicitly, the use of the term in this connection may suggest somewhat too readily that the fixing of exchange rates is the exact equivalent of currency unification in the traditional sense. In the latest edition of his standard textbook on international economics, Professor C.P. Kindleberger succinctly summarizes what is presumably a widely held view: [2]

> "A system of permanently fixed rates is equivalent to the existence of a single world money. A system in which exchange rates can alter, on the other hand, divides the world into separate moneys."

Because a common standard of payment and exchange is undoubtedly an important factor facilitating trade and capital movements, this line of reasoning tends to favor the conclusion that any move away from exchange-rate pegging would, whatever its other merits, be a step toward disintegration of the world economy: [3]

> "The major argument against the freely flexible exchange rate is that it cuts off national economies from one another."

Elsewhere, I have cautioned against the identification of currency unifica-

---

[1] R.A. Mundell, "A Theory of Optimum Currency Areas," *American Economic Review* Vol. 51 (1961), p. 657.

[2] C.P. Kindleberger, *International Economics*, 4th ed., (Homewood, Ill.: Richard D. Irwin, Inc., 1968), p. 517.

[3] C.P. Kindleberger, *International Economics*, op. cit., p. 514.

tion with the fixing of exchange rates. [4] An equally important characteristic of a common currency area (in the customary sense, not that defined by Mundell) is the assurance of perfect convertibility at all times. [5] A third requirement would be the absence of banking and brokerage fees for currency conversion. In many respects, there are also important differences between an area that has a single central authority for the conduct of monetary policy and one in which there are several and institutionally independent central banks, even though all the other criteria listed here may be fulfilled.

The last two characteristics can obviously never be attained by the mere fixing of exchange rates as long as two currencies remain distinct. The assurance of convertibility at fixed rates is possible in theory, but it is considerably more difficult in practice. As every observer of monetary events during the past few decades knows only too well, fixed exchange rates have a most annoying habit of forcing governments to apply intermittent (and often permanent) infringements of the freedom of international payments.

The least that can be said, therefore, is that greater constancy of exchange rates is not a sufficient indicator of a move toward currency unification (in the traditional sense). As usual, the real world offers such a variety of aspects to be considered that we can rarely expect to find a clear-cut case. In this paper, a listing of all the relevant considerations for judging concrete examples is attempted. The question is not entirely academic. In the European Common Market, for example, currency unification is an avowed objective, and it may be useful to have at least a vague idea whether certain measures bring the community closer to its goal or move it away from it.

Convertibility restrictions take so many and varied forms that it is practically impossible to devise a scale according to which their intensity could be gauged. Apart from the extreme case of general prohibition and licensing of every individual transaction, there is a whole spectrum of possibilities with global permissions for the acquisition of foreign exchange for certain types of transactions, prohibition or licensing of others. But there is also an infinite variety of more subtle forms of interference, such as moral suasion by central banks to discourage commercial banks from rendering certain services to their customers, or the mere chance that such steps might

---

[4] "The Assignment Problem", in *Monetary Problems of the International Economy*, ed. R.A. Mundell and A.K. Swoboda, Chicago: University of Chicago Press, 1969, esp. pp. 192–194.

[5] The need for assuming a convertibility guarantee in addition to the fixing of exchange rates was mentioned once by R.I. McKinnon in his contribution to the discussion. "Optimum Currency Areas", *American Economic Review* Vol. 53 (1963), p. 717. McKinnon did not elaborate further on this point.

be taken in the foreseeable future. It is therefore all but impossible to imagine a measuring rod that would permit a construction such as an "indifference curve" between degrees of currency inconvertibility on the one hand, degrees of exchange-rate variability on the other, along which an "index of currency unification" would remain constant (quite apart from the inevitable subjectivity of such an evaluation). But a vague image of something of this sort must inevitably be in the back of one's mind when discussing these questions. Certain economic phenomena are no less real and important for being immune to attempts at exact quantitative measurement.

Because the concept of convertibility is such an elusive variable, we might hope to fare better with the degree of exchange-rate variability. But, again, difficulties are much greater than they are usually made to appear. It is not permissible to argue that any change of Article IV of the Articles of Agreement of the International Monetary Fund to extend the maximum band spread of exchange-rate movements beyond the present 1% to either side of parity, or even the complete elimination of the margins, would necessarily increase an acceptable indicator of exchange-rate variability. It is small comfort to know that exchange rates normally move only within the present narrow limits if these limits can occasionally be changed without advance warning by an unpredictable amount that may exceed 10 or 15% from one day to the other. It can stand repetition that the Bretton Woods' system is not one of unalterably fixed currency parities and that the presumed advantages of a common currency can, for this reason alone, with no stretch of the imagination be claimed for it.

By contrast, a widening of the band together with the possibility of more frequent, hence minor, parity changes may be desirable precisely because it can serve to avoid the need for major and abrupt exchange-rates adjustments. Contrary to superficial impressions, the exchange risk may thus be reduced by permitting greater flexibility. It is the reduction of exchange risks that is presumably the principal goal of any move toward currency unification.

It should also be borne in mind that what reduces risk is not necessarily the relative *constancy* of an economic variable but its *predictability*. A situation in which the exchange rate were known exactly for every single day during the next five years would, as far as exchange risks are concerned, not differ in any material way from one in which these future rates are known to be exactly equal to the one ruling today. By the same token, a system with a "guaranteed parity path" that preserves the present narrow-band spread around the parity holding on any given day [6] would not represent a material

[6] A system of this type was discussed as a possible solution in the third annual report of the German *Sachverständigenrat*. See *Expansion und Stabilität*, (Stuttgart, Kohlhammer, 1966), pp. 157–159.

difference to a modified Bretton Woods system with truly guaranteed parities (a feature that is, as pointed out earlier, not part of the present one).

Most of the advantages of genuine exchange-rate predictability could be secured for traders even without any official fixing of exchange-rate parities and margins by simply letting forward exchange markets develop in a system of perfect currency convertibility. If there were no restrictions on convertibility in a system of flexible exchange rates, there would be no imaginable reason why exporters and importers should not be able to secure forward cover, at least for commitments in the major currencies, even for maturities of several years. With the assurance of convertibility, there would be a strong tendency for all forward markets to be always closely linked to spot markets through covered interest arbitrage, forward premia, or discounts (on an annual basis) corresponding to the interest differentials between any pair of countries. The desire of exporters of machinery to sell foreign exchange earnings expected in two years' time would, if it happened not to be matched by the simultaneous wish of other traders to buy an equivalent amount of this currency forward for two years, lead to a sufficient depreciation to make forward purchases combined with spot sales by arbitrageurs profitable. It appears likely, at least for the major currencies, that alert bankers would take advantage of these profit opportunities until the differences between the covered yields (net of exchange risk) of comparable investments is reduced to a minimum.

The question immediately poses itself why these opportunities for forward coverage do not develop to a greater extent under the present system. The answer is simple: covered interest arbitrage is effectively discouraged by even the subtlest varieties of convertibility restrictions, and many of those practiced today are anything but subtle. It suffices that administrative interference with the free flow of international payments is not even in existence but is only anticipated for the future to make bankers hesitant to acquire forward positions (or to assume forward liabilities) in foreign currencies even when they are matched by an equivalent spot commitment in the opposite direction: The imposition of exchange controls at a later date (but before a forward contract matures) may prevent the fulfilment of contractual obligations just as effectively as if these controls had already been in force at the beginning. Governments and central banks frequently feel that the curtailment of transactions on capital account, and especially of short-term money flows, is a relatively innocuous matter by comparison with inhibition of current-account transactions. This was the basic philosophy of the founding fathers of the International Monetary Fund. It has in recent years led the British government, for example, to proscribe all forward-

exchange deals that do not constitute covering of current-account transactions. Such a measure not only makes purely speculative transactions more
difficult or impossible — its announced objective — but also covered interest
arbitrage. An important group of potential partners of commercial hedgers is
thus removed from the scene. This is the basic reason why forward markets
are such relatively unsatisfactory instruments for covering exchange risks
under the present system, particularly at times when the danger of a parity
adjustment appears imminent and covering opportunities would be needed
most, for it is at such times that convertibility restrictions are an almost
inevitable necessity.

If proper attention is paid to the markedly different climate for the
development of active forward markets under the alternatives of pegged and
flexible exchange rates, it should be easier to appreciate the fact that a
loosening of exchange-rate pegging might under present conditions in many
cases be a movement *toward* currency unification rather than away from it.
The absence of balance-of-payments problems under flexible rates would
allow maximal freedom of international payments and, as a consequence,
maximal flourishing of forward-exchange markets. [7] There is hardly a better
indicator of monetary integration than the degree to which regional interest
rates for comparable investments converge toward each other, but we should
beware of the money illusion inherent in a concentration on *nominal* interest
rates in this connection. A full development of forward markets for as many
maturities as possible in a regime of full convertibility provides the best
guarantee that the structures of *real* rates of interest, the variables that are
alone relevant for the allocation of resources, in different countries will tend
toward equality. Apart from the mechanism of covered interest arbitrage that
tends to equalize forward premia and interest differentials, the interplay of
the factors operating in the money and capital markets will also work toward
an adjustment of nominal interest rates in each country in such a way that
anticipated differences in rates of inflation are taken into account. Finally,
the structure of forward rates will tend to conform to the anticipated

---

[7] In theory, credit transactions might accomplish the same purpose as forward
exchange deals for commercial hedgers. Apart from the fact that this alternative is
usually considerably more expensive, it is normally thwarted equally effectively by
exchange controls.

To say that covering opportunities for commercial trade are welcome in a world
where risk averters are in a majority is not to claim that a trader might not frequently
earn higher profits if he does not cover. Risk evasion implies the avoidance of potential
profits as well as of potential losses.

evolution of spot rates for the various maturities which, in turn, will be influenced by anticipated differences in rates of inflation. [8]

This interplay of market forces will, over the long run, in most cases be gravely disturbed under a regime of adjustably pegged exchange rates. Given differences between rates of inflation in different countries — and only the most incurable romantics can believe that they will not occur in the future as they have in the past — the tendency of adjustment of the structure of forward rates to nominal interest differentials and to expected price-level movements will be gravely disturbed. The same will generally follow even without marked differences between the speeds of inflation whenever substantial structural adjustments within a country affect its trade flows. Difficulties of adjustment will be accentuated by the interference with convertibility that becomes mandatory when certain currencies become progressively overvalued. Covered interest arbitrage can then no longer operate effectively to diminish real interest differentials between countries, and the tendency toward unity of capital markets that would arise with free exchange markets is broken.

Let it be emphasized, to avoid all possible misunderstanding, that forward coverage by anybody who wants to take advantage of it (for traders' as well as for capital transactions) is not merely possible but possible without an additional cost in the nature of an "insurance premium" when currency convertibility is assured beyond the shadow of a doubt. What to some people occasionally appears as "prohibitive risk premia" under the present system (excessive forward discounts considerably exceeding the international interest differentials for currencies for which devaluation is universally expected) can only arise when covered interest arbitrage is impaired by exchange controls. This phenomenon is thus a characteristic feature of the present monetary system that cannot be extrapolated to one in which payments imbalances and the associated convertibility restrictions do not arise. [9]

The possibility of eliminating (without additional cost) the exchange risk for any *given* trade or credit transaction does not yet answer the argument that risks are nevertheless increased in a system of flexible rates because

---

[8] For more details, see my *Theory of Forward Exchange*, Princeton Studies in International Finance Section, 1966, chap. 4, esp. pp. 27–28, reprinted in my *Flexible Exchange Rates*, revised ed., (Chicago: University of Chicago Press, 1969), pp. 97–112, esp. pp. 106–107.

[9] To be sure, only one market side finds hedging expensive when excessive forward discounts arise. But it is normally only this side of the market that is interested in hedging at all when expectations about possible parity changes are asymmetrical.

long-term planning of investment and production for foreign markets are handicapped by the uncertainty about the *future* development of exchange rates (spot as well as forward).

This argument would be entirely correct on the assumption that everything else were to remain unchanged and provided that exchange rates were indeed immutable. *Ceteris paribus* is, however, a particularly unrealistic assumption in this connection. Flexibility of exchange rates has never been advocated for any other purpose than to make possible the elimination of a multitude of other disturbances that disrupt the normal evolution of international trade and capital movements as well as of employment and aggregate output. Previous sections of this paper have already elaborated on this argument with respect to currency convertibility. A proper consideration of all relevant types of risks should convince anyone that it is impossible to conclude that business risk is increased when exchange rates are allowed greater freedom of variation.

It should also be recalled once again in this connection that flexibility must never be identified with instability. We need not enter into a discussion about the probable behavior of speculators at this point; suffice it to say that direct intervention on the foreign-exchange markets is by no means the only instrument available to central banks for preventing unwanted oscillations of exchange rates. The ordinary tools of monetary policy that are used for guiding the evolution of short-term interest rates should be perfectly sufficient to ensure that exchange-rate movements are gradual enough to prevent rather than provoke distortions that would otherwise arise from the divergent evolution of economic variables in different countries. If inflation proceeds at different rates, relative prices in world trade become progressively distorted, and resources are misallocated if exchange rates are artificially *fixed*. Allocative optimality can in that case only be preserved by letting exchange rates adjust smoothly over time.

It has sometimes been proposed to pool the foreign-exchange reserves of the member countries of the EEC, or to establish a regional reserve bank modeled after the International Monetary Fund. Many observers see another step toward currency unification in such a move.

To the extent that the availability of additional sources of foreign exchange for financing deficits (and any pooling of reserves would normally have this effect) reduces the danger of infringements of convertibility or of parity adjustments within the Community, this view is justified. When balance-of-payments deficits can be incurred more easily, the need for harmonizing monetary policy is weakened, on the other hand. Interest rates in the member countries can diverge more from each other than they otherwise could. This aspect clearly constitutes a move away from the conditions of a unified currency area.

This is only a difference of degree, of course. Even without a common reserve pool, institutionally independent central banks are able to pursue independent policies as long as the payments imbalances they may cause can be covered out of their own stocks of foreign exchange. Only the complete centralization of monetary policy in a single central bank would remove this residual degree of independence. But this is undoubtedly a rather marginal aspect of currency unification by comparison with the others.

Of the features we recognized as the distinguishing characteristics of a unified currency area, the one that is of overriding importance as a factor integrating commodity and capital markets in the member regions, is unquestionably unimpeded freedom of monetary transactions. Even if everything else could be kept unchanged − an assumption that is widely at variance with the conditions we are likely to find in the real world − the integrating power of constant exchange rates may be considerably less than what has generally been assumed. There has, to my knowledge, never been any attempt to investigate their quantitative importance empirically. We can only speculate about whether the abandonment of exchange-rate pegging would, *ceteris paribus*, be the equivalent of a 5% tariff, a 2% tariff, or a tariff of 1/100 of 1%. My own estimate would be that it is probably closest to the last of these figures. It would, of course, also depend on the size of the country (where a measure of size should not only take the geographical area, but the economic importance of a country into account). If each township had its own currency, the benefits of unification over a larger area would probably be quite substantial. I would, however, tend to question their importance already for a relatively small country such as Switzerland. More empirical research on this issue, difficult though it may be, is badly needed.

Given the present sizes of currency areas (in the everyday sense of the term) I have the impression − and it cannot be more than a mere impression − that the absence of banking charges for currency conversion in a unified currency area may in most cases be of greater quantitative significance for the flourishing of trade than the constancy of exchange rates. In this case, the estimation of the tariff equivalents is a simple matter since statistics on the average value of this cost item in international trade are easily available. Although they amount to mere fractions of 1% of trading value, they unquestionably constitute a positive obstacle to foreign as opposed to domestic trade. Again, the size of a country will determine how often its inhabitants will have to exchange currencies and how much of a burden the cost of currency transfer are consequently felt to be. I suppose this factor is the main explanation why countries such as Liechtenstein or Monaco do not have their own currencies (we might, for all practical purposes, have added Luxembourg) while Switzerland or Denmark do.

As was already briefly noted earlier in this paper, the fixing of exchange rates between distinguishable national currencies does nothing to eliminate this obstacle to international trade. It does not, in all probability, even reduce it in the slightest. It is this factor rather than the question of exchange-rate variability that should have been the principal focus of interest in the debate on optimum currency areas. The only way in which the advantage of zero conversion costs for payments within a unified currency area can be secured − together with its disadvantages − is the abolition of national currencies. The emphasis on exchange rates in the debate over optimum currency areas has, I believe, been a case of barking up the wrong tree, or, to mix metaphors in a more appropriate fashion in this context, of a false issue having gained currency.

PART 8

TRADE, AID, AND DEVELOPMENT

CHAPTER 19

EXPORT-LED GROWTH AND
THE NEW ECONOMIC HISTORY *

Richard E. CAVES

"Expanding exports can stimulate economic growth or retard it."

Charles P. Kindleberger

A leading exponent of the New Economic History has noted that the approach of this school to economic theory and measurement "represents a reunification of economic history with economic theory" and heals the split that opened in the nineteenth century when the discipline of economic history arose in "revolt against the deductive theories of classical economics." [1] During its sojourn in the wilderness, however, the older economic history did construct some models designed to explain observed historical patterns — models that amount to coherent, if not elegant or fundamental, theory. One prominent example is the "staple" or "export-led" model of economic growth, developed in the research of Harold A. Innis and other Canadian economic historians. The theoretical properties of this model only attracted attention long after it gained wide acceptance as a useful framework for interpreting the pattern of Canadian economic development. [2]

* This manuscript was completed while I served as a Ford Rotating Research Professor at the University of California, Berkeley; preliminary research was supported by a Social Science Research Council Faculty Research Fellowship. Donald F. Gordon supplied valuable comments that helped to improve the estimates reported in Section 19.1 and to reduce (although not eliminate) our differences. I am also indebted to Robert W. Fogel and M.C. Urquhart for encouragement and comments, and to Ronald W. Jones for discussion that has clarified various points.

[1] See Fogel [23]. Full citations are given in the bibliography at the end of this paper.
[2] See Baldwin [1,2], North [50], Caves [11], and Roemer [57, Chap. 3].

The model describes a sequence of events whereby the rapid expansion of some commodity export, requiring a substantial input of natural resources but relatively little local processing, induces higher rates of growth of aggregate and per capita income through a higher rate of capital formation, inflows of capital and labor to the region, and expansions of output and productivity in other sectors via various linkages, externalities, induced innovations, and the like. The resource-based product is called a staple, and this term is used equivalently to name the model.

My reading of the various studies employing some form of the export-led growth model suggests that it has proved quite useful for explaining variations over time in the rate of aggregate growth of certain groups of countries and regions, or differences between the growth rates or patterns of growth of selected countries or regions. [3] Yet the present state of our knowledge permits a good deal less than a full appraisal of its usefulness. Here are some of the lacunae:

1. Quantitative studies either of some countries or regions to which the model would seem likely to apply, or (alternatively) of those to which its application seems dubious but possible.

2. Comparisons of the explanatory power of the model against other theories or models that purport to explain the same growth variables.

3. Careful consideration, in the light of the appropriate "positive" evidence cast up by studies of these types, of the implications of the model for economic policy and the settings in which they might be put to use.

The export-led growth model can easily be stated in terms of hypotheses about the relation among various statistical time series. For that reason it would seem likely fodder for the computational skills of the new economic historians. On the other hand, its theoretical underpinnings may lie somewhat far from the neoclassical heartland to attract their interest. This paper discusses the problems that arise in using the export-led model as a hypothesis and framework for research, primarily in economic history; the boundary between economic history and economic development, however, will prove difficult to respect (or even detect). This volume's dedicatee has taken a frequent interest in the model and maintained toward it a consistent attitude of skeptical interest; [4] I shall join him in this posture. Following his example,

---

[3] This paper does not attempt to provide a survey of the literature, but casual references will be made to a number of relevant sources.

[4] See Kindleberger [28, Chap. 14], [29], [30], [31, Chap. 12], [32], and [33, Chap. 12].

I must start by eschewing any personal claim to the status of economic historian; I do not doubt that economic historians will find it less difficult to accept this caveat than Professor Kindleberger's corresponding disclaimer in his *Economic Growth in France and Britain, 1851–1950.* [5]

The first section of this paper consists of a case study in the use of the model to measure the contribution to Canada's economic growth of the wheat boom at the turn of the century. The second part discusses more generally the problem of where and how to use the model.

19.1. Measuring the wheat-boom's contribution to Canada's growth

Since the Canadian economy can justly claim to have inspired the export-led model, Canada provides a fitting case for applying and testing the model as adapted to the concerns of the New Economic History. The staple model has been proposed and, to some extent, formally tested as a *descriptive* model explaining the overall rates of growth and change of the economy as a response to disturbances in the export sector. Prior to a recent paper of Chambers and Gordon [13] however, it was neither specified nor tested with comparable care as a *normative* model, identifying the relations between export disturbances and real income per capita, and providing a basis for calculating the contribution of staple growth to personal income. In undertaking these tasks, they have taken a substantial step toward bringing the model into practicable use along with other theoretical tools used in the New Economic History. Although I shall argue that their specification omits important links between export growth and real income, which raise considerably its estimated contribution to income growth, their service in providing a simple, operational model for the calculation should be recognized.

19.1.1. *The Chambers-Gordon model*
Their theoretical model is designed to permit an unambiguous measure of gain in real income under plausible assumptions. Chambers and Gordon suppose that the Canadian economy during the period 1901–1911 consisted of the wheat industry (resource-based production of exportables), a domestic sector manufacturing "gadgets" in competition with the world market (the price of its output set by world prices), and a sector producing domestic goods ("haircuts") that are sheltered from trade by high transport costs. The supply of domestic labor depends on the real wage; the supply of capital can

[5] See Kindleberger [33, p. 1].

be thought of either as fixed or as perfectly elastic at the world rate of interest – the analysis works out similarly under either assumption. Suppose that the wheat boom of 1901–1911 can be associated with some combination of exogenous disturbances – improved terms of trade for wheat, innovations in wheat production, innovations in transportation technology, and the like. The marginal product of labor in the wheat industry increases. Labor is drawn from the "gadget" manufacturing sector (where its marginal product is constant); wheat production expands, but the real wage does not increase so long as the labor supply in gadget manufacturing can still be drawn down. An increase in real income occurs because of the rise in rents in the wheat industry. This increase will be spent partly in the sheltered-goods or haircut sector, which Chambers and Gordon assume to be constant cost; the expansion of this sector comprises an additional draft upon the labor supply in the manufactures sector, but this shift does not affect the outcome of the analysis so long as the fixed marginal product of labor in gadget manufacturing continues to peg the real wage level.

With the real wage unaffected by expanding wheat production, and with the real return to domestic capital locked in place by the assumed international mobility of capital, the real-income gains associated with the wheat boom appear principally as increased rents to the owners of wheat land. This rise in rents is not measured by their actual change between the early (1901) and late (1911) years of the boom, however. Without the boom, exogenous productivity increases in the manufacturing sector would have increased the level of the real wage and thereby reduced (*cet. par.*) the rents accruing in the wheat industry. To estimate correctly the contribution of the wheat boom to income per capita, the proper deduction from total rents accruing in 1911 is therefore the rent that would have been imputed in the absence of the boom, allowing for the effect on rents of rising real wages stemming from higher productivity in gadget manufacturing. A secondary source of real-income gain stems from the fact that the Canadian gadget sector in fact was protected by substantial tariffs during this period; allowance therefore is also made for a gain in the form of tariff revenue collected on the extra imports that flowed into Canada as the wheat boom pulled labor out of the gadget manufacturing sector, where its use is inefficient in the sense of comparative advantage.

Chambers and Gordon conclude that this increment to income caused by the wheat boom accounted most probably for 6.1% of the increase in real income per capita in Canada during the decade 1901–1911. [6] On the basis of

[6] I have taken their amended figure of 1.4% of total 1911 income as due to the wheat boom, compared to their estimated increase in income per capita of 23% over the

this finding they suggest that "when successful exporting economies simultaneously experience a rise in per capita income, most of the latter may, as in
the instance we have measured, be attributed to other factors." [7]

This paper raises two broad groups of questions about the substance of the
export-led or staple model and the appropriate procedure for testing and
using it. Although the first group is general and methodological, the second
specific and substantive, both in the end point to the need for further
evidence on the same group of empirical issues.

19.1.2. *Uses and limitations of the model*

One of the general and methodological issues was raised by Dales,
McManus and Watkins [17] in their reply to Chambers and Gordon. This
issue is whether economic historians and others employing the staple theory
have been concerned with extensive (national income) or intensive (income
per capita) growth. Both sides have resorted to what strikes me as a sterile
exercise in quotation snipping from the original sources in order to support
their views, and neither relates its position to the process by which the model
emerged from earlier historical research. The operative categories and magnitudes that play a role in the export-led model are all aggregative rather than
per capita. Anyone who has employed the model as a research tool has
perforce been dealing with extensive magnitudes. It also seems abundantly
clear that the model evolved as a positive or analytical tool, designed in the
first instance to explain extensive patterns. To give Chambers and Gordon
their due, however, it is also clear that users of this positive and aggregative
model have often slipped into suggesting normative conclusions that, on any
reasonable interpretation, must address themselves to intensive growth. But
these adherents of the export-led model — and this point has been lost sight
of in the debate — believed that extensive growth associated with staple
expansion and intensive growth were closely correlated. They certainly face
criticism for failing to make these assumed connections clear and, above all,
for neglecting to test them empirically. But they have been guilty neither of
simple confusions about what constitutes intensive growth nor simple

1901–1911 decade; see Chambers and Gordon [14, p. 882]. This figure appears to
represent their final judgment, including the increased rent on wheat land and increased
tariff revenue but not an allowance that they calculated for associated gains in
economies of scale; that factor is discussed later. Note that they compare the boom's
contribution to *1911* income with the total increase on a *1901* base; in the calculations
reported later I employ a 1901 base throughout.

[7] Chambers and Gordon [13, p. 328].

transgressions in moving from aggregative analysis to policy — charges might be brought if these links between extensive and intensive growth are neglected.

These links between aggregate and per-capita growth constitute the basis for criticizing Chambers and Gordon's specification of the staple model and will be discussed in detail below. It is useful, however, to list some of them and to speculate on the circumstances of their omission or exclusion. The connections between aggregate and per-capita growth include:

1. A negative relation between the rate of expansion of exports and the level of unemployment;

2. A positive relation between the rate of expansion of staple production and the rate of domestic gross saving; and

3. A positive relation between the rate of expansion of staple production and the rate of productivity growth in certain domestic sectors, especially manufacturing and distribution.

The potential relevance of these connections to the export-led model is immediately clear if one recognizes that the uniqueness of this growth process derives from two of its properties: (1) previously idle or undiscovered resources are drawn into use creating a rent and "venting a surplus" through trade; (2) during the period when these resources are absorbed, the rate of economic expansion is not subject to the long-run constraints of "balanced growth" but rather involves the progressive elimination of a disequilibrium, with windfall profits or quasi-rents accruing along the way. If export-led growth is seen only as the venting of surplus resources in the long run, as I believe Chambers and Gordon tend to see it, then the real-income gains reduce primarily to rents on perpetual assets, and other effects that have been hypothesized within the framework of the model are disposed of as inconsistent with long-run purely competitive equilibrium. But are the significant welfare gains associated with rapid economic growth only those that are consistent with movements between positions of long-run equilibrium? The answer to this question lies only in the data; at this stage I shall assert only that the question is an important one. [8]

---

[8] That the model could be reduced to an assertion of preference for rent-yielding activities as a principal source of gains in real income should convey a hint of paradox to anyone reflecting on the history of economic thought, wherein diminishing returns have had a bad press from Ricardo up to the present (e.g., Baldwin [3, p. 3]). This paradox can be easily resolved, of course, by noting that Chambers and Gordon are dealing with an open economy. Nonetheless, something a bit deeper may be involved. Many a statement has been made of the side conditions that must be fulfilled for a particular rise in income, or in income per capita, to count as "modern economic growth" (Kuznets

19.1.3. *Additional effects of the boom*

These general comments indicate both some qualifications upon Chambers and Gordon's findings and, more constructively, some additional calculations. Their measurement provides a valuable contribution so far as it goes, since the role of rents accruing to the owners of natural resources in transmitting the income gains as a result of staple growth has, to my knowledge, been previously noted only in theoretical work on the export-led model [9] and not considered in empirical studies except for its role in permitting the recipients of income from expanding staple production to increase their aggregate expenditure. Furthermore, the statistical procedures employed by Chambers and Gordon seem predominantly reasonable, although one would wish for confirmation of the appropriateness of the census rent figures as measure of the surplus per acre of gross revenues over all economic costs. As an example of possible difficulties, rents conventionally stated as crop shares may have lagged in adjusting to the new prosperity.

As Section 19.1.2 indicated, however, some additional effects of export-led extensive growth on the increase of income per capita should be taken into account for a full test of the model's explanatory power and the welfare significance of the wheat boom. I shall advance several extensions of Chambers and Gordon's calculations, each implying some adjustment to the actual net national income and population of Canada in 1911 to fabricate an alternative economy in which the wheat boom had not occurred. These changes can then be totaled, and an alternative figure computed for net national income per capita in the absence of the wheat boom.

1. Induced immigration

As Chambers and Gordon point out, within their framework of measurement, an increase in the amount of immigration imputed to the wheat boom *by itself* reduces the boom's contribution to income per capita. This is because the real gains which they estimate are independent of the size of the population; therefore any increase that it induces in population just spreads these fixed gains over a larger number of individuals. Because I shall argue that significant influences of immigration and extensive growth on intensive growth may have been omitted, however, the level of immigration provides a useful starting point.

[35]), or "economic progress" (Youngson [71, Chap. 1]). The extent to which export-led growth possesses any special virtues in furthering sustainable growth remains to be demonstrated, but any that it possesses seem unlikely to derive from the creation of rents.

[9] E.g., Caves [11, pp. 99–101].

Chambers and Gordon hold that migrants came to Canada for the wages they could earn there and not because of the wheat boom except to the extent that they were lured by the opportunity to capture some of its rents. On that assumption they quite reasonably impute an inflow of 200,000 to the wheat boom. This is hardly a maximum estimate. The general evidence that is available on the determinants of international migration supports the primacy of the quest for higher personal income, but it also gives great weight to the short-run influence of job availability and a low rate of unemployment. In countries like Canada and the United States, wages per worker probably stood significantly above their levels in at least some of the major countries of emigration and were certainly rising more rapidly. It becomes quite reasonable to attribute to disturbances such as the wheat boom, which had sure if unquantifiable effects on the employment rate and public assessment of income expectations in Canada, a "multiplier effect" on immigration beyond the jobs created directly.

This suggestion is hardly inconsistent with the data on migration. Canada's share of intercontinental migration rose steadily after the turn of the century. The percentage contribution of net immigration to Canada's population growth was four times as large in 1901–1911 as in the two succeeding decades, and it was negative in the preceding decade. [10]

The inducement effect of the wheat boom cannot be estimated as a process of market adjustment, except for the jobs created directly, but some idea of its total (direct and indirect) effects can be gained through an employment-multiplier formulation. Prairie agriculture was not the only sector that acted as an exogenous source of opportunities for prospective immigrants. Employment growth in the other primary sectors and some portion of manufacturing and construction must be treated as comparable to agriculture as independent sources of employment opportunities. (I assume that all farm employment growth was in prairie agriculture.) Employment growth in agriculture was 55% of a total including other primary sectors, one-half of construction, one-fourth of manufacturing, and one-third of unallocated laborers. Applying this agriculture percentage to Keyfitz' estimate of net immigration during the decade [11] indicates total immigration as a

[10] Calculated from Firestone [22, Table 83].

[11] Unfortunately the lack of evidence on the determinants of international migration forces this kind of rough estimate rather than one based on market factors. An alternative rule-of-thumb approach might involve the assumption that net immigration during 1901–1911 bore the same relation to Canada's net natural increase as it did during the next two decades; this procedure yields a higher estimate of immigration caused by the wheat boom – about 600,000.

result of the wheat boom of 392,000, which implicitly includes the 200,000 estimated by Chambers and Gordon as the direct increase.

2. Labor-force participation of immigrants

Chambers and Gordon assume that the labor-force participation rate for immigrants to the prairie was the same as for the prairie population as a whole. For the nation at large, this is clearly incorrect. The immigrants were heavily weighted toward males in the working ages, so that any estimate of their contribution to the labor supply (and thus to wage income) must allow for their higher participation rate, which would appear to be the principal cause of the jump of 13% (4.6 percentage points) for the overall Canadian rate during the decade. [12] Suppose, as a maximum, that net immigration were the sole reason for the excess of the 1910 labor-force participation rate (39.4%) over a 1910 trend value in the participation rate calculated by interpolating between Firestone's 1900 and 1920 values (36.2%). This assumption would imply a participation rate in 1910 for these immigrants of just over two-thirds. This figure would not be unreasonable for new immigrants to Canada in the postwar period, when the number of primary migrants (presumably nearly all seeking employment) has been more than double the number of their dependents. [13] By the end of the 1901–1911 decade, however, earlier immigrants had sired some children and diluted their initial participation rate, so I shall use an arbitrarily lowered value of 60%; this also makes some allowance for an undoubted bias of immigrants with larger numbers of dependents toward agriculture. It is only the higher participation rate of the immigrants induced by the wheat boom, of course, that is relevant to our subsequent calculations.

3. Scale economies associated with aggregate growth

Chambers and Gordon employ Denison's estimate of the rate at which scale economies accrue to increases in total output in the sheltered haircut sector. They do not seem disposed, however, to count this as part of their final figure for real gains caused by the wheat boom. I would argue that, for lack of a better measure of this gain, it should be included. If enterprises are adjusting over a decade to a market that is growing in size and density, it

---

[12] A possible offset to this upward adjustment of the productive capacity brought by the immigrants would be required if their endowment of educational capital was on the average lower than that of the labor force resident in Canada in 1901. Cf. Denison [19, pp. 177–178].

[13] Rates are taken from Firestone [22, p. 58].

seems quite reasonable to suppose that the average firm may be switching between positions of short-run equilibrium that involve an increase of output and economies of scale.

Since the application of Denison's figure for the rate of accumulation of scale economies to Canada at the turn of the century is obviously no more than a shot in the dark, [14] it is worth noting some evidence that associates expansion in the scale of manufacturing enterprises directly with the growth of the prairie economy and thus helps to eliminate the possibility that it would have occurred in any case. During the decade 1901—1911, the average size of manufacturing establishments employing five or more persons grew at about 1.5% per annum, which is roughly the same growth rate that such enterprises showed over the longer subsequent period 1915—1950. [15] This rate of growth was significantly higher for manufacturing establishments located in the parts of Canada most affected by the prairie wheat boom, however. Against 16% for the nation as a whole, the figure was 20% for Ontario, 75% for British Columbia, 100% for Alberta and Saskatchewan, and 145% for Manitoba. Scale gains do appear to be associated with the wheat boom and should be credited to it.

4. Efficiency gains in the gadget sector

Chambers and Gordon would perhaps accept this scale gain but would apply it only to the extra output of the sheltered domestic haircut sector. A case can be made for applying it also to the gadget sector, where they would deny its operation because the component industries are assumed to be in pure competition facing a price determined externally on the world market.

The gadget sector in Chambers and Gordon's model fills two important roles in justifying their approach to the measurement of gains from the wheat boom. First, because it is in competition with gadget producers worldwide,

[14] See Denison [19, Chap. 16]. I would only note that if it is correct for the United States, 1929—1957, it can hardly be excessive for the smaller Canadian economy in an earlier period. There is ample qualitative evidence that greater density of settlement throughout the country significantly lowered the weight of various social overhead costs. Cf. Mackintosh [44, p. 24].

[15] Figures for 1901—1911 are taken from *Fifth Census of Canada, 1911* [10, Vol. III, p. ix]. The figure for 1915—1950 is calculated from Urquhart and Buckley [65, p. 489]. Some doubt exists about the comparability of figures from the 1901 and 1911 censuses with those of other years, and certainly a comparison with years before 1901 would be unwarranted. After 1915 it appears that the growth rate of the average size of manufacturing establishments declined, so that a shorter period following 1915 would show a higher growth rate.

the occurrence of a terms-of-trade change affecting the calculation of real income is averted; and second, this property plus constant returns to scale permit the labor supply to the wheat sector to be perfectly elastic. To satisfy these assumptions, the gadget sector's organization must be either that of pure competition or (under restrictive assumptions) the Chamberlinean large-group equilibrium. Neither type of market structure would be expected to accrue scale economies as a result of the general growth of the Canadian economy, and therefore Chambers and Gordon do not apply the Denisonian measure of scale-economy gains to the gadget sector.

I do not wish to question the logical role of the gadget sector in Chambers and Gordon's model or its empirical capacity to fill the two requirements just noted. I am doubtful, however, about the implication drawn from the concept that scale-economy gains would not have been induced in a significant portion of Canadian manufacturing. First, producers in certain industries will face downward-sloping demand curves because of transport costs for their product — even in an atomistic market structure and with a homogeneous product sold. By increasing the density of settlement, one shifts the demand curve outward for the individual producer and permits a larger scale of output (or higher utilization of capacity, in the short run). The wheat boom unleashed a number of spatial effects — concentrating population in some areas and inducing the construction of lower-cost transport facilities as well as spreading settlement westward across the prairies. One can only conclude that some industries or firms must have been favorably affected.

Second, as D.F. Gordon has pointed out to me, industries characterized by Chamberlinean large-group equilibrium could still have enjoyed scale economies as a result of increased size of the domestic market and the induced entry of new firms. Especially in a tariff-protected industry, such an increased number of firms and product varieties could have the effect of raising the elasticities of substitution between competing producers, flattening out their respective demand curves, and inducing increases in scale, utilization, or both.

One can test the significance of these propositions by inquiring whether changes in establishment size differed significantly between manufacturing industries which Chambers and Gordon nominate as gadget and the rest of the manufacturing sector in the way their theory predicts. During the years 1901–1911 both groups were presumably affected by randomly distributed technical changes which altered the shapes and positions of their plant average unit cost curves. Since Chambers and Gordon hold that the haircut sector also enjoyed scale gains while the gadget sector did not, it is implied that the average size of establishment in the gadget sector rose less over the decade than the average size of establishment in industries that Chambers and Gordon did not list as members of this sector. To test this, I calculated the change in the average size of establishment in Canadian manufacturing 1901–1911, both for gadget industries listed by Chambers and Gordon and for manufacturing as a whole. [16] Substantially greater gains in fact accrued to the gadget sector, where the weighted average size of establishment increased by 49.8% against 18.7% for Canadian manufacturing as a whole and 12.9% for the nongadget residue of the manufacturing sector. The increase for the median gadget industry was 30.0%. [17] The gadget sector hardly appears so tightly locked in the grip of spaceless pure competition that it could not enjoy scale economies associated with the extra expenditure generated by the wheat boom.

It is also noteworthy that measured productivity gains were about the same for the two groups of industries, a weighted average of 50.5% for Chambers and Gordon's list of gadget-type industries, 57.2% for the rest. [18] Finally, one might expect that total output of the gadget sector would have grown less rapidly than for the rest of manufacturing, since in Chambers and Gordon's model it releases its labor supply to permit the increase of domestic labor inputs into the wheat industry. In fact the growth of total gross value of output between 1901 and 1911 was 160.8% in gadgets and only 136.8% in the rest of the manufacturing sector.

This evidence suggests that we should expand the portion of the Canadian economy assumed to enjoy scale economies as a result of the wheat boom. Chambers and Gordon provide no elaborate description of the activities they suppose to comprise the haircut sector, but from their description and the actual distribution of gross national product by industry in 1910 given by Firestone [22, table 89] I suppose it to include the service industries, construction, and a minor portion of manufacturing. This would be consistent with their assumption that the marginal and average propensities to spend on haircuts both equal one-half. Including all of the manufacturing

[16] Chambers and Gordon [13, Appendix C]. Chambers and Gordon doubtless do not intend their list as exhaustive of gadget-type industries, but it does comprise a quarter of total manufacturing output in 1911. Data used in the calculations described in the text are drawn from *Fourth Census of Canada, 1901* [9, Vol. III, Tables VIII, XI] and *Fifth Census of Canada, 1911* [10, Vol. III, Table I].

[17] Four industries on Chambers and Gordon's gadget list were not included in the 1901 census list of industries and thus were omitted from this calculation.

[18] The productivity figure is simply labor productivity — total gross value of output divided by total number of wage and salaried employees.

sector, following the argument developed above, would raise the spending propensity to 0.61.

5. Capital brought by immigrants

At least some immigrants to Canada during 1901–1911 brought substantial amounts of capital with them, especially American and British farmers and farm laborers expecting to purchase farms. Viner estimates the average holdings of each class of immigrants from various contemporary sources; from his data one can calculate a weighted average figure for immigrant capital of $ 153 per person. (Emigrants from Canada apparently departed with smaller sums on the average, therefore applying this figure to net immigrants does not create an upward bias.) [19] Just as induced immigrants contributed to the total size of the economy, their capital contributed to its capital stock. Using Viner's average figure (and making no allowance for the higher average that would probably be appropriate for immigrants planning to buy farms), the induced 392,000 immigrants would have brought $ 60 million with them. An appropriate estimate of its contribution to 1911 net national income would be interest on its (undepreciated) value. Its rate of return should have been somewhat higher than the corporate bond rate, which was 5.12% in 1911. [20] Using the arbitrarily elevated figure of 7%, the contribution of immigrants' capital is $ 4.2 million.

6. Induced domestic saving

Additional gains in real income may also have resulted from the extra saving and capital formation undertaken by Canadians as a result of the wheat boom. Between the turn of the century and World War I Canada's rate of capital formation rose to a strikingly high level, largely financed by a great increase in the volume of foreign borrowing. In the period 1911–1915 53% of gross private domestic investment appears to have been financed from abroad. [21] No real income gain for Canadians was associated with this inflow, however, except to the extent that its marginal product can be shown to have exceeded the interest and dividends paid to foreigners for its services. In view

[19] Viner [67, pp. 41–57]. An overestimate occurs to the extent that immigrants had borrowed their capital abroad.

[20] This is the Wood, Gundy corporate bond yield, which had averaged slightly but not significantly higher over the preceding half-decade. See Urquhart and Buckley [65, p. 274].

[21] Buckley [7, p. 63].

of the circumstantial evidence often noted that foreign borrowing during these years may have been excessive in relation to the needs for which it was undertaken, no *prima facie* case seems to exist for an overall premium of the yield on foreign borrowings over their cost. [22]

Extra domestic saving during the decade that can be imputed to the wheat boom did augment the real incomes of Canadians, however. Its contribution to net national income at the end of the decade can be approximated by multiplying its total undepreciated value (I shall neglect the refinement of compounding) by a rough long-term rate of return, as was done earlier for immigrants' capital. [23] It is, unfortunately, impossible to produce a convincing estimate of the extra domestic saving associated with the boom on the basis of a Canadian marginal propensity to save. The two modern estimates of national income for the period, Buckley's quinquennial averages and Firestone's annual figures for census years, disagree wildly. Both are consistent, however, with a significant increase in the years 1906−1910 over the first half of the decade and over the long-term trend as well. Lacking a direct estimate of the marginal propensity to save out of net national income, I shall simply assume the ratio of 10%, often accepted as a long-term figure for mature countries, and apply it to the increase in net national income from the sources identified above, including those noted by Chambers and Gordon. By the end of the decade this would have amounted to $ 186 million annually. Assuming (for simplicity) that one-tenth of this gain accrued in each of the decade's ten years, the total saving would have been $ 102.3 million; interest on this at 7%, including an allowance for scale economies induced by its expenditure, was $ 7.6 million.

We can now combine these figures to provide a revised estimate of the minimum income per capita that might have prevailed in Canada in 1911 without the wheat boom, following Chambers and Gordon's methods as

[22] See Buckley [7, Chap. 6]. One possible reason for such a differential would be Canadian taxes on the earnings of foreign capital. Since the total provincial revenue from corporation taxes in 1911 was only $2,088,000, we can ignore the portion of this imputable to direct investment from abroad. See Urquhart and Buckley [65, p. 217].

[23] I maintain Chambers and Gordon's assumption that capital was in perfectly elastic supply to Canada on world markets, therefore variations in the rate of domestic saving had no effect on the foreign supply price. If they had, the wheat boom should be charged with any extra cost of the amount of foreign borrowing that would have occurred in its absence; but the extra domestic saving should also get credit for driving down the rate of interest and thereby the real cost of foreign borrowing.

closely as possible but making the changes listed earlier. [24] They estimate net national income in 1911 (current prices) to have been $ 2,081 million, and average population for the year was 7,214,000. [25] Income per capita was thus $ 288.47, an increase of 23.6% from the 1901 figure of $ 233.33. [26] Without the boom, the 1911 net national income would have been reduced by the loss of the extra immigrants' wages ($ 118.5 million) [27], interest on capital brought in by immigrants ($ 4.2 million), land rents as a result of the boom ($ 40.4 million), tariff revenues on imported manufactures ($ 13.0 million) [28], scale economies associated with expenditure from these income flows ($ 9.9 million) [29], and interest on domestic savings ($ 7.6 million). Net national income would have been $ 1887.4 million. Population, augmented

[24] I have not included an estimate of the output that would have been lost in 1911 because of higher unemployment in the absence of the wheat boom. Estimating what percentage of the work force was actually unemployed that year is speculative enough; estimating what it would have been goes farther still. Nonetheless, an illustration may be of interest. Firestone guesses that employment was 4% in 1900, 3% in 1910 on the basis of qualitative information (Firestone [22, pp. 58, 310]). Probably 1911 was not much different from 1910. If we suppose that absence of the boom would have resulted in an extra 1% of unemployment in manufacturing, construction and the service industries, and that their contribution to GNP would have been reduced proportionally from its implicit full-employment value, the loss would have been about $14 million.

[25] Population figures are mid-year averages based on Firestone [22, Table 83].

[26] I assumed that real net national income increased over the decade in the same proportion as Firestone's estimated gross national product in constant dollars. See Firestone [22, p. 276].

[27] The number of induced immigrants multiplied by their participation rate and Chambers and Gordon's figure for annual wages in manufacturing ($504). As Gordon has pointed out to me, figures presented by Urquhart and Buckley [65, pp. 84, 99] seem to indicate a figure for annual wages that is nearly 20% lower. It is probably impossible to reconcile this with Chambers and Gordon's figure for income per capita of $288.47, however; multiplied by the average Canadian rate of labor-force participation, it implies an income per capita for families dependent on wages in manufacturing just over one-half that of the average Canadian! In any case, the effect of reducing Chambers and Gordon's figure for 1911 annual wages would be to lower (or eliminate) the gain owing jointly to immigration and scale economies and raise the gain owing to rents.

[28] In principle, this figure should now be reduced slightly, since some of the induced immigrants not employed directly in agriculture were presumably employed in the tariff-protected manufacturing sector. I have not attempted such an adjustment.

[29] By applying the scale gain to expenditure from the extra tariff revenue one implies that it was rebated or used to reduce other taxes.

by 392,000 fewer immigrants, would have been 6,822,000 [30], and income per capita $ 276.66. The wheat boom thus accounts for a maximum addition of 5.1% to the income per capita that Canadians enjoyed in 1901, or 21.4% of the total increase that took place during the decade. This is more than double the maximum estimated by Chambers and Gordon, who indicate a 2.3% addition to 1901 income, accounting for just under 10% of the total increase. [31] My procedures, like theirs, aim at a maximum estimate; for instance, "excess supply" disturbances in other countries increasing the flow of migrants to Canada tend to make my estimate of induced immigration too large.

Incorporation of these effects of the boom on factor supplies and the scale of production increases the portion of the income gain imputed to the boom but still does not make it the predominant source. There is no denying Chambers and Gordon's conclusion that advances in technological knowledge and its application, moving almost costlessly across national boundaries, are likely to comprise the main source of income gains for small nations. [32] Yet, I wonder how often any *other* source can be found that accounts for as much as 21%. Furthermore, if one's interest in measuring the respective contribution of different sources of growth lies in the resulting lessons for policy options open to the small country itself, the gain from such an *internal* source as growth in the export sector should perhaps not be compared with an *external* source such as the gains from the international diffusion of technological knowledge. The latter can ordinarily be enjoyed freely by the small but developed nation, and no special policy choice is involved except

[30] Other allowances might be made for the effects of this great inflow of migrants. Their propensity to save might have differed significantly – either higher or lower – from that of 1901 residents; if so, an adjustment should be added to or subtracted from (respectively) the estimate. No allowance has been made for any gain in real income that the migrants may have enjoyed in moving to Canada, although this could be estimated in various ways: (1) excess of output per worker in Canada over countries of emigration could be multiplied by the number of emigrant workers; (2) the migrants' gross gain in real income over their previous level of personal consumption was surely no less than their annual remittance to relatives abroad (and more than this amount, if they enjoyed some increase in their standard of living), although remittance as a measure of their gross gain would have to be reduced by an estimate of the (smaller) amount of support that they would have provided to their families had they remained at home.

[31] By their estimate, population in 1911 would have been smaller by 200,000 (hence 7,014,000), net national income by $40.4 million in rents, $42 million in immigrants' wages, and $13 million in tariff revenue ($1,985.6 million); income per capita would have been $283.09.

[32] Chambers and Gordon [13, pp. 327–328].

that of refraining from interference with this flow. In some contexts, it would be appropriate to estimate the proportional contribution of exp. rt-led growth to Canada's expansion during 1901—1911 by comparing it not to Canada's *total* growth per capita but rather to the nation's *excess* growth per capita over that enjoyed during the same years by large countries with equal access to technological advances. The United States, which provides the obvious basis for comparison, enjoyed an increase in real income per capita of about 15% during the same decade.[33] The Canadian growth that I have attributed to the wheat boom (5.1%) constitutes 59% of the excess of Canada's per capita growth rate (8.6%) over the U.S. figure.

Some doubts may have assailed the reader over the significance for Canadians' economic welfare of some of the supplemental sources of income gains per capita enumerated earlier. An economist of neoclassical persuasion may be dubious about the contribution of the immigrants' high rate of labor-force participation[34] or of induced domestic saving[35] to the economic welfare of individuals, just as the economist interested in sustainable processes of economic growth may have reservations about the ultimate value of resource rents. The measurement of changes in economic welfare remains a slippery matter — a finding that should astonish no one.

19.2. General problems in using the model

The export-led growth model has evolved to explain particular patterns of historical experience — primarily Canada's development, although closely related ideas have sprung up independently to explain changes in several other regions and times as well. The model is employed in Ragnar Nurkse's

[33] To derive this figure, I used Martin's estimate of privately produced income in 1911 and 1901, deflating by the Bureau of Labor Statistics wholesale price index (the various retail price indexes available would have imposed a larger deflation). Population was assumed to increase between 1901 and 1911 in the same proportion that it increased between 1900 and 1910. Figures were taken from *U.S. Bureau of the Census* [64, pp. 14, 25, 233, 235].

[34] On the ground that it represents no gain to the working individual and results only from differences in age and sex composition of the immigrants. On the other hand, we noted that Chambers and Gordon's analysis assumes that no gain in real income accrues to the average migrant.

[35] On the ground that at the margin the disutility of current saving should just offset the discounted utility of the expected future stream of income (and output), leaving any net subjective gains to depend on intramarginal surpluses.

interpretation of the international economy in the nineteenth century. A short-run version has been used to explain the differences among the growth rates and foreign-trade performance of the European countries since World War II. [36] The model has never pretended to the status of a general theory. Nonetheless, an analytical cat that has lived this many lives may look forward to a few more. Where else, and how, can the model be used? I propose now to consider more broadly the problems of and prospects for employing this model as a research tool in economic history. The discussion can be organized around two broad questions: (1) To what cases or bodies of data might it fruitfully be applied? (2) What problems of specification and inference arise in fitting data to its component functional relations or in otherwise relating the theory to the facts?

19.2.1. Possible cases for study

Much of the controversy over this model and its uses boils down to the question of its "realm of validity." To what countries or situations should it apply (i.e., explain a substantial portion of the level and fluctuation of the rate of extensive or intensive growth)? If it proves able to conquer some historical terrain, what cases might lie near the boundaries of its applicability, thus offering a chance to test its explanatory power against competing hypotheses? What sorts of cases lie outside its reach? I should like to suggest two principles that seem useful for screening cases of historical experience into those to which the model is and is not likely to enjoy fruitful application.

The first principle is simple enough, although all its implications may not be immediately obvious. It is that substantial shifts in the gross value of exports that a region can profitably sell externally, at least some of them favorable to the expansion of exports, must comprise a major portion of the disturbances impinging on the region's resource allocation and pattern of rewards to factors of production. The justification for this principle is directly clear if the model is being put primarily to positive or analytical uses. It specifies both a source of disturbance and a response mechanism and cannot be expected to show any explanatory power unless both are present. This requirement becomes crucial when one considers the problems of testing the export-led model against alternative explanations of the course of an area's development. Take, for instance, the proposition of Chambers and Gordon that the growth rate of industrial productivity in the Canadian case constitutes both the principal source of intensive growth and also the main

---

[36] Nurkse [52, Chap. 11]; Beckerman [4,5]; Lamfalussy [38].

explanation of how that growth rate varies over time. Rapid growth of industrial productivity raises wages and cuts into the rents yielded by exportable resource-based products; Chambers and Gordon's model would predict a negative correlation over time between the growth rate of industrial productivity and the growth rate of staple outputs, because wage increases would tend to wipe out the rent earned by marginal enterprises engaged in staple production when industrial productivity is growing fast. The staple model, on the other hand, predicts a positive correlation over time between the growth rates of staple production and industrial productivity. This prediction rides not only on the assumption that the growth rate of industrial productivity is endogenous and responsive to general economic growth but also on the presumption that the disturbances affecting the growth rate of staple production are large compared to the exogenous disturbances that affect the growth rate of industrial productivity directly. If this assumed relation between the size of disturbances from the two sources of exportable production and industrial technology fails to hold, then the positive correlation can no longer be predicted.

Does this first principle generate any rules of thumb about cases in which the model would be likely to apply? Note that it does not merely formalize the proposition that a nation regularly exporting a quarter of its gross domestic product is a likely candidate while a nation exporting a twentieth is not. Under some assumptions, it is possible indeed for external disturbances to provoke stronger income and monetary responses in countries with small rates of participation in trade than in those with large trade shares. [37] Nor is it just a matter of small countries versus large countries, although presumptions favoring greater incidence of trade disturbances for small countries can be established in various ways. [38] It seems difficult to develop useful rules of thumb, apart from the principle as stated. The relative strength and magnitude of disturbances affecting a particular country's production for export, as compared to those affecting production for the domestic market, will reflect a host of considerations including the commodity composition of these two streams, the nature of the country's comparative-advantage position in world commerce, and the like.

One proposition that does seem useful in picking instances for possible

---

[37] E.g., McKinnon and Oates [46].

[38] It is not necessary to appeal to the lumpiness of natural resources in order to reach this conclusion, only to the greater proportion that a large country's output stream occupies of total world output. The implications of this phenomenon of relative size have been worked out by Kuznets [36].

application of the model is that as one disaggregates a nation more finely into regional subdivisions a stage will eventually be reached where the predominance of disturbances in "export" markets is attained. Indeed, much of Douglas North's work with the model has emphasized its usefulness as an alternative to traditional location theory in explaining the interactions among the various regions of a country. [39] But as the model surely becomes applicable at this stage for explaining the extensive aspects of regional growth, it also becomes less apt for explaining intensive growth and fruitfully suggesting ways to identify "linkage effects." As a nation is disaggregated more finely into regions, the rising predominance of export disturbances and increasing shares of regional production for export are likely to be matched by increasing average and marginal regional propensities to import. Although not all of the inducement linkages suggested by the export-led model depend on expenditure circuits, it is clear that most of them dry up as the marginal propensity to import of the region under study increases. [40] Establishing that the model gives a good fit for explaining the extensive aspects of the growth of regions of a country thus leads no presumption for its power to explain the growth of the aggregated activity of the country as a whole. This is not only because these regional aggregates wash out as national averages but also because interregional offsets are involved; export-led growth has its zero-sum aspects, and export-led growth for one region can induce export-led contraction for others, such as those whose regional exports are close substitutes in the rest of the nation.

The second principle for locating applications of the export-led model reflects a lesson drawn from the preceding discussion of the Canadian case, namely, that the most difficult step in judging the normative significance of the model is that of predicting and measuring the linkages between the extensive growth identified by the model and growth of income per capita. The principle is that among those instances in which export growth displays some power to explain the rate of expansion of aggregate income flows and factor supplies, interest attaches both to those cases in which per capita income is also increasing and those in which it appears largely unaffected. The

[39] North [50,51]. See Tiebout [63].

[40] One might be concerned that the same problem would affect the study of the influence of export expansion on the growth of small nations. It certainly does in some cases: see Wallich [68, Chap. 12] on Cuba. One statistical study shows, however, that the size of the national economy, while a significant determinant of trade participation and the average propensity to import, only explains a small portion of the international variation of these magnitudes. See Lloyd [40, Chap. 2].

export-led model, at least as set forth by Baldwin and Kindleberger, contains not an unqualified prediction that fast extensive and intensive growth will coincide but rather a taxonomy of traits of the production process of the staple export(s) that suggest what strength, if any, the relation between extensive and intensive growth will show.

The practical significance of accepting this principle and recognizing this taxonomic element in the model becomes immediately apparent when one considers the prospect of applying it both to successfully developed and to less-developed countries. Baldwin [1] suggested that the differing consequences of wheat booms and tropical plantation agriculture for generating modern economic growth might lie in differing characteristics of the production functions and input requirements of the two groups of products, the wheat being capital-intensive, requiring skilled labor, and lacking substantial scale economies, tropical plantation crops involving low capital intensity but also significant scale economies and requiring little if any skilled labor. Implicitly, by this argument, the model might claim to explain overall success or failure in attaining a high level of development. Yet the critical difference might in fact lie not in traits of the production functions of the principal exports but in the presence or absence of general preconditions for successful development in the characteristics and education of the indigenous population, institutional structure, rate of domestic saving, and the like. One can obviously devise research strategies to get around this dilemma, such as studying the consequences of different staple exports developed in the same country, either at the same time or without temporal separation by major institutional changes affecting the viability of sustained development. This is a matter of the tactics of research design rather than the strategy of selecting cases on which the export-led model might shed light, but it illustrates the principle that the relevant cases are not solely those of "successful development."

Let us turn now to some of the particular problems of specifying the model and selecting data for its empirical testing and use. A natural instinct of statistically inclined economists is to formulate it in terms of static and cross-national relationships. I shall argue that attempts to generalize it along those lines are usually dubious on a priori grounds, although they have in fact produced statistical results that credit the model with some explanatory power. If rapid growth of exports is supposed to favor rapid growth of income per capita, should one expect that wealthy countries at any point in time would trade a larger share of their gross output than do poorer countries? This hypothesis asks a great deal: not just that the model correctly identify one significant determinant of intensive growth in some set of national economies, but that it be the principal determinant of growth for the higher-income countries *and* that the poorer countries suffer no preponderance of growth failures — cases in which rapid trade expansion has led to high trade levels without corresponding growth per capita. Kuznets finds, after making adjustment for the relative size of countries in world commerce, that nations with higher income per capita in fact do have larger trade shares, but he quite reasonably attributes this to the results of the development process itself, the increasing span of the market economy and improvements in transport and communications. [41] There is also evidence that this relation between exports and income per capita holds in something approximating a first-differenced form: growth rate of real exports and growth rate of real GNP per capita. These variables are significantly related across a sample of 50 countries for the period 1953–1963; furthermore, the relation is found to hold more strongly among the industrialized countries (those with incomes per capita greater than $ 900 in 1964) and, among the less developed ones, more strongly for those with smaller concentrations of exports in food products. [42] This test likewise is quite indecisive about the hypothesis. It confirms only the general prediction of the model that export growth and intensive growth are related, and not the mechanism by which the relation is supposed to operate. The correlation in question thus might result from some other set of relationships. Over a period of 11 years, it is quite likely that any factor contributing to an unusual increase in real GNP would raise both income per capita and the capacity to export, thus producing the observed correlation. Cross-national analyses of this type probably can serve not to confirm the export-led model but rather to rule out any broad and systematic inconsistency of its predictions with the facts.

19.2.2. *Testing the model on historical data*

Tests of the export-led model, then, must intrinsically involve country case studies — present industrial countries, or now-wealthy nations in their years of rapid growth, or of presently underdeveloped countries. I shall concentrate here on the economic historian's problem of applying the model to the earlier stages of development in the high-income countries, although (as mentioned earlier) the model has been used in other settings as well. On the showing of Kuznets' research, after all, the years 1800–1913 appear to be highly promising for patterns of growth taking the export-led form. He estimates

[41] Kuznets [36, especially pp. 11, 25].
[42] Emery [21] ; Syron and Walsh [62].

average decennial growth rates of world income per capita during that period of 7.3%, of world trade 33%. The ratio of trade to world gross product was apparently increasing every decade by 24.1%, or from a level of about 3% in 1800 to about 33% in 1913. After 1913 the ratio behaved irregularly but declined overall to 22.2% in 1963. [43] For the older developed countries prior to World War I, the trend in the trade-to-income ratio was generally and significantly upward, not downward. In the regions of recent settlement, including such countries as Canada and Australia which are generally regarded as prime examples of export-led growth, the trend was actually less clear. [44] In short, export-led growth seems a matter of reasonable concern for the economic historian — some might say, only for the economic historian. [45]

Let us now turn to the problems of inference and research design for applying the model to explain the growth of a particular nation or region. These can be considered in relation to three of its functional aspects: (1) the incidence of disturbances in the export sector; (2) the link between exports and aggregate income or capacity; and (3) the link between aggregate and per capita growth. Particular emphasis is given to the problem of testing the export-led model against competing substantive hypotheses, rather than implicitly against a statistical nul hypothesis.

1. Exports as a source of disturbance

The theory underlying the model yields a list of disturbances tending to speed (or, symmetrically, delay) the expansion of the export sector. These

---

[43] Kuznets [37, especially pp. 7—10]. Although trade per capita grew slower than income per capita for the developed countries after 1913, it is not clear that the same holds for the less developed countries. Only for Latin America can a clear decline be shown. (*Ibid.*, pp. 17—18.)

[44] Kuznets [37, pp. 18—25]. Lack of a rising ratio of trade to income is no proof that export-led growth is inoperative; on the contrary, a sufficiently strong growth stimulus stemming from the export sector could raise income sufficiently to leave the ex-post ratio unaltered. Kuznets supplies another relevant factor: The regions of recent settlement were among the fastest growing countries in the world during the nineteenth century, therefore for their trade-to-income ratios to rise, very substantial resource allocations toward the export sectors of their slower-growing trading partners would have been required.

[45] Even for recent times, with many countries following conscious policies of import-substituting industrialization, the countries with faster growing exports remain those that also enjoy faster growing industrial production. Using data for the period 1937—1938 to 1955, Maizels [45, Chap. 5] found that countries with faster industrial growth tended if anything to increase their shares in world markets for their exports.

can include any force that raises the world price of, or shifts the foreign demand curve for the country's exportables, plus any domestic disturbance such as a natural-resource discovery or an important invention that produces a similarly discrete shift in the supply curve. Much of the burden of Kravis' evidence of the model's failure to explain the development of the United States in the nineteenth century rests on the absence of such disturbances, relative to the incidence of analogous changes encouraging the development of import-substituting activities. Changes in the terms of trade present a complex picture, but they were dominated by reductions in the price of imported manufactures rather than any recurrent favorable movements in export prices. There was no increase in the share that exports comprised of national product, which remained low throughout the period. The long-term trend from a passive to an active trade balance, which Kravis notes could hardly have been an independent major factor influencing growth, probably reflected changes in the volume of long-term capital inflows. Each of these findings conveys a presumption against a significant influence for export movements; a finding that seems to clinch the matter is a lack of any relation between annual series of exports and national income when exports lead by one year or coincide, only when they lag by one year. [46] Kravis' data begin in 1834; for the early years of the century, however, North's evidence gives the impression that movements in export proceeds did dominate the disturbances impinging on the economy. [47] North's evidence also indicates strongly that regional exports dominated patterns of extensive regional development during the first half of the nineteenth century.

On the other hand, statistical and descriptive analyses of several "regions of recent settlement" such as Canada, Australia, New Zealand, and South Africa make it clear that through much of their history the export sector has provided the primary source of disturbances to the economy. This is shown both by general analyses of eras of rapid and slow extensive growth and by statistical analyses of short-term income fluctuations, in which one can trace the influence of variations in exports on employment and the rate of capital formation as well as on the growth trend of national income. [48]

Relatively simple price-quantity data should often suffice to show whether the growth of exports conveys a foreign disturbance to the economy or rather

---

[46] Kravis [34, pp. 9–16].

[47] North [51, Chap. 5].

[48] Analyses in the short-run framework are offered for New Zealand by Simkin [60], for South Africa by Woods [70], and for Canada by various authors (see Caves and Holton [12, Chap. 3 and references cited therein]).

results from the expansion of domestic capacity. If disturbances arise predominantly from external demand, price and quantity changes should be positively correlated; if the disturbances arise from shifts in domestic supply, the correlation would be negative (zero if foreign demand is perfectly elastic). Technical information on the supply lag in export production can often be used. Application of these simple tools of price theory must avoid the automatic use of the assumption that equilibrium is quickly reached, however; North shows convincingly that that expansion of cotton production in the U.S. South continued for a long time without eliminating excess profits at the margin of cultivation. [49]

2. Export growth and aggregate domestic growth

If export disturbances can be shown to dominate the movements of selected measures of a country's aggregate economic activity, the next question becomes just which aggregates are most vitally affected by export growth and how these relations can be measured. The relation between export expansion and the growth of aggregate factor supplies acquires particular importance when one looks ahead to testing the explanatory power of the export-led growth model against models embodying other hypotheses about the determinants of growth. Why emphasize the expansion of factor supplies — an input measure of growth? The export-led growth model is but one of a class of models that relate variations in the rate of extensive economic growth to some "strategic factor," especially a component of aggregate demand. Other approaches emphasize the growth of supplies of factors of production as primary determinants of growth. When these latter explanations are pressed to their Denisonian [50] conclusion, all strategic factors tend to disappear, and the growth of the economic whole becomes the definitional sum of the growth of its parts. These two approaches seem quite at variance with one another. [51] They become complementary, however, if one restricts the role of "strategic factors" to governing the change in aggregate supplies of factors of production, particularly the rate of accumulation of capital (in its various forms), the rate of resources transfer from inefficient sectors, and the rate of technological advance. Hence the impor-

---

[49] North [51, pp. 123–125]. Also, see Gunewardena [26, p. 56].

[50] Denison [19] and Denison with Poullier [20].

[51] Attempts to explain differing rates of growth among the industrial countries since Worl War II have tended strongly to fall into these competing groups. For a summary of some of the principal contending approaches see Cornwall [16].

tance of the relation between export expansion and these various components of factor supply and organization is manifest.

Once again, the "regions of recent settlement" have demonstrated the connection between export growth and the expansion of total factor supplies in the form of international flows of capital and labor. Study over the years of the process of international capital transfer to such countries as Canada, Australia, and Argentina has shown that classical transfer theory, treating the capital movement as an unexplained disturbance, would generally not provide a satisfactory interpretation of the facts unless one alters the model to allow for its dependence on an export-led domestic boom. [52] One problem of inference arises regularly because of the large portion of foreign borrowings that have frequently supported governmental and social-overhead capital formation rather than export activities or production facilities linked directly to them. This raises the problem, noted earlier, of deciding to what extent export prospects sustain not only the borrower's confidence in the productivity of "domestic improvements" but also the lender's confidence that the borrowing country's foreign balance will permit remission of interest and principal. [53] The amount of inducement that can be credited to export booms is obviously restrained to the degree that investments in the primary exporting sector and in sheltered industries or social-overhead facilities can be shown to be seriously competitive with one another in the short run either for foreign funds or current domestic inputs. [54] It is also restrained if levels of public borrowing that occur during export booms, and apparently because of the prospects and incentives that they generate, are sustained by other needs and enthusiasms when the rate of export growth is curtailed. [55]

As was noted in the evaluation of the wheat boom's contribution to Canadian real income, the welfare significance of foreign and domestic saving are not the same, and the latter can prima facie claim a more important role. The effect of export expansion on the domestic saving rate is thus a topic deserving more research than it has received; unfortunately, primitive estimates of national incomes for years long past make this difficult, and institutional analysis of the sources of financing for particular activities would be necessary.

[52] On Canada, see Meier [47].

[53] On Australia see Robinson [56, p. 70], and Butlin [8, pp. 408–417].

[54] Butlin [8, pp. 376–379; 391–398].

[55] Studies of New Zealand (Simkin [60, p. 440]) and Australia (Butlin [8, *loc. cit.*]) indicate at least moderate independence of foreign borrowing from export movements, although a major export slump is sufficient to kill off new public borrowing abroad.

The effect of export-led growth on international migration seems well established for certain countries. For Canada, gross immigration has been found statistically related to gross domestic business investment, and gross emigration related to previous levels of immigration and to the growth rate of incomes in countries supplying and competing for migrants. [56] As with Canada, the flow of migrants to New Zealand has been found sensitive enough to fluctuations in export prospects for net emigration to occur in depressed times; such a pattern is less clearly evident for South Africa only because of the intervention of policy decisions. [57]

In exploring the relation between expansion of the export sector and the growth of aggregate domestic output, it often appears fruitful to employ that once-respected art form, business-cycle analysis. In countries most clearly matching the export-led growth model, the rate of export expansion appears to be connected to the movements of at least some of the following variables; rate of capital formation, money supply, rate of domestic saving or capital inflow, unemployment or net immigration, and the growth of the import-competing manufacturing sector. In the case of Canada, for example, up to the 1950's national income and capital formation seemed more closely related to exports in the previous year than to current exports; the exports-investment relation clearly embodied an accelerator-type relation, with exports of goods alone related more closely to capital formation than were exports of goods and services taken together. Australia seems to show the same pattern, including notably a positive correlation between the growth of farm (staple) income and the growth of manufacturing output. [58] Where foreign ownership is common in the export sector, short-run effects on the domestic economy may be related not to gross sales of exports but rather to the export sector's domestic outlays (current and capital) for factor payments, intermediate goods and taxes — what Reynolds calls "returned value" in his study of the Chilean economy. [59]

This short-run statistical "accelerator" relation between exports and

---

[56] Caves and Holton [12, pp. 129–140 passim].

[57] On New Zealand, Condliffe [15, Chap. 1]; on South Africa, de Kock [18]. This relation is likely not to hold over very short periods; cf. Simkin [60, pp. 48; 162–165] on New Zealand.

[58] Caves and Holton [12, Chap. 3] on Canada; Robinson [56, p. 70] on Australia.

[59] Reynolds [55, especially pp. 273–278]. Reynolds also shows (pp. 334–341) that in sectors such as copper mining where investment projects are large and "lumpy" no short-run relation between export sales and capital formation may appear, although a long-run one is clearly involved.

investment may answer one question often raised about the significance of export growth in a maturing economy: As an increasing share of capital formation consists of residential construction, social overhead facilities, and import-competing or sheltered activities, how much importance can we ascribe to export growth as a stimulus to investment? On the one hand, the levels of these activities are not directly determined by the level of export production; on the other, their movements (and thus the long-term level of capital formation) may be strongly affected by swings in "business confidence" that in turn rest on the condition of the export sector. [60] Behavioral evidence on the general tone of discourse on commercial prospects may be worth something for testing the latter hypothesis, but in the last analysis it is a statistical question of the foreign-trade accelerator relation. [61]

The information required for short-run analysis of this type may tax the quantity and quality of the national-income data available for many countries in earlier years. Proxies, however, can often be devised. When most capital goods are imported, data on their volume and its relation to consumer-goods imports can answer questions that would otherwise be addressed to the behavior of domestic investment and consumption. [62]

3. Export growth and growth of income per capita

The final link in the export-led model runs from variations in the growth of the export sector, or variations in aggregate expansion induced by the export sector to variations in the growth of income per capita. As appeared from the discussion of Chambers and Gordon's contribution, this connection has received the least successful treatment in empirical research using the model, partly because the appropriate theoretical reasoning was not developed explicitly, partly because of difficulties in securing the necessary empirical data. At least some of the critical causal connections running from export expansion to various sources of intensive growth should prove reasonably easy to test. One type of causal connection is the inducement of innovation, either in the export sector itself or in domestic sectors sufficient-

---

[60] For an Australian discussion along these lines, see Butlin [8] and Robinson [56].

[61] Underlying this discussion or the business cycle generally, and the accelerator in particular, is the assumption that fluctuating export growth leads to a higher average growth rate of aggregate demand over time than would otherwise prevail, and also a higher rate of capital formation. It is unlikely that fluctuations are good for intensive growth per se, although recent research fails to confirm the opposite prediction; see MacBean [43].

[62] Cf. Simkin [60, Chaps. 1,5].

ly affected by export growth to produce a visible increase in the prospective profits from innovation or discovery. Such linkages may also affect other determinants of productivity (broadly defined), such as the attainment of economics of scale and the extent to which optimum technical efficiency ("X-efficiency") in the combination of inputs is achieved. Real-income gains per capita may also result if export expansion is explicitly linked to any form or aspect of capital accumulation, including not just an increased rate of domestic saving for physical investment in the export or related sectors but also induced investment in human resources (including the supply of entrepreneurship) or social overhead capital that are attributable to expansion in the export sector. Export-led growth may also be linked to intensive growth simply because it contributes to extensive expansion of the economy, and extensive expansion from whatever source declares dividends (perhaps at a constant Denisonian rate) in intensive growth. This linkage commands less claim to attention for the export-led model than those previously listed, however, since it allots export expansion no more role than any other source of extensive growth in raising income per capita.

The simplest of these links to intensive growth is that between expansion of the export sector and induced innovation in that sector itself. Descriptive and qualitative evidence of this is fairly persuasive in a number of cases. Youngson's case studies of economic progress in Britain, Sweden, and Denmark stress the inducement of productivity-increasing changes by the rise of new market opportunities or contacts in export markets. The changes take numerous forms: technological innovations, changes in production scale, changes in the organization of production or marketing activities, or the installation of facilitating types of social overhead capital. [63] Kindleberger's review of the evidence on Britain's growth in both the late eighteenth and mid-nineteenth centuries also credits much to technological innovation associated with opportunities to enter expanding foreign markets. [64] In the Canadian case and others like it, the discovery and diffusion of innovations both seem in numerous cases to be bound up with the expansion of various resource-based exports. The evidence of available secondary sources is often less than convincing, however, that specific discoveries were purposive rather than random, and that diffusion occurred more rapidly than it would have in the absence of profits from export sales inflated by a high price or rapidly expanding demand. There is certainly nothing inevitable about induced innovation, and Kindleberger's reading of British industrial histories in the

[63] Youngson [71, Chaps. 6, 8−10, pp. 270−273].
[64] Kindleberger [30, pp. 290−291]; Kindleberger [31, pp. 196−197].

late nineteenth century reveals to him little if any relation between rates of export expansion and innovation. [65]

An important contribution to theoretical synthesis of the export-led model was Baldwin's [1] suggestion that the effects on an economy of the development of a particular export can be associated to a large extent with the traits of its production function – the particular inputs required, the conditions and location of their use, the incidence of scale economies and the like. Comparing one staple's production function and its economic consequences with those of another staple provides a particularly effective way to evaluate the effects of the expansion of particular exports on intensive growth. Historical studies of today's less-developed countries may prove as rewarding for this purpose as research on the presently developed nations, because of the relative preoccupation of some of the former economies with single staple exports and the absence of complementary stimuli for change from other sources. On the other hand, if one is inquiring whether the cultivation of wheat or bananas is likely to contribute more to a nation's economic development, a false inference might well result because bananas have been cultivated only in regions unreceptive to development stimuli for other reasons, wheat only in highly receptive regions. The development and change induced by the expansion of any given export-oriented activity will surely depend both upon that sector's particular input requirements and conditions of production and the extent to which the surrounding economy has achieved any general preconditions for growth needed for it to receive the message. Consider, for example, the finding often stated in the literature on economic development that resource allocations to certain export staples become habituated and resist reassignments clearly indicated by current and prospective opportunity costs. Does this ossification result from the characteristics of production of these products or from general social conditions in the economy that produces them? Did "sugar economies" fail to diversify because sugar is like bituminous coal in its conditions of production, or because sugar was produced in backward economies? [66] Evidence from the less-developed countries must clearly be used with care.

---

[65] Kindleberger [30, pp. 296–197]. Also see Parker [53]. Schmookler's important study [59] ascribes to output growth and capital formation a dominant role in determining the rate of invention.

[66] Wallich [68, pp. 12–13]; Frankel [24, pp. 130–134]. In his study of the behavior of Europe's terms of trade, Kindleberger [27] found that deterioration of national terms of trade had been associated not with the production for export of primary products but with production by underdeveloped economies.

To develop quantitative measures of the linkages between a given export activity and sources of intensive growth involves many practical difficulties, and most historical research proceeds by qualitative comparison of the consequences of different resource-based exports. This exercise holds particular interest when a single country (or its various regions) have experienced the expansion of a number of different export-based sectors, so that the analysis can proceed relatively unhampered by the difficulties that plague inter-country comparisons. [67] If successful, it should provide at least a ranking of resource-based exportables in terms of their contribution (per value unit of output) to intensive growth through any given linkage.

I shall list some of the channels that appear to be more broadly significant and indicate the nature of their connection to sources of intensive growth. Some comments will also be included on the problems of inference that arise in measuring these linkages and on the extent to which they are likely to depend on general environmental conditions as well as on the production process for the particular staple. The list omits those linkages that seem important only for a few products or that hold interest mainly in context of the presently less-developed countries. [68]

1. More favorable linkages stem from exports that require skilled labor than those using unskilled labor. The influence of skill requirements may operate in a number of different ways: (a) Greater incentives are provided for capital formation through education; (b) On-the-job training in the export sector may be disseminated at little real cost through the movement of workers into other sectors or occupations; (c) Skilled workers may be a source of entrepreneurship; (d) Skilled workers may save more of their wage incomes than unskilled workers. North reports a marked contrast between southern cotton and western wheat on this and other attributes in the development of the United States during the early nineteenth century, [69] and the failure to inculcate labor skills is a trait often ascribed to tropical plantation agriculture.

2. An absence of substantial economies of scale in the production of the export staple seems to favor its contribution to intensive growth. Scale economies tend to imply large capital requirements for establishment of enterprises, hence extraregional or foreign borrowing (with no incentive for

[67] Cf. the summary of research on regional development in the United States provided by Perloff and Wingo [54, pp. 199–204].

[68] The latter are discussed by Baldwin [2] and Myint [48, Chaps. 3, 4]. Also see Levin [39, Chaps. 3, 4]; Watkins [69, pp. 145–152].

[69] North [51, pp. 133, 154].

local saving), absentee ownership and no contribution to the supply of local entrepreneurial talent or profit income available for local reinvestment. North also finds this contrast between the staples of the south and west, and it can be drawn among the various staples exported by various less-developed countries. [70]

3. Staples tend to favor intensive growth if they encourage the construction of social overhead capital. This proposition is probabilistic rather than necessary, because a staple could detract from real income if it encouraged excessive or premature construction of social overhead facilities, yielding a social rate of return at the margin less than that on alternative commercial investments. This caveat underlines the case for retrospective measurements of the rate of return on transport facilities and other improvements that may be motivated by the development of certain staple exports. In any case, without making these measurements, various scholars have given favorable marks to export products that have clearly encouraged the construction of railroads and other common-use facilities. [71]

4. Various characteristics of the transport facilities needed to produce and export a staple may affect its linkages to the economy. A commodity that is perishable or weight losing in processing for final consumption encourages the development of local processing industries. The presence or absence of this feature is clearly important for explaining contrasts in patterns of extensive development; whether it matters similarly for intensive development depends, however, on the extent to which the resulting industrialization generates external economies and other real gains through manpower training, commercial specialization, and the like. In any case such "forward linkages" tending to encourage the establishment of processing industries have been noted for numerous temperate-zone agricultural products and some minerals. Contrasts between staples developed within a single country or region have been noted. [72]

5. Another relevant trait of the transport requirements of a staple is its relative bulk, i.e., the volume of shipping space required per unit of FOB. value, in comparison with the volume required by an equivalent value

[70] North [51, pp. 125, 154–155]; Levin [39, pp. 145–147]; see Gunewardena [26, pp. 25–28, 76], for a comparison of tea, rubber and coconuts in Ceylon.

[71] See North [51, p. 125] on cotton in the United States; Neumark [49, Chap. 11], and de Kock [18] on Africa; and Butlin [8, pp. 301–303], on Australia.

[72] See Caves and Holton [12, pp. 179–180] on Canadian regional contrasts; Condliffe [15, pp. 240–241] on New Zealand; Stewart [61, p. 126] on the contrast between phosphate and agricultural staples in Morocco.

unit of the goods for which it is typically traded. Bulky cargoes tend to generate excess capacity on the backhauls and, hence, transport costs at or near the level of marginal costs for the producing region's imports. For better or worse, this means no "natural protection" for import-competing producers in the region. As with the previous trait, of weight-losing processing, the significance of a staple's relative bulkiness cannot be predicted a priori. If the absence of natural protection averts the establishment of a complex of import-competing industries that would in turn generate favorable externalities or linkages, then the effect may be negative. North suggests this for the cotton industry in the U.S. South. [73]

6. The capital-intensity of a staple's production process does not in itself seem to point in any definite direction for predicting its linkages to intensive growth. A high capital-output ratio may interact favorably with other traits, however. One such combination is high capital intensity with an absence of scale economics. This package tends to encourage a high rate of regional capital formation and saving by entrepreneurs and others. [74]

7. High capital intensity can prove unfavorable when combined with other attributes. To invert the previous case, combined with significant economies of scale, it forces dependence on external entrepreneurship and provides no incentive for domestic saving. If, as is likely but not necessary, it is associated with the use of highly complex machinery, it may fail to encourage the development of local production and servicing of machinery and sustain dependence on imported capital goods. [75]

8. The expansion of an export staple raises productivity in the economy at large if it brings previously underutilized factors of production into fuller use, i.e., creates rents or quasi-rents. Chambers and Gordon properly emphasize the primary rent created in resource-based production. The same kind of gain can accrue in other forms, however. Agricultural staples' requirements for labor normally have seasonal patterns which may complement those of other rural occupations, raising the average level of labor utilization. Of course, the seasonal peaks of different activities might also coincide. Where a productive resource is partly utilized in another activity, the creation of a rent depends on a fortuitous dove-tailing of use patterns. As with natural-resource rents,

---

[73] North [51, pp. 126, 153–154].

[74] Caves and Holton [12, pp. 175–178].

[75] See North [51, pp. 131–132] on the U.S. cotton economy; Levin [39, pp. 154–164] on entrepreneurship in the "export economies." The same points are often noted in connection with petroleum and similar staple exports from the present less-developed countries.

the gains from fuller utilization of labor, transportation facilities and the like offer interesting possibilities of measurement that do not seem to have been exploited. Where natural-resource rents accrue as profits to foreign entrepreneurs, the critical question for national welfare is the extent to which they are recaptured via taxation. [76]

9. The level of entrepreneurial skill required for the development of a staple export contributes the most effective augmentation to the region's factor supply if it is high enough to offer challenges and instill abilities useable in other sectors but not so high as to require the importing of a transient class of skilled managerial labor. Just as petroleum extraction is often criticized for offering no chances to native entrepreneurial talent, other staples have demonstrated entrepreneurial requirements that do seem to raise the effective skill level of the local entrepreneurial class and thus contribute to a general increase in the level of productivity. [77]

10. A staple tends to contribute to a region's intensive growth if the distribution of personal income associated with its pattern of factor use and factor payments tends to raise the region's propensity to save. This general criterion is evident enough, but it is not an easy source of operational criteria. Should it yield an uneven distribution of income by utilizing unskilled labor and large masses of capital? Or should it tend to provide broadly based incentives to save by requiring skilled labor and ingesting capital in small quantities? The first pattern may be unfavorable to national capital per worker, and thus income per head, if the capital is imported (and capitalist incomes exported). If only domestic factors are involved, then the case is not so clear and comes to depend not only on the input requirements of the individual export project but also the factor endowment and institutional saving and investment patterns of the region in which it is produced. [78]

11. Its pattern of geographical dispersion or concentration of staple production may affect the contribution of a particular export to general

[76] The theoretical argument underlying this paragraph is elaborated in Caves [11]. For examples respectively of complementary and competing patterns of labor utilization see Lockwood [41, p. 197], and Wallich [68, pp. 12–13]. Reynolds [55, Chap. 2] provides an excellent analysis of the role of taxes in recapturing resource rents in the Chilean copper industry.

[77] Lockwood [41, pp. 213–214]; Gunewardena [26, pp. 25–27; 75–76]; Simkin [60, pp. 169–171].

[78] See North [51, pp. 52; 131–132]; Levin [39, pp. 177–179]. Brazil in the 1880s seems to represent a case in which staple growth yielding unequally distributed income did generate substantial saving; see Loeb [42, p. 88]. For a related theoretical analysis see Galenson and Leibenstein [25].

productivity. The usual argument favors geographic concentration on account of the low-cost reallocations between sectors and the common use of specialized facilities that become possible in an "industrial complex." Quantitative evidence on this effect would surely be difficult to establish, but comparison of regional development histories within a nation is likely to prove enlightening. [79]

This list of possible linkages between the expansion of staple production for export and sources of intensive growth indicates the range of consequences that export-led growth may have, depending on the product in question and the traits of the economy in which it is produced. However, it omits one alleged consequence of export-led expansion for intensive growth — one that is difficult to measure but analytically important. The model identifies the uniqueness of the export-led stimulus with the discovery or innovative use of some resource, or more generally with the discovery of a comparative advantage that makes profitable a substantial expansion in the output of some export activity. While the economy is responding to this stimulus, it may in some sense be in short-run but not long-run neoclassical equilibrium. In a developing economy where many saving decisions and investment commitments rest on hunches and "animal spirits" rather than cold calculations of the marginal efficiency of investment, such a growth process is likely to spur a larger quantity of capital formation and more diverse types of projects, than a growth process not attended by windfalls and an apparent backlog of opportunities. After the event, some of these commitments may prove to have been unwise, and real costs of misallocation will have been incurred. Many may have been right, however, and result in surplus-yielding activities that would otherwise have been delayed or neglected.

Students of export-led growth processes have taken general note of this phenomenon, but I know of no attempt to show to what extent these induced flurries of activity do result in new projects or activities that subsequently fulfill their promise by yielding normal or greater rates of return. It might be fruitful to study the results of an analogous but sharper disturbance that has strongly affected the growth patterns of nations such as Canada and Australia: major wars in which they were not involved as primary combatants but which denied them access to many imports while creating inflated markets for their exports. A massive incentive results for innovation

[79] Lockwood [41, pp. 233–234; 318; 373].

and expansion in both export- and import-competing sectors, especially for manufactured goods, and new industries spring up. After peacetime conditions return, some of these new activities prove viable, some do not. War is often a more powerful but a more transitory disturbance than the development of an important export staple, in the extra demands for both final and intermediate goods that it generates. If activities born of wartime booms often achieve long-run survival in countries where export-led growth processes appear to have operated, then similar (if smaller) gains can be attributed to the booms stimulated by export expansion. [80]

19.3. Summary

The export-led, or staple, growth model emerged from research in Canadian economic history primarily to explain variations in the growth of aggregate economic activity, including factor inflows, in relation to swings in the export of staple products. Chambers and Gordon have recently extended this model by producing an operational method for calculating the effects of an export boom on welfare, i.e., income per capita. The sources of gain that they identify for Canada's wheat boom during the years 1901–1911, additional rents on wheat land and tariff revenue on imports, contributed only 10% of the total increase in real income per capita over that decade. This figure can be raised to 21.4%, however, when other linkages between aggregate growth (induced by the boom) and income per capita are taken into account.

General reflection on the export-led model as a research tool suggests that appropriate statistical cross-country tests are difficult to devise. It is more appropriately tested on national or regional historical data. Operational methods that respect the scarcity and weakness of historical data can be employed to test each of the major segments of the model: the predominance of export growth as a source of disturbance; the relation between export growth and aggregate domestic growth; and the relation between export growth (or induced aggregate growth) and the growth of income per capita.

---

[80] For discussions of the effects of wartime disturbances, see Vernon [66] on Mexico; Lockwood [41, pp. 262–263] on Japan; Loeb [42, e.g., p. 98] on Brazil.

References

[1] Baldwin, R.E. "Patterns of Development in Newly Settled Regions." *Manchester School* XXIV (May 1954) 161–179.

[2] Baldwin, R.E. "Export Technology and Development from a Subsistence Level." *Economic Journal* LXIII (March 1963) 80–92.

[3] Baldwin, R.E. *Economic Development and Export Growth: A Study of Northern Rhodesia, 1920–1960.* Berkeley and Los Angeles: Univ. of California Press, 1966.

[4] Beckerman, W. "Projecting Europe's Growth." *Economic Journal* LXII (December 1962) 912–925.

[5] Beckerman, W. "The Determinants of Economic Growth," *Economic Growth in Britain,* ed. P.D. Henderson. London: Weidenfeld & Nicolson, 1966, pp. 55–83.

[6] Berrill, K. "International Trade and the Rate of Economic Growth," *Economic History Review* XII (April 1960) 351–359.

[7] Buckley, K.A.H. *Capital Formation in Canada, 1896–1930.* Canadian Studies in Economics, No. 2, Toronto: University of Toronto Press, 1955.

[8] Butlin, N.G. *Investment in Australian Economic Development, 1861–1900.* Cambridge, England: At the University Press, 1964.

[9] Canada, Census Office. *Fourth Census of Canada, 1901.* 4 vols., Ottawa: King's Printer, 1902–1906.

[10] Canada, Census and Statistics Office. *Fifth Census of Canada, 1911.* 4 vols., Ottawa: King's Printer, 1912–1914.

[11] Caves, R.E." 'Vent for Surplus' Models of Trade and Growth," in R.E. Baldwin *et al., Trade, Growth, and the Balance of Payments: Essays in Honor of Gottfried Haberler.* Chicago and Amsterdam: Rand McNally and North-Holland Publishing Co., 1965, p. 95–115.

[12] Caves, R.E. and Holton, R.H. *The Canadian Economy: Prospect and Retrospect.* Harvard Economic Studies, No. 112, Cambridge, Mass.: Harvard University Press, 1959.

[13] Chambers, E.J. and Gordon, D.F. "Primary Products and Economic Growth: An Empirical Measurement." *Journal of Political Economy* LXXIV (August 1966) 315–332.

[14] Chambers, E.J. and Gordon, D.F. "Rejoinder." *Journal of Political Economy* LXXV (December 1967), 881–885.

[15] Condliffe, J.B. *New Zealand in the Making: A Study of Economic and Social Development.* Rev. ed., London: George Allen & Unwin Ltd., 1959.

[16] Cornwall, J. "Postwar Growth in Western Europe: A Re-evaluation." *Review of Economics and Statistics* L (August 1968) 361–368.

[17] Dales, J.H., McManus, J.C. and Watkins, M.H. "Primary Products and Economic Growth: A Comment." *Journal of Political Economy* LXXV (December 1967) 876–880.

[18] de Kock, M.H. *The Economic Development of South Africa.* London: P.S. King & Staples, Ltd., 1936.

[19] Denison, E.F. *The Sources of Economic Growth in the United States and the Alternatives Before Us.* Supplementary Paper No. 13, New York: U.S. Committee for Economic Development, 1962.

[20] Denison, E.F., with Poullier, J.P. *Why Growth Rates Differ: Postwar Experience in Nine Western Countries.* Washington, D.C.: The Brookings Institution, 1967.

[21] Emery, R.F. "The Relation of Exports and Economic Growth." *Kyklos,* XX, No. 2 (1967) 470–486.

[22] Firestone, O.J. *Canada's Economic Development, 1867–1953.* International Association for Research in Income and Wealth, Vol. 7, London: Bowes & Bowes, 1958.

[23] Fogel, Robert W. "The Reunification of Economic History with Economic Theory." *American Economic Review* LV (May 1965) 92–98.

[24] Frankel, S.H. *The Economic Impact on Under-developed Societies: Essays on International Investment and Social Change.* Oxford: Basil Blackwell and Mott, Ltd., 1953.

[25] Galenson, W. and Leibenstein, H. "Investment Criteria, Productivity, and Economic Development." *Quarterly Journal of Economics* LXIX (August 1955) 343–370.

[26] Gunewardena, E. *External Trade and the Economic Structure of Ceylon, 1900–1955.* Colombo: Central Bank of Ceylon, 1965.

[27] Kindleberger, C.P. *The Terms of Trade: A European Case Study.* Cambridge, Mass., and New York: The Technology Press of M.I.T. and John Wiley & Sons, Inc., 1956.

[28] Kindleberger, C.P. *Economic Development.* New York: The McGraw-Hill Publishing Co. Inc., 1958.

[29] Kindleberger, C. P. "International Trade and Investment and Resource Use in Economic Growth," *Natural Resources and Economic Growth,* ed. J.J. Spengler. Washington, D.C.: Resources for the Future, 1961, pp. 151–187.

[30] Kindleberger, C.P. "Foreign Trade and Economic Growth: Lessons from Britain and France, 1850 to 1912," *Economic History Review* XIV (December 1961) 289–305.

[31] Kindleberger, C.P. *Foreign Trade and the National Economy.* New Haven and London: The Yale University Press, 1962.

[32] Kindleberger, C.P. "Foreign Trade and Growth: Lessons from British Experience since 1913," *Lloyds Bank Review* No. 65 (July 1962) 16–28.

[33] Kindleberger, C.P. *Economic Growth in France and Britain, 1851–1950.* Cambridge, Mass.: Harvard University Press, 1964.

[34] Kravis, I.B. "Trade as a Handmaiden of Growth: Similarities between the 19th and 20th Centuries." University of Pennsylvania, Department of Economics, Discussion Paper No. 105, October 1968.

[35] Kuznets, S.S. *Six Lectures on Economic Growth.* New York: The Free Press of Glencoe, 1959.

[36] Kuznets, S.S. "Quantitative Aspects of the Economic Growth of Nations: IX. Level and Structure of Foreign Trade: Comparisons for Recent Years." *Economic Development and Cultural Change* XIII (October 1964) Part II.

[37] Kuznets, S.S. "Quantitative Aspects of the Economic Growth of Nations: X. Level and Structure of Foreign Trade: Long-term Trends." *Economic Development and Cultural Change* XV (January 1967) Part II.

[38] Lamfalussy, A. *The United Kingdom and the Six: An Essay on Economic Growth in Western Europe.* Homewood, Ill.: Richard D. Irwin, Inc., 1963.

[39] Levin, J.V. *The Export Economies: Their Pattern of Development in Historical Perspective.* Cambridge, Mass.: Harvard University Press, 1960.

[40] Lloyd, P.J. *International Trade Problems of Small Nations.* Durham, N.C.: Duke University Press, 1968.

[41] Lockwood, W.W. *The Economic Development of Japan: Growth and Structural Change, 1868–1938.* Princeton, N.J.: Princeton University Press, 1954.

[42] Loeb, G.F. *Industrialization and Balanced Growth, with Special Reference to Brazil.* Groningen: J.B. Walters, 1957.

[43] MacBean, A.I. *Export Instability and Economic Development.* London: George Allen & Unwin, Ltd., 1966.

[44] Mackintosh, W.A. *The Economic Background of Dominion-Provincial Relations.* Appendix 3 to Report of the Royal Commission on Dominion-Provincial Relations. Ottawa: King's Printer, 1939.

[45] Maizels, A. *Industrial Growth and World Trade: Empirical Study of Trends in Production, Consumption and Trade in Manufactures from 1899–1959 with a Discussion of Probable Future Trends.* National Institute of Economic and Social Research, Economic and Social Studies, No. 21. Cambridge, England: Cambridge University Press, 1963.

[46] McKinnon, R.I. and Oates, W.E. *The Implications of International Economic Integration for Monetary, Fiscal, and Exchange-Rate Policy.* Princeton Studies in International Finance, No. 16. Princeton, N.J.: International Finance Section, Princeton University, 1966.

[47] Meier, G.M. "Economic Development and the Transfer Mechanism: Canada, 1895–1913." *Canadian Journal of Economies and Political Science* XIX (February 1953) 1–19.

[48] Myint, H. *The Economics of the Developing Countries.* London: Hutchinson & Co. (Publishers) Ltd., 1964.

[49] Neumark, S.D. *Foreign Trade and Economic Development in Africa: A Historical Perspective.* Miscellaneous Publication No. 14, Stanford, Calif.: Food Research Institute, Stanford University, 1964.

[50] North, D.C. "Location Theory and Regional Economic Growth." *Journal of Political Economy* LXIII (June 1955) 243–258.

[51] North, D.C. *The Economic Growth of the United States, 1790–1860.* Englewood Cliffs, N.J.: Prentice-Hall Inc., 1961.

[52] Nurkse, R. *Equilibrium and Growth in the World Economy: Economic Essays.* Harvard Economic Studies, Vol. 118. Cambridge, Mass.: Harvard University Press, 1961.

[53] Parker, W.N. "Economic Development in Historical Perspective." *Economic Development and Cultural Change* X (October 1961) 1–7.

[54] Perloff, Harvey S. and Wingo, L., Jr. "Natural Resource Endowment and Regional Economic Growth." *Natural Resources and Economic Growth,* ed. J.J. Spengler, Washington, D.C.: Resources for the Future, 1961, pp. 191–212.

[55] Reynolds, C.W. "Development Problems of an Export Economy: The Case of Chile and Copper," in M. Mamalakis and C.W. Reynolds, *Essays on the Chilean Economy,* Homewood, Ill.: Richard D. Irwin, Inc., 1965, pp. 203–398.

[56] Robinson, A.J. "Exports and Economic Development." *Quarterly Review of Economics and Business* VI (Autumn 1966) 63–74.

[57] Roemer, M. "The Dynamic Role of Exports in Economic Development: the Fishmeal Industry in Peru, 1956–66." Ph.D. dissertation, Massachusetts Institute of Technology, 1968.

[58] Romans, J.T. *Capital Exports and Growth among U.S. Regions.* New England Research Series No. 1, Middletown, Conn.: Wesleyan University Press, 1965.

[59] Schmookler, J. *Invention and Economic Growth.* Cambridge, Mass.: Harvard University Press, 1966.

[60] Simkin, C.G.F. *The Instability of a Dependent Economy: Economic Fluctuations in New Zealand, 1840–1914.* London: Oxford University Press, 1951.

[61] Stewart, C.F. *The Economy of Morocco, 1912–1962.* Harvard Middle Eastern Monographs, No. 12, Cambridge, Mass.: Harvard University Press, 1964.

[62] Syron, R.F. and B.M. Walsh. "The Relation of Exports and Economic Growth: A Note." *Kyklos* XXI, No. 3 (1968) 541–554.

[63] Tiebout, C.M. "Exports and Regional Economic Growth." *Journal of Political Economy* LXIV (April 1956) 160–169.

[64] United States Bureau of the Census. *Historical Statistics of the United States, 1789–1945.* Washington, D.C.: Government Printing Office, 1949.

[65] Urquhart, M.C. and Buckley, K.A.H., eds. *Historical Statistics of Canada.* Cambridge and Toronto: Cambridge University Press and The Macmillan Co. of Canada, Ltd., 1965.

[66] Vernon, R. *The Dilemma of Mexico's Development: The Roles of the Private and Public Sectors.* Cambridge, Mass.: Harvard University Press, 1963.

[67] Viner, J. *Canada's Balance of International Indebtedness, 1900–1913.* Harvard Economic Studies, No. 26, Cambridge, Mass.: Harvard University Press, 1924.

[68] Wallich, H.C. *Monetary Problems of an Export Economy: The Cuban Experience, 1914–1947.* Harvard Economic Studies, No. 88, Cambridge, Mass.: Harvard University Press, 1950.

[69] Watkins, M.H. "A Staple Theory of Economic Growth." *Canadian Journal of Economics and Political Science* XXIX (May 1963) 141–158.

[70] Woods, I.R. "Some Aspects of South Africa's Foreign Trade in Relation to Her Aggregate Income, 1910–1954." *South African Journal of Economics* XXVI (June 1958) 136–151.

[71] Youngson, A.J. *Possibilities of Economic Progress.* Cambridge, England: Cambridge University Press, 1959.

CHAPTER 20

SOME ASPECTS OF THE BRAZILIAN EXPERIENCE WITH FOREIGN AID *

Carlos F. DIAZ-ALEJANDRO

Disenchantment with foreign aid is shared by both donor and recipient countries. The purpose of this paper is to explore some of the sources of this mood in the case of one large country, Brazil, which during 1964—1967 ranked only behind India, Pakistan, and South Vietnam as a recipient of net official aid flows. [1]

No attempt will be made to cover all aspects of the Brazilian foreign aid experience; discussion will center on topics that have received relatively little emphasis in the aid literature. These include difficulties imposed by the initial conditions on the achievement of large real transfers, the discontinuity of aid and its frequent changes of objectives, disbursement lags, and the relevance of Brazilian experience to the program versus project debate.

Brazil has relied on foreign sources during most postwar years to finance current account deficits in its balance of payments. The algebraic sum of those deficits from 1950 through 1960 reached $2.8 billion; the corresponding figure for 1961 through 1968 was $1.5 billion. External financing has taken many forms, many of which cannot be labelled aid.

* I am grateful to Edmar Bacha, Werner Baer, Jagdish Bhagwati, and Albert Fishlow for helpful comments. Remaining errors and opinions are my sole responsibility.

[1] Net official flows to Brazil from bilateral and multilateral donors during 1964—1967 amounted to $222 million per year. See *Partners in Development*, Report of the Commission of International Development, Lester B. Pearson, Chairman (New York: Frederick A. Praeger, Inc., 1969), p. 392, Table 27.

20.1. An outline of pre-1961 Foreign Financing of the Brazilian Balance of Payments

Before 1961, marking the birth of the Alliance for Progress, Brazil relied for its external financing mainly on private sources, including suppliers' credits, and on bilateral and multilateral public institutions lending at near-commercial rates, such as the U.S. Export-Import Bank (EXIMBANK) and the International Bank for Reconstruction and Development (IBRD). The pre-1961 experience left a legacy of financial commitments that had a marked influence on the post-1961 years, when aid became a more important element in external financing. A closer look at the pre-1961 capital account is therefore warranted.

A summary of the Brazilian balance of payments during the 1950s is presented in Table 20.1. During those years, the net capital inflow represented 17% of merchandise imports and more than 5% of gross fixed investment. The average figures hide considerable fluctuations in the net capital inflow; current account deficits larger than $450 million were

Table 20.1
Brazilian Balance of Payments, 1950 through 1960
(Annual averages, million current dollars)

Current Account	
Exports, FOB	$1,430
Imports, CIF	−1,480
Net nonfinancial services and private transfers	− 65
Net income payments on direct investments	− 79
Other net factor payments abroad	− 60
Net Capital Inflow	−$ 254
Capital Account	
Public transfers	$ 5
Net direct investments	106
Net short term capital, including changes in net short-term assets	97
Medium and long-term capital, net	77
Loan drawings ($260)	
Amortizations (−183)	
Errors and omissions	−30

Negative sign implies a debit.

Sources: Basic data obtained from International Monetary Fund, *Balance of Payments Yearbook* (several issues).

registered in 1951, 1952, and 1960, while 1950, 1953, and 1956 witnessed current account surpluses.

Net direct investments, going mainly into the rapidly expanding manufacturing sector, accounted for a substantial share of the capital inflow. [2] More remarkably, short-term borrowing by the public and private sectors was roughly as important as direct investments as a source of finance. Large commercial debts, including important ones with oil suppliers, were accumulated, especially toward the end of the decade. The EXIMBANK and the IBRD were the major (although often reluctant) external public lenders to Brazil before 1961. The former authorized long-term loans for more than $900 million, while the latter's gross lending to Brazil reached $267 million. [3] Other medium- and long-term capital came from suppliers' credits, many of which involved high financial charges.

Interest payments on these debts became stiff; factor payments abroad, excluding those on direct investments, rose from an annual average of $23 million during 1950–1952 to $99 million during 1958–1960. Amortization obligations also rose, and it became clear toward the end of the decade that Brazil faced a serious foreign debt crisis. Debt service charges, including amortizations on medium- and long-term debt plus interest on all debt, rose from 13% of merchandise exports in 1955 to an unusual 44% in 1960.

The Alliance for Progress in Brazil, then, opened under peculiar conditions. Thanks in part to the net capital inflow, the country had been able to achieve from 1947 through 1960 an annual growth rate in its real gross domestic products of about 7%, with industry expanding at more than 9% per annum. This was accomplished even though the 1955–1959 volume

---

[2] Those direct investments originated not only in the United States but also in Western Europe and Japan. According to the U.S. Department of Commerce, U.S. direct investments in Brazil during 1950 through 1960 amounted to only $43 million a year. See U.S. Department of Commerce, *Balance of Payments,* Statistical Supplement, Revised Edition, (Washington, D.C.; Government Printing Office), 1963, p. 176, Table 49.

[3] Data obtained from Agency for International Development, *U.S. Overseas Loans and Grants and Assistance from International Organizations,* March 1968, pp. 33 and 161. During U.S. fiscal years 1946 through 1960, EXIMBANK long-term loans to Brazil were $970 million. IBRD loans were granted as follows: $117 million during 1949–1952; $52 million during 1953–1957; and $98 million during 1958–1959 (dates refer to U.S. fiscal years). Brazilian domestic financial policies were viewed with disfavor by major external donors during those years; Albert Hirschman considers that period as one of the major missed opportunities of international cooperation for development.

of all merchandise exports was 16% below that of 1948—1949. But by 1961, the Brazilian external debt (including undisbursed) had surpassed $3 billion. [4]

20.2. External Financing During the Alliance for Progress Years; An Overall View

A summary comparison of post-Alliance Brazilian performance with that of the 1950s is at first blush somewhat disconcerting. It is not just that overall growth dropped from around 7 to less than 4% per annum and that industry during the 1960s grew no faster than the total product; more puzzling at first sight is the decline in the net capital inflow, as shown in Table 20.2, at a time when foreign aid was becoming more plentiful. The decline in what is often called the "resource gap" (the current account deficit excluding financial services) is even more striking, going from a resource gap

[4] Data on national accounts, exports, and debt were obtained from *International Financial Statistics*, Fundaçao Getulio Vargas, and IBRD.

Table 20.2
Brazilian Balance of Payments, 1961 through 1967
(Annual averages, million current dollars)

Current Account	
Export, FOB	$ 1,492
Imports, CIF	−1,360
Net nonfinancial services and private transfers	− 57
Net income payments on direct investments	− 88
Other net factor payments abroad	− 134
Net Capital Inflow	$− 147
Capital Account	
Public transfers	$ 25
Net direct investments	131
Net short-term capital including changes in net short-term assets	− 63
Medium- and long-term capital, net	98
Loan drawings ($511)	
Amortizations (−413)	
Errors and omissions	− 44

Sources: Basic data obtained from International Monetary Fund, *Balance of Payments Yearbook* (several issues).

of $115 million during 1950–1960, to a "resource *surplus*" of $75 million during 1961–1967. [5]

Some forms of aid did become more plentiful to Brazil after 1961. As shown in Table 20.3, the U.S. Agency for International Development (AID), and the newly created Inter-American Development Bank (IADB), lent substantial sums to that country after 1961, and the U.S. Food for Freedom program and the World Bank group increased the level of their grants and loans.

When the 1960s are compared as a whole with the 1950s, if one uses aggregate balance of payments statistics, the main accomplishment of this increase in development loans and grants appears to be a tidying up of the Brazilian foreign debt. The short-term commercial debts and suppliers' credits piled up during the 1950s were either paid up or refinanced under better conditions, with the help of U.S. and multilateral lending institutions. A good share of Brazilian economic authorities' time during the early 1960s was spent on short-term debt management or, in the phrase favored by financial writers, in keeping the country from "going bankrupt." Major agreements with a group of creditors (the Hague Club) on debt reschedulings were reached on May 1961 and July 1964. On both occasions creditors chose to keep Brazil on a "short leash," and the reschedulings served only as stop-gap measures. [6] But by 1967, the structure of the Brazilian foreign debt was much healthier than that of 1960; average conditions on interest rates, grace periods, and amortization schedules were softer. The participation of suppliers' credits in total debt had decreased, and short-term commercial

---

[5] The practice of subtracting current financial services (interest payments and profit remittances) on past capital inflows from fresh capital inflows can be, and is often, abused for journalistic and propagandistic purposes. But in some cases it can be defended. Take interest payments on development loans. Such payments are generally justified by creditor or donor countries not as market returns to lending but as designed to teach less developed countries the virtues of financial responsibility and to induce them to use aid funds wisely. Otherwise, they could simply transfer the grant element of loans to less developed countries, as straight grants. Under these circumstances, subtracting interest reflows on development loans from fresh disbursements of those loans (already net of amortizations) is much more justifiable than subtracting profit remittances from new net direct foreign investments. I owe this point to Goran Ohlin.

[6] At the time of the 1964 debt rescheduling, it was generally expected that another such exercise would be needed in 1966. But as will be seen later, surprising current account surpluses in 1964 and 1965 allowed Brazil to pay off more debts than thought possible in 1964. Regardless of the general desirability of such a development, this was a welcomed relief to Brazilian officials who had gone through previous rescheduling ordeals.

Table 20.3

New Loans and Grants to Brazil Authorized by Major Donors

(Annual averages; million current dollars)

	U.S. Fiscal Years 1946 through 1960	U.S. Fiscal Years 1961 through 1967
U.S. AID and predecessor agencies	$ 3.1	$148.8
U.S. Food for Freedom and pre-decessor programs	10.5	75.5
U.S. EXIMBANK long-term loans	64.6	34.7
U.S. Other economic programs	3.0	3.0
U.S. military assistance	8.3	20.9
World Bank group	18.5	35.8
Inter-American Development Bank	–	64.9
Total	$108.0	$383.5

Source: Agency for International Development, *U.S. Overseas Loans and Grants and Assistance from International Organizations* (Washington, D.C.: 1968), pp. 33 and 161.

"World Bank group" refers to IBRD and the International Finance Corporation (IFC). Inter-American Development Bank loans include those of the Social Progress Trust Fund. EXIMBANK loans exclude $397.2 million of refunding loans made by that institution to Brazil during 1961-1965.

Besides the long-term loans shown, during 1961 through 1967 (calendar years) Brazil obtained a total of $195 million from the International Monetary Fund and $129 million from the U.S. Treasury in (disbursed) compensatory loans, for a combined annual average of $46 million. Data on European and Japanese loans are not available in comparable form.

debts were being met regularly, the arrears having been liquidated. Debt service payments, in absolute amounts, were not much higher during 1967–1968 than what they had been in 1960–1961; thanks to an expansion of merchandise exports, the debt service ratio was reduced to 34% in 1967.

All of this is pleasing. But one may wonder what would have happened if AID, IBRD, and IADB loans had not been available in the amounts indicated in Table 20.3. One possibility is that Brazil would have had to "tighten its belt" further during the 1960s to meet its foreign debt obligations. Argentina, after all, from 1963 through 1967 registered current account surpluses adding to $930 million, under the pressure of external debt obligations. Thus it could be argued that the increase in external official inflows shown in Table 20.3 made possible a larger current account deficit, or a smaller surplus, than would have taken place in the absence of official assistance. The fact that such a deficit during the 1960s was smaller on the average than that registered in the 1950s could then be considered irrelevant. In other words, a country can be receiving aid, defined as grants and loans under concessionary terms not available to it from commercial markets, without necessarily registering current account deficits. [7] However, under Brazilian political conditions (of which more will be said later), the realistic alternatives to an increase in external official inflows were either a unilateral moratorium on debt servicing or more debt rescheduling. The prestige and credit standing that Brazil preserved in world financial circles by avoiding those alternatives can be credited to the availability of external official flows. To most Brazilians, unaware or uninterested in the mysterious mores of international bankers, this is probably not a very exciting contribution of foreign aid.

From the Brazilian viewpoint, the desirability of the financial juggling accomplished during the 1960s partly depends on the legitimacy of the old debts and on the economic and other conditions attached to new gross inflows. Little solid information exists on the suppliers' credits and commercial arrears accumulated during the 1950s; the usual stories of high-pressure selling with hints of corruption are heard. More fundamentally, one may question the desirability of mechanisms used in industrialized countries, first to promote their exports of capital and other goods by liberal use of official insurance and credit schemes, and then to pressure recipient countries to consolidate private bad debts that are thus transformed into public debt. On both the exporting and importing sides, this system reduces entrepreneurial incentives to refine cost-benefit calculations and objectively to evaluate commercial risks. [8] The major responsibility for screening what suppliers' credit is accepted for official repayment guarantees naturally rests with the receiving country. But industrialized countries that officially encourage their exporters to push their wares aggressively are not without responsibility when the time comes to consider bad debts.

The terms of the official flows going into Brazil during the 1960s were on the whole more favorable, at least regarding maturities, grace periods, and interest rates, than those of external credits received during the 1950s. But at

---

[7] It may be noted parenthetically that aid literature has yet to integrate the Pincus-Ohlin definition of aid with the older, Chenery-style definition, which concentrated on estimating the foreign exchange gap generated by the current account.

[8] The system has also generated frictions among industrialized countries. The United States has felt that much of its net official flows to Brazil and other Latin American countries has gone to pay off European suppliers' credits of doubtful developmental effectiveness.

an aggregate level, it may be noted that the "tying" characterizing U.S. flows reduced their contribution to Brazilian debt management. Debt servicing is of course untied and must be financed from the general pool of foreign exchange. While imports financed with tied aid presumably free foreign exchange for debt servicing, the substitution is not perfect, especially in the short run; and (even when successful) it taxes the accounting and financial ingenuity of economic authorities, diverting them from considering development problems.

To summarize: During the Alliance years, Brazil received substantially larger official inflows, or aid; but because of unfavorable initial conditions (a large external debt with short maturities) and Brazilian policy choices on how to deal with them (i.e., a reluctance to lose financial respectability by heavier reliance on debt rescheduling), such inflows resulted in a lower transfer of real resources than had been accomplished during the 1950s. The net capital inflow from 1961 through 1967 amounted to about 11% of merchandise imports and to less than 5% of gross fixed investment. In per capita terms, or as a percentage of gross national product (GNP), its contribution seems even smaller. [9]

20.3. The Continuity and Objectives of Foreign Aid

Treating the post-1960 years as a whole misses many of the difficulties surrounding foreign aid to Brazil. The major problem has been Brazil's political and economic instability during the 1960s. Decisions by both bilateral and multilateral donors have been taken with the political and economic short run very much in mind.

After less than one year in office, President Quadros resigned in August 1961. Vice-President Goulart succeeded him; but under military pressure, a parliamentarian-type government was adopted, reducing the powers of the

---

[9] As in other large developing countries, such as India and Pakistan, the per capita aid received by Brazil is below the average for developing countries as a whole. According to the OECD, for example, the per capita receipts of net official assistance during 1964–1966 (annual averages) were $3.0 for Brazil, $13.9 for Costa Rica, $15.7 for Chile, and $18.6 for Panama. For Latin America as a whole the average was $4.4, slightly higher than the $4.1 for all recipient countries. See Organization for Economic Cooperation and Development. *Development Assistance*, 1968 Review (December 1968), p. 271.

presidency. In January 1963, a plebiscite led to a return to a full presidentialist regime. In April 1964, President Goulart was overthrown. Since then, although the military have been in effective command of the government, several political crises have erupted, the most severe in December 1968. Economic policy emphasized stabilization during April 1964 to April 1967 (the term of President Castello Branco) and expansion since then.

Before April 1964, U.S. aid programs followed a zigzagging course, buffetted by Brazilian political changes, and hoping in turn to influence them. The "stop-go" decisions of those years make dizzying reading. In May 1961, AID agreed to lend Brazil $100 million in balance of payments assistance, as part of a package including the International Monetary Fund (IMF), European creditors, EXIMBANK, and the U.S. Treasury. The loan was suspended with Quadros' resignation. However, later on AID agreed to release $75 million from that loan between November 1961 and April 1962. Disenchantment with Goulart led to a new temporary suspension of further disbursements, but the Bell-Dantas agreement of April 1963 resulted in the disbursement of the remaining $25 million. Shortly after that date, AID gave up hope on the Goulart regime and adopted an "islands of sanity" strategy, calling for cooperation with selected state governments (Brazil being a federal republic), autonomous public agencies, and the private sector "to the extent that this was possible." Answering criticisms of the U.S. Government Accounting Office (GAO) regarding project loans made before April 1964, U.S. AID admitted that "... overriding U.S. policy considerations ..." and not just developmental criteria weighed heavily on its decision making. [10]

The point was forcefully, although with some factual inaccuracies, ex-

---

[10] See AID statement reproduced as Appendix II in *Review of Administration of United States Assistance for Capital Development Projects in Brazil*, by the Comptroller General of the United States, B-133283, May 16, 1968. The AID statement reads, in part (p.70):"... the selection of projects which is considered by the GAO as "representative" of the capital development program for Brazil consists exclusively of projects which were prepared for authorization in calender years 1962 and 1963. This was the period in which relations between the U.S. and the Goulart government in Brazil were most difficult.... Yet, for overriding U.S. policy considerations, AID undertook a project lending effort which involved all but one of the loans selected by the GAO for review. Seven of the 11 loans were extended to fulfill a $131 million diplomatic agreement for financial assistance to the Brazilian Northeast region within a specified 2-year time limit."
See also pp. 11 and 76–77 of the same document. The overthrow of Goulart, in fact, made unnecessary the massive implementation of the "islands of sanity" strategy.

pressed by Thomas C. Mann, then Assistant Secretary of State for Inter-American Affairs, testifying in Congress in May 1964: [11]

> "We were aware in January by the time I got there – I do not know how much earlier – that the erosion toward communism in Brazil was very rapid. We had, even before I got here, devised policy to help certain state governments. We did not give any money in balance of payments support, budgetary support, things of that kind, which benefit directly the Central Government of Brazil. That was cut back under Goulart. In my opinion, sir, and I think this is the opinion of many people who are informed about Brazil, the fact that we did put our limited amount of aid in the last year of the Goulart administration into states which were headed by good governors we think strengthened democracy."

Since April 1964, U.S. aid to Brazil became steadier, and greater attention was given to economic, rather than political, criteria. Most of the program, however, was aimed at supporting short-term stabilization measures. Talking early in 1969 about the U.S. AID programs in Brazil, Chile, and Colombia, James R. Fowler, Deputy U.S. Coordinator for the Alliance for Progress, stated: [12]

> "On looking back, as I have recently, over the years of the Alliance in these major three countries, it seems very clear to me that conscious decisions were made that the resource input and the assistance in the first instance would go to try to bring some stability into these economies."

The emphasis on inflation control was particularly strong in Brazil, where the cost of living rose by 89% between the second quarters of 1963 and 1964. The major innovation in AID's Brazilian activities, the program loan, became the key lever for supervising Brazilian use of its monetary and fiscal instruments. Between 1964 and 1968, funds from program loans were only released subject to *quarterly review* of Brazilian policy performance which AID judged satisfactory. After the April 1967 change in Brazilian administration, disbursements from program loans were in fact held up from July until the end of that year, because of disagreements between AID and the new finance minister on economic matters, showing that the quarterly reviews were no mere formality.

---

[11] Reproduced in Appendix II, page 21, of *Unnecessary Dollar Costs Incurred in Financing Purchases of Commodities Produced in Brazil,* By the Comptroller General of the United States, B-146820, March 19, 1965.

[12] Ninety-First Congress, *New Directions for the 1970s: Toward a Strategy of Inter-American Development*, Hearings Before the Subcommittee on Inter-American Affairs of the Committee on Foreign Affairs, House of Representatives (Washington, D.C.: U.S. Government Printing Office, 1969), p. 619. After the 1964 coup the U.S. speedily granted Brazil "emergency" stabilization loans, but on condition that Brazil first settled its differences, inherited from Goulart, with some U.S. investors.

Political considerations, somewhat different from the pre-1964 ones, again interfered with the continuity of U.S. aid flows late in 1968. After the Brazilian military brushed aside, in December 1968, some of the flimsy post-1964 constitutional legality, AID placed "under review" further disbursements from its last program loan (signed in May 1968), as well as project and sector loans that had previously been authorized but not signed. However, disbursements from project and sector loans already signed went ahead.

Discontinuity in lending operations to Brazil has not been the monopoly of AID. As shown in Table 20.3, the EXIMBANK sharply curtailed its gross lending to Brazil during the Alliance years. The reasons for this behavior are not clear. During the early 1960s the EXIMBANK apparently felt that too much of its portfolio was being taken up by this risky borrower. Later on, perhaps because of bureaucratic rivalries, it failed to coordinate its program with that of AID. The World Bank group also followed a stop-go policy in its Brazilian operations; during 1960 through 1964, it did not authorize a single loan to Brazil. This was followed by authorizations of loans amounting to a total of $251 million from 1965 through 1967. After showing some interest in making a loan to a public sector steel company, the IBRD abruptly dropped the matter, limiting its 1965–1967 loans mainly to electricity. The record of the IADB has been steadier; from 1961 through 1964, it authorized loans to Brazil averaging $56 million a year, increasing to $101 million a year from 1965 through 1967. Authorizations on the Food for Freedom program were often erratic, as in 1967, raising serious doubts in Brazilian minds as to their reliability.

The stop-go authorization policies of the EXIMBANK and the IBRD yielded an ironic result. During 1961–1963, when Brazilian economic policy was presumably at its worst, *net disbursements* (gross disbursements to Brazil minus Brazilian amortizations) amounted to a total of $208 million for the EXIMBANK and $26 million for the IBRD. During 1964–1967, when major efforts were made to stabilize the Brazilian economy, net disbursements from both institutions were *negative*, reaching −$119 million for the EXIMBANK and −$30 million for the IBRD. [13] The withdrawal of these institutions from the Brazilian scene during the early 1960s, furthermore, hampered rapid and efficient identification and execution of new projects after 1964. The variable

---

[13] Estimates of the Secretariat of the Inter-American Committee for the Alliance for Progress, made for the 1968 Brazilian country review. Document CIAP/298 (Spanish), October 17, 1968, pp.199–200.

lag of disbursements behind loan authorizations, especially important at a time when the aid pipeline was being built up as it was in the early Alliance years, thus compounded the instability and unpredictability of actual aid receipts. [14]

Whether or not the political and economic judgements that gave foreign aid to Brazil its unstable and short-run character were correct, it is reasonably clear that they sacrificed the contribution aid can make to sensible long-range planning, at least in a few isolated but critical sectors, not to mention the more ambitious social reform targets also contained in the Charter of Punta del Este.

20.4. Loan Authorizations and Disbursements: A look at time profiles and implications for the grant element

Standard calculations of the grant element in development loans implicitly assume that the funds are fully disbursed at the time the loan agreement is signed or that repayment schedules begin to apply only after the funds are disbursed. [15] However, while disbursements will in fact be spread out over several years, loan agreements typically specify that repayments of principal will begin a certain number of years (about 5 years for IADB and IBRD loans and 10 years for AID loans) after their signing, or at best after the first

---

[14] A full consideration of the external aid lags should take into account: (a) The time elapsed between the presentation (by, say, Brazil to AID, IADB, or the IBRD) of a given project and the decision by those institutions whether to accept it or reject it. This may take as much as two years of technical and economic studies. (b) The time elapsed between authorization of the loan by the institution and the signing of the loan agreement. The loan may be authorized, but subject to certain actions by the receiving country which must be taken before the signing of the agreement. (c) The time elapsed between the signing and the actual disbursement of funds. Some institutions prefer to shorten lag b at the expense of lengthening lag c by making disbursements, rather than the signing of the agreement, subject to the more difficult measures to be taken by the receiving countries. The whole process is usually surrounded by a considerable amount of paper work and shuttling, at which, however, the receiving countries are becoming increasingly more adept.

[15] See Goran Ohlin, *Foreign Aid Policies Reconsidered*, (Paris: Development Center of the Organisation for Economic Co-operation and Development, 1966), pp. 101–110; John A. Pincus, "The Cost of Foreign Aid", *The Review of Economics and Statistics*, November 1963, pp. 360–367; Jagdish N. Bhagwati, "Alternative Estimates of the Real Cost of Aid", (Working paper #37 of the MIT Department of Economics, February 1969; to appear in Paul Streeten (ed.), *Essays in Honor of Lord Balogh*, London: Weidenfeld and Nicolsen Ltd., 1970).

disbursements, *regardless of the pace of disbursements*. Although interest is charged only on the disbursed amounts, loans made by the IADB and the IBRD carry a "commitment charge," often of three-fourth of one percent per annum, to be paid on the undisbursed amount of the loan. [16]

Both the disbursement lag and the "commitment charge" reduce the grant element of loans below what is estimated in standard calculations by an amount to be determined in this section. In what follows, attention will be centered on the grace period, assuming that loans are fully disbursed within that time. No change in the standard calculations for the post grace period is necessary.

Assume for simplicity that a loan is disbursed in equal parts throughout the grace period. Use the following notation: L = face value of the loan, q = rate of discount, G = grace period (number of years), and t = time.

The present discounted value of the disbursements at the time of signing will be

$$\int_0^G \frac{L}{G} e^{-qt}\, dt = \frac{L}{Gq} (1 - e^{-qG}) . \qquad (20.1)$$

The value of Equation 20.1 is naturally lower than that of L. Assume that $G = 5$ years and $q = 10\%$. Then the value of Equation 20.1 will only be 79% of L. In other words, this factor alone reduces the grant element of a loan by 21 percentage points.

There is some offset to this; during the grace period, interest will not be paid on the whole face value of the loan but only on its disbursed amount. On the other hand, the penalty charge on the undisbursed balance will chip away at that offset.

The present value of interest payments regarding loan disbursements during the grace period under the new assumption will be

$$\int_0^G \frac{L}{G} it\, e^{-qt}\, dt , \qquad (20.2)$$

---

[16] When disbursements turn out to be especially slow, *ad hoc* postponements of the repayments schedule have sometimes been granted. But the basic loan agreements usually specify that the borrower shall repay the principal in accordance with amortization schedules spelled out with fixed dates. Some IBRD loan agreements allow recipients to postpone interest payments until the project is completed, capitalizing the postponed amounts at the interest rate used for the loan. This tends to increase the grant element.

where, in addition to previous notation, i = interest rate on the loan.

The present value of the penalty charges on the undisbursed amounts during the grace period will be

$$\int_0^G Z(L - \frac{L}{G} t) \, e^{-qt} \, dt \, , \tag{20.3}$$

where the new symbol Z refers to the penalty charge rate.

Combining 20.2 and 20.3, one gets

$$\int_0^G [(i-Z)\frac{L}{G} t + ZL] \, e^{-qt} \, dt \, . \tag{20.4}$$

This expression may be compared with the standard estimate of the present value of interest payments during the grace period,

$$\int_0^G iL \, e^{-qt} \, dt \, . \tag{20.5}$$

If the penalty charge rate were to reach the interest rate, the two expressions would be identical.

Solving equation 20.4, one obtains

$$\frac{i-Z}{q^2} \frac{L}{G} \, [1 - e^{-qG}(qG+1)] + \frac{Z}{q} L(1-e^{-qG}) \, . \tag{20.6}$$

Equation 20.6 can be compared to the solution for 20.5:

$$\frac{i}{q} L(1-e^{-qG}) \, . \tag{20.7}$$

So long as Z is smaller than i, the value of 20.6 will be smaller than 20.7, thus "putting back" some of the grant element taken away in Equation 20.1.

Assume i = 5% and Z = three-fourth of 1%, and other parameters as above. Then Expression 20.6 will become $0.106L$. Expression 20.7 becomes $0.197L$.

In the numerical example given, then, the *net* effect of the new assumptions, as compared with the standard ones assuming instant disbursements and no penalty charges, is to reduce the grant element by about 12 additional percentage points. In other words, if in using standard assumptions the grant

Table 20.4
Average Disbursement Profiles of Project Loans to Brazil
(As cumulated percentages of loan principals)

Disbursements by December 31 of:	IADB	IBRD	AID
Year of signature of loan agreement	6	1	7
First full calendar year after agreement	21	9	24
Second full calendar year after agreement	50	37	49
Third full calendar year after agreement	70	63	76
Fourth full calendar year after agreement	81	88	80
Fifth full calendar year after agreement	88	96	90
Sixth full calendar year after agreement	94	99	100
Seventh full calendar year after agreement	100	99	100

Sources and Method: For the IADB, the calculation includes loans made from Ordinary Resources, Special Operations and Social Trust Fund from 1961 through 1968. Basic data obtained from the *Annual Reports* of that institution (Statements of Approved Loans). IBRD loans include those made during 1958 and 1959 plus those granted from 1965 through 1968. The averages shown for this institution, therefore, are probably less representative than those for the IADB and AID. (IBRD loans made during 1958–1959 were disbursed rapidly, while 1965–1968 loans have had very slow disbursement rates.) Basic IBRD data obtained from its *Monthly Statement of Loans*, December issues, mimeographed. Calculations for AID include only project loans made from 1962 through 1968; basic data obtained from AID, Office of the Controller, *Status of Loan Agreements*, December issues.

element of a loan was 35%, under the modified assumptions the grant element will be 23%. [17]

Table 20.4 summarizes the disbursement rates of project loans made to Brazil by the IADB (57 loans), IBRD (16 loans) and AID (39 loans). No institution had disbursed, on the average, more than 50% of the principal of its loans 2½ years after the signing of the loan agreements. [18] About 80% or more of the principal became disbursed only after 4½ years following the loan agreement. These lags are to some extent inevitable: Equipment has to be ordered, projects will run into unexpected technical snags, receiving countries may fail to put up their share of the funds at the required time, etc.

[17] This wrinkle in the grant element calculation has been independently worked out, under more general assumptions, by Victor Tokman, in his "On the measurement of Aid: A methodological refinement," (Mimeographed; Washington, D.C., Pan American Union, September 1969).

[18] Assuming signatures of loan agreements are evenly spread through the year.

Bureaucratic delays, by both recipients and donors, often complicated by policy disagreements, also add to disbursement delays. But regardless of their justification, it is clear that this type of development loan does not provide cash on hand as a bond sale could.

A more realistic example of grant element calculations, with and without the wrinkle developed in this section, can be given, taking into account Table 20.4. Assume an IBRD-IADB type of loan, with an interest rate of 5% per annum and a 5 year grace period followed by 20 years of amortization of the principal in equal amounts. Using a discount rate of 10% per annum, the grant element of that loan, using standard procedures, would be about 35%. When a "commitment charge" of three quarters of one per cent, and disbursements of 10, 20, 30, and 40% of the loan for the first, second, third, and fourth years following its signature are taken into account in the calculation (leaving other assumptions unchanged), the grant element drops by about half to 18%. [19] The latter calculation, of course, assumes that the

[19] Using discount rates between 7 and 9%, the Secretariat of the Inter-American Committee for the Alliance for Progress (CIAP, using Spanish initials) has estimated grant elements for 1961–1967 capital flows to all Latin America, by major sources, as follows:

Loans	Percent
AID	68
PL480 (Title IV)	46
IADB (all programs)	33
IBRD and International Development Association	24
EXIMBANK	16
PL480	
Title I	100
Title II and III	71
Other U.S. grants (Peace Corps, etc.)	100

See Document CIES/1382, *El Financiamiento Externo para el Desarrollo de la América Latina*, May, 1969 (mimeographed), Table II-3. These estimates do not take into account the negative effects of "tying" of AID and some IADB loans.

Determination of the correct discount rate is complicated not only by whether one is trying to measure benefits to recipients or costs to donors but also by the need to take into account inflationary trends in the world economy. From the viewpoint of the recipient, the expected trend in its export prices should be used to modify current borrowing costs in world markets. In the Brazilian case, dollar export prices rose by 23% between 1960–1963 and 1964–1967, or at an average annual rate of more than 5%. If such an increase can be considered permanent, it has clearly reduced the real burden of future servicing of the foreign debt.

repayment profile on the total loan is fixed regardless of the disbursement rate, an assumption that seems realistic for most IBRD and IADB loans.

20.5 The Experience with Program Loans and Other Aid Practices

Not all loans to Brazil share the slow disbursement rates indicated in Table 20.4. The AID program loans, in particular, have been disbursed more quickly (typically within two years), especially when no policy disagreements arose between the Brazilian and the U.S. governments. This section will discuss other characteristics of U.S. program loans to Brazil, as well as the newer concept of sector loans, and other features of project loans.

Program Loans

For many years economists praised the advantages of program over project loans, especially in the context of development planning. More recently, reflecting Latin American experience, program lending has come under professional criticism; Albert Hirschman and Richard Bird claim that, para-doxically, program aid is fully effective only when it does not achieve anything, in the sense that in these situations the donor rewards what he considers virtue where virtue appears of its own accord. [20] It is argued in this section that Brazilian experience with AID program loans does not shed much light on the project versus program debate, because AID program loans to Brazil have little in common, except for their label, with the program loans that economists have in mind. Brazilian experience is more relevant to a discussion on the desirability of linking aid to short-term or stabilization performance.

From 1961 through 1968, program type AID loans to Brazil worth $625 million were authorized and signed; $100 million of which were granted before April 1964. Those pre-1964 loans, however, were given as general balance of payments support in the midst of difficult political conditions and generated much U.S. congressional opposition to this aid form. Partly to persuade the U.S. Congress and the White House that funds would not be wasted, the

---

[20] See Albert O. Hirschman and Richard M. Bird, *Foreign Aid. A Critique and a Proposal*, Essays in International Finance, Princeton University, No. 69, July 1968, especially pp. 7—9. These authors also suggest that the administration of program loans will exhibit a built-in tendency to deflect attention from long-term economic and social progress criteria to the much more easily ascertained and quantified short-term monetary and fiscal indicators (see their pp. 10—11).

post-1964 program loans were accompanied by a system of quarterly review, to which reference has been made earlier. Latin American program loans took on a character different from those made to the more "reliable" India. Those reviews, replaced since 1968 by semi-annual sessions, often involved as many as 30 people each on the U.S. and the Brazilian side and went into many detailed aspects of the Brazilian economic policy, even though AID had other ways of obtaining the desired information. Many Brazilian officials found them not only humiliating but also counterproductive. [21] They created an atmosphere encouraging rationalizations and double-talk and were not conducive to frank discussions of aid and development policies. The reviews concentrated on monetary and fiscal instruments, including exchange-rate policy, rather than on targets, in a fashion not unlike that of the International Monetary Fund (IMF). To many, in fact, AID program loans differed from IMF stand-by agreements only in the much more generous financial conditions involved in the former, with the offsetting cost that the latter involved major review sessions only once a year with officials who stay in the country just a few days. Instead of the yearly "letters of intention" required by the IMF for stand-by credits, AID program loans required (or, more diplomatically, were accompanied by) letters from Brazilian economic officials to the chairman of the Inter-American Committee for the Alliance for Progress, with detailed quantitative targets in the fields of credit and fiscal policy. In other words, instead of committing program loans to support a 5 year development plan, AID used 1 year pledges to back 1 year financial and fiscal policy packages. To paraphrase Hirschman and Bird, AID program loans attempted to reward virtue of a very particular and fragile species.

Under pressure from the U.S. Treasury Department, and much to the annoyance of AID, "additionality" requirements (aimed at going beyond standard tying procedures and assuring that program loan dollars would be spent on additional Brazilian imports from the United States) further complicated program loan reviews. Paradoxically, at a time when the United States was promoting the liberalization of the Brazilian import and exchange control system, special regulations had to be introduced by Brazil to encourage the diversion of import demand toward U.S. sources. These

---

[21] Overstaffing at both AID/Brazil and in the Brazilian government, it is said, contributed to the attendance of these sessions. Even sympathetic Brazilian officials complained of the "invasion" of Brazil by AID. AID/Brazil personnel has been cut from 408 (in June 30, 1967) to an estimated 267 in U.S. fiscal year 1969. See U.S. House of Representatives, *New Directions for the 1970s: Toward a Strategy of Inter-American Development*, op. cit., p. 590.

regulations went against the spirit, if not the letter, of postwar agreements against trade discriminations. For example, 6 month credits at low rates of interest (negative in real terms) were granted to importers of certain narrowly specified goods, which happened to be available only in the United States. Since the adoption of a flexible exchange rate, which is depreciated in small but frequent doses by the Central Bank, importers of "allowable" U.S. goods were promised that they could pay for those imports at the going *spot* exchange rate, even though the imports were not likely to materialize for 6 or more months. Other importers, of course, would have to pay a premium on forward dollars to cover themselves against exchange risks.

Until 1968, "allowable" imports from the United States under aid funds were regulated by an extensive *negative* list, including, besides luxury goods, commodities for which the United States already enjoyed a large share of the Brazilian market. In 1968, the system was tightened by the change to a *positive* list of allowed imports, increasing the time devoted by Brazilian and AID officials in wrestling with U.S. Treasury officials about which goods could or could not be imported. A good day in aid administration became one in which AID could convince the Treasury officials that traditional Brazilian imports from Chile should be left out of the positive list. Additionality was finally abolished in June 1969.

It appears that the implementation of additionality caused fewer problems in Brazil than it did in Chile and Colombia. Incentives to Brazilian importers of U.S. goods were so strong that funds moved quickly, unlike Chile, where program loans funds have gone unspent on several occasions. [22] For whatever reasons, which may include the Brazilian import liberalization program and its impact on imports of durable consumer goods, the U.S. share in total Brazilian imports rose from 32.3% during 1961–1965 to 36.7% in 1966–1967. Detailed data are not yet available for judging the extent to which this was the result of trade diversion induced by tying and additionality. But one real cost of additionality, perhaps its greatest, is clear: it used up

---

[22] Apparently Chileans found that increased real costs forthcoming from "additionality" and other tying regulations were sometimes greater than the grant element in AID loans. Jagdish N. Bhagwati has pointed out to me that Thailand has refused to accept PD 31 benefits (i.e., tendering for USAID contracts) extended to some less developed countries by the U.S. government, because it would have involved the use of restricted-account arrangements, contrary to principles of non-discriminatory multilateral payments. For a review of different forms of aid tying, see his "The Tying of Aid," in United Nations Conference on Trade and Development, Second Session, New Delhi, Volume IV, *Prob'ems and Policies of Financing*, (New York: United Nations), 1968, pp. 45–71.

an inordinate share of the time of both Brazilian and U.S. officials dealing with aid and reduced the credibility of AID officials arguing that the funds were given to promote Brazilian development. This is a far cry from the ideal program loan that economists contrast with project lending.

Defenders of the AID program loans argue that, given the mood of the U.S. Congress, only short-term commitments keyed to anti-inflationary efforts and surrounded by the paraphenalia of rigorous quarterly reviews were politically feasible, if aid to Brazil was to be raised quickly after April 1964. It is further argued that the review mechanisms have helped Brazilian planning (at least of a short-term nature), by forcing that government to marshall its data and thoughts regularly and by providing for expert foreign counselling. Although the alleged goal of these loans is not to force conditions on an unwilling government but to strengthen the hand of the "good guys" within that government, who without prodding agree with AID prescriptions, it is considered that the "good guys" can benefit from the discipline of frequent reviews and, depending on the political climate, from the chance to blame foreigners for the need to take unpopular policy measures. Hirschman and Bird have pointed out the difficulties in these arguments; difficulties which, it may be added, become more serious when the policy debate takes place in a bilateral framework and deals with short-run policies that are easily reversible.

There is polite disagreement between AID and Brazilian officials regarding the impact of post-April 1964 program loans on Brazilian economic macro-policy making, especially during the first 3 years. Having sold program loans to Congress at least partly on the basis of the "leverage" they give over short-run macroeconomic policies, AID naturally likes to hint, with great discretion, that the loans gave the "good guys" the critical margin to push through their policies. Brazilian left-wing critics of aid, of course, agree with this evaluation, which they express in a somewhat less polite language. The "good guys," in the Brazilian case an impressive group of economists, although grateful for the additional funds, usually claim the macro-policies would have been the same without them. As far as an outsider can judge these subtle matters, the latter appear to have the better case, at least for 1964–1967. In more recent years, the mechanisms of program lending may have played a more important role in strengthening the hands of those within the government wishing to maintain the momentum of the stabilization plan and to adopt a more flexible exchange rate policy. [23]

---

[23] See "The Impact of AID Program Lending on Brazilian Economic Policy and

Flexibility in the granting and speed in the disbursement of AID program loans to Brazil have been their most impressive features; these are consistent with their stabilization goals. In the early stages of the anti-inflationary program, as that adopted in Brazil after April 1964, those features can be particularly important in mitigating the harshness of the impact of austerity measures. Much of their potential advantages, however, were wasted. During 1964 through 1966, Brazil accumulated a current account *surplus* of $230 million dollars, while projections made during 1964 had expected substantial current account deficits. For 1965 and 1966, current account deficits of $300 and $400 million were forecast; in fact, 1965 registered a surplus of $250 million and 1966 a deficit of $70 million. The major surprise was the low level of merchandise imports, in turn reflecting an unexpected contraction in the levels of investment and general economic activity. [24] As U.S. officials, worried about the U.S. balance of payments, watched nervously, the assets of Brazilian monetary authorities, rather than Brazilian imports, rose steadily from $170 million at the end of the second quarter of 1964 to $505 million at the end of 1965. To avoid this embarrassing surge in reserves, plans to arrange for new debt rescheduling meetings in 1966 were abandoned, and substantial debt repayments were accomplished. [25] Tied AID program loans were substituted for another form of short-term "program lending," having the advantage of freeing untied foreign exchange, i.e., debt rescheduling. The

Performance", presented by AID to Hearings before the Subcommittee on Inter-American Affairs, where it stated:

> "The GOB's [Government of Brazil] indication of its intent to adopt a policy of smaller, more frequent exchange rate adjustments was a major factor in our decision to proceed with the 1968 program loan."

House of Representatives, *New Directions for the 1970's: Toward a Strategy of Inter-American Development*, op.cit., p. 599. The use of counterpart funds generated by program loans is supposed to be the immediate political lever helping the "good guys." The fact that these funds can be channelled to the private sector rather easily via credit institutions has also been used to persuade the U.S. Congress of the advantages of program in contrast with project lending, because typically large projects are found mainly in the public sector.

[24] Merchandise imports, FOB, had been forecast late in 1964 by the CIAP Secretariat, in consultation with the Brazilian government, to reach $1,450 million in 1965 and $ 1,600 million in 1966. The figures actually registered were $ 941 million in 1965 and $1,303 million in 1966. During 1960–1963 the corresponding figures averaged about $1.3 billion.

[25] The debt service during 1964 amounted to about $410 million; the corresponding figure for 1966 was $570 million. Since then, AID has tried to insure that its loans do not go simply to pay off debts of other institutions and countries.

role of AID program loans as cushion against the negative short-run effects of stabilization was much less visible. Per capita real absorption during 1964—1966 fell slightly below the levels reached during 1961—1963. Some urban real wages also fell during 1964—1966, but this may have been limited to the best organized and paid urban workers.

To summarize: Brazilian experience is more relevant to a discussion of lending for stabilization versus lending for development, or more precisely, to the establishment of priorities among short- and long-term goals, than to the project versus program debate. [26] This experience shows the limitations of stabilization aid. While the gradual elimination of inflation and distortions in relative prices certainly deserved high priority, it appears in retrospect that it would have been wiser to have earlier devoted a greater share of development assistance to obtaining at least a few key long-run economic and social objectives, independently of short-term political and economic circumstances. The argument that *nothing* worthwhile could be done along these lines in Brazil until either government instability or inflation were eliminated is not convincing. After all, inflation during 1966—1967 was not that much smaller than in 1961, and the question of whether the present regime is more stable (or democratic) than earlier ones is very much a moot one.

Sector Loans

During more recent years, AID has given greater attention to long-term development goals, such as improving Brazilian agriculture and the educational and health systems. The macroleverage provided by its program loans has

---

[26] Two additional points may be considered in this debate, one favoring project and the other program lending. As project lending is typically accompanied by recipient's commitments to put up part of project costs from their own savings, and as the project will not advance if those funds are not forthcoming, pressure will be maintained on the recipient to keep up its savings. Program loans, on the other hand, are given on the basis of estimated current account deficits, which may be compatible with very many aggregate consumption—investment mixes; the one in fact realized (and its corresponding level of national savings) will only become known long after the fact. Suppose that all projects undertaken in a given country have the same share of foreign project lending element, which will be disbursed only when the local share is put up. Then aid disbursements will be proportional to domestic savings, something that cannot be said for program loans.

Countries with large external debt servicing, however, can run into difficult administrative problems if gross aid inflows only come in project form, with disbursements subject to the vagaries of project implementation, while debt obligations have to be met regularly with free foreign exchange (or "program repayments").

been found unsuitable to promote sectoral reforms, and a new form of lending, sector loans, has begun to appear. [27] Authorized loans for secondary education and for the establishment of a Brazilian national fund for water and sewerage projects are examples of this type of lending. As the direct import content of these activities is minimal, sector loans share with program loans the feature of providing foreign exchange, tied only to purchasing from the United States. As Brazil has already developed a diversified capital goods industry, it may be noted that external financing of only direct import requirements of machinery and equipment has become an increasingly unsatisfactory way to transfer real resources into that country. In fact, a recent AID loan to finance U.S. capital goods into Brazil has moved slowly owing to the keen competition (and political pressure) of Brazilian capital goods producers. In contrast with program loans, sector loans include fewer but more pointed preconditions of a sectoral, rather than of a macroeconomic character. In this respect, they are closer to, say, project loans for electricity which carry as preconditions changes in public utility rates and the organization of public electrical enterprises. It is likely that institutions with experience in project lending, like the IBRD, will expand more and more into sectoral loans in areas such as industry, agriculture, and education, by liberalizing their policy on financing domestic costs while insisting on more general policy commitments.

It is too early to evaluate the performance of sector loans in Brazil. They do get into more sensitive areas than project loans (education versus electricity), raising Hirschman and Bird difficulties. It is already known that negotiations over the secondary-education sector loans have been slow and painful. They have been further complicated by the constitutional need to deal in this matter both with several state governments and with the federal

---

[27] Counterpart funds generated by program lending were used, among many other things, to try to promote sectorial reforms. But in the attempt to achieve many targets with a single program loan, such efforts became ineffectual, and it became obvious that priority was given to the anti-inflationary goals. PL-480 loans and grants could have been labelled "sector loans" in that, at least in theory, they were given on conditions that improvements were registered in Brazilian agricultural production. However, it is doubtful that they were used for that purpose. In fact, they discouraged Brazilian corn exports, by debitting them against PL-480 wheat available to Brazil, ton for ton. (Corn is a promising activity within Brazilian agriculture.) They also tended to hamper agricultural integration between Brazil and Argentina, at a time when promotion of Latin American integration became U.S. policy. PL-480 wheat flow, however, has declined as a share of total Brazilian wheat imports, from about half during 1960–1962 to 30% during 1963–1966.

government of Brazil. Other AID plans to devise sectoral loans for university education were aborted for political reasons. Although it is doubtful that this type of loan can succeed in transferring large amounts of resources *and* promoting badly needed institutional changes within a bilateral setting involving the United States and the present Brazilian regime, [28] it represents, at least, an effort to use aid to support policy changes with substantial long-run implications (i.e., educational reform, which has been badly needed in Brazil for many years) rather than those which may be easily reversible (i.e., a few percentage changes in credit expansion or in the exchange rate).

Project Loans

As indicated earlier, Brazil has received a large number of project loans from AID, IADB, and IBRD during the 1960s. Conspicuously absent from among donor institutions is the International Development Association (IDA), dispensing untied soft loans. This institution has ignored Brazil as too rich, leading some to recommend facetiously a secession of the Brazilian northeast as a way to increase the inflow of aid. As in other countries, project loans signed during 1961 through 1967 by the IBRD were predominantly for electricity, while those from AID, and especially the IADB, were more diversified. [29] The geographical diversification within Brazil of the two latter institutions is also greater than that of the IBRD, which has concentrated its activities in the relatively prosperous south. But more recently the trend is for

---

[28] An AID sector loan to Chilean education has met with few difficulties. But given the interest of the Chilean government in education, this may be a good example of the Hirschman and Bird point that program (or sector) aid is fully effective only when it does not achieve anything, except transferring resources.

[29] Expressed as percentages of total value of loans signed, the sectorial breakdown was as follows:

	IADB	AID	IBRD
Agriculture	12	14	15
Industry	20	4	–
Electricity	24	51	85
Transport	5	21	–
Housing	5	–	–
Education	6	–	–
Water, sewerage, and health	21	3	–
Multisector and other	8	7	–

Data was obtained from the CIAP Secretariat. The IABD includes the Social Progress Trust Fund.

the portfolio of these institutions to become less differentiated, as the IBRD gets ready to expand into transport, industry, agriculture, and social sectors, while the IADB, its Social Trust Fund exhausted, increases its loans into traditional social overhead fields.

If project loans made during 1961 through 1967 by these institutions are part of a coordinated development strategy, that strategy is not at all obvious. Until very recently, lack of a Brazilian long-range development plan, and the understandable Brazilian reluctance to have those loans coordinated by foreign institutions, partly account for the ad hoc procedures used to evaluate projects by each lender. Well-known tying procedures on AID and many IADB loans, the impact of which could only be mitigated in part by Brazilian maneuvering as to where different projects were to be financed, reduced their economic value and biased investment policies. U.S. legislation requiring that at least 50% of the tonnage financed by AID loans be shipped on U.S. vessels, for example, caused serious delays during 1964/1965 for at least one AID fertilizer loan, as a result of which a crop year was missed. Projects involving large direct imports from the United States, such as capital-intensive highway maintenance, which opened possibilities of diverting Brazilian imports from Western Europe toward the United States, tended to be favored over higher priority projects involving a high share of local costs. [30] These biases received their main support, it should be noted, from the U.S. Treasury.

More generally, the fact that until very recently bilateral and multilateral donors concentrated their project lending on large infrastructure units biased investment in their favor. Knowledge that external finance is more available for certain types of projects is bound to exert an influence over investment plans, especially bearing in mind the costliness of project preparation. Ideally, Brazil should have a plan whose priorities were established independently of external financing possibilities. In that case AID, IADB, IBRD, etc., could pick from the plan whatever projects and sectors they preferred to finance,

---

[30] William S. Gaud, chief AID Administrator until early 1969, stated the point explicitly:

"In 1965 we further modified our financing policies to include U.S. export promotion as an explicit criterion for selecting capital projects and commodities for AID financing. Moreover, we have been giving increasing weight to choosing capital projects which have a "follow-on" export potential".

See Gaud's statement before the Subcommittee on International Exchange and Payments of the Joint Economic Committee, January 14, 1969, reproduced as appendix 6 of *El Financiamiento Externo para el Desarrollo de la América Latina, op. cit.* Aid loans also appear to favor projects involving U.S. direct investments as well as U.S. consulting firms.

each according to its own interest. But in fact, no such strong planning mechanism exists as yet in Brazil, and the investment pattern ends up reflecting to some extent the lenders' ad hoc preferences. If those lenders fancy dams and dislike education loans, Brazil will tend to invest in dams and neglect education.

One of the best features of project lending (i.e., the encouragement it gives to sectoral project preparation, financial planning, and institution-building) also tended to perpetuate the traditional allocation of project loans. Electricity grew increasingly attractive as a candidate for loans, while less traditional borrowers, such as education and health, had to wait for major policy changes before they could hope for a share of external funds. Furthermore, the institutional strength generated by external support made it easier for the favored sectors to claim higher shares of *domestic* resources. Donor reluctance to lend to public enterprises engaged in manufacturing and mining has also contributed to investment biases, and to occasional political frictions. In short, administrative ease, short run politics (including at least regional and national Brazilian politics, plus those within the U.S. government and others involving international agencies), and export promotion considerations seem at least as important as developmental criteria in the explanation of which Brazilian projects receive external finance.

20.6 Concluding Remarks

Although this essay has attempted neither an exhaustive treatment of foreign aid to Brazil nor an analysis of Brazilian economic conditions during the 1960s, it may be misleading to finish without indicating some of the achievements of post-1964 policies. A gradual reduction in the rate of inflation from its 1963–1964 levels has been accomplished. Year-over-year percentage price increases are shown in Table 20.5. [31]

Controlling inflation has taken longer than expected; the inflationary impact of correcting long-distorted relative prices, or what has been dubbed corrective inflation, was underestimated. Supply responses to relative price increases were often disappointingly sluggish, while those to decreases were frequently quick. Yet, since 1964, each year has witnessed lower inflation. The creation of a new Central Bank and budgetary and fiscal reforms have

---

[31] Data from the IMF's *International Financial Statistics.*

Table 20.5
Percentage Price Increases

	Wholesale Index Excluding Coffee	Consumer Prices
1961	40	38
1962	51	52
1963	75	72
1964	82	87
1965	53	61
1966	41	47
1967	27	30
1968	23	24

expanded and improved the public sector instruments for seeking macro-economic equilibrium, as well as for expanding public savings.

Other institutional changes, such as the creation of a planning ministry and a central mortgage or housing bank have improved the machinery for long-term national and sectorial planning.

Not without some setbacks and waverings, domestic relative prices have moved closer to reflecting real opportunity costs, making them better guides for resource allocation. Changes in policies toward foreign exchange, interest, and public utility rates, plus a program of import liberalization started in 1966 which helped to rationalize the protectionist system (although import duties remain high), have contributed to this purpose. The domestic capital market was encouraged, and it is now perhaps the most active in Latin America.

Measures to help the Brazilian northeast, already started before 1964, were continued and extended. Indeed, the "aid program" of the Brazilian south to its north, relying mainly on tax incentives, dwarfs that of the rest of the world to Brazil. [32]

---

[32] See Albert O. Hirschman, "Industrial Development in the Brazilian Northeast and the Tax Credit Scheme Article 34/18", *The Journal of Development Studies*, Volume 5, Number 1, October 1968, pp. 5—29. The tax incentive scheme was established by law in December 1961 and modified in June 1963. Brazilian help to its own northeast is often given as a reason by AID and IBRD for the relatively few loans these institutions have given to that part of the country. See *New Directions for the 1970s: Toward a Strategy of Inter-American Development.* op. cit., p. 586, comments by Mr. William A. Ellis, of AID. Incidentally, the published versions of these hearings on U.S. aid are liberally sprinkled with "Security deletions." On the other hand, they provide some light reading, as in the following interchange between Congressman Gross and Mr. Ellis (p. 585):

Agricultural and export diversification have been encouraged. Non-coffee merchandise exports, which during 1962—1963 averaged $615 million a year, reached $1,028 million a year during 1967—1968. Finally, while the overall growth rate hardly stayed ahead of population expansion through 1963—1966, it has risen substantially during 1967—1968. The recovery of investment during recent years has also been strong.

These, then, are the major accomplishments achieved at respectable social, political, and economic costs. Those costs have been borne unequally by different social groups; masses of Brazilians have received little tangible immediate help, or hope of future help, from the economic reforms. Under these circumstances, it remains to be seen how permanent they will prove to be.

The role of foreign aid in inducing these reforms and softening their negative short-run impact has been, as discussed earlier, very modest. But the clearest benefit to Brazil from aid received during the 1960s, i.e., an improvement in its foreign debt situation, facilitates future Brazilian policies toward external financing which may avoid its past shortcomings. Assuming the continuation of vigorous export promoting policies and the strengthening of its planning mechanism, Brazil should be able during the 1970s to rely to a much larger extent on international private capital markets for external financing of either its program or project needs. Two other large Latin American countries, Argentina and Mexico, have already started issuing long-term bonds in world capital markets, while several less developed countries have recently obtained suppliers' credits (as well as the more desirable buyers' credits) under conditions which favorably compare with those now available from international organizations, thanks to tough bargain-

Mr. Gross:	Earlier, one of you spoke of the Constitution of Brazil. That has been shredded a good many times, hasn't it?
Mr. Ellis:	Yes, sir.
Mr. Gross:	A constitution does not mean to them what it means to us in this country?
Mr Ellis:	The last constitution was that of 1967 and some of the basic elements of that have been suspended.
Mr. Gross:	We get a lot of coffee from Brazil, do we not?
Mr. Ellis:	Yes, sir.
Mr. Gross:	We pay for it, do we not?
Mr. Ellis:	Yes, sir.

ing and judicious shopping.[33] The disbursement of these program and project loans are likely to be faster and involve less political friction than those given by major aid donors. Their degree of (ex-ante) tying will also be smaller, assuming that world capital markets will continue their process of expansion and liberalization started in the 1950s. On balance, the real cost of borrowing from world capital markets is likely to remain higher than borrowing from bilateral and multilateral donors, although to countries such as Argentina, Brazil, and Mexico that additional cost may be relatively small. Tying, disbursement delays, and administrative complications have lowered the real grant element involved in official aid. On the other hand, competition among exporters of goods and money capital from industrialized nations has increased in the 1960s relative to the 1950s and is likely to further increase during the next decade. High interest rates in world capital markets (reflected in any case in the rates of multilateral loans from the IBRD and IADB) are likely to decline in the future. Under these circumstances and at least for a share of external borrowing, the additional costs to Brazilian direct borrowing in world markets may be more than offset by the benefits of greater self-reliance. As with several other Latin American countries, Brazil should be getting ready to eliminate the middlemen in its dealing with external sources of finance.

Does this mean a partial retreat from the role for external financing envisioned in the Charter of Punta del Este? It does. A possible conclusion to this review of difficulties of foreign aid to Brazil would be to suggest the obvious ways in which it could be improved (put it on steadier, longer term bases, avoid political meddling and breathing down the recipient's neck, increase the role of multilateral aid, eliminate red tape and tying, etc.). One could call for a return to the principles and the spirit of the Alliance for Pro-

---

[33] It is not clear whether the preoccupation of some U.S. officials with European suppliers' credits is more a result of paternalistic concern with the welfare of developing countries than of their export-promoting interests. Note the following remarks of William A. Ellis, AID Mission Director in Brazil:

> "....the European and the Japanese have been very aggressive in providing supplier credits in Brazil. These are on fairly short terms, and we think they have compounded the balance-of-payments problem. We discouraged that. They are ready to move in, and sometimes the rates are, from a commercial standpoint, very attractive. For example, they got some very large British supplier credits at 5 or 5½%. Today that is very attractive money. The British are prepared to subsidize their exports to that extent."

See *New Directions for the 1970's: Toward a Strategy of Inter-American Development, op. cit.,* pp. 591–592.

gress. But there is little reason to think that what worked badly in the 1960s will work much better in the 1970s. Large and semi-industrialized developing countries, such as Brazil, and industrialized nations with "thick" capital markets and the will to live by the market rules of the game they so frequently preach to developing countries, would do well to ponder Professor C.P. Kindleberger's recent words: [34]

> In a world increasingly attracted by decentralization and local responsibility, the possibility of returning to the impersonal forces of the international capital market inevitably suggests itself. If the complex apparatus of intergovernmental and governmental aid and lending is not working satisfactorily, perhaps the time has come to revive the mechanism which it replaced. If the second-best machinery is poor, can we repair the first-best?

[34] Charles P. Kindleberger, "Less Developed Countries and the International Capital Market." Mimeographed, Massachusetts Institute of Technology, 1969.

CHAPTER 21

INTERNATIONAL TRADE AND UNEVEN DEVELOPMENT

Stephen H. HYMER and Stephen A. RESNICK

21.1. Introduction

In his article "Group Behavior and International Trade," C.P. Kindleberger traced the effect of the fall in the world price of wheat after 1870 on the trade and production of several European countries.[1] He found that England, the Netherlands, Belgium, and Denmark followed the classical economic model by allowing imports of wheat to substitute for domestic production. Germany, France, and Italy, however, raised tariffs to counter the effect of the change in the terms of trade. Because of this difference in response, Kindleberger concluded that it was necessary to analyze group behavior, i.e., class struggle and alliance, in predicting how an economy reacts to changes in price or other economic variables. "For accurate prediction and policy-formation, an adequate theory of the behavior of large groups and their components is needed as an adjunct to the analytical tools of the market." [2] In technical terms, the usual economic model of international trade is misspecified because it deals only with market relations and omits important social and political equations. It therefore yields biased estimates and wrong predictions. The model, for example, takes into account the effect of tariffs on the distribution of income but not the feedback of a change in income distribution (real or threatened) on the setting of tariffs.

---

[1] C.P. Kindleberger, "Group Behavior and International Trade," *The Journal of Political Economy* Vol. LIX, No. 1 (February 1951). Both of us read this article as graduate students at M.I.T. but only many years later came to realize how deeply it had influenced us. Another important influence was a conversation one of us had with Samuelson in which the following question was posed: "What is there in Marx that is (a) valid and (b) not included in the M.I.T. Graduate Economics Curriculum. His reply was "The Class Struggle."

[2] Kindleberger, *Ibid*, p. 46.

More recently, Harry Johnson has also stressed the importance of the missing political equations in international trade theory.[3] In his theoretical model of economic nationalism, he argued that many countries have a preference for industry over agriculture, government ownership over private ownership, national ownership over foreign, and import substitution over export expansion. These preferences determine a pattern of behavior quite different from that predicted by international trade theory. Instead of choosing the point on the production possibilities curve that maximizes the value of output at world prices (i.e., a point where the marginal rate of transformation equals the international price ratio), they use tariffs, subsidies, and other instruments to bias production away from Pareto optimality and to satisfy their given "noneconomic" preferences, e.g., they sacrifice real income in order to increase the share of manufacturing in national production or the share of nationals in the ownership of the capital stock.

In a similar vein, our recent analysis of government expenditure policy in underdeveloped countries stressed the importance of explicitly introducing government utility functions and tax equations into economic analysis.[4] We argued that the government is the main provider of a large portion of the capital stock of a country (both physical and human) as well as the sole provider of certain essential support services. Since the government does not usually use market criteria for its production and pricing decisions, the observed level of production and consumption in an economy will depend not only on private tastes, technologies, and factor endowments, as theory suggests, but also on the preferences and decision rules used by the government, i.e., on political as well as economic equations.

Given these considerations, our goal in this paper is to analyze the historic origins of underdevelopment using a framework that includes political as well as economic factors. Our purpose is to explain why the growth of the international economy over the course of the last few centuries has failed to equalize factor prices but instead has created a dualism between the developed and underdeveloped areas of the world.

Among other things, we want to show the frail base upon which rest so many of the orthodox economists' policy recommendations for development. Since international trade theory tells only a portion of the story of the gains

[3] H.G. Johnson, "A Theoretical Model of Economic Nationalism in New and Developing States," *Political Science Quarterly* Vol. LXXX (June 1965).

[4] S. Hymer and S. Resnick, "Interactions Between the Government and the Private Sector in Underdeveloped Countries: Government Expenditure Policy and the Reflection Ratio," Ian Stewart, ed., *Economic Development and Structural Change (Edinburgh: Edinburgh University Press, 1969)*.

and losses from trade, it is seriously misleading when used by itself in empirical analysis and policy prescription. As the following simple econometric model of supply response demonstrates, the cost of ignoring political factors is an inability to identify economic relations and, therefore, an inability to make policy recommendations.

Equation 21.1 describes the usual economic supply function. Equation 21.2 is a political equation relating government policy to world price.

$$x_t = a_1 + b_1 P_t (1 - t_t) + u_{1t} \tag{21.1}$$

$$t_t = a_2 + b_2 P_t + u_{2t} \tag{21.2}$$

where: x_t is exports in real terms, P_t is the world price, t_t is the net tax rate, i.e., taxes less subsidies including expenditures on infrastructure, and u_{it} is the error of the ith equation.

Solving these equations yields the reduced form,

$$x_t = a_1 + b_1(1 - a_2)P_t - b_1 b_2 P_t^2 - b_1 P_t u_{2t} + u_{1t}$$
$$= a_1 + B_1 P_t + B_2 P_t^2 + u_t \tag{21.3}$$

The first problem encountered in any attempt to evaluate the parameters of supply response in this model, is the difficulty of obtaining data on t. One can sometimes measure tariffs and taxes accurately, but it is almost never possible to estimate other government instruments, e.g., the value of subsidies contained in the wide variety of services offered by the government to the private sector at reduced prices. Where t cannot be measured, one cannot estimate the structural equations of the model but must confine the analysis to the reduced form. This is not adequate for policy. To formulate policy (i.e., to decide how best to alter the decision rule implied by Equation 21.2), a government must know the value of b_1 and cannot rely merely on the reduced form estimates B_1 and B_2 so long as b_2 is not small.

Thus the question of whether "power" relationships should be included in economic models is an empirical one and not a matter of convenience or of specialization between economists and political scientists. Since economists usually ignore political factors, structural estimates are not available and policy is often severely hampered. Empirical work on input/output tables provides an important example of information based only on reduced form estimates. The coefficients of these tables, so frequently used by planners, are derived from the actual flows in a given year and do not reflect technological linkages alone, as they purport to, but also the tastes, interests, and limitations of the previous governments' decision rules. Thus there are good econometric reasons for a government interested in overcoming underdevelopment, i.e., changing policy and structure, to be wary of them.

This model also points to another important problem for policy making even where accurate estimates of t are available. Suppose that a previous government had been characterized by a decision rule which attempted to stabilize price to producers by varying t inversely to P (e.g., through a marketing board). This would reduce the observed variance of $P(1 - t)$ and increase the difficulty of estimating the coefficients of Equation 21.1 thus making it difficult to use past experience as a basis for future policy. More generally, when a government attempts to change (i.e., develop) the structure of an economy, it often finds the data generated by the previous structure (i.e., the historical facts) to be unhelpful as a basis for policy. Revolution, by definition, implies values of a and b outside the historical sample, and only under very special conditions would the statistical estimates of those coefficients apply to nonmarginal changes. Ideology supplies the strength to ignore the facts. One of the important purposes of historical analysis is to show how power relations in the past constrained the full development of the productive potential of the economy.

This essay is divided into three parts corresponding to the three major stages of the international economy: *Mercantilism* (late 15th to 19th century), *Colonialism* (1870 to 1939), and *The Present.* For convenience we call these Mercantilism I, Mercantilism II, and Mercantilism III, respectively, since they represent successive stages of unequal trade and uneven development. The argument is conducted heuristically, but our hope is to proceed at a later point to theoretical and econometric models using sets of interdependent political and economic equations.

21.2. Mercantilism I: 15th Century to 1870

The Mercantilist period created the first truly international economy. The oceans were transformed from a barrier separating Europe from Asia, America, and Africa, to a medium of exchange, and new dimensions for commercial intercourse were created. Ironically, the global integration that created *one world*, unified by mercantile and political relationships, also led to the fragmentation of its parts into a small set of developing countries and a large group of stunted and deformed economies which became the underdeveloped areas of the world. It is this historical process of uneven development that we will focus upon in the following analysis.

International trade theory [5] predicts that in a market system the fall in

[5] By trade theory we mean the classic law of comparative advantage. (Continued on next page.)

transport costs created by the age of exploration would lead to an increase in trade and improved welfare for the world as a whole as well as for each of its trading countries. Individuals and groups within a country may, of course, gain or lose depending on their ownership of the factors of production. In an egalitarian peasant economy, for example, all individuals will be better off, since they share equally in the resources of the country. In a more highly developed civilization such as existed in parts of Asia and South America, labor will lose and land will gain since imported manufactures will substitute for crafts and services while increased exports of primary products would raise the value of natural resources.

Our model yields different results, because it takes into account political as well as market relationships. Mercantilist trade changed the power structure within and between countries, and this radical break is of greater importance in explaining the patterns of trade and income distribution than is the market reaction to price focused upon in the orthodox model.

Figure 21.1 is a device to illustrate the employment structure of the traditional economy and the changes that occurred as a result of Mercantilism I trade. The diagram is based on an equation linking food production (and consumption) per capita $\bar{f}$ to: output per man hour in agriculture a, hours per man in agriculture h, and the percentage of persons engaged in agriculture n.

$$\bar{f} = ahn \qquad\qquad (21.4)$$

For a given per capita food standard, Equation 21.4 traces out a rectangular hyperbola AA, describing possible distributions of the work force of a

"Under a system of perfectly free commerce, each country naturally devotes its capital and labour to such employments as are most beneficial to each. This pursuit of individual advantage is admirably connected with the universal good of the whole. By stimulating industry, by rewarding ingenuity, and by using most efficaciously the peculiar powers bestowed by nature, it distributes labour most effectively and most economically: while, by increasing the general mass of productions, it diffuses general benefit, and binds together, by one common tie of interest and intercourse, the universal society of nations throughout the civilised world. It is this principle which determines that wine shall be made in France and Portugal, that corn shall be grown in America and Poland, and that hardware and other goods shall be manufactured in England."

David Ricardo, *The Principles of Political Economy and Taxation*. (London: J.M. Dent & Sons Ltd., 1948) p. 81. Since Ricardo's time, numerous qualifications have been added to his statement, and now the orthodox model recognizes exceptions to the "gains from trade argument." These qualifications are not the ones we shall be concerned with in this essay.

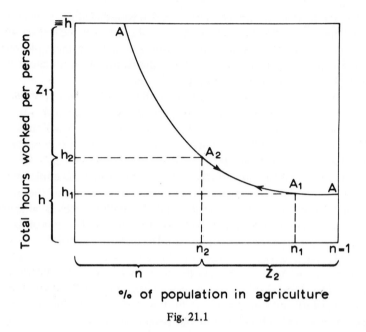

Fig. 21.1

traditional society. It is assumed that a is unaffected by h and n. [6] At a point such as A_1 (which we shall argue represents one of the prevalent African modes of production) nearly the entire population is engaged in the agrarian sector (n approaches 1), but the hours worked per man in agriculture are low. At a point such as A_2 (Oriental Despotism), a much larger fraction of the population is outside the agrarian sector, while those engaged in agriculture are more fully specialized and work substantially longer hours in farming in order to produce an agricultural surplus for the remainder of the population.

The distribution of time in nonagricultural activities can be illustrated in Figure 21.1 by dropping perpendiculars to each axis. The vertical distance between the total hours of labor per worker $\bar{h}$ and the actual hours worked in agriculture per worker h represents the time available in the agrarian sector for the production of household goods and services [7] ($Z_1 = (\bar{h} - h)n$ where Z_1 refers to hours per capita spent on rural household goods).

---

[6] It is unlikely that h and n are independent, but it is convenient to postpone discussion of this until after the model is presented.

[7] S. Hymer and S. Resnick, "A Model of an Agrarian Economy Including the Production of Non-Agricultural Goods," *American Economic Review* (September 1969).

The horizontal distance between the total population ($n = 1$) and that fraction engaged in agriculture n represents the proportion engaged in what the physiocrats called the unproductive sector, i.e., the aristocrats, soldiers, servants, officers, clerks, traders, and artisans associated with the state sector. The size of this sector (per capita) is $Z_2 = \overline{h}\,(1 - n)$.

The African case was characterized by a small state sector, because its egalitarian political structure inhibited the appropriation of the surplus by a small group. Most families had full rights to land and paid little, if anything, in the way of rents or taxes either in kind or in labor services. The fraction Z_2 was, thus, very small (in many cases even the chief's family grew its own food), while the portion of time spent on Z_1 was large, much of it was devoted to leisure and ceremony. [8]

An opposite pattern is found in the Asian case. Because of the great power of the state to extract a surplus, Z_2 is large and Z_1 is small. A large number of people are engaged in extracting the surplus from agricultural workers, managing the affairs of the bureaucracy, and providing consumption goods and services for the state. In order to meet their taxes, the agricultural population must reduce their consumption of Z_1 and devote their time to producing an agricultural surplus. In addition, the requirements of corvée further reduce the time available for household production.

In Figure 21.1, as we have drawn it, the standard of life for the majority of the population is clearly superior in the African case. Food consumption per capita is the same in both cases by assumption, while Z_1 is much greater in Africa than in Asia. This result depends crucially on the assumption that AA is a rectangular hyperbola. In reality, there are several reasons for believing that agricultural labor productivity associated with the Asian mode differs from that found in Africa. The advanced civilization associated with Oriental despotism was based on a hydraulic society which implied investment of resources in irrigation and other infrastructure to increase agricultural output. If a was sufficiently higher as a result of this investment, it would be possible then for h (hours per worker in agriculture) to be the same in both cases even though the Asian mode had a larger Z_2. This would have happened if the state in practice charged a tithe exactly equal to its social productivity so that the agricultural population did not suffer because of its existence. There is no historical reason to believe this was the case. Studies of Oriental despotism suggest that the state attempted to maximize the surplus and to reduce income in the agricultural sector to the minimum necessary for survival, and

---

[8] See S. Hymer, "Economic Forms in Pre-Colonial Ghana," *The Journal of Economic History* (June 1970) for a discussion of the African case.

sometimes not even that. [9] Moreover, some of the government infrastructure was needed merely to compensate for diminishing returns resulting from the use of a higher labor/land ratio. [10]

The revolutionary impact of the new trading possibilities introduced by Mercantilism I led to the growth of the state in certain African economies and to a movement towards the Asian mode; while in certain Asian economies, it led to a decline in state power and a movement away from their original position. This movement is shown by the arrows in Figure 21.1. In both cases, there is a dramatic change in the composition of output and its distribution even though national income did not necessarily increase and in some cases fell.

In the African case, the new opportunities for foreign trade provided both an incentive and the means for the growth of a state sector. Economic factors were not the sole cause of state formation but were an important contributing factor. A military group that succeeded in monopolizing coercive power in a given area could establish peace and security for traders and levy taxes accordingly. The state, in a word, substituted tolls and tariffs for banditry. The larger the area brought under control, the greater the taxes that could be charged, and the more powerful a military and bureaucratic establishment that could be supported. The strength of the state could also be used to capture slaves, to organize slave production of exportables (in gold mining for example), or to meet food requirements. It was thus possible to expropriate a surplus through exploitation of labor as well as through taxation of trade.

The impact of Mercantilism I on income in Africa and its distribution was very complex. The local elites benefited, as did both the plantation owners in the new world and the merchants who organized the elaborate mercantile system based on the slave trade. To the extent that it participated in the upsurge of economic activity on a voluntary basis, a certain portion of the population at large also benefited by trading food or manufactures for imported goods. Nonetheless, gains were in no way commensurate with the enormous dead weight loss associated with the capture of slaves and their

[9] K.A. Wittfogel, *Oriental Despotism* (New Haven: Yale University Press, 1967).

[10] Three men working one-third of the time can nearly always duplicate the work patterns of one man working full time. The opposite is not true. For example, one full-time agriculturalist cannot be in more than one place at one time. If ϵ_1 is the set of activities achievable under part-time work in the African mode, and ϵ_2 is the set possible for full-time specialists in the Asian mode, then $\epsilon_1 C \epsilon_2$ but $\epsilon_2 \not\subset \epsilon_1$. The African societies could spread themselves over the land and take advantage of nature, while Asian societies had to concentrate around the river where it was possible to grow water-crops which allow for more equal spacing of work over time.

exploitation in plantations. As regards Africa, therefore, the production possibilities of society shifted inward as a result of those losses from trade. Among those who remained, there was a reallocation of labor into Z_2 owing to the growth of the state (it is assumed that Z_2 includes plantation production) and out of Z_1 as free men substituted imported goods for domestic manufactures. The distribution of employment resembled more closely that of the Asian society, but the distribution of income among the living was quite different. The standard of life of slaves were repressed below the preceding levels; but the standard of life of free men was increased, because their marketed surplus was compensated by imported goods rather than simply taken away through taxes.

In the Asian case, the coming of the West led to the undermining of the power structure in countries or regions characterized by the Asiatic mode of production. The steady penetration of Western traders from the 16th century onward eroded the political and economic relationships based on Oriental despotism. In terms of Figure 21.1, there was a decline in Z_2 and an increase in Z_1 as labor was freed from activities serving the state. Thus the Asian mode moved somewhat in the direction of the African as the influence of the state declined and that of the West increased. The impact of Mercantilism I trade thus at first led to an improvement in welfare as the decline of Z_2 and rise in Z_1 distributed income in favor of the long exploited peasant. The decline of Oriental despotism with its unproductive class of retainers and its demands for corvée labor meant that the wage-rental ratio for the society as a whole rose contrary to the predictions of the classical model.

In some areas a new Z_2 arose in connection with the expansion of commercial activity as new trading routes to the West replaced the historical trade among China, India, and Southeast Asia. The flourishing of this trade, during the 17th and especially the 18th century, led to the growth of Western controlled coastal regions and port areas and the demand for a food surplus to service traders, soldiers, and consuls. In these areas, Z_2 (the new sector specializing in commercial activity) rose while Z_1 declined, replaced by imported manufactures, as the hinterland specialized in food or export production.

Through time, the West pushed steadily inward and established a new system of political control. The tendency to improve welfare increasingly came under pressure as the West increased its ability to control the indigenous work force, to enforce tribute, and to levy taxes. As the West's ability to extract a surplus grew, the share of the gains from trade going to the vast majority of the population declined, and only a small class of foreign traders and rulers or, in some regions, local elites benefited substantially. The peasant, freed from Oriental despotism, found himself increasingly bound to a new master, and there was once again a tendency for Z_2 (including plantation labor) to rise and for Z_1 to fall.

The Western impact in Latin America (Mexico and Peru) was different in that the existing political structure was quickly taken over and the population exploited at a maximal rate. So ruthless was the appropriation of the surplus in gold and silver mining that a large percentage of the population soon died. The complex pattern of Western rule and colonization that existed in Asia was, therefore, not duplicated in Latin America. There was a total collapse of society and enormous losses from trade.

Our models of trade in Mercantilism I have emphasized shifts in the power structures rather than movements along the production possibilities curve and have yielded quite different predictions about changes in production, employment, and distribution of income than those of international trade theory. Our analysis can be summarized in the following simple balance equation of the gains and losses from trade (providing one is willing to accept, for the sake of argument, the measurability of changes in welfare):

$$\begin{array}{ccc} \text{Gains to elite} & & \text{Gains (or losses) to} & & \text{Gains from} \\ \text{in Europe} & + & \text{majority in Europe} & = & \text{trade} \end{array}$$

$$\begin{array}{ccc} & \text{Gains to elite} & & & \\ - & \text{in underdevel-} & + & \text{Losses of} & - & \text{Deadweight} \\ & \text{oped countries} & & \text{exploited} & & \text{loss} \end{array}$$

The crucial feature of Mercantilism I is that the overall gains from trade were small and the deadweight loss was large. It is hard to imagine any reasonable set of calculations that would show that the value of the increase in world income during the 16th, 17th, and 18th centuries could offset the tremendous costs associated with the murder and enslavement of Africans and Americans. This is true even if one were to argue that there was a net gain in welfare for those Asian countries in which the population was freed from Oriental despotism. [11] Many of the gains accruing to the elites in the underdeveloped world and Europe (and possibly to workers in Europe) arose

[11] The Asian case is, however, complex even if, on balance, there was a net improvement in welfare. An interesting example is provided by India. The India ruling class began to decline prior to the coming of the West and Indian society might have been in a state of transition that would have led to the growth of indigenous merchant-capitalism. Although there is some historical evidence supporting this view, colonialism in fact ended the possibility of such a path and created an underdeveloped country.

mainly from the shifts in power and increased exploitation rather than from increased productivity. This slash and burn capitalism was possible only because Mercantilism I was able to use the human capital accumulated over previous centuries and did not worry about maintaining its reproduction.

If Mercantilism I caused an inward shift in the production possibilities curve in parts of Africa and America, it also caused an outward shift in Europe. Again, changes in the distribution of income and power were the crucial factors. It is not necessary to postulate that Europe as a whole (or even England as a whole) gained from Mercantilism I to explain the phenomenal rise in savings, investment, and income in the 19th century. The important feature is that some groups benefited and that a new class was formed out of the gains from trade. In other words, in place of the usual neoclassical formulation for investment $(I = sY)$ we would substitute the equation $(I' = s'Y_c)$ where I' refers only to investment in industry, Y_c refers to the income of the capitalist class, and s' refers to the capitalist savings rate. An increase in industrial capital could then occur even if Y fell, as long as Y_c/Y rose sufficiently. Empirically, it is difficult to estimate what happened to Y, but it is clear that Mercantilism I led to the growth of capitalist income and power in Europe.

The steps in this process are interesting. At first, the merchant capitalist class had little power and was subjected to discrimination by the feudalistic state. However, the new possibilities of maritime commerce and exploitation led to an alliance between the state and merchants (in some cases pirates). It was highly profitable for the monarch to subsidize international trade and offer it protection because of the profits to be gained. Thus the state and the emerging capitalist class grew in step, though much of the increased national power was dissipated in international rivalry. Eventually the capitalist class became sufficiently strong to take power and to switch government expenditure away from the agrarian sector, remove agrarian preferences and protection, and to increase agrarian taxes. This further enhanced the industrial capitalist class and led to its further growth. During the 19th century, industrial capital emerged triumphant, dismantled the corn law structure and the rest of the Mercantilist framework, and created a new technology based on iron and steam, and a new set of government policies (so called laissez-faire) with which it conquered the world and laid the basis for the second international economy. A total restructuring and reorganization of the hinterland occurred in Mercantilism II as Europe formulated a single strategic conception for the development of the world economy and planned a new division of labor. Many of the mainstays of Mercantilism I were cast away, like the first stage of a rocket, and new enclaves of growth were created.

Mercantilism II began as an unequal partnership based on the asymmetrical results of Mercantilism I, and during the course of its lifetime, it further widened the gap between Europeans and non-Europeans.

21.3. Mercantilism II: 1870 to World War II

The period from 1870 to the 1920s was characterized by a fall in international transportation costs and an increase in the variety of manufactured goods available for trading. Trade theory predicts these events would cause the hinterlands of Africa, Asia, and America to expand export production and to replace the production of home goods by imported manufactures. The outward shift in the production possibilities curve would imply an increase in national income but not necessarily a corresponding improvement in welfare of every subgroup. The initial impact of this trade could, for example, lower wage rates and the standards of living of large parts of the population as production of labor-intensive home goods declined and the production of land-intensive export goods increased. Through time, however, the level of income would be expected to rise for everyone. Increased income would lead to increased savings and investment, and an outward shift in the production possibilities curve. A rise in wages would occur as the capital/labor ratio increased.

Broadly speaking, this scenario fits a large number of countries. It explains the great expansion of trade, the emergence of surplus labor, the strengthening of the landowning class, and the growth of mercantile capitalists. Furthermore, it also predicts the eventual investment in industry after the 1930s, the growth of the industrial labor force, and the emergence, in the late 1960s, of manufacturing exports. Even the attraction of foreign investment finds support in the predictive power of the theory because of the increased infrastructure and human capital financed by the export economy.

This scenario, however, should not be used in trade classes to illustrate the benefits of greater integration into the world economy, because it omits "power" equations and incorrectly identifies the structure of the system. Because so many underdeveloped countries with such diverse backgrounds followed the pattern outlined here indicates common biases in government policy rather than the power of the trade model. Neoclassical theory would predict a much greater variety of growth patterns given the great diversity of initial conditions and is to some extent falsified by this common experience. We suggest that the expansion of exports reflected in large part the similar policies of colonial rule, while the growth of manufacturing reflected the growing strength of the indigenous capitalist class associated with the "national independence" movements after World War II.

Colonial strategy squeezed the traditional economy to create an elastic supply of labor and biased infrastructure toward exports in order to transfer the surplus to the center in the form of lower prices. The specific labor policies used conformed to no single pattern, rather a variety of devices emerged to deal with the variety of initial conditions. In some cases the government levied labor taxes or poll taxes to stimulate an exodus from the "traditional" economy into the "commercial" economy. In other cases, the government seized the land or created a landlord class thus reducing the opportunity cost of wage labor. The fostering of a proletariat for the export sector (including the food surplus to feed it) was also stimulated through land concentration, intensification of tenure arrangements, and the growth of indebtedness. National and international mobility was encouraged as the government helped in recruitment and enforcement of contracts thus making possible vast transferences of population within continents as well as from Asia to Africa and America. In this way, labor and exports were generated in each colony.

The gains from trade generated during Mercantilism II were shared unevenly. Initially, there was a decline (sometimes drastic) in the standard of living for many people as they were coerced into export production. Through time, this decline tended to be reversed as new opportunities were made available in the commercial economy. Increased specialization led to new divisions of labor and created new dependencies as resources were reallocated from the traditional economy to export production and the personalized society of the village was fragmented. The striking feature of Mercantilism II, however, is that the standard of living for the vast majority of the population of Africa, Asia, and America rose very slowly in sharp contrast to the progress at the center.

Although exact statistics are not available, evidence suggests that the real wage for unskilled labor has risen slowly over the last 50 to 100 years, and this wage can be taken as a proxy for the level of income of perhaps two-thirds of the population. Moreover, other evidence suggests that debt peonage and tenure arrangements increased in the agrarian sector as peasants found themselves increasingly bound to money lenders and absentee landowners. No doubt there was some improvement in consumption patterns as superior European manufactures increasingly replaced native rural industry. However, the displacement of rural industry and traditional activities also led to the fragmentation of the agrarian society, and in many countries, especially those in which export specialization proceeded most rapidly, there was a serious deterioration of the social life of the society. [12]

The gains from trade were partly captured by local elites (some of whom were foreigners from the mother country) who accumulated land, capital, education, or the rights to higher paying employment in the government bureaucracy or in the commercial economy. Often an alien complex of production was established where the peasant cultivated the soil or worked in the mines, a foreign mercantile class grew in strength (in Asia, Chinese, and in Africa, Indian), and the Europeans controlled the import-export trade as well as determined colonial expenditure and labor policies. The distribution of income reflected the political power of this economic structure. Much of the gains from export growth went to the government (in the form of increased revenues), to the urban centers (where services and industry grew based on export growth), and to local and foreign elites of one type or another.

In part, the gains were passed abroad in the form of lower prices. The division between the metropole and the local elite depended largely on the propensities to import. If surplus receivers had a much higher propensity to import than the population as a whole, the "cheap labor" policies followed would be export biased to the benefit of the mother country. On the other hand, if local elites spent a high proportion of their income on local services, they would divert labor from export production. This would still involve an international transfer of surplus, since a high proportion of this elite income went to foreign settlers and colonial officials from the mother country. The surplus would, however, tend to be consumed locally rather than in the center.

This possible antitrade bias was offset, at least in the initial phase of colonialism, by a number of other policies designed to specifically encourage exports. Many labor policies directed labor towards particular industries, e.g., mining, whose only function was production for exports. Similarly, infrastructure was heavily biased towards export production and neglected the production of home goods or placed it at a disadvantage. In other words, the steps taken to produce cheap labor were combined with steps taken to induce it to flow into exports.

The observed high elasticity of exports in this period thus reflects government policy as well as market response. A high export price resulting

---

[12] For an historical account of the decline of traditional life and the effects on the distribution of income brought about by the export economy, see S. Resnick, "Decline of Rural Industry under Export Expansion: A Comparison among Burma, Philippines, and Thailand, 1870–1938, " *Journal of Economic History* (June 1970).

from an expansion of demand would induce an increase in private investment because of high profits. It would also provide the government with extra revenue (since trade taxes were the dominant source of funds) and thus lead to the improvement of infrastructure and other support services which would further stimulate international supply because of their export bias. Thus a strong tendency towards immiserizing growth was built into the system, for any rise in price would trigger an expansion of export biased investment until price fell sufficiently.

An alternative development strategy would have allocated a greater share of public investment to home good industries and produced a more balanced investment program. This would have a substitution and an income effect. The substitution effect of removing the export bias in infrastructure might bias production away from exports, but this might be offset by the income effect from growth if importables were highly income elastic. Moreover, the development of the hinterland would have increased the variety of possible exports and provided new opportunities for mutually beneficial trade.

A more forward looking policy would have directed a large flow of funds from the center to the periphery for investment purposes. The dominant feature of Mercantilism II was the global capital market centered in London. For the first time in history, investment decisions throughout the world were coordinated in one place and subjected to a single strategic conception. It thus became technically possible to spread capital evenly throughout the world. In other words, capital accumulation after 1870 could have proceeded via capital widening rather than capital deepening, i.e., the capital/labor ratio could have remained constant and a far larger number of people activated as industrial workers. This would soon have exhausted the metropolitan labor force and either capital would have had to move to the hinterland or labor move to the center. This, combined with efficient trade, would have produced factor price equalization on a global basis. In other words, had this strategy been followed, industrial capitalism would have reproduced for the entire world population the higher level of living it achieved for Europeans. (The term Europeans is used to include people of European descent in all continents.)

The whole pattern of production and trade would have been quite different in such a system. Manufacturing production would have spread throughout the world, earnings and output per worker *employed* would have been much lower, but both the work and its fruits would have been shared equally. The structure of manufacturing output would be altered towards the mass production of basic consumption needs rather than towards the high income goods that account for most of industrial output. Instead of this, capital accumulation proceeded via capital deepening in the industrial countries and led to a widening differential in production and income between the center and the hinterland. Thus, the returns to labor were not equalized despite the great expansion of trade after 1870 and large migrations of Europeans, Asians, and Africans.

Capital per worker was raised and the expansion of the industrial labor force slowed down. This created a radically different structure of demand from the egalitarian one just described and led to an economy based on continuous "creative destruction" to use Schumpeter's phrase. Because the capital/labor ratio increased steadily, the producer good sector had to continuously innovate labor saving machinery. Raising per capita income for a small, favored group meant a continuous change in the basket of goods consumed since, according to Engel's law, people tend not to consume more of the same as they get richer but reallocate their consumption patterns away from old goods towards new goods. Thus, toward the end of the 19th century, product innovation and marketing became the dominant problems of business enterprise rather than the mass production of goods. Instead of applying the achievements of science widely and solving the basic problems of subsistence for the majority of the world's population, attention was focused on creating "new products" and lightening the work load of the privileged under the guise of technological change.

Why was the second path chosen rather than the first? It could have been the result of the exogenous factor of technological change or differences in production functions, as many economic models imply, but we would argue that political factors were an important if not dominant determinant. In our view, the observed uneven development represented uneven power, and the resulting distribution of income and demand was a social phenomenon rather than a technical one.

The control device was government expenditure. Private capital was highly mobile during this period and flowed to wherever profit could be made. But the rate of profit or the demand for investment in any country depended upon the extent of public investment in infrastructure and human capital. The colonial system centralized power over government expenditure policy and insured a much higher rate of public capital formation in the center than in the hinterland. This biased distribution of public capital provided "external economies" in the center and directed private industrial capital away from the hinterland.

That this policy neither maximized world income nor distributed it equally is not surprising. The imperial system did not weigh people equally in its social welfare function. Political power was used to foster the growth of the capital of the mother country (i.e., the capitalists), subject to the constraints of class conflict. Using Kindleberger's group behavior approach, we might analyze the policy of this period in terms of the alliances and coalitions formed between the following groups:

	Center	Hinterland
Capital	C_1	C_2
Land	T_1	T_2
Labor	L_1	L_2

Let us first examine trade between Europe and the areas of European settlement in America, Oceania, and Africa. According to the theory of the time, colonization, i.e., the migration of Europeans to other continents, was a method of expanding land and warding off the tendency for profits to fall because of diminishing returns in agriculture. The resulting pattern of international trade initially involved the exchange of manufactures for raw materials because of two important historical advantages associated with the mother country: (1) a large domestic market giving rise to internal and external economies, and (2) a strong capitalist class (or stock of entrepreneurship). Through time, the colony developed its own manufacturing sector (aided perhaps by tariffs or other government instruments) as the internal market expanded and as the indigenous capitalist class acquired the strength and resources to engage in industrial activity. Two-way trade in manufactures could then begin based on differences in comparative advantage and tastes.

As Kindleberger noted, the smooth working of this model would only take place under specific political conditions. Since trade would tend to reduce rents, it could only occur where the resistance of landlords was weak. In England, where the industrial classes had reached a position of dominance, this condition prevailed and free trade allowed the importation of wheat which helped to complete the liquidation of landlords as the most powerful economic group in Britain.[13] But in Germany, the agricultural class was sufficiently strong to stop this development from taking place. Ironically, growth and development proceeded much more rapidly after 1870 in Germany than in the rest of Europe, perhaps because of the balance struck between agricultural and industrial classes. The fusion of rye and steel created a powerful alliance that could use the state's power to pursue a growth-oriented strategy.

In terms of the earlier framework, the major conflict was between T_1 and

[13] C.P. Kindleberger, *Op. cit.*, pp. 32–33.

T_2. The politics of labor were relatively unimportant, because it was not yet well organized and, in any case, labor tended to benefit from the cheap wheat. It also could migrate to the hinterland when severely hurt at the center (see Kindleberger's discussion of Italy). The conflict between C_1 and C_2 was also muted in the early stage because of the low degree of capitalist development in America.

After 1870, this power structure changed drastically. The landed classes became unimportant as a separate interest group (in the center), because they were destroyed or absorbed into industrial capital. The English capitalist class lost its hegemonic position as native bourgeoisies arose on the continent, in America, and in Japan. Rivalry between C's became a dominant element in the foundation of Mercantilism II.

Equally important, labor became a powerful force as it became concentrated in industrial centers. The class consciousness was accentuated in England because of the shock of the great transformation out of agriculture and into the city as a consequence of wheat imports.

The result of these changes was that the imperial centers were in no position to embark on a "big push" in the hinterland. Their main concerns were to ward off rivalry from competing centers and to satisfy the growing demands of labor. Their policies tended to be defensive rather than offensive, mercantilist (i.e., protectionist) rather than free trade: ironically Edwardian England revived the paraphernalia of the landed aristocracy it had just destroyed.

Many of the policies of Mercantilism II thus slowed down the rate of growth and prevented the full development of the potential created by the scientific revolution. The fact is masked by growth statistics that show what happened instead of what could have happened. Unlike Mercantilism I, where the dead weight losses exceeded the gains, technological achievements of the 19th century were so great as to overwhelm the inefficiencies and retarding elements of Mercantilism II.

Instead of promoting the growth of enterprise in the hinterland, colonial policy arrested the development of native capitalists by failing to provide positive incentives and by the application of negative measures including, in some cases, outright destruction of burgeoning enterpreneurship. For similar reasons, they preferred low-wage/low-productivity labor in the hinterland over high-wage/high-productivity workers, because the latter would have been a potential political threat. The dual of this policy was to create a labor aristocracy in the center and to protect it through tariffs and immigration policy. Education programs and expenditures were unequal being biased towards labor in the center. The two parts of the labor force must be seen as one if this period is to be analyzed properly.

Finally, the center had to devote an increased share of government activity to military and other nonproductive expenditures and had to rely frequently in the hinterland on an alliance with an inefficient class of landlords, officials, and soldiers, to maintain stability at the cost of development. A great part of the surplus extracted from the population was thus wasted locally.

The ideology of Mercantilism II, as reflected in economic theory, was capitalism triumphant. By the early twentieth century, nearly all of the components needed to solve mankind's material problems had been discovered. The only task left was the systems analysis problem of organizing and applying them. Mercantilism II began with great promise, but after a brief time span became seriously troubled and increasingly characterized by war, depression, the breakdown of the international economy, and war again, rather than by free trade, pax brittanica, and material improvement.

21.4. Mercantilism III

Political change, i.e., national independence, is clearly at the heart of the policy changes that ushered in Mercantilism III. The depression and World War II weakened the center allowing the national bourgeois class (C_2), born in the colonial export economy, to assert independence and to divert government expenditures to their own ends. Their control was, however, far from complete, and the restrictions and biases of the international economic system governed much of their actions. They did not, for example, face perfectly competitive markets in which they could trade freely with other countries. Instead, they frequently encountered large oligopolistic corporations with whom they had to bargain for needed investment goods and technology. Moreover, the governments in the advanced countries, though no longer possessing legal control, continued to exert pressure to keep the hinterland open to capital and manufactured goods from the center. Finally, the tariff structure used by the center effectively closed the rich industrial markets to manufacturing exports from the hinterland.

The set of policy options open to the newly independent countries were thus severely restricted (especially with respect to their control over the export staples and the accompanying network of financial intermediaries) while their targets and search procedures reflected and were limited by their disadvantaged past. The national bourgeois were, in effect, middlemen who did not understand the wider system above them and who could not mobilize the people below them. Given the limited vantage point of their past, they became imitators rather than innovators; they were children of the Europeans, an underdeveloped middle class. Forced industrialization became their strategy and the goal was to create a national capitalist class by using protection and import-substitution policies. The result was uneven development.

Although there seems to be a variety of experiences in the postwar period, as each country endeavored to formulate a national policy peculiar to its circumstances, a common theme is found in the tendency to reproduce on a national scale the pattern of the international economy evolved during Mercantilism I and II. Capital formation is concentrated in urban centers resulting in rising capital/labor ratios, productivity, and per capita income for a small group of people. The neglect of the agrarian sector leads to rural stagnation and an unlimited supply of labor at low wages. An income and class gap emerges parallel to the international gap between European and non-European, previously decribed.

Basically, the import-substitution policies result in a rapid growth of manufacturing, centered in urban areas with little generation of employment. The economic reasons usually given are the labor-saving nature of foreign technology coupled with imperfections in the factor market that cause the imported price of capital to be too low and lead to a steady increase in the organized manufacturing sector's capital/labor ratio.

Although we cannot analyze this system in detail here, we do want to point out, in the spirit of this paper, that the reasons behind this scenario lie as much in the "power" equations as the market equations. The biases in economic structure come from the governments' attempt to favor one sector over another. The devices used to protect the national capitalist class have long been studied by trade economists, i.e., the instruments of tariffs, quotas, exchange controls, import licensing, and internal subsidies. Less fully analyzed but equally important are the biases in government infrastructure towards urban industrial needs, the establishment of a discriminatory educational system, and the use of the police power of the state to suppress the rural population and maintain the surplus of labor at the existing wage. It is these policies and the political relationships involved, and not merely the shape of production functions, that help to explain the output mix, factor proportions, and factor prices observed. The symbiosis, between the national bourgeois and the state, favored capital and a select group of urban labor at the expense of the population as a whole, and this resulted in a rapid growth of manufacturing, an increase in industrial wages rather than employment, and an excess demand for jobs. It also resulted in an output mix aimed at the few, emphasizing import substitution rather than import displacement. [14] In other words, the "independence" strategy accepted foreign tastes and foreign

[14] For footnote see next page.

technology and tried to reproduce them on a miniature basis instead of adapting to local needs and local endowments.

There is reason to believe that this strategy is reaching a turning point as it encounters increased imbalance in the labor market and the foreign exchange market. A new solution is therefore needed to deal with the crisis in population, employment, and balance of payments that result from growing political pressure from the excluded population and the international economy. The basis for it seems to be an alliance between C_2 and C_1, the native capitalist class and the multinational corporation. This new group behavior, if it continues to develop, will lead to new economic configurations and a new international division of labor. We cannot analyze it in detail here but we might conclude the essay with a few conjectures about the next round of Mercantilism III.

We argued that Mercantilism I led to the formation of C_1, while Mercantilism II broke down, in large part, because of rivalries between subgroups of C_1, i.e., the various national capitals of the center. In the first round of Mercantilism III, C_2 succeeded in establishing itself as a minor partner, secure but in no way powerful enough to challenge or replace C_1. Meanwhile, a new relationship has appeared within C_1 in the form of a growing trend towards multinationalization of private enterprise. Mergers and foreign investment by American and European firms are leading to interpenetration of markets and the weakening of links between particular countries and particular firms.[15]

Thus the stage is set for a new international industrial structure dominated by 300 to 500 large North Atlantic oligopolistic corporations that operate on a global basis in cooperation with smaller national firms who serve as suppliers, distributors, licensees, and in some ways, as competitors. The trade pattern associated with this international hierarchy of decision-making will lead to an exchange of goods and services based on skill differentials. The center will specialize in complex manufacture and high-level technology, i.e., systems design, research, marketing, finance, while the hinterland will specialize in labor-intensive production. The multinational corporation, if it

[14] We are grateful to Lloyd Best of the University of West Indies for this distinction. See Lloyd Best and Kari Levitt, *Externally-Propelled Growth and Industrialization in the Caribbean*. Mimeographed, September 1969.

[15] These issues are discussed more fully in S. Hymer and R. Rowthorn in "The Multinational Corporation and International Oligopoly: The Non-American Challenge" in C.P. Kindleberger, ed., *The International Corporation* (Cambridge: The M.I.T. Press, 1970) and S. Hymer "The Multinational Corporation and the Problem of Uneven Development" in J. Bhagwati, ed., *Economics and World Order* (New York, MacMillan & Co., 1971).

succeeds, will reproduce on a world level the centralization of control found in its internal administrative structure.

Three major political questions dominate any attempt to predict the future course of the international economy. First, will there be some sort of alliance of L's to match the alliance of C's? Second, will multinational corporations be able to construct multinational political institutions to replace the nation-states whose power they are eroding? Third, will it be possible to resolve rivalry between the capitalist and socialist block and within the capitalist block itself (e.g., the problem of Japan and Germany)? The progression from Mercantilism I to Mercantilism II to Mercantilism III has seen an increased complexity of political and economic linkages between countries. Modern communications and the multinational corporations are increasing interconnectedness to so great an extent that a qualitatively new system is emerging. The greater the interactions between countries, the greater the interdependence, i.e., the higher are international multipliers and the lower are national multipliers. If we were dealing purely with market relationships, this would not present analytical problems, since a great deal is known by economists about the self-regulating properties of general equilibrium systems involving many decision units. These stability properties do not hold on the political plane where tariff struggles and "beggar my neighbor" policies, etc. lead away from Pareto optimality. International trade theory, because it does not include these political factors, is misleading in analyzing the current world economy.

CHAPTER 22

TRADE AND TECHNICAL EFFICIENCY *

Staffan B. LINDER

Between international trade, on the one hand, and technological advances and technical efficiency, on the other hand, there are interesting mutual relationships. In this paper, it will be suggested that additional explorations into these relationships could be made to some advantage for an understanding of the effects of international trade.

22.1. Theoretical suggestions

The selection of the best input combinations for the producion of particular output levels is a question of economic efficiency and depends upon input and output prices. Technical efficiency, however, requires that maximum output quantities be secured from given input quantities. There can be two different types of reasons for technical inefficiency; (1) there are managerial slacks of a general kind, and (2) the best available technology is not utilized. "The best available" does not necessarily mean the most advanced but rather that the choice of technique has been made on the basis of complete knowledge of the available alternatives.

The marginalist theory of the firm, which plays a central role in the theory of production, pays little attention to factors affecting technical efficiency and technical progress. In this static theory, there is assumed to be a given state of the art. It is also assumed that firms run under conditions of technical efficiency, there being no managerial slacks and technological oversights. Firms operate according to a production function that presupposes technical efficiency.

* The author wishes to express his thanks to Clark W. Reynolds, Jagdish Bhagwati, and Murray Kemp for criticism and comments.

The omission in this way of all technical matters from economic analysis represents, for many purposes, a useful simplification. In other contexts, however, it has been found to be a severe restriction on economic analysis. Efforts have thus been made to incorporate a theory of technical change into economics. There are various discussions of the effects of exogenous technological progress on such matters as business cycles and growth. There is also a growing literature treating technical progress in the form of invention, innovation, imitation, diffusion of knowledge, and learning by doing as an endogenous process. In growth theory as well, the necessity of explaining "the residual," i.e., the amount of growth not explained by changes in factor totals, forces attention in this direction. [1]

Interest in technical efficiency and technical change also comes from economists that want to construct a theory of the firm capable of describing behavior under uncertainty. In the marginalist theory of the firm, the assumption that producers are omniscient must mean that information costs are treated as being zero. However, as has been argued, information costs are anything but zero and the establishment of technical efficiency as well as the development of new techniques is not just a technical problem but a highly economic one. Some economists try to introduce modifications within the neoclassical framework in order to allow for nonzero information costs. [2] Others take a more dramatic step and try to construct a new theory of the firm referring to this alternative as a "behavioral theory of the firm." [3]

This theory of the firm describes the entrepreneurs' choice among alternatives as a *search process*. As a result of information costs the search process gives a decision when a satisfactory solution has been found. This solution may well be associated with managerial slack in the organization and with the use of suboptimal techniques, in other words with technical inefficiency. The solution adopted may also be marred by economic inefficiency. Once such a solution is found, the search process may or may not continue depending upon the circumstances.

---

[1] See, for instance, F.H. Hahn and R.C.O. Matthews, "The Theory of Economic Growth: A Survey." *Economic Journal* (December 1964), pp. 779–902.

[2] See, for instance, George J. Stigler, "The Economics of Information," *Journal of Political Economy* (June 1961), pp. 213–225.

[3] This new approach has been inspired in particular by Herbert A. Simon. See, for instance, his "Theories of Decision-Making in Economics and Behavioral Science." *American Economic Review*, (June 1959), pp. 253–283. For a more elaborate treatment the reader may be referred to Richard M. Cyert and James C. March, *A Behavioral Theory of The Firm* (Englewood Cliffs, N.J.: Prentice-Hall, Inc., 1963).

On the relative merits of the marginalist and behavioral theories of the firm, there is an extensive discussion. [4] Some have taken the eclectic position that the predictions made by the two theories converge. The conclusions that can be derived from the behavioral theory become identical with those of the marginalist theory if information, not immediately available for free, gradually amasses and is put to use through some simple learning mechanism and if "survival of the fittest" means a weeding out of those not capable of learning. [5] With this kind of convergence, the behavioral theory merely amounts to the introduction of a number of complicating factors representing a sociological description of what actually takes place during a process of adaptation of entrepreneurial behavior.

However, such convergence seems likely only under the conditions for which the marginalist theory is constructed. It is probable that, through the price mechanism, information will be forced upon the firm making it behave in a way that is economically efficient. But this does not ensure *technical* efficiency. True, the learning-by-doing process leads to some limited improvement in technical efficiency but only within the given production process and within the technology actually being exploited. The process does not ensure any search for new, unknown heights. Survival of the fittest brings about competitive pressures that force firms not to settle down, but there is nothing to guarantee that the fittest firm itself is not technically inefficient in a constantly changing world. The behavioral theory has the advantage in that it suggests that technical inefficiency may well be the rule rather than the exception.

Anyhow, whatever language is chosen, the analysis must take into account that there is a considerable amount of technical inefficiency in the production processes. Furthermore, growth studies reveal that technological progress and changes in technical efficiency are of great importance in explaining the growth performance of the various economies. [6] In the theory of

---

[4] F. Machlup, "Theories of the Firm; Marginalist, Behavioral, Managerial," *American Economic Review* (March 1967), pp. 1–33, is an attempt by one of the defenders of the marginalist approach to sum up this discussion.

[5] For an argument of this kind see, for instance, Armen A. Alchian, "Uncertainty, Evolution and Economic Theory," *Journal of Political Economy* (June 1950), pp. 211–222, and Richard H. Day, "Profits, Learning, and the Convergence of Satisficing to Marginalism," *Quarterly Journal of Economics* (May 1967), pp. 302–311.

[6] Differences in levels of technical efficiency are discussed by E.E.G. Salter, *Productivity and Technical Changes* (Monographs 6) (Cambridge, England, At the University Press, 1960), appendix to chapter VII. Edward F. Denison, ("How to Raise

international trade, not much attention is given to the effects of trade on technical efficiency. [7]

This means that trade theory does not contribute much to one important component of growth analysis. In trade theory, a great many efforts are certainly made to elucidate the effects of trade on growth. There are studies of the effects of improved economic efficiency on the accumulation of factors of production; of the relationships between growth and terms of trade change; of the contribution to growth of capital imports, capital exports, and labor movements; of the staple theory of growth and the "vent-for-surplus" theory. How important these writings are is difficult to determine. It may be noted that they are left out of the Hahn and Matthews survey of growth theory. That this can be both possible and convenient may, however, indicate no more than that growth theory proper is on a more esoteric level and, thus, difficult to review together with more applied studies. More disquieting for trade theory is the fact that an empirically minded researcher such as Denison in his *Why Growth Rates Differ* finds, it seems, little use of the growth aspects of trade theory. An explanation for this is that, in trade theory, little

the High-Employment Growth Rate by One Percentage Point," *American Economic Review*, Papers and Proceedings (May 1962), p. 75) refers to better means for disseminating information and alertness in "adopting it" as an important source of economic growth. In his great study *Why Growth Rates Differ* he devotes considerable attention to "technological and managerial knowledge" as a source both of differences in growth and income levels. For instance:

"... output per unit of input in Northwest Europe in 1960 was more than one-quarter below the United States even after eliminating the effects of economies of scale, over-allocation of resources to agriculture and self-employment, and differences in the rate of utilization. Thus, there appears to be opportunity for the European countries to add substantial increments to their growth rates by imitating and adopting American practices."

[E.F. Denison, assisted by J.-P. Poullier, *Why Growth Rates Differ*. Postwar Experience in Nine Western Countries (Washington, D.C.: The Brookings Institution, 1967) p. 283.]
Richard E. Caves (and associates), in *Britain's Economic Prospects* (Washington, D.C.: The Brookings Institution, 1968), also give great weight to problems of technical efficiency.

[7] Two exceptions to this rule are provided by Charles P. Kindleberger, *Foreign Trade and the National Economy*. Studies in Comparative Economics 2 (New Haven: Yale University Press, 1962), esp. chaps. 6 and 7; and H. Leibenstein, "Allocative Efficiency vs. X-Efficiency," *American Economic Review* (June 1966), pp. 392–415. The infant industry argument also concerns problems of technical efficiency. This argument has lived a long, although analytically isolated, life in trade theory.

attention has been devoted to the effects of trade on technical change and efficiency. [8]

Using the language of the behavioral theory of the firm, the question then is: how does international trade affect the search process? It will be argued here that this process can be affected in positive as well as negative ways.

The search process could be stimulated for the following reasons:

(a) The *cost of searching* for improvements will be lower or, in other words, the *supply of knowledge* will be improved. The reasons for this are the demonstration effect of foreign goods and foreign methods established through foreign trade. According to sociological literature, the suasion effect of personal contacts may be of particular importance in the diffusion of knowledge. [9] The network of personal contacts will be widened through international trade.

(b) The *profits of searching*, i.e., the *demand for knowledge* of new ways, will be improved. The bigger the market is, the greater the opportunities of recouping the search costs and making a net profit. The rewards, but not the costs, of search will be a function of the length of production runs. This will stimulate both the search to establish technical leadership through invention and innovation and to make rapid imitations, for instance, to take advantage of lower factor costs. The importance of the profitability considerations in adopting new knowledge is stressed in a number of studies, for instance by Schmookler, Mansfield, and Griliches. [10]

---

[8] That economists are well aware of these growth effects of international trade but at the same time abstain from bringing them explicitly into the analysis not receiving any guidance from trade theory can be instanced in the following quotation:

"In considering international trade restrictions, we have to pass over their significance for competition and for the flow of information about production processes and methods of industrial organization,"

(Moses Abramovitz, in "Economic Growth in the United States," a review article on Denison's study of the sources of economic growth in the US, *American Economic Review*, September 1962, p. 774).

[9] See, for instance, E. Rogers, *Diffusion of Innovations* (New York: Free Press of Glencoe, 1962). Also J.S. Coleman, *Introduction to Mathematical Sociology* (New York: Free Press of Glencoe, 1964), chap. 17; and K.J. Arrow, "Classificatory Notes on the Production and Transmission of Technological Knowledge", *American Economic Review* (May 1969), pp. 29–35.

[10] J. Schmookler, *Invention and Economic Growth* (Cambridge, Mass.: Harvard University Press, 1966); E. Mansfield, *The Economics of Technological Change* (New York: W.W. Norton & Co., 1968) and *Industrial Research and Technological Innovation* (New York, W.W. Norton & Co., 1968); and Z. Griliches, "Hybrid Corn: An Exploration in the Economics of Technological Change." *Econometrica*, October 1957, pp. 501–522.

(c) The *penalty of not searching* for information to carry out improvements will rise. If the incentive of greater profits from search is not enough, the penalty of greater loss from nonsearch should stimulate demand for information. The carrot is the chance that one's own search efforts are successful; the stick is the risk that the search efforts of the competitors are successful. Through foreign trade, the combined amount of search that an entrepreneur will encounter against him will increase and make it necessary for him to increase his own effort in order to ensure survival. The grace period for firms tolerating too much slack will be shorter, the more intensive the competition. The risk that a given amount of slack will prove to be too much slack will increase and there will perhaps not be time enough to adjust once difficulties have emerged. Thus, through an energetic search, difficulty must be prevented from emerging at all.

These penalties may also be useful to stir up firms from what could be called a "learning-by-doing inertia." Through learning by doing, a firm will be able gradually to improve its performance within a given activity. Various kinds of defects in the product can be attended to, workers acquire new skills and management learns to handle its various functions. However, as Domar has pointed out, this increased technical efficiency may make management unwilling to face the uncertainties and unknowns of unfamiliar activities into which an application of the results of a search process would throw them. [11] The proudness of craftsmanship may make labor resist new ways and methods. Learning by doing could thus, in the long run, prove to have a negative effect on technical efficiency. The penalty of not searching will make a firm less inclined to settle down in the warmth of the well known.

But success in the search process is not guaranteed. The fact that there is a penalty to such failure must mean that there are risks for the firms engaged in international trade. However, as we know from the comparative cost theory and from the adjustment mechanism theory, the risk is not that all the economy will collapse if competitive pressures are not met. Trade theory only recognizes certain reallocation problems that may be painful but are not impossible to solve. However, the additional question exists of whether the search effort may not be impaired in comparison to what it would be under some other commercial policy regime. If entrepreneurs in their search efforts are unsuccessful and they have to fall back on a passive adjustment of input prices, the edge of initiative may be cut. Future search efforts may be less

[11] E. Domar in a discussion on "Theory of Innovation," *American Economic Review*, May 1969, pp. 44–46.

energetic through an intimidation that was the result of stifling previous search efforts. It is important to note, however, that whereas the positive effects of trade on technical efficiency can be spread to all trading partners, the negative effects can hit only certain countries or regions: in the competitive search process only some countries or regions can possibly be on the losing side and these may not even be exposed to this intimidation effect.

That such a negative effect of the competitive process may in fact occur is indicated by certain empirical research. C.F. Carter and B.R. Williams in their study of innovating and investment in some 250 British companies found that in some industries keener competition will act as a positive stimulus to search and investment, whereas in other industries, greater protection and less competition, "so that a longer view may be taken," will be beneficial to the level of technical efficiency. They conclude that no general rule applies. Investment in innovation, they argue, is not a necessary consequence of competition. "Competition may lead to technical progress if it is supported by a supply of scientists and technologists and by an appropriate provision for research and development, and if its stimulating effects are not outweighed by the uncertainty it creates". [12]

22.2. Tariff Policy

If trade has an effect on the process of search for technical efficiency and technical progress, it has, according to growth theory, an important effect on economic growth. If the impact of trade on the search process is an either/or situation, this means that one faces an intricate problem in trade policy to determine the best strategy for growth. It will be argued that such considerations have been important in applied policy considerations and that a discussion of them could contribute to our understanding of tariff policy.

In current theory of tariff policy, the effects of trade on *economic* efficiency are important. Trade is taken to have beneficial effects on economic efficiency, and there is thus a general case in favor of trade.

---

[12] C.F. Carter and B.R. Williams, *Investment in Innovation* (London: Oxford University Press, 1958), p. 48 and p. 142 and by the same authors *Industry and Technical Progress* (London: Oxford University Press, 1958), Chap. 15. The two quotations are from the first work p. 142 and p. 48, respectively. A writer who early took an interest in problems of response to competitive pressures in the context of international trade was Erik Hoffmeyer, *The Dollar Shortage* (Amsterdam: North-Holland Publishing Company, 1958).

However, in analyzing the effects on economic efficiency various kinds of second-best considerations have to be taken into account. [13] Trade has both positive and negative effects on economic efficiency, and the problem of trade policy is to strike the correct balance.

For any student of practical matters, this kind of tariff theory makes a nonworldly impression because of the highly esoteric character of second-best theory. I would venture the assertion that parliaments have rarely acted under the impression of such a theory. Thus, irrespective of whether actual tariff policy is wrong or right, a different theory is required to explain the thinking that underlies it.

On the basis of the previous arguments the following tariff theory could be outlined: The beneficial effects of trade on technical efficiency provide a strong argument for trade. However, for certain countries or regions, unrestricted trade could stifle the search effort and yield negative effects on technical efficiency. In formulating a tariff policy, a balance must be struck between the positive and negative effects.

However, in this balancing act, considerations of economic efficiency must also be taken into account. If, presently, too little attention is given to technical efficiency in trade theory, in correcting for this one must not lose sight of economic efficiency. If trade results in no negative effects on search and no second best considerations have to be made, there is a double case for free trade. If, however, there is a negative effect on search or if second best considerations have to be made, there is a conflict between technical and economic efficiency requirements, and an optimum must be sought out. If there are both negative effects on search and second best considerations to be made, there may or may not be a conflict. For instance, protection of industry may be called for, both to stimulate search and to correct a marginal inequality between wages in industry as compared to agriculture.

Actual tariff structures could be interpreted in this light. Tariffs are low where the economic efficiency gains are of dominating importance. Thus they are in the production of primary products. Tariffs are high where the risks of being exposed to a passive adaptation owing to the foreigners' successful search are high, in relation to the gains in economic efficiency from a lowering of trade barriers. This would be the case for manufactures. As is readily seen, the one tariff argument concerned with technical efficiency

---

[13] See Harry G. Johnson, "Optimal Trade Intervention in the Presence of Domestic Distortions", in Essays in Honor of Gottfried Haberler, *Trade, Growth, and the Balance of Payments* (Chicago: Rand McNally & Co., 1965).

considerations in the theory of tariff policy, (i.e., the infant industry argument) fits easily into this approach.

Many economists have tried to calculate the economic efficiency gains from an additional freeing of trade. [14] They have invariably reached the conclusion that such gains are insignificant and have reluctantly tended to conclude that trade policy is less important than one may think. Yet, in actual fact trade policy has attracted much attention. This again could be explained in terms of technical efficiency. This brings us to the problem of customs unions that has been so important in recent commercial policy considerations.

Peculiarly, as long as we discuss the effects of trade only in terms of economic efficiency, it is hard to find a rationale for customs unions. According to current doctrine, customs unions are suspect animals. They may or may not lead to any gains as second-best theory tells us. [15] The losses of trade diversion may swamp the gains from trade creation. Furthermore, as C.A. Cooper and B.F. Massell have pointed out, all the economic efficiency gains that a customs union could lead to could, in fact, be secured through appropriate changes in the most-favored-nation rates. [16] Thus, it would be possible to have the economic efficiency gains of customs unions without forming customs unions and without being exposed to the efficiency losses which customs unions would entail. For good reasons, these two authors complain that customs union theory does not make it possible for us to understand why customs unions are formed.

However, when we take technical efficiency into account, a better understanding of the drive toward customs unions may be gained. The formation of a customs union may be viewed as a method of increasing the level of competition within a group of countries which are similar enough for the pattern of adjustment on balance to become active rather than passive. Disadvantages in the way of stifled search effects can be avoided, and the beneficial effects of stimulated search for improved technical efficiency can be obtained. Customs unions viewed in this way are not a perfect substitute to reciprocated reductions in most-favored-nation rates.

[14] For references, see Bhagwati's survey of trade theory: "The Pure Theory of International Trade: A Survey," *Economic Journal* (March 1964), pp. 1–84.

[15] See R.G. Lipsey, "The Theory of Customs Unions: A General Survey," *Economic Journal* (September 1960), pp. 496–513.

[16] C.A. Cooper and B.F. Massell, "A New Look at Customs Union Theory," *Economic Journal* (December 1965), pp. 742–747.

22.3. Comparative Advantage

Trade will affect not only the general intensity of the search effort but also the direction of the search. The work of J. Schmookler on invention and economic growth is of great interest in this context. Schmookler rejects the hypothesis that inventions come in some neat succession where the one invention not only makes the other one possible but also stimulates its actual delivery. He also finds no empirical support for the widespread idea that in given economic areas there will be gradually rising costs of inventions, the fund of technological possibilities eventually drying up alltogether. Instead inventive activity is influenced by demand conditions, i.e., the size of the market for the inventions. When this demand rises, inventive activity rises and vice versa.

It is likely that what holds for search for inventions will hold for search for improvements in general. However, if the direction of the search effort is demand oriented, the question is demand *where*. Schmookler does not take up this question explicitly, but it is abundantly clear from his presentation that it is demand in the market surrounding the entrepreneur rather than in some geographically very distant market. This means that the search will proceed differently in different countries depending upon demand conditions. One explanation for this can be given in terms of information costs, i.e., a factor which is an important determinant for the process of search as already argued. The search costs will rise with the distance from the entrepreneur. As a result we will get a pattern of comparative advantages that will be determined by the demand structures. This kind of theory agrees with the growing literature that tries to find other explanations of the pattern of trade than the factor proportions account which is built on the marginalist theory of production, assuming technical efficiency and the same production functions in all countries. [17]

Because the search process has these characteristics, the theory of comparative advantage is of less generality than is usually thought. The comparative cost theory was originally set out to explain why countries on

---

[17] See Staffan B. Linder, *An Essay on Trade and Transformation* (New York: John Wiley & Sons, 1961), chap.III; M.V. Posner, "International Trade and Technical Change," *Oxford Economic Papers* (October 1961, pp. 323–341); Charles P. Kindleberger, *Foreign Trade and the National Economy*; R. Vernon, "International Investment and International Trade in the Product Cycle," *Quarterly Journal of Economics* (May 1966), pp. 190–207; and G.C. Hufbauer, *Synthetic Materials and the Theory of International Trade*. (Cambridge, Mass.: Harvard University Press, 1966).

different levels of productivity could nonetheless trade with each other to mutual advantage. However, different levels of productivity result in different demand structures. It is logically possible that the demand structures become so different that there are no overlapping demands. At least for a country on a very low productivity level, it may be impossible with positive factor rewards to produce goods asked for in countries on high productivity and income levels. In this case the conclusion — generally held to be truistic — of the comparative cost theory does not hold. This theory by assumption neglects the possibility of nonoverlapping demands. Portugal and England in the example of Ricardo were both, in the pretrade situation, producers and consumers of both wine and cloth. The problem may be of some importance in practice, i.e., in the trade relationships between developed and underdeveloped countries. [18]

[18] This possibility has been explored at some length by the author in *Trade and Trade Policy for Development* (New York: Frederich A. Praeger, 1967).

CHAPTER 23

ON MISUNDERSTANDING THE CAPITAL CONSTRAINT IN LDCs: THE CONSEQUENCES FOR TRADE POLICY

Ronald I. McKINNON

Very few observers of decision-making processes in developing countries have eyes as keen as those of Charles Kindleberger. Few, if any, can match his insight into the way capital markets function internationally or domestically. This essay spans both fields and attempts to build on some of the intellectual capital he has already provided.

23.1. The Intervention Puzzle

Public policy in underdeveloped economies is now one of pervasive intervention, particularly in those that have guided their own development for several decades, such as South America, Turkey, Iran, the Philippines, India, Pakistan and Ceylon. Intervention typically spans all sectors of the economy, leading to mispriced scarce resources and ubiquitous excess supplies or excess demands in both commodity and factor markets. The foreign trade sector has been particularly vulnerable with a variety of restrictions on both imports and exports.

Observers are familiar with high nominal tariffs amounting to several hundred percent on certain classes of imports, largely consumables or "inessentials", whereas tariffs are low or waived altogether for imports of many "essential" intermediate inputs and capital goods used by favored domestic industries. The pattern of direct (nontariff) controls usually accentuates the marked discriminatory impact of nominal tariffs. In addition, export taxes or prohibitions are used to lower the domestic prices of raw materials or wage goods that would otherwise be sold internationally.

Thus industrial protection results both from keeping competing foreign products out and, equally importantly, from cheapening intermediate products used by favored domestic industries. In economies where restrictions on competitive imports are so high and extensive as to leave much redundancy in the tariff structure, the allocation of foreign exchange and tariff exemptions can be the more important instrument of public policy. By its nature, it is also more discriminatory because allocations are frequently made to particular producers, whereas tariffs on competing imports could protect any domestic producer in the sheltered industry. Indeed, an import license for intermediate inputs or capital goods may be the "ticket" that an entrepreneur needs to start domestic production.

What sense can one make of all of this analytically? There is now an extensive, elegant, and useful literature [1] on the relationships of domestic distortions to foreign trade restrictions. It is set in the familiar neoclassical framework where labor and capital are symmetrically treated as highly aggregated factors of production and the economy is neatly divided into sectors according to the commodities produced, each with its own economic characteristics — some of which may be designated as "distortions".

Briefly, this neoclassical literature demonstrates that restrictions on foreign trade will never be a first-best compensation for domestic distortions in product and factor markets. Trade restrictions intended to be compensatory could easily reduce welfare. More recently, this literature has shown that many trade restrictions and internal distortions can make economic growth "immiserizing".

The neoclassicists suggest that domestic distortions should be directly offset by taxes and subsidies in the markets where the distortions appear. Only if a country has monopoly power in the foreign trade of specific noneconomic objectives directly affecting foreign trade — such as self-sufficiency — can one make an economic case for interfering with trade flows. Even then, the concern has been with protection from competing *goods* rather than foreign exchange allocations to particular *producers*.

How then can the limited role for trade restrictions within the neoclassical model be reconciled with the morass of restrictions observed in practice? Must one "write off" what governments do as being purely political in dividing spoils among adherents or, worse, as being quite irrational?

In this paper, no attempt is made to deny the importance of politics or illusions — both are important in advanced as well as in poor countries. However, there is an *economic* explanation of existing intervention in less

---

[1] The most recent results are nicely reviewed in J.N. Bhagwati, "The Generalized Theory of Distortions and Welfare," Chapter 4 in this volume.

developed countries (LDCs) which is outside the standard neoclassical framework. Once this alternative explanation is understood, the appropriate role of the government in dealing with domestic "distortions" can be shown to conflict with current practice and *also to be different from the tax-cum-subsidy recommendations of the neoclassical model as they affect product and factor markets.*

23.2. The Capital Constraint

I hypothesize that the economic profile of underdeveloped countries is dominated by fragmentation in the markets for land, labor, and capital, as well as fragmentation in the distribution of knowledge and technical opportunities. There is a wide variety of returns to be earned on existing and potential investments which cannot be easily delineated by type of product or sector. This dispersion of returns in capital markets may be classified as a "distortion," but there is no tax-subsidy arrangement by which governments can costlessly compensate for it, given the great uncertainty involved in identifying entrepreneurs with access to profitable investments. Only if the institutions of an effective capital market are developed, can distortions in the factor markets be efficiently offset. Indeed, the process of "economic development" is, in an important measure, the reduction of this dispersion in rates of return.

Uncertainty confines economic units to self-finance in capital accumulation. Correspondingly, labor and land are also imperfectly mobilized because of the absence of complementary investments, and they remain attached to family enterprises in suboptimal uses. With a large self-financed household or "unorganized" sector and an imperfectly financed corporate or "organized" sector, there is little use emphasizing a class structure based on the functional distribution of income among wages, profits, interest, and land rents, with established rates of return to each class. Nor is there much gain to be had from sharply distinguishing a saving class from an investing class, and both from a laboring class. There are many entrepreneurs who provide labor, make technical decisions, consume, save, and invest. I suggest that the efficiency of all these operations is heavily influenced by the capital constraint on individual enterprise which need not accurately reflect the scarcity of capital in the economy as a whole.

In contrast, the neoclassical model does specify a functional distribution of income with *uniform* returns to factors producing a single output. Fragmentation or distortions in the factor markets are confined to intersectoral differences based on output produced. For example, it is often posited that the returns to labor in industry may be higher than in agriculture and the returns to "capital" in industry may be lower. Hence, taxing the use of capital and subsidizing the use of labor in industry is the optimal policy. Other combinations of tax subsidies in factor markets could be desirable within the neoclassical model.

However, if the actual factor markets are fragmented as per my hypothesis and the functional distribution of income cannot even be established *within* sectors, then a tax-cum-subsidy to highly aggregated factors is a nonoperational concept. It would be nonoperational even in the unlikely presence of an administratively efficient fiscal apparatus for collecting taxes and paying subsidies. Usually, the government's fiscal apparatus is quite weak and brings with it distortions of its own. Instead, institutions of the capital market — such as banks and financial intermediaries — should be designed to channel capital from inferior to preferred uses, and only incidentally would this be associated with intersectoral transfers.

Making domestic capital markets function effectively encompasses the whole of monetary and financial policy as well as the theory of uncertainty. Such an investigation is outside the scope of the present paper, [2] and I shall not attempt to elaborate systematically what "first-best" policy in LDCs should be. *Our intent is simply to establish the importance of the capital constraint for the complex of foreign trade policies actually followed.* It is important to recognize how manipulation of the foreign exchanges is, in considerable measure, an attempt to replace a functioning capital market by second-best techniques. This is manifest not only in favoring one industry against another but in giving monopolistic advantages to particular firms and in lowering the costs of capital goods or intermediate products for the economy as a whole.

In treating this rather diffuse but important subject, the plan of this paper is:

1. To show how authorities respond at the microeconomic level to imperfections in the capital market. "Infant-industry" and "learning" arguments for protection are examined in some detail, but the analysis is, initially, confined to individual producers or industries.

---

[2] Many of the ideas in this essay are part of a longer treatise — *Money, Foreign Trade and Taxation in Developing Economies* — to be published by the Oxford University Press. I am indebted to my colleague and collaborator in that venture, Edward S. Shaw, for his kind consent to have this essay separately published. By now, his ideas on this subject cannot be distinguished from my own.

2. To show how a complex of interventions to protect individual producers can have unexpected macroeconomic repercussions of *unprotecting* important segments of the economy such as agriculture and the production of intermediate products. However, even when unprotection becomes very marked, it may be tolerated because of the inadequacy of the capital market.

3. To analyze perversities that arise in manipulating the foreign exchanges, with or without capital transfers from abroad, in order to cheapen imports of intermediate inputs and capital goods in lieu of providing direct access to financial capital by individual enterprise.

The emphasis throughout is on the inefficiency of manipulating the foreign exchanges in response to the internal capital constraint, thus setting up the presumption that such policies are inferior. However, the case is not proven, because the real costs of providing institutions which channel funds directly from low- to high-return activities are not analyzed. Indeed, they would vary with the level of development. [3] Nevertheless, the direction of further research is established, as is the nature of the "vacuum" that would be created if existing interventions were suddenly removed without appropriate compensatory action to provide alternative financial channels.

23.3 The Infant-Industry Argument for Protection

The traditional infant-industry argument is essentially based on imperfections in domestic capital markets. It is frequently alleged that some new industries need protection to cover the initial losses, although ultimately they will be privately profitable at world prices. A "temporary" tariff on competing imports will raise the price of domestic output and provide a source of "self" finance to domestic firms during the early period. But, as Harry Johnson has pointed out, [4] a *perfect* capital market would provide funds for the lean years (months) until the industry matured. Indeed, only repayment of principal and interest in the absence of protection would vindicate the new industry since early losses must be held to social account.

---

[3] Again, another strand of neoclassical literature, "growth theory," is of no help because it assumes that capital markets operate costlessly to equalize returns everywhere. This is tantamount to assuming away the development problem.

[4] H.G. Johnson, "Optimal Intervention and Domestic Distortions," pp. 22–29 in *Trade, Growth and the Balance of Payments,* Essays in Honor of Gottfried Haberler (Chicago; Rand McNally & Company, 1965).

However, uncertainty as to yields of financial and tangible assets shortens, sometimes drastically, the time span over which finance is available on terms satisfactory to both lenders and borrowers in underdeveloped countries. The choice of technique is related to this myopia, as some entrepreneurs must get a quick return to shallow investments or be completely excluded by the short-term nature of the capital market. Extending horizons of investors, savers, and financial institutions can be a superior alternative to tariff protection. Unfortunately, protection is the common response.

Tariff-setting machinery has not the discipline of even moderately efficient capital markets in identifying those activities that really are socially profitable. Once chosen for protection, the *techniques* used by the favored industry will reflect the myopic nature of a still distorted capital market operating at short term. Only by the most subtle manipulation may the tariff authority lengthen the term over which the protected industry can obtain finance and still phase out protection so that there is at least some chance it will eventually become competitive at world prices.

Moreover, a high output price as a result of tariff protection reduces domestic sales of the protected commodity and lowers welfare by penalizing users — a result well-known to trade theorists. At the microeconomic level, authorities may compensate for this by singling out particular "infant" producers for tariff exemptions or foreign exchange allocations with which to buy intermediate products (inclusive of capital goods) at low prices. This enables final product prices to be lowered either through internal price controls or through lowering the protective tariff on competing imports. Cheaper inputs are a common source of short-term finance to "infant" producers which can partially replace finance through higher output prices.

Additionally, an import license can permit tne licensee to raise finance from outside his enterprise. The short-run myopia of the capital market is reduced if exclusive licenses provide lenders with evidence of viability. Such licenses may be issued along with domestic bank loans or be part of a package deal to attract foreign direct or portfolio finance. Indeed, a surprisingly large number of "infant" producers in LDCs are the local subsidiaries of large international corporations, with well-established importing rights for intermediate products. *Effectively, import licenses are used as monopoly cnarters in order to ameliorate the capital constraint.*

One important opportunity cost is the problem of monopoly control. Price ceilings over the protected output or allocations of foreign exchange to an uneconomically large number of domestic producers are common responses to the control problem. These do not work well. In a wide variety of less developed countries in Asia and Latin America, noncompetitive domestic cartels are maintained by their connection with the license-issuing authorities. Clearly, a preferable solution is a capital market that suppresses inefficient activities and draws resources at long term toward enterprises with high real rates of return.

23.4. Learning and Enclave Effects

If the time-span argument for protection proves ineffective, recourse can be had to the learning effects associated with infant or mature industries which are somehow external to the participating factors of production. Labor-force training is frequently cited. Following conventional analysis, [5] we can distinguish labor-force training specific to the particular enterprise in which training occurs from generalized training which the workers can apply outside the firm.

Specific labor training can be financed by capital available to the particular enterprise since it stands to capture the benefits of increased worker productivity. [6] The training itself represents a real investment, with a time lapse between cash outlays and returns, which can be as important as the acquisition of durable capital goods. Moreover, whether or not it is undertaken depends on profitability *and* on the capital constraint binding the individual enterprise.

Even generalized technical training — plumbing, carpentry, etc. — is specific to a particular individual, increasing his real productivity. His ability to undertake such training (apprenticeship) would then depend on his own personal capital constraint.

It may be justifiably argued that complete removal of the *personal* capital constraint is beyond the capability of even highly developed capital markets. However, a wide class of underdeveloped economies with "lumps" of labor, capital, and land attached to small independent enterprises can *internalize* most of the returns to labor-force training. Enterprises may be run by an extended family — Chinese style — at lower levels of development; or the existing labor force may be considered an unalterable fixture of the firm as in the more advanced Japanese case. In this situation, a loosening of the capital constraint on individual enterprises may have far-reaching effects on the

[5] Gary S. Becker, *Investment in Human Capital* (New York: National Bureau of Economic Research, 1964).

[6] There may of course be some bilateral bargaining between firm and worker over the division of the increased productivity.

learning process. An important part of the "profit" of such indigenous enterprise will be on returns to investments in a more highly trained labor force.

As in the case of the infant-industry argument, the predilection of authorities is to use tariffs, allocations of foreign exchange, or other ad hoc subsidies to promote "learning." Paradoxically, the ultimate effect of these policies may be to fragment labor and capital markets even further by having protected sectors (enclaves) exerting substantial monopoly power to extract much higher returns than those prevailing in the rest of the economy. Rather than "distortions" being offset as per the neoclassical model, they are accentuated.

The splitting apart of the Colombian wage structure has recently been studied in detail. [7] "Elite" urban groups appropriate, behind a tariff barrier, much higher wages than those in the surrounding economy. The pressure for additional tariff protection is then redoubled by firms having to pay higher wages which reduces their ability to compete with imports — thus offsetting the initial tariff protection. A spiraling of enclave tariff protection and wage increases ensues. The high wages inhibit the absorption of labor into new industry, aggravate the unemployment problem, and further bias the choice of technique. In many countries now, on-the-job training is confined to a nongrowing band of high-wage urban workers in the subsidized activities. The problem of labor absorption has been one of the most pressing recent concerns in the development literature.

How should learning effects, including general technical change, be dealt with? Suppose we drop the neoclassical view that learning externalities can be classified by sector and are proportional to the output produced. There are, however, entrepreneurs with the information and the opportunities to exploit technological gaps in the way existing resources are employed as compared to best-practice techniques in advanced economies. For example, there may be firms with a wide variety of techniques, reflecting their differential access to capital, all producing the same output. These opportunities are scattered throughout the underdeveloped economy, some possibly in the government sector.

Furthermore, we posit that exploitation of these opportunities usually requires new investment or a significant restructuring of existing capital assets. The purchase of equipment, new construction, or even the shift from subsistence to commercial agriculture have large *indivisible* investments

[7] R. Nelson, P. Schultz and R. Slighton, *Colombian development Policy*. (Santa Monica, Calif.: The Rand Corporation, 1969).

associated with them. The introduction of commercial agriculture may require a complete package of new seeds, pesticides, and fertilizer for which finance has to be found. One then concludes that the potential rate of return within individual enterprises is as good as any single measure of the learning potentialities within the economy. There are external spin-offs when other entrepreneurs copy innovators, but these show up as higher profits there. [8]

If learning effects are positively correlated with potential rates of return rather than levels of output — assuming the absence of tariffs or other distortions in the commodity markets — then government policy in dealing with one phase of learning is enormously simplified. The channeling of funds to high-rate-of-return activities and the reduction of short-run myopia, automatically identifies and subsidizes the learning process. No formal decisions have to be made to protect manufacturing at the expense of agriculture, one industry at the expense of another, or import substitution at the expense of export expansion. Even the neoclassical case for direct intervention in product markets tends to be weakened since learning externalities are not linked to particular outputs per se. Learning can be widespread without those interventions behind which enclaves can form.

23.5. The Macroeconomics of Unprotection

While policymakers respond imperfectly to individual producers constrained by capital availability, they are only dimly aware of the general equilibrium consequences of intervention. Except in the uninteresting case where the relevant economic resources have been completely idle, *every direct act of "protection" of some activity is also an indirect source of "unprotection" to others.* Therefore, to evaluate the overall impact of a complex of trade restrictions, one must have at least a rough idea of where "unprotection" is focussed. One can then judge whether toleration of this unprotection is related to the capital constraint.

Suppose there exists a differentiated tariff structure or direct import controls where: (a) imports of consumer goods are kept out; and (b) intermediate products, including capital goods, enter freely at the existing exchange rate. Compare the resource allocation of this differentiated tariff structure with that under free trade. The external value of aggregate imports

---

[8] Of course, there are still the conventional cases to be made for government-financed research and development expenditures and public support for general education, both of which are very important in poor countries.

is assumed to be equal to aggregate exports in both cases. Then, one can see intuitively that the differentiated tariff structure is discriminatory against:
1. Producers of exports;
2. Domestic producers of intermediate inputs and capital goods; and
3. Consumers of "inessentials".

As a formal theorem, it has been shown that a tariff on one class of imports of rate "t" is actually equivalent to an alternative policy of taxing exports and subsidizing the remaining imports at the same rate "t". [9]

This symmetry theorem holds quite generally and is, surprisingly, independent of the way intermediate inputs are used in export or import competing products. Thus one cannot overcome anti-export bias by allocating imported intermediate products to exporters. To expose this common fallacy, suppose we consider the extreme case where all imports of intermediate products enter export activities as under entrepot trade.

If all intermediate products are re-exported in some form, a differential tariff is equivalent to taxing *value added* in export activities at the tariff rate applicable to imports of final consumption goods. Intuitively one can see this by noting that value added in pure entrepot trade (net foreign exchange earned) is spent abroad and is effectively taxed by the import tariff on the return flow of consumer imports. In short, special foreign-exchange allocations to exporters may ameliorate export repression, but they can never completely offset it.

Inflows of foreign capital, which themselves may be responses to malfunctioning domestic capital markets, can accentuate the unprotective effects of a differentiated tariff. As a general proposition, absorbing external capital in "real" terms increases imports relative to exports and has the immediate impact of unprotecting the production of tradable goods as compared to nontradables. If imports are broadly spread, the negative protective impact on any one industry is not too serious. However, if we have a sharply differentiated tariff structure with few holes through which the transfer can take place, then unprotection can be sharply focussed. Not only are actual and potential domestic producers in the open categories for intermediates sharply unprotected, but the real price of foreign exchange vis-a-vis the domestic price level would be driven down more than it would be under free

---

[9] See the present author's "Intermediate Products and Differential Tariffs: A Generalization of Lerner's Symmetry Theorem," *Quarterly Journal of Economics*, (Novermber 1966), for a much more complete analysis of general equilibrium repercussions.

trade. Thus, the profitability of exporting also declines as a result of the transfer. [10]

Apart from domestic trade controls, externally negotiated agreements can also sharpen the absorptive impact of a capital transfer. Government-to-government aid, foreign direct investment, or foreign supplier credits are frequently "tied" to the importation of specific intermediate products.

Much of this indirect unprotection is an unexpected and unwanted byproduct of protecting *individual* producers, which we analyzed earlier. However, tolerance by the authorities of some very marked unprotection can be explained by our main hypothesis of imperfectly functioning capital markets, as shown in the next sections where the unprotection of agriculture and welfare implications of cheapening imported capital goods are analyzed.

23.6. Agriculture and Its Terms of Trade

The differential tariff structure described in the preceding sections was largely developed to protect industrial enterprise in urban areas. Insofar as poor countries have been largely primary product exporters, indirect unprotection has fallen pretty heavily on agriculture. In addition, *direct* unprotection via export restrictions was surprisingly prevalent. For example, beef exports were curtailed in Uruguay, Argentina, and Brazil in order to keep urban food prices low; and raw jute and cotton exports were curbed in Pakistan to provide cheap inputs for manufacturing activities. The results have been devastating to rural incomes in many countries with, for example, complete stagnation in Brazilian land productivity in the postwar period, and no perceptible increase in the living standards of Pakistani peasants in the last 20 years.

Putting aside the political struggle over income distribution, an important economic intention was to mobilize the agricultural "surplus" for industrial development on the apparent presumption that internal channels of finance would be inadequate to do the job. The resource transfer can be very large for

---

[10] Of course, if the foreign capital flows into export activities, the adverse absorptive impact could be overcome with exports eventually expanding. The postwar evidence, however, seems to point in the opposite direction, as indicated by B.I. Cohen, "Relative Effects of Foreign Capital and Exports on Economic Development", *The Review of Economics and Statistics* (May 1968) pp. 281–286. LDCs receiving large aid injections were poor exporters.

many poor countries, although not necessarily for others. It depends on: (1) the involuntary transfer directly via the terms of trade change; and (2) resources "voluntarily" tranferred via a trade balance surplus of agriculture with the rest of the economy because profitability in agriculture was artificially depressed while that of industry was raised. In Pakistan in 1964–1965, an estimate of total resources transferred out of agriculture to urban areas was approximately twice as high as the total flow of private saving everywhere in the economy for that year. [11] The amount of slippage in this transfer process is high; there is no assurance that funds flow from low- to high-productivity pursuits, and savings — voluntary — are not adequately rewarded.

In the middle 1960s, there has been a significant reaction against the old policies so that the terms of trade of agriculture have been partly restored. [12] There are, of course, gains to be had from this partial restoration even though, at the micro level, detailed interventions remain. The "green" revolution makes agricultural investments look more attractive to policy-makers. However, the basic problem of improving financial channels to control adequately the flow of savings to the most efficient enterprise in agriculture *or* industry has not been effectively dealt with. Until this capital constraint is relaxed, the temptation to manipulate the agricultural terms of trade in an oscillatory fashion will continue as a substitute for a functioning capital market.

[11] A.N. Chowdhury, *Direct Controls in Foreign Trade and the Strategy of Economic Development in Pakistan*; Ph.D. Dissertation, Stanford University, 1968, Chapter IV. Chowdhury gets a measure of the total resource transfer in world prices by applying rough data to the following relationship:

$$\frac{E}{P_e} - \frac{M}{P_m} = \frac{E-M}{P_e} + \frac{M}{P_m}\left(\frac{P_m}{P_e} - 1\right)$$

where E and M are the exports and imports of the agricultural sector valued at current domestic prices; and P_e and P_m are the ratio of domestic prices of exports and imports to corresponding indices of world prices. Thus, if $E = M$, the first terms on the right-hand side will be zero, but still there can be significant resource transfer due to the second term (terms of trade loss) if the ratio of P_m to P_e exceeds unity. This relationship would be complicated if world prices were sensitive to changes in Pakistani agricultural output.

[12] See for example, Joel Bergsman, "Commercial Policy and Industrialization in Postwar Brazil," (Mimeo) November 1968; Carlos F. Diza-Alezandro, "An Interpretation of Argentine Economic Growth Since 1930", *Journal of Development Studies*, Part I (October 1966) and Part II (January 1967); S.R. Lewis, Jr., "Effects of Trade Policy on Domestic Relative Prices: The Case of Pakistan," *American Economic Review* (March 1968).

23.7. **The Cheapening of Capital Goods**

In the minds of authorities, there is a strong semantic association between "capital" accumulation — leading to growth — and the acquisition of "capital goods." Differential tariffs and tied transfers of foreign capital generally cheapen the domestic prices of foreign capital goods (inclusive of many intermediate inputs) far beyond specific protective agreements with individual producers. Viewed most favorably, such a policy is a second-best way of subsidizing growth by trying to relieve the constraint of a fragmented domestic capital market. Less favorably, it may actually have a negative impact.

In order to conceptualize the various distortions involved, let us begin with a hypothetical subsidy system, then proceed to embellish it with greater realism. Suppose a government with a distortion-free fiscal system (based on lump-sum taxes) could raise a surplus of revenues over expenditures. It designates an extensive list of durable producer goods — machinery, possibly structures — as "capital" goods eligible for subsidy. No distinction is made between those that are domestically produced and imports. A uniform ad valorem subsidy, say 20%, on the purchase of these goods by all domestic users, private and public, is paid out. The effective price that domestic producers "see" then falls by approximately 20%.[13]

This "pure" subsidy is one technique by which the government can inject its own surplus into the accumulation process. Its efficiency is marred by the fact that it is necessarily discriminatory. Durable producer goods have to be arbitrarily identified as such. For example, sewing machines or refrigerators may be vital inputs into certain classes of small industry but are normally considered "consumer" goods in wealthy urban households. The capital stock at any point in time consists not only of fixed assets (durable producer goods) but inventories of raw materials, goods in process, and finished goods. Subsidies give incentives to overuse "fixed" capital as compared to "working" capital. Indeed, most observers are struck by the abundance of excess capacity in plant and equipment in poor countries in the "organized" industrial sector and the absence of multiple shift work.

Moreover, a high proportion of saving and investing can take place *within* household enterprise — both rural and urban — sometimes referred to as "unorganized" activity. In India in the early 1960s, this household invest-

---

[13] The exact amount of the price fall would depend on the supply response in the case of domestically produced goods; but the price fall would be 20% for those goods which have their prices determined in foreign markets.

ment accounted for perhaps 50% of total investment in the Indian econo-my.[14] Much of this internalized savings-investment flow does not pass through an organized market and would be ineligible for formal subsidy. For example, the internal use of labor services for construction work — urban building or rural farm improvement — would be ineligible. Additionally, important investments in labor-force training and learning-by-doing, as dis-cussed previously, would also escape the subsidy in both organized and unorganized activities.

The notion of subsidizing the acquisition of capital goods is not confined to policymakers in less-developed countries. Academic learning models have been constructed that suggest that gross investment should be subsidized in order to achieve social optimality[15] — at least for certain industries. Among other things, such an approach assumes a perfect capital market where private rates of return are everywhere equalized. High-learning industries can then be identified by "other" technological characteristics and an efficient fiscal subsidy can be devised.

In contrast, the theme developed here is that any surplus of public capital is best channeled to investment opportunities where rates of return are high — irrespective of the particular physical embodiment. In a fragmented world, high learning will be better correlated with high real rates of return than with any other economic indices, such as cumulative gross investment or current output, which purport to take external effects into account.

23.8. Discrimination Between Domestic and Imported Producer Goods

Let us now drop the assumption of distortionless government "financing" of the subsidy. Subsidies are rarely paid out directly. They may be given in the form of tax rebates where firms in the organized sector are allowed to "write off" substantially more than the purchase price of durable equipment. Government-owned utilities or steel plants may sell their outputs at less than the long-run marginal cost of production. However, the most common technique for "financing" the subsidy is to manipulate the foreign exchanges through the differential tariff system.

From our symmetry theorem, we know that exporters and domestic

[14] C.T. Kurien, "Indian Economic Crises: A Diagnostic Study," (Mimeographed) 1969, p. 97.
[15] See K.J. Arrow, "The Implications of Learning by Doing", *The Review of Economic Studies*, (June 1962) pp. 155—173.

producers of capital goods implicitly pay much of the effective subsidy. The disappointing export growth of most poor semi-industrial countries is well known, and the implications of agriculture were discussed in the preceding section. Here I concentrate on the distortions involved in suppressing domestic production of capital goods and intermediate products, either for internal use or for export.

Cheap imports of capital goods can affect domestic entrepreneurship and learning processes in a subtle way. Most foreign equipment is built for advanced economies where factor and commodity prices are very different — in particular, where labor is much more expensive. Indeed, learning in more advanced economies, in part, lowers the foreign-exchange cost of machinery and equipment to poor countries. It would be foolish, of course, for poor countries not to take optimal advantage of these advanced technologies where unit costs are further reduced by great economies of scale. However, there is an underlying investment allocation problem. One can invest in advanced technologies embodied in foreign capital goods *or* invest in domestically produced equipment and labor-force training. In the absence of other distortions in factor markets, e.g., high urban wages, the latter could more nearly reflect real factor and commodity scarcity in the economy in question because of better information on local needs. At the margin, there is an optimal division of the economy's investible funds, and one does not want to inhibit product development in the domestic industry by subsidizing foreign competition.

I have already noted how the capital constraint impeded certain kinds of on-the-job training, particularly in indigenous enterprise. However, when one adds the large real subsidies to imports of foreign capital goods, then a serious bias is induced toward overuse of foreign plant and equipment relative to broader use of domestic skilled and semiskilled labor and relatively simple domestic inputs. With the "seed-fertilizer" revolution in agriculture, B.F. Johnston and J. Cownie [16] have analyzed the possible perversities of the increased cash flow in peasant agriculture being used for substantial mechanization to replace labor, when in fact the basic technology could absorb much labor at greatly increased levels of productivity. If imported tractors or other fairly sophisticated kinds of agricultural equipment are made to look inexpensive, this could result in substantially accelerated migration towards urban areas where the absorption problem is already acute.

---

[16] B.F. Johnson and J. Cownie, "The Seed-Fertilizer Revolution and Labor Force Absorption," *American Economic Review*, (Sept. 1969) pp. 569–582.

In the industrial sector, the cheapening of foreign capital goods and other intermediate products yields a competitive advantage to foreign over domestically owned enterprise for *operating* directly in the domestic economy. That is, foreign-owned firms have intangible but significant investments in the use of foreign technologies where the marginal cost of incremental applications in underdeveloped countries is small. This "natural" advantage is artificially accentuated by the policy of cheapening foreign-produced intermediate products. In many cases, these intermediate products are outputs of the foreign "parent" company. Foreign enterprise already has an advantage because of inadequate domestic financing available to indigenous entrepreneurs. The further distortion in the commodity market accentuates this effect, to the detriment of domestic entrepreneurial development.

These generally adverse effects, the failure to develop backward linkages, plus the evident unprotection of specific domestic capital goods producers, eventually calls into play a protective response. The Brazilian "law of similars" is an example. If a domestic producer can show adequate "availability" of his intermediate product, competing imports will be curtailed. Yet the bureaucratic procedures are sufficiently complex that only producers in fairly large established companies, many of which are foreign, find it feasible to be represented before the tariff board. The small machine shop operator covering only a tiny proportion of the market is unlikely to find it economically feasible to bargain for protection — not that a general widening of tariffs would be socially desirable, given their negative effects on exports. Thus, the generally adverse impact on domestic production of producer goods is likely to bear heavily on small indigenous enterprise.

23.9. The Rationing of Scarce Inputs

So far we have discussed distortion at two levels arising out of attempts by authorities to cheapen capital goods and other intermediate products. Under the "pure" subsidy, there was discrimination among forms of capital accumulation. Second, when the subsidy was "financed" by exchange rate manipulation to lower prices of some foreign producer goods, an additional bias against domestic capital goods industries and learning processes was introduced. A third level of distortion exists when the subsidy is not completely "financed" and rationing is employed in order that lower prices to *some* users can be maintained.

Even with high tariffs or other restrictions on imports of final consumer goods, there is frequently inadequate foreign exchange to support potential demand for imports of intermediate products. The low price for foreign exchange in these favored categories requires rationing, in the form of exchange controls, among potential users. The licensing procedure here can be complex but again militate in favor of the "organized" sector or "essential" industries. To obtain licenses, direct "need" has to be shown, together with fairly large-scale usage. The function of carrying inventories of materials and equipment is shifted to the final manufacturer who applies directly for import licenses. Considerable time may elapse between permission to import and the actual importation itself, and the whole process of license granting is subject to uncertainty.

The efficiency of investment in inventories of materials and equipment is correspondingly impaired. Final users overstate "needs" to the governmental authorities because of uncertainty, black-market profits to be made, and the time lapse. Independent merchants can no longer legally hold inventories of imported inputs for serving large and small enterprise. Economies of scale in inventory holding are lost. We have the paradox that attempts to relieve the capital constraint through the cheapening of producer goods via a disequilibrium exchange rate lead to the holding of capital in very inefficient forms in some areas with shortages in others.

23.10. Concluding Comment

Evidently, much hinges on how domestic capital markets operate or fail to operate. Yet this critical issue has received little systematic attention in the literature of economic development. On the contrary, much of the theoretical discussion has taken place as if one were dealing with a unitary state where the government had the fiscal power and the information to costlessly replace capital markets. However, most underdeveloped economies are highly pluralistic with divisions between rural and urban, organized and unorganized, etc. To treat the government as omniscient is to invite intervention and resource misallocation.

Assuming omniscience, the neoclassicists advocate "first-best" tax-cum-subsidy policies in domestic product and factor markets in order to overcome the distortions commonly found in the underdeveloped environment. Excluding administrative costs, these are usually preferable to tariffs or other interventions in foreign trade. However, just as the literature on technological externalities and the provision of public goods has begun to discard the tax-cum-subsidy recommendations of the old Pigouvian welfare economics, so might foreign trade theorists discard taxes and subsidies in dealing with economic development. The main problems are not so much fiscal as financial.

Perhaps the appropriate compromise between direct intervention and doing nothing is for the state to recognize explicitly its own role in constructing institutions necessary for a capital market to work. In particular, the monetary and financial systems require state sanction and a degree of state control. (Optimal financial policy for development requires a larger treatise outside the confines of the present essay.) Encouraging efficient capital markets and withdrawing from manipulation of the foreign exchanges would be mutually supporting economic policies.

PUBLICATIONS OF CHARLES P. KINDLEBERGER

Books

International Short-Term Capital Movements, New York: Columbia University Press. 1937, 252 pp. Reprinted, Augustus M. Kelley, Inc., 1966.

The Dollar Shortage, Cambridge, Mass.: Technology Press and John Wiley & Sons, Inc., 1950, 271 pp.

International Economics, Homewood, Ill..: Richard D. Irwin, Inc., first edition 1953, 530 pp.; revised edition 1958, 636 pp. third edition 1963, 686 pp.; fourth edition 1968, 611 pp.

The Terms of Trade: A European Case Study (With the assistance of H.G. Van der Tak and J. Vanek). Cambridge, Mass.: Technology Press and John Wiley & Sons, Inc., 1956, 382 pp.

Economic Development, New York: McGraw-Hill Book Co., first edition 1958, 325 pp.; second edition 1965, 425 pp.

Foreign Trade and the National Economy, New Haven: Yale University Press, 1962, 265 pp.

Economic Growth in France and Britain, 1851–1950, Cambridge, Mass.: Harvard University Press, 1964, 378 pp.

Europe and the Dollar, Cambridge, Mass.: M.I.T. Press, 1966, 297 pp.

Europe's Postwar Growth: The Role of the Labor Supply, Cambridge, Mass.: Harvard University Press, 1967, 270 pp.

American Business Abroad: Six Lectures on Direct Investment, New Haven: Yale University Press, 1969, 225 pp.

Power and Money, New York: Basic Books, 1970, 246 pp.

(editor) *The International Corporation*, Cambridge, Mass.: M.I.T. Press, 1970, 415 pp.

Articles

1934–1943

"Comparative Currency Depreciation between Denmark and New Zealand," *Harvard Business Review*, Vol. XII, No. 4 (July 1934), pp. 416–427.

"The Theory of Inflation and Foreign Trade," *The Economics of Inflation*, H. Parker Willis and John M. Chapman, eds. New York: Columbia University Press, 1935, pp. 371–379.

"Flexibility of Demand in International Trade Theory," *The Quarterly Journal of Economics*, Vol. LI, No 2 (February 1937), pp. 352–362.

"Speculation and Forward Exchange," *Journal of Political Economy*, Vol. XLVII, No. 2 (April 1939), pp. 163–182.
"The Economic Tasks of the Postwar World," *Foreign Affairs*, Vol. 20. No. 3 (April 1942), pp. 466–477. With Alvin H. Hansen.
"International Monetary Stabilization," *Postwar Economic Problems*, Seymour E. Harris, ed. New York: McGraw-Hill Book Co., Inc., 1943, pp. 375–399.
"Planning for Foreign Investment," *American Economic Review*, Vol. XXXIII, No. 1 (March 1943), pp. 347–354.

1944–1950

"The Foreign-Trade Multiplier, The Propensity to Import and Balance–of–Payments Equilibrium," *American Economic Review*, Vol. XXXIX, No. 2 (March 1949), pp. 491–494.
"Germany and the Economic Recovery of Europe," *Proceedings of the Academy of Political Science*, Vol. XXIII, No. 3 (May 1949), pp. 68–82.
"International Disequilibrium," *The Canadian Journal of Economics and Political Science*, Vol 16, No. 4 (November 1950), pp. 529–538.

1951–1955

"Bretton Woods Reappraised," *International Organization*, Vol. V, No. 1 (February 1951), pp. 32–48.
"Group Behavior and International Trade," *The Journal of Political Economy*, Vol. LIX, No. 1 (February 1951), pp. 30–47.
"European Economic Integration," *Money, Trade and Economic Growth (in honor of John Henry Williams)*, New York: The Macmillan Company, 1951, pp. 58–76.
"The Mechanism for Adjustment in International Payments – The lessons of Postwar Experience" Papers and Proceedings, *American Economic Review*, Vol. XLII, No 2 (May 1952), pp. 332–344. With Emile Despres.
"L'Asymétrie de la balance des payments et le problème du dollar," *Revue Economique*, Vol. V, No. 2 (March 1954), pp. 166–189.
"German Terms of Trade by Commodity Classes and Areas," *The Review of Economics and Statistics*, Vol. XXXVI, No .2 (May 1954), pp. 167–175.
"Anciens et nouveaux products dans le commerce international," *Economie Appliquée*, Vol. VII, No. 3 (July-September 1954), pp. 281–297.
"Les termes d'échange de la Belgique entre 1870 et 1952," *Bulletin d'information et de documentation*, Vol. II, No. 3 (September 1954), pp. 1–10.
"The Position and Prospects of Sterling," *Journal of Political Economy*, Vol. LXIII, No. 1 (February 1955), pp. 70–74.
"Industrial Europe's Terms of Trade on Current Account, 1870–1953," *The Economic Journal*, Vol. LXV, No. 1 (March 1955), pp. 19–35.
"Economists in International Organizations," *International Organization*, Vol. IX, No. 3 (August 1955), pp. 338–353.
"The Regional Approach to United States Economic Foreign Policy," In Foreign Economic Policy, *Hearings* before the Subcommittee on Foreign Economic Policy of the Joint Committee on the Economic Report, Congress of the United States, 84th Congress, Washington, D.C., 1955.

1956–1960

"Tariff Policy for the United States – A Strong Rich Country," Proceedings of the American Farm Economic Association, *Journal of Farm Economics*, Vol. XXXVIII, No. 2 (May 1956). pp. 309–315.

"Aspects sociaux de la formation de capital dans les pays sours-developées," *Cahiers* de l'Institute de Science Economique Appliquée, Serie F., 3 (August 1956), pp. 35–51.

"Partial vs. General-Equilibrium in International Trade," *Indian Journal of Economics*, Vol. XXXVIII, No. 148 (July 1957), pp. 31–38.

Fluctuations cycliques internationales," *Revue Economique*, Vol. VIII, No. 6 (November 1957), pp. 927–938.

"Imports, the Tariff and the Need for Adjustment," In *Foreign Economic Policy*, a compendium of papers presented to the Subcommittee on Foreign Economic Policy of the House Committee on Ways and Means, 85th Congress, Washington, D.C. (December 1957), pp. 73–87.

"The Terms of Trade and Economic Development," *Supplement to Review of Economics and Statistics*, Vol. XL (February 1958), pp. 72–85.

"The Dollar Shortage Re-revisited," *American Economic Review*, Vol. XLVIII, No. 3 (June 1958), pp. 388–395.

"New Trade Channels," *Challenge*, Vol. 7, No. 5 (February 1959), pp. 64–69.

Statement on International Aspects on Employment, Growth and Price Levels, Testimony before the Joint Economic Committee, Congress of the United States (June 30, 1959), pp. 954–958.

"United States Economic Foreign Policy: Research Requirements for 1965," *World Politics*, Vol. XI, No. 4 (July 1959), pp. 588–613.

Statement on "Implications for the U.S. Resulting from Gold Outflow," before the Joint Economic Committee, Congress of the United States. *The Commercial Chronicle*, Vol. 190, No. 5864 (July 16, 1959), pp. 1, 30–32.

"International Political Theory from the Outside," *Theoretical Aspects of International Relations*, Wm.T.R. Fox, ed. Notre Dame, Ind.: University of Notre Dame Press, 1959, pp. 69–82.

"The Technical Basis of Economic Integration," *World Politics*, Vol. XIII, No. 3 (April 1960), pp. 562–567.

"International Trade and United States Experience: 1870–1955," *Post-war Economic Trends*, R.E. Freeman, ed. New York: Harper & Brothers, 1960, pp. 339–373.

1961–1965

"La fin du rôle dominant des Etats-Unis et l'avenir d'une politique économique mondiale," *Cahiers* de L'Institut de Science Economique Appliquée, Serie P, No. 5 (May 1961), pp. 91–105.

"The Problem of World Liquidity and Payments," A statement included in "International Payments Imbalance and Need for Strengthening Financial Arrangements," *Hearings* before the Subcommittee on International Exchange and Payments of the Joint Economic Committee, Congress of the United States (May 16, June 19, 20, 21, 1961), pp. 283–285.

"Obsolesence and Technical Change," *Bulletin* of the Oxford University Institute of Statistics, Vol. 23, No. 3 (August 1961), pp. 281–297.

"Foreign Trade and Economic Growth, Lessons from Britain and France, 1850–1913," *The Economic History Review*, Vol. XIV, No. 2 (December 1961), pp. 285–305.

"International Trade and Investment and Resource Use in Economic Growth," *Natural Resources and Economic Growth*, J.J. Spengler, ed. Washington, D.C.: Resources for the Future, Inc., 1961, pp. 151–190.

"Tariff Reductions to Correct Balance-of-Payments Difficulties," *Industrial Management Review*, Vol. 3, No. 2 (Spring 1962), pp. 1–7.

"Protected Markets and Economic Growth," In *Factors Affecting the United States Balance of Payments*, Compilation of Studies Prepared for the Subcommittee on International Exchange and Payments of the Joint Economic Committee, Congress of the United States, Washington, D.C.: U.S. Government Printing Office, 1962, pp. 159–173.

"Foreign Trade and Growth: Lessons from British Experience since 1913," *Lloyds Bank Review*, No. 65 (July 1962), pp. 16–28.

"The Postwar Resurgence of the French Economy," In S. Hoffmann et al., *In Search of France*, Cambridge, Mass.: Harvard University Press, 1963, pp. 118–158.

"Flexible Exchange Rates," In *Monetary Management*, A Series of Research Studies Prepared for the Commission of Money and Credit, Englewood Cliffs, N.J.: Prentice-Hall, Inc., 1963, pp. 403–425.

"European Economic Integration and the Development of a Single Financial Center for Long-Term Capital," *Weltwirtschaftliches Archiv*, Band 90, Heft 2 (July 1963), pp. 189–210.

"The Prospects for International Liquidity and the Future Evolution of the International Payments System," *International Trade Theory in a Developing World* (Proceedings of a Conference held by the International Economic Association) R. Harrod and D. Hague, eds., New York: St. Martin Press, Inc., 1963, pp. 273–292.

"Short-run Measures to Strengthen the Dollar," Included in "The International Monetary System: Functioning and Possible Reform," *Hearings* before the Joint Economic Committee, Congress of the United States, 88th Congress, First Session (November 12, 13, 14, and 15, 1963), pp. 383–390.

"Terms of Trade for Primary Products," *Natural Resources and International Development*, Marion Clawson, ed., published for Resources for the Future Inc. Baltimore, Md.: Johns Hopkins Press, 1964, pp. 339–366.

"All About United States Foreign Investment," (review article). *Economic Development and Cultural Exchange*, Vol. XII, No. 3 (April 1964), pp. 325–328.

"Reflections on the Present United States Position on East-West Trade," In *East-West Trade* A Compilation of Views of Businessmen, Bankers, and Academic Experts, Committee on Foreign Relations, U.S. Senate, Washington, D.C. (November 1964), pp. 268–272.

"Trends in International Economics," *Annals* of the American Academy of Political and Social Science, Vol. 358 (March 1965), pp. 170–179.

"Balance-of-Payments Deficits and the International Market for Liquidity," *Essays in International Finance*, International Finance Section, Princeton University, No. 46 (May 1965), pp. 1–26.

"Mass Migration, Then and Now," *Foreign Affairs* Vol. 43, No. 4 (July 1965), pp. 647–658.

"Emigration and Economic Growth," Banca Nazionale del Lavoro *Quarterly Review*, No. 74 (September 1965) pp. 235–254.

"The United States Balance of Payments in the Nineteenth Century, A Review Article," *Explorations in Entrepreneurial History*, Vol. 3, No. 1 (Fall 1965), pp. 50–55.

"The Economics of 2001," M.I.T. Alumni Association *Technology Review*, Vol. 68, No. 1 (November 1965), pp. 25–26, 64.

"Germany's Persistent Balance-of-Payments Disequilibrium," *Trade, Growth, and the Balance of Payments*, Essays in Honor of Gottfried Haberler, Chicago: Rand McNally & Co., 1965, pp. 230–248.

"Integration vs. Nationalism in the European Economy," *The Reporter*, Vol. 33, No. 10 (December 2, 1965), pp. 38–40.

"European Integration and the International Corporation," *Columbia Journal of World Business*, Vol. 1, No. 1 (Winter 1965), pp. 65–73.

1966–1970

"The Dollar and World Liquidity – A Minority View," *The Economist*, Vol. CCXVIII, No. 6389 (February 5, 1966), pp. 526–529. With Emile Despres and Walter S. Salant.

"Capital Movements and International Payments Adjustment," *Konjunkturpolitik, 12.* Jahrgang, Erstes Heft 1966, pp. 10–30.

"Le rôle des États-Unis dans l'économie européenne," In *L'Europe du XIXe et XXe Siècle*, Milan: Marzarati, 1966, pp. 417–451.

"International Monetary Arrangements," The English, Scottish and Australian Bank Research Lecture, Brisbane, Australia: University of Queensland Press, August 1966, pp. 1–20.

Statement in Contingency Planning in U.S. International Monetary Policy, Joint Economic Committee, Congress of the U.S. 89th Congress, 2nd Session, Washington, D.C.: Government Printing Office, 1966, pp. 49–62.

"The Contribution of International Trade Theory to Regional Economics," In *Capital, Income & Regional Development*, report of a conference sponsored by the Agricultural Policy Institute and the Department of Economics, North Carolina State University (October 1964), API Series 21 (October 1966), pp. 17–27.

'Professional Education: Toward a Way of Thought," *Technology Review*, November 1966, pp. 29–32, 49, 50, 53, 54.

"The International Monetary System – Strengths, Weaknesses and Possible Improvements," In National Industrial Conference Board, *International Financing 1966*. Addresses before the Third International Financing Conference, November 22, 1966.

"Public Policy and the International Corporation," A statement in *International Aspects of Antitrust*, Hearings before the Subcommittee on Antitrust and Monopoly of the Committee on the Judiciary, United States Senate, Part 1, Washington, D.C.: Government Printing Office 1967, pp. 148–173.

"The U.S. in World Markets," *The Changing American Economy*, J.R. Coleman, ed. New York: Basic Books, Inc., Publishers 1967, pp. 210–220.

"French Planning," *National Economic Planning*, Max F. Millikan, ed., A Conference of the Universities-National Bureau Committee on Economic Research, New York: Columbia University Press 1967 pp. 279–300.

A.I.D. Discussion Paper No. 14, "Liberal Policies vs. Controls in the Foreign Trade of Developing Countries," Alliance for International Development, April 1967.

Testimony on the Economic Report of the President and the Annual Report of the

Council of Economic Advisers before the Joint Economic Committee, 90th Congress, 1st Session, Hearings, May 1967.

"The State of Economic Partnership Today," *Interplay*, Vol. 1, No. 1 (June-July 1967), pp. 19–21.

"A Monetary Policy for an Interdependent World," *The Lamp*, Summer 1967, pp. 20–22.

"The Politics of Money and World Language," *Essays in International Finance* (Princeton) No. 61 (August 1967), pp. 1–11.

"The Pros and Cons of an International Capital Market," *Zeitschrift fuer die Gesamte Staatswissenschaft*, Vol. 123, No. 4 (October 1967), pp. 600–617.

"The International Firm and the International Capital Market," *Southern Economic Journal*, Vol. XXXIV, No. 2 (October 1967), pp. 223–230.

"Study Abroad and Emigration," *The Brain Drain*, Walter Adams, ed., New York: The Macmillan Co. 1968, pp. 35–55.

"Commitment to Responsibility," *World Politics*, Vol. XX, No. 2 (January 1968), pp. 357–367.

Testimony before the Senate Committee on Banking and Currency in "Cold Cover," *Hearings* before the Committee on Banking and Currency, United States Senate 90th Congress, 2nd Session (February 1, 1968), Washington, D.C.: U.S. Government Printing Office, 1968, pp. 166–167.

"The Marshall Plan and the Cold War," *International Journal* (Canada), Vol. XXIII, No. 3 (Summer 1968), pp. 369–382.

"The Euro-Dollar Market and the Internationalization of United States Monetary Policy," Banca Nazionale del Lavoro *Quarterly Review*, No. 88 (March 1969), pp. 3–15.

"Investissements et matières premières," *Esprit* (France), No. 380 (April 1969), pp. 630–636.

"Is Time Money?" *Interplay*, Vol. 3, No. 20 (August–September 1969), pp. 40–42.

"Princeton *Essays in International Finance*," *Journal of Economic Literature*, Vol. 1, No. 3 (September 1969), pp. 807–810.

"Measuring Equilibrium in Balances of Payments," *Journal of Political Economy*, Vol. 77, No. 6 (November-December, 1969), pp. 873–891.

"Le Prix de l'or et le problème du N-1", *Economie Appliquée*, Tome XXIII, No. 1 (1970), pp. 149–162.

"The Case for Fixed Exchange Rates, 1970," *The International Adjustment Mechanism*, Monetary Conference, October 1969, The Federal Reserve Bank of Boston, pp. 93–108.

"Toward a GATT for Investment: A Proposal for Supervision of the International Corporation," with Paul M. Goldberg. *Law and Policy in International Business*, Vol. 2, No. 2 (Summer 1970), pp. 295–325.

"Less Developed Countries and the International Capital Market," in *Industrial Organization and Economic Development*, Essays in Honor of E.S. Mason, Jesse W. Markham and Gustav F. Papanek, editors, Boston, Houghton Mifflin Company, 1970, pp. 337–349.

"An Economist's View of the Euro-dollar Market: Two Puzzles," in *The Eurodollar*, Herbert V. Prochnow, editor, Chicago, Rand McNally & Company, 1970, pp. 257–271.

"The Dollar System," Federal Reserve Bank of Boston, *New England Economic Review*, September/October 1970, pp. 3–9.

SUBJECT INDEX